Wait for Me

The Americanization of Tamara

Tami McIntyre

VANTAGE PRESS
New York

Some names have been changed to protect the identities
of the actual individuals represented.

In loving memory to
John Calvin Ferguson,
from his "Girlie"

To a Child Innocent of Time

Filled with the infinite of infancy,
Life was your banister to slide down on;
You with sweet graveness in your flippancy,
You lived a game of checkers, and you won.

To Tamara,
John Simon
Harvard University, 1944

Contents

Introduction

Before you begin to read this book, especially if you were born after 1945, I suggest that you first consider placing yourself into a time zone when there were no computers, television sets, video recorders, plastics, frozen foods, polio vaccines, contact lenses, ballpoint pens, dishwashers, clothes driers, air conditioners, camcorders, organ transplants, cellular phones, plus other recent inventions that we, in the nineties, take so much for granted. Oh, and I must not forget the PILL.

It was a time before man learned to split the atom, before laser beams came on the scene, before man walked on the Moon. It was the time of the Roaring Twenties, when Lindbergh flew the Atlantic, and Babe Ruth hit his famous "60 home runs" in a single season and Mickey Mouse started his career in *Steamboat Willie,* when silent movies became "talkies," and Herbert Hoover became president, and the Depression became a reality.

Then followed the memorable thirties when the Empire State Building, then "the tallest building in the world," was opened and the "Star Spangled Banner" became our national anthem, and F.D.R. was the American president and his "Fireside Chats" became an institution. It was a time when nylon became patented, and "The Hit Parade" became the top radio show. Tommy Dorsey, Glenn Miller, Benny Goodman, Harry James, and Gene Krupa were some of the well-known bandleaders of the era.

Finally, it was the forties, the time of World War II, when the World's Fair celebrated its second year in New York, when bulldog-faced Winston Churchill became Britain's prime minister and proclaimed to his countrymen that he had "nothing to give but blood, toil, tears and sweat." Pearl Harbor now became more than two words on a map, American women put on military uniforms, and ration stamps limited the distribution of scarce foods. Bob Hope, Frank Sinatra, and other popular celebrities toured the battlefields to cheer American men overseas. Back home the residents of each community united to help the war effort. Doolittle, Eisenhower, MacArthur, and others became household names. So did war heroes: 1st Lt. Audie Murphy, Howard Gilmore, the five Sullivan brothers, and others too numerous to mention. *Oklahoma* and *The Voice of the Turtle* opened on Broadway. *Casablanca, The Human Comedy,* and *For Whom the Bell Tolls* were some of the movies people flocked to see. "As Time Goes By" became a haunting melody on lovers' lips.

How did couples live together before 1945? Well, unlike the nineties, they married first, then lived together, most of them reasonably happily ever after. Divorces, frowned upon by society, were rare.

We shopped in the new five-and-ten stores where attractive or useful items cost either a nickel or a dime. For that matter, that is what ice cream cones, public phone calls, streetcar rides, movie tickets, and Cokes cost. Miracle of miracles, we could mail a letter and two postcards all for the price of one nickel! Gasoline cost eleven cents a gallon, and prices of cars advertised in the papers cost hundreds of dollars, not thousands.

People smoked cigarettes then, unfiltered ones at first: Lucky Strikes, Marlboros, Chesterfields, Pall Malls, Camels, Old Golds. Words like "coke," "pot," "grass," "aids" meant exactly this: Coke to drink, a pot to cook in, grass to mow, and "aids" meant helping.

However, please bear in mind that my generation was not all that backward. We did know the difference between the sexes. One happy Frenchman had even exclaimed, "Vive la différence!" Sex changes were unheard of until George Jorgenson became a woman named Christine. On the whole, people had to be satisfied with what God had given them. If they did deviate from the man-woman combination, they did so in the privacy of their most private chambers. As for the remainder of this old-fashioned and unbelievable generation, the women—believe it or not!—actually felt that in order to have a baby, you had to get a husband first.

The first seventeen years of my life were spent in a walled-in Chinese house in the old walled-in capital of China, Peking. It was within these walls that I first learned to live within three cultures. From the Chinese and my Russian papa, I learned to revere my elders and to seek knowledge. From my stoic Bulgarian mama, I learned to believe in truth and perseverance. From our American neighbor and friend, Dr. Ferguson, I learned, first, to believe in myself, and second, to know that there was a much larger, more beautiful world outside the walls that surrounded me. Later, on my own, I found out that living within these ivy-covered walls did not necessarily protect me from evil.

Papa had settled in Peking a few years before the Russian revolution, bringing with him his beautiful, aristocratic bride and his own desires to pursue his Far Eastern studies as well as to teach Russian in the great National University of Peking.

After Ivan and I were born, our parents needed much larger quarters. Fortunately, Papa learned of a house in the Chinese quarters of the city. Formerly owned by a wealthy Mandarin, this estate, with its three homes in separate compounds, had been bought by an American scholar-philanthropist, Dr. John Calvin Ferguson. Papa had been pleased with the modest rent and had leased the third home from the American.

"There used to be a big willow tree right here in the front courtyard." Vanya kicked at some weeds to show me the spot. "Did you know that?"

I shook my head.

He looked at me with pity. "Of course not. You were too little."

"Did the tree die?" I asked. Vanya knew everything.

"No, Papa had it chopped down. Dr. Ferguson said he could." "Why?"

"Why do you ask why all the time, Tamara?"

"I want to know. That's why. Tell me."

His eyes narrowed. "Cuz there was supposed to be a fox living in the hollow tree trunk. The superstitious Chinese believed that a fox changed into human form at night, enticed his victims, then destroyed them. Understand?"

"But Papa didn't believe that," I persisted.

"Papa is not Chinese, stupid. Chinese servants wouldn't

Mama in the Central Courtyard with
Beba, Peking, China

Papa in His Study

work in a haunted house. That's why the willow tree was chopped down. No more fox. Now plenty servants. See?"

From his book-lined study, Papa had ruled our family like a gentle autocrat. He always saw to it that we had books to read, paper, pencils, and, for me, Chinese brushes. He encouraged us to read, write, draw, and paint.

"Always remember, Tamara," he had once stressed to me in his quiet, convincing voice, "here in my study a whole world lies before you. These books are our treasures. There is so much to learn. With books you can never be lonely."

His own world had revolved around his Asian studies, his Russian lectures at the National University of Peking, his students and colleagues. He often allowed me to sit in his study while he and some scholar associate discussed pedagogical topics or events of the day. Whenever Dr. Ferguson came to visit him, I made sure to be there too. I liked the tall, white-haired American who came to see Papa.

"Ah, there's my Girlie. And how's my Girlie today?"

It puzzled my parents, especially Papa, when Dr. Ferguson inquired about me. After all, I was just a little girl. The tall American was an important man, well-known throughout the Far East for his erudite writings on China's past and its treasures. After all, he had been president of Nanking University and Nanyang College. Many came to see this great man to learn from him. Even Papa felt humble in his presence. Not me, though. He became my dear friend, my very first American friend.

Except in unusual circumstances, Papa's sphere of influence ended outside his study door. Beyond that door, Mama ran the household with a firm though gentle hand. At first she had found it difficult to communicate with the servants. Fortunately, our amiable cook spoke pidgin Russian and translated her orders to the other servants, or else Vanya or I did.

I found Mama's world quite exciting: tea parties, getting ready for dinner, the theater, ballet . . . clothes . . . old Russia . . . conversations . . . the poor czar and the czarina . . . the princesses . . . little Crown Prince Alexei . . . his illness, his bleeding. So tragic . . . the royal family's sad end. Often Russian phrases interspersed with French. The latest styles, cloche hats, flapper dresses, long, long strings of pearls. Coty perfume. If I kept quiet, I could sit by Mama's side and listen.

"Did you see Garbo and Gilbert in *Flesh and the Devil?*"

"But *mais oui.* Oy, that Garbo. *Elle est tres belle, n'est ce pas?*"

"*Oui.* They are all beautiful, those stars. Look at Swanson, Negri . . . our own Nazimova."

"And don't forget that . . . that 'it' girl. What's her name?"

"Clara Bow?"

"What is 'it,' Mama?" Laughter. Amused looks.

Mama's friends. Bobbed, marcelled hair except for Mama's, which was coiled into a chignon at the nape of her neck. Smoke from cigarettes in jade or ivory holders. Mama didn't smoke. "Hush, *dochenka* [little daughter], grown-ups are talking."

Alone with us, Mama was different. If she had time she played games with us, cards, dominoes. Or told riddles, stories, fables. As we got older, she taught us more.

"Soon you'll be going to a real school, and you'll learn many things that I can't teach you. Papa and I want you to learn Russian. And after Russian comes French."

"Why French, Mama?"

"It's a beautiful language."

"I hate the French verbs, Mama."

"They're easier than Russian verbs, Tamara." Mama was firm.

"But I know Russian verbs."

"Tsk," her finger pressed to her lips, "Papa said you will learn French, and you will."

Early in my life I had learned not to trust Vanya. It had been a terrifying incident that even now I cannot forget. I was four; Vanya, six. Mama usually bathed Vanya and me in the guest-house bathroom. She bathed one of us first, called Papa to come fetch, then bathed the other one. This one time, however, she had been in a hurry. She and Papa were going out.

"I'm going to put the two of you in the tub together."

Vanya had climbed into the tub by himself. Mama lifted me and placed me in the tub in front of him. I had laughed, enjoying the idea of taking a bath with my big brother. He had stared at me, then had grinned.

"Chort!" (the devil!)

Mama glanced at us, annoyed. "Vanya, I've forgotten the soap. Look after her, will you, while I run to the main house?"

Vanya had smiled, eyes gleaming as he looked at me. Mama had opened the door, and momentarily I felt the chilly air on my back. The bathroom was warm; so was the water.

Vanya's right hand had reached out to me slowly. He placed it on top of my head, then crossed his other hand over it. At first I had thought he was playing. He was bending my head down into the water. I tried to wrench away. I heard his quick intake of breath as he pushed me farther into the bath water. Water went up my nose. I couldn't breathe. I felt water gurgling in my mouth; I choked on it in my throat. Too much water, warm water. Suddenly he let me go, and I was sobbing. Mama stood there holding the soap.

"Vanya, whatever happened to her?"

His voice was calm. "She slipped, Mama. She slipped."

Mama never bathed us together again.

At times things that I couldn't understand had happened at home. One day, all of a sudden, Aunt Raisa and my two cousins were living in the back quarters behind our main house. Aunt Raisa, a shorter mama with bobbed hair; Yura, a quiet, bashful eight-year-old; and Peter, a year younger. Mama had been all smiles. Her sister joined her in the dressmaking business. Yura and Peter enrolled in the Peking American School.

I especially liked my cousin Petya. He shielded me from Vanya's sneak attacks. Petya never called me little or stupid. One day I asked him, "Why are you all living with us?"

"Uncle Sergei sent for us." His face had clouded. "My papa is dead. The Bolsheviks killed him. That's why Uncle Sergei got us out of Russia."

So that was what had happened.

Everything had gone well until the day Peter had his accident. Somehow he had fallen off the high Russian stove in our living room. Something terrible had happened to his leg. He had been taken to the PUMC (Peking Union Medical College). Papa had been a thundercloud. Mama's eyes had been red. Vanya had been unusually quiet.

"Mama, is Petya coming back?"

"Hush, child." Absentmindedly, she had patted my head. "What? Oh, yes, he'll be coming back. Sometime later, not now."

Peter did return...on crutches...but not for long. Soon after, he, Yura, and Aunt Raisa moved out. Then Papa summoned all of us into his study. Even I, little as I was, saw that Papa was very angry but trying desperately to be calm.

"From now on," he had glared at Vanya and me, "I don't want their names mentioned...ever again. I shall pay the hospital bill, but that is it, Vera." His voice had hardened. "That's the last time we shall deal with them. Do you all understand?"

I hadn't understood, but it was not the time to ask him why.

Because Vanya preferred to stay by himself, it was not too difficult for me to avoid him. Then, too, at Dr. Ferguson's suggestion, Papa had enrolled him in the American School.

My world expanded when I too, became old enough to go to PAS (Peking American School). I liked everything about the school. For the first time in my life I was among children my own age. We shared books, studied, and played together. I learned to tell the kids apart. Missionaries or legation kids? British? American? More than half were Americans. Printed dresses, puffed sleeves, ribbons in their hair. Pretty girls, lively boys. Upper-crust Chinese, most of them reserved, polite, intelligent. A few French and German children. Russians? Four of us, three boys and me.

I liked the Americans, but they could tease.

"Why do you call my brother 'Bowlegs'?"

"Because he is," they told me.

I felt sorry for Vanya. That he couldn't take their taunts had made them tease him even more.

In the second grade I met Dorlise. Like most of the students she was an American; however, she belonged neither to the clannish missionaries nor to the transient legationers.

"Name's Dorlise. Named after Aunty Dorothy Louise. See? Dor-lise. Who're you?" I liked her abrupt way of speaking.

I never wanted to tell my name to foreigners. "T'mara," I mouthed it quickly. Then I waited. Usually the person smiled in amusement and then asked, "Which is it? Tomorrow? Or today?"

Instead, Dorlise had smiled. "That's a pretty name and unusual like my own. What are you?"

I regretted that I couldn't say American. To me Americans were the luckiest people in the world. "I'm Russian," I told her.

"Good. I like Russians. They're nice."

Whether she had ever met any Russians before me I never asked. I was happy enough to have found a good friend my own age.

In PAS I learned about Abraham Lincoln, George Washington, the Indians. My third-grade teacher taught me about Charles Lindbergh, Admiral Byrd and the South Pole, Will Rogers and cowboys. I became a Brownie, then a Girl Scout. In school Dorlise and I planned for the summer. In summertime we waited impatiently for PAS to start.

Part I
Peking, China
1935–May 10, 1939

1

Uprooted

Actually, the Rosencrantz piano started it all. Mama had wanted a piano for such a long time. Then, suddenly, or so it seemed to me, Papa bought her one. I hadn't even known that it was coming. Three Chinese coolies, groaning and cursing under its weight, carried it through the two front courtyards. Carefully they set it down by the backyard window of our living room. After they had gone, we all stood around admiring its ebony beauty. There were even two gold candelabra attached to it. Mama's face was flushed as she sat down on the round stool. Smiling, she lightly fingered the keys.

"The tone is superb," she murmured. "But my fingers are so clumsy. It's been years since I last touched a piano." She looked up at Papa. "Thank you, Serioja. It's beautiful."

Then I made my mistake. Had I kept silent, it wouldn't have happened, but I did open my big mouth and impulsively blurted out, "Mama, will you teach me how to play?"

She was still fingering the keys, humming softly to herself. "I've already thought of that, Tamara. You'll be taking piano lessons at the convent. They're good, not too expensive."

That was all right with me. My friend Dorlise was excited when I told her. "Just think, Tamdee," she exclaimed. "You might become a concert pianist and travel all over the world, maybe even to America! And I'll be your impresario!"

It was generous of her to offer her services; I was all for it. After I touched the piano, however, the playing part did not seem quite so attractive. "I'm scared," I confided to her. "Mama said

3

that I am going to have a nun for a teacher."

"Oh, God, no!" Dorlise gasped. "They remind me of penguins, eh?"

I had already lost my enthusiasm for playing the piano.

Meeting Mother Hildebalde depressed me. I had ridden to the convent in a ricksha, all by myself. A young nun had pointed out the door where Mother Hildebalde gave lessons. "Just knock once," she told me. "Mother will hear you."

Mother Hildebalde was waiting. When I entered the cavernous room, I noticed the black-cowled form sitting hunched over on a straight-backed chair next to the piano bench. Her back had been turned to me; her head, bowed. I thought of Dorlise's penguins and suppressed a giggle. The nun turned. She was a tiny, very fragile old lady. Her baby-pink face looked as if God with a supernatural tweak had used his thumb and index finger to pinch in her nose, her chin, and her cheeks. In her hands she held a rosary, rotating it slowly. I had interrupted her prayers.

Frankly, I did not know how to behave with a nun. Dorlise and I had smiled over that problem.

"Just look angelic," my friend had advised. "After all, nuns are human, too."

The nun beckoned me forward. I walked towards her slowly, feeling the saintliness radiate from her presence.

"Tamara Rubleva?" She gave me a quizzical look. I noticed how pale and watery her eyes were behind the rimless glasses. Her voice was soft, with a slight accent. She motioned for me to sit down on the bench. "Shall we begin? Ah, I forget something." She smiled sheepishly, then took my right hand in hers. She looked at my fingers carefully. "It's good. You have long fingers; that's good. *Eh bien!* Now place your fingers here. *Comme ça!*"

My piano lessons had started. Twice a week, for half an hour, lessons with a copper coin atop the back of each hand took place. Scales to practice, Hanon to play over and over again while the clock ticked by ever so slowly. Little time was left for other, more pleasant things.

Dorlise missed seeing me. "You're always so darned busy," she moaned. "Now I don't see you anymore except at school."

It was true. The only time we were together was in the classroom at PAS. On weekends I had to practice longer hours, or my parents had guests and we absolutely had to be present.

Then the bombshell dropped! Father explained it to me one evening after supper. I had already suspected that something was afoot by that insufferable smirk on Vanya's face. He always relished any discomfort that might come my way.

Papa had cleared his throat. He did that when he started his lectures or had something important to announce to us. This time he turned to me. "Tamara, you'll be going to the convent to study. They've raised the tuition at the American School, and we can't afford to send you there anymore."

Instinctively I glanced at my brother. His head was lowered, but he was smiling.

"What about Vanya?" I asked. "Why only me?"

"Sacred Heart's only for girls; tuition there is half as much," Mama interjected quietly. "Besides, it's a very good school, and, Tamara," Mama, seeing that I was about to protest shook her finger, "just think, you'll be learning French!"

"We have French at PAS," I mumbled. I felt the tears welling up. It just wasn't fair!

"Well, it's done," Papa said coldly. We got up from the table. "You're already enrolled there; that's all there is to it." His tone was final.

Didn't they realize what they had done to me! No more would I be in school with my friends, my teachers, even the strict principal, Miss Moore. I loved them all! Who would now draw the Honor Roll on the blackboard? Who would now sit in back of Dorlise instead of me?

It was useless to plead with them. The worst thorn in my side was Vanya's triumphant glee. I resented him now more than ever. He was more important to my parents than I was!

I didn't like going to the convent school. Even now I cannot recall having learned much in its hallowed classrooms. I was now in the seventh grade along with five other girls. All of us had to wear ugly uniforms made of scratchy navy wool with prim, high-necked blouses and black stockings. Our black shoes couldn't be patent leather because they'd reflect our underpants. Dorlise had doubled up laughing when I told her that.

5

Sacred Heart School

My five schoolmates weren't too bad, though. There was Denise, a chubby Greek girl with pimply cheeks; Alicia Wang, the tall Chinese girl with intelligent, black eyes; Lillian Ito, the complacent Japanese girl; Lisa, a beautiful Russian with the fleeting smile, and poor Helen, also Russian. Helen was a pale, plump orphan whom the Sisters had taken in. If Helen hadn't been in the class, I would have been totally depressed. As it was, she was so comical at times that she made even studying at the convent more bearable. Her pitiful attempts at memorization kept us all in a helpless state of silent laughter.

Of course, most of our teachers were nuns. Several novices taught some classes. Every day I marveled at their patience. They had totally rejected the real world.

"Can you believe it?" I told Dorlise. "They're going to live in that convent all their lives. No movies, skating, or dancing. Some of the novices are as young as you and I. Helen told me she is going to be a nun."

Dorlise kept me informed about her school activities.

"Boy, Tamdee," she gushed one day, "We've got a new man teacher, Mr. Huit. Gosh, is he handsome! All us girls in class have a crush on him, even some of the teachers!"

In turn, I told Dorlise about Mother Joseph-Helen. "She's part Indian and part English. She's one, no, the tallest nun in the whole darned convent and thin as a rail. Boy, is she strict! Br-r-r!" I shuddered, picturing my homeroom teacher. "Dorlise, she's like a ghost, pale as ashes! She's got this straight, long nose; narrow, shapeless lips, and her eyes look right through you. You can't escape her; I think she even reads my thoughts!"

The longer I studied at the convent, the more I hated it. Lessons with the nuns were primarily memorization exercises from ancient texts, books that the Peking American School would have discarded long ago. Physical geography, Mother Joseph-Helen's pet subject, was the worst. The only good thing about taking PG was that it followed catechism. Alicia and I didn't have to take catechism since we weren't Catholic. Thus, we had an extra half hour to refresh our memories. I became quite adept at this memory game. The only trouble was that if I forgot a line while reciting a passage, I'd have to start over again from the very beginning. I also would not have been able to explain in my very own words what I had memorized. Whether Mother Joseph-Helen ever thought about that I don't know. I received a good grade from her; that was all that mattered to me.

At least Dorlise and I were able to compare notes on our schools and visit each other. It was good to be her friend. She had entered PAS when I was in the second grade. Somehow we just clicked, the shy little Russian girl and the mischievous American, daughter of a young marine and a military attache's secretary. I still remember the day she came into our class.

We had all taken our seats that morning, and Miss Kelso, who doubled as teacher and choir director, had taken the roll. She was just about to begin our lesson when the door opened, and Miss Moore came in with a little girl.

I had never seen this girl before. She must have just arrived from the States. While Miss Moore conferred with our teacher, we all looked over the newcomer. She had a Buster Brown haircut just like mine, except that her hair was chestnut in color while mine resembled flax. Her eyes were her best feature, brown with a darker center. Her cheeks were the shade of ripe peaches; her lips were full and rosy. She seemed bashful, but no wonder, I thought. The whole class was staring at her. There was something unusual about the way she was dressed. Most American girls wore flower-print dresses with tiny, puffed sleeves usually edged in lace. Store-bought clothes from the United States! I had often wished that I could have just one dress like that instead of the ones Mama had made for me. Dorlise's dress was special. It was of the palest lavender cotton with a big collar on which were appliqued flowers in darker shades of purple. Her socks matched her dress. Her shoes were of patent leather!

Miss Kelso tried to make her feel at home. "Welcome, dear," she bent down towards the newcomer. "Miss Moore tells me that your name is Dorlise." She pronounced it slowly. "Door-lizz."

Miss Moore had given the class a stern look and then left.

Dorlise's face reddened. "It's Dor-leeze," she corrected. "My auntie's name is Dorothy; my middle name is Louise. Put them together, and you get Dorlise. It's that simple." She looked at the class defiantly.

There was only one empty seat, and that was in front of my desk. Miss Kelso led her to it. We became friends at recess.

Dorlise Krenz, Peking, China

Maybe it was because both of us were different from the other girls, many of whom came from either military or missionary families. During class she turned to look back at me a couple of times, and I had smiled. The second time she too had smiled. When the bell rang, she had stood up and held out her hand to me.

"I'm Dorlise Krenz," she said gruffly. "What's your name?"

"Tamara," I pronounced it slowly, waiting for her reaction to my unusual name. "I'm Russian."

"Good," she withdrew her hand. A merry glint came into her eyes, transforming her whole face. "I like Russians. I'm glad your name is unusual too. I really get mad when they mispronounce mine. Will you be my friend?"

So we became friends. Dorlise had a big brother and a little sister. That Vanya and I didn't get along surprised her. "Why, Henry's the best brother a girl could have," she told me once. "He always looks out for me. He has to because my father's not here."

"Well, my father is," I retorted. "There's something not quite

9

Tamara on the Beach, Tsingtao, China, 1938

right about Vanya, I believe. He is so sneaky about things. And he hits me a lot when no one else is around." It was good to have someone to share things with, to have a friend.

After six years in PAS, I now had to change schools. That for me was the supreme tragedy in my life. That change, along with the alarming news printed in the *Peking Chronicle*, as well as the special radio bulletins, jolted me out of a routine, complacent childhood.

Circumstances beyond my control soon brought my lamented school days to an abrupt end. A year before, Papa had made one special purchase, a small radio shaped like a miniature Gothic cathedral window. That radio completely changed our lifestyle. Instead of going into our own rooms after dinner, we now gathered in the living room around the Philco radio to listen to the local station, the *Voice of Service*. It was our main contact with the outside world.

Lately, the news had become disquieting. Newscasters' words became more solemn and foreboding. China's neighbor, Japan, had become a major source of anxiety and concern.

I must have been too engrossed in my own activities. At that time of my life, politics held no interest for me. World affairs were adults' concerns, not mine. My own private world revolved around my schoolwork, painting, and doing things with Dorlise and my other friends. There were books to read. I had started reading Charles Dickens and Jane Austen. There were bicycle trips to take, some even as far as the Western Hills. Of course, there were piano lessons and exercises to practice. Mother Hildebalde was, contrary to her appearance, a harsh taskmaster! Vanya, however, kept up with world events, reading the *Peking Chronicle* avidly. Such was the business of men!

"You know," he informed me one day, "that we might go to war. Papa is worried about the situation here in Peking."

If Papa was worried, then it had to be serious. Come to think of it, Papa had been preoccupied these past few days. I'd thought it was because of the dwindling student enrollment in his Russian classes. These days few students were interested in studying the language, much less its literature. One evening, when Mama had asked him a question about the situation, he had

11

made it clear to us. I found myself becoming interested, as well as concerned, in spite of myself.

"What, Serioja, is this North China Autonomous Region? Why does China object to its establishment?"

Papa's face had been calm, but his words had sent a chill down my spine. "It's what the Japanese are planning," he said. "They wish to bring all of North China under their control."

"Can they do that?" Mama was confused. "How?"

"Simply by bringing together the five provinces: Chahar, Shansi, Suiyuan, Hopei, and Shantung under their control in one consolidated region." Papa even brought out a map from his study to show us the five provinces.

This kind of talk I didn't like. It was too foreign, too grim and threatening. What Vanya had told me was apparently true, and the Japanese were an enemy to be feared. Strange! I had always thought of them as picturesque people clad in colorful kimonos. The women carried flowered parasols and wore snow white, one-toed socks and lacquered wooden shoes, walking pigeon-toed. And then, the toys made in Japan always broke easily. That I learned from my own experience!

Events moved rapidly after that. On July 8, 1937, the *Peking Chronicle* featured bold, heavy headlines on the front page: "LUKOUCHIAO, CENTER OF CLASH BETWEEN CHINESE AND JAPANESE FORCES!" Lukouchiao was not far from Peking! The Marco Polo Bridge was there. Marco Polo himself had crossed this same bridge in the thirteenth century and had written enthusiastically about it: "When you leave the City of Cambulac (Peking) and have ridden ten miles, you come to a very large river called Pulisangkin. . . . Over this river there is a very fine stone bridge, so fine indeed, that it has very few equals" ("Guide to Peking," *Peking Chronicle Press*, December 1938).

That evening, the *Voice of Service* broadcast news just as grim. The clash had occurred some time around midnight on the seventh of July. Some had accused the Japanese of firing the first shot. Others swore that it was the Chinese. No matter! What did matter was that some soldiers had been killed. This then was the opening for undeclared war!

In August the Japanese attacked Shanghai. A full-scale war had begun in earnest. It was still difficult to believe; yet it was true. It was our new servant, Boy, who had alerted us. Mama had hired him recently, after our other servant had had to leave. Although Mama thought the new fellow lazy, we found him to be likable and friendly.

One day he came up to Vanya excitedly. "Listen," he urged, holding up his hand. Vanya listened, then yelled for me to join them. He and Boy were standing in the central courtyard. They motioned for me to be silent. I stood with them, my heart thumping faster when I heard the sounds. Boom! Boom! The far-off sounds were all too clear. No one could mistake the sound of shells exploding. Both Mother and Father rushed outside. They too listened in startled silence. The sounds of war were near.

"Why would the Japanese want to take over China?"

"They seek power," Papa had answered. "The Chinese and the Japanese have always been enemies. Just like the Russians and the Germans. We Russians don't like the Germans. The Japanese and the Chinese are the same; they don't like each other."

As a child I had learned a ditty Mama had laughingly taught me: *Nemetz-Peretz-Kolbasa; skushal loshad bez hvosta* (German pepper sausage ate a horse without a tail). I'd chant it over and over again while I played, mainly because it rhymed so well. Now I knew its real meaning; although it didn't make much sense, it insulted the Germans. Were the Germans, too, repeating their own offensive ditties about us Russians?

I didn't feel that way about German people. In fact, my parents had quite a few German friends. *However*, I thought to myself, *I don't care for the Japanese. They've been copycats for centuries, copying what the Chinese invented, always attempting to make whatever they copied better than the original.* Father's best friend, Takahashi, had been Japanese, but he had been different. I think that I disliked the Japanese because I had been born in China; I was Chinese even more so than Russian.

Ten days after the Lukouchiao incident, as it was now called, Generalissimo Chiang Kai-shek announced that the final moment had arrived. "We are at war with Japan," he was said to have declared, "and there is no alternative to victory. There is to be no compromise, for if we do that, then our very existence will be compromised."

13

The Japanese proposed peace negotiations, but as expected, the Generalissimo rejected them. It was not too long after hostilities had begun that Peking and Tientsin were captured. Even inside our home we heard the distant cries of *Banzai!* as the triumphant conquerors entered our city.

In spite of the occupation, we still led somewhat normal lives. The only change at first was that Mama had given up her dress salon. In its place she decided to rent the guest house to a single person. The income from room and board would nearly equal what she had earned from sewing. Best of all, she now would have much more time for us.

Our first tenant was a fastidious young German, Herr Hermann Gunther. As Mama described him, he was like a German god—blond, blue-eyed, and muscular. He had been quiet and courteous, and we rarely saw him.

After he left, an American jockey, Mr. Carter, was our next tenant. He asked Mama if he could take his meals with us since he was studying Russian and wished to practice speaking the language with us. Mama agreed, although it became a bit complicated for her. We had to be more formal now in our table settings and our deportment. This formality pleased Papa.

"And also Mama can practice her English," he chuckled.

Kenneth Carter was a man of persistent habit. He insisted on eating corn flakes every morning along with whatever food our cook had prepared. Kellogg's Corn Flakes could be bought only at Slon's, a gourmet store with gourmet prices to match. The corn flakes cost a lot, and Mama had sternly warned both Vanya and me not to ask to eat any. I remember sitting across from Mr. Carter and watching him cut up bananas into his cereal. It looked so tempting compared to my own watery oatmeal. So this was what Americans ate! Lucky people! No wonder all Americans looked so happy and well-fed.

Our next tenant after Mr. Carter was Capt. Paul Viaud, a young French army officer. I gushed about him to Dorlise. "Oh, if you could only see him! He's so tall, and what a handsome man he is in that grey uniform! Dorlise, he has these steely, grey-blue eyes that look at you and just melt your insides! And you should hear him speak with that glorious accent! He sounds just like Charles Boyer!"

Captain Viaud had told Mama that he was a nephew of Pierre Loti, the French novelist. Loti was one of Mama's favorite authors; she liked his sensuous and impressionistic novels set in foreign lands. Poor Dorlise! She visited our house nearly every day in the hope of catching a glimpse of our dashing tenant. No such luck! He was either gone or, if at our house, he was inside his rooms. There was no way we could get him to appear without doing something drastic and creative.

"Maybe I could swoon on his doorstep," Dorlise suggested once. Mama overheard her and laughed.

"You silly girls, he would know what you were up to." She turned serious. "Don't you two try anything wild. That'd be embarrassing to all of us, especially to that poor man."

So we were left to languish in vain. Then other things came up to divert our attention and interrupt our disappointment in not seeing Monsieur Viaud.

During the summer the *Voice of Service* was sponsoring a contest for a new name for the radio station. Whoever submitted the new name would win a small camera. Dorlise, Vanya, and I decided to enter the contest and try our luck at winning. We sat at the dining room table with paper and pencil, thinking up different names.

"How about *China Speaks?*" Dorlise asked.

Too general. We thought of *Peking News,* but that sounded more like a newspaper. Even Mama tried to think of a name. Each suggestion was written down and eventually crossed out.

It was getting dark. Dorlise, unwilling to leave us, stood up. "Darn it! I've got to go. I'll keep thinking at home," she offered. She gave Mama a loud kiss on the cheek. "Bye, all."

"How about the *Voice of Peking?*" I asked. The name had just come to me out of the blue. The minute I said it I knew that it was good. They all looked at me in surprise.

"That's it, Tamdee; it's pur-r-fect!" yelled Dorlise.

Vanya looked at me in envious admiration. "Hey, that's good, Sis. Let's mail it in right away." He wrote the name down on a postcard, signing his name at the bottom. Then we walked Dorlise to the front gates. "Here, Dorlise, please mail this on your way home," Vanya said, giving her the postcard.

Dorlise smiled. "Sure thing, Vanya."

I objected. "But I'm supposed to sign it, not you."

"Tamara!" Vanya stopped me from taking the postcard from Dorlise and patiently explained. "If we win, it'll have been a joint effort since we were all cooperating. Right? So don't worry; you'll get the prize if we win."

Soon I was to find out what "cooperating" with Vanya really meant. On the radio a week later, it was announced that we indeed had won. "It is our pleasure to announce that from now on the official name of this radio station is the *Voice of Peking*. It was, we are happy to announce, Ivan Rublev who submitted that name. As the winner, Ivan, you will be getting your prize in a few days."

We thought that the prize would come in the mail, but it didn't. A few days after the announcement, the doorbell rang. Soon we heard Boy's footsteps running. He entered our living room all out of breath. "There's a young man at the gates. He'd like to see *Shao ye* [the young gentleman]." With a pleased grin he handed my brother a visiting card. Vanya read the name.

"I don't know him," he said puzzled. "What's he look like?" Vanya asked Boy.

"About your age, maybe one or two years older. He says he comes from the radio station."

"Oh," Vanya's face brightened, "show him in, Boy."

"What's his name?" I asked.

Before Vanya could answer me, the door had opened, and Boy was ushering in a young man. He was about Vanya's height, five foot six or seven. His face wore a pinched expression; his pale blue eyes darted about the room taking in all of us and everything else in a rapid survey. Outwardly he was what I would call an ordinary, unremarkable young man until he smiled. Then his whole appearance changed. His eyes sparkled; his cheeks filled out; he made us feel as if we had known him all our lives. At least, that's what I thought when I met him that first time.

"I'm Mischa," his voice was pleasant. There was the slightest trace of a Russian accent in his English. "I've come from the *Voice of Peking* to thank you," he announced, giving my brother a low, exaggerated bow. "Our station would like you to accept this humble gift from us." He held out a small package wrapped in red wrapping paper.

16

"Here's your prize, Mr. Rublev."

I wondered whether Vanya would tell the truth. When would he mention that I was the one who had really thought of the prize-winning name?

"Thanks, thanks a lot," Vanya answered, taking the package and slowly unwrapping it.

I could feel the resentment stirring within me. It wasn't the prize that mattered. I didn't care a hoot for the little camera that he was now so carefully examining. I already had my Brownie Junior that Papa had gotten me last year. It was enough for me, but Vanya could at least have explained that it was I who had thought of the name for the radio station.

The young man looked around towards Mama, who had been sitting on the sofa reading a magazine. She actually was quite aware of what had been going on. I noticed her watching Vanya. Mischa went over to her, offering his hand.

"My name is Mischa Dubinsky," he said gallantly. He bowed. "I want to congratulate you for having such a smart son. He came up with a great name for our station. In fact, his name got everyone's vote."

Mama smiled and withdrew her hand. *Merci,* Mr. Dubinsky."

And that was how we met Mischa, that ingratiating Russian lad who insinuated himself into our family's life, little by little. Reflecting on it now, I am still upset at how we all could have been so naively stupid, innocent, and gullible.

In the days that followed, Mischa regularly visited our home. If neither of us was at home, he unabashedly attached himself to Mother, questioning her about her youth in Russia, how she had met Father, how they came to settle in China.

"He is so romantic," Mama observed at the dinner table. "He wanted to know all about you, Serioja, and me." She had been flattered by this young man's attention.

"I think that you'd better not be so talkative with this Mischa." Father warned, putting down his fork. "I think he is being a little too inquisitive. These days, we can't be too careful." He looked at Vanya, then at me, and finally asked us, "What else has he been asking you two?"

His anxiety didn't surprise me. I knew that Father didn't approve of Mischa. For one thing, Mischa was much too bold. He often roamed about our home, going into any room whenever he wished, not even knocking on the door beforehand. He acted as if he were an actual member of our family!

"He's asked questions about you, Papotchka," answered Vanya. "How many classes you teach; what books you buy; what you do in your spare time. But, Papa, he just likes and admires our family a lot. I know that he does."

"I'm sure he does," answered Papa. "It may be completely innocent. But I'd prefer that you be more cautious in telling him about us. Remember, we know nothing about him except his name; if that really is his name."

"Why not ask him about himself then?" I suggested.

"If you wish. I know you like to go out with him because he's so generous. Have you ever wondered why he is always treating you two, or," Papa paused, "*where* he gets his money?"

Vanya's face reddened. It always did whenever he got upset. He liked Mischa because Mischa was always telling him how intelligent and well-read he was. He also flattered me, but I didn't pay much attention to it. I had a feeling that Mischa flattered everyone for Mischa's own purposes.

"He works hard," Vanya declared, pushing his plate back. "Papa, he does odd jobs, he told me, besides being errand boy for the radio station."

"And he spends half his day at our home," added Father rather abruptly. "Do you realize how often he comes here? Almost every day! If it's not at breakfast time, then it's at lunchtime. I don't mind company, but this is really getting out of hand. Your whole vacation time is being wasted. Instead of reading good books or painting or practicing your piano lessons, you two spend your precious time walking the streets of Peking, going from one ice-cream parlor to the next. Am I not right?"

We both nodded. Mama was silent, her face almost as flushed as Vanya's. Father was right; yet it was difficult to think of giving up our ice-cream trips. Mischa always treated us. He thought nothing of spending money on us. After the first few feeble protests on our part, we had gone right along with him, accepting his treats without question or even mild protests. I felt that Father was being too suspicious about Mischa, but he was absolutely right about our wasting our spare time. Father had always insisted that we use our time wisely.

"We're going out with him today," Vanya remarked. "He told me that he'd like to take us out to this special restaurant. After that, we'll taper off with him. Is that all right, Papa?"

Father approved. "Yes, I think it'll be better all around if you don't see him all the time. Limit yourselves to once or twice a week."

It wasn't as difficult as I thought it'd be. When we were sitting at the newly decorated restaurant, I began to quiz Mischa about his family and life in Harbin. My interest in him and his family surprised him. Usually, he was quizzing us about ourselves and our family.

"There's not much to tell," he said musingly. "My father was killed by the Reds. There're just me and Mama."

"Why did you come to Peking?"

Mischa looked startled; then he shifted around in his seat, turning his head to catch the waiter's eye. "It's time for us to leave," he explained, not bothering to answer Vanya's question. "Let me pay the check; you two just go on outside and wait for me. I'll be along shortly."

His abrupt behavior surprised us. No longer was Mischa the genial host; he had suddenly become an aloof stranger. His face had become pinched and taut. He now looked older than his eighteen years. Vanya and I walked on past other tables towards the door.

"I'm going to the WC," I whispered to Vanya. "You go on." I quickly turned and headed for the restroom behind the beaded curtain. From there I had a clear view of Mischa. He had left our table. Instead of paying the cashier, he walked towards the kitchen. A man dressed in a black Western suit was leaning against the door, apparently waiting for Mischa. I saw Mischa hand the man something, say a few words, then head on out towards the front door. I hurried out to join Vanya.

"Mischa didn't pay the cashier," I whispered breathlessly. "Something mighty strange is going on here. You know he was just talking to a man who looked as if he owned this place."

Vanya scoffed at my amateurish sleuthing, "So what?"

"Well," I replied triumphantly, "the man was Japanese."

Just then Mischa came up to us. "Oh, you're here. I was

19

delayed; sorry." He smiled his dazzling smile. He was now the congenial old Mischa again.

When we got home, Mama was sitting in one of the wicker chairs in the central courtyard. She was waiting for us.

"Ah, Mischa! I'm so glad you have come in with them. I thought that you would. That's why I came out here to wait for you. I thought it would be nice for you to have dinner with us tomorrow night. Ta Shih Fu is making beef Stroganoff, and we'd like to invite your mother and you. It's about time we met your mother, don't you agree?"

Outwardly, Mischa had seemed delighted. However, as I watched him closely, he struck me as being somewhat uneasy and uncomfortable. Perhaps our questions at the restaurant and now Mama's invitation had made him suspicious; I thought I detected a wary look in his eyes. We must have put him on his guard.

He quickly assumed his customary friendliness. "Thank you, it would be a pleasure. I'm sure Mother will be happy to come. She has wanted to meet all of you for some time. Of course, I've told her all about your fine family."

The next evening he was slightly late for dinner, out of breath, and, of course, without his mother. Neither of my parents had actually expected her to come. Mischa himself was dressed in a grey flannel suit and had on a blue silk tie. He looked quite the gentleman! His blond hair was slicked down with pomade, and there was a strong aroma of cologne around him.

"You look nice, Mischa," exclaimed Mother as he came inside. "But where is your mother? We've been so anxious to meet her."

A pained expression came over his face. "When I got home yesterday, Mother was complaining of a terrible headache. You know she gets these migraines often ever since Father died." He shrugged his shoulders. "So here I am, alone as usual."

The dinner was superb. Of course, we all liked Ta Shih Fu's beef Stroganoff, but this time he had outdone himself. When dessert time came, he served us Peking Dust, that special concoction of ground chestnuts with whipped cream.

Mischa wiped his mouth, shaking his head in awe. He turned to Mother. "That was a superb dinner, Madame Rubleva. My congratulations for having such a good cook."

Mama, pleased at the compliment, offered him more. He shook his head and excused himself for not staying longer. As he explained it, he had to be with his mother.

After Mischa left, it dawned on me how much of our time he had been taking up. I was also surprised at how quiet Papa had been all evening. At the dinner table Mischa had asked Mama what she thought of the Japanese occupation of Peking.

"I don't know, Mischa. I'm sorry for the Chinese, of course. Peking is their capital city, and the Japanese took it without a struggle. In other parts of China, however, there is fighting. I hate war, any kind of war, anywhere."

"And you, Professor?" Mischa turned to Father. "What about you? Do you think the Japanese will win?"

Papa had stared at the young Russian. "I can't foresee the future," he had answered coldly, "nor can I predict that which is so uncertain. I, too, hate war. I don't like aggression. However, this struggle is between the Chinese and the Japanese. Since we are neither, I feel it is not up to us to judge them."

I was surprised at Father's answer, knowing how he really felt about the war. He had been broken-hearted about the fate of the Chinese who, as he had reiterated so often, were *his* people. He felt strongly that the Japanese were cruel invaders, plunderers, rapists, murderers. Who wouldn't feel that way? Why was it that he had evaded answering Mischa's questions? He really didn't trust this young man, did he? I looked at Father, studied him carefully, and was saddened by what I saw.

Too often we take our parents for granted, I thought to myself. *We see them merely as figureheads of love, security, and discipline. We don't actually see them as human beings.* This time, as I looked at his tired face, slumped shoulders, and intelligent eyes, I saw Papa in quite another way. I noticed the worn serge suit, faded and ill-fitting. The skin on his face, especially on his chin and neck, now hung loosely; once it had been smooth with hardly a wrinkle. How was it that I hadn't noticed how old he had become? In fact, Papa resembled Alexei Grigorievich, Porfirieffa's old husband who was seventy-five. I quickly did some mental arithmetic. Papa would be fifty-two five days before my own sixteenth birthday on September the seventh. Suddenly I felt a special tenderness for him.

21

Several days later, when I was sitting on my favorite bench in the painted pavilion, I learned part of the answer to Father's weary appearance. I had been deeply absorbed in reading *Pride and Prejudice*. Dorlise had already read it and had suggested that I read it right away. "Tamdee, you'll love it! Wait till you meet Fitzwilliam Darcy, the proud one. The prejudiced one is the beautiful Elizabeth Bennet. It's a terrific love story!"

She had certainly been right. I read through this book faster than I had ever read any other novel, not skipping any lines for fear that I might miss something. So it was some time before I realized that my parents had been talking just outside the pavilion's red gate. They were talking in low, urgent tones. Papa had been firm; Mother, fearful. Quietly, I closed my book, making sure that my bookmark was in place so that I could open it exactly to the page I was reading.

"But I can't do that, Serioja." Mother was not usually frightened, but now she sounded as if she was scared. I bent my head to the wall to hear better. What couldn't Mother do?

"You're a brave woman, Vera. You've got to tell them." Father was emphatic. "We have to do it tonight; tomorrow may be too late."

For a time there was silence. I wished that I could see their faces; yet I dared not show myself. There was serious, maybe even dangerous, trouble brewing.

Mama had pleaded with Father. "Serioja, how can you be so sure? Let's just wait, just one more day."

Papa's voice had been urgent. "No, it has to be done tonight, Boy's night off. We just can't take any chances, Vera."

It was then that I noticed the large pot of geraniums in front of the pavilion. If I crouched down beside it, they wouldn't be able to see me. Carefully I slid off the bench and crawled towards the pot. I scrunched myself real tight and squeezed between the red pillar and the pot. This way I could see them better, but they couldn't see me. It was still twilight, and I could see that Mama was worried as she clutched Papa's arm. There were tears in her eyes. Papa shook her hand free, but his voice was gentle.

"Verotchka," I strained to hear him, "I'm going back to the study now. There's a lot to do, so very much to do." He sighed. "Remember one thing though, no matter what happens, life still is wonderful. Of that there's no doubt." He laughed at that, somewhat sardonically, I thought, watching his unhappy face. Then he bent over to kiss her.

I watched him walk back to his study, a short, sturdy figure, his head held proudly high, his lips tightly closed.

In no time it was after supper. Ta Shih Fu had silently cleared the table, cleaned up his kitchen, and was now gone for the day. Mama, not to my surprise, indicated that we were to remain seated at the table.

"We have some important matters to discuss tonight," she told Vanya and me. I searched Vanya's face to see if he had any inkling of what she was about to say. Apparently not. He just stared at her. Papa sat in his chair, silently waiting, watching Mama intently. Since I had eavesdropped, I had a sinking sensation in the pit of my stomach. Whatever Mama would say would be unpleasant. These days, nothing much was pleasant. It was peaceful in the dining room. Here we had had many happy gatherings. In the good old days, we had joked and laughed around this table. Here, too, we had played charades with Dorlise, and Mama had laughed in delight like a young girl once more. An unfamiliar sadness overwhelmed me as I thought about all those events. Just a few months ago everything had been normal. Now everything was insanely confused. It was whispers, suspicions, thoughts of unforeseen dangers! Why had everything changed so suddenly in such a short space of time?

I stared at the lovely lampshade above our heads. It had cost Mama a lot of money. She hadn't been able to resist its octagonal shape, the royal yellow silk shade with the hand-painted, Ming-blue dragons eternally chasing each other. Below them dangled the yellow fringe that edged most of the lampshades of that time. Yet its subdued, soft glow could not extinguish the lines in my parents' faces nor give us much comfort.

Mother placed a platter of peanuts in the center of the table, then gave me plates for Papa, Vanya, and me. Her voice was low. "We've a great deal to talk about today. Father and I are going to need your help. You two are almost adults now, and we expect you to act accordingly. What Papa has to tell you is very important. Now listen carefully."

Papa had cleared his throat. *Now he's about to lecture,* I

thought to myself. I remember hiding outside the windows of the schoolroom in the back courtyard, peering inside to see the students seated at their desks. Papa, the Professor, was standing on his podium, Napoleon-like, clearing his throat, then sounding out for all to hear; *"Eto stol!"* (This is a table!) Then his students would repeat the phrase. Now, however, it wasn't students listening; it was his wife and two children.

"Mama and I have been mulling things over," he said thoughtfully, toying with a pencil in his right hand. His brown eyes were fixed on Vanya, then shifted to mine, softening their gaze. "We have to share with you what has to be done and why. We are a unit," he straightened himself, sitting upright in his chair, his back ramrod-straight. "We are a family, and more than ever we must now act as one. You have to know what is going on." There was complete silence. I looked over at Vanya. His dark eyes were bright, mirroring his growing inner excitement. I wondered how much of all this he already knew. As for me, I was completely confused. This was a new experience for me, this awesome feeling of an overwhelming fear of the unknown. I listened for Father's next words, hoping that they, at least, would be comforting, telling me that life was once again wonderful, that there was no doubt! However, it was only a fleeting thought; his next words were ominous.

"You know," he proceeded thoughtfully, "that we've had quite a few visitors lately. They're good friends of mine who want me to move to Chungking where it is safer. They tell me that I'm in danger." He smiled. "I don't feel that I am in danger, and I have told them not to worry about me. As you already know perhaps, even Professor Brunnert came here yesterday to warn me."

I remembered seeing the German professor from my perch by the living room window. Ushered in by Boy, he had entered Papa's study but had stayed there only a short time. I also recalled that Papa had been somewhat irritated by his visit. I had heard him mutter *"Chudak!"* to himself later. Why had he called that dignified old man a weirdo?

Papa went on. "I've been warned by professors from Pei Ta, by my students, even by some of the White Russians here. The Japanese want me to join their White House. I told Herr Brunnert that I would join only whenever my body becomes cold and lifeless!" His voice became edgy. "They're cowards, all of them! They're selling their souls to the devil; that's what they're doing. No honesty, no loyalty! Just plain hypocrisy and cowardice, trying to save their own thin skins!" He seemed to have forgotten us; it was as if he were talking to himself, his voice almost inaudible.

"Papa, just what is the White House?" I interrupted.

He reached out to pat my hand. "I'm sorry, *dochenka*. I should explain. The White House is an association organized recently by the Japanese. Its members are those White Russians who will from now on pledge allegiance to the Japanese. In other words, these poor exiles of the czarist regime will be forced to cooperate with the Japanese. Were I to become a member of this exclusive club," his voice turned bitter, "then Vanya would be mustered into the Japanese army to fight the Chinese. How would he like that?" He looked at Vanya, then back at me. "And what would become of you, Tamara? I hate to think! No, I didn't have to think *twice* about my answer to their kind invitation. I'll never join their association. Never!"

"But what are you, Papa? Where do you belong?" I persisted; I was puzzled. If Papa wasn't a White Russian, was he then a Red? A Red meant being a Communist, and I knew for sure that Papa wasn't that. If not Red, what then?

He chuckled, looking at Mama. "I'm a scholar, not a White nor a Red, nor a Pink, if there are any Pinks. White Russians are those who immigrated to other countries to escape the Bolsheviks. Some fled to Europe; many settled in Paris. Others came out east; many settled in Harbin. The Reds are those who fought against the czarist regime. I didn't fight against the czar. I left Mother Russia long before the Revolution. Once I set foot in China, I found the land where I wanted to live. This, I promised myself, was the land where I would work, bring up my children, and be buried in its soil. My life belongs to this city, Peking! I need nothing more than you three who are so dear to me, my books and papers, and my work. I need no White House, no alliance with the Japanese. I need peace so that I can work and study; therefore, I have chosen to remain here. I want to be sure, however, that all of you agree with me. Mama has told me that I am right in my decision. You two are old enough to have your own say in a matter as serious as this. Should I become a member of the White House?"

Both Vanya and I agreed that he shouldn't become a member. I felt terribly important, knowing that Papa wanted my vote; I was now an adult, a voting member of our family!

"Won't the Japanese be angry if you refuse to join their association?" Vanya asked.

Father shook his head. "I doubt it," he answered. "Everybody knows that I'm a scholar. I have never dealt in politics. Of course," he added hastily, "I don't condone what the Japanese have done, warring with China. It'll all be smoothed out eventually. In time the Japanese will retreat, and China will become China once more. It's too big a country to be defeated forever. I, for one, am not worried."

He paused momentarily, then held up his hand for attention. "There is something that Mama and I have to do, and we need your help. It is important that only the four of us know about it, not one other soul." He turned to me. "Not even Dorlise, though she is like a sister to you. Absolutely no one else!"

I knew then that this must be what I had heard Mother and Father whispering about so mysteriously by the red pavilion. I watched Father's face, uneasily feeling that something even more dangerous, more frightening was about to happen. He had looked so sternly first at Vanya, then at me. I sensed his urgency, the importance of what he was about to demand of us.

"I want to emphasize only one thing to you. One word of this to anyone, and we might all of us," again that unfamiliar steely gaze, "be put to death, shot by a firing squad or even worse!"

This couldn't be happening! Not to us! I glanced over at Mama. Her face was pale.

"You know that I've been receiving books and publications from the Soviet Union all these years," Papa paused, as if waiting for his words to sink in.

I had been aware of that. Sometimes I'd get the packages from the mailman and carry them into Papa's study myself. The cardboard wrapping had a peculiar smell to it. The books themselves never looked attractive. The paper on which they were printed was cheap and fragile. There were few illustrations except for indistinct photographs of Lenin or other members of the Bolshevik Party. They weren't books that I wanted to read, although I had seen Vanya take some of them into his room.

"Some of these books may be political in nature. Many of the books may cause me trouble. I had ordered them because I've always been interested in my motherland." He lifted his hand proudly. "I don't have to approve of a political situation, but I do have to know what is going on. Well, to explain it as briefly as I can, the Japanese don't agree with me. The Soviet Union, in their opinion, is a formidable enemy. Books about the Soviet Union or anything printed there—stories, poems, essays, whatever—are all considered to be propaganda and therefore dangerous. Anyone owning such books is automatically a Communist." He said the last word in a menacing way; hearing it, I shuddered.

"But you aren't a Communist, are you?" I dreaded asking, but I felt that I had to know for sure. In my mind Communists were extremely dangerous persons. I hoped Father wasn't one; Communists were shot without question and with no trial!

He quelled my fears. "Of course not," he assured me. Again, he patted my hand. "However, that is not the case here. The important thing is that I have incriminating material in my library. The books that I have ordered from the Soviet Union could label me a Communist in their eyes. I could be in grave danger if they ever decided to search our house, especially since I haven't cooperated with them or joined their White House."

How complicated life was getting to be! What was Father going to do now? Suddenly I wished that we didn't have to live like this. Why couldn't we all be American like Dorlise? Then we wouldn't have to worry about the Japs or our security and safety. All we'd need to have was the American flag on our ricksha or hanging in solemn glory from our gates. The last time Dorlise had come to visit us, she had proudly pointed to the ricksha where that small, powerful flag was waving in the breeze!

"This flag protects me from everything!" she had bragged.

But we weren't Americans; we weren't even genuine Russians, not having even their protection. *How terribly, terribly unfair,* I thought. I hoped that Papa, at least, could keep us safe.

"In short," Papa continued, "we've got to burn the books."

"What about Boy?" Vanya asked. The enormity of the hard work before us was beginning to hit him. Where did Papa plan to do all this? What about the smoke and the ashes?

Mama smiled. She seemed very calm now. I could feel my own heart thumping away. I didn't relish this kind of excitement.

"You know Boy won't be here; it's his day off. That's why we have to do this task tonight. Right away!"

Papa smiled. "Now that you two know what has to be done, let's get right to it. Okay! Into the backyard we go. I've got the books stored in the little courtyard behind my study."

Papa had been very thorough. When we entered the narrow courtyard we saw the books, piles of them, neatly stacked.

"Where are we going to burn them?" It scared me to hear my own voice. Already, I was imagining all sorts of Japanese shapes and shadows looming in the darkening twilight. All of this couldn't be happening to us. It was just a bad dream. But it wasn't a dream; it was all too real! There was Mama grasping the big shovel. She had begun to dig in the flower bed by the acacia tree. Papa held another shovel; Vanya had one too.

"And what am I to do?" I asked in a small voice.

"You're to shred the books. Like this," Mama whispered hoarsely. Her forehead was covered with beads of sweat. Soon the three of them had dug a deep pit in what had once been the flower bed. Luckily, it had been an easy task to scoop out the soft ground.

"Now all of us will start shredding," ordered Papa. "Tear them up right into the pit."

We tore away at the books, one by one. How many there were I couldn't count. All I knew was that my fingers became numb, that I wanted so badly to stop and call it quits, but I couldn't. Mama, Vanya, and Father were shredding, not saying a word. One, two, then the fast ripping of pages. It didn't matter if the books were stories or textbooks; they all had been printed in the Soviet Union. They were Communist! They all had to be thrown down into the pit, be burned, and then buried.

Then Father lit the match. There was a spurt of fire, then a growling roar as the pages burst into flame and glowed in the darkness. There was an eerie silence in the backyard.

"What if Colonel Stilwell's family smells the smoke?" I asked. The Stilwells lived right next door. Sometimes, if their voices were raised, we could even hear their conversations.

"That's a risk we just have to take," Papa stated calmly.

"The Americans are good; they won't denounce us. Don't worry."

What a dirty business this was! We were tired, blackened with soot, smelling of smoke. We were finally done by midnight. Mama told us to go inside and get cleaned up. She and Father would finish the task.

Vanya and I did as she had ordered. Both of us were now too exhausted to do anything but go to bed. I had never seen Vanya look so beat!

"Hey, we did it! We're a team! *That's* what I call cooperation," I teased him. "Why do you look so woebegone?"

"I'm worried about Papa," he told me. "Oh well, you're too young to understand." He waved his hand halfheartedly and went on into his own room.

Even in times like these he could insult me and be condescending. I stuck out my tongue at him and his room and muttered, "Smarty-pants, you think you're something, don't you?"

Once my head hit the pillow, I knew no more. It had been quite a day and night. I was glad that it was over! But it wasn't really over. The next day we had to bury the revolvers; Mama had insisted on that.

In Vanya's room in the back courtyard there was a huge Chinese armoire, black-lacquered with big brass knobs. Here all our winter clothes, blankets, odd bundles of old tablecloths, and pieces of material for future use were stored. At the bottom of all this were two revolvers!

These old revolvers had always intimidated me. I remembered vividly when Papa had first showed them to us. Vanya and I had been very little. He had taken each of us by a hand and had led us into the backroom. "There's something important I have to show you. Listen closely to what I have to tell you."

I must have been nearly five then; Vanya was seven. I felt so important to be getting all this attention from Papa. He was usually too busy to spend much time with us, but here he was taking his valuable time to explain the seriousness of what he was about to allow us to see. At the armoire he unbolted the brass locks, swung open the massive doors, and moved the winter clothing aside until we could see the wooden bottom of the cabinet and the cloth-wrapped bundle resting there. He lifted the bundle out carefully.

"Now," he cautiously unwrapped the cloth, "I want you to look at what's inside!" After what seemed an eternity to me, he had them uncovered. Frightened, I stared at the two revolvers in his hands. They looked heavy and old; on the carved surfaces was some rust. Papa handled them reverently as he showed them to Vanya and me. "These belonged to my brothers," he explained in a low voice. "Mischa and Kolya were officers in the army of Czar Nicholas II. They are both dead, and the revolvers are mine now."

He gently took my hand in his, guiding it over one gun. "See how hard it is? Well, Tamara, this gun can kill. It's a very, very dangerous thing. It is loaded. That means that there are bullets in its chambers. If you pull on this," he pointed to the trigger, "you can kill a person. Do you understand?"

He then looked at Vanya and told him too how the revolvers operated. When he had finished, he warned us firmly, "I want you two always to remember that you are *never*, I repeat, *never* to touch these revolvers. If you do, you could kill, either yourself or, worse yet, someone else."

Father had never been so adamant or severe. He really convinced me that day. Ever after, when I passed the armoire, I gave it a wide berth and regarded it with fear lest my very breath might set off those hidden revolvers.

Like all the other things that had happened to us so rapidly, we now had to do away with those fearful weapons. The very next night, we buried them in the little back courtyard behind Papa's study.

Now that all of the damaging evidence had been disposed of, we felt that we could relax. Vanya returned to PAS. I had had to quit the convent school because Father could no longer afford to pay the tuition.

"You can stay home," Papa had told me. "Tsinyushka will teach you how to write Chinese characters, a much better exercise for you instead of memorizing useless misinformation. He's an excellent calligrapher."

Tsinyushka was Father's male secretary; he'd been with him ever since I could remember. Father had taught him Russian; English he had learned on his own. He was like a member of our family—eating with us at times, staying up late with Father to work at compiling the Russo-Chinese dictionary. I don't know how Father had found him, but suffice it to say the Tsinyushka was Father's man Friday. Other servants came and left. Mr. Tsin (his real name) stayed on, ever loyal, devoted, hardworking. In my mind's nose, I can still smell that rancid Chinese paste he always used to affix Chinese characters alongside the Russian words they defined.

I was relieved not to have to go back to the convent school. Dorlise was envious when I told her. "God, Tamdee," she blasphemed, "I wish Mother would let me stay home. I hate to go to school these days. Except for Huie, it's so darn boring. God bless him!"

"Huie" was that self-same Mr. Huit, the new math teacher at PAS. According to Dorlise, all the girls still had a crush on him. Even she did!

"Oh, Tamdee, he's so good looking!" she moaned. "Can you just picture him? Dark brown hair, blue eyes, and just perfect features!" Her eyes were swimming in ecstasy. I tried to see him with her words. She gushed, "He looks Irish, so romantically, desperately handsome!" It was impossible to talk to her about anyone else. Mr. Huit was on her mind, night and day and even at noon.

While she dreamed of Mr. Huit, I brushed away with my *mao bi*, forming Chinese characters, much to Mr. Tsin's delight. "She will become a great calligrapher," he assured my parents. Father was quite happy with my progress.

At times I felt that I was suspended somewhere in limbo, not really here nor there nor anywhere. Everyone else had a goal in life. Dorlise had classes to attend; Vanya did too. Papa had students to teach, even if no new ones enrolled. Mama had the house to look after as well as us. My goal? I was really doing nothing. Writing characters with Chinese brushes was fun, but it wasn't getting me anywhere. Everybody else was doing something constructive except me. I didn't even want to think about my future. Formerly, I had had many dreams. I would marry a Yankee-man some day. Yes, some day that handsome American would appear. He and I would travel everywhere: Mongolia,

Tibet, Manchuria, perhaps Siberia and Russia. Finally, he would take me to his home in America to live. Nowadays, I couldn't even dream anymore.

I realized that Dorlise too would eventually return to America. Others, except for my Chinese friends, would also go back home. They had their lives to live. Vanya would be graduated from PAS and would likely go either to Yenching or to Tsinhua, the two good colleges here in Peking. And what would I be doing? I couldn't even finish at PAS or the Sacred Heart Convent school! Evidently, my parents hoped that I would marry eventually. That was it. The whole idea was wholly depressing.

Enough about the future! I had to think about the present. These days we didn't go out much. With the Japanese occupying Peking, it was no longer the same. Besides, it wasn't safe, especially since our family was under no country's protection.

It was Dorlise who kept us well informed. "Boy, you should see Hatamen Street right now," she'd exclaim as she burst into the living room, out of breath and excited. "Mama, you should see the geishas; they're painted something awful!"

I had seen them whenever I rode my bike through the city. They sat in shiny new rickshas, wearing colorful kimonos. They certainly made quite a sight in their carefully combed coiffeurs, their stark white faces, almost masklike, and their dainty feet encased in lacquered sandals. They all looked alike to me, almost unreal in their doll-like beauty. I had read about them, but even those descriptions didn't do them justice.

Indeed Peking had changed. It was heartbreaking to see how it had changed. Soldiers strutted everywhere. Ugly, grim-faced, arrogant, despicable conquerors, they frightened anyone who dared cross their paths. How I hated them! I couldn't help it. My heart went out to my Chinese neighbors whom I now no longer saw. Chinese house gates remained closed. Happy pig-tailed children no longer played hopscotch in the streets; old men carrying bluecloth-covered bird cages no longer sauntered by for their daily evening stroll. Housewives, some bound-footed, others more modern with their bigger, clumsy feet, did not stop anymore to pass the time of day with their neighbors. No longer did we hear nor see those familiar, multivaried sounds and sights of Peking.

I really didn't know too much about the Japanese. The one Japanese we did know had been Mr. Takahashi, and he had been Father's good friend.

Papa had met him many years ago when he had first arrived in Peking. Both men had been students then. Father had helped him with his Russian; Takahashi had taught Father Japanese. Through the years, they had remained good friends and had kept in touch with each other. Then one evening Father had read in the paper that Takahashi had died.

The Japanese who paraded on the streets of Peking were of a different breed. Gradually, Peking streets emptied. The Chinese women disappeared along with the children. Finally, only men who had no alternative walked their usual routes, their eyes alert, ready to face the arrogant enemy, unwillingly bowing their heads in humiliation and shame.

Everything had changed! Now the Japanese flag flew from the rooftop of the Chen Kwang Theater where once Dorlise and I had watched Johnny Weissmuller court Maureen O'Sullivan on film. How I detested that blood-red symbol on the white background! For me it portrayed China's sorrow.

Before we even realized it, the facades of the stores had changed. I could no longer read the inscriptions over their entrances. The characters were now Japanese, not Chinese. Peking had become a silent city in stark contrast to the noisy, bustling metropolis whose gaily clad inhabitants strolled by on thoroughfares or unpaved *hutungs*, bowing to each other with their inbred courtesy, always ready to take time out to stop to talk. Even the familiar beggars who lined the walls of each bystreet had moved away. Only the mangy, half-starved dogs roamed the *hutungs*, unafraid of friend or foe, roaming around, always waiting to find the scrap that wasn't there.

Mischa too appeared to have abandoned us. Ever since that day when Mama had invited his mother to have dinner with us and she hadn't come, he had visited us less frequently and finally his visits ceased altogether. I can't say that we missed him.

Now winter was coming. Summer had been hot and dry. A windy autumn had followed, and the first snowflakes had fallen in November, ushering in the cold.

It was Vanya whose schedule seemed virtually unchanged. Every weekday morning he rode his bicycle to Kan Mein Hutung. There were different teachers. Perhaps he had a little more homework, but that was it. By dinnertime he was usually done, ready to join us by the little radio, to huddle around with us, to listen to the latest news.

Papa didn't look good, but he had been like this ever since the Japanese had taken over Peking. He was preoccupied, silent, and unlike his usual, happy self. He had lost weight, but it didn't seem to bother him. He now no longer rode to the university. The only class that he taught was in the schoolroom in our backyard. Just a few Chinese students came to learn Russian. Eventually, even those dropped out, one by one.

Mother let our amahs go. We now had only Ta Shih Fu and Boy to help us. Ta Shih Fu cooked; Boy served. Boy was a poor servant, and I thought it would be only a matter of time before he too would be let go.

Fortunately, Paul Viaud still lived in the guest house and took his meals with us. That enabled Mother to pay the servants, and we were surviving. Dr. Ferguson, our kind American landlord, suggested that Father forgo the rent.

"I know that times are hard, Professor," he had said one day. He didn't want to make Father feel obligated, but he knew our situation. "When all this is over, you can repay the rent."

The winter, when it came, was a cold, hard one. Vanya was home again. It was Christmas vacation time. Our thoughts were often on the coming New Year, hoping that this time it would be a better one, bringing with it hope, peace on earth, and good will to men.

2

The Arrest

Recalling and reliving those incredible events that occurred on the seventeenth of December and the days that followed is still difficult for me. That night is as clearly etched in my memory as if it had happened yesterday. The ugly, gnawing gut-wrenching fear has disappeared, but the pain will always be with me. I try not to dwell on those times since they now belong to a long-gone past and should be laid aside to rest. For one last time I shall brace myself to endure the stress of bringing out into the open those sharply etched pictures for all to see.

In the beginning that evening was much like the others before it. The routine we followed these days was dull but pleasant. The weather had turned colder. The air had an icy chill, and it felt good to be inside the warmth of the living room. In happier times before the occupation, it was the time to plan for Christmas; to think of the Christ child; to buy gifts; to decorate the house. There definitely wouldn't be a tree, not after that night when the candle fell causing the fire. Soon the snow would be piling up, and Vanya and I would get out our sleds to pull each other through the two backyards, going in and out through the old moon gate. Then we'd have a worn gray, sloshy railroad path in the snow. What fun we'd have! Dorlise would join us there as she had in the past. Maybe we could make a skating rink again! Last year we had made one by throwing buckets of water in the corner of the farthest backyard. Since the water froze quickly, we soon did have a rink. At PUMC the rink was often crowded, and the ice had cracks that often caused stumbles and falls. We preferred our own homemade rink.

Now Papa was shoveling more coal into our big, cast-iron Russian stove. I liked to watch him do this, to see the tiny red sparks flying around, crackling noisily, flying crazily upward like minute lightning bugs! With the stove door open we could feel the heat from the red-hot coals. How beautiful and comforting those orange, blue, and yellow flames were, darting in and out like so many forked tongues!

The *Voice of Peking* was now broadcasting its classical music hour. Ta Shih Fu had cleared the dinner table and left for the day. This was really our favorite time, when each family member settled down comfortably to his favorite task. Papa remained at the dining room table to work on his dictionary or lectures. I usually painted at this time, sitting in Mama's place across from Papa. Mama always made herself comfortable on the couch near the radio. She loved the music that was broadcast at this time and wanted nothing to distract her from it. She was totally absorbed while listening. I enjoyed watching her because she looked so beautiful and serene. Her head rested on the back of the sofa, eyes closed, a smile of contentment on her face. Whatever pictures she was seeing in her mind's eye must have been glorious to make her look so lovely. Vanya was usually immersed in a *National Geographic*. Imaginatively, he had already traveled around the world through the pages of this magazine.

This one evening Ludwig von Beethoven's music mesmerized us. Even now when I listen to his *Moonlight Sonata*, I can't help thinking of that fateful December night. The piano music had begun so softly, repeating the notes, running and flowing, almost like rippling waves at low tide. The first movement lulled me into a sense of tranquility; I was completely at peace. Then the tempo increased; the second movement became agitated. The music became louder and more brusque. Suddenly, almost in time with the crescendo came the piercing sound of the doorbell waking us from our euphoric states. Mother jerked her head, a look of angry annoyance crossing her face.

"Who can it be at this hour?" she looked questioningly at Father.

Looking as puzzled as Mother, Papa shook his head. Next we heard Boy running and his soft knock on the living-room door.

When I opened it, he stood there all out of breath.

"Xiao Jie [Miss], I'd like to speak to Lao Ye," he said excitedly. I thought his face unusually flushed, but it could have been from the cold. I could feel that icy wind rushing past me from the outside.

"Come in, Boy," Mother said. "There's no need to leave the door open."

Boy entered hesitatingly. There was something awkward about his behavior, as if he knew something we didn't know. He saw Papa at the table and went over to him.

"Lao Ye [Old Gentleman], there is a young man who says he's from the university. He says he wants to ask you about a Russian dictionary."

Papa got up from his chair, slipping on the jacket that was hanging over the back of his chair. "Show him into the study," he directed.

The music again became soft and peaceful, but our listening mood had been broken. Why should someone come at nine o'clock in the evening to inquire about a dictionary? It all seemed strangely unusual. Had it been someone whom Papa knew, it might make sense, but, no, apparently this was a stranger.

Just then Father came back into the living room. Again, the cold air entered the room with him. It must be really chilly outside, I thought. How lucky we are to be inside in the warmth and security of our home. Papa sat on the sofa; he was upset.

"Who was it, Papotchka?" asked Vanya, laying down his magazine.

"Just some fellow from Tung Bei [the northeast]. I don't know why, but people from that part of the country seem more audacious. He comes from another stock of Chinese. He was really insolent to me, almost rude!" He shook his head in disbelief. "You know what he wanted? To see if I sold dictionaries! Unbelievable!"

Mama smiled, patting his hand. "Relax, Serioja, and let's enjoy the music. There are all kinds of people in this world of ours. Don't let a person like him bother you. Maybe he's planning to take Russian lessons and just wanted to see what you were like."

"I wouldn't want him for a student," Papa answered. He was

going to say something more, but again there was the bell, three loud, ear-piercing rings that shattered the silence of that cold winter night.

Father rose from the sofa, really annoyed this time. "What in God's name is that fellow up to?" He hurried to the front door. He had hardly touched the knob when the door flew open!

We heard them then—the running footsteps. There were many of them, almost like an army, running on the walkway of the front courtyard, hard soles on hard cement. They came closer, through the moon gate, on into the central courtyard, milling around in the glassed-in veranda, and finally all converging before the front door of the main house, the door that had burst open just as Father was about to open it himself.

Before we even realized what was happening, our two rooms were swarming with men. *They're Chinese,* I noticed to my relief, *not Japanese.* It's strange that that's what came into my head at that moment. Some had on the black and white uniform of the police; others wore western clothing; a few had on the long Chinese robes. Some looked like students.

I watched Father's face, unable now to take my eyes off him. He had turned pale, but outwardly he seemed calm and in control of himself. He had one arm around Mother's waist; Mama seemed calm and unafraid at this unexpected invasion of our privacy. Vanya and I moved closer to our parents; their nearness made us feel more secure. Vanya acted as if he too weren't afraid. Was I the only coward in the family? My knees felt as if they were going to buckle under me at any moment.

I heard Father's whisper to Mama, "That student who came before is here. He's the one in the long blue gown, the tall one." I followed Papa's gaze and saw a young man talking to another Chinese who seemed to be the one in authority. The student wore his hair rather long for a Chinese. It was combed straight back without a part. His cheekbones were high and prominent, but it was his eyes that caught my attention. They were large, almond-shaped, but the insolence and hate that I saw in them scared me. I had never before seen a Chinese show his feelings so openly nor stare so brazenly. I felt that he looked familiar. Where was it that I could have seen him previously? Where had it been? Where? Then I realized that he looked like Boy. This man and Boy could have been brothers they looked so much alike. Boy's eyes were like this man's, but Boy's weren't filled with so much hate.

Watching them while they surveyed the four of us, I started to look around the rooms. The Chinese in the robes had formed a circle around us; behind them were the students; then the police on the outside. To my horror I caught sight of the hateful olive-drab uniform of a Japanese soldier. He must have been lurking in the background. Apparently Mama and Papa hadn't seen him yet. Was there more than one? I couldn't tell because so many people were milling around us.

Ironically, the radio kept on playing. The *Moonlight Sonata* was at the end. The music had just risen to the powerful notes of the coda when someone turned off the radio. Except for the muffled shuffling of feet and my own beating heart, there was a cold, deadly silence.

An older Chinese, the one wearing the gray, padded gown and Western hat, seemed to be the one in authority. It was he who stepped out of the crowd, approaching Father.

"We shall have to ask that the four of you go into that room." He pointed towards Mama's bedroom. "We have some things to take care of."

As we filed into the bedroom, there was already someone there—a policeman who had moved a chair near the door. He was to guard us! Were we now prisoners? What had we done?

The policeman motioned my parents to sit on one bed. As I moved to sit next to Mama, he held up his hand. "You and your brother sit across on that other bed." Although his voice was gruff, I didn't think he looked too frightening.

"What is this all about, do you know?" I whispered to Vanya. "What are they going to do to us?"

The policeman raised his head. He had begun reading a magazine. Although I had whispered, he had heard it.

"*Bu yao shuo hua. Bu xu!*" (Don't talk. You mustn't!) he growled. Papa looked at me sympathetically but said nothing.

Occasionally I felt an involuntary shudder go through my whole body. Now it seemed as if I couldn't stop shaking. My teeth chattered, clicking together. Vanya took off his leather jacket and put it over my shoulders. I was grateful to him, but it didn't stop my shivers.

Now Father was whispering in hushed tones. The policeman was too absorbed in his reading to notice. "Should they take me, and I have a feeling they might, you must go straight to Dr. Ferguson and tell him everything." He looked directly at Vanya. "Dr. Ferguson is the only one who can help us now."

Mama put her arm around him. "It'll be all right, won't it, Serioja?" She sounded worried. "What are they doing out there? There seems to be so much activity."

"They're probably searching through my books and papers," Father sighed, looking down at his hands. "I honestly don't know what they want or what they're looking for, but apparently it's something that I have." He stopped talking, listening now to sounds coming from outside. "Can you hear someone digging? Isn't that the sound of a shovel in the backyard?"

We froze, listening. It did sound like something scraping the ground.

"It could be the wind," Mama surmised. "It's very windy outside. Have you noticed how cold it's gotten?"

"If they dig in the dirt...?" I was going to mention the books we had buried a few weeks ago, but Mother's stern glance effectively stopped me in midsentence. Father nodded, smiling at me as if he had read my mind.

"The ground's too hard and frozen," he whispered. "Don't worry about that."

The policeman looked up at us, then seeing that we were quiet, resumed his reading.

Although my parents' outwardly calm behavior made me feel less apprehensive, I still couldn't stop shaking. My ears were concentrating on catching every bit of noise that came from outside the bedroom. I thought there were steps coming from all directions. I heard books being thrown on the floor; furniture being shoved back and forth. Occasionally, I heard digging. Everything was beginning to close in on me. It was as if I were caught up in a nightmarish whirlwind! It gradually dawned on me that this was all too real. It was no dream.

It was just too much for me. An uncontrollable urge to cry and to scream my head off overwhelmed me. I gulped down my saliva, feeling the lump in my throat growing larger till I was afraid that I'd choke. I kept swallowing faster, sucking in my cheeks to keep from making even one sound! I couldn't do this to the family; I couldn't let them know that I was the one who was scared to death! But the tears welled up in the corners of my eyes, blurring my sight, and rolled on down my cheeks. Still, I kept shaking. I blinked back the tears. I lectured myself sternly. *Tamara, take hold of yourself! You're no cry baby! Besides, everything will turn out all right.* That was Papa's motto, especially whenever things started to go awry. I closed my eyes, repeating that motto to myself again and again, silently, in my thoughts and with my lips.

The clock on the dresser sounded the quarter hour. *What time is it?* I wondered. I looked at the dial hand. It was already a quarter to four. It was nearly daybreak! If it really was that time, I should be sleepy, but I was wide awake, and so were all the others.

Suddenly there was no more noise. The silence was even more frightening and ominous than the varied sounds we'd been listening to throughout the night. Then we heard someone talking in a low voice. Again the silence! Then there was a sharp rap at the bedroom door.

At the signal, the policeman rose quickly, motioning for us to do likewise. *"Lai!* [Come!]" he ordered, opening the door wide for us all to go through.

The Chinese in the Western hat was standing in the center of the room. There were probably fifteen men around him. The others must have gone, or were they lurking in the courtyards?

"We are sorry to intrude upon your family, Professor," the Chinese apologized. He bowed his head in a brief salutation.

"My dear," Father spoke, turning to Mother, who was holding on to his arm, "this gentleman is Mr. Hsu, the prefect of police. I'm sure you have heard me speak of him."

I marveled at Mama's composure. She inclined her head to one side, and the shadow of a smile crossed her face. "I had a feeling that we had met before," she said calmly. "It must have been at the university, a faculty tea perhaps?"

The prefect nodded. "It must have been. I couldn't forget such a charming lady!" Then the tone of his voice changed abruptly; he had business to attend to! The exchange of courtesies was over and done with. Now Mr. Hsu took charge. "This is not a serious matter, Madame." He had been speaking in Russian; now he reverted to Chinese for the benefit of the others. "We've got to clear up some things and feel that it would be best if you, Professor Rublev, accompany us to the police station."

When I heard that, my legs grew weak. Vanya's face turned white. His eyes, peering out from behind those hideous glasses, stared worriedly at Papa. Father, however, showed no sign of alarm. He bowed to the prefect, his face a pleasant mask.

"I shall be pleased to accompany you, Mr. Hsu. However, could I not wait until morning so that I can make suitable arrangements for my wife and children?"

Mr. Hsu paused. "There's no need of that, sir." He raised his voice slightly. "You need only to answer a few questions."

The circle forming around us grew smaller, hemming in the four of us tightly. I could feel the tension in those around us. What was going to happen now? Was Papa to be arrested? Was this all because Father had refused to join the White House? Or was there some other reason for this surprise invasion of our home?

Mother's behavior changed when Mr. Hsu insisted that Father go to the police station. She tightened her hold on his arm. "If he goes, then I too shall go with him."

Mr. Hsu hadn't expected this. Nor had the others. Wives were usually submissive and obedient not only to their husbands but also to men in general. He stared at Mother. Vanya and I did too. How well I knew that cold look in Mama's eyes! It was the same as when I had lied about using her sewing machine. There was a determined firmness not only in her eyes but also about her clenched mouth, her straight back, her feet ready to move in step with Father's. The police prefect shrugged his shoulders.

Mother also shrugged hers. "Then there is no problem. I shall go with the professor. The children will see us in two days. That is right, isn't it?"

Mr. Hsu nodded curtly.

"Then I take you at *your word*." She emphasized the last two words. If he were an honorable man, he would not want to lose face in front of all these people.

Mr. Hsu was silent. She had called his bluff. He bowed. "You may come with your husband," he conceded.

Father had listened silently to this interchange. With his left hand he reached into his trousers' pocket, took something out, and handed it to Vanya. "It's all I have with me," he said apologetically.

Mr. Hsu reached for Vanya's hand. "Let me see what your father gave you." Vanya opened his fist. In his palm lay three crumpled Chinese dollar bills. Mr. Hsu appeared satisfied.

But I wasn't! I had to do something for Father and Mother! I broke through the circle of men and ran into the dining room. A few followed me. In one buffet drawer Ta Shih Fu kept our bread. I opened the drawer, found part of a loaf, and hurriedly wrapped it in a napkin. Then I ran back to Father.

"Here, you might need this." I thrust it into his hand, giving old Hsu a scornful look. Amazingly, my shivers had ceased, and I no longer was afraid. "It's bread for my parents. Is that all right with you?" The Chinese nodded.

When I put the bread in Papotchka's hands, I hugged him hard. "I love you both so much, Papa." I turned to Mother, hugging her tight. "Don't worry about us," I whispered. "We'll talk to Dr. Ferguson as soon as it turns light."

Mama blinked away her tears. "I'm crying only because I have to leave you, but I do have to go with Serioja. You do understand, don't you, Tamarotchka?"

"Of course, Mamotchka, we love you so." I knew tears were in my eyes, but I wasn't going to break down in front of these hateful men, I told myself firmly. Absolutely not!

Vanya hugged them too, whispering words of encouragement. Then the men hastily surrounded our parents and herded them out the door. We could see only the tops of their heads as they went out into the front courtyard through the red pavilion. Again there was an uneasy silence except for shuffling feet and the sound of the front gates being unbarred.

Out in the street a long black car was waiting, its motor idling. Hsu led my parents towards it, seating them in back. Then two figures climbed in to sit on either side of them. I could see the profile of the one nearest the window. He had a beard and then with a pang of fear I saw the olive drab cap on his head. He was Japanese!

Then Mr. Hsu got into the front seat beside the driver.

Miraculously, the other men had disappeared. Vanya and I stood on the front steps straining our eyes to catch a last glimpse of our parents. It was still too dark. As the car sped away, we saw only the silhouette of their heads. Soon the car became a tiny black dot and turned the corner. Somewhere a rooster crowed.

We stood there silently, staring out into the empty street, hemmed in on either side by brick walls. At intervals red or black wooden gates disrupted this gray facade. Behind those walls and gates families were sleeping soundly, unaware of our misfortune. We were about to turn back into the front gate pavilion when Vanya looked to the left.

"Tamara, look!" He pointed down the street.

I strained to see. It was still dark, but I could just make out the tiny white speck disappearing in the distance.

"That's Beba!" I cried. There was no mistaking that bushy tail and those short legs, running as if his very life depended on it, running away from our house. Beba was our dog, and of all the dogs that we had had in our family he was the special one, all white, a mixture of several species, an indeterminable breed. Pure mutt, Mama would say, but he had *charisma*. He was sly as a fox, wise as an owl, lovable as a child. In short, he was the fifth member of our family. With the coming of the police and all the tumult that had followed, we hadn't even thought of him, much less missed him.

Now that we were alone and had seen that familiar white blur, we realized what must have happened. With men streaming in and out the front gates, he must have sneaked outside to satisfy his curiosity. Just like Beba to sniff things out for himself! The street had always lured him before, but it was always a harsh "No! No!" Now with no one to watch over him, he could do his own investigating. After all that had happened, we couldn't lose Beba too.

"I'm going after him," Vanya shouted as he sprinted down the steps, two at a time. "Don't bar the gates until I come back." He ran down the street, pulling up his jacket collar. Beba had turned his white puff of a head around. Seeing Vanya coming behind him added speed to his feet. I knew that that imp of a dog was laughing to himself, his pink tongue out, his slanting, almost human little eyes blinking with amusement.

"Darn that dog!" I vented my anger in oaths. "Darn that darned dog!" I hoped that Vanya could catch him. I wanted so much to feel that warm, wriggly body close to me, to feel his tongue lick my hand. Oh, Beba, please come back. Vanya too had now disappeared from sight. I felt abandoned, cold, and alone. I didn't want to go back to the empty house by myself. All I could do was just stand there on the top step, seeing the grayness of the dirt on the street, the gray brick walls, and the awakening winter sky. I was empty inside, devoid of any feeling whatsoever, completely numb!

Then I heard the sound, just one soft footstep followed by another, right behind me. Turning around, I saw a Chinese policeman with a revolver in the holster suspended from his white belt.

"What are you doing here?" I demanded. My gruff, coarse voice surprised me. I spoke as I felt, cold and unfeeling.

The man's shrewd eyes appraised me. His voice was low, strictly impersonal. "I'm here to guard you and your brother and your home," he stated. He made no other moves, just stood there. I decided then to remain exactly where I was until Vanya returned with or without Beba.

Subtly the grayness of the sky faded. Even in my despondent state I couldn't help observing the changes going on above me. The sky had suddenly transformed into a light blue cover with slender tongues of pink and yellow scattered about. *How absolutely clean and glorious those colors are,* I thought to myself. *How can God, if He really is omnipotent, how can He make everything else so ugly? How can He make human beings hurt each other? Today He has made this wonderful dawn. Why couldn't He have made MY dawn today as beautiful as yesterday's when I was happy, safe, and secure with my parents in our home?* I heard the door of the servants' quarters open quietly. Through the corner of my eyes I glimpsed another policeman coming out to join the first. Then there were at least two of them! No one spoke a word. The three of us just stood there, motionless. A half hour must have gone by. It was even lighter now, but not yet daybreak.

Suddenly, there was Vanya coming around the corner. What a welcome sight! In his arms was a fluffy white bundle with a continuously wagging tail. He soon reached the front steps. "Whew!" he exclaimed, all out of breath. "What a chase this imp led me on!" Then he saw the men in uniform. His voice changed. "What are they doing here, Tamara?" he asked angrily. We mounted the steps, bypassing the guards.

"They're here to take care of us, dear brother," I informed him sarcastically. "They're staying in there with Boy!"

"With Boy?"

"Yep, with Boy," I answered as cheerfully as I could, but I certainly didn't feel that way. I stopped in my tracks; a thought had struck me. "You know, after that Tung Bei student saw Papa the first time, Boy disappeared. That's strange, isn't it? I'll bet you *anything* that he's with them."

The minute we passed the open door of the servants' quarters we noticed Boy, his hunched-over form sitting at the table by the window. Someone else was sitting across from him. Both of them were so wrapped up in their conversation that they didn't notice us. I tried to catch a glimpse of the stranger's face, but Boy's body was in the way.

The policemen had followed us back into the gate-pavilion. They now took up the heavy wooden log and slid it into the brass rings at either end of the closed gates. To me it seemed strange that men who didn't even belong here were barring our front gates. Boy should have been doing that task, but Boy was busy with someone else.

Whom were these policemen really protecting? Us two? I laughed to myself. From what were they protecting whom? The policemen had walked over to the open door of the servants' quarters. Without even glancing at us they stepped in and shut the door. Vanya and I walked down the steps into the front yard where the poplar trees stood silent in their lonely vigil.

We would have gone straight towards our own rooms in the main house had we not noticed the light in the guest house. Paul Viaud, as usual, had gone to Tientsin for the weekend. I myself had caught a glimpse of his tall, strident figure leaving with his canvas valise to get into the ricksha waiting at the front gates. I remembered that the guest house had been dark when our parents were being escorted to the street by Mr. Hsu.

"I'm going to find out what is going on in there," Vanya said.

He was irritated, to say the least! "Nobody should be in there."

I followed him up the steps into the vestibule that led to Paul's living quarters. An uneasy feeling came over me. Looking at Vanya's face, I realized that it was now the two of us against the world. It was not a pleasant thought.

To our surprise we found the white French doors wide open! Even more surprising were the three figures sprawled over the living-room chairs, their feet brazenly resting on Mama's rosewood tea table. The student from Tung Bei was there. There was no mistaking that evil face!

We entered the room. The students paid no attention to us; they didn't even shift in their seats.

Vanya surprised me with his outburst. "Get out!" he shouted. His eyes flashed with anger. He looked at the trio scornfully. His voice was harsh, icy. I sensed his outrage. He then took a step towards the Tung Bei student. "Get out. You have no right here! Out of this house! Right now!"

They stared at us insolently, looking us up and down, as if we were things on sale. From inside his robe the Tung Bei student took a pack of cigarettes. He slowly withdrew one, not taking his eyes off Vanya's face. With a malevolent smile, he took out a matchbox, withdrew a match, slowly and deliberately taking his time. During all these elaborate motions, he stared unwaveringly at Vanya. He then struck the match on his shoe sole, lit the cigarette, and inhaled and exhaled slowly. With a quick movement he flung the dead match onto the carpet, inhaling again with a smug, self-satisfied look. He blew a cloud of thick, blue smoke directly at Vanya, watching his reaction with amusement. Poor Vanya! Involuntarily, he tried to stop coughing, but he couldn't. He had inherited Mama's allergies to different things, and of all things, cigarette smoke was for him one of the worst.

This humiliation infuriated him even more. Choking back his coughing, he stepped towards them. He calmed his voice and again warned, "I told you before to get out of here immediately. Otherwise," he looked in the direction of the front-gate pavilion, "I shall have to ask the police to put you out."

At that, the students merely laughed. My heart sank.

Then, all of a sudden, the Tung Bei student rose. I hadn't realized how tall he was! He looked around the room, then rested

47

his eyes on Vanya. The others, following his lead, got up too.

He walked towards the French doors. As he passed us, he lifted his hand, clenched it into a fist, and shook it in Vanya's face. He spat on the floor, then spoke softly. "You haven't heard the last from us, you *Kung Chang Tang!*"

Vanya slammed the French doors shut when they left. I shuddered, still feeling their evil presence even after they had gone.

"What did they call us, Vanya? What does *Kung Chang Tang* mean?"

Vanya looked out towards the front yard. It was empty; the men were gone. "Tamara, it's bad," his voice broke. "He called us Communists!"

"But we aren't Communists. Papa said so." I protested.

"But *they* think we are. If that's what they believe, then Father is in de–e–e–p trouble."

With heavy hearts we walked back towards our own living quarters. Naturally, the old Russian stove had gone out long ago. It was frigid inside the house, almost as cold as outside. The stove, however, was the least of our worries. What did dismay us were the ugly reminders of what had gone on during the night. We realized now that while we had been imprisoned in the bedroom, the police had been busily searching for something. What it could have been we had no idea. Father hadn't known either. I remembered having asked him.

"It must have been something important that they were looking for." Vanya must have read my mind.

The rooms were all in shambles! The police had been quite thorough, to say the least. Over Mother's prized Imperial dragon carpets they had scattered piles of books, magazines, and papers. Sheets from Father's dictionary that he and Tsin had labored over for years were wildly strewn all over; some were even in Ta Shih Fu's kitchen!

Poor Papa! I couldn't help thinking. Again, hot, scalding tears streamed down my cheeks. "How could they ever do that to him?"

The cabinets, the cupboards in the dining room, all had their doors and drawers open, their contents lying all over the floor! Father's study truly looked like a disaster area, as if a

48

deadly typhoon had razed it. His ceiling-high bookcases had been completely emptied. The books lay on the floor; some were open, their pages showing the traces of muddy footprints where the men had trampled. Papa's desk had been rifled, the drawers lying empty on the floor.

Only the three wooden figures, the ancient carvings of the Chinese war gods, still stood in their places on top of one bookcase. Their mask-like brown faces grinned with a horror that matched our own!

Vanya shook his head in disbelief. "How could they have done this?" He looked around, downcast. "I wouldn't know where to start cleaning up this mess, would you?"

"No, but I do know what we need to do, Vanya. Let's go back into the living room, sit on the sofa, and decide what we have to do first, then the next thing, and so on. We've just got to get ourselves organized!" I surprised myself by the words that poured forth. It was true; that's what we had to do. If anything was in a mess, we had to clean it up. Papa had always insisted on that!

"At times you amaze me, Sis," said Vanya, his voice full of admiration. My brother was proud of me for once!

I was flattered by his compliment, but I also knew by now to beware of Vanya's compliments. "We've got to remain calm and think things through, and you, Vanya, have to do your share of the work. Cooperation now is a fifty-fifty proposition!"

We returned to the living room, stepping gingerly over piles of books and other things that the police had scattered about so haphazardly. It was still somewhat dark outside and deadly quiet. Beba lay on the floor next to the sofa on which we now sat. Every so often he would lift his head and look up at us with his wise, blinking eyes. He too sensed that something was dreadfully wrong!

"The first thing that I'm going to do when it gets light is see Dr. Ferguson." Vanya was twisting his clasped hands, rubbing the bottoms of his palms together. "It's those darned guards at the gate that bother me," he complained. "Father hadn't considered that. I don't know how we're going to tell the Fergusons."

Neither did I, but we had to come up with some way of letting the good American know. We sat there considering our options and priorities. In the back of my mind I had an uneasy feeling that we were being watched. There were too many shadows around here! We couldn't turn on the lamps; anyone could then see us plainly. Sitting there in semi-darkness, we watched the different shadows, trying to figure out what they would turn out to be in the daylight. I kept listening for strange sounds.

Occasionally, Beba's tail thumped on the floor. Even those thumps made me jump! Our nerves were surely taut. I knew better than that; Beba would yap furiously if any stranger attempted even to come near us. If nothing else, Beba was a superb watchdog! I reached down to pat our furry friend.

At least, I reflected, I'm not alone in this misfortune. I shot a grateful look at Vanya. He and I would solve our problems. Once we had somehow let Dr. Ferguson know, the good American would take charge from then on. Dr. Ferguson was a powerful person, more so even than Father. Everyone in Peking knew Dr. Ferguson. He was an American! Our problem was that we couldn't think of any way to let him know!

It must be nearly five o'clock now. All the clocks in the house had stopped; there had been no one to wind them. It was still too dark to go awaken the Fergusons. It would be terribly impolite!

I got up to stretch my legs, feeling stiff from having sat in one position for such a long time. The cold was beginning to get to me as well. It was insidiously seeping into my bones, making me shiver. How could I be so tired and yet not sleepy?

I tiptoed to the front door, careful not to let my footsteps alert someone unfriendly who might be close by. Anyone could be lurking somewhere. There were so many shadows at this time of night! Or was it now day? Frankly, I didn't care. At least, I could try looking out through the glass panes of the door.

My eyes gradually became accustomed to the different shapes of things. I could see out through the open gates of the red pavilion, past the moon gate, on to the guest house in the front courtyard. There was the door in the middle of the vestibule; there were the steps leading to the inside. I strained my eyes to see more clearly. With a shudder, I froze! What was that shadowy form standing beside that door? It was definitely something. Was it a soldier standing on guard with a rifle? Could I be mistaken? I bit my lips, opening my eyes wider. Maybe if I blinked, the form would disappear. It was still there, darker than the house! Worse yet, it was motionless, rigid. I couldn't believe it! A soldier standing at attention with a rifle! I was too terrified to turn away from the apparition.

"What is it?" Vanya had been watching me and was alarmed.

"Sh-sh! Be quiet," I whispered urgently. "Get up very slowly and stand here beside me. It looks as if someone is watching us. Whoever it is hasn't moved an inch!"

"I'm right behind you, Sis." I could feel his breath on the back of my neck.

For what seemed like hours we stood there, motionless, our eyes fixed on that immobile figure. I could sense my brother's heart beating as fast as my own.

"It must be one of the guards; you're right," he whispered.

It was getting lighter. Little by little the shadows of the night began to disappear. Odd forms took on their familiar shapes once more. The moon gate became clearer and, sure enough, there were the graceful twigs of the lilac bushes stretched out against it. The grayness grew less monotonous, taking on colors that had been cloaked over by the night, objects now assuming their natural hues.

The motionless form still remained, but it too had changed from dark to a color! Bright red! To my chagrin, I realized that the phantom sentinel had really been one of the wooden columns that supported the closed-in porch of the guest house! We turned away in relief. Night can really transform things into more of a nightmare than they really are. If I hadn't been so tired and miserable, I would have laughed at my own silly fears. Now with the dawning of a new day the cobwebs in our minds had cleared, and we both knew what we had to do.

Vanya turned to me, inclining his head toward the kitchen. Softly he whispered. "Tamara, in back! That's the way to the colonel's house!" Amazing! We both had had the same thought.

"Exactly what I was thinking," I exclaimed loudly. I came to my senses with a shock when I realized that anyone hiding nearby could have heard us talking. "The colonel will surely help us," I lowered my voice to a whisper.

Our next-door neighbor was an American colonel. He and his wife and five children lived in Dr. Ferguson's middle compound. We knew them only by sight. Whenever we glimpsed them on Magpie Street, they were usually either getting in or out of their car. We had learned a great deal about them, though. Servants are apt to gossip about their masters, and their amahs and ours were friends. We knew that there were two sons in the family; the younger, Amah had told me, was named Benjy. There were three girls, one of them my age.

It was not only through Amah's gossip that we had learned about them. We had discovered that if we stood in the back courtyard, we could hear them talking. We heard the colonel's wife giving orders to her cook, for their kitchen was on that side, close to the wall. Sometimes we heard Benjy bouncing a ball against the wall. Mama used to marvel that the oldest daughter continuously played the piano. She played Brahms' *Lullaby* rather well. Sometimes we heard another daughter playing the violin.

"What an industrious, talented family they must be!" Mama would often comment, eyeing me with a sly look. "I am sure that *their* daughters do not watch the clock when they practice."

The parents seemed busy too. Once I saw the colonel's wife get into the car. The chauffeur had gotten out to open the rear door for her. She was a tall woman, very dignified. She was wearing what Mama considered "the height of elegance," a simple dark dress with a beautiful multi-strand of pearls next to her throat. On her wrists were matching bracelets. She resembled the women pictured in Mama's French fashion magazines.

We rarely saw the colonel. He was quite distinguished-looking, very tall and spare. His features were sharp, and his pale blue eyes were sheltered behind rimless spectacles that gave him a somewhat stern appearance. Ta Shih Fu had told us that the American officer was a good man. The servants respected him because he knew their language and spoke it well.

In the middle back courtyard, beside the wall that separated our two homes, there grew a tall tree that Papa called the *ook-sosnoe* (vinegar) tree. I always meant to ask him why. Its long branches with their lacy, fernlike leaves curved downward, two of them right over the wall and into the colonel's backyard.

Vanya and I each had had the same idea. In the past we had often climbed this same tree. It was sturdy, and from its higher branches we could easily survey our own home and the courtyards around it, each courtyard separated by a wall, each with its own special doorway, whether moon gate or arch. Mama had been shocked when we told her we could look into Colonel Stilwell's backyard and right into their kitchen! She had ordered us never to climb that tree again.

"Their house must have a big, red gate inside their front courtyard, like ours. I'm sure there must be one since originally all these houses belonged to one Mandarin with his different wives and concubines. Ours has always been barred because it leads into the colonel's quarters. If there is such a gate leading into Dr. Ferguson's house, then I wouldn't even have to step into the street once I got into the colonel's compound."

"I thought of that too," I said. "You'd better get cleaned up a bit," I suggested, examining him as a stranger would. "Boy, you sure look bad."

"You need to take a look at yourself before criticizing me," he retorted.

Vanya looked better once he had shaved. I watched him while he combed his hair. Afterwards, he rehearsed to me what he would tell the Americans. Make it brief and to the point, I advised him. Vanya sometimes could drag on and on. I also asked him to be sure to tell the Fergusons that we were okay.

We walked into the kitchen. It was deserted. Normally Ta Shih Fu would already be here, lighting the stove, getting our breakfast ready. He hadn't even shown up! Was he in on it too? I was sure that Boy was.

"I'll bet he won't," Vanya declared, echoing my thoughts. He opened the door into the back courtyard. The acacia's huge gnarled branches stretched up high, almost like an airy roof over the whole yard, casting eerie shadows on the ground. I grabbed Beba, holding him close. I didn't want him to start barking. Should the guards be asleep, his barking would awaken the whole street! Right now, all was quiet and peaceful.

We walked to the trunk of the vinegar tree and stood there listening. Not a sound came from the colonel's kitchen. Even though the servants must have been asleep, Vanya and I could no longer wait. He scaled the tree with ease, just like a monkey. No wonder! Ever since early childhood we had climbed trees. Why not? There were trees in every courtyard of this house. That was one of the things we both liked to do. How free I'd feel when I'd finally reach the tiled roofs after climbing higher and higher, struggling from one branch to the next one above. I'd jump on to the roof, scamper up the slanting tiles to the very top. From there I could look down into Magpie Street or into some neighbor's yard.

Vanya was quick. I watched him climb to the sturdiest branch from which he'd swing into the colonel's backyard. Vanya laughed when I warned him that they might think him a thief.

"That'll be too bad for me, won't it? I doubt it, Sis; the servants know me." With that he swung over the wall.

I felt lost when he disappeared from sight. Beba was getting restless and struggling to wriggle out of my grasp. I couldn't let him go because he would bark, and his shrill yap would not only waken the guards but also all of Magpie Street.

What was that hissing sound? I dared not move. Beba's warm body had stiffened; his ears perked up.

"Pssst!" There it was again. It was Vanya on the other side of the wall. "Tamara," his voice was a stage whisper.

I came closer to the wall. "What's the matter?"

"I'm okay. I slid down the coal pile against the wall. I just didn't want you to worry. Are you and Beba okay?"

"I'm not worried, but thanks for thinking of us."

"All right, I'm on my way." Footsteps, then silence.

Beba was a comfort, but not completely. To the left of the colonel's wall on our side another wall with a moon gate in the middle set off the farthest backyard in our compound. Here were the quarters in which Aunt Raica and our cousins had lived at one time. Here also was the storeroom that Father had had converted into a schoolroom for his private students and the area where we had made our skating rink. There was a grapevine too that in summertime was entwined into the framework of a bamboo arbor under which, if the evenings were balmy enough, we would eat our meals. Now the grapevine was lying dormant, its sleeping branches buried in the ground to protect them from Peking's harsh winter. The mound over it was high, resembling the Chinese burial mounds we had often passed on our way to the Western Hills. This too was a burial mound. Here, in the past, we had laid to rest the dogs, kittens, chickens, and even turtles that during our growing-up years had been a vital part of our lives. Once they died, Vanya and I made up solemn funerals and performed their last rites before burying them here.

Now, this backyard beyond the moon gate scared me. I knew that the ghosts of departed pets were watching me. More than that, I sensed that if I should turn around, I would find a guard hidden behind some tree, waiting to catch me by surprise. Perhaps Boy was lurking here as well. There was something about that fellow that bothered me. Was it his uncanny resemblance to that student? No, that wasn't it. In a moment it came to me! Boy had known darn well what was going to happen at our house last night. He hadn't acted surprised, just excited. Besides that, he was a poor servant. He hadn't even known how to build a fire in the stoves. Ta Shih Fu had had to teach him! I had also seen him talking to someone in the servants' quarters, someone whom we couldn't see. Then my mind took a giant step. Could it have been Mischa in the servants' quarters? Now that I thought of it he and Boy had seemed too friendly with each other. Why couldn't we have figured out that Mischa didn't have to deliver that small camera to us! It could have been more easily sent through the post.

Why then had Mischa arranged to visit our house? He had been so curious, not only with us but also with Mother and Father! Why hadn't we sensed right away that there was something about him that didn't ring true? He always had money and always insisted on treating us. He had visited us at odd hours, not at the customary visiting hours in Peking. He must have been checking out what we did every day; that must have been it!

Father hadn't liked him, and he was a good judge of character. Yes, it only seemed logical that Mischa had been with Boy in the servants' quarters! He hadn't visited us for nearly a month. He had known what was about to happen! I couldn't wait until Vanya returned to see what he thought of my deduction. I had to be right. The more I thought of it the more convinced I became. I suddenly wished that Dorlise were here with us; she'd agree with me. She hadn't liked the Russian jerk, as she called him, either. In fact, she had asked Vanya once what he ever saw in him. Well, unfortunately, she was not here.

I thought I heard footsteps and froze. Beba, however, was quiet in my arms. He and I had remained in this one spot ever since Vanya had disappeared over the wall. I dared not move an inch. The very thought of having to reenter the house alone petrified me. Never again would I go back in there alone! No, I'd just wait right here till Vanya came back. If he didn't come back soon, I'd have to scale that tree myself and jump over into the colonel's backyard. I just couldn't remain here alone, not even with Beba!

Suddenly, I heard someone scrambling on the other side of the wall. Soon Vanya's grinning face peered at me from its top. He turned his head back, waving farewell to someone below him. With an agile leap he caught a branch of the vinegar tree and was soon swinging down the trunk, Tarzan-like, to land beside me. He was out of breath, but happy with the outcome of his errand.

"They'll be coming to see us shortly," he whispered quietly.

"Who?"

"The Fergusons. Dr. Ferguson and Mary." He looked at me strangely. "Are you all right?"

I was, now that he was back. "Yep." I answered. "It was just sort of scary being here by myself. I was afraid that Beba would start barking. Gosh, it's really eerie here in the yard when you're by yourself. I kept thinking all sorts of things!" I wanted to tell him about my suspicions of Boy and Mischa, but that could wait. I wanted to know all about what had happened at the Fergusons.' As we walked to the kitchen, he started to tell me but changed his mind.

"How about cocoa?" he asked. "I'm starved, aren't you?"

I hadn't really thought about eating, but now that he had mentioned it I realized how hungry I was. *Maybe that is what is wrong with me,* I thought.

In the wooden icebox I found a bottle of milk, three-quarters full. In one of Ta Shih Fu's cabinets I found the cocoa. We mixed it, drinking it cold.

"Mrs. Stilwell was already up, thank goodness. She heard me." He smiled at the recall. "She was in the kitchen talking to their cook. Then all of a sudden they saw me coming down, sliding down their coalpile. After I told her, she was really terrific. You were right. They do have gates in their front courtyard, just like ours, only theirs aren't barred. Apparently, they're all good friends because they called each other by their first names. She and I just walked over into the Fergusons' front yard, and the servant took us into their main living quarters."

"What did Dr. Ferguson say when you told him?"

Vanya grinned. "You wouldn't believe it. He was upset that I hadn't come right away, as soon as the students had left. When I told him that we couldn't think of disturbing his family during the night he was even more annoyed. But do you know what? His servant had to waken him when Mrs. Stilwell and I first arrived."

"What else?" I wanted to know if Dr. Ferguson would be able to get our parents released.

"He said that he'd have to contact the head of the Chinese police to find out about them. He seemed most encouraging. Told me that we've got to get busy and start cleaning up this mess so that Papa and Mama would not be too horrified when they return."

That was consoling, and he was right; that was exactly what we should do. Where were we to start? The living room seemed logical. We agreed that Vanya should go into the study to go through the books and put them in some sort of order. I would gather the remainder of the books scattered about in the living and the dining rooms and carry them to him in the study. Perhaps by the time the Fergusons came, we would be able to have the living room at least fit to receive visitors.

Dr. Ferguson and his daughter had no problems with our guards when they rang the doorbell. They were Americans, citizens of a powerful country that had the respect of both the Chinese and the Japanese. Besides, Dr. Ferguson was known throughout Peking not only as a noted scholar but also as a great philanthropist.

We heard his familiar, booming voice at the front gates and rushed out to greet him. Mary ran down the steps from the gate-pavilion and gave me a big hug.

"So sorry, dear," she spoke quietly. "This must have been such a terrible shock for you children." Her eyes behind the severe rimless glasses were kind. We walked arm in arm through the moon gate towards our living room. Dr. Ferguson fol-

Dr. John C. Ferguson

lowed; Vanya trailed behind. Unlike me, Vanya was ill at ease with the old missionary.

Dr. Ferguson sat in one of Mama's slip-covered armchairs and looked around. Mary made herself comfortable on the sofa, motioning me to sit beside her. She put an arm around my shoulder. Vanya alone remained standing, his back against the piano. His face looked drawn.

"I see that you've been quite busy," the American observed approvingly. "From Vanya's description it must have been quite a mess!" He shook his head, puzzled. "It really took us by surprise when we heard what had happened, and I can't for the life of me think why they should wish to question your father. I have known him all these years!"

Mary interrupted. "And to think your mother has been arrested too!"

Dr. Ferguson turned to Vanya. "Am I to understand that your mother insisted on going? That she went of her own volition?"

Vanya nodded his head, reddening. "Yes, sir. She felt that we could take care of ourselves, but that Father needed her. We *can* take care of ourselves." He sounded almost defiant when he uttered the last sentence.

The American was thoughtful. "She certainly is a brave lady," he said admiringly. "Your mother is not only beautiful but immensely loyal." He rose from the chair, looking at each of us encouragingly. "I don't want you young folks to worry one whit. I'm going to look into this matter right away. I know some people to contact." He paused, thinking. "Yes, I know exactly the person to contact. I'll find out why they have arrested your father. Now, what I want the two of you to do," his voice trailed off as he looked at me from under those bushy eyebrows. He was trying to be severe, but I couldn't help smiling at him. "You just finish cleaning up as you were doing. When your parents come, they'll be pleasantly surprised at what you've done. And, oh, yes, clean yourselves up, and get some rest!"

We walked with the Fergusons to the front gates. At the gate pavilion the three policemen and Boy had come out and were standing in a row, eyes looking down, bowing politely to the Americans. Dr. Ferguson acknowledged their salutations with a brief nod, and then he and Mary walked home.

"Strange that Ta Shih Fu hasn't shown up," remarked Vanya thoughtfully. "I wonder if he, too, has been in on all this."

"Could be," I answered. Ta Shih Fu had been with us for as long as I could remember, but who knew? He could have been bribed.

"You never know," said Vanya, again echoing my thoughts. "In wartime things are different. Sometimes even families turn against one another." Vanya was bitter because of all that had happened. I, on the contrary, felt optimistic. Now that Dr. Ferguson had taken charge, things would be all right. How little I knew about the real world and human nature, including my own!

We continued to clean up the rooms. It had taken a long time to put all the books back, but we finally managed to fill the empty shelves. We packed into a carton Papa's dictionary, which was two thousand or so loose pages onto which had been painstakingly glued character inserts. We labeled it "Father's Dictionary." It would take months to get those papers all straightened out! The notes, letters, bills, and other papers from Papa's desk we put back in drawers. He could sort them out himself later on. We cleaned up his desk, replacing the blue cloisonne vase that contained his pens and pencils back on the right-hand side where it had always been. His large half-moon ink pad was on the left. By evening his study looked almost normal. Vanya and I were extremely pleased with our handiwork.

We also felt happy because of something else. Mr. Hsu had said *two days*. Therefore, they would be released tomorrow. Mr. Hsu would not break his word.

I awakened on Monday, feeling elated. Today was the day when Mama and Papa would return home! They would be so surprised at all we had done! I smiled to myself thinking about it. The past two days had been terrible! I couldn't believe what horrors we had lived through, but all this would come to an end today! Our lives would once more resume their normal routines, and I soon would be regaling Dorlise about all that had happened. She wouldn't believe it! No, indeed, she wouldn't!

Then the doorbell rang. Vanya and I both ran towards the front yard. At the moon gate we heard the Frenchman's melodic voice. I had forgotten all about him; he was returning from his weekend in Tientsin. I had thought it was our parents.

When Vanya saw my disappointment, he comforted me. "They'll come; don't worry, Tamara. They'll probably be here by noon." Mr. Hsu had promised us that they'd return in two days. I kept recalling his words.

A few minutes later Boy knocked on our front door. His rosy face seemed to deepen in color as I opened the door. Out of his lowered lids he gave me a sly look. I couldn't hide my dislike for him.

"What is it, Boy?" I asked coldly. He looked so insufferably smug, so absolutely sure of himself!

"The Frenchman sends you his compliments. He would like to see both you and *Shao Ye* [the young gentleman]." I was startled by the insolent leer Boy directed at me and by his impertinence.

"Tell him we'll come," I said, closing the door. I couldn't abide this fellow! I used to like him, I remembered. How could I have been so dumb? I was now firmly convinced that he was a spy working for the Japanese. He was too much like that Tung Bei student; they could have been brothers!

When we were ready, we walked over to the guest house. Monsieur Viaud stood waiting for us at his front door. What a reassuring sight! Hollywood-movie-type dashing he was in his blue-gray uniform, and so aristocratic in his bearing! Had I been older, I was convinced, he would have taken my hand and pressed it to his lips. As it was, he still behaved like a gallant Frenchman. He nodded politely to both of us and, sweeping his hand out in a welcoming gesture, he bowed!

"Come in; come in." How romantic-looking he was! That accent was charming! I couldn't wait to tell Dorlise about him. I could just see her, listening to my every word!

He seated us in the same rosewood chairs over which the students had sprawled. Once we were seated, he himself sat down on the sofa.

"I was . . . how you say?" He spread out his palms in a helpless gesture.

"Astonished!" I interjected.

"Yes, that's it, thank you. Astonished to see the policemen. Three of them! But why?"

"We don't know, Monsieur Viaud." My brother shrugged his shoulders.

"But what happened? Boy said that your parents are arrested. Is it true? And these men are here for what?"

"To guard us," I said biting my lower lip. His concern and sympathy were beginning to get to me. I didn't want anyone to be kind. That made me want to cry.

"We're almost as much in the dark as you are," Vanya answered, giving me a warning look. "They came here last Saturday evening and locked us in the bedroom till about three o'clock in the morning. Then they arrested the folks, taking them away. You should have seen the house! They practically turned it inside out, searching and digging outside."

"For what?" the Frenchman asked curiously.

Vanya laughed cynically. "Search me. But after my parents were gone, we found three of them here in your living room. I chased them out, but before they left, their leader called us *Communists!*"

"*Mon Dieu!* Why? But that is impossible!" He got up from the sofa and paced up and down in front of us, once in a while giving us a quick, sharp look. "*Im-po-ssi-ble* [he pronounced it in French] that they would suspect that good man. *Mon Dieu!*"

We watched him pace. Suddenly he stopped in front of Vanya. "Do you know where your father is?" he asked.

Both of us shook our heads.

"*Bon!*" He then told us the decision he had reached. "I shall not go to Tientsin for the weekends any more, that is, until your parents return home. I shall remain here in Peking. If there is anything I can do . . ."

"Thank you," I interrupted. "We are okay."

"Okay?" For a moment he looked mystified. "Oh, yes, *très bien!* But money, do you need money?" At a look from my brother, he added, "I'll be glad to lend you whatever you need until your parents return."

My brother rose. "Thank you, Monsieur. Papa gave us money before they left."

I too got up. I wished that I had worn something prettier than this old woolen skirt and sweater. He turned to me, his tall form bending in a courteous bow. I gave him my hand.

"Monsieur Viaud?" It was a good thing that I had remembered this! "Our cook has not come back. We don't know what happened, but we just can't feed you any more. If he returns, then we'll let you know. I'm sorry."

He laughed, shaking my hand. "That's the least of my worries, Mademoiselle. I just wish I could do something for you and your brother."

We felt better after leaving him. What a fine man! And Boy had complained that the French officer was bad-tempered! He certainly had been as courteous and handsome as a Frenchman could possibly be. It was good to have him here with us!

In the late afternoon Dr. Ferguson came to see us. His face was grave as he sat down in the armchair. I had a sinking feeling that he had some bad news for us. In a way I was partially right. He wasted no time to tell us that he had been trying to find out where they had taken our parents. He frowned, shaking his head. "I hadn't realized it would be this difficult."

"Why, Dr. Ferguson?" I asked. "Couldn't you have asked Mr. Hsu? He told Mama that they would question Father for two days. After that,"—I was so positive about this!—"After that, he promised me that they would be released."

The American remained quiet for a moment. His wonderfully kind eyes studied my face. He took my hand. "Girlie," he said seriously, "it's not so simple as that. Hsu is just a pawn in this game. It is the Japanese who instigated this arrest. They are the ones who want your father, not the Chinese."

Although his voice was gentle, his words cut into me like a knife! Vanya paled.

"Why do they want him, sir?"

"Well," he focused his gaze on the dining-room lamp; he was finding it difficult to explain things to us. I interrupted his "well."

"What I would like to know, Dr. Ferguson, is whether Mischa had anything to do with Father's arrest." I could feel the heat rising from my neck to the top of my head.

He nodded his head. "Yes, Girlie, Mischa is one of them, working for the Japanese. You were absolutely right in your suspicions. His orders had been to find out all about your family's living habits. He was to examine the contents of each room in this house, to meet your family's friends. That wasn't all." He angrily emphasized the next words, "You, and by that I mean *all* of you, have been followed wherever you have gone. Even you, Girlie!"

I couldn't believe this! Why?

"How did you find this out?" Vanya asked the American.

"I have ways," Dr. Ferguson replied quietly. "But I want both of you to forget that, along with Mischa. You no longer have to worry about being followed or having the Russian boy spy on you. There are much more important things to think about." He stretched his arm out to encircle my waist and brought me close to him. "I have learned," he was looking at Vanya now, "that they separated your parents right away. First, they went directly to the Chinese police station where they apparently dropped off your mother. Your father?" He looked at me and his eyes were full of sympathy. He patted my hand. "They took your father somewhere else. I'm afraid that he is in the hands of the Japanese. These are the military Japanese, and their ways are very secret. We don't know where your father is. That is what I aim to find out!" He heaved a deep sigh.

"But why separate them?" I asked.

"Your mother was not supposed to be arrested in the first place, but she insisted on going with him, that brave lady! Now that they have her, they can't release her until your father's questioning has been conducted and the whole affair resolved. They will then question her, most likely to see if their stories coincide. I think I'd better clear up something for you. I've just found this out myself. The problem, as I have been told, really concerns the Japanese." His eyes from under the bushy white brows looked sharply at both of us in turn. He wanted to make sure that we were paying attention! He didn't have to worry about that!

He continued, "I was able to find this out when I visited the Japanese Embassy yesterday after church. I know two of the people who work there. They made some inquiries and then informed me rather regretfully that there was not much that they could do since your father is being held by the militarists. These are the Japanese who have taken over Peking. They are the ones who are bent on *cleaning up* this city. The embassy people and the militarists do not work together. Therefore it will be rather difficult and may take time for us to find out things. But

I'm sure that *my source* won't fail. He's an admirable man. He promised me that he will try, in the next day or two, to find out where the professor is and under what charges he is being held prisoner."

"Charges?" I asked him incredulously. "Why charges? My father hasn't done anything wrong or opposed them."

"Not in your eyes, child, or mine, but in their eyes, yes. That may be his trouble, that he didn't do anything! He did not register in the Japanese White House. All the other White Russians did."

"But, Dr. Ferguson," I protested, "he is not a *White* Russian. He left Russia before the Russian revolution even began! You know that he's a scholar. He just wanted to study linguistics and compile his Russo-Chinese dictionary. He taught Russian because he had to earn money. Why should he join some club?"

He smiled. "There, there, Girlie, don't get all fired up. I realize this and so do a lot of other people. With the Japanese, however, it is: 'If you are not with us, then you are against us.' Do you understand?"

I stared at Vanya, and he nodded his head in agreement. As usual, we had both thought of the same thing!

"So that is why that Tung Bei student called us Communists!" I told the good doctor what had happened at the guest house.

He stood up, taking up his cane. "Don't let this lower your spirits, children. Let's not worry yet. I have a good feeling that this will soon be straightened out. Just you two keep your faith in the Almighty. Remember, your father is innocent.

"Oh," he smiled, remembering something. He bent forward towards us, lowering his voice, "We're going to have to outsmart these policemen who are guarding you." His white moustache twitched. "I talked with Miss Moore today. She's going to be sending your school lessons and homework home with me. Every morning I shall bring it to you, Vanya, under my overcoat. You are to do the homework for me to return the next day; so no matter what happens, you'll be able to graduate this year!"

Vanya was touched by the American's thoughtfulness. "I'd thought of that, sir, but I didn't know what to do about it. This is most kind of you."

"Well, it's the least thing I can do." He started towards the door, then turned. "Any questions to ask? Anything bothering you?"

I had millions of questions, but I knew that he would not be able to answer them. Remarkably for me, I kept silent.

At the gate-pavilion the guards were lined up to pay their respects. They bowed at his appearance. He nodded to them, then turned to give me a sly wink.

"See you both tomorrow." He lifted one foot to step over the brass threshold. "Oh, by the way," he let his foot remain on the stoop, "do not, and this I am adamant about, do not let anyone come into the house to see you. Do you realize that they've already taken into custody most of the visitors who have appeared at your gates?"

"No!" Both Vanya and I were surprised.

The missionary nodded. "They chose a good time for this to happen, just before Christmas and New Year's when many friends would be apt to pay their respects to your parents."

I had a horrifying thought! "Then Dorlise might have been arrested!"

Dr. Ferguson laughed, shaking his head. "She's American, dear. Only Chinese and Russians can be arrested, nobody else."

"One more question, Dr. Ferguson." I was hesitant about asking him this, but I just had to know. "How long do you think it'll be? I mean, how long—maybe no more than a week?"

His face as he looked at me was grave. So was his voice. "That I can't say, Girlie. It could be a week. It could be a month. I just don't know." He seemed in a hurry to go.

We followed him down the gate steps to the bottom step and watched the tall, dignified figure walk the few short steps to his house, swinging his cane as usual. How considerate and thoughtful of him! Were it not for him, Vanya and I would be completely alone, on our own to do whatever we could to solve our problems.

After that the days passed slowly. It was now no longer living from day to day, counting the minutes and hours for our parent's return. A week had passed since that terrible night! Dr. Ferguson visited us faithfully every day. Every day we heard his cheerful, "No news is good news." He brought Vanya's homework and took back to Miss Moore what my brother had finished the night before. Often, he spoke to us about his beloved wife.

"She's been ailing for nearly a year now," he told us one day. "Now she has to have bed rest, or so the doctor has ordered."

How sad it was for him! I wished that we could do something to make him happier. He was so kind to us even with his own troubles and misfortunes.

I remembered Mrs. Ferguson well. Sometimes when Dr. Ferguson would pick me up in his car if he saw me walking on Magpie Street, Mrs. Ferguson would be sitting next to him. She was such a sweet lady, just like the pictures of American grandmothers that I had seen in the magazines that we bought in Tung An Shih Chang, the big market. Her hair was fluffy white and wavy; she had pink and white skin; her gentle, kindly blue eyes looked at me through her rimless spectacles. She had such a sweet voice and always inquired how Mama was. She was so tiny compared to Dr. Ferguson. Anyone, even me, could see that he loved her very much.

Once I dared ask him what ailed her. His face had clouded over. "It's her heart, dear child. She can't exert herself, and sometimes she thinks she's stronger than she is."

"Will you please give her our love?"

"She is always asking me about the two of you, Girlie. If she were able, she'd be here herself. Of course, I will."

Sometimes when I was painting, I would paint pictures for her and send them to her with Dr. Ferguson. One day Dr. Ferguson came to the house with someone else. Trailing behind him was his number-one servant, wearing a spotless white gown and carrying in both hands a huge basket wrapped in red paper. This he formally deposited on our tea table. Then smiling broadly, he bowed to both Vanya and me and returned home.

"What is this?" I gasped. I knew that it was a present for us, but why? "Is this for us?"

Dr. Ferguson looked especially fine today. He was wearing a dark blue suit, and his light blue silk necktie matched his eyes perfectly. There was something special about him today, something about his attitude as well. He was happier, more joyous! My question surprised him.

"Don't you two know what day it is?" he asked us in surprise.

More than a week had gone by since Mama and Papa were taken away, I thought. No, he couldn't be happy about that. I must have looked really puzzled.

"Why, Tamara and Vanya, it's Christmas!" His voice rang out through the two rooms. "This basket is from Mrs. Ferguson, Mary, and me!" He pointed to the basket, looking somewhat embarrassed. "I'm sorry. I realize it won't be a happy time without your parents, but at least you'll have something good to eat! I have to leave now; we're all going to church. Mrs. Ferguson feels up to it." He seemed so happy about her improved health that I went over to him and hugged him, tears in my eyes.

"I'm so glad she's better, Dr. Ferguson. Our thanks to all of you for thinking of Vanya and me."

We wished his family a Merry Christmas and just like the days before we walked him out to the gate-pavilion. After his departure we unwrapped the basket. What was in it was unbelievable! An array of American goodies surrounded the snow-white plucked chicken that lay in the center! There were cans and more cans of food, similar to what we had seen advertised in the American papers that Ta Shih Fu used to bring home from market. We had never thought that we'd see the real things right before our eyes! And to think, they'd been given us for our very own. We stacked the cans on the dining-room table. Underneath those cans were more cans, and then there were packages. There was a large can of cookies. There were candy bars with strange names like Baby Ruth and Butterfinger. At the bottom was fruit: shiny red apples, grapes, bananas. They were so perfect that they didn't look real, but they were! Finally, there were two cans of salted American peanuts!

"Can you believe all this?" I asked Vanya.

"We'd better put this chicken in the ice-box. We've got to cook it or it'll spoil." Vanya lifted it out of the basket. "It must have cost a lot!"

"How do we cook it?" I asked him. "I don't know how."

"Let's not worry," he told me. "I'll put it away. Maybe they'll be here tomorrow." He spoke wistfully, "Mama, I'm sure, will know how to cook it."

"We'll put all the other stuff away too," I told him. "We'll save it and share it with Mama and Papa. We don't need to eat them now."

We carefully stacked the cans in the buffet. I could imagine how delighted our parents would be when they saw all this expensive American food.

After that we settled down at the dining-room table. It was time to draw a Christmas card for the Fergusons and to thank them for their wonderful gift.

The next day I awakened refreshed and filled with a buoyancy I hadn't felt before. Why was I feeling this way? Then I recalled what had happened yesterday. Yesterday had been Christmas and in a few more days would come New Year's Day. Surely the Japanese would release our parents by then.

Vanya and I got busy. We cleaned up the entire house, shaking out the rugs, polishing Mama's Rosencrantz piano till we could see our faces in it. The rooms sparkled!

After we had finished our cleaning we went to the kitchen to make some cocoa. Vanya had figured out how to light the stove. It was cozy and warm with the stove lighted and hot cocoa on the table in front of us.

"I found Mama's *Malhovitz Cookbook*," Vanya informed me, taking it out of a drawer. "It'll tell you here how to roast the chicken."

There was nothing that we had to do to the chicken but place it in a roasting pan and slide it onto the middle rack of the old coal stove. It wasn't long before a wonderful odor permeated the kitchen. Both of us breathed deeply, relishing the aroma. I didn't realize how hungry I was for some really good food. We had been living on Chinese *shao-bing* (sesame rolls) and noodles long enough!

Vanya kept opening the door to the oven, inspecting the browning chicken. "It's almost ready," he announced. The chicken had been in for almost an hour and was golden brown.

"It's ready," I agreed.

I had set the table in the dining room. It was chilly in there, but the chicken warmed us up. That was all that we ate, not wanting to waste any American canned food for ourselves.

"When Mama and Papa come home, we'll celebrate," we told

each other. This was one thing Vanya and I could agree on. No matter how hungry we were we would not touch the canned food. The chicken and fruit had to be eaten, but the other food would keep for the homecoming celebration in the future!

3

The Facts of Life—the Hard Way

The days passed slowly for us even though we tried to keep busy. There was always plenty to do. The house sparkled with our constant washing and polishing, but now we tackled painting! I had found some light green paint in a can on the pantry shelf. The kitchen window frames needed a new coat. While I painted, Vanya cleaned the yard, sweeping the snow away from the walks, especially in the front courtyard. If Monsieur Viaud left the guest house for the day, Vanya went in there and gave it a good cleaning. There was firewood in the shed, but it had to be chopped. Vanya shaped the coal dust in the little yard next to the kitchen into coal balls for the kitchen stove. The stove in the living room used too much coal, so we decided not to light it any more. We stayed in the kitchen most of the time anyway. To keep ourselves warm, we wore heavy jackets, even in our living quarters. We were finding it to be all too true that one could get used to almost anything!

Boy had kept his distance for a few days. Now, however, he was coming around to see if we could use his help. That was a laugh! He didn't act like a servant. Last week he had refused to make coal balls or do other dirty work when Vanya asked him, saying that he was here against his will. That was a joke! Often I'd heard him laughing in the servants' quarters with the police! He was their friend, an ally, a spy, that's what he was!

Vanya still thought that I was being too hard on Boy. In fact, to my utter disgust and disappointment, Vanya and Boy had

71

Under House Arrest, Peking,China

become quite friendly. Often, I would hear voices and then see Vanya awkwardly sweeping or cleaning up out in the yard; Boy meanwhile was crouched on his haunches watching my brother doing the work that Boy should have been doing. No wonder his rosy, good-looking, yet insolent face was wreathed in a big smile.

I tried to reason with Vanya, telling him my fears and suspicions. Vanya then became condescending and shrugged his shoulders. "Boy is imprisoned here just like us. He has a wife whom he misses, but he cannot leave our house. I feel sorry for the poor guy."

"Then if he's so nice, why doesn't he work? We still have to pay him his wages; yet we do his work. It's not fair! Here we are starving ourselves because we're existing on Paul Viaud's rent money. Part of that money goes for Boy's wages! It's an outrage, an injustice! Why can't you understand that, Vanya?" How my brother could be so absolutely stupid was beyond me!

Vanya was resigned to doing nothing about Boy. "There's

nothing that we can do. Even Dr. Ferguson told you that. Boy is here against his will."

"I won't believe that," I cried out angrily. "He's a spy, and the sooner you believe it, the better it'll be for all of us. You're being a traitor when you pal around with him, can't you see that?"

"No, I can't."

I avoided Boy. It was humiliating enough that we were working hard while he "partied" with our guards. Most of all, Vanya's conciliatory attitude towards him enraged me. How could he be so friendly to this traitor? I had seen Vanya's poor sore hands, red and cracked from shaping coal balls. No matter how he washed his hands, the dirt remained in the cracks. Still he palled around with the fellow. When I pointed that out to him, he had grinned.

"I don't mind it, Sis; honest I don't. Boy has helped me."

I didn't ask him how.

A few days later Boy came into the kitchen. He was on his best behavior, I noticed grimly. He knew very well that I had no use for him; he had even told Vanya that for a young girl my temper was too strong!

Boy told us that Monsieur Viaud wished to see us. We hadn't seen him for several weeks now, almost three weeks in fact. With a start I realized that my parents had been gone for even longer than that!

When Paul Viaud came into our living room, I noticed that he had surreptitiously glanced at everything in the two rooms. Everything sparkled! Vanya and I smiled at each other, proud of our housekeeping abilities.

"Would you like some tea?" I asked, after the Frenchman had seated himself in Dr. Ferguson's favorite armchair.

He shook his head. *"Non, merci, Mademoiselle."* He looked at me thoughtfully. I was somewhat embarrassed at his studying me as if he were appraising me.

"Is there something you need, Monsieur Viaud?" asked Vanya. "If we can, we shall be glad to do it, but as you know, we are without our parents, and under home-arrest . . ." My brother spread out his hands, showing his palms helplessly.

I couldn't take my eyes off the handsome officer. How sad it

73

was that he had to pay attention to me under these conditions. Had our parents been at home, then he wouldn't even have known that I existed. I wondered what it was he wanted. I would soon find out!

He shifted uneasily in his chair. "Mademoiselle," he hesitated. How steely his gray eyes were, even if his voice was kind. I surmised that the aloofness went with being an officer. "Mademoiselle, I have thought about how to ask you this," his gaze softened. Oh, how I wished Dorlise could have been here now to see this.

"As you may remember, before your parents were..." he paused, "eh, before they were taken away by the Japanese, I had meals served in my quarters. I realize now that you do not have a cook, but..." Here his face became flushed; his eyes lost their chilliness and became gentle, almost pleading, "I was wondering if you could manage to make dinner for me in the evenings? I would be more than happy to come to your quarters here and eat with you. That way it wouldn't be so much trouble, *oui?*" He talked quickly as if he were afraid I might interrupt him before he laid out his proposition. As it was, I was too flabbergasted. He went on, "Of course, I shall pay you extra for board."

I looked over at Vanya who was gazing open-mouthed at the Frenchman. What could I say? This we had not expected. We could use the extra money, but I had to be honest with him.

"Monsieur Viaud," I started out shyly, "thank you for your offer, but I am only sixteen years old, and I know little about cooking. Also, Boy our only remaining servant, is worthless. Even though I would like to accommodate you, I just can't."

He raised his hands in protest, smiling. I noticed his white, even teeth. This man could be a movie star he was so handsome! How could I ever cook for him?

"Please reconsider. I am not a fussy man, and I will be most patient, I promise. I will eat what you eat. You two have to eat, don't you?" Again, those disturbing eyes of his pleaded with me.

How could I ever refuse him! However, I thought of the noodles and *shao-bing* that we had been eating. One time when I had asked Boy to get us some *wo-wo-toh*, the millet bread that the poorest of the poor Chinese eat, he had absolutely refused. He wouldn't be seen buying such miserable food!

74

"You can do it, Tamara," urged Vanya. "It's not that hard. Besides, you've got Mama's *Malhovitz.*"

How easy for him to say! I wanted to glare at him. What a louse he was to say that, but then I should have known! That was so typical of Vanya's "cooperation." Come to think of it, though, I had cooked the chicken. I could follow directions. It wouldn't hurt to try. If it didn't work, then I would quit. I had now come full circle from wanting to refuse the officer's request to accepting his offer. After all, we needed the extra money!

"All right, Monsieur. I'm willing to prepare evening meals for you." I could see the relief in his face. I should have bitten my tongue, but like an impetuous fool, I went on, "If you will be patient, I'll do it. If you're not satisfied, we'll stop. Please don't get angry with me because you're the one who asked me to do this. All right?"

I knew that I was letting myself into something I might later regret, but it would be seven dollars more for us. Vanya smiled with relief at my words.

The Frenchman stood up. How tall he was! Not ever having been this close to him before, I hadn't realized that he was such a tall man. That blue-gray uniform looked as if it had been especially tailored for him; it fit so perfectly. His eyes were the same blue-gray, so romantic-looking and distant. He really didn't belong here, I thought; he should be leading the French Foreign Legion somewhere out on the Sahara Desert. To top it all off, he bowed, then saluted me by touching the edge of his kepi gallantly, as only a Frenchman could!

"Mademoiselle, I congratulate you on your wise decision. Believe me, I think you might even come to enjoy the experience of cooking. Think how much you will learn!"

"*Merci, Monsieur,* and I'm sure that you'll learn much too." I was trying to be gracious in the same way Mama would have been. Inside, however, I was rather scared and disgusted with myself for agreeing to this outrageous proposition.

When he had left, I went to the kitchen right away and began to study *Malhovitz.* It had been Mama's cooking Bible; in fact, she swore by *Malhovitz!* It was a big book, almost six hundred pages of complex Russian recipes. I blew the dust off the green cover and unhappily began to thumb through it. What was it that Ta Shih Fu used to cook for us? It all seemed so long ago now. His meals had not been simple. Every meal had been special: fish with white Bechamel sauce, meats with thick, brown sauces and mushrooms, or raisins, or whatever! Then there had been stuffed chickens decorated with curlicued carrots and green onions. I groaned with despair as I turned the pages. How could I have gotten myself into such a mess!

Paul Viaud had suggested that I start giving him meals on Monday; I had the whole weekend during which I could plan. When Dr. Ferguson came, I told him of my new venture.

"Why, good for you, Girlie!" He was full of enthusiasm. "That's a wonderful idea. I'm proud of you, Tamara." He then suggested that his number-one boy, Chang, could do our shopping for us, if that was agreeable.

"Just let him buy the groceries for you. Make out your list; then give it to Boy to bring over to Chang. Chang is a good shopper."

That solved part of my problem. According to Boy, he was not allowed to go to the real market. He was permitted to go only to the corner Chinese stores or restaurants, always accompanied by one of our guards. Whether this was merely to prove to us that he was a prisoner too or an excuse not to go shopping for us did not matter to me. Vanya and I ate the Chinese noodles and bean cakes he bought for us. That food satisfied our needs, simple as they were nowadays.

I had thoroughly checked the wooden icebox. There was absolutely nothing in it but the large squares of ice lying in the tinned-off section of the top compartment. Well, at least our iceman had not been arrested, I thought grimly.

Paul had given me our next month's rent in advance plus the extra seven dollars for board. I wrote a short list of groceries for Chang. Not knowing what the market prices were, I had limited my supplies to the basics. My first attempt would be simple. After that, we would see.

Vanya had informed Boy that Mr. Viaud would now be eating with us. This meant that he was to wear his white coat over his padded blue jacket and trousers. Later, Vanya told me that Boy had not liked this news. However, since the French officer was involved, there was nothing that he could do. The Frenchman's very presence scared him.

When I learned how Boy felt about Paul, I was in a much better frame of mind about this cooking deal. On Monday I set the table, using Mama's good Chinese tablecloth. Vanya and I had polished her silverware and were using her crystal glasses instead of the old ones.

I had carefully worked out the menu: soup for the first course; then wieners with mashed potatoes and tomato sauce. I remembered how pretty the dish had looked when Ta Shih Fu had served it. There was even a side dish of string beans for color! For dessert I would make a custard. That was no problem.

Monday evening came. I had been busy in the kitchen since morning, studying *Malhovitz,* carefully going over my recipes step by step. Boy had come in towards dinnertime. He offered to mash the potatoes; that delighted me since it was one less thing for me to worry about. Everything else was ready. Boy, wearing his white gown, looked every inch a well-groomed servant!

Vanya and Monsieur Viaud were already seated at the table. I had declined to join them, not only because I was worried and uneasy, but also I didn't wish to see the effects of my cooking upon them. Most of all, I was really busy in the kitchen!

It was already too late to remedy the blunder I had made. I should have known better and checked carefully, but my inexperience and ignorance contributed to the mistake. On Ta Shih Fu's butcher-block table next to the stove were two old blue-and-white honey jars. The honey had long since been eaten. In one jar was sugar; in the other was salt.

The soup, when I made it, had tasted good. When I tasted it later, I thought it needed a bit more salt. Just at that moment, Boy came in with a tray, ready to get the soup.

"Wait a minute, Boy; let me add a bit more salt." I took a bit of what I thought was salt and added it to the soup, then tasted it.

"It still needs more salt," I added more from the jar.

"Xiao Jie, they're waiting," said Boy impatiently. He took the spoon from my hand. "The Frenchman will get angry."

I dished out the soup into bowls and let him go. Then, without even thinking, I licked the spoon that I had used to dip into the honey jar. It tasted of sugar. I had confused the two jars. My heart sank! I imagined the Frenchman and Vanya spluttering, choking on that sweet soup. It was tragically funny! The more I thought about it, the more comical it appeared to me. I could picture Vanya's discomfort and the Frenchman's distress! Well, they were getting what they deserved! They had insisted that cooking would be no problem for me. I doubled up with silent laughter, tears coming to my eyes. Boy found me like that when he returned to the kitchen.

"The second course, Xiao Jie. Are you ready to put it on the tray?" He put the empty soup bowls on the table.

I couldn't believe it. "You mean, they ate all the soup?" I couldn't believe it!

Boy looked at me strangely. "Why wouldn't they? The Frenchman really liked it."

I dished out the wieners, potatoes, and the vegetables onto the oval serving plate. In a trance I poured the hot tomato sauce on the top. *This is unbelievable; I'm becoming a chef!*

Dessert was custard with burnt sugar sauce. The clean plates that Boy brought back told me that my efforts had been worthwhile. I sat down on the kitchen stool and wiped my forehead with a dishcloth. *Today at last is over; it is now time to plan tomorrow's meal!*

I was beginning to enjoy this cooking business. Monsieur Viaud had even insisted on increasing the board payments to ten dollars! He explained this generosity by saying that he realized how much prices of food had risen.

Our lives had now fallen into a more definite routine. Cleaning the house, planning menus, making out grocery lists, Vanya working on his studies, and both of us reading through the books on Father's shelves kept us busy. But it was not a happy or settled life. Always lurking in the background was the big question: Where are our parents? Gradually, as time passed, we began to have serious doubts. Were they still alive, or were people around us, even Dr. Ferguson, lying to us about our parents' fate?

Our lives had been centered upon our living quarters and the guest house where Monsieur Viaud stayed. We had not gone out to the back courtyard since that dawn when Vanya had climbed the vinegar tree to get to Dr. Ferguson's compound. One day we decided to go out there, to see again the schoolroom where Papa had taught his private students. We had been avoiding it because it reminded us of him. I could envision him now; he looked the way I had seen him when, after having sneaked up towards the window, I had peeped in. There he would be, standing at his podium, a short, portly, but thoroughly imposing figure of a man. Holding up his pen in his right hand, he stood poised to teach. The students in front of him, seated two by two on the plain wooden benches, silently watched his every movement.

Papa should have been an actor! His voice belied his size, for it rang out loud and clear, every word an elaborate, artistic endeavor!

"This," he would intone in his rich baritone, "is a pen!"

And like a well-trained chorus, the students echoed the sentence in unison.

Now the schoolroom, except for the thick dust on the furniture, was chilly, quiet, and empty. Father's desk without him behind it looked rather forlorn. What was it about the room, though, that didn't seem quite right? Both Vanya and I noticed it almost at the same time. Something was missing from the room!

Then we realized what it was. To the right of Papa's desk, and above it, was the darkened outline of the school clock. The wallpaper around the clock had faded. There was only the telltale newness of the paper where the clock had been hanging.

"It's gone!" Vanya stared open-mouthed at the empty spot.

"Stolen!" The thought nauseated me. Hadn't they taken enough from us already? Of course, Peking had thieves, just like any other city. But we had never had anything stolen from our house before! Thieves wouldn't want to climb over our walls whose tops had sharp fragments of glass imbedded in them. They'd be cut to pieces if they tried. With a sickening feeling I realized that this was an inside job!

"Maybe it was stolen the night of the arrest," suggested Vanya. "I'll mention it to Boy."

It was probably Boy who stole it, I thought, but I said nothing.

"You know, it could have been that a policeman stole it."

Vanya's face was speculative. "Some policemen are poor enough to want to steal when they have the opportunity, and a clock like that one would bring in quite a bit of money."

I recalled how Papa had been so enthusiastic when he had bought the clock. Rearranging this storage room, into which all sorts of junk had been cast away all these years, and transforming it into such a pleasant and airy schoolroom had filled him and Mama with vitality and happy thoughts for the future. Hanging that clock had been the final touch of class! The clock had made the schoolroom official!

Vanya told me that when he reported the theft to Boy, the servant, much to my brother's surprise, had collapsed in a fit of laughter.

"What's so funny about having something stolen?"

"You are fortunate," Boy had told him. "In your house it was only a clock that was stolen, but the colonel's family next door are still making out the list of what was stolen from them! Why, as Wang, their old gate-man, has informed me, their jewelry, silverware, and many curios were stolen. In fact, the whole family has been so upset over all this that they have instructed one of their servants to sleep outside the girls' bedroom door. They think that the girls need protection. Any bad person, in order to get to the girls, would have to step over the servant's body first."

"I assured Boy that we didn't have things of value here in our house," Vanya continued. "Come to think of it we really don't, do we? There're Father's books, but they're important only to him or to a few other scholars, not to an illiterate thief!"

"I guess you're right." I still couldn't get over the fact that a thief had been in our house. As usual, we had been sitting at the kitchen table, drinking cocoa.

Suddenly we heard the door being rattled. Boy came inside, his face red, his teeth chattering from the cold. I noticed right away that he was in one of his more expansive, affable moods. He was quite an actor, this fellow. I looked him over coldly, wondering what it was that he could be up to now. As usual, Vanya treated him cheerfully.

He came over to the table, resting his hand on the edge. He addressed Vanya, "You know, Shao Ye, what you told me about the stolen clock started me thinking. I worry about you two.

80

After all, my quarters are not close to yours. There must be quite a gang of thieves around. You know it's a known fact that they come back to a house once they've staked it out. I just have a bad feeling that you and Xiao Jie are not too safe by yourselves." He looked at me through lowered eyelids.

At this declaration of his concern, I couldn't help laughing. "Are you trying to scare us, Boy?" I asked him scornfully. "I'm not afraid of thieves."

He became apologetic, almost humble. His face was flushed. His eyes glistened with an inner excitement. He shook his head vehemently. "Oh, no, Xiao Jie," he protested. "Please don't think that I'm bad. I admire you both. The two of you have been so brave facing all the unhappiness that has descended upon you. I'm just trying to think how best to help you."

He looked at me earnestly. His eyes appeared as guileless and innocent as a baby's. What beautiful features he has, I thought. What a spectacular portrait in charcoal I could do of him, were he a different type person! I quickly switched back to reality. He had paused for a moment, his broad forehead broken by the two frown lines between his eyes.

"You know what?" He suddenly looked up at us as if the idea had occurred to him only at that very moment. Whom did he think he was kidding? Perhaps Vanya thought him pleasant and worth cultivating. I had no use for Boy. He knew it since I didn't hide my dislike for him. He bit his underlip, thinking hard. "Perhaps I should sleep outside your bedroom door. Just to protect you from any thieves. Once a thief has acquainted himself with a house and its plan, he often comes back." He shook his head sorrowfully. "These are bad times, my friends."

Vanya turned to me. "I think it's a good idea, Sis," he agreed in a low voice. "At least we'll be safer."

"We have enough protection from the police," I spoke in Chinese so that Boy would understand. "The Stilwell family might need a servant's protection, but I'm not afraid of thieves."

"Aw, c'mon, Sis, Boy wants to help us, can't you see?"

I shook my head. "We're as safe as we can be," I insisted stubbornly. "Listen," I turned angrily to Vanya. "We aren't safe anywhere, can't you see that? If we're Russian, we're already in trouble. There is no difference between us and the poorest Chinese beggar! The Japanese would as soon kill us as they would a Chinese! Why should we worry about thieves?"

"Because," Vanya was being obstinate too, "because both of us are such sound sleepers. We didn't hear anyone steal the clock, did we?"

"Of course not," I snapped, reverting to English. "It was in the backyard. Who could hear all the way back out there? No, I don't want Boy here guarding us."

By Boy's reaction I knew that he understood me. He had really looked embarrassed when I had spouted off to Vanya. *Why should I care how he feels? I'm the important one in this case.* I continued more calmly. "Did Boy protect us from the police when they came? He knew darned well when he opened the gates that first time that they were there. Did he warn us?"

"He had to let them in."

"Baloney!" I replied disgustedly. So far as I was concerned, the interview with Boy was concluded!

Vanya argued with me. I was surprised how insistent he could be. Finally, more because I was tired of all this bickering back and forth, I gave in, despite my misgivings. After all, I reasoned to myself, Vanya is two years older than I am; maybe he's right. When Vanya informed Boy that he could guard us, the servant grinned from ear to ear.

"I'll get my bedding roll!" he chortled happily. He padded silently out the door.

When he came back, he put his bedding roll neatly on top of Mama's sofa, which was situated right up against the bedroom wall. It was the same bedroom into which all of us had been herded on the night of the arrest. In it were two double beds. I slept in the one against the living-room wall; Vanya had taken over the one across from me.

Boy had now become chummy. "I'll come back at nine o'clock," he informed us cheerfully. "If you're asleep and hear any noise, don't worry. It'll only be me. I'll try to be as quiet as I can. And. . . . " Here he looked directly at me. His eyes were so frank and friendly that I couldn't help smiling. He noticed that and laughed gleefully. "You'll be safe from harm, Xiao Jie, I promise you."

By nine o'clock Vanya and I fallen asleep. We didn't hear him enter the house.

It was really strange, my waking up in this way. I had had such a weird sensation! It was as if I were still sleeping, half dreaming of something that now was becoming very real! Could it be that I was awake and that my half dream was not really a half dream?

I had been lying on my back. Slowly I raised my eyelids to see if I was really awake. It was pitch dark. Not a sound could be heard except for Vanya's breathing in the next bed. But it was there still, this inquietude. Something was dreadfully wrong right here, right in this bed where my body lay. What was happening? I opened my eyes wide, seeing nothing but that absolute darkness. Or was it all so black, without any shadows or highlights? Suddenly, a wave of horror swept over me, engulfing all of my being. Where were my hands? Desperately, I wriggled my fingers. Yes, my hands were encircling my head on top of the pillow. My whole being froze when I felt hands moving over my body, up my thighs, coming to rest on my pubic hairs, gently feeling me there, moving back and forth as if performing some strange kind of ritual!

For sure, this was not a dream! There was someone right here, crouching on the floor beside my bed, his hand stretched out beneath my heavy feather quilt, under my flannel gown, feeling the most private part of my *own* body. Who dared do such a thing?

With a wild scream I kicked off the quilt, flailing madly at the intruder, kicking at him with my feet! By now my eyes had grown accustomed to the darkness. I was able to distinguish the familiar surroundings as well as discern the crouching figure of a man who was softly stealing towards the living-room door.

Quickly, I jumped out of bed. "Vanya, turn on the light!" Darn! The light switch had to be on his side of the room!

All I heard in answer was a loud snore.

"How the devil can you sleep at a time like this?" I sprinted to his bed, scrambling over his motionless form to find the switch. Once the room was bathed in light I felt better. In disgust I stared at Vanya's peaceful countenance.

I grabbed both his shoulders and shook him. He merely turned his head, burrowing his face deeper into his pillow, the trace of a smile on his face.

"Vanya! Vanya!" I felt like screaming, but I knew that my screams would serve to scare only myself, no one else. I shook him harder. "Wake up, Vanya, for God's sake. Someone has been in here and was feeling me all over my naked body!"

Vanya groaned, then sleepily turned towards the sound of my voice. He cautiously opened his eyes, then blinked when the light blinded him and shocked him out of his dream-filled stupor. "What's all the fuss about? What's wrong with you? What time is it? Can't you let me sleep? Let me alone!"

This was my protector, my dear brother, who cared only that he be allowed to sleep in comfort, no matter what.

"Please, Vanya, wake up! There was someone in this room, and he had his hands on my . . . naked bottom parts." I was too ashamed to go on. Ugh! I shivered remembering that hand moving over my naked body!

He finally managed to waken and sit up in bed. "You look awful," he observed critically. "What do you want me to do?"

I tried to remain calm. "Are you awake enough to understand what I've been telling you? Do you realize that someone was in here by my bed feeling me under my nightgown?"

At last he was awake! His eyes opened wide. When I knew that he understood, I was relieved. Before he had a chance to dive under the covers again, I ordered him to get dressed in a hurry. "I'm too scared to go into the living room by myself. We've got to see where our bodyguard, Boy, is." I couldn't help my sarcasm.

Vanya pulled on his worn wool knickers over his pajama bottoms. When he had pulled on his jacket, he was ready. "Okay, let's go." His voice was hoarse and sleep-scratchy.

Now that I reflect on all of this I marvel that I had not been more terrified than I was. Even though I was sixteen years old at the time that this happened, I had absolutely no knowledge of sex. It was only the shameful fact that someone had *touched* me on my vagina that had shocked me. As to any other thoughts of being molested or raped, such possibilities never even entered my mind. It was just simply that I didn't know that such sexual activities existed.

Mama had warned me about something though. I was never to mention genitals nor talk about certain body functions except to her or my amah. Those words were "impolite" and not to be used in front of men or company. As for the word *sex*, it was not in my vocabulary then.

That someone had touched me on my vagina disgusted and frightened me. I wanted now to find out where the culprit was so that he could be captured and hopefully punished.

Vanya and I stole into the living room on our tiptoes. When we switched on the light we found the sofa undisturbed. There was no bedding roll on it, nor was Boy anywhere in the room!

"Why that sneaky thief!" I exclaimed furiously. "Why that darned cowardly pig! Can you believe it? He was the one who did this to me, Vanya! I just know it was him, and it's your fault because you insisted that he should sleep in the next room to guard us! Some guard he's turned out to be!" I was shaking with rage and frustration.

Vanya was embarrassed, and well he should have been! *My God!* I thought to myself in horror. *He's uncomfortable because this has happened to me. There's no sorrow or sympathy for me! He's uncomfortable because it's something that we shouldn't talk about in public! What a weakling he is!* I was surprised that this was all the backbone he had.

"I want you to confront Boy about this," I ordered him sternly. "You are my older brother. Boy has done something very ugly to me. Father himself asked you to look after me. Is this the way to carry out your promise to him?"

In reply he looked down at the ground, biting his lips nervously. "It won't do any good, you'll see," he said half-heartedly. "He'll deny everything. He'll just say that he didn't do it. You'll be the one to lose face."

"I'll never lose face!" I countered savagely. "But you'd better do this. He has insulted me. By insulting me, he has insulted you, our whole family. Don't you see?"

I was sure now that it had been Boy. I kept seeing that crouching figure slinking off. Even in the darkness, there was no mistaking that square head and the broad shoulders. Boy was proud of his physique. He was always exercising around the gate pavilion in the mornings.

Finally, Vanya agreed that he would confront Boy and called him into the kitchen. When the servant finally showed up, his rosy face was all aglow with good humor and friendliness. His audacity amazed me. When he saw me leaning against Ta Shih Fu's work table, he nodded politely as if nothing had ever happened! What kind of stupid fools did he think we were? Could he not sense how angry I was? No matter what, he was not going to get away with this indignity!

"A good morning to you both," he said pleasantly. "Did you want something?" Impertinently he turned to me. Was there no limit to his brazenness? I couldn't believe that a Chinese person could act like this one. Papa had often talked to us about Confucius, teaching us about filial piety and all those other principles of proper behavior. I thought that all Chinese had been instilled with the Master's words. Not Boy, though!

Vanya had been rubbing his palms together, his usual behavior when he was ill at ease or at a loss for words. Not once did he look directly at Boy, eye to eye. His eyes just strayed off to some unseen point. My own anger was mounting by the minute. *He is just a coward, that's all. He can't even defend his sister against an evil fiend like Boy!*

Thus it was that I walked up to Boy, my hands on my hips. I know he didn't expect me to look directly into his startled face. I stared into the sullen, sleepy-looking eyes. He looked at me indolently, smiling that despicable, scornful smile as if to say, "And what are you going to do about it?"

"How dare you!" I shook so with fury that I could scarcely speak. "Here you are, promising to guard us from thieves, and what do you do? You creep like a snake into our bedroom and feel my body. Have you no face?"

It was Vanya who let out an involuntary gasp. My brother didn't know me very well! I could've laughed in his face to see his shocked expression, but it was Boy with whom I was at war!

Boy, too, was surprised. He stood there staring at me in open-mouthed astonishment. I stared right back at him, mustering all the hate and revulsion that I could into my expression. He finally lowered his eyes. His smile was contemptuous, though. "What is it that you are trying to tell me, Xiao Jie?" What an actor!

"You heard what I said." I decided that the best way to handle him was to remain calm. I too could act. "You, Boy, were in my bedroom last night, touching and feeling me. I saw you."

Boy then shifted his gaze to Vanya, shook his head, feigning bewilderment. "I think your sister has had too much misfortune, and it is beginning to tell on her." His eyes now became compassionate, almost luminous, in their sympathy for me. "She must be losing her mind; don't you think, Shao Ye?"

"I was sound asleep," explained my brother. "I really didn't hear or see anything."

Couldn't he see how amused Boy was? And how humiliating it had to be for me? How could Vanya be so dense? Or was it that he was just being honest? He hadn't seen anything, hadn't heard anything, nor could he say anything. *Just like the proverbial monkeys*, I thought to myself bitterly.

Boy now relaxed, knowing that Vanya was not taking sides. "Your sister must rest; she's been working too hard."

"I shall rest," I informed him coldly. "Then I shall inform Dr. Ferguson about you. I'm sure you'd like him to know what kind of person you are!"

With that I stormed out of the room, knowing that if I stayed there any longer I might break down and cry. It wasn't pleasant to be so helpless and alone.

Impatiently, I waited for Dr. Ferguson to come. Every time the bell rang, I hastened to the door. However, it was either the policemen changing shifts or some poor unfortunate who happened to ring at our gates.

Finally I heard his cheerful voice in the front courtyard and saw him coming through, tapping the cement walk with his cane. Once he was comfortably settled in his favorite chair, I dragged up the hassock and sat down near him. I began to tell him, hesitatingly at first, for it was difficult to begin, and I certainly didn't want to break down in front of him. He listened gravely as I talked. There was just one problem with my story. I couldn't bring myself to tell him where exactly it was that Boy had touched me. I could not mention that word out loud, least of all to Dr. Ferguson.

The American was sympathetic, nodding his head. It relieved me to be able to confide in someone who would understand. But he didn't understand. Far from it! I had hoped that he would see to it that Boy was fired and would finally leave our house. That, however, was not to be.

The American's voice was calm. "Tamara, dear Girlie." How kind and gentle he was! Whenever he was here I always felt safe. "I shall talk to Chang and have him talk to Boy. This you must understand. Boy, like you and Vanya, is under house arrest. He is not here of his own free will. The Japanese have ordered him to remain here so there is absolutely nothing that we can do about it. We have to make the best of things, my dear, even though at times they are unpleasant to us." His bushy white eyebrows twitched. His blue eyes bored into mine, kind but intent in their seriousness. "When your folks return, then it will be an entirely different matter. They can fire him. None of us, not you or I or Vanya, can."

I hadn't expected this from him; I had thought that he would summon Boy into the room and fire him. Later on, however, thinking it over, I realized that he still had not comprehended what it was that Boy had actually done. Nor could I, under any circumstances whatsoever, have brought myself to tell him in detail how or where the servant had fondled and caressed me.

I was glad that I had talked with Dr. Ferguson, though, because it helped me come to terms with myself. From then on I was prepared! I slept with a baseball bat within reach on my side of the bed. As for Boy, I stayed away from him as much as I could. I spoke to him only when he was in the kitchen with the tray, waiting for me to dish out Paul Viaud's dinner.

Vanya, poor soul, got from me the silent treatment that I had learned from Mama. It didn't last long because he was so dejected and pathetic. I, too, was feeling lost, having no one to talk to. Before long, we became friends once more. After all, what he wanted most, poor guy, was to be left alone with his *National Geographic* magazines, his telescope, and those disgusting glassy medical slides that he so expertly maneuvered under the microscope. Let him find comfort and solace in his darkened room! Let him examine those wriggly, scraggly pieces of bacteria or whatever it was that squirmed under the power of his lens!

At times it irritated me that I was sorry for him, but it was the truth! Whenever he handled things, he always managed to do them in a clumsy, stupid way! He worked diligently to clean the house with me, but it was not in him to clean a house. He would dust the bookshelves, then find a book or magazine that interested him, and the dusting was completely forgotten. If he cut firewood, I was always on the alert, knowing that it was not in him to chop wood. Sure enough, one time he almost lost his thumb! When he formed coal balls out of coal dust, I knew that his soft hands would get infected. Just as I thought, they did!

I must admit that he never complained. He went about his work, becoming more introverted, slinking into himself, muttering or whistling softly under his breath! He seemed to like Boy's company, but with me he was different. He didn't trust me and treated me warily, as if I were the hostile one to beware of. Although he was my brother, I felt he had become a stranger. Did I really know and understand him? No!

Then sometimes things would change. After a few days spent alone, he would emerge from his cocoon a changed, much happier individual. It was during those interludes that he called me "Old Pal." It was then that I was the one who had to be wary!

With the American missionary, another daily pattern took shape. He still came to visit us; every single day, no matter how cold, how ugly the weather, or what troubles he might have had at home, he always came. And always he comforted us, encouraged us, never failing to remind us over and over again that "No news is good news." Every day, too, once he was in the safety of our inner quarters, he fished out Vanya's homework and extended the other hand for the previous homework Vanya had completed. Every single day he bowed formally to the waiting policemen, calmly walking past them, a dignified, black-coated American gentleman, swinging his cane, Vanya's completed homework safely tucked inside his coat!

He had discovered also that the postman always came at a certain time to deliver our mail. Our good neighbor by chance began to come to our house at the same time. Often he intercepted the mail, taking it before the policemen could confiscate it. He also informed us that some people—our parents' friends—had been arrested because they happened to ring our bell at the front gates.

Dr. Ferguson didn't have much use for Boy. Nothing was ever said, but I could tell. He simply acted as if the young servant didn't exist. His ignoring Boy convinced me that he believed me, but he was powerless to do anything about having him fired.

One evening I questioned Vanya. It was when both of us were in our beds, ready to go to sleep. "Whatever do you see in Boy? Why don't you stay away from him as I do? Can't you see that it was he and Mischa who helped put our parents in prison? Can't you see that?"

I should have known what his reaction would be. He just glanced towards me with that sidelong, supercilious look of his. Then he looked away. Vanya could never look me directly in the eye; it was the same with others I had noticed.

I knew he didn't like my nagging. Gritting his teeth in an attempt to control his temper, he smiled contemptuously. "Tamara, I'm not lowering myself to argue with you. You just don't know nor understand what our situation is; it's way beyond you." I could tell he was now on the defensive.

"I'm not arguing," I answered quietly. "It's just that I believe you're not doing Papa or Mama any good by playing up to Boy. You know very well that he is working for the Japs."

At that my brother smirked. "Sometimes, Sis, you underestimate my intelligence. Why do you think I'm being nice to Boy? He is, you know, the only link we have to our enemies. You act shamefully towards him. I'm the one who treats him with respect; in your opinion, I'm therefore the dumb one. Well, put this in your little skull, little sister. I learn things from him that you never could!" On his face was that self-satisfied expression that was so familiar and at the same time revolting to me.

"And what do you learn from him?" I persisted in cornering him, hoping to convince him eventually that he could be wrong.

He squinted at me to see if I was serious. "Oh," he eyed me craftily, "the stuff he tells me would certainly not interest you. In fact, your highness would be horrified! You're such a goody-goody you wouldn't even believe it when I told you."

"Like what?" I kept on because I believed that he was itching to tell me. He was teasing, trying to make me squirm and cajole to find out. It had always been thus, ever since we were children.

I wondered if I should persist, but my curiosity won out.

"All right, tell me."

He shook his head.

"Is it about Mama and Papa?"

"No, not exactly." He shook his head, grinning maliciously.

"C'mon, Vanyushka." It was time to coax now. I had softened my voice to a feline purr.

He kept on grinning. Something was really amusing him. So be it. I wasn't going to annoy him further. He was waiting for me to beg. He would have to wait a long time for that. I snuggled under my quilt, asking him to please turn off the light.

He did so without a word.

Each of us knew that the other was not asleep. I heard him chuckling to himself. *I can wait*, I told myself patiently; yet I was angry with myself for being too curious for my own good.

Suddenly I heard his low voice. "Aren't you the least bit curious, Sis?"

I pretended to be sleepy. "'Bout what?" I asked, yawning.

"'Bout what Boy and I talked about."

I moved my head deeper into the pillow, pulling the quilt over my ears. "Good night, Vanya," I said sleepily. I knew he really wanted to tell me.

He switched on the light, sitting up cross-legged on his bed. His black hair was tousled, almost covering his eyes. *Darn*, I thought to myself, *it's time to cut his hair again.*

I too sat up, yoga-style, facing him. His face looked so young, and with a pang, I noticed how lost and unhappy he was. He started talking. "Boy told me the other day how the Japanese torture prisoners, and, Sis," his eyes revealed his wretchedness, "it's not pleasant what I'm about to tell you. Are you sure you want to hear?"

I hadn't expected this. I didn't want to hear; yet I *had* to hear. I knew for sure that I would have nightmares over this, because I would imagine that everything he told me was what they were actually doing to our parents. If the Japanese tortured people, then they would certainly torture Mama and Papa in the same way. Or maybe they were being treated even worse. But I had to hear whatever it was! Reluctantly, I agreed to listen.

His eyes now narrowed mysteriously. He was telling it in the same way Boy would have told him, not applying the story to our own situation in any way. In that way it would be easier for me to listen.

"Tell me," I urged him gently.

He lowered his eyes, making patterns with a finger along his quilt. For a second or two he hesitated, as if trying to determine where to begin, then, having made up his mind, he started, his tone even, almost chilling in its impersonal aloofness.

"The Japanese use these sharp spikes made from bamboo. They are like long needles, you know. These needles, they slowly and deliberately slide under the nails of a prisoner. They push them in slowly, little by little, until the prisoner can't stand the excruciating pain and faints. They revive the prisoner, then start all over again, until all the fingers have bamboo needles sticking out of them!"

"Oh, no," I whispered softly. "How could they do that?"

He smiled, looking grotesque, grinning masklike in his misery. "They do other things that are even more horrible!" He gave me a quick, appraising glance to see if I could take it. I boldly stared back at him.

"Do you know that they pour a pitcher of kerosene into a prisoner down his throat! They just hold his mouth open and pour the liquid into him. When they think that he's had enough, they . . . " Vanya twisted his face hideously, trying to hide, even from himself, the awful vision. "Tamara, from the other end of the prisoner, the rectum"—he waited for his words to sink in—"they pump air up the prisoner until he, or she, blows up!"

I screamed; I couldn't help it.

"I don't want to hear any more!" I shivered. I could envision Papa being tortured in this way. No, I didn't want to hear another word. I wished Vanya hadn't told me about these tortures in the first place!

Vanya didn't stop; he continued like a demon obsessed! "Then they take a prisoner and pour water into his nostrils, on and on until the person's lungs are full. He dies, drowning, according to Boy."

"No more, please, Vanya." I tried to calm myself. "Vanya, please, I won't be able to sleep! They can't be that cruel!" I whispered in horror.

Tonelessly he chattered on, like a mechanized robot pro-grammed to complete his assignment. "If the prisoner has not died by that time, he is then carried to the Heavenly Bridge, Tien Tiao. There, before sunrise, before the first rooster crows, the trussed-up unfortunate is thrown to the ground. With one blow of a sword, a soldier hacks off his head. Whoosh! The head rolls on the ground, and justice, Japanese style, is served!"

Afraid of hearing my own words, I whispered, "Boy told you all that?"

He nodded, satisfied that he had justified his "cooperation" with Boy by learning about Japanese methods of torture.

I stared at him, fearing that my own eyes might be jarred out of their sockets in my horror. I wanted to sink deep into my bed, cover myself completely with the quilt, and hide myself from this awful, unbelievable truth. I cursed myself for my outrageous imagination! Why did my mind visualize so clearly such horrible pictures? All of this was plainly rumor, gossip, propaganda: Papa bound hand and foot in a truss; gasoline, kerosene poured into him through a funnel; Papa choking, gasping, dying! I shook my head back and forth, closing my eyes tightly and frowning des-perately as I tried to shake off this maddening, horrible sight!

I dreaded the remaining darkness of night. Even worse, I feared the dawn. That was the time when they took the prisoners to the Heavenly Bridge, all trussed up. One slash of a sword! Off with his head!

Out of a deep sleep I heard the train whistle. I knew that it was now dawn at Tien Tiao. *My dear God,* I prayed, *When will all this end and things return to normal?* Vanya's words and the bright light shining through the bedroom window combined to awaken me.

"Did you sleep well?" My brother sounded mighty cheerful.

"After what you told me last night?" I groaned, putting my hands to my head. It felt heavy as if a sandbag had been lying on top of it all night. "I dreamed that Mama and Papa had been tor-tured, then shot, then beheaded! It was awful, Vanya! I've never had such nightmares before." I shuddered at the recollection.

He sounded sympathetic. "I'm sorry, Tamara. I've had the same kind of dreams. They're terrible, aren't they?" He looked at me sympathetically. "Imagine how Boy feels and what *he* dreams of! He told me that he had actually seen two Japanese soldiers hack an old Chinese man to pieces right here on Magpie Street. They were drunk, of course, but that doesn't excuse their actions."

"I'm not surprised," I said dully. "Nothing surprises me anymore."

"Do you know why they killed the old man?" he asked.

"No, why?"

" 'Cause he didn't move fast enough for them! He was in their way."

Vanya and I were once more in a "truce" period. We had not argued since that day I had confronted Boy. We had been polite with each other. Now I noticed that Vanya was beginning to share more, to be more friendly. He needs me, I realized with cautious amusement. In fact, he was becoming quite palsy-walsy with me lately. What was it that he was after? I hated myself for being suspicious of his actions towards me; yet I learned that my intuitions about him usually proved to be indubitably correct.

Vanya had risen earlier than I. When I finally wakened for good, after my fitful and nightmarish sleep, I realized that it was already past daybreak. It was time to get up and start the new day! What would today bring? Good news? Maybe even a snippet? Something telling us that our parents were alive, even though in prison? I wasn't going to raise my own spirits, then have them dashed back to their present low state! I dressed automatically, putting on the checkered wool skirt that I had worn day in, day out, all these winter months. I slipped on the green sweater, smelling my own sweat under the armpits. If I washed the sweater it would take several days to dry. *Let it be,* I thought to myself. *It's my own smell.*

I finished dressing, then joined Vanya in the kitchen. He had lighted the stove. It was warm and cozy. *Our life these days sure is strange,* I thought. *In the days gone by, Ta Shih Fu would have thrown a conniption fit if we had even entered his domain. Now God knows where he is. Vanya and I are now the masters of this room! Ha!* The kitchen stove, black wrought-iron with its curlicued designs, a stranger in bygone days, was now our dear friend, keeping us warm and full! We had learned how to humor the old thing. With one of those round, black iron lids, we would fan the smoldering coals gently until the fire grew brighter. Finally, the flames would shoot upwards, hungry as always! We had learned how to cope with its hunger for coal balls.

I was surprised and puzzled by Vanya's attitude these days. He actually wanted to talk things over with me. I knew that he was still seeing Boy, sharing things with him, but now he was acting as if I were really important. I couldn't believe his attempt at reconciliation! Did he really want my friendship? It was strange, this approving look that he often bestowed upon me. He was looking at me with different eyes, as if I were someone completely different from the sister he had previously detested.

We now sat at the kitchen table. He had heated the cocoa, even buttered some toast for me. Now he watched me bite into the toast as if he were seeing me for the first time as a distinct individual, not someone attached to him like a parasite.

"You know, Old Pal . . . " Then he took a deep gulp of cocoa. I watched his Adam's apple move up and down.

"Please; no more tortures, Vanya," I objected firmly.

"It's not about that." He laughed heartily, but his eyes were watching me carefully.

How well I knew my brother!

"All right, then, what is it that you want to tell me?" I was all patience, but he had become embarrassed, scrunching his shoulders. He remained silent, studying me.

"Well then," I said as I slid off the stool. "If you won't tell me, I'm leaving. I have things to do."

He put out his hand to stop me. "Tamara, don't leave. It's just that you sort of surprised me. I thought you wouldn't want me to tell you what other things Boy had said. They're really repulsive!"

I couldn't imagine what in the world he was up to this time. All at once he got hold of himself. "It's about . . . " He paused dramatically, studying my face, wondering whether he should go on, but I was all ears, waiting for him to continue.

"Well, Boy told me something most interesting, but it's hard to believe. Did you ever wonder how we came to be born, Tamara?" His skin was turning red the way it always did when he was ashamed or had lost face.

"No, I didn't." I hadn't thought of that in a long time. Then I recalled having asked Mama once where I had come from. I remembered her face then. We had been sitting in the central courtyard under the acacia tree, she on the settee and I on the wicker ottoman leaning against her legs. I had been six or seven.

"Where did I come from, Mama?" It was just a question that had come to me out of the blue; like other questions, it popped out of the mouth unexpectedly.

She had looked at me with such good humor and delight. She gave me a stupid answer. "You came out of my vagina, baby. That's why you are such a stinky little girl!"

I had known all along that she was teasing me. No matter how I nagged at her, she kept repeating the same silly answer. I didn't bother asking her anymore. Besides, I existed; that was what was important. People existed. When they didn't, it meant that they died. It was sad because you didn't see them anymore. Porfirieffa's husband, for example, had been old, had died, and therefore, had ceased to exist!

Vanya was persistent. "Do you know *how* we came to be born?"

"No, does it matter?"

"Aren't you curious about what makes you be born?"

I had never thought of it that way. "Why? What's so strange about being born? Everyone is born."

"But how do babies *get* to be born?" he asked me. "Do you know how they get into their mothers' stomachs?"

"They just get there somehow," I told him wisely. "Then they grow in there until they are ready to be born. I really don't care how they get there."

"I'll bet you'd care if you knew." He gave me a strange leer, which I didn't like. It was like the look Boy had given me one time. "What if I told you that to get us Papa put his penis into Mama's vagina and pumped her till his semen spilled into her. That stuff just mixed up inside her and made each of us grow. That's God's honest truth. Boy told me." He slid off his stool, his eyes triumphantly fixed on mine. "What, Tamara, do you think of that?"

I knew that he was lying. Definitely, he was. I could tell it by the way his cheeks were flushed and the way that devilish half-smile played on his lips. He was just trying to embarrass me by telling me things which in Mama's presence he would never dare to utter. Then I began to wonder. He couldn't have made all that up. Even with Boy's imagination to help him, he couldn't have imagined all that. It was so disgusting, so revolting, so preposterous! But what if it were true?

"You're lying," I whispered unconvincingly.

"So Boy told me, and he's a married man."

I arched my back, biting my lips in disdain. "There you go again, quoting that liar. Can't you understand what a hold he has on you?"

He shook his head stubbornly.

"You're the doubter. I believe him. Besides, he showed me some photographs."

"What kind of photographs?" I asked.

He grinned. "You wouldn't believe it. They were postcards of a sort. One showed a woman lying on her back in a bed. There was a man lying on top of her. They were completely naked. There was his penis just poking into the space between her legs, like a bullet going in! Boy explained that all women have a hole in their vaginas especially for the semen to go into. That way it mixes in with her juices and then a baby is formed somehow. The photographs he showed me were pretty interesting."

"Ugh!" That was all I could say. How terribly disgusting. I wondered if Dorlise knew anything about such things. No, if she had known, she would have told me. Then I thought of my parents. That was what convinced me. Not my sweet, gentle Mama. She would never lie under Papa's weighty body. Never!

"No matter what you think, it's true." Vanya had been expecting my negative reaction. "I know. You can't believe that of Mama and Papa. It's true, Tamara, believe me. They had to do it to get you and me. They did it at least two times. Think of it, all through the ages man has lain on top of a woman so that they would have children." He waxed dramatic. "Just think," he repeated in a more subdued tone, "all through these centuries!"

I'd had enough of this nonsense. I couldn't listen to him anymore. It was not something that I wanted to discuss. Then I began remembering certain vague memories of events, and I realized that, whether I liked it or not, he just might be telling the truth.

97

I remembered when I was little, about five years old, Papa had taken me up on his lap in his study. He had a big book laid out in front of him on his desk. I had been playing with an eraser or something like that on his desk, not paying much attention to what he was doing, just content to sit on his lap. He had been really engrossed in this book, studying it, leafing through its pages, sometimes turning them back to take another look. Somehow my eyes had strayed to this book. I had been surprised to see pictures of naked men and women; then there were pictures of their naked parts, genitals and all. I had wondered to myself what Papa thought pretty in those pictures and bent my head to look more closely. At that, Papa had put me down, closing the book.

Another thought struck me like lightning, and this one made me numb! *Was that what Boy was about to do to me when I awakened?* I shuddered at the very idea.

Vanya had been quietly observing me with a strange, calculating look in his eyes. "You know, I think that somewhere in Papa's library there is a book about reproduction."

"What's reproduction?"

"That's the business of begetting children, Tamara. Even I know that," he told me haughtily.

"Where's the book?" If he was bluffing, I'd find out.

"We'll have to look through his books, but I remember seeing it one time. H. G. Wells wrote it, I think."

It would take a lot of looking, I told myself. Papa had so many books! We both walked towards Papa's study. Vanya was quite familiar with the shelves; he had put all the books back in order. He kept searching, fingering the books lightly, until he came to one shelf.

"I think it's here. Ah . . ." He pulled out an enormous volume, almost like an encyclopedia. "Yep, here it is. By H. G. Wells, just as I thought." He took the book over to Father's desk and put it on the blotting pad.

We looked under "reproduction." We found several paragraphs on the intriguing subject on the various pages that we flipped through. We couldn't make any sense of the article. There were too many unfamiliar scientific words. I soon lost interest. There were not even pictures to examine.

"You said Boy showed you pictures?" I challenged Vanya.

"Yes, he did." Vanya grinned. "There were quite a few. They really were postcards, showing men and women in different positions, but there was always the man's penis in the woman's er—ah, you know . . . " he finished lamely.

"Different positions? What do you mean by that?" I asked.

"Ooh, why, a man could lie down with the woman on top of him, just so long as they are hooked together. You know . . . " he added significantly.

I took up a pencil and made a rough sketch. "Like this?"

He examined it critically. "Yes, sort of," he replied.

What was I doing drawing stuff like this? Ashamed, I quickly tore the paper into small pieces.

"What'd you do that for?" objected Vanya. "That was good."

"I'll never, never get married!" I declared. "No man'll ever do that to me."

Vanya grinned again. "Never say *never*, Old Pal."

We went to bed later than usual. Vanya had more than the customary batch of homework to do for the next day. I thought that he would like company for encouragement, so I stayed up with him. I had tried reading, but it only made me sleepy. Instead, I turned to practicing calligraphy with the *mao-bi* (Chinese writing brush).

When we finally did go to our respective beds, I could hardly crawl under the blanket, I was so tired. I fell into a deep sleep, thankfully without anymore nightmares.

I awakened with the sun filtering through the paper window. There was an unpleasant sensation between my thighs, a sticky, unfamiliar wetness on my pubic hairs.

When I went to roll over, something prevented me from doing so. With a growing uneasiness I turned my head to that side. There was Vanya. He was lying there, not in his own bed, but next to me, his arm flung out in a dreamless sleep. His ugly, wet penis was resting against me. Sickened and infuriated, I pushed at him with all my might, kicking at him, until he plopped onto the floor. He was now wide awake, rubbing his eyes.

Grinning sheepishly, he whispered in a conspiratory tone, "That was nice, Sis, but I wish you'd been awake enough to enjoy it."

I could barely see him for my tears. Running to the bathroom, I washed his filth off me. Then I really sobbed my heart out, sitting there on the toilet seat behind the locked door. Now there was really no one for me. God was the only One to Whom I could talk now.

4

Visitors Not Welcome

Nearly six months had passed since the arrest. We knew no more than the same old refrain: "No news is good news." This time last year Mama and the servants had been doing the annual spring cleaning. This time this year, Vanya and I had learned a great deal, not much of it pleasant!

One afternoon Dr. Ferguson sent word by Chang that he was bringing three Chinese officials to visit us. Would I please have tea ready for them?

Had it been anyone else who had asked this of me, I would have refused in no uncertain terms. I could not feel civil towards anyone who had an official title here in Peking. Any Chinese official remaining here was a traitor working for the Japanese and would naturally be hostile towards not only our parents but also to us. However, out of respect for the kind American, I set up the tea table and prepared tea in the way Ta Shih Fu had once taught me. We had no sweet food except the can of American cookies Dr. Ferguson had given us for Christmas. The Chinese would have to go hungry for sweets; in no way would I serve them those!

Vanya and I cleaned ourselves up as best we could. Our clothes were worn but clean. We sat in the living room thumbing through magazines, waiting for the sound of the bell.

Once more, Vanya and I were back on speaking terms. I had no other choice. I did insist, however, that he sleep in the living room from now on. I no longer trusted him. Every night I pushed Mama's heavy dresser against the door.

I no longer cared how chummy he got with Boy. My main goal

was to keep on cooking for Monsieur Viaud so that he wouldn't complain. So long as the plates came back empty, I remained satisfied. That ten dollars for his board surely helped us!

There were many things to occupy my time: books to read, the piano to play, pictures to paint. At night I knelt beside my bed and spoke very plainly to God. I explained to Him that it had really been such a long, long time without our parents, and I was terribly tired and depressed, but I thanked Him for His wonderful servant, Dr. Ferguson.

It was not long that we had to wait for our guests. Soon we heard the good Doctor's cheerful voice followed by the tapping of his cane. We also heard some muffled voices; his three companions were now following him through the little red pavilion towards our quarters. Vanya rose to hold open the door for them. I waited curiously for them to enter, wondering what the purpose of their visit could be.

The officials wore Western clothing. Apparently they were members of the Chinese diplomatic section, not police officials. They were friendly enough, making themselves immediately at home. They were interested in how we were occupying our time. One of them even asked to see my artwork. I knew then that Dr. Ferguson had told them about us.

They were impressed with my Chinese calligraphy, shaking their heads in approval, pointing out to each other the perfection of my brush strokes!

They questioned Vanya about his hobbies. At first, he was rather reticent. However, when he found out that Mr. Chen knew something about astronomy, my brother even brought out his telescope to show it to the older man.

I served the hot tea, apologizing that I had nothing more to offer them. It was a very proper, semiformal kind of tea party, and I felt proud of both of us. I knew that the Chinese could find nothing wrong in our behavior. Dr. Ferguson had left the entertaining to us. Today he was more the observer, watching us from afar, not really taking the lion's share in all of this. After a time, after I had filled the teapot once more and they had drunk their fill, Dr. Ferguson rose, taking up his cane. This was the signal that it was time for everyone else to rise and speak their farewells. There was much bowing and placing both fists together, Chinese salutation-style.

Whether it was an inspection or merely curiosity on the part of the Chinese, we never did find out. Dr. Ferguson's hug at the front gates made me feel great, however. There was a big smile to accompany it.

Another time, some five months after the arrest, we had three other visitors. It was towards the end of May, when the lilacs, forsythia, and my favorite, purple daisies, were a mass of blooms in the front courtyard. With winter behind us, I began to feel more optimistic. At times, I had been so desperate and discouraged; I was sure that there was no longer any hope of our parents' being alive. I felt in my heart that this kind of living was just a big charade as far as Vanya and I were concerned. Life was just a dramatic production with Dr. Ferguson, the good director, and the Japanese, the evil producers. I was sure that Mama and Papa had long before been killed off. In time, they would get rid of us too. It would just take a bit more time because the good American was in the way! And then, of course, there was the Frenchman who kept an eye on us!

The day that the three women barged into our living room so unceremoniously startled Vanya and me so completely that for a few minutes we could only stare at them open-mouthed. I had been playing records on the old Victrola in the corner of the dining room. Vanya had been doing his homework, and his papers were scattered all over the dining-room table. Somehow they had managed to enter the main house unannounced. There was no Boy to escort them in after they had entered the front courtyard. The policemen never allowed visitors to enter but had in the past escorted them straight to the police station for questioning. Apparently, this time the policemen had let them enter because they were Americans who had insisted on seeing us for their own special reasons.

Vanya and I remembered what Dr. Ferguson had made us promise him; we were *not* to let anyone inside our quarters! Here they were, these women, uninvited and unannounced. What were we to do? The women were almost as startled at seeing us as we were at seeing them. One of them looked vaguely familiar although, for the life of me, I couldn't figure out where I had seen her before.

They looked like American missionary women. They were motherly looking, their clothes similar—formless flowered prints that most American women favored, unless they were members of the more stylish diplomatic section, which focused more on socializing than proselyting.

They were missionaries. Hastily they introduced themselves, apologizing for barging in on us like this. The taller one was their spokeswoman. The other two were both short and rather stout. They stood in the middle of the living room, curiously surveying us and the two rooms.

Neither Vanya nor I remembered their names. We gawked at them at first in surprise, then in hostility, and finally in suspicion. The tall woman's concern didn't touch us at all.

"We just had to come over to see for ourselves that you children were all right. There's so much gossip these days, such intrigue! One doesn't know what's real any more, does one?"

The other two women nodded assent. I followed their glances, trying to look through *their* eyes at what they were seeing. The house was clean. There was even a large vase of purple lilacs on our tea table. The Rosencrantz piano shone. We two looked fairly presentable, although Vanya's knickers were worn at the knees, and my darning had made them look even worse! The tall woman had been talking to me. I nodded mechanically at her, wishing she'd go away.

"Pardon me?" I was embarrassed; I hadn't been listening.

Her eyes were gray behind her horn-rimmed glasses. Wispy strands of pepper-colored hair straggled out from under her floppy, white hat. "I was just saying that we've heard that such awful things were happening to you. Whatever did happen?"

Vanya didn't have to look at me that way! I wasn't that dumb that I'd tell all, at least to these three women.

"I'm sorry, ladies," I drew myself up as tall as I could. "We have been forbidden to talk to anybody. As you can see, we are all right. Thank you for coming. We'd appreciate it if you would leave now that you have seen us and our home."

I felt rather sorry for them. Vanya had given me a big grin after my speech. The ladies had looked at each other in bewilderment. They hadn't counted on our being this unfriendly and inhospitable. But what could we do? For all we knew they could be spies for the Japanese; the stories they would repeat, should we talk to them, might mean death for our parents and jail for us.

They turned back towards the door, walking out in single file. The tall one was the last. Before she left, she bent her head towards me, then whispered softly into my ear, "If there is anything that we can do for you, let us know. We realize you're under guard."

I smiled then, in case she genuinely meant it, and nodded my head. It didn't really matter whether they were well-meaning missionary ladies or not. The assistance we needed wouldn't be theirs to give.

The following day when Dr. Ferguson visited, we told him about the ladies. He was astonished and irritated at this intrusion. "I've told Boy, and the policemen, countless times that no one was to see you unless it was Mary, your French tenant, or I myself." His eyebrows twitched in annoyance, and the kind blue eyes looked worried. "They might be, and probably were, some do-goody ladies from the church, but these days, even do-gooders are under suspicion." He then winked, once more becoming his cheerful old self. "But you both were right to behave as you did, politely but firmly not doing or saying anything!" He chuckled at the thought. "I can just imagine those three going back to the other ladies of the church and telling them about the two of you! There'll be even stranger rumors going in those circles, I'll bet!" As he walked back to the front gates with us by his side, he tapped his cane on the brass of the threshold and said, "You did the right thing, but I'm sure those ladies meant well." With that, he waved his cane in the air, went through the front gates, and walked away up Magpie Street.

We had another visitor in June. She too had been wholly unexpected and even more unwelcome! Vanya had adamantly told Boy that he was not to let any stranger come into our quarters.

We had heard the bell ring but paid no attention, even though the ring was loud. It had sounded as if someone was pressing the bell with all his might! Dr. Ferguson had already been here once; I figured whoever it was at the gates would have business with Boy or the guards, not with us. I was wrong.

This time it was Boy who ran in through the living-room door. He was flustered and worried. "There's a young lady outside, sitting in a ricksha. I think she's Russian. She's very upset and insists on seeing the two of you." He was breathless, still huffing from his exertion.

"Send her away," Vanya told him brusquely. "You know very well that we must not see her."

"She's looks frightened, Shao Ye," the servant whispered, his voice pleading. "What harm is there in seeing her? She said she had just arrived from the railway station from Tientsin."

"We can't, you know that. She'll probably be arrested if she's Russian," I said. I didn't want him telling us what to do; all of us had been told not to let strangers into our living quarters.

"Let her in but explain that it's only for a moment," Vanya ordered. We hurried after Boy to the gate pavilion. We could see her through the opened gates. She was getting out of the ricksha. In her arms she had a large handbag and several packages. She rushed up the steps, her face hidden by her brown felt hat. As she entered the pavilion, she raised her head, smiling shyly. She attempted to free one hand so that she could shake ours, but dropped a package in the effort. Vanya stooped to pick it up.

Why, she's not much older than Vanya, I thought. She would have been pretty if she hadn't been so confused.

"I'm Natasha." Her voice was soft. "Natasha Gavriluk," she explained. "You are the professor's son and daughter. Right?"

Vanya and I nodded. I changed my mind about her age. She had to be around twenty-three or -four, I decided, when I studied her face again as we walked down the steps into the front courtyard. Her hat looked funny, pulled down over her ears. There was some mousy fur on the edge, quite improper for June weather. Her hair was reddish; I could see tiny curls from under the brim. Her eyes were a beautiful blue, her most attractive feature.

Suddenly, she paused by the moon gate. She looked back towards Boy, who was standing inside the gate pavilion looking silently down at her. We had been walking with her towards our own quarters.

Her eyes widened. "Wha-what's the matter?" She stared from Vanya to me. "Why is your servant watching me?"

I motioned her quickly inside. Once we stepped into the living room I took her bundles from her, placing them on the sofa. "Sit down," I told her sternly. "I don't know who you are or what you are or who sent you here to us. Anyway, Vanya, my brother, and I are alone in this house. Our parents are not here."

Vanya sat down beside her. "It's best for you to leave our house," he warned her.

"But you don't understand!" She placed her gloved hand on his arm. "I'm a friend of the Yasakoffs," she whispered. "They're the ones who told me to come here." Suddenly her face blanched. "Is there trouble here?"

Just then we heard the sound of our gates being barred. My heart sank. The policemen had returned. They were the ones who always barred the gates! Apparently she had noticed my alarm.

"What is it? Tell me!" Then she leaned back against the sofa, placing one hand across her eyes. "Oh, my dear God, what have I stumbled into?" Her voice lowered to a whimper, and she sat thus for five full minutes, her face hidden, her body shaking, murmuring, "Oh, my God, my Holy Saviour, save me!"

I learned the full meaning of "misery loves company." The poor young woman was stranded, helpless, and she was seeking help from us, two helpless, even younger strangers. Strange as it may have seemed, her tragic situation made me feel like laughing. She was so pathetic in her misery. She turned a tear-lined face towards me. "What about you two? Why, you're nothing but children!" She stood up, her hand to her mouth. "Dear God, what have I done?"

Calling us children really irked Vanya. "We're not children," he objected. "I'll be eighteen in October, and Tamara here is sixteen."

I don't think she heard him. She started to gather up her things, tearfully muttering to herself. Then she walked towards the door, biting her lips. She turned. "I think I'd better go. I shouldn't have come, I know that now. I brought you gifts from the Yasakoffs." She dropped two packages. "Here they are. I'm going now."

"We can't take anything from people," I explained to her. I felt sorry for her then. She was genuinely frightened out of her wits.

"Have your parents been arrested?" Her eyes nearly jumped out of their sockets when she realized they must be in prison.

I laughed nervously. "Yes. We're under arrest too."

"Oh, no! My God!" She backed towards the sofa, almost swaying as she fell on to it, scattering her bundles. There was no life in her anymore.

"What shall we do with her?" I asked Vanya helplessly. When I said that, she sat up, shaking her head as if to clear it. "I'm scared to death," she moaned softly. "You've got to help me." The look in her eyes was wild. Her hands clenched and unclenched themselves. She was extremely upset. *Does she have something to hide?* I wondered.

"You've just got to help me," she repeated. She was now more in control of herself.

"We can't help you," I told her quietly.

She nodded as if she understood. "I know; I know," she murmured. Vanya tried to reassure her.

"One good thing, Natasha, you don't know our family personally. That's in your favor."

"But I'm Russian!" she replied.

That was when she really paled. Like a caged animal she ran first to the windows, then the door, looking out towards the moon gate. "Can they see us? The guards, I mean?" She seemed calmer now, but it was only for a moment.

"The guards are probably in the servants' quarters now. You shouldn't have insisted on seeing us," I told her somewhat rudely.

She panicked. "How could I have known? They're back, are they?"

"The guards?" asked Vanya.

"Yes." She was like a trapped bird, fluttering.

When he nodded, she ran to the kitchen door. "Is there a way out of here from the back? I've got to get out! Oh, dear God! They mustn't find me."

There was something awfully suspicious about her. Both Vanya and I silently had agreed that we couldn't help her. She could be a spy! I thought bitterly of Mischa.

"There is no other way out," I told her firmly. "The policemen know that you're here. Your rickshaman is still in front of our house. They would find you anyway."

Again there was a fresh deluge of tears.

"You'd better go now," Vanya spoke gently, taking her arm. "If they even think that you know us, it might be worse for you."

Numbly she let him steer her towards the door. When he turned the knob, however, she stepped back. Opening her purse quickly, she took out a thin green booklet. "Here, take this!" she whispered, trying to give it to me.

I backed away from her, shaking my head in refusal. "I can't; I'm sorry," I apologized.

"Please." She shoved it towards me, her eyes pleading. "It's my Soviet passport." I ignored her. "If they find me with it, then I'll really be in trouble!"

"What are you?" asked Vanya in surprise. "You mean you have two passports on you?" He whistled.

"Father had no passport. That's why they arrested him," I informed her coldly. "With two you really should be safe." I couldn't help being mean to her. She didn't *have* to come!

She was too terrified to listen. She had seen the Russian stove by the door. Opening the little door, she tried to throw the green booklet inside. I was quicker, however, and slammed the door shut before she could do it.

"Not here, you don't," I told her angrily. "Look, we don't know who you are. We happen to be in enough trouble already without you making it any worse for us. Take your two passports and leave us in peace."

She ignored me, running like a hunted animal towards the dining room, muttering and praying to herself, clutching her purse to her breast. Then I noticed that as she ran, she was tearing her passport apart, dropping the pieces onto the floor. Finally she slipped the rest of it behind a chair cushion. "Please, let me hide it here." Her eyes looked much too miserable for it to be an act.

"All right," I agreed, convinced that she must really be in trouble. Tears welled up in my own eyes. "Don't worry," I whispered to her as we accompanied her to the front. "They won't arrest you. You're too young."

I was wrong.

They were waiting for her by the red gates. Although they did not tie her hands with rope like a common prisoner, two of

109

them did escort her down the steps onto Magpie Street. There, a different ricksha, not hers, awaited her. After making sure that she was seated, the policemen jumped on their black bicycles, one on either side of her, to take her away.

Our last glimpse of her was when she turned her tear-stained face towards us, giving us a helpless and mute farewell.

It is strange how unforeseen events often shape a person's character or even develop their hitherto dormant traits. Nearly nine months had dragged by since that horrible, unforgettable December night. Already I felt years older! Life and its complexities these days bewildered me.

When I stopped to look at myself in action, I realized that most of these days I was more or less behaving like Kate in Shakespeare's *The Taming of the Shrew*! In the past, people would often comment upon my sunny disposition, a trait that had been molded into shape by my favorite amah. I remember so well when that molding actually began!

When I was eight or so years old, Mama on this one particular day had called me *ugly*. I now know that she hadn't really meant it. Once in a while she would say things teasingly, but to me, this one time, *ugly* had sounded real. I ran tearfully to hunt for Amah, who, I knew, would comfort me. I found her sitting on the kitchen stool talking to Ta Shih Fu while she mended our old socks. When she saw me in tears, she laid aside her work, encircling me affectionately. "And why are you crying, Xiao Mei [little sister]? Did big brother hit you again?"

Between sobs I told her what Mama had called me. Amah gently rubbed my back. When I had finished my tale of woe, she moved me away from her so that she could look directly into my eyes.

"Little girl!" Her small eyes, so wise-looking and kind, seemed to crinkle at the corners when she smiled. "Tell me, child, do you know why we Chinese call you Mei Li?"

I shook my head.

"*Mei* is a character that means beautiful; the character *Li* means the same thing. Placing the two characters like these side by side means that you are doubly beautiful. When Chinese people name a person, they take their time. Do you think they would call you Mei Li if you were ugly?"

I smiled through my tears. "No, Amah," I admitted.

"Well, then, let me tell you a little secret. You know when you are most beautiful to people? It's when you smile, just as you are doing now. Your Mama was teasing you, so don't cry any more. But remember; if you want to live up to your name and be doubly beautiful, you *have to smile!*"

I've never forgotten that one wonderful amah nor her wise counsel. That advice has served me well on so many occasions. Even in my enforced isolation, I recalled that time and smiled to myself. Once more I realized it was up to me and only me. To mold myself into the person that I wished to become and to survive this living nightmare, I *should* smile!

Shakespeare's Polonius had maximized it well: "This above all: to thine own self be true." How often lately I had repeated those lines to myself. "And it must follow, as night the day, Thou canst not then be false to any man." Shakespeare and Amah! They had little in common, but they surely knew their fellow human beings!

Indeed, I was most fortunate. How much my dear parents had already bequeathed to me! Mentally, my mind made a list: their own love for books, art, languages, and music had stimulated our minds. We had to keep our hands busy in order to survive physically, but with us in that old house on Magpie Street was a vast store of knowledge that opened doors to the world. If Dickens, Thoreau, or Swift didn't fit our mood or fancy, there were other authors who would. From around the world they appeared! Russia's Tolstoy calmed me with tales of simple peasant faith; de Maupassant left me dreaming of love and sacrifice; Louisa May Alcott made me wish that I could be one of her *Little Women*.

At other times I sat on the dining room floor beside the mahogany gramophone. Searching through the piles of heavy albums, I found favorite selections for listening. There were La Scala operatic records. I listened to Enrico Caruso, Chaliapin, who was Mama's favorite, and John MacCormack, whose tender songs blended with my own girlish dreams and made them one.

The music lifted me into a totally different world that was filled with love, wonder, and joy.

I withdrew more and more into myself those days and valued my moments alone. I was happiest reading books. Deep involvement in reading a novel transported me into a completely new world. For a time, I could forget all the ugliness around me. Away from books, I remained suspicious and cynical towards anyone who spoke to me. Only the American missionary had a place in my heart, but he too at times was subjected to my cynicism and suspicion.

There was one lovely summer's day I remember well. I was curled up on the wicker settee underneath the sheltering branches of the white acacia tree in the central courtyard. The acacia was in full bloom. Its branches bent down, loaded with cascading, fragrant clusters. Every once in a while I closed my eyes and lifted my face upwards to inhale the heavenly scent. Then I raised my eyelids to look at that mind-boggling, limitless blue expanse of sky above me. How I would like to be a bird and soar away from all this unhappiness! How peaceful and lovely nature is! Man alone is deliberately cruel to his fellowmen!

I hadn't realized that Dr. Ferguson had come into the courtyard, nor did I know how long he had been standing there, in the little red pavilion, watching me. A slight cough alerted me to his presence. He was chuckling, regarding me with affectionate amusement.

"Enjoying this delightful weather we're having?" He cast a glance up at the sky, then stepped down, walking towards me. He pulled up a chair close to the settee. "I'm glad to see you relax for a change." He laid his cane across his lap, giving it a pat. "How are you, my dear?" He bent his head towards my face so that he could look directly into my eyes.

Our eyes met. How blue and clear his eyes were! *What a truly wonderful face he has,* I thought to myself. The bushy, twitching snow white eyebrows, the aristocratic nose, and most of all his smile beneath the thin, white moustache altogether represented to me a kindness and concern that I could find in no other single face.

Should I ask him? I wondered. We were alone, so this was the best time to talk with him. Vanya was in his backroom examining things through his microscope.

"You're thoughtful today, Girlie. Have you something to tell me?" His fingers tapped a tune on his cane.

I kept my hand on my open book so that I wouldn't lose my page. Doing this also gave me confidence. "It's not really that important, Dr. Ferguson; I've just been thinking about things."

"Anything concerning you, dear, is important. What is it, my child?"

That was what made the good American so special to me. He treated me like an adult, even if he often did call me "child." I could talk to him person-to-person, not the way most grown-ups talked to me, as if I didn't know enough or weren't equal to them. With Mama and Papa I had to listen to what they told me; rarely could I tell them what I thought or what was in my heart! With Dr. Ferguson, however, I felt equal and at ease, even though he was the tallest man I had ever seen. He did not ridicule me, nor mock, nor belittle! With him I felt as tall as he was!

"It's just that I've been thinking a lot about things lately. Something *has* been bothering me; you're right about that. I think all the time about my parents, but lately I've been wondering what Vanya and I'll do if we never do see our parents again. If you know . . . " I couldn't complete the sentence.

I had to talk on while I had this opportunity with him. "If our parents don't ever return, what happens then, Dr. Ferguson? What will become of Vanya and me? We can't live here in this house forever. Where do we go? What shall we do?" Suddenly, I stopped, realizing that this shouldn't be his worry. He had enough troubles with his wife being ill. I had no right to burden him with all this. "I'm sorry, Dr. Ferguson," I apologized. "This is my worry, not yours."

He laid both hands on me. "Don't you *ever* say that, Girlie. I've worried about what to do in case it ever does happen, although I'm almost sure it won't. You're right, however, to confide in me. I'll do my best to do anything I can to put your mind at ease." His sincerity made me feel that we were a team!

It was a relief to learn that he had been thinking of our plight! Maybe he had even discussed it with his wife or with Mary. He hadn't been at all surprised when I brought up the subject.

He paused. "I haven't talked about your problems or those of your parents for two reasons. In the first place, I think your folks are all right. Secondly, there is little that we can do other than wait to see what the Chinese and the Japanese do here in Peking. However, to alleviate your worries, Girlie, I'll tell you this. If it should ever develop that something should happen to your parents, then I'll send you to my own family in America where you'll be able to study and," here his eyes fastened themselves on mine with genuine love, "become a real American."

"And Vanya?"

A frown wrinkled the American's smooth brow. "He'll have to go to the Soviet Union," he said slowly. "I honestly think that he'll be happier there in the land of his fathers."

I couldn't ask him why he had decided this; in fact, his answer had indeed surprised me, pleased me, and puzzled me. I had always sensed that Dr. Ferguson had disliked Vanya as much as Vanya disliked him. What surprised me was that he had known how much I wanted to be an American. Even more puzzling to me was that he knew that Vanya's pride was the New Russia. He was right; Vanya should go there. If he did, I would never see him again! Whether that was bad or good I couldn't say at the moment. It was all too much! But America? At the very thought an overwhelming radiance flooded over me.

My moving to America could happen only if we lost both our parents. Of course, then, *it must not happen!* But at least I knew now what would be—if the worst should ever occur.

I thanked him then.

"Then it is all right with you?" he asked me, his eyes searching mine this time.

After he left, I started to read where I had left off, but I found myself flipping over the pages mechanically. My eyes had scanned the lines, but my brain cells had been thinking of other things. In disgust, I slammed the book shut.

Life in America! Ah, what a wonderful life that would be! I saw the house we would be living in, a house just like all the other homes in the United States of America. It would be a white house with a brick facade, trimmed in dark evergreen—shutters and all! Rows and rows of Del Monte food cans would line the sparkling white kitchen shelves! There would be a rose garden in front and a green lawn, and no walls at all to shut out the world!

Boy's padded footsteps coming through the red pavilion brought my dreams to an abrupt stop. His ruddy face looked meek for a change. His tone was not as insolent as usual. I still couldn't look into his face without recalling what he had done to me. I gave him an icy stare as he approached. I wasn't one to forgive or forget easily, especially in Boy's case.

"What is it that you want, Boy?"

He came closer, stopping a few feet away from me. He placed his right hand over the left one in front of him.

"Wang the policeman. It's on account of him that I come to you."

I nodded, waiting. I remembered the old man, having seen him several times when we had walked with Dr. Ferguson to the gates. Wang was of the old school, an aged Chinese with gentle manners. His Mandarin was spoken purely, not with the guttural impurities of those who came from provinces other than ours. Wang, however, wore that black and white uniform that now had become to me almost as hateful a symbol as that of the Japanese olive drab.

"He wants a favor from you. May he come to see you?"

I nodded assent, curious indeed to find out what a guard would want of his prisoner.

Boy smiled. As he turned to leave, he paused. "He'll come now. All right?"

"All right," I said curtly. I seated myself in a chair. This was going to be an official visit, so I decided to be properly formal. I wondered if the policeman had secret news. Maybe he had known Papa in the past. Maybe he needed more information. But then he would quiz Vanya, not me. What would he want with me? The more I thought about it, the more curious I became. Was he going to ask me if Papa was a white, red, or pink Russian? That's what most people wanted to know. It's strange how colors had become so important, not only in paintings and clothes but also in politics! Anyway, I couldn't, and certainly wouldn't, give him much information!

Old Wang walked in through the pavilion, his deeply-lined face wreathed in smiles. He was shaking his head, obviously delighted at being able to see me. His cap was in his hands.

"Thank you for so honoring me, Xiao Mei," he bowed low, an unusual action to perform before a prisoner, I thought. "I realize that what I am about to ask you is a most strange request. Were you to acquiesce in this you will have my gratitude and that of my family for generations to come." He bowed his head, his eyes misting.

His humble attitude, especially towards a sixteen-year-old Russian girl who was completely at his mercy, dumfounded me. Like the *Looking Glass*'s Alice, I became curiouser and curiouser.

"May I ask what you want me to do?" I watched his face closely, alert to any change in expression. No matter, I was not going to let down my guard. It would have been good to have Vanya around at a time like this, but naturally he was out of earshot, probably out back.

The policeman straightened himself. Looking at him, I couldn't determine his age. That he was old could be seen by the numerous lines and the fading eyes that now were reflectively scanning my face. I considered asking him to sit down, but I decided not to. After all, he was here as my guard!

"As you know, young lady," he said in a courteous manner (evidently he was better educated than other policemen), "when an individual dies in China, we have a tradition which, to my family as well as that of my ancestors, is most important. At a person's funeral there is placed the portrait of the deceased. This is carried in front of the catafalque so that all the people living can see and remember what the departed one had looked like in life. I am getting close to the age when I know that my time has become short. I have been sorely troubled for a long time. It's difficult, these days, especially if one is as old and poor as I am. I had often thought of getting my portrait taken. Can you imagine how exorbitant a photograph that size would cost?" He came a few steps closer towards me, twisting his cap nervously. Poor man, even his hand was shaking! He looked quite harmless except for that damned uniform. I smiled, trying to ease his discomfort.

"Your servant tells me that you are an artist." He eyed me with respect.

"No," I shook my head. "I'm no artist."

He put up his hand, admonishing me gently. "Xiao Jie, I have seen your paintings." He looked at me hopefully. "I'm asking you to please draw my likeness. Once that has been accomplished, I shall be at peace. I shall have no more worries, knowing that when I pass on, people will be able to see me as the man I once was."

"I am not good at portraits," I objected. "You may not even be happy with the likeness I draw of you."

"I shall; I shall." He gave me a deep bow again. "Does that mean you will do it?"

I told him I would try, and furthermore, we would start on it tomorrow. Strangely, for the first time in a long time I felt good, as if I could breathe again.

The next day I had everything set up and ready for him. He was to sit on a stool on the cement part of the central courtyard. I had the easel set up, my charcoal ready, and some bread, thankfully fresh! Since I didn't own a charcoal eraser, I had learned long ago to substitute. The soft part of fresh, white bread, if kneaded properly, made the best eraser, even much better than a bought one!

The old man was prompt. He was freshly shaven and had even gotten a haircut sometime during the night. The smile on his face was radiant.

"Now remember, you must sit perfectly still," I told him. "You move one inch and you'll spoil the picture."

I hadn't needed to remind him of that. He sat on the hard stool as if he had been molded into it. After a while I worried that he was sitting too still.

At times when I'd sketch someone, no matter how hard I tried, the expression wouldn't be right. I remembered hearing an artist friend of Mama's once explain, "If the eyes aren't drawn right, then forget it. You are no artist!" Her warning was always foremost in my mind when I tackled a portrait. I didn't know how other portraitists worked, but I always had to work on the eyes first. If those turned out right, then I had no problems with the remainder of the portrait.

With Old Wang I was fortunate. I caught the expression right away. Whether it was that I was determined to get it right because of what it would mean for him, or the fact that he sat so still, or a combination of the two, I don't really know. I just transferred to paper that wonderful expression of his: his age, wisdom, suffering, patience, calm anticipation of death to come, all that I saw in him I drew with my charcoal. After the eyes were done, I had him rest for a while and stretch his arms and legs. I wouldn't let him see the portrait until it was finished.

It took us three whole mornings. He was surprised that last day when I finally blew the last of the charcoal dust off the paper and turned to him.

"All right," I told him. "You do not have to sit anymore."

"I can sit longer if you wish." He hadn't understood that I meant the portrait was finished.

I smiled, motioning him forward. "You can see it now if you wish."

It was a large portrait—lifesize. He came around the easel, hesitatingly at first. He looked carefully at himself on the paper and stepped back in admiration. His old eyes widened, and I, looking at the real person and the image I had completed, was surprised at my skill. I couldn't believe that it was I who had really done this! It *was* good!

He stepped away, then stepped up close to it, looking at each line, shaking his head in disbelief. Had I not held him up, he would have knelt at my feet.

"I shall ever be in your debt, Xiao Jie." He lifted the painting with reverence. "You have made it so that I shall die in peace." His eyes grew misty. He couldn't take his eyes off the picture, and neither could I. With joy he had a vision of himself being carried in a coffin, and in the very front that big image of himself in life. He even envisioned his neighbors exclaiming, nodding their heads, remembering. "There goes Old Wang to his ancestors' home!"

He left holding his precious package and backing out through the moon gate, thanking me with every step. "May all the gods look favorably on you, young lady," he breathed. "You are a good person."

I looked up at the clear blue sky. "And please, my dear God," I whispered, "wilt Thou too begin to look favorably upon me?"

5

The Cracked Mirror

Vanya and Boy had become very good friends, especially since I had distanced myself from the two of them. Then one day Vanya told me that Boy had said we should be getting good news soon.

"How does Boy know that?" I asked. "Perhaps he could also tell you where they are. I suspect that he's just playing up to you. Of course, you're falling for it."

Vanya corrected me. "He just told me that we *might* have good news, not *will*. If you don't want to hear the rest of what he told me, that's okay with me. I won't tell you." His lips closed into a thin, stubborn line.

That was typically Vanya. Either do it his way, or he wouldn't play. I was seething inside.

"Whatever you wish," I retorted huffily. "That's your business. As for me, Boy is a liar, a traitor, and more than that, he's despicable. How you can associate with him is beyond me. But then," I looked straight into his face till he looked down, "birds of a feather do flock together, don't they?"

He smiled at me. My words hadn't even fazed him!

"I know. Boy can be full of baloney at times. Honestly, though, Sis, he's quite an interesting fellow. He knows all sorts of things about magic and superstition. Some of the stuff he has told me may be far-fetched, but he told me something the other day that got me to thinking." His eyes clouded over with a faraway look.

"Do you remember long ago when we were very little and moved to this house from Tientsin? Come to think of it, you wouldn't, because you were a baby then. Anyway, in the front

119

courtyard was this huge willow tree. It grew very close to the moon gate, towering over the rooftops. It was a beautiful old tree, hundreds of years old."

I remembered hearing the story.

"Well," his dark eyes showed his excitement, "Father had to have it chopped down. They told him it was haunted, you know."

I nodded impatiently. "I know all that. The tree was supposedly three hundred years old."

"Like our acacia tree in back." He continued as if I had not interrupted him. "Well, that willow tree's trunk was so twisted and gnarled that it just seemed to curl round and round towards this huge deep hollow that was way up where the main branches separated to smaller branches and so forth. Papa told me that an official, a well-respected Mandarin, used to live in this whole compound before Dr. Ferguson bought it. This poor Chinese Mandarin had one misfortune after another befall him. Both of us know how superstitious the Chinese are; well, in those days, they were even more so. They were absolutely sure that a spirit fox lived in this hollow. When night fell onto the city, the fox assumed the shape of a human being. Because of the fox, so the story goes, the Mandarin died; his family was forced to sell the compound and flee the city. They sold it to a *waiguo ren* [foreigner] because no Chinese would buy the place. Because the fox lived in the willow tree here, no one would rent the place either. Until Papa comes along, fresh from a foreign country, ignorant of what is going on here. He rents the house, learns about the fox, has the tree chopped down. The fox disappears. Now there are no problems. Servants are hired; prosperity comes; everything is fine. . . . "

"*Until now,*" I interrupted. "Does Boy say that the fox has come back?" I had read enough stories in *Liao Ch'ai*. I could tell Vanya stories about foxes that he hadn't even dreamed of!

He grinned sheepishly. "No, the fox is gone for good. But, Tamara, the devil is in our house now. Boy is firmly convinced that all of our misfortunes have been caused by the devil, who wants us out of this house so that he can live here. Or, Boy says that things will, for sure, get back to normal if we can get rid of the devil through special procedures."

"And do we chop down the big acacia tree in back to get rid of him, dear brother? Who will do the chopping? Am I to cooperate with you and do the chopping? What kind of fool does Boy think I am?"

Vanya didn't give up; he was bent on convincing me. "Boy said that it really is simple. All we have to do is place a mirror on top of one of the tiles on Paul's roof. The mirror part must face our quarters. This means that the devil will catch sight of himself and when he does see his own image, he will run away as fast as he can. He will never come back. It is only then, Boy says with conviction, that our folks will return. Not until then."

Why, that would be as easy as eating with chopsticks! Boy must really think us stupid, I told myself grimly. Every literate Chinese is sure to have read *Liao Ch'ai*. Foxes and devils abound in those stories. Vanya, who wasn't interested in Chinese literature, hadn't even heard of *Liao Ch'ai*. Still, there might be the slightest chance that it could be true. Even thinking of such a possibility made me feel ashamed. Here I was, proud of doing the right things in the right way! Was Tamara superstitious? No, not on your life! Still, what harm would there be in putting a mirror up on Paul's roof tile in the way Boy had suggested? After all, he was Chinese. It would be an adventure to climb up on Paul's roof tiles and look down onto Magpie Street without anyone else being aware of us.

"I know where there's a little mirror," I told Vanya. Without much ado, I ran towards the bedroom. Sure enough, in Mama's top dresser drawer there lay her old hand mirror, its handle broken off, the mirror cracked in half but still in good enough shape otherwise.

"Here it is." I was panting with excitement when I handed it to him. "How do you plan to secure it?"

He squinted towards the top of the roof where the tiles joined each other, not slanting now but almost perpendicular.

"I'm going to need some string or wire to do this. Wait a minute; I think I've got just the right thing." He fished into his knickers' pocket and withdrew a thin piece of wire almost a foot and a half in length. "It pays to be thrifty," he observed with a grin. "Okay, I'm on my way."

Quickly, he scaled the tree that grew right next to the outside door of Paul's bathroom. He had stuck the mirror down in front, inside his pants' belt.

"Don't drop that mirror," I warned him. "We don't need seven more years of bad luck."

"Besides getting the devil too!" He laughed cheerfully. He was already on the roof and climbing up the tiles towards the top.

"Wait for me." I shinnied up the tree, swinging myself onto the roof. This was fun, just as in the old days. Mama had always scolded us about roof climbing, but she had never climbed herself. She couldn't realize how delightful it was to be on top of the world up here and to look down on the passersby on Magpie Street!

At first we paid no attention to what was going on in the street. We were busily securing the mirror to one of the roof tiles. More than that, we didn't want any Chinese watching us. They would find it really amusing to see *yang kuei tzes* like us foreign devils putting up a mirror to get rid of their own devil!

It was not so difficult to secure the mirror to the tile as we had thought it would be. Once made secure, the mirror's shining surface faced our living quarters. I carefully peeped into it, wondering if besides my own face I would see another face looking into it, wondering if it would be wicked and flame-red, flicking its tongue about. All I could see was the blue sky as a background for my own face.

Our task finished, we could now check out Magpie Street. There were people walking up and down the street, totally unconscious of the two foreign devils watching them from above. They didn't appear to be afraid of our devil-haunted home.

It had been a long, long time since I had seen our street. I was surprised that it still looked the same as before. Because it was just a *hutung* along which people lived, the Japanese invaders wouldn't want to take it over immediately.

Some little children were playing marbles on the other side of the street against the wall that faced our house. One of them happened to look up and see us. When he told the others that he had seen us, they all quit playing and took positions against their wall, staring at us with their delightfully impish faces. Choruslike, they began to chant, as Chinese little ones often did upon sighting a foreigner, *"Yang kuei tzes* [little foreign devils]."

Laughingly we waved at them. *"Xiao Chungguo kuei tze!"*

we shouted in return. Having heard this commotion, an old woman came out of one of the gates to see what was going on. When she saw us on top of the roof, she angrily yelled at the children, shooing them away with her broom.

We could see the colonel's house and, beyond it, the Fergusons'. Another old crone was walking in our direction, holding her steaming supper in front of her. It was a large, blue bowl of hot noodles, some of which were slithering down over the edge looking just like so many wriggly white worms. In her other hand she clutched a short string at the end of which tangled a small bottle of soy sauce. When she got closer, I could see the top of her head, her thinning gray hair held together by a stiff black headband. She was walking quickly, but her steps were short, mincing, making her progress slow and labored. Her feet had been bound at an early age. When she walked immediately underneath us, I noticed that she was actually walking on her heels. In front, each of her tiny shoes was pointing straight up! She looked graceful walking like this; yet what terrible pain she must have endured in having had her feet bound so tightly as a child! *Thank goodness,* I thought to myself, *footbinding is now outlawed!* That is not to say that we, too, don't have our own weird and cruel customs and practices. Mama had worked with Aunt Raica in their dressmaking salon to make corsets for high-fashioned women to bind themselves in mercilessly. High heels tilted women forward so that they would be statuesque and shapely. Are these not barbaric customs and practices too?

Behind the mincing woman was a man with a long, skull-like head leaning forward in front of his hunched body as he walked by. I noticed the braided, ropelike queue hanging down his back. *The queue is going out of style just like the bound feet,* I thought to myself. In one hand he was holding a square birdcage covered with a blue cloth. He and his bird were out for a stroll, I decided. Everything on Magpie Street seemed tranquil.

Several rickshas passed by, some of the men almost sprinting as they ran. Others pathetically gasped for breath from the strain of pulling their heavy human fares. There was a car coming and I hurriedly slid down the other side of the roof, afraid that it might be Dr. Ferguson's. If he had seen us, I know that he would have disapproved. The car continued, however, past our house and went on until it turned the corner.

A beggar shuffled by picking out and counting the coppers at the bottom of his begging can. Magpie Street was slim pickings. He too hurried on.

It was time for us to climb down. We had had our fill of the world outside. In a way, I felt rather relieved that our street had not changed. I knew who had changed though; we had.

I reflected on the little cracked mirror and smiled.

6

The Mirror at Work

"I have a feeling, a very good feeling," Dr. Ferguson told us quietly, a few days later. He was sitting in his favorite armchair in our living room. I had teasingly asked him if he would take a copper for his thoughts. He looked down at the floor and tapped with his knuckles at his heart. "That funny feeling is right in here.

"Now, let's get down to business. I think that maybe it's time to send your parents a CARE package," he suggested.

"What's a CARE package?" I asked curiously. "I've never heard that term before."

The good doctor chuckled. "It's what our Red Cross Association does for people who are in dire need," he explained. "Perhaps the Japanese will permit your parents to receive some food and maybe even a batch of clean clothes. There's no harm in trying, is there?"

Vanya and I looked at each other with renewed hope just as we had done so often in the past. This time though was the first that Dr. Ferguson had suggested we do something constructive. They must be alive then! He wouldn't have suggested the CARE package if he hadn't thought so himself!

"But will they let us do that?" Vanya was dubious.

"No harm in trying," answered our friend. He was silent for a while, then added, "I shall send Chang to get some things that I think might be acceptable. You, Girlie, in the meantime, get some clean underwear together. When Chang brings you the food, divide it into two packages. Don't put in too many clothes, just one change of underwear apiece. Understand?"

We nodded happily, and he rose to leave.

Again, I had the feeling that he knew much more than he was telling us, but I knew that it was useless to ask him. By now we knew him rather well. He was as straightforward and firm in his actions as the first president of his country, George Washington, must have been. Furthermore, we knew full well that he wouldn't raise our hopes with mere rumors. Once he was certain of the truth he would tell us, not before.

When he left, Vanya and I hurried into the bedroom and selected the underwear. When Chang brought the food to us several hours later, we divided it, just as the American had suggested. Before he left, Dr. Ferguson had also cautioned us about sending any messages. "It might cause endless problems if you pull something like that," he had said, shaking his finger at us.

Unbeknownst to Vanya, I had disobeyed. If I send a short note to Mama, no harm will be done, I thought to myself. I wrote down three little words in the Cyrillic alphabet on a scrap of paper and pinned it to her panties. Romanized, the words were "cheep-cheep, Biebee." Those words would assure her that we were all right. As a child I had invented "Cheep-cheep" as a way of saying that everything was all right. Mama still called me "Biebee" (Baby), even though I was now grown up. Reading those cryptic words would comfort Mama, I thought. When the packages had been wrapped and labeled, we gave them to our guards to deliver them.

For the first time in nine months Vanya and I were encouraged. We even celebrated the occasion by taking out a Baby Ruth bar from our Christmas hoard. Cutting it in half, we each savored the nutty sweetness, enjoying each delicious bite.

The next day our packages were returned. There was no reason given. Our guards looked at us silently, unwilling or unable to tell us why the packages had been returned.

When we told Dr. Ferguson what had happened, he was not discouraged. "Don't worry," he assured us calmly. "I'll talk to my contact, and we'll find out what the problem is. Then we'll try again."

When I first examined the bundles, I found that they had been opened and then rewrapped. Now, however, neither Vanya nor I wanted to open them. We just put them up on the pantry shelf where we wouldn't have to look at them all the time.

"I wonder why those packages were returned," Vanya kept repeating; he couldn't forget it.

"Well, one thing I know," I finally told him. "They've been opened, you know."

He looked at me in surprise. "You're crazy, Old Pal. How'd you know?"

I laughed triumphantly. "I tied the string, remember? I always make three knots just to make sure. Well, the strings on these packages have only one knot. Elementary, my dear Watson!"

He had to see for himself. When we brought the packages out into the kitchen, he suggested we open them.

"I wonder why?" He was really worried, I could see. Both packages looked the same inside. The underwear was neatly folded; the soap, chocolate bars were still on top.

Then I remembered what I had done. I reexamined Mama's package. I unfolded her underwear and carefully looked inside her panties. The note wasn't there! Had I forgotten to pin the note? No, I knew that I had. But it wasn't where it should have been. What had happened to it? I stole a glance at Vanya, who was busily tying Papa's bundle, knotting the string three times just as I had done. Should I tell him? I decided I shouldn't.

The next day Dr. Ferguson told us to resend the bundles. This time they weren't returned. Whether they had been received or not, none of us knew, but it did give us hope.

I now began to plan on a second package.

Two weeks later Boy brought us a bundle in return. It was quite a large one, wrapped in what looked like a dirty, camel's hair coat tied with a string. There was a strange, sickening smell of disinfectant about the package.

"Your father is sending his old clothes back," Boy informed me. He was grinning like Alice's Cheshire cat. "You can wash them for him."

Vanya carried the bundle into the cool pantry and laid it gently on the shelf by the window. "Let's wait to open it," he said quietly. "I really don't want to see what's inside."

Neither did I. I was relieved when he said that. We had heard enough stories about Japanese brutality. Both Vanya and I had feared the same thing. What if we found blood spots on Father's clothing? We'd know for sure that he had been tortured. It was better not to know.

That dirty bundle had supernatural power! No matter where I went in the compound I kept thinking about it. Something kept telling me that we should open it, but I felt that I could not. I didn't want to know if there was blood inside! That sickening, medicinal odor was so strong that it permeated the whole pantry. If I opened the door to get something from the icebox, that strange, pervading smell hit me. The bundle may have been Father's, but it was a part of Father with which we were unfamiliar. Could the Japanese have killed him and then given us what the murder mysteries I had read termed "his effects?" I busied myself with other things, and tried to forget the mysterious bundle.

A few days later, the doorbell rang twice, rather insistently it seemed. We no longer paid any attention to its ringing except to listen and then ignore. Dr. Ferguson's ring we knew; his ring was always followed by his loud and cheerful voice. These rings, however, were not meant to be ignored. They were loud, shrill, like those that rang that fateful December night. If I live to be a hundred, I'll never forget them.

Then we heard the missionary's voice, loud and cheerful as always, but he was not alone; someone was with him. I heard him say, "Well, at last! Here we are, my dear."

Both of us walked quickly towards the front courtyard in time to see Dr. Ferguson stepping down from the gate pavilion, supporting his frail companion, whose head was bent low.

How small the person looked. And then I recognized that black print dress with the red border, which was hanging so loosely on the thin frame. Her shoulders were shaking; she clutched the American's arm tightly, looking down so that we couldn't see her tearful face. Her dark hair had been carelessly knotted as if she had not had time nor pins to put it up the proper way.

We stood stark still, unbelieving, feeling joy and sorrow at the same time. "Mama!" Both Vanya and I cried out in one voice. I felt a hard lump in my throat, and the tears came to my eyes. Vanya too couldn't hold back his. Then we ran to her, hugging her, feeling her poor bony self, numbly sharing the heartache that was inside her.

She lifted her head and looked at us apprehensively. Her tears flowed endlessly, but it was not her tears that took us aback! It was the way she had looked at us. We had not expected that strange look of mistrust and suspicion from her. Didn't we matter to her any longer? Or had she stopped loving us? Didn't she recognize us, *her children?*

The good American gently patted her arm. "Come on, dear lady," he had spoken softly, comfortingly. The look he gave us warned us to say nothing. We got his message.

"Your mother has had quite a surprise today," he continued. "All of a sudden they came, got her, released her. It has been quite a shock to her, and she needs time to recover from all this excitement. Let's get her inside the house so that the poor lady can get her bearings."

He gently steered her through the central courtyard towards the living room, Vanya rushing in ahead to open the door. As she lifted her foot to step over the threshold, it seemed to me that a slight shudder passed through her. *She's remembering,* I thought to myself, *the last time she had stepped over this threshold.* She had been holding onto Papa's arm then, and she was stepping out, *not in!* I couldn't stop my own tears from flowing. This Mama was now so different. She had little life in her. Like a helpless invalid she had allowed Dr. Ferguson to lead her to the sofa. He patted her gently on her arm.

"It's time for me to go now," he told her softly. He bent down so that she could see his face. "I'm leaving now, Mrs. Rubleva, but I'll be back to see that you're all right. You're in good hands, ma'am."

She still wept silently, looking down at her hands, which were twisting an already much twisted handkerchief.

"Bu yao sung" (Do not see me to the door). He murmured the traditional, polite phrase of the Chinese. Vanya and I rose to walk with him, his request reminding us of our manners. He lowered his voice and spoke quietly to us. "Don't question your mother right away. Let her be by herself until she gets her full bearings. It's been a long time for her, poor lady!"

Mama had not moved at all, nor had she raised her head. Then she did, turning to stare disconsolately at Dr. Ferguson. He smiled cheerfully. "Good-bye, Vera. I'm going home now."

Her eyes welled up again. Again, though, her demeanor changed. It was as if she had now realized where she was and knew that her situation had changed, that she was free. She slowly got up off the sofa, straightened her back, becoming again her former self, the polite, gracious hostess she once had been.

Her voice low and somewhat hesitant. "You've been very kind, Dr. Ferguson. Thank you for what you've done for us." She gave him her hand, and he took it silently. I know that at that moment he didn't trust himself to speak.

He walked to the living-room door, turned the knob, and we followed him out to the front gate, saying good-bye as he got into his car.

When we returned, she was still standing by the sofa. She had moved slightly aside when I opened the door. As we entered the room, she again sat down on the sofa, hiding her face in her hands. Vanya and I left her there to go into the kitchen to talk.

We sat down on the stools by Ta Shih Fu's worktable. Our cups of cocoa were still there on the table, half empty. I took a sip of mine, making a grimace in spite of myself. There's nothing like watered-down, cold cocoa!

The realization that we now had Mama back with us hit us all at once. It felt strange that she was with us and yet we felt that we were still without her. She was so changed, so different, almost like a stranger. What was it that she had gone through? What had happened to her?

"Dr. Ferguson told us to let her be. It must have been a shock for her to come back here." Vanya's voice was quite hoarse, and there were tears in his eyes. "You know, Tamara, I just can't understand how she can be like this with us. She doesn't seem to care at all, as if we aren't her children anymore. She's just plain unapproachable!"

"I have the same feeling, Vanya." I couldn't understand her behavior either. I thought that she could have been overjoyed to see us, that she would have hugged and kissed us, never wanting to let go of us. That is what both of us had wanted to do to her, but she had stopped us with just one look. What had caused her

130

to look at us that way? Vanya and I sat there, each reliving that unexpected entrance of hers back into our lives after such a long, silent absence.

It began to dawn on me what had happened. It was difficult to imagine what Mama had been thinking and feeling as she came back home to us, suddenly and without warning. The more I thought about it, the more I knew that I was right.

"Vanya," I whispered, "I think I know the reason. She does not *trust* us. I have a feeling that in some weird way she thinks that the Japanese have brainwashed us; that we can't be trusted. You saw that look she gave us when she first came?"

He nodded mutely, miserably. Poor Vanya, Mama's beloved *Kocya*. He couldn't forget that look, that silent rejection of him who had always been her favorite child!

"Don't you think that that might be the reason?" I asked.

"Yes, I think you've hit on the reason." He scooped out the bottom cocoa dregs with his finger. "I guess we'll just have to let her be for a while. Eventually, she'll be convinced that we're okay, not on the side of the Japs. Let's go and rejoin her. She might be hungry."

She was lying on the sofa when we entered the room, her arm shading her eyes as if she were asleep. I tiptoed up to her, wanting to touch her. When I saw Vanya's warning look, I merely slid down to the floor beside her. Vanya sat across in the armchair.

She must have been dozing or maybe just lost in thinking to herself. After a time she took her hand from her face, looking from Vanya to me. It was a serious, unhappy look, not motherly at all. Her somber dark eyes studied us. There was a haunting look in her appraisal, but it was also cold and impersonal. What could have happened to make her look like that? I tried to reach out to her with my love.

"Mama," I whispered, "we've missed you so much!"

She didn't reply, just looked at me. Vanya came forward, taking her thin hand in his. He laid it against his cheek. "Mama," he whispered. I hoped he would not break down. He and I had to be the strong ones.

Her voice was so low that we could hardly hear her. "They've done away with him, haven't they?"

131

"We don't know, Mama." Vanya tried to make his voice reassuring and confident. "Dr. Ferguson doesn't think so. We've been sending him packages every Monday and Friday."

At this news, her face became more alive. Her eyes brightened. "Where did you send them?" Still she whispered. I wondered why. Couldn't she talk in a normal voice?

"The Japanese have him somewhere," I told her, taking her hand. "Now we can send packages to him. The first time we sent packages to both you and him, but they were returned."

She sat up at this. "Returned?" She looked at Vanya for verification. We both nodded, happy to see her show some life at last. For the first time the shadow of a smile crossed her face.

"Some time ago, I received two packages from you. That was such a surprise," she recalled. "Although," she chuckled, "once before they told me that there had been a package, but they wouldn't give it to me." She looked at me intensely. "They showed me a scrap of paper. This bit of paper was what had really caused that flurry of activity. On it were these three words, 'run-run, Biebee.' They thought that you people were helping me plan an escape."

Vanya stared at me in amazement, his mouth wide open. He had no idea what Mama was talking about. Mama's smile widened.

"Gavriluk, you know, the woman you met when she arrived here from Tientsin. Well, she told me all about you then. Poor thing! She was my roommate in the cell along with Miss Yang, the University of Peking's secretary. All of us had huddled and mulled over that scrap of paper, wondering why *run* was written twice. Miss Yang and I had read it in English; Gavriluk didn't know English and read it in Russian out loud. '*Cheep-cheep,*' she read, and when I heard her say those wonderful words I laughed and laughed until the tears ran down my cheeks! They thought that I had truly gone mad! I knew then that the two of you were all right, but it took a lot of explaining to the police to make *them* understand. After that, I received both of the packages you had sent. We enjoyed the chocolates especially. We even shared some with the generalissimo."

"Who is the generalissimo?" I asked. The only one I knew of was the Kuomintang leader.

132

Mama's face hardened. "She was one of the women who guarded us," she whispered. "She was a mean, old Chinese witch, as hardhearted and vindictive as a Russian Baba-Yaga! She would never permit the three of us to talk to one another. That is why we were whispering all the time. She was quite deaf and if we whispered, she couldn't hear us. We even learned to whisper without moving our lips too much. In fact, I'm afraid to talk normally now because I can still see her face." Mama looked around the room as if to convince herself that here, she was safe.

"No fear of that anymore," laughed Vanya. "It's just us in the house and the police in Boy's quarters."

Mama stared at us, her face puzzled. "Police? Why should they still be here?" she asked. Fear showed in her eyes. We told her everything. She listened quietly, interrupting only once or twice to ask us a question. When we had finished, she stretched out her arms to embrace us to her.

"I didn't know, my dears! How the two of you must have suffered, my poor, poor children! I had been told that you were fine, that Dr. Ferguson was looking after you. Why, I even thought that he had taken you home with him." She shook her head in dismay.

"We were all right, Mama," I assured her. "In fact, I've learned how to cook, and Vanya makes the best coal balls in Peking!"

Again, she smiled. This time I caught a glimpse of my old Mama, the way she used to be! "If only I could be sure that Papotchka is all right, then I'll feel much better. It's just this terrible not knowing feeling that becomes unbearable."

It was Vanya who had remembered the bundle. Hesitatingly, he told her about it.

"But we just couldn't bring ourselves around to open it," I explained to her.

At this, Mama had risen, a look of determination on her set face. "Where is this bundle?" she demanded.

"Out in the pantry on the top shelf," Vanya told her.

She went there in a hurry. We tried to keep up with her. I dreaded seeing the contents but knew that Mama was determined to open it. I was right.

She noticed the odor immediately. It didn't bother her,

although to me it seemed stronger than ever. With impatient, trembling hands, Mama turned the bundle. She looked around. "Where's a knife? Get me one please, Vanya."

He rushed into the kitchen, knowing that she was in a hurry. Soon he came back with one. "I'll cut the string," he told her quietly.

While she held the string taut, he cut it. Soon the folds of the camel's hair coat fell apart, revealing the grayish knit underwear that Papa had worn last winter. Mama tenderly lifted up the garments, one by one, caressing them as if they were Papa's hand or cheek. There was a shirt beneath the underwear. The collar was frayed, as if it too had been worn constantly for a long time. Mama held it up to her nose.

"It does not have his smell," she observed as she sniffed. She laid it aside after she had sniffed again. "These clothes could actually belong to anybody."

That thought had never crossed my mind. The only thing that had bothered me was that Papa's clothes might be covered with blood. That would indicate possible torture, and for that reason Vanya and I had not wanted to open the bundle.

"There's a strange medicinal smell to all of these clothes," Vanya reminded her. I know he was trying to make her feel better. "That may account for your not being able to smell any odor that might be his. They likely use disinfectant in the place where he is being held. You know, for lice and stuff."

Mama pursed her lips. She was thinking hard. "It does sort of smell like that *Cascaragrada,* you know, that Japanese medicine Papotchka was always taking. He used to order it directly from Tokyo, remember?"

There was a tiny clinking sound as she rummaged some more among the contents. She felt around with her hands and soon brought out a small, round container made of tin. She held it to her nose.

"That's what it is. This is what we've been smelling. Must have been some medicine he has been taking."

Vanya took the tin from her, examining it closely.

"Mama, it looks as if there's something scrawled on the lid. I just can't make out what it is." He handed it over to her.

I leaned over to get a closer look. Sure enough, there were some scrawls on it as if a pin had been used to scratch out a message. Her face brightened. "I've got it. It says, 'Am well. Not worry.'"

There was no signature, but it still helped in a way. If these all were really Father's things, then we'd have reason to believe that he was alive! But Mama still was not convinced.

In her search she was nearing the bottom of the pile. Some dirty socks lay there. One of them had a large hole in it, showing another sock inside.

"They're almost warm," Mama murmured. She took up the holey one, lifting it up in front of her. Suddenly, she gasped. Quickly, she took out all the socks. Each one, she carefully examined. From each dirty sock she pulled out another one.

Mama flushed a bright pink. Her dark eyes glowed. A smile played on her lips. We stared at her in surprise. To our amazement, she began to laugh. The tears that ran down her cheeks were tears of joy!

"But don't you both see?" she cried. "These *are* Papa's things. There is no doubt that these are his socks. That's exactly the way he takes them off, two in one, two in one! His feet get so cold in wintertime."

"What do you mean?" I asked, completely baffled. "Why should he do that?"

Mama looked at the sock in her hand and laughingly pressed it to her cheek. "Yes, I'm sure these are his things. You see, I used to get so angry at him all the time. I had to get his clothes ready for Amah to wash. And there were always two socks in one, always! He complained that his toes got cold. One sock couldn't keep him warm, so in spite of my nagging, he persisted in putting one sock inside another! My dear God, bless you, dear Father! I know now for sure!"

She embraced us both. Her voice was no longer a whisper. She had suspected us once before, she now no longer did. We were one family now—minus Number One!

We left Papa's clothes there and went into the kitchen where we made her some hot cocoa and toast. We told Mama how much Dr. Ferguson was doing for all of us and how comforting, how encouraging he had been, then we laughed at how Gavriluk had paced back and forth in our living room, trying to get rid of her Soviet passport.

"She was released yesterday," said Mama. "Poor girl, she was absolutely terrified of everybody."

It was then that I realized what relief from continuous worry meant. Small relief medicine though it was, we all had taken a good dose of it.

On the very same day that Mama returned, our guards left, all three of them. Wang, the old one whose portrait I had drawn, requested through Boy that I come into the front courtyard. He met me by the steps, smiling broadly. His yellow teeth with the black gap reminded me how difficult that part of his face had been to sketch correctly. He bowed low to me. This time I smiled and bowed back.

"What can I do for you, Wang Xian-Sheng (Mr. Wang)?" I asked.

He was embarrassed. "I would like to give you a little gift before I leave you." He handed me a small package wrapped in a Chinese newspaper. "I wasn't able to pay you for the portrait, but it would give me great pleasure if you would accept this."

I unwrapped his gift. In the paper lay a lovely celadon brush stand shaped like a lotus bud.

"How beautiful!" I exclaimed. Indeed it was. "I shall always treasure it, and it will always remind me of you. Thank you indeed, Mr. Wang."

"It is I who thank you," he said gravely. Again he gave me that gallant bow, his old face smiling with dignity.

I offered him my hand western fashion.

He shook it several times.

"I am glad to see you leave us," I told him. "Now we may have even better news. I am also happy to know that some of you policemen are human."

He nodded his head in agreement.

"You must not think badly of us, Xiao Jie," His voice had become hoarse. "Most of us Chinese are human, please believe me. We also know that your father has committed no crimes. In China he has been well-known and respected, both for his knowledge and his love for our people." He hesitated. "Perhaps that has been his trouble. He loved our country even more than he loved himself. His guilt lay in the fact that he would not collaborate with the enemy." The old man's eyes filled with tears.

I took a chance. "Would you happen to know where they are holding him?"

He shook his head. "I knew before, when they first took your parents away. However, they separated them on that very night. Your mama has probably told you that already. She was placed in the *Gung An Ju* [the police station], and your father was, at first, taken to *Mei Chia Hutung*, where the Japanese interrogated him." He paused; his eyes filled with sympathy. "I believe they kept him there for several months. Then they moved him somewhere else. None of us knows where."

He took a step back. "Don't worry about your father," he told me quietly. "He will come back to you. The fact that Americans are interested in his welfare means a great deal. The Japanese would not dare do anything to harm him."

That comforted me somewhat. I thanked him again and watched him depart. Then I ran back into our quarters to tell Mama and Vanya what had happened and to show them my unusual gift. When I had finished, Mama sighed.

"Now that the police are leaving, there is something I am going to have to do. I am going to fire Boy. That fellow is not going to stay here one minute longer."

I had told her about his attitude and everything else, except what Boy had done to me that night. Mama had said she couldn't stand him either.

"Would you call him to come here?" she asked Vanya. "I might as well get rid of him right now."

Vanya ran towards the servants' quarters. We waited for a time, then heard the heavy gate bar slide into its rings. Soon Vanya came running back, alone and out of breath. He was grinning from ear to ear. "He saved you the trouble, Mama. Old Wang, the nice policeman, and another of the guards were just about to come back here to tell us that we'd better lock up the gates; Boy left with the guard. The servants' quarters are completely empty. All his stuff is gone. The gates are now barred. Can you believe it, Tamara? We're free at last!" He grabbed me by the waist, twirling me like a dervish!

It did feel good. We walked back into the front courtyard, our arms entwined around Mama's waist. It was quiet again except for the rustling of the poplar leaves and the lone chirping of a bird somewhere. It seemed to me that I had not heard those pleasant sounds for the longest time. Was it that they had been there all this time, but I would not listen? It didn't matter anyway. We walked all the way from the red gates, turning around to stroll back through the moon gate into the painted pavilion, then back into our own private quarters.

"We have to let Monsieur Viaud know that I am back home again," Mama said, once we were inside.

"He probably knows already. I'm sure he must," said Vanya. "He came in late last night. I saw his light on at eleven o'clock when I walked around checking on things. I'm sure Boy or the guards must have told him."

"He'll probably come around this evening to welcome you home. He hasn't been eating his meals here for the past week because he's had some business at the French Embassy. Thank goodness," I sighed happily. "I'm a little tired of cooking every day."

Mama smiled. "I think we'll have to make different arrangements with him. With Boy gone, there is no one to serve him. We'll just have to tell him that we can't give him board anymore."

Later in the day, Dr. Ferguson paid us a visit. He seemed pleased that Mama looked happier. We told him about the bundle and how Mama was sure that those were Papa's things because of the socks. He congratulated her on her clever sleuthing.

In spite of his evident good humor, there seemed to be a sadness about him. He didn't seem to have his mind on us. Mama sensed that something else was bothering him more.

"How is Mrs. Ferguson?" she asked him quietly. We had told Mama that his wife was ill.

His face clouded then. "She's not too good these days, I'm afraid." He shook his head sorrowfully. "The doctor tells me that it's just a matter of time now." He got up, tall and distinguished looking in his finely tailored navy suit and that sky blue necktie that matched his eyes. He picked up his cane and walked to the front door, staring unseeingly through the glass. "We've been together for a long, long time, my wife and I," he murmured softly. Then he turned to Mother, his gaze softening as he looked at her. "But so have you and the professor, haven't you?" He gave her a gentle embrace. "I've got to go now."

As usual, we walked him to the gates. When he paused before stepping over the threshold, he waved his cane towards us. "You know that you are at liberty now to go out once more. There is no one who can stop you now."

Paul Viaud arrived somewhat later in the evening and came over to see Mama. He seemed to me to be even more handsome than ever. He was dashing, as always, in that blue-gray uniform that matched the color of his eyes. He embraced Mama, then turned to me. To him I was now a young lady, no girl.

"So delighted to see you again, Mademoiselle." He made me a gallant bow. It was that well-modulated, British-accented English of his, mixed in with his charming French tones, that had made me blush. How I wish that Dorlise could see me now!

The amenities had been performed. Paul sat down but declined tea. Mama was about to tell him of her decision, I think, when he gently interrupted her.

"Madame, I have something to tell you. I shall be hoping that you understand."

We wondered, watching his face. He looked at her earnestly with those cool, gray eyes, then continued, talking faster as he went along as if he were afraid Mama would interrupt.

"I was ordered out of Peking a month ago. Because I felt your children could use my protection, I asked for special dispensation to remain here as long as necessary. Now, however, you, Madame, are here! The policemen are gone. I feel that I must obey my orders immediately. Therefore, if you agree, Madame Rubleva, I shall give you a month's rent in advance, but I shall tell you my adieus later on this evening." He looked anxiously at Mama. When she smiled, he was relieved. "Am I to understand that you are not angry?"

"But of course not, Paul," she smiled shyly. "I myself have been wondering how to tell you that we couldn't give you board anymore." She bent her head to one side, smiled, then held out her hand. "You've anticipated me. Thank you for being so kind and considerate of my children."

We walked him to his door, watching him lower his head when he had to step inside. He turned the light on in the vestibule. We saw his handsome figure standing rigidly at attention. Then his hand went quickly to his forehead in a smart salute.

That very evening he left, bag and baggage. Vanya and I helped him carry his luggage out to the French Embassy car that had come for him. He seated himself regally in the backseat, and laid his head back for a moment. Then, with a quick smile and a wave of his hand, Paul Viaud was gone forever from our lives.

7

A Taste of Freedom

It was Mama's third day at home. Both Vanya and I noticed the change in her. She wasn't so tense now nor so prone to tears. We had been eager to question her about the *Gung An Ju* but hesitated to do so knowing that the pain of her confinement was still intense. She had just begun to feel at ease with us. Seeing her sweet smile once in a while gave us that patience we needed to wait. When she was ready, then she'd tell us.

What she seemed to enjoy most was just to sit in our enclosed glass veranda and look out into the central courtyard. There the white acacia branches swayed gently towards her as if to greet her. Their delicate aroma filtered through even into her refuge behind the glass enclosure.

It was there that I served her the simple lunch of soup and salad. I had tried to make it an event, bringing the food to her on a silver tray. I had even filled a small bud vase that I had found in the pantry with my purple daisies. These I placed in the center of the veranda table. Vanya had followed me with our own bowls of soup.

"It's so peaceful out here," Mama murmured. "It feels good to have the sun touch my face again." She smiled wistfully. Then, when she noticed the soup in front of her, she began stirring it with her spoon. "I cannot believe that I'm really here." Mechanically, she put down her spoon and placed her head on the back of the chair, closing her eyes.

"Mama, please." I gently touched her on her arm. "Eat while the soup's still warm. You're terribly thin!"

141

She paid no attention to what I had said. Apparently, she was now completely out of our world, just alone with her thoughts and basking in the sun's gentle rays. Vanya and I had already finished our soup. I was taking up our bowls when she spoke.

"We had to speak so softly when those women guards came around, especially the *generalissimo*."

"How old was she?" I asked.

For a moment she seemed lost. "Who? Oh, her?" She paused, in thought. Then with a start she saw the soup in front of her. She took up her spoon, dipping it into the bowl.

"Mm-mn, but this tastes good. Did you make it?" She was surprised when I nodded. Then she settled back in her chair. "I think she was in her sixties. It's difficult to tell a Chinese woman's age. But the *generalissimo?*" Mama's face became grim. "That woman was old. She had a hump on her back. In fact, the witch was all bent over, partly because of her evil soul. My, but she was ugly! Her deformity didn't hamper her actions though. Mm-mn." Mama's eyes strayed once more to the outside. "She had such a sharp, pointed face, just like a fox's. Her eyes, oh, but they were something! Little black beads that twirled around in their sockets, seeing everything. Not a thing escaped her inspections. A real dragon lady she was. Even the other women guards shunned her." Mama shuddered at the recollection.

"Mama," Vanya's voice was hesitant, "where were you after they separated you from Papa?"

Her eyes lost their glow. Her voice reverted to a whisper. "It was on that night," she kept her eyes closed, "that very night when they took us away. It was at the *Gung An Ju*, which is what they call the Chinese police station. When we were seated in the car, I nudged Father and asked him where he thought they were taking us. At first, he had remained so quiet that I thought he hadn't heard me. Poor Serioja!" She shivered slightly at the recollection. "Then he asked one of the guards in front, the one next to the driver. The man was a Japanese, and Papa had, of course, spoken to him in Japanese. The man had been about to refuse, but when he turned to look at us, he changed his mind."

She smiled with a strange bitterness, so unlike her sweet self. "Evidently, we didn't look that dangerous to him. He nodded yes, turning his back to us. I somehow sensed though that he was very much alert. I had the certain feeling that he understood Russian just by the way he leaned back against the seat. I knew that he was listening to every word of ours." She sighed deeply. "Papa took my hand. His own was sweating in spite of the cold." She shaded her eyes with one hand. "They will probably take us in for questioning is what he told me then. Papa's voice had been completely calm."

She laughed. "It was just as if he were giving me a list for shopping. 'I don't know what they are charging me with,' he said, 'except that I didn't join their White House.' "

"That's all?" I asked her.

"That's all. That's what Father told me in the car that night," she answered. "He didn't say much else because the guard on his side looked at both of us so malevolently that he just squeezed my hand hard and ceased to talk. We rode most of the way in complete silence. I kept looking out the window, past the guard on my side. He was like a stone statue, he was. I wanted to see where they were taking us, but it was too dark outside, and I wasn't able to get my bearings. Father held on to my hand. That was comforting."

She stopped then and finished her soup. "You're spoiling me with all this attention. I'm not used to that." She smiled. "Now, you children, I'm going to clean up the dishes."

We refused to let her. "We enjoy doing them," I told her.

Later, in the kitchen, Vanya scoffed, "We do?" He dried the last bowl.

"Sure we do," I answered. "You don't want Mama doing it, do you?"

When we returned to the veranda, she was sitting in the same position. Her eyes were closed, but she was not asleep. The minute she heard us, she stirred and opened her eyes.

"Children, something has been bothering me ever since that first night, but there was nothing else that I could do."

Vanya was puzzled. "What're you talking about, Mama?"

"I really felt bad about leaving the two of you in this house. It was a difficult decision for me to make. There was so little time. I knew though that Dr. Ferguson was close by to take care of you. You would be safe. But poor Papa," her voice softened, "had no one on his side. That's why I had to go with him. I had to show him that I believed in him. I had no idea that they would put you both under house arrest."

She was pleading with us to understand! Feeling the need to go on, she explained, "I could never have imagined that they would do that to you two. When we rode in that black car to God alone knew where, it was much too dark. Only once in a while was there a dim streetlight. I couldn't see anything familiar. The car was going rather fast. There was absolutely no sign of life anywhere, just empty, ghoulish streets and that terrible, dreadful silence. Never in my wildest dreams had I ever imagined Peking at such an hour or under such circumstances! Finally, it dawned on me, the sheer reality, the horror of all that was happening!

"Serioja and I were under arrest. The Japanese, not the Chinese, had arrested us and were taking us somewhere, God and the enemy alone knew where. Only the two of you knew that we had been taken away. We could be killed, and that would be it! Only you children would miss us, no one else. In this big world, who were the two of you? The more I thought about it, the weaker and more numb I became. My head was spinning; my mind was reeling with the enormity of it all. I was in aftershock!"

"How terrible!" I whispered.

"Not really terrible," Mama corrected. She narrowed her eyes. "Perhaps when you think of what has happened, at first you think it rather terrible. Eventually you come to the sad conclusion that in such a situation there is nothing that you can do, absolutely nothing. It is then that your head finally begins to clear. You've gone through emotions you've never experienced before; you're ready to accept and to cope with the inevitable! You decide that you'll cling to life as long and as stubbornly as you can!"

Vanya and I didn't want to interrupt as long as she was revealing so much. "In times like these," she went on, "one always somehow finds the strength to go on. I stole a look at Papa's proud profile as we rode in the car. He was looking straight ahead. He didn't know what they would do to him; yet he kept his head up, his eyes calm. I detected no fear in him. That is what kept me going all this time. I couldn't fail him because he is so brave and good."

"Did you have a chance to talk anymore?" I asked her. I knew now how much she loved Father. I also saw Father in quite a different way now, not as the Papa who told such wonderful fairy tales or who, when angry, could singe the earth with his fiery glance. Dorlise had seen that glance once and couldn't forget it. The Papa I knew and this husband of Mama's were quite different. I was eager to learn more about this other Papa!

"There wasn't much more chance to talk," Mama told us. She had taken the bud vase and was examining the purple daisies. "These are so lovely," she sighed. "I never realized how pretty they are. I remember how you used to play among them as a child, Tamara."

"What happened then?" Vanya asked.

"I kept wishing that we would get to wherever we were going. At the same time I dreaded the end of the journey, not knowing what would follow. The ride was a very long one. Everyone was silent, more like statues than human beings. Suddenly the car turned a corner and slowed down. Papa tightened his grip on my hand, twirling my wedding band with his fingers. Then he gave me last-minute instructions: 'Remember to tell the truth if you are questioned. There is nothing to be afraid of.'" Mama paused and stared gloomily through the window.

"What then?" I was impatient to know.

"The car came to a stop. All of them got out. The Japanese in the front seat was the one in command."

"Where was it that you stopped?" Vanya wanted to know.

Mama shook her head. "I didn't know. It was getting to be daylight. The Japanese signaled for Father and me to get out. We were standing in front of this tall, gray brick building. There were barred windows on the lower stories. Some Chinese policemen stood at the big iron gates, sleepily standing at attention. Thankfully, I saw no more Japanese uniforms." I saw her shiver, and I shivered too! Mama knew she had to continue.

"Out of somewhere appeared several Chinese policemen and a civilian. The civilian was the one in charge and motioned us to go inside the gates. We mounted the steps into the building and found ourselves in what looked like a small theater lobby. Father had gone in first. Almost immediately he was surrounded by guards. When I came up, I could see him looking at me, his eyes giving me a sign of warm recognition. He kept looking at me with those calm, serene-looking brown eyes of his. Seeing him thus, I was filled with a courage that I never could have mustered alone. I wanted so much to run over to him, cover him with my arms, shield him from all this madness. The guards were between us, a silent, hostile barrier. Instead, I just had to stand there, waiting. I thought for a moment of the two of you left at home alone. Then I saw him, so brave, so very much alone." Her eyes filled with tears.

"You needn't have worried about us, Mama," offered Vanya.

"When you're a mother, you do. Of course, I hoped that you would be all right. At first, after Papa and I were separated and they questioned me, they told me that you were fine. Then another examiner told me just the opposite. He told me that you, Vanya, had been inducted into the Japanese army and that you, my little one," she put her hand on top of my head, "he told me that you were in a brothel, a prostitute for Japanese soldiers. When he told me that I thought I'd die, that it was useless to live anymore!"

I shuddered, although I didn't really know what a prostitute was. It had to be something bad if it had to do with Japanese soldiers, nor could I forget the look of horror on her face when she told me. I reminded myself to look up the word in our dictionary when I had the chance.

"Anyway," Mama heaved a sigh of relief, "that part of it is now ended. Let me rest for a while. We have plenty of time to catch up."

"But, Mama," I insisted, "you just can't stop there. We want to know what happened next. Please tell us."

She smiled reluctantly. "All right, I'll tell you then. They separated us then and there. They wouldn't even let me give Serioja a last embrace. While I stood there watching, they led Papa away, a policeman on each side of him and one behind. Imagine! Our dear Papotchka, such a dangerous man that he required three guards! It would have been laughable if it hadn't been so tragic! The last that I saw of him"—her voice dropped to a painful whisper—"was his firm little figure in the midst of three men. He couldn't even turn to say good-bye. He just walked away with them, down the hall, and out of sight. That's all."

146

Vanya and I remained silent. I couldn't trust myself to speak. Mama, however, was calmer. "They led me into a room beyond the lobby, in the direction opposite to where they had taken Father. It was quite dark when we entered through a door. My eyes soon got accustomed to the dimness. The room had seemed empty at first. Then I saw some shadowy figures stirring. At one end of the room was a long, dark shape. I surmised that it was a *k'ang*."

"What's a *k'ang?*" Vanya wanted to know.

Mama laughed. "I would have thought you'd know, Kocya. Boy used the one in the servants' quarters. It's a Chinese bed made out of cement and bricks, with a small opening in the middle. Inside, it's like a small stove. In the winter they build a fire inside to warm the bricks and keep the occupants warm and cozy."

"Did you sleep on the *k'ang?*" I asked curiously.

"I did not sleep on it, Tamara. When the policeman switched on the light and I saw what was in the room, I automatically turned back towards the door. The guard stopped me with his hand.

"What I had seen had filled me with dismay. There were six or seven Chinese women, ragged, unkempt, and so miserable-looking that I had to turn away. Some lay against the wall, side by side, sort of scrunched up. Not even beggars on the street looked as wretched as these women. Two women huddled on top of the *k'ang*. They looked young. Nestling beside them were two infants, apparently newly born. Near them on the floor lay a woman who was big with child. She was staring at me with pain-filled eyes. Suddenly she began to moan, rocking her swollen body back and forth, back and forth. Then she stopped rocking and looked away.

"I turned to the policeman. My face must have shown my pity and horror at what I was seeing. He merely shrugged. His face resembled a stone mask. 'I'm sorry, *tai-tai* [lady],' he told me. 'My orders were to bring you here.' With these words he left, locking the door behind him."

"What did you do then?" Vanya took her hand, pressing it to his cheek. She bit her lip, recollecting. Then she smiled. "I joined them. What else could I do? I found an empty place by the wall and sat down on the floor. Not for long though. Shortly afterwards, the door was unlocked, and two guards came in, lugging an old iron bed and a mattress. They placed the bed across from the *k'ang*. One of them beckoned to me, then pointed to the bed. 'For you,' he told me. With that they left. Again I heard the click of the key in the lock. When they left, they had also switched off the light. Again, we were in semidarkness. One of the babies started to yowl. Its mother quickly put the child to her breast, and we could hear that hungry suckling sound. Soon the infant had had its fill, and the sound stopped. Off and on I heard the stirring and shifting of bodies. One woman sat up, startled. She stared fixedly at me. It wasn't often that a foreigner joined them in prison, so I guess that I was an oddity. There wasn't much more to see. A tiny window just over the *k'ang* provided us with our only light and ventilation.

"I felt the mattress of my bed. It was lumpy and uncomfortable, but that was still better than the floor, even though it was probably full of lice. Soon my tiredness overcame any other feelings I might have had. I threw my coat over me and curled up, pillowing my arms under my head. I heard footsteps outside the door. They grew fainter. I wondered if Father had been taken to their men's quarters or if he were close by. My head was spinning with so many thoughts, fears and apprehensions. I kept talking to myself." She laughed. "I told myself to stay calm, to be brave, that everything would be all right."

She would have continued, but the doorbell rang. We knew who it was even before Vanya had unbarred the red gates. Dr. Ferguson, who else? As usual he visited with us for a bit and complimented Mama on her appearance.

"You're looking prettier and younger every time I see you," he teased her.

She smiled, blushing. "It's my children's good care, Dr. Ferguson. I still can't believe I'm home."

She looked much better these days, she had even put on some weight. We had worried at first about her occasional depression, but Dr. Ferguson had told us that that too would go away.

"She'll get back to her former self," he promised us. "This is to be expected. She misses and worries about your father. Just go along with her moods. You can't expect her to be happy."

After nearly a month at home, Mama changed. It was as though she had had time enough to think and had then made her decision. One day she really surprised us. It was about daybreak, and here she was, routing us out of our beds. I sat up, staring at her bent form as she kept shaking my shoulders. It was not yet daylight.

"What is it, Mama?" I was squinting, still asleep.

Her hair had been neatly combed into a bun. She had on a blouse and skirt but was barefoot.

"Get dressed and come outside." She whipped off the sheet.

"What for?" I asked.

I saw that she was determined that I get up. "You'll see. Just hurry."

I heard Vanya moving about in the next room, stomping and muttering. Looking for his glasses, I'll bet. I grinned to myself. He was always misplacing them, and, without them, he was too blind to see where he might have put them.

When we met her in the central courtyard, Mama was already exercising. When she saw us, she stopped, motioned for us to stand in front of her, just the way Father had led us.

Papa had always believed that an exercised body and a trained mind went hand in hand in life. Early in our lives he had insisted on all of us exercising in the manner of his favorite gymnast, Herr Mueller. Mama often skipped these morning exercises, pleading that she needed extra sleep. Vanya and I, however, were rarely excused. Now Mama was starting this exercise business all over again. I groaned.

"Why, Mama, do we have to do this?" I demanded piteously.

She was almost as stern as Papa had been. "Your knees are bent. Keep your chest out. Now, keep up with me. One, two, three, four." And so it went.

Finally, after half an hour of this we all trooped inside to eat the breakfast she had already prepared for us. Our muscles were sore and we were perspiring, but we felt good. I had to admit that!

There was something that had been bothering me for some time, but I didn't know what to do about it. It was so shameful and humiliating; yet the change was painfully evident to me. I finally decided to confront Vanya. After all, it was his fault.

"Vanya," I looked him directly in the eye as I said it, "I think you've made me pregnant."

He stared at me, his mouth wide open. When he blushed, I really became angry. I remembered that morning when I had awakened to feel his ooze between my legs and had found him in bed beside me. Neither of us had ever mentioned it again; yet I couldn't forget his words or that sly, self-satisfied look. What disturbed me now was that I had noticed how large my stomach was getting. I realized it especially when I lay awake in bed at night and when I awakened in the mornings. My stomach was not getting smaller. For a whole month it had been that way. Had he impregnated me that night? That would be a terrible thing. Hadn't people talked about Jane Ann Houser's pregnancy and the fact that she wasn't married? Anyone who had a baby without a husband was ostracized! What would Dr. Ferguson think of me? What would Mama say? How could this terrible thing have happened to me? I had had nothing to do with it, but here I was, miserably contemplating my distended stomach. And Vanya was the cause of my misery!

He glanced at my stomach. "You can't be," he whispered.

"Didn't you put your darned penis into me?" I asked, ashamed to say the ugly word yet angry enough to utter it in disgust. Moreover, his apparent helplessness and idiotic grin only served to fan my fury.

Finally he shrugged. "I really don't remember, Sis. You were sleeping, and I just poked around you. I never thought the stuff would come out of me. It felt so good at the time. Gee, I'm sorry, Old Pal. Yeah, your stomach does look big."

He had another thought. "You've been stuffing yourself with *lao-bings* lately. That could be it; you're eating too much."

"I'm not," I snapped back. "What am I going to do if I get any bigger? What if I have a baby? Can you imagine what everybody will say about me? Can't you understand?"

"Well, what can I do about it? If you have a baby, then you'll have it. Don't worry."

There was nothing he could do. He was right. I should have known better than talk to him. What a weakling he was! I'd have to think of something else.

150

Mama was sitting in one of the wicker chairs beneath the acacia tree. She had a book in her lap, but her head was resting on the back cushion. Her eyes were closed.

"Mama," I whispered softly. I still hadn't figured out how to phrase my problem to her.

She opened her eyes. "Oh, it's you. I guess that I've been dreaming." Her face was rosy. "What is it, dear?"

I pointed to my bulging stomach. "Mama, just look. See how big my stomach is. Could I be pregnant?"

What Mama might have thought when I asked her this question I had no idea. She had never talked to me about sex except for that comment she had made about where I had come from. I had thought then that she was making fun of me. But this had been the sole extent of my sex education up to the time when Vanya had told me what he had learned from Boy.

Mama looked at my stomach. She was quite matter-of-fact. "Are you menstruating?" she asked.

I told her that I was.

"Then you're not pregnant," she assured me.

I could have hugged her. I could have fallen down on my knees and blessed her. An immense wave of relief now swept over my whole being. My joy knew no bounds. There would be no scandal, no loss of face, no baby! I couldn't be pregnant because I still was having my cursed—no, definitely no, my *blessed* periods!

Not only had Mama started us on an exercise program, but she now took over the kitchen. She examined the cupboards.

"We need some staples," she told me. "Now that we're allowed some freedom, I'd like you and Vanya to go to Wise's, if it's still there. Remember one thing, Tamara, you and Vanya must stay together. I don't want either of you alone on the streets."

"Don't worry about us, Mama. We'll stay together. I promise you. Except when one of us has to go into a store. The other one will have to guard our bikes."

"But of course," she agreed. "You're right. Here is your list of things to get."

We had to clean our bikes first. They looked rather good though, in spite of the fact that we hadn't ridden them for so

151

long. As soon as Vanya and I had pumped up our tires, we started out. When we rounded the corner into Tu Ti Miao Hutung, I was struck by the changes on this small street that joined our own Magpie Street to Piao Pei Hutung. On the right-hand side of Tu Ti Miao there had been a long, red-bricked wall that had always been covered with ivy intertwined with wisteria vines. Formerly, on our way to school we had often stopped to admire it, especially when the wisteria was in full bloom. The sight of those lovely purple clusters was unforgettable! At the end of this wall, close to Piao Pei Hutung there had been a bright green gate. Whenever we passed this place, we had always craned our necks to see if we could get a glimpse of the beautiful mansion inside. It was built in western style, red brick like the wall. There were many glass windows and several chimneys. It was such a contrast to the Chinese homes on the other side. The gates, unlike the ones across from it, were rarely left open. In front of them a liveried servant stood watch, ready to open or close the gates. A black Ford, polished to perfection, stood by the wall, waiting for its occupants.

Once on our way to school we had glimpsed a little girl staring out of one of the windows. She had seemed so alone in that big house.

"That's Olga," Vanya told me. "Did you see her?"

"Yes, I saw her, and I know all about her." I had seen the Konovaloffs' daughter. They were probably the wealthiest Russians living in Peking. They didn't socialize with other Russians in the city. With Mama and Papa they were just nodding acquaintances.

I felt sorry for the little girl. I wondered with whom she played or if she ever had a chance to play with other children. Maybe she wasn't lonely, but she looked it when I saw her at the window of that beautiful big mansion all by herself.

Now, as we passed the red, brick wall, I realized that some things indeed had changed. The gates were painted red and were now wide open. We slowed down to look. There was the imposing old mansion. Yellow chrysanthemums in ornate pots lined the stairs leading up to the house. The garden itself was more beautiful than I had imagined. Out of the center of a small pond to the right sprang a black marble dragon's head. Water streamed out of its mouth. Lovely pink lotus blossoms nodded their petals in mute delight at this constant rain. Beyond the pond was a rose garden. To one side stood a bonsai pine, its gnarled trunk no more than a foot high; yet its evergreen branches stretched out in miniature grandeur. Japanese!

"Beautiful, isn't it?" I whispered, sliding my left foot on the ground. A weeping willow bent its graceful, silvery boughs over the pond and the rocks. Some of its swaying branches dipped into the crystal waters, almost caressing the dragon's head. What a tranquil and delightful scene! Such a contrast to this dusty hutung, devoid of even a single tree.

As we watched, a woman came out of the house, tripping daintily down the steps into the garden. On her back she carried an infant. She made a lovely picture in her flowered red kimono with the ornately embroidered obi around her tiny waist. Her hair was piled high on top of her head, not one hair out of place. Of the child, all that we saw was a doll-like head with a tiny tuft of black hair.

Vanya pressed his right foot on his pedal. "Come on, Sis; let's go," he said gruffly.

Apparently the Konovaloffs had moved out, and Japanese people now lived there. Where was Olga? Had her parents been taken away too because they were Russian?

We bicycled on into Piao Pei Hutung, one of our favorite streets. This was a busy business thoroughfare where bicycle shops and restaurants used to abound. It was the street that led to the wide, well-traveled boulevard, our popular Hatamen Street.

Piao Pei Hutung had always hummed with the loud voices of street vendors, happy children playing, and throngs of busy pedestrians. The street barber had his corner here, shaving his customers' heads; others chatted away, waiting their turn. At the very corner stood the friendly, young peanut vendor who roasted peanuts and those delicious chestnuts in his black cauldrons. What a welcome sight he was as he mixed these with his huge ladle, his round, smiling face red from the heat and blackened with soot. I observed a few rickshamen loafing in front of the gates of one of the houses. They sat idly on the footrests of their vehicles, staring at each passerby in hopes of catching a fare.

They watched us *yang kuei tzes* ride by them in silence. A few smoked their long-stemmed pipes, breathing in tobacco smoke, narrowing their eyes either from the swirling smoke or else the dust around them. Others were busy polishing the brass lanterns on either side of their rickshas. Some just sat.

I noticed apprehensively that there were quite a few Japanese soldiers on the street. They frightened me. I detested the sight of their ill-fitting uniforms almost as much as their faces. To me they all appeared mean and cruel. What a contrast to my beloved Chinese countrymen with their innate quiet dignity, their pleasant courtesy, their respect for their fellow man! Strange that we saw no Chinese women anywhere. It now was a man's world that we had entered. Something else was also missing. Piao Pei Hutung was sadly quiet. There were no vendor's songs, no children's laughter, nothing!

There had been a barber shop on the left-hand side. I remembered that this was where most men usually gathered to pass the time of day, waiting by the red-and-white sign until the barber called them in. I looked for it now. We had just passed it before I realized that that had been it.

"Look, Vanya," I pointed it out to him.

He nodded, "Yep, that's the way it goes."

The red-and-white sign, so familiar to us, was no longer there. Neither was the glass window with all its odd-shaped bottles containing different hair tonics and pomades. The window was now curtained with flowered drapes. Over the closed door a bright red lantern was hanging.

"What is that lantern for?" I asked Vanya. I knew very well that it couldn't be a Japanese barber shop.

"It's a brothel," he informed me, grinning.

When we entered Hatamen Street, I was happy to see that it was, as usual, quite crowded. It was also much cleaner. There used to be many mangy, stray dogs lurking along the store fronts scrounging for food, but no longer. Beggars no longer slinked along the walls waiting for shoppers to come out of stores or the market. Along the sidewalks the trees had been trimmed; the store fronts were newly painted, less gaudy in their choice of colors. Men and women with little ones in tow strolled along, leisurely looking into store windows, eagerly chatting to each other gazing at the other pedestrians. There was a distinct difference nevertheless. These people were different. Their clothing was unfamiliar to me. Their language when we listened to it seemed guttural in contrast to the musical *pu tung hua* that we knew so well. These people gave us glassy stares, as if we were the intruders, not they.

There were few Chinese. There was not even a single Chinese man taking a stroll with his birdcage in hand nor any of the happy, carefree children that we used to see. It was as if a huge mask had been dropped over Peking, hiding its original inhabitants from view. Something was terribly wrong with our city! It was sick, and I could see no cure!

Flags were suspended from almost every new store front: the stark, white rectangle with the round, red ball in the middle. To me it meant that our snow-white Peking had been splattered with the red blood of its people. Perhaps Papa's, too!

At last we reached Wise's.

"Hurry up and get what Mama wants," ordered Vanya. We got off our bikes, leaning them against a sidewalk tree. "I'll wait here for you."

I hastened into the store. I was surprised to see that it was still in business. Its facade had even received a new coat of paint. Beside the Chinese letters were some others in Japanese. "Oh, boy," I said under my breath.

Inside there were more customers and more goods on the counters than in the old days. Wise's had always been popular because there was such a wide variety of products. Foreigners liked to shop here because it was cleaner, and the meats, although expensive, were fresher. They also had sausages and all kinds of pickled things which attracted Mama and her friends.

The customers now were mostly Japanese. There was a soldier waiting impatiently to be served. I was surprised again to see that many of the soldiers had red beards. This soldier wore horn-rimmed spectacles with thick lenses that enlarged his eyes and gave him an even meaner look. He was opening the candy and nut jars, poking around, choosing a kind he liked, and popping it into his mouth. I couldn't help staring at him.

Another foreigner was in the store. She was either French or German. She too had seen the Japanese. When she met my eyes,

155

she shook her head slightly, as if in warning. Whether she thought that I might say something, I don't know. I smiled back at her, nodding my head. If she only knew what had happened to us, she wouldn't have been so concerned. I knew how to keep my mouth shut better than she did. Of that I was absolutely certain!

Finally, it was my turn to order. "One pound of sugar, please. One bag of salt, and four pounds of flour," I told the storekeeper.

He was not the friendly storekeeper we had known before. This one was quite young and spoke Japanese fluently. I checked his features carefully; he was definitely Chinese. Japanese bone structure was sharper.

He placed my purchases in a white paper bag, tying it expertly with red-and-white string. Before he gave me the bag, he stretched out his hand. "One yen, eighty sen."

I handed him two yuan. He opened his cash box and took out some change. I stared at the money.

"What's this?" I asked, without thinking.

"Your change, Miss, twenty sen." His eyes narrowed as he placed the coins in my hand.

The other customers eyed me curiously. Quickly I took the bag and walked out.

Vanya had been looking around. When he saw me, he heaved a sigh of relief. "I thought they must have kidnapped you. How come it took you so long?"

"Never mind." I jumped on my bike. "Come on, let's get out of here. I'll tell you later."

He gave me a quick look and got on his bicycle too. "That bad, is it?"

I was already on my way. "That bad."

When we got home, I told him and Mama all about my experience. Mama looked pale when I told her how arrogant the shopkeeper had been.

"He is probably working for the Japanese. I guess they have to be like that," she said. Then she smiled. "While you were gone, I had a visitor, Dr. Ferguson."

"Any news?" Both Vanya and I said the same thing.

"Not really. I was the one who did most of the talking, telling him about the *Gung An Ju*, the generalissimo, and so on. Best of all, he understood my English!" She laughed at that.

I was pleased to see how her face was rounding out. Her eyes too had regained some of their sparkle and liveliness.

"Mama," I said. "You never told us much about Miss Yang. She was the secretary at the Peking National University, wasn't she? Didn't you say she was your roommate?"

"Yes, she was. There has been so much to tell you that I thought I had already told you about her. She was arrested because she had come to our house with a Christmas gift for us. The police arrested her for that just as they arrested Gavriluk and the others."

"What did you do when you saw Dr. Ferguson?" Vanya asked.

"Oh, you can't imagine how I felt. I thought I was really dreaming! They had led me to the room across from the interrogation room. It was a small parlor. There he was, sitting, as big as life, waiting for me. He stood up when I entered, reached out with his arms, and wrapped me in them so tightly that I could hardly breathe! I couldn't believe it. He kept patting my head and telling me in his gentle voice, 'Vera, I'm taking you home now to your children.'

"When he finally released me from his grasp, I stumbled and almost fell. My legs had turned to jelly, and if he hadn't caught me, I would have crumpled to the floor, I am sure. He kept his arm around me then, supporting me."

"He hadn't told us that you were coming," Vanya complained.

"Why should he have told you? What if he had told you and they wouldn't release me? How would you have felt then when I didn't come? No, he did the right thing." Mama was very positive about that.

"You haven't finished telling us about Miss Yang," I reminded her.

"Ah, yes. Well, I'm sorry to have to tell you that she's still there," said Mama sadly. "What a highly intelligent woman she is, and how badly they had treated her!" She shuddered. "Just because she was acquainted with Papa. That's what is so terribly unfair. She and Papa are innocent of any of the charges against them, but . . . " She made a futile gesture with her hands. "But they believe what they want to believe."

That very day, towards the late afternoon, the doorbell rang.

157

Both Vanya and I rushed towards the gate-pavilion. We doubted that it was Dr. Ferguson. He usually didn't come twice in a day unless it was important. I wondered if possibly the missionary ladies were paying us a return visit. I surely hoped not. It would only put Mama ill at ease. Mama had cautioned us to ask who was at the gate before opening it.

In an unusually gruff voice, Vanya asked, "Who is it? I'm not opening the gates until I know who it is."

We both heard the familiar chuckle. There was only one person who sounded like that.

"If you don't open the gates, you'll be darned sorry, Old Pal. Come on, Vanya, or I'll drop these packages I have."

I helped him unbar the gates. There she stood, grinning like a Cheshire cat, her arms loaded with packages and one dainty foot determinedly placed on the brass threshold.

"I don't believe it!" I cried, giving her and the packages an enormous hug. "Well, you old sweet son of a gun! What a special surprise. I thought we'd never see you again, Dorlise!"

"Big fat chance of that happening," she said, giving me an impish look. How fresh and cheerful she looked, just as always. She stepped inside, looking around. Then she waved her rickshaman off. He had been watching us with a wide smile lighting up his homely face. "Oh, no," she called him back. "Wait for me. I'll be here for a while. Or you can come back in two hours."

She watched us bar the gates. "Hey, you guys are pretty good at that," she said admiringly. "Oh, by the way, how's Mama?"

We told her she could judge for herself when she saw her, and we walked down the front steps. She kept looking at both of us, her face just bubbling with joy. "Gosh, I was so worried about you all. Dr. Ferguson kept us informed, you know. I can't wait to see Mama."

"Well, at first she was not too good; she was moody, suspicious, crying for the slightest reason. She's fine now. In fact, she has us exercising every morning now, just as Papa did."

We walked through the moon gate into the little pavilion. Through its open gates we could see Mama standing in the glass-enclosed veranda, waiting to see who it was. When she saw Dorlise, her face broke into a relieved smile. She came running out toward us. Dorlise and Mama had a special rapport between them. Somehow Dorlise had started calling her Mama and treating her as if she really were her mother. Her own mother was rather strict.

They hugged each other. "I brought stuff, Mama," she said.

"You're my present, Dorlise," Mama said. Her eyes filled with tears. "I thought I'd never be here to see you again."

"Oh, bosh, Mama, of course you would have seen me. Now stop crying so I can show you what I've brought. Vanya, where are the packages?"

We had left them in the gate-pavilion. Vanya ran to get them. Soon she had unwrapped the packages for us, placing the contents, one by one, on the tea table.

"Here are all the American foods you like. Del Monte fruit— your prunes, Tamara—beans, Campbell soups. Boy! Some of the stuff I bought. Other cans," her brown eyes twinkled, "I stole from our kitchen. Nobody will miss them."

"You didn't *steal*, Dorlise?" Mama was horrified.

"Of course," she picked up a can. "Look, Mama, this is what we call *hash*. This is corned beef hash that you eat with eggs, and is it good!"

"Sounds strange. What is it?" I asked.

"Oh, gosh. Why'd you have to ask? Honestly, Tamdee, I think it's meat, but I'm not sure. All I know is that it tastes good."

We thanked her for doing this for us. "Listen," she said. "You're going to share this stuff with me, you know. After all, you're my other family, aren't you?" She pulled us all together, encircling us. "Boy, we're going to have fun now, aren't we?" And then she stopped, her face reddening. "I'm so sorry, Mama. I know how much you miss Papa. We all do," she added softly.

"I know, my dear," said Mama. "Don't feel bad about being happy. You are young; you should be that way. Come; we'll celebrate your coming here with tea and cookies—the ones you brought." She smiled at Dorlise.

When we were sitting at the table, Dorlise told us about our friends, what was happening at PAS and with her own family.

"I would have come to see you sooner, but Mary Ferguson said not to. Now I can come every day! That is," again she blushed, "if you want me to."

She told us that she used to make her rickshaman go by our

159

house. "Usually, the gates were closed, but a couple of times, I saw the police standing there on your steps. Whew! That sure was scary! Weren't you guys scared?"

"Of course," I told her. "But there's nothing that we could do in a situation like that."

"I'd have told them a word or two," she said angrily. "Who did they think they were?"

Mama placed her hand on Dorlise's shoulder. "My dear Dorlise, you could do that because you are American. We are Russian. That is where the difference lies. Russians here have no security at all; we're not like you."

Poor Mama! She had always been so proud of her heritage. There was something wistful in her voice when she told Dorlise that Russians were not protected by their country.

"You're absolutely right, Mama," Dorlise munched on a cookie. "Mm-mn, these are good, aren't they? Oh, by the way, you know I had a feeling that I was being followed when I came to your house. Anyway, I'm going to really watch and see. If I am, by golly, you know what?" She got a naughty look on her face. "I'm, by golly, going to give that follower a merry chase. I'll get Chin to pull me to all sorts of places."

At that we laughed, but I felt sorry for her rickshaman. She was always thinking of places to go to, and it was good that he was young and strong.

After this first visit of hers, we felt good. She was like a refreshing summer rain, fresh and welcome, leaving us revived in spirit. More than that, she had made us feel that we were not alone now; she was our contact with the outside world, a living newspaper!

September came. I turned seventeen. The leaves on the acacia trees were already turning brown. The ivy that climbed the inner walls of our courtyards had put on its autumn colors of red and gold. By October, it had shed its leaves. Only its thin, brown vines rose snakelike from the hard earth, weaving in and out amongst themselves, making sinister black lines against the wall's white plaster. There was a foreboding coolness in the air. Soon it would be time to mix the coal dust and roll it into balls, to gather dead branches and break them down for firewood. Only the hardy chrysanthemums still retained their muted green leaves and sprouted their many-petalled buds.

The first snowflakes fell in November, casting a soft silver-white glow to the rooftops and the ground below.

We continued our lives in much the same manner. Dr. Ferguson came daily, cheerful and encouraging, even though he brought us no news. Dorlise too came often, like a breath of sunshine, her arms always loaded, either with goodies or American magazines. Sometimes she even skipped school, staying with us all day. She told me privately that she felt better being with us and cheering Mama with her hilarious impersonations of different people than she did going to school and studying "the same boring subjects." She regaled us with her one-way infatuation with the handsome history teacher, Mr. White. She loved to join us at suppertime, even though it was often only Chinese noodles with vegetables and a bit of meat.

"I love your cooking, Mama!" Dorlise never ceased exclaiming over Mama, no matter what she was doing. I think that sometimes she did it on purpose in order to bolster Mother's spirits, as well as ours.

One day, when Dr. Ferguson arrived, we could see that something was on his mind. We were even more surprised when he looked at Vanya sternly, then bluntly asked him, "How would you like a job, son?"

"A job?" Vanya had turned pale. He glanced at Mama. "Did you say a job?"

"Why, yes, Vanya." Dr. Ferguson chuckled. "You're now what age? Eighteen?"

"I just turned nineteen in October."

"Well," the American looked searchingly at him, "Don't you think it's about time to start helping your mother out?" He looked at Mama for approval. "What do you think, Mother?"

Mama was silently twisting her handkerchief; she was worried. "But what can he do, Dr. Ferguson?" She turned to look at Vanya.

"I'm sure he's capable of many things," the American assured her. "He's certainly proved it by the way he's acted when you were gone." He smiled at Vanya. "I have an acquaintance, Mr. Werner. He's a fine man, and he needs assistance in his work. He told me that he would be most happy to try out our

161

young friend here. So how about it, Vanya?"

"I'd like that, I think," he answered with some enthusiasm. "I'll try my best, Dr. Ferguson! Thank you."

"Good. I knew you would." The American stood up. He shook Vanya's hand. "Now, it's all settled. Come over to my house at eight-thirty tomorrow morning, and my ricksha will take you to him."

Vanya smiled a broad smile. "I'll be there, sir."

Suddenly Mama too got up. "Dr. Ferguson?" Shyly she reached out her hand to detain him. "I'd like to ask your advice, please."

Our good neighbor turned towards her, his great head bent down towards her own. He had tremendous respect for Mama, I could tell. He admired and respected her courage and her gracious femininity.

"If you're going to ask me about what I think you are, then please, don't worry about it." He laughed cheerfully. "You are my friends."

Mama's face turned scarlet. She was probably thinking about all the rent we owed him.

She shook her head. "No, Dr. Ferguson, it's not about the rent. I realize how good you've been about that, and I have not forgotten how much we owe you. It's this. I've been thinking that I'd like to start my salon once more. I don't have sewing help; so I shall have to go about it slowly. What do you think of that?"

We had not expected that; yet it was just like Mama to do something constructive! The American thought for a moment.

"It may be a good idea, Vera," he mused. "It'll keep you busy, and," he gave me a wink, "it'll keep Tamara out of trouble. In fact"—he seemed to like the idea the more he thought about it—"I'm sure that Mary and Mrs. Stilwell could find plenty of clients for you. It's a very good idea!"

After he left, Mama was full of plans.

"We'll support ourselves. Only all of us are going to have to work hard and help each other. You, Tamara, will have to do the household chores and the cooking since you won't be working at a job."

The next morning Vanya got up early, shaved, and put on his one good suit. The sleeves of the jacket were a bit short. I had not realized how much he had grown and matured this year. He did look rather handsome dressed up. Mama and I both surveyed him rather critically.

"You look nice," Mama said. She straightened the tie he had gotten from Papa's tie rack. "Please, Vanya, don't slouch. You look so handsome when you stand up straight."

I agreed.

After he left, we barred the red gates. Then Mama and I went to clean up Paul Viaud's former lodgings.

"We'll fix it like it used to be in the old days when I had my salon." Mama was all energy. She couldn't do things fast enough. It took us all morning and part of the afternoon. At last, she was satisfied. With pursed lips, she studied the results of our labors.

We had brought back her old sewing machine from its storage place in her bedroom. I had a strange feeling as I looked at this black contraption, remembering that terrible day in my childhood when I had told her a lie. I looked to see if she had recalled it as well. She was too busy, too full of plans, to have thought of it. For that I was thankful!

8

Diversions

Vanya enjoyed his work although he did not talk too much about it. He did tell us about the different people he was meeting, either through work or through other friends. One day he came home much later than usual.

He was apologetic. "Sorry, Mama, but I couldn't help it. I met the most wonderful people today. You wouldn't believe it. He used to be the Chinese ambassador to Mexico, and his wife is Mexican. Mr. Hu is a great guy, really impressive. But it's his wife who is *the* person to know. Gosh!" He shook his head in disbelief. "You should hear her play the piano! She's a tiny lady, but what energy! It tired me just to watch her movements. When she plays the piano, her fingers fly so fast over the keys that you have difficulty keeping track of them. It's amazing!"

"Do they have children?" I asked.

"Yes." He turned back to Mama. "They want to meet you. I told them about you; not the arrest or anything, just how nice you are. Will you go to their house with me?"

Mama shook her head. "Vanya, I have told both of you several times already; I'm not stepping out of this house until Papa is released. I'm sorry."

He looked at me for support. "Can't you convince her, Old Pal? Besides, you must meet them too. They have two handsome sons and two beautiful daughters—our ages."

Aha! So there was a catch to all this, after all! There were two girls in the family. Now I knew why he had wanted Mama to meet the family.

I shook my head. "I agree with Mama. If she does not feel like going, I don't see why you should pester her. I'm not interested either. I'd rather be here with Mama."

Vanya didn't say any more about the Hu family. Mama and I both noticed, however, that he was coming home later each day. I was angry that he was so thoughtless of Mama. It wasn't fair to be gone all the time. When he did come home, it was only to get cleaned up and go to bed.

"You really should spend more time at home, Vanya," I rebuked him. "I know Mama worries even if she doesn't say anything. She works hard all day sewing, making money for us. It appears as if you don't care about us at all. You don't even ask if we've had news of Father."

He glared at me, his face flushing. Then his eyes began to dart all over as they usually did when he was too angry to focus them on only one thing or one person.

"It's none of your business what I do. I give Mama part of the money I earn. You don't earn anything!" He left in a huff that day. However, I noticed that he came home earlier. For two days he came home to have supper with us, acting as if nothing had happened between him and me.

On the third evening I found out why. He brought the Hu boys over to meet us. When I opened the heavy gates at his special knock, I saw the two young men with him. They smiled at my surprised stare. When they had stepped into the gate-pavilion, Vanya introduced them.

"Tamara, I want you to meet George," he nodded at the more handsome but shorter of the two. He had short, curly hair and dark eyes that constantly twinkled. "This guy is the oldest Hu offspring."

I held out my hand; George grasped it firmly. I liked his handshake.

"And this is Reuben," George added laughingly. "He is the dreamer in the family. Don't mind him."

Reuben was tall with smoldering black eyes. *He's the Mexican type,* I thought to myself, *whereas George is a good mixture of both Chinese and Mexican.* Reuben's raven-black hair was combed straight back from his low forehead. There was a dark shadow over his upper lip, the beginning of a moustache. He looked at me silently, nodding his head somewhat curtly. He didn't even smile. *Well, this one is what Dorlise would call a boor,* I decided. He certainly didn't have George's manners.

We sat in the little red pavilion and visited. I explained to them that Mama was busy today. She had a deadline to meet with some party dresses the colonel's daughters had ordered.

"Well, I sure hope we'll get to meet her soon, especially since her daughter is so charming," George replied.

He's the extrovert of the two brothers, I concluded. He was a tease, easygoing and good-natured. Some of the comments he directed to Vanya embarrassed my brother, especially when the name Emily was mentioned. I saw Vanya redden several times, looking unusually sheepish.

"Who is Emily?" I innocently asked.

The two brothers looked at Vanya. George grinned, slapping Vanya playfully on the back. "She's our sister," he explained. "Your brother seems to be very much taken with her."

Reuben said nothing. Somehow I felt uneasy with him. He had been staring at me with those heavy-lidded, smoldering eyes. Was there something wrong with my appearance? I decided to try Dorlise's trick. She had said one time that if people stared at her, she'd return the stare.

"You'd be surprised," she had laughed, "how quickly they lower their eyes."

Well, it worked! He stopped staring. Instead, he looked down at his feet.

"Ah, so!" I gave George a sly smile. "So my dear brother has fallen in love. We'd been wondering, Mother and I, what had been keeping him out so late these days. We knew it couldn't be work."

Vanya flushed. "Sis, Emily is beautiful and pure. You wouldn't understand."

"Touché!" George smiled and looked at me sympathetically. "Come on, Tamara," he suggested, offering me his arm. "I dislike this love stuff, don't you? Let's walk." He winked at me.

We walked back into the front courtyard and stood under one of the poplars. "Is your sister in love with Vanya too?" I asked him curiously. "I've never seen my brother like this."

He shook his head. "Frankly, I don't think Emily loves or is in love with anyone. When you meet her, you'll understand what

I mean." He squeezed my hand which was holding his arm. "You know, Tamara, you really should come and meet the others. We aren't all that bad." He grinned. "My sister Alicia is around your age. I'm sure you both will like each other. She has all the beauty and brains in our family, which I think is sort of unfair. God must have been tired when He was shelling out talents to the rest of us.

"Then, of course, there is Emily. Well, what can I say about her?" He paused, thinking. "She is eighteen, rather on the plump side, nice but not too bright. We do have a lot of fun at the house; everybody sings and plays some sort of instrument. There is usually a concert every night under Mother's direction. The house is always full of friends of the family, so you can imagine. It's a lot of fun."

What he was saying about his family sounded great. At any other time I'd have been delighted to meet them. But now I felt, as Mama did, that getting to know them would be most unfair to poor Papa. Socializing for us was definitely out!

"Some day I will," I answered him. I meant it. I'd have liked to explain to him why; yet something stopped me. It was just as well because Vanya and Reuben had joined us.

"Time to go," announced Reuben brusquely.

George looked at his watch. "Ah, so it is. I'm so glad that Vanya brought us here to meet you, Tamara." He gave me an exaggerated bow. I gave him a curtsy.

"I enjoyed meeting you, too, sir."

"You'll come to visit us?" His eyes looked into mine, attempting a sternness that he couldn't maintain. He smiled and added emphatically, "I mean that."

I nodded, crossing my fingers. Reuben was formal, shaking my hand briefly. His eyes again peered out through those heavy lids, studying my face in a disturbing, almost sinister manner. I was relieved when they finally left. "Ugh!" I couldn't help uttering that.

"What's the matter with you?" Vanya's eyebrows rose in surprise. "Didn't you like them?"

"Oh, George was very nice," I answered. We walked back to the house. "But that Reuben. Ye-ugh! He gives me the creeps." I shivered in mock dismay.

"Oh, Reuben's okay. He'll grow on you. Listen, Sis, you ought to hear him play the piano."

"I prefer George," I said as we went inside. "He's got a good sense of humor."

Mama had put away her sewing for the night and was reading a book when we came in. I told her about the Hu brothers. I was going to tell her about Emily when I caught Vanya's warning look. I paused. He really looked lovesick and miserable. "Poor guy, I won't tease him anymore," I said to myself. But how could he fall in love at a time like this?

In time I did get to meet the Hu family. Vanya had told Dorlise about them. Of course, she was curious to see what they were like, especially Vanya's heartthrob, as she had dubbed Emily. Even Mama insisted that I go, after Dorlise had put the pressure on her.

"Look, Mama," she argued, pinching my cheek playfully, "see how pale and wan your daughter looks. All she does is sit in the house here, either working or reading. She needs to get out to have a little fun. Don't you agree, Mama?" She studied Mama, batting those big brown eyes of hers. Of course, that started Mama laughing.

"Oh, Dorlise, stop that!" Mama's eyes were misty from laughing so hard. "Of course, she needs to get out. I haven't insisted because she didn't want to go anywhere. It's true, though. Tamara, you should see friends your own age." She looked at me affectionately. "I know why you've stayed home all this time. But I'm all right now. I'm fine here by myself. In fact, I'd get more work done if you young ladies were not here all the time making me laugh and cry." She gave Dorlise a wink.

Soon after this, Vanya brought us an invitation from George. Dorlise and I were both asked to come to a Saturday party.

Dorlise came to our house early, bringing some American hash with her. "I'm cooking supper for us," she announced to Mama.

Vanya had bought himself a new shirt and had even visited the barbershop. I sighed with relief. I hated to cut his coarse, thick hair almost as much as he disliked my doing it! When he returned from the barber, I stopped short. His hair had really been cut! When he saw my expression, he went to get a hand mirror. For a time he eyed himself, critically looking at his reflection.

"You really think it's all right, Old Pal?" he asked.

"Sure, it's fine," I said, trying not to laugh. His bluish scalp over the earpart, why, I could almost see it!

"Mama, what do *you* think?"

Mama looked at him. She made him turn this way and that. "You look positively handsome, my dear," she beamed.

When he asked Dorlise the same question, she bent her head to one side, gazing at him critically. Slowly she narrowed her eyes. "Turn around," she ordered. "Hmm...." She pursed her lips, giving me a quick, mischievous glance. "Vanya, you got scalped! My God, Old Pal, what in heaven's name did they do to you? Where'd you go to get such a lou—I mean, such a haircut?"

Vanya panicked. "Mama," he lowered his head in front of her, "tell me, is it really that bad?"

Mama shook her head. Her face was flushed from trying to contain her laughter. She shook her finger at Dorlise and me. "Can't you see that they're teasing you?" She smiled at him. "You're so handsome you look like Cary Grant." She chased us out. "Now hurry and go. I want to lock you people out and then get back to my work. Enjoy yourselves at the Hus.'"

I caught a glimpse of her face before she swung the red gates shut. She was still smiling.

The Hus didn't live too far away from us. Their house was a large one, built in the Chinese style, but inside it was furnished with heavy European furniture: big overstuffed sofas and chairs. On the tops of the huge, ornate tables, which must have been built in Queen Victoria's time, were odd-shaped, fringed lamps, each one brightly lit. Numerous pots and plants stood at different spots on the floor. It was quite an interesting conglomeration of furniture pieces, each one by itself a curious piece. In fact, the Hus' living room reminded me of a museum.

By the French doors stood an old piano, its top piled high with an assortment of music books. When we entered this room from the wide porch, we saw a tiny woman seated on the piano stool, her hands idly fingering the keys. Her face was nondescript, colorless, and finely wrinkled. Her hair was mousy. When she saw us enter, I was surprised at the change in her. Her warm, sparkling eyes seemed to envelop us all with their love and friendliness. Her whole face blossomed into a beautiful smile. She rose from her piano perch and walked towards us with short, brisk steps. Even with spiked heels she was shorter than anyone else in the room.

"At last, Vanya, you've brought them here!" She welcomed us in an accent that was unfamiliar, but then I remembered Vanya's telling us that she was Mexican. I understood now why Vanya liked coming here. All of them—especially Mrs. Hu—made me feel good, as if I had always belonged in their circle of happy friends.

The room was crowded with young people. Some of them sat talking. Others were gathered around the piano. George walked toward us, leaving a boisterous, laughing group of his friends.

"Finally, you've come to our home. Welcome!" He looked at me in mock disbelief. "I never thought we'd ever see you here."

I returned his smile. "You're the one who talked us into coming," I replied teasingly. I surveyed those in the room. Then I saw Reuben, sitting on a hassock, strumming a guitar, oblivious to those around him. I was happy that he hadn't seen us. Even bent over his instrument, he looked morose. *What a strange contrast in brothers,* I thought.

A lovely young girl my own age came over to us, holding out her hand, a model of perfection. Her face was oval; the eyes, almond-shaped, large, and intelligent; the nose, straight; her lips were etched in a lovely smile, showing her perfect teeth. Her gaze was calm and straightforward, reminding me of George's, minus his mockery.

She introduced herself, "I'm Alicia. I've heard a lot about the two of you from Vanya. Welcome to our house."

I had never seen anyone so beautiful or so seemingly unaware of her own loveliness. Her skin was like the finest ivory. There was no tint to it, just the luminous eyes and the perfect features. Everything about her was minute and delicate, like a flower that is too fragile to hold. She glanced about her at the crowd of people, then gave Vanya a dazzling smile.

"I think that Emily is out on the porch," she told him quietly. "If you'd like, I'll go fetch her." She glided out of the room in the manner of a ballerina making a graceful exit.

170

We waited for them there, standing motionless as we continued to inspect the house and the other guests. Mrs. Hu noticed us and came over to tell us, "It's always like this. You see, we enjoy having young people around. We all love music here. Most everyone plays some instrument or sings. While we wait for them, let's go over to the piano. I'll play you a Mexican tune."

She sat down at the piano and began to play. Her tiny hands spilled over the keys as if they were a part of them. She played spirited tunes, some of which I recognized; others were foreign to me. She played music that was soothing, and I felt lulled into a state of dreamless tranquility. Then she changed again to the staccato tempos of her Mexican heritage. When she stopped playing, we begged her to play on.

"Any requests?" she asked, turning to look at us.

"Could you play that piece you first played for us?" I asked. "What is it called?"

She was pleased. "It's *The Mexican Hat Dance,* and everyone likes it," she said.

She played more. Her fingers flew over the keys magically. Faster and faster she played, her bright eyes smiling, encircling all of us in her spell.

I was so engrossed in watching her and listening to the music that when someone tapped my shoulder, I jumped.

It was Vanya. "Tamara, come with me; I want you to meet Emily," he whispered. I had forgotten all about meeting his *heartthrob,* having been so mesmerized by Mrs. Hu.

"Okay, Vanya, where is she?" I followed him towards the armchair in which she sat. As we approached her, I looked at the girl who had stolen my brother's heart. I saw a round, rosy face wreathed in thick, dark-brown hair; regular Chinese eyes, black and slanting; wide, flat nose; full, voluptuous lips.

I was disappointed in Emily. Perhaps if the other members of her family had not been around, I'd have found her more attractive. Of course, I had not yet met the master of the Hu household, but the others' personalities were well-fixed in my mind. Their Mexican mother was a dynamo, small in size but gigantic in her personality. How she had mesmerized us all with her music! All she did was sit at the piano, and the whole room became quiet, waiting for her to touch the keys! The oldest,

171

George, handsome, courteous, most like his mother in spirit and talent! Alicia, gentle, intelligent, lovely! Even Reuben, sullen, dreamy, loving music above all else!

But Emily! I looked at Vanya and thought to myself how true it is when they say love is blind. Her brothers and sister had those unusually attractive features which often result from Euro-Asian parentage. Emily? She was just ordinary when compared to her siblings. She might be called attractive, but there were thousands of attractive girls in China, many much more so than Emily. She was shy, almost painfully so. Or was it that she had nothing to say? She was somewhat plump, and, according to what Dorlise said later, had no more personality than a rag doll. Had Vanya fallen for Alicia, I'd have been the first to applaud his choice. I was really surprised at him and somewhat saddened by his selection. He, however, was completely enamored. After I met her, he took her out to the porch where they stayed by themselves for most of the evening.

Later on, Mr. Hu made his entrance, surveying the guests and his family benevolently. He *did* look like an ambassador, I thought, even though he was now an ex! Mrs. Hu introduced Dorlise and me.

"This is Vanya's sister and her friend, Dorlise," she informed him. He bowed, looking down at us from his towering height. He was a dignified gentleman with high cheekbones and, for a Chinese, a straight, somewhat prominent nose. *There must be barbarian blood in him, probably Manchurian,* I thought to myself. He spoke English flawlessly; in fact, he sounded like a blue-blooded Londoner. Dorlise and I looked at each other in delight. She even nudged me with her elbow. Had he not been looking at me with such graciousness, I'd have been convulsed with laughter. I was already picturing Dorlise later on at our house, mimicking this fine man.

"Chawmed, I ahm shuah!" She wouldn't miss this opportunity!

It was difficult for us to leave. When the clock on their living room wall struck eleven, I couldn't believe it. Time had just flown. We had met many interesting people besides the Hus. There was Freddie, the young man in the traditional Chinese robe. He acted as if he were part of the Hu family. Good looking, very reserved—or else shy—he sat with Mr. Hu at the end of the large living room, surveying the scene but not taking part in it, preferring the company of the older diplomat. There were some attractive girls, friends of Alicia's, who flirted outrageously with George, who took it all in stride, giving one a quick wink, another a peck on the cheek, still another a secretive smile meant only for her. He blessed them all with his attention yet did not single out any particular girl. Dorlise liked him; I could see that. I just hoped that she wouldn't get herself into the same situation as Vanya had. It would really be exasperating to have *two* lovesick romancers around me.

There were some other young men who apparently were either George's friends or admirers of Alicia. I doubted if any other than Vanya had come here for Emily's sake.

Dorlise and I bade our hosts good-bye, loath to leave but already having overstayed our planned first visit.

Mama was relieved and happy when we returned home.

"I hope you weren't worried about us, Mama," Dorlise explained. We both anxiously studied her face, feeling guilty for staying out so late.

Mama smiled wearily. "Just a little bit," she admitted. "But then, I knew that you were having fun. I realize how quickly time passes when you're happy. I was young once." She rubbed her cheek. "I suppose Vanya stayed on."

We then told her about Emily and how crazy Vanya was about her. "Mama, he's just impossible," moaned Dorlise, snuggling up to her on the sofa. Dorlise had sent a message home by her rickshaman that she would be staying with us overnight. She often did that to keep us company. Actually, I think she realized how much we loved her, and she felt that she belonged with us, more so than with her own sedate, reserved American family.

Mama smiled when we had finished our descriptions of the various Hus. She dismissed Vanya's love affair with a wave of her hand. Dorlise and I were surprised.

"Just puppy love," Mama chuckled to herself. "It comes to every boy and girl, sooner or later."

"What's that, Mama?" I asked. "Why 'puppy' love?"

"Because it's the first time a boy or girl falls in love. It is the purest, sweetest kind of emotion. It is the time when adolescents or teenagers experience their first attraction to someone of the opposite sex. It is a beautiful time in a young person's life, and you two will also, I hope, go through it. Some people never forget their first love," she smiled. "I remember mine. Then there are others, of course, with whom you think that you are in love. But finally you meet *the* person," she paused, "and you know that this is the person with whom you want to spend the rest of your life."

"How do you know when?" asked Dorlise. Her brown eyes were wide with curiosity.

Mama kissed her gently on her forehead. "You just know, that's all," she answered quietly. "And now, you girls, it's off to bed with you."

We never heard Vanya come home that night. Mama must have opened the gates for him. At breakfast he appeared sleepy-eyed but cheerful.

I don't remember just when it happened; it had all started out so gradually. Reuben began coming home with Vanya in the evenings. Sometimes he would also drop around during the day, just to visit with Mama and me. If we were busy, he would sit down to play the piano, seemingly happy just to be around where it was peaceful and quiet. Mama enjoyed his presence; he was unassuming and shy. She liked to hear him play while she did handwork on her clients' dresses.

Dorlise was amused. "Oh, Tamdee," she laughed, stroking her cheek with her index finger several times, teasing me as we had done when we were smaller. "Shame, shame," she continued, "*xu, xu, xu!*" She grabbed Mama's arm. "She doesn't even realize that Reuben is head over heels in love with her, does she?"

"He's not, Dorlise." I couldn't stand it if it were true. However, I recalled that several times I had seen him look at me stealthily and intensely. I'd paid no attention to him, but come to think of it, he had been spending a lot of time here.

"Ugh," I spat out in disgust. "Not him, Dorlise. I just can't stand him. He's so . . ."—I searched for the right word—"so insipid, don't you think?"

"Let's face it, mah deah," chided Dorlise, lapsing into Mr. Hu's accent, "You arh sech a sahren, mah deah!"

"Oh, pooh-bah!" I protested. "He's just in love with 'myousheek.' I imitated Reuben's way of saying music.

"Isn't he an absolute scream when he says that!" Dorlise got that mischievous grin on her face. "I just want to keep saying, 'Ick-sheek, myou-sheek, poor Reuben is the Ick-sheek.' "

Poor Mama tried to be serious, but we could tell she was amused. "You ought to treat him better than you do," she reprimanded us. "He is such a gentle, young man. Remember that he can't help it if he feels that way about you."

I groaned. "You too, Mama? Well, I can't help it if I feel the way I do about him. I can't stand him. Why couldn't it be George who's in love with me? Then I wouldn't feel so bad. He's at least normal."

They both laughed at me. Mama even got tears in her eyes.

"Believe me, Tamdee, if Georgie-Porgie were in love with you, he wouldn't act so normal either, would he, Mama?"

Mama wiped her eyes. "You two are impossible. But, to answer your question, Dorlise, probably not. People change somewhat when they fall in love. I can even remember a certain young lady," she gazed pointedly at Dorlise, "who had a passing crush on a certain handsome young teacher."

I laughed, seeing the confused look on Dorlise's face. "Mama, you're right. I had forgotten about that. Yeah, Miz Krenz, ma'am, what about old Whitey-boy? And Huie?"

Dorlise blushed. A secretive look came over her face. "That's all in the dead, dead past," she said quickly. Her eyes became thoughtful. She looked in Mama's direction. Mama was now putting the final stitches on a brocade evening gown for Mrs. Stilwell. She had laid a sheet on the rug so as not to soil the lovely dress. Mama was obviously not listening to us now.

"Tamara?" Dorlise placed her finger on her lips. "I've been thinking of something to do. You know, it gets so boring at times, just sitting around."

"There're books here that you can read," Mama said.

Dorlise groaned. "I didn't think that you were listening. I know, Mama, I read plenty. It's just that it would be sort of fun to do something different."

Oh, boy, I thought to myself. *She's already got something planned.* I knew that ideas were rolling about in her head, hitting and colliding with each other.

"You know the Hus?" she asked.

175

"What a stupid question, silly. Have you forgotten? We were there yesterday evening?"

She grinned. "Well, I've been thinking. Wouldn't it be neat to play a trick on the boys?"

Mama shook her head in despair. She couldn't say anything as her mouth was full of pins. I wondered what Dorlise was up to now. "Okay, out with it, Dorlise. I can see you've already got it all planned."

She sounded excited. "Wait till you hear." She looked to see if Mama was listening, then leaned forward, her brown eyes full of mischief. "You know that we have two rickshas at our house. Auntie said we could borrow hers, and the other one is for my use. So *that* problem is settled."

"Are you sure Auntie said yes?" I asked her doubtfully.

She turned angelic eyes upon me. "Why, Tamara Rubleva, do you think I'd stoop so low as to lie to you? Well, I thought that we could dress up like rickshamen and then go to their house." She looked at Mama pleadingly, "Mama, we're going to need your help in this project."

Mama took the pins out of her mouth. She laid the dress aside, rubbing her eyes. She was amused at Dorlise's enthusiasm. "And what is it that you would like me to do?"

Dorlise hesitated. "You just need to write a note to Reuben and George Hu, saying that you need them to come here and that you've sent the two rickshamen to get them. That's all." She fished in her bag. "I didn't think you'd mind so I just brought some notepaper with me." She held it out.

Mama looked at the pretty notepaper edged in a forget-me-not flower pattern. Dorlise gave her a pen and a scrap of paper. "I just wrote down the invitation for you to copy. Thought it might make it easier for you."

What a conniver! She knew beforehand that we would fall for her scheme! We both watched Mama copy the letter in her handwriting, signing it with her inimitable, flowery signature: *Vera Rubleva*.

Dorlise blew the ink dry, then waved the note in the air. "Good. Thanks, Mama. You're a dear." She hugged Mama affectionately and rose. "I've got to go and prepare the stuff for us. Now, I'll be here tomorrow with rickshas and everything; so you've got to be ready. Till tomorrow then!" She waved her hand over her head just as a matador would after he had gored the bull!

The next day, true to her word, Dorlise came, riding in her own rickshaw, the other one pulled by her Auntie's man. When I opened the gates for her, she was just dismissing the two coolies.

"You can have a good time until ten-thirty this evening," she ordered them sternly. "Then you can wait on these steps until we return. Don't ring the bell here!"

They nodded, grinning as they walked off, leaving their vehicles parked by the front steps.

After we had eaten an early supper, Dorlise showed us the clothes she had brought. I knew these belonged to the rickshamen.

"Did they let you borrow them?" I asked in surprise.

She shook her head, her brown eyes filled with guilt. "I just sort of borrowed them," she confessed. "Tamdee, I *had* to."

Mama joined us in getting ready for our adventure. She kept laughing until the tears rolled down her cheeks. "Impossible," she kept repeating with obvious delight. It was something that she herself would have done when she was our age. What an unbeatable team she and Dorlise would have made!

We were now dressed in coolie clothes, from the dirty bandannas around our black-stockinged heads to the worn Chinese shoes on our feet. Only our faces still looked foreign. Mama, of course, solved that problem for us.

"Tamara, go to the coal shed and bring back some coal dust," she ordered.

"You're like Cinderella's fairy godmother, Mama," said Dorlise approvingly.

"Only, I'm not transforming you into beauties," Mama retorted.

When I brought back the coal dust, Mama mixed it with a bit of water. Soon she had both of us looking like bootblacks. A bit of her dark powder, then some of my charcoal on our eyebrows, and presto! In the twilight hours, anyone now would think us nothing but two somewhat tired and dusty ricksha coolies! Dorlise tucked Mama's note into her jacket pocket.

"Well, I guess it's time to go," Dorlise said.

177

"Okay, Mama, how do we look?"

Mama laughed, "Go on, you two, and leave me with my sewing. You two look perfect. Just be careful with the rickshas."

She was still smiling when she closed the gates behind us.

We walked down the steps to the vehicles. Dorlise got in between the pulling bars and expertly lifted her ricksha. Holding the bars under her armpits, she fished in one of her pockets. "Ah, just what I was looking for." She withdrew a tiny packet and took out a cigarette, placing it between her lips.

"Dorlise! Don't!" I was horrified.

"Don't worry, Tamdee. I won't light it till we get there. Come on, let's go."

I imitated her in holding up my vehicle. For a moment, when I lifted the handles, I was afraid it might upset. It was heavier than I'd thought it would be. However, as I let down the bars, holding them lightly, the vehicle itself became lighter. There was a trick to it, I soon found out. Of course, Dorlise already knew this trick. I quickly sensed that this was not her first time pulling a ricksha.

We walked along Magpie Street, holding onto our rickshas in the same relaxed manner in which we had seen the real pullers do after they had stopped running for the day and were on their way home. We spoke to each other in Chinese, Dorlise using the slangy, picturesque, and coarse dialect of the common Peking folk, who ended their musical syllables in the familiar "er" sound. To all appearances we were just a couple of poor ricksha coolies going home. People passed us by, pedestrians or other rickshamen ignoring us as simply a part of the busy street scene. I heard Dorlise chuckle to herself; I, too, was rather impressed at how well we were pulling this off.

Dorlise's hissing "Pssst!" roused me from my thoughts. When I looked up, there were three staggering figures walking unsteadily towards us. Japanese soldiers! They were walking abreast of each other, blocking the narrow street! Their swords were dangling from their sides; their booted feet tramped through the sloshy mud. They were quite drunk, singing in loud voices that were decidedly out of tune. When they were about ten feet away from us, one of them noticed us. A few harsh words towards his companions and they were all yelling to us, waving their hands, and cursing at us in their guttural tongue.

"They want to hire us," whispered Dorlise in shocked disbelief. "Good God! Tamdee, we've got to get out of here pronto."

I too saw the danger. We had pulled the American flags off the rickshas before we had started out. Now we had no protection. We looked around in panic. The soldiers had quickened their paces, lurching forward, their faces glaring at us in their drunken madness. Their shouts became louder.

By sheer luck we noticed the small, even narrower *hutung* (side street) to the left of us. In the darkness it could easily be missed by a stranger. We, however, now recognized it, having used it many times before.

Dorlise, who was in front, quickly darted into this *hutung,* disappearing into its darkness. I followed her, my heart beating frantically. I didn't dare look back but ran as fast as I could, pulling the vehicle behind me. We heard the befuddled curses of the Japanese as they staggered on, blinded by their fury and inability to find us.

The gathering twilight and that small *hutung* saved us. We kept on running, pulling our rickshas clumsily, for this street was muddier than the one we had left. Finally we came to the end. A larger street crossed it in either direction. It was quiet now except for the loud beating of our hearts.

"That sure was a close shave," I whispered to Dorlise. "Can you imagine what would have happened to us if they had caught up with us?"

She made a swift motion with her hand, slicing her neck. "Just like that!" she turned towards me. "Did you see how long their swords were? Whew!"

Just like that, I thought. Off with their heads, the Red Queen had said. Or was it the white one?

By the time we arrived at the Hus' home, it was nearly ten o'clock. As usual, their car was parked by the gates. There was another automobile behind it. Several idle ricksha coolies sat on their footrests, smoking and talking.

"Well," Dorlise murmured, slowing down. "Here goes!" She got some matches out. On the third try she was able to get the cigarette lit. She puffed at it quickly, sucking in her cheeks to draw in the smoke. Suddenly she started to cough.

179

"Gosh darn!" she whispered hoarsely. "Here, hold this, will you?" She handed the cigarette to me. I was afraid to put it in my mouth. I held it gingerly between my fingers the way I had seen Papa's friends do.

"Aren't you going?" I flipped the ashes to the ground. The cigarette, I decided, was enhancing my coolie appearance.

"Here, give me that." She took the cigarette away from me, again placing it between her lips. I noticed its red glow as she inhaled. Carefully, she laid down the handle bars of her ricksha. Now she was sauntering confidently toward the gates. Then suddenly I heard her "khrrrh," gathering the phlegm in her throat. She stopped to spit it out, just the way a coolie would do. She threw the cigarette down, grinding it with her foot.

She rang the doorbell, tapping her foot impatiently on the wooden threshold. A few of the rickshamen watched her in silence.

The gates swung open. Lao Wang, the Hus' aged gatekeeper, peered out into the street.

"*Shei-ya?*" (Who is it?) he croaked. Then he saw the pseudo rickshaman.

Dorlise narrowed her eyes. "I have a message here for the young masters," she announced in a strange, husky voice. Even though I knew that it was she, I still had my doubts, when I heard the unfamiliar voice. Lao Wang, who knew us well as foreign young ladies, did not even bother to take a second look at her. He took the envelope she offered.

"You wait here in case there is an answer," he suggested, shuffling slowly towards the main house.

"There will be an answer," Dorlise muttered under her breath. She squatted down on her haunches, looked around her at the others, then spat. "Ai-ya, but I've had a hard day today." She dug into her pocket, fishing out another cigarette.

Not too long after that, George and Reuben came out into the street, searching for us. Dorlise slowly got up, eyeing them boldly.

Reuben was already getting into her ricksha. She turned in my direction. "Eh, Lao Yang, lai ba." (Old Yang, come on.) I picked up the handles of the ricksha and sauntered over towards George, trying to appear nonchalant. I set the vehicle down care-

180

fully so that he could step in. All this time I kept praying that I would be able to lift him up and keep from giggling. Surprisingly, I raised the handle bars easily. Soon Dorlise and I were loping at an even, leisurely pace, side by side, while the brothers chatted amiably between themselves.

"I wonder what Mrs. Rubleva wants us for," said George. "Her note sounded urgent."

"She should have sent for Vanya," said Reuben, "if she needs help. I guess, though, that he's not too good around the house since he has fallen for Emily."

Dorlise gave me a sidelong glance.

"He's okay," George answered. He shifted his position, and I almost dropped him. "He's just in love. You ought to know that feeling well, moping around as you do for Tamara. Why are you wasting your time, Reuben? She hardly knows you exist."

I almost dropped him then and there. Both Dorlise and I were now laughing so hard that we thought for sure they would notice it. However, they were too occupied with their own conversation. As long as we kept on running, we were all right.

We had pulled them for almost a block and were about to turn the corner when Dorlise began to cough. "Whoo, ai-ya," she moaned in misery. "Ai-ya, whoo, oo," she sputtered and coughed, bemoaning her sad state. This had been our prearranged signal. She was so genuine about it though that I began to wonder if she really was in distress. Then I caught her wink. She stopped suddenly, and so did I. Reuben nearly fell out of his ricksha.

"What the . . . ?" growled George, but it was too late. Dorlise and I were lifting the handle bars higher and higher, until Reuben and George had their heads touching the ground, their feet up in the air. They had to somersault backwards in order to get out of the rickshas. George stalked angrily towards us, followed by an equally irate Reuben.

Dorlise and I put out our hands in mock protest, pleading in Chinese, *"Bu yao, bu yao da!"* (Don't, don't beat!), while the tears coursed down our cheeks from laughing so hard. When the boys got close to us, they heard our muffled laughter. Puzzled, they came even closer. George scanned my face. I lowered my eyes quickly. Reuben stalked over to Dorlise, shaking the dirt off his trousers. He was furious. When he was about to take her by the shoulders, she pulled off her blue bandanna and the black stocking that hid her hair. Shaking her head, she glanced up coquettishly at him. There were white streaks down her cheeks where her tears had washed off the coal dust.

She bowed to Reuben ceremoniously. "Guess who?" she asked in her normal voice.

The brothers were dumfounded. Even when I, too, took off my head disguise, they had to walk around us, examining us carefully.

George was in awe. "You two girls are positively unbelievable!"

Reuben remained silent. I wondered if he was disappointed in his lady love. Out of the corner of my eye, I could see him eyeing me as if he couldn't decide who I was. I remembered their conversation earlier, and in spite of myself, I began to blush. I was grateful for the makeup so that no one could really see my embarrassment.

The boys walked back to the house with us while we pulled the rickshas. The Chinese standing beside the gates stared at us in amazement, then oohed, aahed, and ai-yaed. When they found out what had happened, they puzzled over the fact that the two foreign misses could pull off such a stunt on their young masters. Inside the house we received much the same reaction. Never had anyone dared do something like this. For a time Dorlise and I basked in this glorious adulation. Even Mr. Hu applauded us when we came into the house. When we told him about meeting the Japanese soldiers, however, his face became grave.

"You could have gotten yourselves into a great deal of trouble," he told us sternly. "First of all, in their drunken stupor, they could have killed you. Secondly, without a flag on your ricksha, you had absolutely no protection. You must remember, young ladies, that these are dangerous times."

I promised him that we would be more careful in the future. Dorlise looked quite penitent. Knowing her, however, I sorely doubted it. She was probably even now thinking up something else, not boring, that we could do.

We came home, tired but happy. It had been quite an evening, and Mama, bless her, had waited up so that she could hear all about our big adventure.

9

Fu Tai Tai

A few days after our ricksha escapade, the front doorbell rang. I ran to unbar the gates and was quite surprised to see Chang, the Fergusons' Number-One Boy. I noticed that he was wearing the unbleached white gown and square cap of mourning. His eyes were red and swollen. He bowed low, asking permission to see Mama.

"But, of course," I answered, leading him towards our quarters. I wondered who had died. It was the custom of servants to come to their employers when some member of their family had died. They always kowtowed, wept bitter tears, and received a gift of money as well as the condolences of their sympathetic masters.

Mama saw him coming and opened the door for him. When he bowed, she returned his bow and stood there silently, waiting for him to speak. For a while he stood there, head bowed, eyes glued to the ground, and tears unashamedly rolling down his cheeks.

Finally Mama touched his hand gently. "I am so sorry for your grief," she said. "How can I help you?"

He lifted his head, revealing his nearly swollen shut eyes. "Fu Tai Tai" (Mrs. Ferguson), he sobbed. "She died very early this morning."

My chest tightened. Cold shivers traveled from the top of my head on down throughout my entire body. Mrs. Ferguson's death had been expected, but now that it had actually happened, there still was shock. I couldn't help thinking of our dear friend. Poor

183

Dr. Ferguson! How could he cope with losing his beloved companion of so many years?

Mama walked over to Chang. She took both his hands in her own. "Please tell Fu Kai Sun that I will come to see him and Miss Ferguson tomorrow to pay my respects. Thank you, Chang, for coming," she told him softly.

He bowed low, backing out towards the door. Vanya opened it for him and escorted him out to the front gates.

"Poor Dr. Ferguson," I whispered. "I just feel so bad for him, Mama."

She nodded, her eyes misty.

"Of course, you do, dear. We all do. But remember, Tamara, Mrs. Ferguson was quite elderly, and she had been sick for such a long time. Now she is finally at peace." Mama looked at me with understanding. "It is your first encounter with death. What you must remember is that she had had a beautiful, long life. Her death is just a sleeping away for her. It is always for the living that we must feel sorrow." Mama patted me on the cheek. "Remember her as you saw her last."

I did remember. Dr. Ferguson had come over one day to see Father about a bronze vase he was examining. I just happened to be in the front courtyard when he was leaving. It had been quite some time ago—three or four years, I thought. Dr. Ferguson had playfully grabbed my hand and winked at Father. "I'm going to borrow your daughter for a short time, Professor. I'm taking her with me," he had explained. His blue eyes had twinkled then. "Come on, Girlie, let's go to my house now and see Mrs. Ferguson. She'll be tickled to see you."

Off we had gone through the gate. I had skipped along beside him, and he, distinguished as ever in his dark suit, had walked along briskly, swinging his cane.

The Fergusons' house intrigued me. It was the most beautiful one of the three in the compound. It was built in the most traditional Chinese style with a goldfish pond in the garden and lotuses and tiny bridges beside picturesque rock formations. There were charming pavilions on elevated, man-made mounds and graceful, curved trees planted in specially designated places where they would appear most advantageously. As we walked along, it was like a Chinese scroll painting being unrolled—simple, natural, lovely, and totally unforgettable.

The house itself was a large one. Inside, the partitions were intricately carved. The furniture, of course, was Chinese in style. Rich teakwood chairs and low tables, majestic scrolls hanging on the walls, their right-hand sides filled with the red seals of their former owners. Some of them even bore the great seals of departed emperors. Porcelains and the good doctor's favorite bronzes stood on carved stands, each one an exquisitely lovely object.

He and I had walked through the garden hand in hand. He stopped to pluck a jujube from a tree and handed it to me.

"Taste it, Girlie. It's good," he had assured me. He himself bit into another one he had picked. When I had finished nibbling at the jujube, I'd wondered what to do with the pit but had finally managed to slip it covertly into my skirt pocket.

We had walked through the long living room, then through a door that led into a hall. He'd turned left, and we'd entered a large, sunny room. In the center, along the end wall, was a high bed, all in pink and white, with a multitude of ruffles. Mrs. Ferguson had lain there, propped up by many white pillows, some of them edged in lace and others embroidered with flowers. She'd had such a sweet face, I remember. Her skin had been just like a baby's, a soft pink. She'd been smiling when we entered the room. I hadn't been able to take my eyes off her. Her hair, snow white and fluffy, had resembled a halo round her head.

"Guess who is here?" her husband had said. He'd taken my hand and led me to her bedside.

She had been sweet and gentle. Her blue eyes had twinkled in much the same way his did.

"Why, it's Tamara! How much you have grown, dear." She'd patted her bed. "Here, jump up and sit and visit with me. I want to hear all about you, dear."

Dr. Ferguson had left us in the meantime. I'd carefully seated myself on the edge of the bed, making sure that I didn't sit too close. I hadn't wanted to jostle her in any way.

I'd told her of my interest in painting, my practicing calligraphy. She'd asked me about Vanya, school, Mama and Papa. She hadn't really seemed too ill then, just frail. She'd laughed often and showed me the pretty things in her room, pointing them out

185

to me. She'd known exactly what would catch a young girl's fancy. Her room had been filled with flowers: roses, lilies, and chrysanthemums of course, yellow, white, and pinkish-purple.

"You see, my dear," she had been explaining when her husband came back for me, "I cannot go outside anymore, so my husband brings the outside in to me." She'd given him a loving glance. Dr. Ferguson had bent over and kissed her, looking at her very fondly. *How good he is to her,* I'd thought to myself. As for Mrs. Ferguson? To me she had been like a fairy godmother: kind, gentle, and lovely in her fragile way. I'd kissed her cheek too when I said good-bye and felt its soft coolness.

Now, however, she was gone. Her room would be empty. I realized that Mama was correct about her dying. Mrs. Ferguson had lived a good, long life. Now she was with God and at peace.

"I'll go there tomorrow morning to see if I can do something," Mama said musingly, "and, of course, to give them our condolences." She walked into the bedroom, leaving the door wide open. I heard her fussing around in there and walked to the door.

"What's the matter, Mama?" I asked. I knew she was upset.

"I think I'm going to sleep early tonight," she replied. "I feel sad about visiting them tomorrow, that's all."

I kissed her good night then, feeling the wetness on her cheek. As for me, I decided to stay up a little longer. I walked out to the glassed-in veranda and sat down on the wicker settee, staring outside at the darkening sky. I kept thinking of the Fergusons and about Papa too, alone somewhere. Had Mama also been thinking of him? Then I realized that Dr. Ferguson might not be coming to see us anymore now or at least not until some time had passed and his sorrow had eased. What if he didn't ever come again? What if he was so shattered by his wife's death that he would forget our troubles, burdened as he was with his own?

The thick, straining branches of the acacia tree were stark black lines against the grayness of the sky. The dark form of a cat slunk slowly out of the hidden enclosure of the roof. Noiselessly, it padded its way across the slanting tiles, disappearing in the neighboring rooftop, lost in the silent darkness. Through the stillness of this lonely night came the weary cry of a peddler trying to sell the last of his wares. I listened to his ghostly wail till it died down in the distance.

A star twinkled behind the topmost branches of our neighbor's willow tree beyond the wall. Another star made its appearance; then, as unobtrusively, a third star emerged. It was cold outside, and once more stillness reigned. Night had pulled close its somber mantle and covered the heart of our city.

I awakened on this special morning with the uneasy feeling that something sad and mournful was going to happen today. Gradually, events of the past two days went by rapidly within my somewhat dreamy state of mind. Then came the stark realization. Today was the day, the day of Mrs. Ferguson's funeral!

I lay in my bed, not wanting to get up, wishing somehow that I could in some magical way put this day away, make it fade into oblivion. I tried in vain to shut out the image that my mind was playing back before my eyes of her lying dead in her coffin. Efforts to make it go away only made me picture her even more vividly.

Somewhere far off, a dog howled. It was not Beba; his barks were short and shrill. Instead, this was the low, mournful howl of a big dog, more like a wolf dog. It was a warning, a menacing alert to an approaching danger. Then, as suddenly as it had started, it stopped. Once more it was quiet.

I wondered what the hour was. The bedroom was now in semi-lightness, as if the sun were trying to steal through the whiteness of the rice-paper windows in order to warm me with its rays. I sat up, rubbing the sleep out of my eyes. Outside my bedroom I heard whispers. Mama and Vanya were stirring in the dining room, speaking in low tones so as not to waken me. I heard the clink of silverware against china. They must be eating breakfast. Good! I wasn't hungry enough to join them. They were going to put her coffin into the frozen earth forever and ever. Ashes to ashes was the Bible's way of describing death.

All at once I wished that I didn't have to go say good-bye to her. After all, this was a ritual performed for the dead by the living. I wanted to remember her as I had last seen her, all pink, happily talking about the beautiful things in life. I didn't want to see her lying dead in a willow-wood coffin.

Why did people have to die anyway? Why? I lay in my bed, thinking about death. What was it really like to be dead? I had

187

never before seen a dead person, that is, someone who was near and dear to me, someone who had "passed away," as they usually explained it in polite, hushed tones. Of course, there were the beggars who lay against the walls that lined Peking's numerous *hutungs*. Some of them had lain there for days, mere bundles of rags topped by a rigid face with staring eyes that saw nothing. Those were the ones who were the *dead* ones. The others, who were not in rags, merely "passed away." The beggars then disappeared leaving only the empty wall as mute testimony that once upon a time this had been their spot on earth. Since I had not known them in life, I did not mourn their departure. Besides, sleeping and dying beggars looked alike. They were all equally miserable. They were all soon forgotten. They were a part of Peking just as were its mangy, starving dogs that roamed the city. Mrs. Ferguson's passing was my first real contact with death at close range. I was most unwilling to meet it.

All of us took extra care with our appearance. After all, this was going to be the first time that all three of us would appear in public. When it was nearly one o'clock, we walked the short distance to our neighbor's house.

Magpie Street was already filled with rickshamen. A number of cars were parked from beyond our own gates almost to the very next corner where the Konovaloffs' mansion stood in its lonesome splendor. Coolies and chauffeurs milled around, talking, smoking, or simply rubbing their hands together and stomping their feet to ward off the winter chill.

At the entrance to the Fergusons' house stood some of their houseboys, unrecognizable in their funereal disguise of coarse, muslin robes. They waited silently, somber-faced and red-eyed, watching for guests they would usher inside.

The outside red gates, so like our own, had now been hidden beneath the elaborate, white pavilion that had arisen overnight, almost like a specter! It was a huge structure that had been built over almost the entire house. Its roof of coarse white cloth turned up at the corners towards the sky. Like a giant square tent, it covered all the roofs of the house, spreading over the rock garden, the pond, and the colorful pavilions, hiding the pale blue winter sky from sight. Only the unbleached whiteness of death greeted us mourners from the inside.

Numerous scrolls were hanging on the walls of this white pavilion. There were long ones, shorter ones, horizontal ones. The black characters on white paper expressed praise and sympathy for the dead, love for the departed, honor and reverence for the chief mourner. At certain spots, more servants stood, bowing their heads in sorrow. Silently they motioned us to move on, to walk through the other smaller pavilions, bedecked with white paper flowers. Finally we came to the door of the enormous living room where the funeral rites were to be held.

On its front steps stood a distinguished group. They are Americans, I thought, judging by their bearing and fashionable dress. People went up to them, shaking their hands, saying a few words, then moving on inside. They all seemed to know one another. Mama with Vanya and me in tow bypassed this group and went straight towards the white-draped doorway. Faithful Chang stood in front. His familiar and ample girth was engulfed by the unbleached whites of mourning. His usually genial expression was now solemn as he greeted us, bowing low, his hands fisted against each other in humble salutation. His eyes, almost swollen shut from weeping, welcomed us when he saw who we were.

"Ai, Tai-tai, it is good of you to come and share our sorrow when you also have so much sorrow to bear." He moved forward, motioning to Mama. "Come with me, please."

He led us into the living room. I couldn't believe that it was the same room I had seen two or three years before. It now looked more like the chapel at the French convent. It was filled with folding chairs; most of them already were filled with the Fergusons' friends. Some had their heads bent low; others looked stonily ahead. Chang led us down the center aisle. He seated us a few seats behind the first row. Then he walked slowly back to his post.

When we were first seated, Mama in the middle and Vanya in the aisle seat, I didn't dare look around. Out of the corner of my eye, I watched Mama's behavior, so I could do likewise. She was sitting with her hands clasped and her eyes closed, as if in prayer. An old man in his sixties sat to my left. He, too, sat with folded hands, his venerable white head bowed, his lips moving silently. I took off my gloves, laying them down in my lap. Then I, too, folded my hands. Slowly, with my head bent low, I raised my eyes to look at the people in front. To my amazement I noticed that some of them were talking, softly it is true, but they were acting normally! They even appeared at ease! I searched the rows looking for our old friend. I didn't want to see him sad; yet I had to see him. Ah, there he was in the very front seat with Mary close beside him. His wonderful white head was bowed, oblivious apparently to the sympathetic friends around him, lost in his silent grief. When I saw him like this, I wanted to cry, not for his wife but for him because of his great sorrow.

Crowded into the spacious, quiet room were several hundred people. Behind us, several seats to the left, sat our neighbors: the Colonel, his gracious wife, and their children. She had gently tapped Mama's shoulder, smiling her greeting. All around there was the scent of flowers, the strongest being that of the lovely tuberoses, those graceful narcissuslike flowers I liked so much. The pungent fragrance of the white, tear-dropped petals was hauntingly sweet but had always been associated with the dead.

I looked beyond the chairs and the guests towards the very front of the room where there was a mass of flowers. Among them I distinguished the casket, almost concealed by the blanket of flowers covering its lid. As I looked, I became conscious of the music that had slowly and unobtrusively broken into that awesome, unnatural stillness. The music was mournful, majestically slow, and repetitious! Its haunting refrain repeated itself in my head long after the music itself had ended.

A gray-haired man wearing a black suit came out of a side door and stood in front, his back to the casket. Chang suddenly appeared, placing a lectern in front of this man. I recognized Reverend Brown, pastor of one of the Protestant churches of Peking. He was the father of one of my former PAS classmates.

Reverend Brown turned to give the casket a long look. Then he turned back to the audience, welcoming us in this last farewell to his friend and ours, Mrs. Ferguson. In a quiet, comforting voice he addressed the husband, the daughter, and those there who were her other relatives. He spoke with joy of her youth, as if he himself had known her, and of her marriage to the handsome, young Scottish missionary. He spoke of her innate goodness, her delight in her children and in all things living. He told us of her devotion to her husband, her generosity to all, and, most of all, her love for her fellowmen. I listened to his every word, wishing that I had known her more, yet grateful that I had known her at all. I wondered to myself, as I listened to this gentle preacher, if someone would also speak of me like that when I lay dead. It would be good to have been loved so much!

He ended his words with a well-known Psalm. We all stood up as one, and I mouthed the unfamiliar words as if I, along with the others, had learned them by heart in my childhood. Once more, the organist began to play. Later, when I asked her, Mama told me that this haunting music was Chopin's *Funeral March*. I have heard it many times since played at other funerals that I have attended. Still, whenever I hear that sorrowful march, it is her casket that I picture, the pink roses on top and the lowered head of my grieving friend.

Six young men, dressed in somber dark suits, walked slowly up to the coffin. Carefully they lifted the sad burden onto their shoulders. As one we all stood, watching that slow march down the aisle, step by step, as they walked in cadence to the doleful music, each ringing organ note striking a painful blow to us all. Then our good friend took his place behind the group, held up by the loving arm of Mary. Then came Reverend Brown, his calm gaze looking over the mourners, blessing them in silence for their presence here. On this special day these were all his sheep. And some—like me—were lost.

Death too passed away, as silently as the night that falls and brings with it the coming daylight and the sun.

10

The American Way

Two days after the funeral of his wife, Dr. Ferguson came to visit us. We were quite surprised, for we had not expected him to return to see us so soon. However, surely enough, here he was, sitting with us in our living room, drinking the tea that Mama had hastily brewed. He was apologetic for not having come sooner. There had been many things to do, but he would certainly not neglect us. As he explained to us, we were important to him; he was concerned not only about us but also about Father. In fact, he told us his wife, even as she lay dying, had made him promise that he would take care of us!

I couldn't get over that—a person on her deathbed had been so concerned about others in trouble!

"I was going to anyway," Dr. Ferguson said softly, "but all three of you had been on her mind before she passed away."

How good these Americans are, I thought to myself. My heart was full of love for this kind man and his family. He sat in the white, slipcovered chair that he had adopted as his own nearly a year ago. He was eyeing me thoughtfully, and I sensed that what he would say next would most likely concern me.

As always, his tone was affectionate. "How would you like to have a job, my Girlie?" he asked.

I thought I heard Mama gasp. She still wouldn't acknowledge that I was no longer a little girl. "I believe that I'd like it," I answered right away. I wondered what kind of work he had in mind for me. He smiled. His face was still somewhat pale, I noticed. His eyes no longer twinkled as they had, but they still showed his concern and kindness. Never, never would I disappoint him. Never!

"There is an American at our embassy," he continued slowly. "He is the second consul there, a fine man." He looked at Mama when he said this. "He and his lovely wife, Marianne, have two children. They need someone now to teach and work with the children." He turned to me. "Girlie, Mr. Clubb wants his children to learn Russian and French. You know these languages, don't you? You could teach these languages to them, couldn't you?" He looked at me questioningly.

I do know those languages, I convinced myself. Russian was my second language. And in spite of myself, I had learned French at the convent. Could I teach these languages to two small children? I hadn't ever thought of doing anything like that.

After a little thought, I answered dubiously, "I know Russian rather well, but my French is a bit rusty. I haven't been to school for so long, you know. But I'll be glad to try, Dr. Ferguson."

"That's my Girlie," he commented.

Although he seemed satisfied, I surely wasn't. "You'll have to explain to Mr. Clubb that I'm a bit rusty in French. Please?" Already I was beginning to feel queasy.

He gave me an admiring glance. "I think you're too modest, Tamara. I'll tell the Clubbs. I'm sure they'll be happy."

He left us then, giving Vanya a hearty handshake. Mama got a brotherly hug. I was given a wink and a gentle pat on the shoulder. We walked with him down to the front gates. As we watched him walk toward his house, I noticed with a pang that his gait was not so jaunty, nor did he swing his cane as he used to. *Poor man,* I thought. *There is only his faithful daughter, Mary, now. No lovely wife to share his life and thoughts.* That pushed me to thinking about my own future. For the very first time in my life I would have a job! Like Vanya, I too would be giving money to Mama. All three of us would now be contributing to the family income. It was a big, big step for me, but I was eager and ready. At least, I would be trying my darndest!

It amazes me at times when I realize how, in this world of ours, the life of one person is somehow structured to fit into the whole scheme of life. Looking backward now into time almost convinces me that I should believe in predestination, Dr. Ferguson's Presbyterian religious code. People and events follow one another within a certain pattern leading the individual from one stage of life into the next. It seems to have been so ordained, as if it had been ordered to be so! So be it! Amen!

In taking a position with the Clubbs as governess for their small children, I had begun to shape my own destiny as well as fulfill my job requirements. Step by orderly step, the web of life had begun to spin its intricate threads, gathering each one to meld with the other, culminating in a final, unifying effect, for better or for worse.

Dr. Ferguson's chauffeur drove me to the Clubbs', a large, comfortable house furnished with deep-pile carpets, slipcovered armchairs and sofas, and bookcases filled with books. I was ushered into the living room by a square-faced old amah, who appraised me rather dourly. She apparently was not pleased with what she saw. She then ushered me into what I gathered was the children's room. There she stood by, watching me silently, her eyes narrowed and most unfriendly.

As soon as I entered, I saw the two children. They were standing close together, their eyes already alert to inspect me. Golden-haired, rosy-cheeked, and blue-eyed, they were to me what American children should look like. The little girl, her face wreathed in a shy smile, looked to be five years old. She was dainty, with fine features. Her golden hair was like Shirley Temple's, framing her face like a halo. Her eyes, as they watched me with friendly fascination, were a greenish-blue. The boy was older, tall, well-built, and blond like his sister. He was either nine or ten and surveyed me with serious but not too friendly eyes. *He will have to get to know me before he makes up his mind about me,* I decided.

So be it. *I'll have to be careful with these children, especially the boy,* I cautioned myself.

The little girl came up to me. She looked up, her clear, blue eyes innocent of anything except a loving kind of curiosity.

"I'm Zoe," she squeaked. "You're going to teach us, aren't you?" she asked. She took hold of my hand.

I looked down at her. I hadn't been this close to a little girl before. She seemed such a lovable child, all trusting, ready to take me to her heart. I looked at the boy. He had not seemed too

194

happy with my appearance. My imagination may have been working overtime, but I thought I had detected a scowl on his face when he'd first caught sight of me. This young man, I concluded, was going to need my especial attention. He was already against me; why, I couldn't determine.

He walked up to me, his hand out for me to shake. "I'm Oliver Clubb," he said formally. This one was much wiser than his nine or ten years, appraising me in much the same way his old amah had done, only somewhat more discreetly.

"Is it true that you know how to speak Russian and French?" he asked.

I liked the way he looked at me. His gray-blue eyes were clear and honest, looking directly at me. *I'm going to like him,* I told myself, *but he's going to be a handful. He's intelligent, curious, and determined. I'll really have to be on my toes with him.*

My thoughts were interrupted at this time by the appearance of the children's mother. I guessed that she must have just come from a reception, as she was exquisitely dressed in a grayish suit with a fur piece casually draped over her shoulders. She was tall and had large, candid blue eyes. Her straight, blonde hair was severely combed back with a chignon on the nape of her neck, just like Mama's. She was the Nordic type, I guessed. Mama might have described her features as classic. She could have been the perfect woman for the cover of *Vogue* or some other ultra-chic fashion magazine. All of this came into the room with a quick, long-legged stride.

"I see you've met the children." Her voice was low and even; her smile, gracious. Her manner put people at ease. I liked her immediately.

"They are delightful children, Mrs. Clubb!" I couldn't help adding, "Indeed, I look forward to working with them."

"I don't know whether Zoe is ready to learn much at this time," she said, picking up her daughter and giving her a big squeeze. "Oliver, however, is ready and willing, aren't you, dear?" She smiled at him.

Oliver nodded silently, looking down at the floor.

Just then Mrs. Clubb noticed the amah hovering by the door.

"Oh, Lao Ma," she said pleasantly, "I was about to call for you. Please see that Miss Rubleva and the children have their tea in here, will you?" She turned to me, "I can see that the children like you already. We're looking forward to your stay with us." She quickly hugged her children and, taking up her purse, she left the room.

Lao Ma started to follow her, but not before she had turned back to give me a strange look.

She doesn't like me, I suspected. I could cut through her antagonism with a knife. I wondered why she felt like that towards me. She and I certainly had never met before. It was either that she disliked Russians, or she might have heard that my father was in prison. Well, I shrugged my shoulders. I'd have as little to do with her as possible.

During teatime Zoe told me all about herself. She was a beautiful child and very talkative, chattering away a mile a minute in her sweet, baby tones. She told me what she liked and didn't like to eat; what her daddy did, and how Mommy was busy all the time.

Oliver, on the other hand, drank his milk slowly and took bites of his sandwich in between. I could sense his serious-looking eyes studying me, examining me from head to toe. When Zoe stopped to catch her breath, I turned to him.

"And what is it that you like to do, Oliver?"

He finished chewing before answering me. "I enjoy world geography," he told me primly. He pointed to the large globe sitting on the windowsill. "I also like languages. Daddy knows a few. He can speak Russian, you know."

"How about you?" I asked.

He shook his head. "That's why my father hired you. To teach us Russian and French."

Was there something superior in his tone? I glanced at his face. I couldn't be sure. It was serious, unsmiling. *That could be because he's shy,* I thought.

I laughed. "All right, shall we begin? Let's see which one of you can say, *"Otchen horosho, spasibo."*

Both children repeated it flawlessly.

"What does it mean?" asked Oliver.

"Very well, thank you, that's what it means. If I ask you how you are feeling, that's what you would reply to me."

Oliver repeated the short phrase to himself. Zoe looked up

at me with adoring eyes. I could see that she and I were going to be good friends.

"Now, I'll teach you how to say hello," I told them. I saw their eyes look past me towards the doorway.

He had come in quietly and stood in the doorway, watching us. My back had been turned to him so that I realized he was there only when Zoe excitedly cried, "Daddy," as she jumped up from her chair and ran into his outstretched arms. He picked her up and, smiling rather shyly, approached the table.

I had expected him to be taller, considering how willowy his wife was. He was of medium height and dark-haired, with a square face, broad, high forehead, and eyes that looked out from behind rimmed glasses. They were looking at me now, appraising me, much in the same manner that his son had been appraising me. I felt quite uncomfortable under his obvious scrutiny.

"You understand, Miss Rubleva, that we wish you to teach the children French and Russian," he said abruptly after we had shaken hands. "I expect that after you get used to us here, that you will set up a schedule for them. Allot so much time for certain studies. I am sure you understand." He then asked me suddenly, *"Parlez-vous français, Mademoiselle?"*

It had startled me when he so abruptly switched into French. *Ah, so he is testing me,* I thought to myself with amusement. Like son, like father. Although I had not expected such a test, nor for it to be given in such a manner, I was able to regain my composure right away.

"Mais oui, Monsieur, un peu," I answered. *"Ya sluishu shto vui govorite po Russki"* (I hear that you speak Russian). It was tit for tat. I could test him as well.

At that he laughed.

"Konetchna, no ne otchen horosho" (Of course, but not very well).

He then showed me textbooks, which he suggested I use. "Why don't you take these home with you. Then you can make up your lesson plans." It was an order. With that, he bowed and left me with the children.

I felt depressed and let down after his brief visit. The children and Mrs. Clubb I liked. Mr. Clubb was a different story. He had an uncanny way of making me feel unsure of myself, and that was something that I wasn't used to. Then, too, with him, as with his son Oliver, I felt that I was not a friend who would be helping them but someone hired to work as their servant. I was to do what was required of me, I would be paid, and that was the end of said economic relationship. I'd be getting twenty Chinese dollars a month, which I'd hand over to Mama. Not only that, I had to submit a schedule for the time I was being paid!

So that was the way it was to be! If the American diplomat wanted things done in that way, I'd do them that way. I knew both languages, Russian better than French. I'd teach his children, but my early enthusiasm for the challenge was waning fast. What had I fallen into? No matter, that twenty dollars was going to help us a great deal. Mama had been pleased to learn that I'd be paid so well.

When it was time to leave, Zoe hugged me as if I were going away forever. Oliver shook my hand politely and gave me a thin smile. With him, I knew that I was on probation. I already adored Mrs. Clubb and planned to pattern my behavior after hers. As for Mr. Clubb . . .

"Well, Mr. Clubb," I whispered to myself as the ricksha stopped at our gates, "you shall have your pound of flesh!"

It took awhile for me to feel more comfortable in the Clubb household. The children were as sweet and helpful to me as they could be. Oliver became an apt pupil, although he despised learning the French verbs, and I equally disliked teaching them to him. I couldn't see the sense of studying these verbs through memorization. To be learned properly, they had to be used in context.

Sensible or not, I taught Oliver in much the same way that I had been taught physical geography by Mother Joseph Helen; learning by rote was the only way I could teach the verbs because I had been taught to learn unpleasant material that way. While Zoe happily played with her toys and listened to us, Oliver and I struggled through those horrible French verbs. When the teaching was over and done according to schedule, all of us felt quite relieved. It had been a struggle, but now we'd have fun. I read stories to the children, anything I could find among the many good books on their shelves. At times, I sensed that Mr. Clubb was standing in the doorway listening. Whether he was pleased or not with my performance as a servant-teacher, I couldn't really tell. Evidently, he was a person unaccustomed to giving praise, even if deserved. I learned to be grateful that he didn't criticize my work. Often, I wished that I could teach these children more. If only I had known how to then! However, I consoled myself that I was doing my best, not for the salary, but for the children's sake.

In time, even Lao Ma became more pleasant. I really think that when I arrived she was alarmed that her position as guardian of the children was being threatened. When she realized that I was not about to usurp her position but, on the contrary, respected her not only for her age and wisdom but also for her long tenure here, gradually, she began to tolerate me.

I often wondered to myself if the Clubbs had any inkling about Papa's imprisonment by the Japanese. They had not mentioned my family to me or even professed the least interest in my private life. All they were interested in was my ability to perform the task of teaching their children.

Now my life was divided into two, very well-defined halves. With Mama and Vanya I lived my Russian life. Poor, overworked Mama was sewing till late at night on formal gowns for Mrs. Stilwell and her daughters. She sewed till the needle punctured her fingers, and her eyes could focus no more. Vanya was still, as he woefully put it, slaving away for Mr. Werner, unhappy in that work and spending every precious hour that he could with his beloved first love, Emily Hu. Dr. Ferguson was still making his no-news visits; I gave Mama my twenty dollars and felt guilty that I often ate good food at the Clubbs' house while she existed on scanty rations of millet and fatty meat. This was my Russian life. My other life, the American one, was spent at the Clubbs', beginning with early breakfasts!

The American food advertisements that Vanya and I had mulled over in our kitchen sanctuary and dreamed of eating someday were now a reality for me. I ate Del Monte canned fruits, poured delicious, creamy thick Pet concentrated milk over my Kellogg's Corn Flakes. I ate real butter, spreading thick slabs on the hot corn muffins that the Clubbs' cook brought to the table. I ate almost as many of Aunt Jemima's pancakes with real Vermont Log Cabin syrup as had Little Black Sambo! I remained at the Clubbs' home until after the children's suppertime, eating together with them. Then I came back home to my Russian life with Mama.

How I wished that Mama could share with me this American life! Nevertheless, she seemed quite content. The demands of her clients made time pass quickly for her; the harder she worked, the less time she had to worry and fret about Papa.

In the evenings at home, if it were not too cold outside, Mama and I would sit under the acacia tree. I described to her how the Americans lived. It must have sounded unbelievable to her. Or it may have rekindled thoughts of those years so long ago when she was a carefree, young girl in her father's house.

I had now worked for the Clubbs for several months. Winter had passed; spring was now ending. Peking was already getting a preview of how hot summer would be. The Clubbs, as was their custom, were making plans for their summer vacation in Tsing-tao. One day Mrs. Clubb surprised me by inviting me to come along with them on vacation and take care of the children.

Dr. Ferguson was ecstatic. "Girlie, what a wonderful opportunity for you. You need some sun on that pale skin of yours." He tweaked my cheek playfully. "Mother," he turned towards Mama, "don't you think she ought to go?"

At first Mama had hesitated, but when she saw the American's approving expression, she nodded her head. "If you think so, Dr. Ferguson."

"I think so," he had echoed after her. "I really think so."

And so it was ordained!

I didn't want to leave Mama, knowing that Vanya would not be spending much time at home, since he was so involved with his beloved Emily. It was Dr. Ferguson who practically ordered me to go. Even Vanya told me not to worry, that he would take care of things. His words were of little comfort, for I knew that nothing, not even Mama's welfare, could overcome his obsession with Emily. But at Mama's urging, I finally decided to go.

11

Harder Facts of Life

What a completely different world Tsingtao was! I was reminded in a way of our early summers at Peitahe when Mama and Vanya and I had stayed at the Porfirieffs' dacha. But this was so much more! The Americans really knew how to spend their summer vacations. They, of course, had the best of everything!

There were quite a few American Embassy families staying in Tsingtao for the summer. Of course, the husbands had to remain in Peking to work, visiting their families only on weekends.

We ate our meals in a separate building, a huge cavernous building called "the mess hall." *Strange name for a dining room,* I thought. Mrs. Clubb, the children, and I sat at one of the long, wooden tables. A beautiful, dark-haired lady took the empty seat beside me. I had not met her before.

"This is Elsie Lyons," Mrs. Clubb told me. Elsie smiled graciously, extending her hand.

"And this is Tamara," Marianne Clubb said in a low voice. "You remember, I told you about her."

I had never before seen such a beautiful woman! I now looked forward to mealtimes just so that I could sit next to her and admire her classic profile.

She and Marianne Clubb were close friends. Although Mrs. Clubb resembled a Nordic goddess, Mrs. Lyons could be likened to no one in her beauty, charm, or sweetness. Her perfection was unparalleled! Dark hair; skin like ivory with a tint of pink akin to that found on a seashell; eyes a bluish-gray; thick, darkened eyebrows; eyelashes the color of midnight—I could go on listing her perfections, but in my eyes there was no one more lovely nor so perfect in every way as she was. I felt honored to be sitting right next to her. Moreover, she always made sure that I got the salt or cream that had been passed to her. She and Marianne Clubb were like night and day; each was perfection in her own way!

From that time on, Elsie Lyons accepted me as a friend. Her attitude both pleased and surprised me but placed me in an awkward position. Although Mrs. Clubb, my employer, was pleasant, I could feel a distinct barrier between us: gracious employer, obedient employee. With Elsie it was different; she was a friend. I had never met anyone like her.

In time she asked me about myself. She was so genuinely interested that I told her everything, things I couldn't even think of telling the Clubbs! I told her about Papa being in the Japanese jail, wherever that was. I told her how Mama worked night and day, about our wonderful Dr. Ferguson, who was so helpful and comforting, and poor Vanya, who was so much in love that nothing else mattered to him. She listened quietly to everything that I had to say. I was surprised that Oliver and Zoe listened too. Usually they were too busy with their own projects to be able to be quiet any length of time. I really think they were surprised to hear me talk so much. As I talked on and on, I realized that even Mrs. Clubb had been listening to me. When I finally stopped talking, I was embarrassed. That had never happened to me before. Mrs. Lyons just had the knack of drawing people out.

I also realized that no one else had been talking except me. Why had they listened so intently? How could they possibly understand what was in my heart, how much pain and loneliness there was, how hopeless I sometimes felt, how much I missed and wanted to see my father? Why should it affect those who were rich and had everything in life that anybody would want? I felt guilty knowing that I had, in a way, ruined their afternoon.

I caught the eyes of the children.

"May we be excused?" I asked Mrs. Clubb. "I thought we'd walk down to the beach and look for seashells."

"Of course, Tamara; the children need the exercise."

We walked down to the beach, Oliver, Zoe, and I. I knew that Mrs. Clubb and her friends would still be in the mess hall, drinking their coffee and talking about people and things. They talked about such things as the cost of coffee, the servant situation, the next party at the country club, and the newcomers in the legation from abroad. *How easily these embassy women solve matters,* I thought. *While the Americans relaxed, Mama sewed dresses and waited for news of Papa. Why was I born a Russian in China? How do Americans live so well? Why can't I have been born a Ferguson? Why is Papa in prison?*

My thoughts were interrupted by a tall young man in swimming trunks. He had been walking on the beach. When he saw the children and me gathering seashells, he came towards us. "Would you mind if I talk to you?" he asked. He seemed rather shy.

I was startled; I had been too engrossed in my own thoughts to have seen his quiet approach. He was so friendly, however, that I smiled up at him.

"Let's sit down on the sand," I said, slipping down even as I said those words. The children happily settled down beside me and immediately began to dig.

The young man looked at me. "Is it all right if I sit beside you?" he asked. I liked him. He was so big, so muscular, yet so gentle. Carefully, he sat down on the sand beside me.

"My name is Richard O'Dowd," he said quietly. He took a slow appraisal of me. "Dick, to my friends," he added, holding out his hand.

"Pleased to meet you," I answered, smiling as I shook his hand.

"You don't know me," he said seriously, "but I sure know a great deal about you." His blue eyes studied my face intently.

"What do you mean?" I asked curiously. "What is it that you know about me?"

He didn't look as if he was one of the young men who ate in the mess room. I would have remembered seeing him.

"I'm one of the marines stationed here," he explained. He was a handsome, young man, very tall, over six feet, I imagined.

I knew that I shouldn't be talking to him. All of my life it had been drummed into me. Beware of American marines! They are bad. They will hurt you. Your reputation will be ruined if you even say "hello" to a marine! And here I was, talking for the first time to a real live marine! Mama would have been horrified, had she known! I looked at this Richard O'Dowd and didn't think him frightening at all. In fact, I liked him!

He had a strong face, a ruddy complexion, curly blond hair, and was blue-eyed. He was what I thought a young American man should be, what Oliver would look like when he grew up. He was watching me, his eyes troubled.

"I've never talked to a real American marine," I told him.

He smiled. It was a warm, friendly smile. He didn't look harmful at all. He would get along well with Vanya—maybe.

"I really don't know how to tell you this. . . . " He hesitated, sounding quite embarrassed. I stared at him, puzzled. Why, he didn't even know me! What was it that he wanted to tell me that could be of any consequence?

"What is it that you want to tell me?" I tried to help him get his thoughts together.

"It's just this." His eyes, frank and intent, bored into me. "I'm sorry. You aren't at all what I expected you to be. Well . . . ," he drew in the sand with his finger, outlining a mountain, "well, there are some Limeys here in Tsingtao too," he said lamely.

"Limeys?" I was ashamed to be so ignorant.

He smiled. "They're Britishers," he explained. "I don't know if you know"—he glanced at me quizzically—"but there is a bar down in the village. I just happened to be there the other day, and I heard these Limeys talking. They were discussing you. And what they said was scary. So"—he looked at me compassion-ately—"I thought I'd better warn you. I could not live with myself if I didn't."

I didn't understand what he was trying to tell me. Why should he look at me with such concern? Why should he pity me? Why should he have to warn me about anything? There was nothing that I could say. I just couldn't figure out what he meant about the Limeys and what they were planning to do to me.

"You're a Russian, aren't you?" he asked me.

"Yes," I answered him, "and you're an American. So what does that have to do with anything?"

Again his blue eyes studied me. He bit his lips. "One of the Limeys—mind you, he may have been drunk—told the guys at the bar something, and they all became quiet and listened. He told the fellows that your father is a dangerous criminal, who is now being held in prison. He said that you are a *cheapie*, and that he's going to really go over you. When he is finished with you, he told them, no one else will ever want you. He even boasted drunkenly to those around him that he would throw you into the ocean for the fish to finish you off." Dick's voice softened as he spoke. His face became flushed.

"I'm sorry," he said. "I just felt that you should be warned. That fellow, drunk as he was, meant what he said." He looked at me, worried. "Is this true? Is your father really in jail?"

I told Dick what had happened to us, all of it, from the very beginning. I told him how I came to be here with the Clubbs in Tsingtao.

Dick shook his head. "Jeepers," he exclaimed, "am I sure glad that I did come to you. I was debating about it; then I thought that you should at least be warned about this Limey. I'm sorry." He really looked worried. "Now that I've met you, I want to help you. We've got to do something." He looked at me earnestly.

I was too upset by his words to think clearly. From what I understood there was a crazy Limey who wanted to murder me. The children, too, had been listening, but I doubted if they understood much. I just didn't know what to think! It was all incredible! Why would anyone want to hurt me? What had I done to them?

"I guess I'd better tell the Clubbs," I said. I wasn't sure that the Clubbs would take me seriously. It all sounded too weird. Why should anyone who didn't know me want to harm me?

Mrs. Clubb, however, was very still when I related what the marine had told me. As I kept talking, I noticed that she became tight-lipped and serious. I stopped, wondering if I should go on.

"What else did he say?" Mrs. Clubb's voice sounded strange.

"He said that I should just tell you this. That I shouldn't go out alone anymore." I told her. That sounded strange to me too. Why shouldn't I walk alone wherever I pleased? The children did. So had I.

"This Richard O'Dowd is absolutely right," Mrs. Clubb said.

She looked thoughtful. "From now on you stay around here, Tamara. Stay here with the children, until we decide what must be done. We must not take any chances."

Even though I was puzzled, I did as she told me. I played and read to the children, using the mess hall as our place of refuge. Sometimes, we went to see Lao Ma in the servants' quarters. Lao Ma, once I really got to know her, wasn't that bad. Just crabby because she was old, that's all.

A few days later, Mrs. Clubb sent for me. Her lovely face looked serious but not ominous. She motioned me to sit down beside her.

"Tamara, I had a talk with our chief officer here at the marine base about what this Richard O'Dowd told you. I want you to know," she said as she studied me thoughtfully, "that he assembled all the men stationed here in Tsingtao—Britishers and Limeys included—and announced that our part of the beach is absolutely off limits to them. They are not, if they see you, to talk to you or have any contact whatsoever with you. No one, absolutely no one, is to approach you on the beach, the streets, or anywhere else! Disobedience of this order will result in their being court-martialed." Her eyes flashed. "Not only that. You shall have a bodyguard wherever you go, and it will be that young man you met, Cpl. Richard O'Dowd. He's been checked out. He's a fine, reliable young man, and he will accompany you wherever you go. Is that understood?"

I nodded. What else could I say? This was so much fuss about nothing, really! Some drunken Limey had made threats. What could he possibly do to me? Frankly, I thought all this was making a mountain out of a molehill. If Mrs. Clubb felt that way, however, I'd go along. She, of course, knew better than I.

So it was that whenever the children and I went to the beach, Dick O'Dowd appeared out of nowhere. There he was! He'd sit beside us, shaping strange, grainy creatures out of the sand. Sometimes he lifted Oliver, or Zoe, up on his muscular shoulders so that they could see the whole beach and the ocean as well.

Sometimes he took Oliver out into the ocean. He was a powerful swimmer, and the children loved it when he held them over the pounding waves. I couldn't swim and wasn't even interested in the water. I liked to stretch out on the sand. "Teach them, Dick," I'd murmur lazily, digging my fingers into the sand. So they frolicked, the three of them, and I watched and basked in the warmth of the sun.

Sometimes Dick talked to me about his home state of Idaho. I felt confused. There was America; then there were the states that together made up America. His Idaho was one of the states. It was all so complicated!

Dick told me that he liked being a marine. "There's something special," he boasted, "about being a marine. You have to be really strong to be one."

I thought of what Mama and Papa had told me about American marines. I couldn't believe that about Dick; he was kind and considerate to me, a really gentle man. Mama had never known a marine!

He told me about his "hometown." I found out that everybody in America had a hometown! In Idaho they grew corn and potatoes as well as other crops. Dick missed his home. It was a good life, he said, where people worshipped God and lived a simple life.

"When I go back home, I'll write to you," he promised.

Time passed quickly in Tsingtao. It had become a regular routine for the children and me. Beach after breakfast, then rest and lunch. More rest and beach, then supper and sleep for the night. It was a routine, simple and lazy, but pleasant.

Too soon, our holiday ended. Mr. Clubb arrived and helped us pack. We said goodbye to Elsie Lyons. I gave Dick O'Dowd my address and thanked him for being nice to me. I couldn't wait to come back home to see Mama again!

Mama looked tired but happy when she greeted me at the front gates. It had been only a month that I'd been gone, but it had seemed to me more like a year. I had learned much in that short a time. More than ever now, I wished that I could go to America to live.

At home, there was nothing new that Mama could tell me. As usual, Dr. Ferguson didn't miss a day. Mama told me that she thoroughly enjoyed his visits.

He had also told her how pleased the Clubbs were with me. This had been a surprise. Of course, they had been quite kind, thoughtful, and had treated me well. This, however, was the way they treated Lao Ma and the others in their employ. Although I didn't tell Mama this, I had, in a way, felt inferior when in their midst. Whether it was the fact that Papa was in prison and that we all had to scrimp for everything, I don't know. It was that same uncomfortable feeling I had had when I had wanted to be a part of the American girls' group at PAS. They too had been friendly, but I'd never felt that I truly belonged. Dr. Ferguson, Dorlise, and others we knew didn't make me feel that way. *Why,* I wondered to myself, *why should this be so?*

I did tell Mama about how the Americans spent their vacations, the rich foods that covered their dining tables, and the many servants that silently did their impromptu bidding. Mama listened eagerly, smiling and nodding her head. I imagine that she was recalling the good times of her youth.

One thing I didn't mention was the Limey episode. She had enough worries without my adding more. When I asked about Vanya's romance, her face had clouded. She complained that he was away so much of the time that she didn't know what was happening with him. I could see that she was upset about this.

Once again, Vanya had made me a promise he couldn't and didn't keep. Had he no idea of responsibility? Maybe I was the one who was wrong. I kept thinking about it, and the more I thought, the more angry I got. Here Papa was suffering at the hands of the Japanese; brave Mama was working and slaving for all of us, alone, sad, and unsure of the future. Her son—who should have been the strength and backbone of the family—was absent, lovesick, and worst of all, jobless.

Mama told me Vanya's sad story. He just had to quit working for Mr. Werner because the German was too demanding of him. I was furious, but I didn't let her know how I felt. She told me that Dr. Ferguson had been disappointed that Vanya hadn't stayed on the job.

"Poor Kocya," Mama murmured. "He is so sensitive!"

That he is, I thought bitterly, *and he gets away with it!*

Several days after I had come home, Dr. Ferguson came with some news. I had been delighted to see him again. I couldn't help it; when I first saw him, I flung myself into his arms, hugging him tightly.

"My, oh my, my," he laughed, quite pleased with my demonstration. "What a special welcome for an old man. Well, Girlie," he began, his eyes twinkling merrily, "I hear that you all had a good time in Tsingtao. You certainly are a sight for sore eyes."

"Sore eyes?" I asked, puzzled.

Again he laughed. "My dear, that's an American expression. It means that you look good."

"Oh," I placed my arms around Mama's shoulders. "I'm happy to be with Mama again."

"Of course, you are." The American turned to face Mama. His face had become serious.

"Vera," he said unhurriedly. "I believe that soon we'll be able to arrange a visit for all of you with the professor." I sensed that he had not wanted to startle Mama with this announcement, so he had been careful how he phrased it.

Still her face had turned pale, and her eyes filled with tears. She stared at the American in disbelief.

"You mean that I really will get to see Sergei? He's coming to see us?" She had many more questions to ask, I know, but the missionary stopped her.

"Not so fast, my dear," he laughed. "You'll be going to see him, not the other way around." He turned to me. "How would you like to see your father again, Girlie?"

I couldn't believe that he'd said that. All this time I had been wondering if Papa were even alive! The fact that we might see him soon boggled my mind!

"It's partly on account of you, my dear," he told me. "You know Elsie Lyons, the daughter of our American ambassador to Japan? Well, Girlie, she was quite interested in you. I honestly think that both she and the Clubbs had a lot to do with all this. They are wonderful, wonderful people. Anyway, I think that Ambassador Grew, her father, had a hand in this too. They've ways of finding out things which I don't. So-o-o . . ." His eyes fixed themselves on Mama. "I'm not promising anything. All I want right now is for all of you to be on the alert. Understand?"

He got up slowly, reaching for his cane. "One of these days soon, I hope, I will be coming here to tell you that my car is at your disposal." He winked at me.

Mama went up to him shyly placing her hand on his arm.

"Have you been able to find out where they're holding him?" Her voice quivered.

He paused for a moment, idly tapping his cane. The blue eyes beneath the heavy, white eyebrows narrowed as he looked through the glass window of the door.

"I think I do know," he replied. Then he frowned. "Let's put it this way. *Pei Ta*—the university where Sergei taught for eighteen years or so—is now being used by the Japanese as barracks for their military personnel. From what I've been able to gather, he is now being held in the basement. They've converted that part into detention quarters for political prisoners."

I heard Mama catch her breath. Vanya had stood by silently, watching the American's face. Ever since he had quit working at Mr. Werner's, he had been ill at ease with the missionary. I gulped, sensing the terrible irony of it all. For almost twenty years Papa had taught at *Pei Ta* (Peking National University). Now he was imprisoned in the basement!

Before the American left, he cautioned us. "Remember, we have to deal very carefully with these people," he told us quietly. "They are different from us; their ways are alien to ours. One false move and everything that we have worked for can be undone."

"I still don't know why they arrested him," Mama said in a low voice. "What harm did he do them?"

"He did not join them," said the American softly. "That meant that he was against them."

After he left, we all joined hands and danced wildly down the poplar alley. Mama was laughing and crying at the same time.

"Ach, how good it will be when we're all together again," she said excitedly. "I never thought the day would ever come."

That night, I'm sure, we all slept better than we ever had for a long time. The next morning Dr. Ferguson came earlier than usual. His face was beaming.

"I've just seen Nakamura from the Japanese Embassy," he told us. "He's been my contact all this time. Well," he said as he studied the tip of his cane, "Nakamura and this man, Suzuki, who is the military chargé d'affaires in Peking, got together—finally." He heaved a deep sigh. "They've set up your reunion for

210

next Monday at two o'clock in the afternoon."

Mama put her hands up to her face. "I just can't believe it," she whispered.

The American chuckled, his eyes misty. "It's coming to an end, my dear." He reached over to pat her back. "I'll see you Monday morning anyway. We'll decide how to proceed at that time."

He shook hands with Vanya. As I walked out with him to the front gates, he stopped. He put both his hands on my shoulders, his blue eyes grave and piercing.

"Take charge of Mother, my Girlie," he said. "She needs to rely upon your strength; be there to support her whenever she needs you."

I nodded silently, my heart filled with too many different kinds of emotions to answer him properly. Quickly, I bolted the gates after him.

These ups and downs of life were really trying for me. One day I felt on top of the whole world; the next day I couldn't sink much lower in my misery. All the problems had to do with Father. Was he alive? Was he being tortured as Boy had once so picturesquely described to us? Had the Japanese stuck bamboo needles into his fingernails until they bled? Had they pumped water into him until his stomach swelled to the size of a nine months'-pregnant woman's stomach? Had he been tortured at all? If so, he must have withstood it to still be alive. What would he look like? Fifteen months was a long time to be jailed in a Japanese prison. The Japanese certainly weren't known for their humanity. How much weight had he lost?

These are some of the questions that I mulled over whenever I laid me down to sleep, and whenever I rose up to face the day, the questions still remained. I could imagine how Mama must have turned over the same questions in her mind. For her, facing up to them would be even more difficult. I wakened on this Monday morning and felt that I had not slept at all.

Dr. Ferguson had cautioned us yesterday. "You will have only one hour." He had stressed the word *hour.* "Don't ask him, please don't, about his treatment while in prison." (That comment of his made shivers travel down my back.) "Just tell him what all you have been doing, what you've read or done, about your studies, Vanya, and you, Tamara, about your work. And if

211

he talks, just listen. Remember; one hour is not a long time."

I put on my old plaid skirt and white shirt. I had worn it for most of the year. The shirt collar was frayed, but my hair hid it. After I washed my face, I stared into the mirror critically. My face was pale. My brown eyes, looking so intently into themselves, appeared haunted and lost.

"Comb your hair more," my alter ego commanded me, and I obeyed. I took out Mama's old tortoise-shell comb and began running it through my hair, watching the individual hairs flare out in electric sparkles, then gradually fall back into place. I brushed my teeth, knowing even then that I would have to do it again after breakfast. Anything to make time pass. Now my face was washed, hair combed, teeth brushed, hands scrubbed. That done, I went to join Mama and Vanya.

Mama was strangely calm and unhurried as she drank her coffee and watched us eat our oatmeal. If she was tense or excited, she certainly didn't show it. She insisted on cleaning up the kitchen without our help, even to the point of scrubbing the hardened soot off the German stove. I hovered over her, leaning my elbows on Ta Shih Fu's worktable.

"Come on, Mama, let me help," I pleaded. There were beads of sweat on her forehead. She mopped her brow with her sleeve.

"Go find something else to do, Tamara." Mama was on edge.

"I'll sweep," I insisted. I had seen the broom in the corner.

She didn't answer. She finished the stove and was now studying it intently, a scowl on her face. *What is so important about shining up a stove?* I thought to myself. *No, that's not it. She wants to keep busy so that she doesn't have to think.* That's what I often did myself.

Mama appeared satisfied. Now she was moving towards our little storage cupboard. Opening it wide, she surveyed our meager hoard. It was made up of the part of the food we'd received from Dr. Ferguson that Vanya and I had saved.

"Mmm," she took out a bar of Hershey's chocolate and a small box of soup cubes.

"What's that for?" I asked her.

She looked at me sheepishly. "I just thought we'd make up a little package for Father," she answered. "What else do you think he'll like?"

"Raisins, Mama?" I took out the red box. "Those are good for energy." Then I thought of something. "You know, it might not be a good idea to give him anything. They might think that we've written a message or something."

She pressed her lips together, clenching her teeth. Her chin stuck out stubbornly. "I'm going to try," she said.

I would have hugged her for her mulish stubbornness, but I knew that any show of sympathy or kindness would weaken her. She was strongest when the going was toughest, and by golly, she needed all her fortitude now. *If I am feeling so queasy about seeing Papa, imagine how she must feel,* I told myself.

"All right, Mama, you try. But you'd better wash all that dirt off you. Dr. Ferguson said twelve sharp, remember? You've got to look your best for Papa." I grabbed her shoulders playfully. How thin she was! Her shoulder blades were bony to my touch. Quickly I removed my hands.

That was another thing about Mama. She would never complain about herself. She endured her suffering in silence; I too will be strong, I promised myself.

"I'm going out back," I told her. "The stone walk needs sweeping."

She nodded, her eyes understanding. "And I'll take your good advice and get cleaned up."

I went back and began to sweep the walk. I came to the wall that Vanya had scaled in order to get to the Colonel's on that fateful December night. As I went on sweeping, my broom hit something hard. I bent down to look and thought it was a large, oval-shaped stone. But there were dark brown designs on the top with a tiny head sticking out. I dropped the broom, running towards the kitchen.

"Mama, Mama, the tortoise has come back!" I yelled. She ran out of the kitchen, and I pointed out to her the slow-moving creature. He inched his way closer to the wall, hiding beneath the fallen leaves.

"You're right, Tamara," she said, "but he never really left. He was just somewhere else; that's why we couldn't find him. Besides, his colors blend so well with the soil that he may even have been here all this time." She gave him another look, then, smiling, ran back inside the house.

213

I knew that tortoises could live for a hundred years and more. Papa had bought this tortoise when I was just a little girl. At first we had seen him every day. Then somehow we forgot about him, or maybe he had just disappeared for a time. I don't remember which came first, but we had often wondered what had become of him. After all these years the old fellow was finally back, looking none the worse for his travels. It gave me a joyful feeling to see my slow friend again. It could even be a favorable omen!

I quit my sweeping and walked back into the house. Vanya might be interested in hearing about the tortoise. I had to step over the ground where Mama used to have her pansies. This was the spot where we had buried the ashes of those books we had burned. Some tall weeds were growing there now. I glanced quickly into the small side yard in back of Papa's study. That was where the revolvers were buried. I was still afraid of them. I wouldn't go into that yard by myself for anything. It was best to let them be.

Vanya had shaved and was dressed up. His knickers were thin at the knees, but he preferred wearing them. He seemed taller, and I noticed that he was not slouching now as he usually did.

I was glad that I didn't have that problem of slouching. I was like Papa in that respect. He always carried himself proudly, his way of compensating for his unusual stature.

What was I doing, thinking about all these different things in the past? Was I trying to calm myself? Stopping myself from thinking about Papa? Was I fearful of seeing him and the dreadful changes I might find in him? I wondered whether his guards had told him that we would be coming to see him. An uncontrollable shiver coursed down the length of my spine. I thought I would collapse to the ground because my knees were buckling under me. But I didn't; I realized time was passing quickly, and it would soon be time to go.

Even though Mama had heated soup from one of the cans that Dorlise had brought, no one ate it. We sat in the living room, leafing idly through magazines, not seeing either the words or the pictures inside them. All of us remained silent, tense, and most apprehensive. All of us waited for that moment, that ominous minute of time when the bell would ring!

Promptly at twelve we heard the loud banging of the brass knockers. We had not been listening for that and were startled. Quickly, we hurried out to the front gates. Mama was behind us, clutching her purse and the cellophane package. Her face was drawn, and I felt my heart beating faster, almost pounding. It was not from my running.

When we opened the gates, we saw Dr. Ferguson, sitting in his parked car. He was looking out the side window, his kind face wreathed in smiles. Wang, his chauffeur, was standing by the car door. When we came up, he bowed, helping Mama inside to sit beside the American.

We had not expected Dr. Ferguson to be here. He chuckled when he became aware of our surprise. "Don't worry," he explained. "I'm not going along with you. Just part of the way. Now, Girlie, you sit here beside Mother. Vanya, you sit in front with Wang." He leaned back in his seat, giving Mama a sharp glance.

"By the way," he added, once we had been seated, "I've asked Chang to stay in your house till you get back. It's not a good idea to leave the house empty and open."

He motioned Wang to start driving. The car's motor had been purring when we seated ourselves. Now it was gathering speed. Before we realized it, we had already passed the Konovaloffs' mansion and were heading towards Hatamen Street. Dr. Ferguson patted Mama's hand.

"We still have quite a way to go," he told us. "I'm on my way to see Arthur Ringwalt, the American consul here. He's your Mr. Clubb's boss," he explained, looking past Mama towards me. "Things are moving along quite well. In fact, Vera, I don't think that I'm being too optimistic when I say that we're moving at a good speed towards your husband's release."

Mama heaved a long sigh. I sensed that she could be close to tears and hoped that she wouldn't break down now of all times. I just couldn't bear to see that. I suspected, however, that she couldn't maintain this passive calm of hers forever.

Dr. Ferguson's next words startled all of us. Never in my wildest dreams would I have thought that this could ever happen!

215

"Perhaps I should have told this to you folks earlier, but I didn't want you to raise your hopes and then have them dashed to the ground. You remember when Mother was away and I came to see you both?" He glanced at Vanya, who had turned towards the back seat. "Well, I would often meet the postman on my way to your house. He and I would both be heading towards your house from opposite directions." He couldn't help chuckling to himself. "God really smiled on all of us this one special day! It just so happened that there was this invitation from Harvard University in Cambridge, Massachusetts, in America."

He looked past Mama to me, his eyes twinkling merrily. "They were most interested in having your father and all of you come to the States as soon as possible. Of course, Harvard didn't know of the trouble you all are in right now. Anyway, they want to employ your father to work on a long-term project."

"And what project is this, Dr. Ferguson?" asked Mama. Her voice was shaking. This unforeseen bit of good news had really astounded her.

"Harvard University will be compiling a dictionary in English-Chinese and Chinese-English. They need the professor's experience, expertise, and knowledge. I apologize for intercepting your husband's mail and, especially so, in opening it." He winked at me. "That, you know, is a federal offense in the United States." He touched his moustache, twirling its ends. "Better that it came into my hands than those of the Japanese. We would never have known about it then."

Once again I felt a twinge of foreboding! It was that same strange sensation of something about to happen that I'd had when Mama came home after we had put up the cracked mirror.

Dr. Ferguson patted his pocket.

"The letter's right here. Mr. Ringwalt is quite anxious to see it. In fact, I took the liberty of writing to Harvard and telling them of the situation here in Peking. Not too long ago they wrote me that, if the Japanese do release your father, they will be most happy to employ him and have even offered him three hundred dollars a month!"

"In gold?" exclaimed Vanya, his eyes wide.

The American smiled. "Yes, Vanya, in gold. That's why Arthur and I are going to have this meeting. There is the *quota*

216

problem to consider, however. That is the big *if*."

"What do you mean by the *quota* problem?" Mama asked.

"Well, Vera, the American government can let in only a certain percentage of different nationals. If their quota, say, of Russians is lower than it should be, then you all will have no difficulty being allowed to enter. Don't worry, though, Arthur and I will see to it that you get your visas."

"Does Father know anything about this?" asked Vanya.

Dr. Ferguson shook his head. "No, he doesn't. Well, here's where I get off." He gathered his light topcoat, his hat, and lifted his cane. He looked mysterious, like an agent on a secret mission. All in all, he was immensely pleased with himself and had every right to be.

We hadn't been watching the streets, so engrossed and excited had we been by the American's surprising news. The car had now stopped. We were in front of the American Embassy. On either side of the gates stood a tall marine, motionless, strong, and silent. I looked at both of them and then at the striped flag with the rectangle of bright stars in its corner. How much that glorious banner symbolized! How beautifully it waved in the breeze!

The car moved on as soon as Dr. Ferguson had gotten out. He gave us a quick wave with his gloved hand and turned to walk through the ornamental wrought-iron gates. Wang stepped on the gas, and the car sped through the quiet Foreign Legation street and once again entered the bustling Chinese thoroughfare. It was filled with pedestrians of all shapes and sizes, walking, running, stopping to chat away in their many-dialectal, musical tongues.

Soon we arrived at the great city gates. Wang drove through their high arch where immediately the landscape changed. We were now on a rough country road with fields and paddies on either side. Once in a while we passed a bus or tiny roadside noodle eatery. The ride was now no longer smooth. Mama and I bumped into each other several times.

After riding for twenty more minutes, we came to a long, extensive, gray wall. Behind it towered a huge building. Wang drove along the wall until he came to its wide open gates.

In the street, sprawling against the wall, as well as milling inside the gray inner yard, were several hundred Japanese soldiers. Wang carefully and slowly came to a stop. He glanced back at Mama, his sympathy showing in his eyes. Patiently he waited for us to get out of the car, not getting out himself. In spite of the American flag on the car, he must have felt himself in enemy territory.

Some of the soldiers stared at us. When they saw the American flag on the car, they turned away. Vanya got out of the car first, coming around to the back to help Mama out. I stepped down after her, taking her cold hand in mine.

The building itself was high and well-built with many windows. Some Japanese soldiers were leaning out of lower windows, looking down on the scene below. I glanced at the smaller, barred windows at the base of the building. Some scrawny bushes were struggling to grow in front of them. Those must be the basement windows, I thought. They were dark, and no faces stared out of them. I wondered if Papa could be somewhere in there, perhaps even looking out. I couldn't know, seeing nothing, no one.

We had to walk the length of the yard to get into what looked like a ticket booth in a theater. We passed the olive-drab uniformed men who looked at us silently, watched us covertly. Soon the whole yard became quiet, and the sound of our footsteps on the concrete walk was the only sound to be heard. The silent, unfriendly faces watched us as we moved along, their black eyes bright, some suspicious, some curious. I can still envision that silent horde. I was not afraid of them, but I did know that they were my enemy, not China's alone. I straightened my shoulders, holding on to Mama's hand. Then, suddenly, I remembered why we were here. It was *here* that Papa was! Right here, among all these unfriendly men! One little man, my father, among so many enemies!

We were now at the ticket booth. Vanya was in front, and a Japanese soldier sat inside. His cap was pulled down over his brow. To be at our eye level, he had to raise his head. He was definitely hostile, but Vanya was polite. He apologized for bothering him, gave him Papa's name, telling him that we had an appointment with Father at two o'clock.

The Japanese looked past Vanya to Mama and me. All this time his hands were busily shuffling papers. Then he looked

218

down, leafing through them quickly. Every once in a while, he glanced up to see if we were still there. Finally, he reached the end of the pile. He shook his head vehemently.

Some of the soldiers had come closer, pressing forward to see what was causing the commotion. They had nearly surrounded us. I glared at them, trying to shield poor Mama from their shoving rudeness. She was about to crumple!

Vanya, bless him, remained persistent. "We do have an appointment. It was made by Mr. Suzuki, your chargé d'affaires, and Mr. Arthur Ringwalt of the American Embassy. Who is the officer in charge here?"

Vanya had asked the wrong question. The Japanese vigorously shook his head, muttering to himself in Japanese. I heard some loud snickers behind us, and then someone spoke to the man in the booth. He removed his cap, scratching his reddish hair. His beady eyes looked sinister.

"No, no." He waved his hand at us. "Go! No one by name of Rublev. No one here called Rublev."

At that we turned as one towards the gate. The soldiers made way, watching us curiously.

Wang had seen everything. By the time we reached the car, the motor was running and the doors were open. As soon as we had seated ourselves, he drove off, faster than he would have had his employer been in the car.

When we got home, Chang and I both went back to the Fergusons. I told Dr. Ferguson and Mary what had happened. I had never seen our neighbor so angry. His usually good-natured, cheerful face had reddened.

"No," he roared. "It had been arranged! Why do they have to do this to your poor mother?" He paced back and forth, his hands behind his back, his white eyebrows twitching. Suddenly, he stopped in front of me.

"Go to your mother, Tamara, and tell her not to worry. I'm getting in touch with Arthur Ringwalt right away. We're going to get to the bottom of this mess if it's the last thing we do."

I ran back home. Mama and Vanya were still in the gate pavilion waiting for me. Mama looked upset and dejected.

I told them what Dr. Ferguson had said.

"I surely hope he can do something," Mama said sadly. There

219

was no conviction in the tone of her voice.

Later, when I was in the kitchen, cleaning up after our early supper, I heard voices in the living room. *Who could be here at this time?* I wondered. I tiptoed to the door, placing my ear against it. It was Dr. Ferguson. Quickly, I wiped my hands and opened the door.

"Ah, there she is, my Girlie," laughed the kindly American. "There's my dear Girlie!" *What a contrast to his previous outburst,* I thought. I wondered what had happened now. Then I looked over at Mama, and saw her smiling. She was calm and happy. What was going on?

"We're all going tomorrow," Mama told me. "Vanya, you, Mr. Ringwalt, the American consul, and I—we're all going together. This way, they can't turn us away!"

I looked dubious. Dr. Ferguson laughed. "Don't wear that long face, dear. Mr. Ringwalt had quite a talk with Suzuki. Both of them will be going with you. If there is a problem, Mr. Suzuki will have to handle it. So put on your prettiest dress tomorrow, my Girlie. Give your father something to see for his sore eyes!" He gave Mama a hug, then left us.

That night, we all slept quite fitfully. When morning came, however, we all felt more encouraged. At least we now had reinforcements. I put on my plaid skirt and white blouse, a little worse for yesterday's wear. However, that was all I had to wear. My teeth were clean; my hair was combed; my face was washed. I stood in front of Dr. Ferguson when he came, smiling at his inspecting look.

"Good girl." He approved. "Come on; let's get going. Chang will stay here to guard the house."

We followed him, as he walked on, swinging his ivory-tipped cane, marching like a general in front of his troops. His enthusiasm was infectious. All of us felt better in spite of yesterday's fiasco. At least, today, we would not be alone. Suzuki would be with us, and even more importantly, an American diplomat would be at our side. They could not rebuff him in the way they had treated us. He was an *American!*

Mr. Ringwalt did not keep us waiting. As Wang neared the American Embassy gates, we noticed a slight man, dressed impeccably in a dark suit, carrying a black briefcase. He was walking slowly back and forth between those two tall marine sentries who looked straight ahead of them, not to the right, nor to the left, just straight ahead. Anything or anyone below the level of their eyeballs, I guessed would be overlooked. The flag was still there, resting at ease without the winds of yesterday.

"Ah, there's Arthur," Dr. Ferguson rapped on the window of his car, smiling broadly. The American consul nodded in return. He walked quickly for a short man. In fact, all of his movements were rapid, as if the White Rabbit himself were holding his watch in his paws, clocking him. "You're late; you're late," I could almost hear him say, "for a very *important* date."

He was already seated beside Wang before I realized that he was inside the car. I hadn't even seen him open the car door! He turned, took off his hat, nodding to Mama politely and acknowledging both Vanya and me. I had never before met a man in such a hurry! He had a no-nonsense way about him. I was surprised at myself for analyzing this man's personality. I found myself doing this quite often these days. I wondered if others tried to figure out why people acted the way they did. How would someone analyze me?

Mr. Ringwalt interrupted my thoughts.

"This time, Madame Rubleva," he began emphatically, "we *will* see the professor." He himself talked like a professor, pronouncing each word separately and distinctly. Whether he was speaking this way so that Mama could understand him or merely that this was his own way of speaking, I had no way of knowing.

The ride to the university this time seemed much shorter than yesterday's. Perhaps it was because we were more relaxed, knowing already what the university surroundings would be like. There was that long, gray wall. Wang parked beside the gates. He got out and came to Mama's side, opening the door for her.

Mr. Ringwalt got out from his side of the car and gallantly waited for Mama to step down. He took her hand, helping her out of the car "Here we are, Ma'am," he said quietly.

Dr. Ferguson looked at her anxiously. "Are you all right, Vera?"

Mama smiled, lifting up her face to his. "Thank you, I am."

Then Vanya and I got out, joining them.

"Aren't you coming, Dr. Ferguson?" asked Vanya.

The American missionary shook his head. "No, son, I'm not. You're in good hands with Mr. Ringwalt. And there is my friend Suzuki waiting for you by the booth." He nodded his head at the nattily dressed Japanese who was standing on the steps, holding a grey felt hat in his very, very white gloves.

12

Father

Dr. Ferguson waved a kiss to Mama and me through the window. Then he leaned back, spoke to Wang, and the car sped away. I did not feel apprehensive today. Mr. Ringwalt had taken full charge. He was now making his way towards the Japanese civilian, ignoring the staring soldiers by the simple act of looking towards one man. He was also holding Mama's arm, speaking to her in a low voice. Vanya and I walked behind them, feeling completely safe knowing that the American was with us. I even managed to outstare an inquisitive soldier who finally lowered his gaze to inspect the rifle he had been polishing. The basement windows looked the same, still dark and half hidden by the untended shrubs.

We had now come up to the Japanese. Mr. Ringwalt spoke to him quietly. Then he turned around to introduce us. Mr. Suzuki grinned, showing his large square teeth. He held out his gloved hand to Mama.

"So honored to meet you, Madame," he said, in his precise English pronunciation. "I regret that it is under these circumstances," he added sorrowfully, his voice lowered to give his words the proper dramatic effect.

"So am I," Mama answered. She too wore gloves. Her face looked serene and lovely. She smiled at Mr. Suzuki as if they were meeting at some faculty reception, not in this dusty yard filled with enemy soldiers. Watching her, I marvelled at the change in her. I could tell that Mr. Ringwalt liked her just by the way he protectively hovered around her.

I also realized why Mr. Suzuki was a diplomat. In the first place he knew how to dress. There was not a wrinkle in his clothing. His trousers were ironed and creased to perfection. His snow-white shirt was starched, its collar properly stiff. His tie was the color of his suit but had enough contrasting shades to make it enhance his total appearance. His shoes, adorned with gray, black-buttoned spats, shone to reflect the sky. His language was courteous and tactful. His manner was subdued. Once, I thought I saw him give Mama a cold look; yet I could have been mistaken. It was my old, suspicious self hard at work once more!

"If you will excuse me," he said, bowing politely, "I shall go first to see if everything is ready."

We all returned his bow. Dr. Ferguson and Papa too had taught us long ago to be more polite to our enemies than to our friends. For me that had been a difficult lesson to learn.

Mr. Ringwalt took Mama's hand, patting it comfortingly. "It won't be long now," he assured her quietly. "Don't worry about anything, please. I'm right here beside you."

The man in the booth was the same one who had turned us away yesterday. At Suzuki's approach he pushed back his cap, peering through the glass. The diplomat shoved some papers through to him, speaking to him in Japanese. He was polite but haughty in his manner. I was amused to see the soldier look abashed. Indeed, he rose from his seat and started to bow, grinning respectfully. Several times he nodded assent as Mr. Suzuki spoke. Afterwards, he glanced over at Mr. Ringwalt. Then he came out of the booth, holding his cap. He bowed once more to the civilian and walked towards the back.

Mr. Suzuki came back to our little group. "Just a few more minutes," he said, looking at Mama sympathetically. He took off his gloves, carefully folding them in half.

The soldier returned, motioning for us to follow him. We entered a large room resembling a theater lobby. Across from us were stairs leading up to the next floors. To the right of them were steps leading down to the basement. I stared at those steps, wondering if that was the way that Papa would come to meet us. We turned left and walked down a wide corridor with doors on either side. There were many doors, probably former university classrooms. He stopped in front of one of these doors, opening it slowly and looking inside. Then he beckoned us to enter.

The room in which we found ourselves was not very large. It was bare except for a circle of straight-backed chairs. Mr. Suzuki bowed to the soldier and invited us to sit. The soldier again bowed to us, closing the door softly as he slipped out.

Mr. Ringwalt motioned Mama to sit next to him. He eyed her with concern. She had not said much during this time; she just did what he asked. She had lost some of the composure she had shown outside.

Vanya and I did not want to sit down just yet. We stood for a time, getting our bearings. Mr. Suzuki also stood. His hands were clasped behind his back. He had lifted his pale face towards the stark-white ceiling above him, gazing intently at some undiscernible spot.

"I think you'd better sit down now," Mr. Ringwalt said quietly. "Vanya, you sit here next to me. Tamara can be beside Mother." He smiled encouragingly at us.

I heard the creak of the door as it opened. Mama had not moved an inch since she had taken her seat between us. Her back was ramrod straight; she stared unflinchingly at the doorknob. I saw that her eyes had brightened, and I too fixed my attention there. Through the door appeared several Japanese, wearing those hateful olive-drab uniforms. They nodded solemnly to Suzuki but ignored all of us, even Mr. Ringwalt. They walked to chairs immediately across from us and sat down. Their short, stubby legs in the clumsy-looking, black boots were spread apart; their hands rested on their laps; their faces impassively gazed past us at the empty wall beyond. I looked at each one of them in turn, trying to find a semblance of humanity in at least one of them. They too, I thought, must be family men; they must have wives, children. They must have some kind of compassion in them. I could see nothing. In those yellow, masklike faces I saw no evidence of kindness or sympathy. Seeing nothing, I veiled my own self, for I too had been brought up in Oriental ways. My face too became masked!

Mr. Ringwalt broke the silence. "Remember; you have only one hour," he cautioned us. He smiled at Mama. "You're okay, aren't you?"

She nodded slightly, without speaking, still staring at that shiny round doorknob. In fact, all of us on this side, as well as Mr. Suzuki sitting next to me, were mesmerized by that knob.

Again, the knob was turned. I almost jumped up; I was so sure that it was Papa. Mama too started up, her eyes anxious now and apprehensive.

Three more Japanese entered. They all wore Western suits, not uniforms. They filed in one by one, then took their places beside their countrymen. There were few empty seats left. I didn't realize there would be so many people at this one-hour reunion!

One of the men was old and apparently very important. He had a long, white beard. His forehead was high; his yellow, taut skin stretched glazedly over his prominent cheekbones and aristocratic, almost Occidental nose. The Japanese had all arisen at his appearance, bowing low to him. Only after he had seated himself did they resume their places. He acknowledged their respectful greetings, then proceeded to take stock of us. There was no hostility nor antagonism in the look that he gave Mother, not even curiosity or scorn. It was just a penetrating, all-knowing, and reserved inspection. His shrewd, impersonal eyes flickered for a moment on Vanya and me, then lingered on Arthur Ringwalt, who nodded his head with a tactful courtliness. The other two men, who were quite a bit younger, held papers and pens on their laps. They, I surmised, were his secretaries; both of them were scribbling away.

It was difficult waiting for Papa to come, to watch for that doorknob to turn. Each second of the endless waiting became in my mind one long hour. In fact, the waiting became just another period of the waiting that I had been doing all my life. I had waited to grow older so that I could go to school. I had waited to become a Brownie so that I could recite their motto and wear that cute, brown uniform topped by the elfin hat; then it was time to wait to become a Girl Scout and work for different badges. Then I had to wait to go to scout camp, wait for the holidays, wait for my breasts to develop to show that I was becoming a woman like Mama. After one waiting period had ended, another had begun, and so it would be, I imagined, forever and ever. This period of waiting for the doorknob to turn, though, was the worst one yet!

Finally the doorknob did turn, ever so slowly. The door

opened, revealing three men. Two of them were dressed in olive-drab uniforms. Between them stood an old man with a long, gray beard. His pepper-colored hair was neatly combed back, revealing a high, broad forehead. The hair was long, falling in soft waves upon his shoulders. Looking upon his calm face, I had a fleeting thought of seeing Jesus as an old man. The skin on the face was the color of old ivory. He had high cheekbones made even more prominent by the contrast with his dark brown eyes that seemed to shine with an inner serenity. His appearance was sad-looking. His dark suit, several sizes too big for him, was hanging loosely upon his thin frame. The old shirt underneath his jacket was collarless. His trousers bulged out at the bottom like those of a circus clown. He paused for a moment, as if he were disoriented, as if the unfamiliar white glare of the walls was too strong for eyes that hadn't seen the light of day for some time. Then his eyes turned to us. Slowly a slight smile formed on his face. His eyes studied each one of us, becoming more tender and loving as he shuffled towards us, his arms outstretched.

He first embraced Vanya, then me. Not a word was said. I felt tears blurring my vision and blinked them away. "Oh, Papa!" I said softly. I felt the stonehardness of his body. There was no extra flesh on him, just muscle and bone. He patted me gently on the back. He held me off from him, looking deeply into my eyes.

"You've become a young lady," he declared. I noticed happily that his voice was strong, firm, and clear. There was also a new note in it, a certain quality of patience and meditative tranquility that had not been there before.

Mama had been standing all this time, waiting for her turn to hold and be held. Her face had been on him ever since he had entered the room. Silently she looked at him and wept.

He went to her then. Wordlessly he held her in his arms. I heard her try to stifle her weeping. Papa gently comforted her.

"Verotchka, don't cry, my dear one. I am fine! I am strong."

All those tears that Mama had quelled inside her during all this time had finally let loose, flowing as quickly and freely as her eyes could release them. She couldn't say a thing except his name, softly repeating it between her sobs, "Serioja, Serioja!"

Finally it was Papa who set her back down in her chair, then sat down beside her.

"Don't cry, Verotchka—please." He took her hand in his own pale one. "As you see, I've been treated most kindly by these people. They've been good to me." He looked straight into her eyes. "I'm in good shape. You know, I exercise every single day. Just feel how strong my muscles are." He flexed his right biceps proudly. "Here, feel," he told us.

Vanya and I both took turns feeling it. I was surprised at how hard it was, as hard as stone! He smiled at us.

"You all look so good to me," he said contentedly. "I've missed all of you. Vanya," he said looking at him proudly, "you've become quite tall." He turned suddenly to the Japanese official, "How good of you, sir," he stood up, bowing humbly to the old man, his arms down by his sides. "You have bestowed such a great privilege on me by giving me this opportunity to see my family again."

The Japanese looked at him with no sign of emotion. He nodded his head slightly, acknowledging Father's gratitude. A sour taste formed in my mouth, as if I had swallowed vinegar. Why did people act this way? All of us except Mama were hiding our real feelings and playing out actors' roles in this drama. Mama was honest enough to let her tears flow unashamedly. But poor Papa! Never would I have thought that he could be so humble and submissive!

Suddenly I was filled with anger towards this old Japanese, whoever he was. It was he, I was sure, who had turned Papa into this passive imitation of his former self. I wished that I could go up to him and berate him for all this suffering that he and his countrymen had inflicted upon us.

Of course, I did no such thing. I was a hypocrite too, playing my role. My forehead was as smooth and placid as Papa's. I even had a half-smile on my lips, just like his. Wasn't I my father's daughter? He and I both knew well the strange ways of the Orient, better than Mama or Vanya ever could.

"It is towards the enemy that you must be polite," he had told me once. "The worst thing you can ever do is show loss of self-control."

How well I recalled those words. I looked at the Japanese without resentment. Miraculously it seemed to me, my eyes glazed themselves with tranquility and calmness. I was now in full control of myself! I looked at Papa. Our eyes met. His lips, under that scraggly gray moustache, twitched at the corners. That movement made me feel somewhat better. He too was role-playing!

Mr. Ringwalt got up at this moment. He extended his hand to Father. Mama half-rose from her seat. Her face was reddening from embarrassment.

"Oh, Mr. Ringwalt, I'm so sorry. I forgot to introduce you!"

He smiled. "Under any other circumstance I would have considered it a *faux pas*," he explained jokingly. "Under these circumstances, though, you are forgiven." He then smiled at Papa. "I'm Arthur Ringwalt, sir. I've been looking forward to meeting you, Dr. Rublev."

Addressing Father so courteously with his title had really startled Papa. He looked around quickly. Then he relaxed. He extended his own hand, bowing politely.

"My pleasure, Mr. Ringwalt." Although Father spoke haltingly, his English was well-spoken.

Mr. Ringwalt asked Papa to sit down, then sat down next to him. He looked at Mama encouragingly. "You have probably already been informed by Mr. Yukimaro here,"—he nodded in the direction of the old Japanese—"that you will be released in the near future."

Father was holding my hand. I felt the increased tension and pressure when the consul had ended his message. Otherwise, outwardly, there was no visible reaction from him. He fixed his steady gaze on the American's face, searching for the correct words with which to reply. He knew very well that the Japanese would be most interested in what he had to say.

"I have understood so," he replied politely.

There was one disturbing thing that I noticed when he first began to speak. He had a slight stutter. *Perhaps he has been isolated and is not used to talking much,* I thought to myself. There could be many reasons for this. Maybe he was ill at ease speaking in English. He did think in Russian, that I knew, but he hadn't used to stutter, or had he? Then I recalled how in the old days he had often recited long poems and excerpts from dramas. There had been no stuttering then.

Mr. Ringwalt took out some papers from his briefcase. "I

realize, Dr. Rublev," he went on quietly, "how much you'd like to talk with this delightful family of yours, but, sir, our time here is getting short. We have only one hour for this interview, and there are a few matters that need to be settled today in order to facilitate your release. First of all, you have to choose between two options, sir, if you are released. The people in charge now do not wish you to remain in China. You can choose to go either to the United States of America or return to the Soviet Union. It is your choice to make." When he had finished speaking, Mr. Ringwalt regarded Father searchingly and somewhat sternly.

This dramatic turn of events must have appeared like a bolt from the blue for Papa; yet he, more than any of us, remained calm. For a moment he looked down, as if studying his hands. He seemed thoughtful. Was it that difficult a choice to make? *Please, God,* I prayed silently and desperately, *help him to make the right decision!*

Inwardly, Papa must have been overwhelmed by the enormity of all this. Everyone's attention was focused on him, awaiting his reply. Slowly he raised his head. He faced the consul, his eyes steady. Then he smiled and breathed a sigh of relief.

"Mr. Ringwalt, sir," he said, so quietly that we had to strain to hear his words, "there is only one decision that I could ever make. I would like, if I am released, to go to the United States."

His reply elated me. Belief rushed in to crowd out disbelief. My dream that I might go to America was really, really coming true!

Even Mr. Ringwalt was relieved. He took a deep breath. "Good! I was hoping you'd say that," he answered lightly. "You and your family will be heading for the United States soon." His eyes crinkled at the corners. "Welcome aboard!" He looked at us, then back at Father.

"I have the further privilege, Dr. Rublev," he continued, "of announcing to you that Harvard University in Cambridge, Massachusetts, has sent you an invitation to do research work at their Harvard-Yenching Institute. They will be compiling an English-Chinese dictionary, and because of your expertise, they are interested in having you work on this project. As soon as we have your visas, we will let Mr. Yukimaro know. Then you, Mrs. Rubleva, and your daughter will sail for the United States." He raised his head and looked at the Japanese official. The old man nodded in agreement. "Good, then it's settled."

He placed his hand on Father's shoulder. Even though he himself was not a tall man, he still had to look down at Papa. "Your son will follow after he gets the rest of your affairs here straightened out. He will pack your library with the assistance of your good neighbor, Dr. John Ferguson. We just want to know if you have anything else to add, question or do you approve?"

Father nodded. I don't think that at that moment he trusted himself to speak.

Mr. Ringwalt selected some papers from his briefcase. "In that case, I have here," he passed them over to Father along with his pen, "some papers that you should read over very carefully. After that, you may sign them. The gist of them is that once you have set foot in the United States, you promise that you will never publicize your experiences here." He pronounced the last sentence very distinctly, almost severely. I think that he was giving Papa a dire warning.

Then he laughed dryly. "I think that we have enough witnesses here to attest to your signature on these documents."

Papa took the papers and the pen and looked over the papers carefully. He took his time and finally signed them with his full name in a strong, steady hand and returned them to the consul.

"Congratulations, sir." Mr. Ringwalt stood up and shook Papa's hand. "You will be starting a new life in a wonderful new country. Good luck to you and yours. God bless you, sir."

I marvelled at Papa's composure. He, too, had risen. His countenance was so serene. He was now a man who had made his peace with the world; former worries and problems no longer existed for him!

"Thank you, Consul Ringwalt." His voice grew stronger. "You have done much for me and my family. I don't know how to thank you except with words. I shall forever be in your debt." He bowed, not humbly this time but as an equal.

"I thank *you*," said the American good-naturedly. "It will be an honor for my country to have you in our midst." He turned, hearing the slight cough that had arisen from Mr. Suzuki's throat. "I'm afraid, sir, that this meeting is now at an end."

I hadn't realized that the hour had gone by so quickly. It had seemed too short a time. Mama hastily rose and put her arms around Father, her face nuzzling his neck. Vanya and I jointly embraced the two of them.

"How can I let you go, Serioja?" whispered Mama sorrowfully.

"Now, now," he said. He moved his lips against her hair. "Just a while longer, my dearest Verotchka, and we'll all be together once more. You have been patient this long; be patient a little bit longer, won't you?" He cupped her face in his hands, studying her lovingly. "I love you very much."

There were footsteps outside the door. Papa stepped back. *"Do Sveedan'ya,* my dear ones, until we meet again."

Once more he shook the American's hand. Then he turned his back to us. He bowed three times to the still-seated Japanese. Yukimaro lifted his hand to stroke his beard. He regarded his prisoner in silence. The two soldiers who had escorted Papa from his cell now stood at the open door.

We watched his short figure shuffle slowly towards his guards. What, in Heaven's name, could be so dangerous about this little old man with the long, gray beard and unflinching eyes, wearing a suit that was miles too big for him? I wanted to run after him, to drag him away from all of them. Instead, I stood there with Mama, waiting for him to leave.

He did not once turn his head to look back. He just stepped out of that door. Once again, he calmly walked out of our lives.

13

Peking, Good-bye!

"What am I going to do without you, Tamdee?" Dorlise's voice sounded mournful when I told her the news. She wanted to hear all about Papa.

"Did he look as if he'd been tortured?" she asked, when Mama was out of earshot.

I tried to recall exactly how he had looked. "I don't honestly know, Dorlise. He's dreadfully thin, just skin and bones. But you know what? I just couldn't get over the serenity in him. His eyes looked so at peace, as if nothing worried him at all. In that whole room he was the most unruffled one, except for that mean old Japanese." I couldn't help shuddering. "I can just imagine how cruel that Yukimaro can be, and he wouldn't even bat an eyelash. Just think; Papa had to bow before him!"

I wanted to forget the Japanese, so I changed the subject. My friend understood. "Tell me, Dorlise, what America is really like, please. I can imagine that to us it will seem like Paradise after all this!" It was good that we had started talking about something else because Mama came in just then.

Dorlise wrinkled her brow. "Gosh, I'm trying to remember." She laughed, somewhat ashamedly. "Would you believe, Tamdee, that I honestly can't tell you? I was just a wee little tyke when we visited there. In fact, *you* will be telling me all about it in your letters. You *will* write to me, won't you?" She went over to Mama and embraced her. "You'll see that she writes to me, won't you? I'm so afraid that she'll meet others and will forget all about me."

Mother gave her a big hug. "There's no chance of that, ever!

233

She *will* write to you, I promise you that. It's rare to have such a loyal friend as you've been, not only to Tamara but to all of us. Besides, you'll be going there soon yourself, won't you? After you finish school here."

"Uh, I might. And then again I might not. I don't honestly know." She placed her hands on her hips. "Now, let's get down to business. Remember; I came here today to help you guys pack. What do you want me to do? I'm playing hooky from school today; so you'd better give me a good excuse for my absence."

Mama shook her head. "You're incorrigible, Dorlise!" Dorlise and I both laughed at that.

"Well!" Dorlise looked at Mother. "What can I do?"

"We can't do any packing until we get some boxes and newspapers. Do you know if you can get me some?"

"No problem." Dorlise's eyes were glistening with excitement. "Do you want me to get them now?"

"No." Mama smiled at her exuberance. "Tomorrow, or even the day after will be fine. I'd really appreciate that."

"Whew, you've got all of Papa's books to pack too, don't you?" She looked around, aghast. "That's going to be a dilly of a job!"

"Vanya will be doing the books," I told her. "We just have the curios, rugs, and pictures that Mama painted. Actually, we don't have much of anything else. Not many clothes, you know."

Suddenly an idea struck Dorlise. Her eyes brightened and a big smile wreathed her rosy face. "Hey, Tamdee, Mama! Why doesn't Tamdee stay here and let Vanya go in her place? Then she can live with us, and I'll help her pack the books. Won't that be swell?" She realized by our expressions that that wouldn't do.

"Vanya has to go to America on a student visa, Dorlise, since he's over eighteen," Mama explained. "His visa takes much longer to obtain. We'll be going under what is called the 'Protectorship of the United States.' It's as if America has become our foster country, our guardian angel, so to speak. It's all been arranged. Besides, I'd never want Tamara to travel alone."

Even though Dorlise and I felt I would be perfectly capable of traveling alone, we dropped the subject. Instead, Dorlise shrugged her shoulders, saying gamely, "Okay, ladies, I'll get the stuff for you and help you pack. Anything else that you want, need, or would like to have?" She smiled impishly at Mama.

It was fun to plan. Mama had become a completely different person ever since that interview with Father. Her energy was boundless.

With undisguised delight, she finished sewing her last dress for the Colonel's daughter. With a sigh of relief she had written a short note, which she had enclosed with her bill. "Dear Mrs. Stilwell, soon we'll be leaving for the United States. I regret to inform you that my salon is now closed. I will no longer be taking orders for dresses. Thank you for your patronage." She had signed it with a flourish of her pen.

What should we take and what would we leave behind? That was the problem. So many things to think about and decisions to make. Dr. Ferguson had told us that our passage would be paid in full. Many Americans had contributed to a going-away fund for us. He had given Mama a list of the contributors.

"When you get to America, you folks could write to thank them," he suggested. We scanned the list, seeing many familiar names, as well as some unknown ones. Mama was deeply touched.

"Never in my life did I think that so many people could be this generous," she exclaimed. "Just think, we're perfect strangers to many of these people. We'll not only thank them, Dr. Ferguson," she continued earnestly, "but as soon as we are able to, we'll repay them. You have my word on that."

There were many things that we wouldn't be able to take with us. We went about weeding through all our treasured possessions. I couldn't take my doll house nor my carved teakwood chest where I had kept all my treasures. I was quite upset that Mama had to leave so many of the beautiful Chinese things behind.

"Can't we take the dragon lampshade in the dining room? And the big yellow platter? Mama, we've had that beautiful Chinese plate ever since I was a baby! I can't believe you want to leave all the china behind too!"

She had looked at me quite sternly. "Tamara," she bit her lips, "we're fortunate to be leaving here. We are even more fortunate that Papa is alive and will be joining us. Yes, these Chinese

235

things are beautiful, and we've enjoyed them all these years, it's true. However, I'd much rather have Papa than them, wouldn't you?"

We did pack some things. The two big vases had to be packed very carefully. Mama wrapped the smaller Chinese rugs around them. She was truly a master packer. She wouldn't let us help her except to bring things to her, run errands, but *only* she packed!

"I know how to conserve space," she told us firmly. She bent over the suitcases, folding things, rolling clothing and stuffing them into bowls and things; her face was flushed, determined, and sometimes dreamy. Her energy was boundless. If we suggested she rest, she would straighten up, wipe her forehead with the back of her hand, and look at us as if we had gone mad.

"Rest? When all this has to be done? I shall rest only when we are on the ship. I'll have plenty of time then. Not now. There is work to be done."

Even though Vanya offered to help, she chased him away. "Go on to your Emily," she told him gruffly. "You'll have enough to do after we're gone."

Mama was truly considerate of him. She realized that the poor fellow was being torn apart these days. Here he was in love with Emily and soon would be leaving her. This way she made him feel less guilty when he was gone. Mama felt for him.

The weather went along with our happiness these days. If it rained, it rained just enough to cleanse the air and renew the greenness that was sprouting everywhere. It was springtime. The world around us had awakened from under its melting blanket of snow. It was filled with a new beginning, new leaves, new flowers, and, of course, for me, new dreams, new hopes!

These days I wakened eagerly. The faster the days went by, the sooner we would see Papa and America. What else could a lucky girl like me want? Soon our family would be together once more, free to live as we so chose.

Dr. Vergil Bradfield from the Peking Union Medical College had been in charge of the arrangements for our trip from the fund-raising of our expenses to our trip by train to Tanku where we were to take a small ship to Kobe. After a short stay in Kobe, we were to board the MS *Hikawa Maru* on May 24, 1939, and to land in Seattle some twenty days later. We were to travel third class on this huge, Japanese oceanliner. The total cost for the three of us was $339, including the head tax. In Kobe we were to stay at an American Tourist House that was run by a Mr. Sanford. Everything had been planned down to the most careful detail. Had we planned such a trip on our own, I doubt if we could have done any better.

Of course, all of us were excited. More so, we actually received a short note from Papa. It really was just a list of things he needed, but it was definitely in his handwriting.

"I am requesting that the following things be sent from my home: (1) warm jacket or sweater; (2) carbolic soap; (3) insect repellent; (4) underwear; (5) a Japanese textbook compiled by *Galichem* or *Spaldwin* (maybe both); (6) chocolate bar; (7) soup cubes."

We had also been given a paper delivered by the Japanese Consulate. It named the three of us, giving us permission to leave China.

We were to leave Peking on May 10th. This way we could have some time to sightsee in Japan. Neither Mama nor I were too thrilled about this.

"Oh, I'm sure you will enjoy it," said Dr. Ferguson when he had handed Mama our tickets and the itinerary. "Besides, it'll give your husband time to rest and get reacquainted with you ladies." He gave Mama a mischievous wink, and she blushed.

"Mary is going to be in Japan in May, too," he added. "There's a PUMC convention of some sort. Wouldn't that be something if you people bumped into each other? Who knows? It might happen."

Everything that could be packed by Mama, Dorlise, and me was now packed and ready to go. Mama had tied all the boxes and even our old, worn-out suitcases with the strong Chinese rope that Dorlise had brought to us. Vanya and I made the labels.

I had a hard time sleeping these days. It was exciting enough to know that soon we would have Papa with us. But to be also going to America! That was much too overwhelming! Of course, there was that envelope with the tickets, right there on top of Mama's bureau. I don't know how many times I went there to look at them, to finger the tickets, just to make sure that it wasn't all a dream!

Again, my waiting game began. I kept thinking that soon, on one of these days in Peking, I would no longer be here. I'd no longer see these multicolored, glass-topped walls, or moon gates, or red pavilions, or anything Chinese. It was hard to imagine that. Instead, I'd have to learn to speak English all the time with an American accent. Away with my British accent mixed with a Chinese sing-song expression! Well, time would tell! A lot of foreigners lived in the United States Dr. Ferguson had told me; so many other people had had the same problems I'd have.

I found myself dreaming of eating ice-cream cones topped with whipped cream and a red cherry, just like the magazine ads had pictured. There I'd be, sitting on a drugstore stool, letting my tongue flicker on three scoops: one brown, one pink, and one white. Mmm! It was difficult for me to believe that American drugstores sold things other than evil-smelling, medicinal drugs.

With the packing done there was not much left to do except wait. Time lies long in idle hands! It seemed as if the tenth of May would never come. Mama had made me a pretty suit out of some purple material that she had stored away from her salon days. For herself she chose to make a dark blue serge one. When she modeled it for me, I couldn't get over how pretty she looked.

Finally, the day arrived! The tenth of May! I wakened shivering with suppressed excitement. This would be my last day in this bed! In this house! I jumped out of bed. Quickly I dressed in the new suit that I'd laid out last night. I combed my hair carefully, smiling at my reflection. I just couldn't help smiling all the time! *Today, Tamara, my girl,* I told myself, *today you'll be leaving for the United States.* I savored those words. How good they sounded on my tongue! Of course, I always knew that I would go there someday! *If you dream hard enough, your dreams will come true.* I remembered that Dr. Ferguson had told me that one time. Now that that one dream is coming true, why not keep on dreaming? *Some day,* I promised myself, *I'll marry a Yankee man! I know for sure I'll marry a Yankee man now,* I told myself. That's the main thing. *To believe.* To thine own self be true, and it shall follow . . . as night the day . . . Oh, how glorious life was!

Vanya and Mama were already at the table. Mama was beautiful today, prettier than I'd seen her in a long, long time. That navy suit was really becoming on her, but it was the radiance in her face that took my breath away. She had taken pains with her hair, making those two waves on either side of her face. It softened her prominent cheekbones, giving her a classic look. She wore what Papa called her "gypsy earrings," pretty golden loops with a tiny diamond in the center.

"Well." Vanya gave me a cool, appraising look. "Hey! you look good for a change."

I thanked him for the compliment, biting into a piece of toast.

"Mama, I still can't believe we're leaving today," I murmured. There was that funny, tickling, quivery sensation at the pit of my stomach. I always got that when I was excited.

Vanya was wearing his knickers and the leather jacket that long ago had lost its luster. I was sorry that he couldn't be with us or see Papa when we would.

"What's the matter?" he asked me. "Why'd you look at me like that?"

"I just felt sad that you weren't coming along," I told him. "What'd you think I was looking at you for? I just wished that you were going, that's all."

He grinned. "No need to feel bad for me, Old Pal. I'm looking forward to being my own master for a few days. Besides, there'll be plenty of work left for me. Who's going to pack the books and clean up the house, eh?"

Mama gave him a quick glance. "Who's going to be visiting Emily, eh?"

"Tell the Hus good-bye for me, will you?" I asked him. I wanted them to know that we were leaving. Dorlise and I had been so busy helping Mama that we hadn't even seen them. Poor Reuben! Ah! Ik-sheek would never forgive me for not telling him that I'd never see him again. Maybe he already knew. Vanya must have told Emily. Oh, well, he'd soon get over me and find another girl to moon over. Ugh! I smiled to myself. Dorlise would write to me about him. Of that I was certain.

"You write to me, Tamara," ordered Vanya. Any other time I'd have resented his commanding tone.

"I sure will, Old Pal. I'll write about everything."

"And I'll write about the home fires here," he promised. "Don't worry, Mama, I'll take care of things; I will."

I *still* couldn't believe we'd be leaving.

"Tamara, hurry," Mama started to rise, looking around the room. "It's time for us to be going."

Just then the doorbell rang. Vanya ran to open the front gates. Mama nervously started to pin on her hat. I grabbed my bulging purse.

We heard Dr. Ferguson's boisterous laugh as he made his way into our living room.

"Well, are you ladies ready?" He sat down in his armchair. It'd be the last time I'd see him here. "Why, hello, hello, hello, Girlie." His eyes were as blue as the heavenly sky outside. "What's all the excitement about?" He beckoned me towards him, then settled me on his lap. It took me back to the old days when I was a little girl.

"I sure am going to miss you, my Girlie," he said softly. I kept my head turned away so he couldn't see my tears.

"Mother," he said, turning to her, "we've had quite a time together, haven't we? All these years! You know, you've been like my second family. I've grown to love all of you. My goodness! How long have you lived in this house?"

"About sixteen, seventeen years, I believe," said Mama slowly. "I don't know how we could have survived all this if it hadn't been for you." Her eyes filled with tears.

He shook his finger at Mama. "Now don't you turn on the water faucets." His voice was hoarse. "I don't want any weeping around here."

But Mama was persistent. "They're tears of joy, Dr. Ferguson." She stood, drew herself up to her full height, her hands folded in front of her. She always positioned herself thus if she had something serious or dutiful to say.

"Dr. Ferguson," I knew she was trying to phrase her thoughts in English.

"Yes?" He was amused by her formality.

"I can't begin to thank . . . "

"Then don't, my dear," he interrupted. "Anything I, and the other people who helped, did, we did because you are dear to us.

You would have done the same had we needed your help, wouldn't you?"

Mama, not trusting herself to speak, nodded yes.

"There is one thing that you both can do for me though." His eyes twinkled. "Whenever you see someone in trouble whom you can give a helping hand, do so, and that would be your *thank you* to me." He looked at his watch. "Hurry, my friends, it's twenty past six and your train leaves in about one hour."

"May I say *good-bye* please," I whispered, suddenly overwhelmed by the thought that I would never again see this home of ours. I ran out to the kitchen and on to the backyard. "I won't be long," I called back, running quickly, knowing that this would be my very last look ever again!

It was quiet and peaceful here, as if the yard too was bidding me farewell.

The enormous trunk of the old acacia tree stood there surrounded by the rotting, circular bench. How often Papa had sat there with us, telling us stories beneath its shade. How often I had laid my precious childhood treasures on that very bench to examine.

And that little wall there, between the living room windows and the kitchen door, that was where Yura, my older cousin, had asked me to pull down my pants so that he could stick his penis at me while Vanya and Petya had looked on curiously. Luckily for me, Ta Shih Fu had seen us and had then called Mama. Yura had been punished.

Next was the garden circle where Wang used to plant pansies and where, almost two years ago, we had burned and buried the shredded books. Here I had found the tortoise crawling near the vinegar tree. It was now even taller, that tree that Vanya had climbed on that cold December night while I had waited with Beba below. Had it been all that long ago?

I ran through the moon gate into the very back courtyard where the grapemound lay, still undug, with the grape trellis there but now bare. There were no grapes, of course, only the mound covering the huge vines and the pets that lay buried there.

I quickly said a silent farewell to Cookie, Vanya's pet rooster; little Goolinka, our sweet-faced Pekinese; the many many cats

241

whose names I couldn't remember; and, last of all, to my Prince, proud son of Tibetan pastures. I remembered Prince's dying in my arms. His once silky white fur, then matted, his thin body shaking, then quiet. Good night, sweet Prince.

"Good-bye, my friends," I whispered to everything around me and ran back to the house. There were just too many memories, most of them dear, but I had no more time for farewells.

I didn't see too much of Peking as we sped to the train station in Dr. Ferguson's car. The excitement of leaving and the thought of seeing Father again crowded my thoughts. Besides, Peking was not my Peking any more. It was now a Japanese city, filled with soldiers and heavily made-up women wearing brightly flowered kimonos.

Dr. Ferguson led us to our train. It was already crowded with milling passengers carrying their bundles and roped-up, old suitcases. Their offspring clung tightly to their parents' trousers, looking up with frightened, tear-stained eyes.

Dorlise was already there, impatiently waiting for us on the platform. "Thank goodness!" she had shrieked when we finally showed up. She hugged me close to her as if she would never let me go. Even the presence of our dignified neighbor couldn't curb her picturesque language.

"Damn it, Tamdee, I really thought you'd get here at a decent time, not just before the train is about to shove off. Here's something for you," she thrust a huge round, unwrapped box into my hands. "Toffee," she grinned.

Then she slipped a smaller package into my pocket. "This you open after the train starts moving. The toffees are good," she told me impishly. "They're English. The best! In fact," her face reddened slightly, "I had some while I was waiting for you all." She laughed somewhat sheepishly, glancing shyly at Dr. Ferguson.

"Thanks, Dorlise," I looked at her lovable face. "I'm surely going to miss you. You know that, don't you?"

"Yep, I know it," she said brusquely. "Hey, you'd better go. Mama just got on."

I gave her one last hug, and one for Dr. Ferguson as well. "Hurry," Dorlise cried, shoving me up the steps to the train.

Once we were seated, we both looked out at those wonderful

faces. They kept on smiling, waving their hands frantically, while more and more passengers piled into the car. It became fuller than full, with people standing next to us.

Suddenly the train gave a sharp jerk; then there was a lurch, and somewhere far off a whistle blew. We heard the screechy grinding of wheels and saw the long, moving swirl of thick black smoke as it spouted from the black engine way out front.

"Good-bye," we mouthed, waving to them.

"Kiss Papa for me," yelled Vanya. He was smiling, as were the others around him.

The train lurched once more and slowly began to move. The waving figures grew smaller and smaller until they were mere dots in the landscape, rapidly fading away, then they were no more.

14

All Aboard!

It took us about four and a half hours to reach Tanku. The train was crowded with mostly Chinese travelers and enemy soldiers. The Japanese were everywhere, strutting about the aisles or sitting in the best compartments; their yellow faces, smug and self-satisfied. Fortunately, for the first part of our journey, we had a pleasant Chinese peasant family sitting across from us. They didn't talk much, being busy with their three little ones, who would not keep still. However, they left us when the train stopped in Tientsin.

A lone Japanese student now took up their bench. He placed his books beside him, taking up one and holding it close to his thick spectacles. His lips moved in silence as he read. Mama sat by the aisle, either watching the other passengers or just dozing. She was exhausted. I sat by the window staring out; never again would I see these paddies or fields, nor the huts among them. If I felt the Japanese student's eyes on me, I played Dorlise's old trick. I eyed him down until he lowered his eyes. Hmm! I thought bitterly, just another spy watching us.

Finally our train arrived in Tanku. The station was like the others, just as dirty and crowded with people. Their blue cloth-bound bundles and bulging baskets lay on the ground beside them. They too were waiting, always waiting, either to go elsewhere or to return to their humble hovels to continue living their simple lives.

We were constantly on the lookout for Papa, straining our eyes to see if he could be that long-bearded man sitting way off to the left or whether he was the man just coming through the gates from the station platform. Mama looked in one direction; I, in the other. We scanned every bearded man we saw. Papa was nowhere to be seen.

Heartsick, we walked onto the pier, carrying our purses and the small suitcase that contained our essentials as well as the few valuables my parents owned. We found the river steamer that was to take us on to Kobe. The baggage was being loaded on it. We watched, searching for our own huge, rope-secured suitcases. We hoped the rusty locks would not break under the weight, but there were too many suitcases and trunks. Many of them had been tied in much the same way that Mama had secured ours, so we finally gave up looking, hoping the locks and ropes would hold.

Both of us were tired. I was hungry too, but when I asked Mama if she was, she shook her head. I could see that her spirits were sinking.

"All of this could be a Japanese trick," she had murmured one time. "They're just trying to get rid of us."

"Let's get on board ship," I suggested. "We are just idly standing around here. You know, Mama, he may already be inside our cabin." I caught the glimmer of hope in her eyes and prayed that my words would prove true.

"Yes," she said eagerly, but I could see that she was still worried. "He probably is there waiting for us."

She took my arm, and we walked toward the ship. A few foreign nationals were headed the same way, carrying their smart bags and conversing excitedly with one another. Most of them, I guessed, were returning home to the United States after having toured the Far East. What a carefree people they were, enjoying their pleasures like children, with not a worry in the world!

As we walked on, we heard footsteps hurrying toward us. We both turned our heads and stopped. A grinning Japanese, dressed in Western clothes, also stopped. He bowed from his waist down. Like many of the Japanese men we had seen, he was wearing black-rimmed spectacles with thick lenses that gave his eyes an enlarged, unnatural appearance that reminded me of the political caricatures I'd seen in the *Peking Chronicle* before the occupation.

He addressed Mother by name. Her face paled.

"Yes, that is my name," she answered. "Do you know where my husband is?"

He shook his head solemnly, again bowing profusely, his mouth wide open and showing his large, uneven white teeth.

"So sorry. Not now," he answered politely. "You go on *Hikawa Maru* in Kobe?"

I nodded. Mama was too upset to answer him.

He looked at her carefully, nodding, as if to himself. I could hear his unspoken *ah-sodeska*. I really didn't know what it meant, but I'd heard many Japanese saying it on the train. It must have meant *"ah so,"* or some expression to that effect. It really was of no consequence.

He bowed again, still grinning. *"Sayonara,* Madame. Soon you see the professor, your husband." He turned to leave.

"When shall we see my father?" I demanded, looking straight into those magnified eyes.

"Ah-h-h," he pointed to the gray ship. "Maybe one hour, maybe two. You see him. Sure." He put his hand up as if he were taking an oath. Then he changed the gesture to a wave. *"Say-onara,"* he called out, grinning as he turned away.

"Sayonara," I answered. I went to join Mama, who had gone on ahead. I'd have liked to have thanked the Japanese in his own language. I remembered that *arrigato* meant *thanks.* However, he hadn't really done anything except worry Mother a bit more, so I didn't.

The little ship was beautiful, her decks shiny and spotless. The courteous, uniformed man who took our tickets led us through a narrow hall past several cabins until he came to the last door.

"This one is yours," he bowed to Mama, opening the door into an immaculate cabin. I could see an upper and a lower berth, a table, and the porthole with its tiny curtains tied back. "Your husband will be sharing this with you," he said politely.

He didn't ask Mama where her husband was. I wondered if he knew. If he did, there was no evidence of it in his manner. Then he walked back to the cabin next to Mama's, unlocking the door.

"This one is for you, young lady," he smiled at me. I liked

him. Although Japanese, he wasn't like the soldiers.

My cabin was similar to Mama's except that it was already occupied. A large lady, whose back was turned at the moment, was busily removing some dresses from the open suitcase lying on the lower bunk. The Japanese closed the door again, softly.

He looked over his passenger list. "You will be sharing this cabin with . . . ah, here it is, Mrs. Richardson," he murmured. "American lady. Ver-r-r-y nice." He smiled at me, handing me the key. Then, bowing to Mama and me, he left.

Together we returned to Mama's cabin. I certainly didn't want to join the plump American matron. At this moment Mama and I needed only each other's company.

It felt good to shut the cabin door and take off our jackets and shoes. We were still tense, even though we were now by ourselves. We carefully listened to every single sound that penetrated the small cabin. We learned to distinguish the soft footsteps of stewards from the sharp, quick steps of passengers. We eagerly listened to the different muffled voices in the hope that a certain one just might be Papa's. However, there were only confused passengers searching for their cabins; others were laughing, greeting friends, or exuberant about returning home.

The ship was scheduled to sail at six-thirty the next morning. It was now nearly four in the afternoon. Already, we had had a long, tiring day. Mama took a seat facing the door in case it should open. I sat on the tautly folded blanket on the lower berth. The bed was narrow but comfortable, the mattress firm. The cabin was attractive. In examining it, I noticed the sign on the back of the cabin door.

"Mama, these are first-class cabins!" She didn't answer.

When I went to the tiny bathroom with a miniature toilet and sink, I felt how soft and luxurious the carpet was. Everything was so sparkling clean and looked like new. Even soap and toothpaste had been laid out for us as well as fluffy, white monogrammed towels.

"I think I'll wash my face," I said, getting up off the berth. The soap smelled so good. It made my face tingle after I had washed it. I looked out at Mama. She hadn't moved. She had dark circles under her eyes. Her face looked drawn. She wasn't interested in the cabin at all!

247

"Mama," I went over to her and sat down on the rug at her feet. "Mama, he'll be here. Don't worry, please!" I put my hands in her lap, pressing my chin against her knees.

She sighed. "I hope so, Tamara." She stared at the door. "He should have been here already. I just have the most uneasy feeling."

"About what?" I tried to sound unworried.

"I told you before," Mama's voice shook. "I feel that they're trying to get rid of us by sending us out of China. I doubt if they'll ever let Papa go."

"Oh, Mama!" I exclaimed. "They can't do that to us. They've given their word to the Americans." In trying to convince her, I was trying hard to convince myself.

My outburst comforted her somewhat, or at least she seemed to be more at ease and gave up her watching post to go into the bathroom and get cleaned up.

Sometime later we heard the musical tinkling of the dinner bell. "If you want to go, go ahead," Mama told me. "I'm staying here."

I refused to go, not wanting to miss Papa if he should come. I also knew that Mama needed me more than I needed food.

"There's Dorlise's toffee on the bed. Oh, I forgot! She gave me another little package." I rummaged in my purse until I found it.

Quickly, I unwrapped the package. Inside the little box there was a gold heart pendant. In the center was a mother-of-pearl background. On top of that were two roses, entwined. One was in pink gold; the other, white gold. The card said simply, "Love, Dorlise."

Mama took it in her hands, admiring it. "You're the one rose; she is the other. What a dear girl she is!" Mama handed it back to me. "I hope you'll always keep in touch with her, wherever you both may be."

I placed the little locket back in my purse. It would accompany me wherever we went on this long journey to America.

It was eight o'clock now and still no sign of Papa!

"Perhaps," Mama looked at me with concern, "You'd better go to your cabin and get settled. Your cabinmate may wonder why you still haven't shown up. If Papa should come, then I'll knock on the wall three times. What do you think?"

"I don't like to leave you by yourself," I told her. I was also not that anxious to be with the fat American lady.

"I want to get some rest, Tamara," Mama said firmly. "We've had a long day. I promise you I'll call you right away."

I left her, rather unwillingly, after giving her a hard squeeze goodnight.

When I opened the door to my cabin, I had to get accustomed to the semidarkness. Only the light over the lower bunk was lit. I saw Mrs. Richardson's ample form ensconced in her bunk. She wore a delicate, satiny bed jacket that had ecru lace bordering the sleeves. Her hair was hidden in a blue hairnet. She had on weird-looking spectacles that perched halfway down her nose. She held a magazine in her hands. More magazines were on her blanket. When I entered the cabin, she stopped reading and peered at me through her glasses. Then she took them off and surveyed me more openly, her smile quite friendly and pleasant. Her face was unusually shiny in the glow of the ship's tiny lamp. Then I saw that she had lathered her face in cold cream.

"You must be my roommate," she said in a husky voice. "Welcome aboard, my dear. I'm Emily Richardson from Spokane, Washington." This time when she smiled I saw that her teeth were stained by her bright orange lipstick, a weird sight.

I didn't wish to talk, but I could see that she was curious about me. All I wanted to do was to crawl into my bunk. Unfortunately, it was the upper bunk above hers. If she kept on talking, I wouldn't be able to hear Mama's three knocks.

"I'm happy to met you," I said politely. When I told her my name, she showed no surprise.

"I had hoped to meet you sooner, but now that we've met, I'm sure we'll enjoy each other's company, won't we?"

To that I nodded, but she kept on quizzing me. "Are you traveling alone? No, you couldn't be. Why you're just a child."

That remark set me off. "I'm seventeen, and I'm not alone."

"Oh, that's fortunate for you!" she said with relief. I felt I had to explain my situation to her. How could I shut her up without being rude? What would Dorlise do?

"I'm here with my parents," I told her politely. "My father is not well; that's why I didn't come to my cabin earlier."

She nodded sympathetically. "I understand, dear; most people's stomachs and the sea waves often don't mix too well." Then she asked me in alarm, "You're feeling all right, aren't you?"

I quickly reassured her. "I'm just terribly tired. I don't get seasick." I hoped I didn't; I didn't even know what being seasick involved. I climbed into the upper berth hurriedly.

"Tell you father to eat plenty of grapefruit, if nothing else." She placed her glasses on her nose.

Relieved, I took off my clothes. She turned off her light. I lay in the semidarkness, waiting for Mama to knock. Every once in a while, in spite of myself, I dozed off. I wakened to hear soft snoring beneath me. I hurriedly dressed in my bunk. By the dim light of the porthole I was able to climb down the ladder, keeping an eye on my cabin-mate's sleeping face. I had made sure that I had my purse and keys with me. I tiptoed out of the cabin, carefully closing the door and noiselessly heading for Mama's cabin.

Mama was wide awake when I opened the door. When she saw that it was not Papa, her face fell. "Only me, Mama," I whispered. "I just couldn't sleep."

"Neither could I," she whispered in return, moving over to make room for me on the lower bunk. Why we were whispering was beyond me; there was no need for that.

"It's nearly six o'clock," I told her unhappily. "The ship sails at six-thirty."

A dreadful feeling of being lost and abandoned overwhelmed me. I knew Mama was right. We were going to leave for America on this ship; Papa had been disposed of by the Japanese; and—as Dr. Ferguson had once told me—Vanya would be sent to Russia!

We had really been naïve and gullible! Was Dr. Ferguson in on their plans? I couldn't, I didn't want to believe it, but how could it be otherwise? What were Mama and I going to do? There wasn't even Dr. Ferguson to comfort us or advise us. Well, I concluded, it's now up to me. At least we were on our way to America or *were* we?

Suddenly, far off, we heard the long eerie sound of the foghorn. Out of the dawn's silence, breaking into the sleeping ship's tranquility, came the first warning alert. Soon the ship would sail on for Kobe, leaving forever the shores of Tanku! All aboard! All passengers going to Kobe should be aboard ship; those who weren't would be left behind. There was no way to make a ship wait!

Mama started to pace back and forth, wringing her hands. "There's not much time left. Oh, my God, he's still not here!"

The musical tinkling bell passed our door, ringing out loudly the first call to breakfast. It faded away as the steward went on throughout the ship. I heard my own cabin door open, then close. I'll bet Mrs. Richardson is now on her way, I thought with amusement. She wouldn't miss a meal for anything! I wondered what she had thought when she saw my empty berth.

Once more, the foghorn sounded, as mournful and as eerie as the first time. It was now a quarter after six, and still no sign of Papa!

People walked by in the corridor; some were talking in low, conversational tones. Once we heard a child's excited babbling; then a woman's soothing tones reminded us that, in spite of our own problems, the world was still continuing on its course, most of its people living life as usual.

In fifteen more minutes the horn would blow its last sad call, and the ship would sail for Japan. Mama and I had been so disheartened that we hadn't even heard the door open.

He had entered the cabin as quietly as he had come into the room at the Peking University, that momentous moment when the soldiers had escorted him into the room where we had been waiting. Only when I heard Mama's loud gasp did I realize that he was here inside our cabin with us. I half turned, afraid to look lest again I would be discouraged and disheartened.

But he was here this time all right, the same short-statured figure in the suit that was miles too big; the long gray beard curling at the ends; and those wonderful brown eyes that glowed with such serenity and love.

At first he came towards us hesitantly; then suddenly he was right there with us, enveloping us silently in his arms.

Then I heard the soft footstep and turning my head saw the same Japanese man who had met us on the pier. He was standing by the door, watching us, his face one big grin.

Papa let go of us. He bowed low before the Japanese. It infuriated me that he was again humbling himself before one of those who had treated him and his family so unjustly.

"Kind Yamamoto-san, allow me to present you to my dear wife and daughter." He urged me forward with his hand behind my back. Mama nodded to the man, her eyes already glistening with tears.

"Ah, Mr. Yamamoto brought me here," Papa explained. He looked at the stranger gratefully. "He has been so good to me."

I'll bet, I thought dryly to myself. He could have told Mama that Papa would come aboard just before sailing time and saved us all that worry. Personally, I saw nothing for which we should be grateful. However, having been brought up in my father's pseudo-Oriental tradition, I kept my thoughts to myself. My face was properly bland.

Mama had been staring at Papa as if he were a ghost. Now she had shaken herself out of the trance and remembered the civilities and courtesies that had to be performed. She held out her hand graciously and smiled her most dazzling smile. Her dark eyes, strained and tired from a long night of sleeplessness, could not match the warmth in her voice.

"Thank you very much, Mr. Yamamoto," she said in her soft, musical voice. "I am so grateful to you for returning my husband to me. We shall forever be in your debt."

If they had asked for my opinion, I'd have said, "Baloney."

The Japanese shook Mama's hand heartily. Then he bowed himself out, but not before bestowing a toothy smile in my direction. I was relieved when he at last closed the door after himself.

"Who is he?" I asked Papa.

Papa was emphatic in his enthusiasm. I was surprised. "He is a very fine man," Papa stated. He then turned to Mama, his gaze calm and loving. "He was the one who came all the way with me from the university to the ship. Of course, I told him all about you. He said he wanted to meet you two. A fine man," he repeated as if he were trying to convince himself of the fact.

"Ah-h . . . " Papa backed away, smiling. "Let me feast my eyes upon the two of you. I couldn't imagine that you would look so good, but you both look healthy and well. I am too." He took off his jacket.

Immediately I smelled that medicinal odor about him. Without his jacket he looked even thinner. I could see Mama's eyes fastened upon him. She too was aghast at the mere shadow of the man she loved.

He laughed suddenly, a happy chuckle really. "I know I may look bad to you, but I am better than the time you saw me last. Really, I'm in better shape now than ever. Believe me, I am." He thereupon flexed his arm muscles.

Mama and I played along with his fantasy. With a growing horror I began to wonder if he was in his right mind.

"Here, feel." He offered us his flexed right arm. Mama and I both felt the stone-hard biceps.

"That's terrific," I exclaimed, whether in real awe or make-believe, I myself couldn't tell.

Papa smiled through his beard. It was strange to see him like this when once he had been clean-shaven and short-haired.

"It was because I exercised constantly," he explained. "Sit down and let me tell you what has happened to me all these months that I've been in prison."

Mama objected. "Serioja," she told him gently, "you must rest. You are safe now; you will always be safe in America."

He nodded impatiently. "Yes, yes, I know that. I am safe, but I'm not tired. I want to tell you both this. You see, I built myself up all the while they were trying to break me down. I want you to know right now what happened to me."

He was eager to have his say. He must have been so alone, poor Papa! He kept on talking, stuttering at times, but triumphant and proud that because he had exercised he had thereby survived!

We let him talk.

"When I was separated from you, Mama, they took me to Mei Chia Hutung, the Japanese headquarters for the military at that time." His face became grim. "It was also their grilling headquarters. My first sight when I was being led to my cell was of two Chinese girls who had been interrogated. Apparently they were being led back into their cells. They showed signs of having been beaten savagely. Their faces were red and swollen; their eyes were puffed up and half-closed as the soldiers dragged them past me. Needless to say, that was a most sinister and terrifying introduction to my new surroundings."

Mama poured him a glass of water. He drank it thirstily,

smacking his lips. His eyes expressed his gratitude to her. Then he put down the glass and continued.

"The first night they let me sleep, although it was difficult to do so, since a bright light was on all night. There was no bed to lie on, only a blanket on the cement floor. I used it for a cover as it was terribly cold. The next day they took me into another room. That was where they questioned me.

"Serioja," Mama hesitated. She was scowling. "I don't understand. What is it that they had against you?" Her lips were quivering with emotion.

Papa laughed mirthlessly, then drank another sip of water.

"They had five counts against me, all fabricated lies, of course. In the first place, they said that I was anti-Japanese because I wouldn't register in the White House." He grinned with amusement. "Then they *knew* that I was really very wealthy. They were *sure* that I was the one supplying the generalissimo with money to buy arms to fight them. Me!" He pointed to himself, and we smiled with him. "But that's what they believed, and they couldn't be convinced otherwise. Next, they were convinced that I was in some way tied up with the Communists. Do you know how they knew that?"

"How?" Mama asked.

"When they searched our house, they found some red-covered books, which they confiscated. These had to be, they thought, propaganda, because they were red in color!" He shook his head sadly. "They also were sure that we had ammunition hidden in the house that was to be distributed to Chinese students."

"We did have Uncle Kolya's revolvers," I offered.

Papa laughed. "Yes, that was all our hidden ammunition. You didn't bring them, did you?"

"No," I told him, "definitely not. I wouldn't even walk into that little yard where we had buried them."

"Ah, well, someday someone will dig them up, and wonder how they got there. They were the only things I owned that had belonged to my brothers. Such is life!"

"How could they believe such drivel? They had no evidence."

"They don't have to have evidence. They believe what they want to believe, that's all there is to it," Papa said simply.

Something had bothered me for a long time, and I felt that now was as good a time as any to find out the answer from Papa.

"Why did we have to burn all those books?" I asked him. "Wasn't that propaganda?"

Papa shook his head. "Not really, Tamara," he replied. "They were mostly Russian textbooks, stories, novels, poetry, and such. However, because they had been printed in the Soviet Union would have been cause enough for them to have brought charges against me. The fact that I'm a scholar meant nothing to them. I actually laughed when I saw Krilov's *Fables* in their hands. That book was dangerous, they knew, because its covers were red! And now, about your good friend, Mischa!"

I snorted contemptuously. "Not my good friend, Papa. He was really Vanya's friend."

"Well, he was working for them. I had a feeling that he had been asking too many questions. He was supposed to find out all about our living habits and to meet as many of our friends as possible." He placed his finger alongside his nose. I smiled to myself seeing this old habit of his return once more.

"I don't think Mischa could have given them much information." His face clouded as he thought about Mischa. "It seems such a shame to me that a young man like him would lower himself to spy for the Japanese. But that's Mischa for you."

"He's despicable!" I blurted out. "We all had been so nice to him too! Why was he such a traitor?"

Papa was patient with me. "For money, security. You must remember that some of these poor Russian exiles have nothing but memories of a Russia that is no longer there. What do they have in China? They must try to get any kind of job, just to keep the wolf away from the door. Look how many Russian girls worked at Soochow Hutung selling their bodies to rich American marines, to Limeys, or to gallant French officers. Where did these poor girls end up? Sick with syphilis, shunned by the very families that had sent them out to Soochow Hutung in the first place. Relatives happily enough took their money even after these poor girls had been stripped of their pride and their honor!"

He looked at me tenderly. "We, as Russians, were more fortunate, that is, until the Japanese came. We can't blame Mischa too much; his life is miserable enough. In the long run, he will find that the Japanese too will forsake him. There is little left for him on which to survive." Papa then changed the subject, returning to his own experiences. He had to rationalize for himself some kind of absolution by talking all this out with us and by reliving it one more time!

"Do you know what they told me one time?" He looked at me curiously, as if puzzled over how much I knew about life. "They told me that you too were in Soochow Hutung, selling your body to *their* soldiers." He began to stutter. "I al-al-al-mo-mo-st-st lost my mind wo-or-ry-ry-ing ov-ov-er you. But then," his look hardened, and he managed, "I-I-I kn-kn-ew i-i-i-t couldn't b-b-be true. Not with your high morals and ideals." He added, as if to himself, "You can be talked into almost anything if you are weak enough to submit to someone else."

Mama hushed him. She spoke to him tenderly. "We've all the time in the world now. Let's all rest awhile from these awful horrors. Later, when we have more energy, we'll talk again. You've suffered much," she sighed. "So have we all."

He nodded his head just like an obedient schoolboy. "One more thing, Mama." He was looking at her with such humility that she began to laugh. He started to untie the sash that was looped through the belt bands of his trousers. "I brought a gift for Tamara. I want to give it to her now."

I was surprised, even more so when his trousers began to slide downward. He chuckled to himself then, standing in front of us in a wrinkled, collarless old shirt and the new white underpants we had sent him as he had requested.

"I appreciated these so much, Mama." Impishly he pointed to them. Then he probed under the elastic band around his waist till he found the string for which he had been looking.

"In the last cell that I was in," he explained, "there was this wonderful old Chinese gentleman imprisoned with me. He was in his late seventies, I guess—a dignified, fine gentleman of the old school. Of course, he did not expect to survive his imprisonment. The Japanese were holding him for ransom because they believed him to be quite wealthy. Once they got what they wanted, he felt that they would do away with him. He and I had many philosophical discussions together. I was comforted and encouraged by his amazing attitude towards life. His wife had died long ago, but he had two sons and a daughter who were living. He told me that he himself was not afraid of dying; he had lived a most full and useful life.

" 'I've seen the mountains, the lakes, and the wonders of nature in my beloved land,' he told me. 'I've met people from every province. With them I've discussed many subjects. I've asked innumerable questions in my lifetime, but I have found few real answers. I had a delightful woman to share my youth and the beginning of my old age. My children are now grown. They have their own families to rear, to worry about.

"I had to leave my old home and all the treasures therein, except one. This one special ornament had belonged to my wife, and she had worn it continuously from the time that I had presented it to her on our betrothal until the moment of her death. You have told me of your young daughter who, as you have said, is a bud about to flower. Some day soon she will bloom, and you will bask in her radiant beauty. I want to present to you this remembrance of my good wife, for you have become to me a brother. Please give it to your girl-child, and tell her this from me.

"If she is ever in a desperate condition, let her sell this bauble so that she may keep on with her station in life. But let us hope that she will be able to keep it; to hand it down to her daughter, and from that daughter on to the granddaughter so that all the women down the line will wear it for generations to come, mindful that an old Chinese gentleman had wished it to be so.' "

Papa then pulled out the string and at its end dangled the most beautiful bracelet of jade that I had ever seen. He untied it and gave it to me.

"I was fortunate that they didn't think to search me," he chuckled. "Enjoy it always, my dear. I wish that my old cellmate could know that I have fulfilled his bequest. Perhaps he does."

I held it in my hand, surprised at its hard coldness. It wasn't just one color of jade. It started from an almost pure white towards a lighter sea green, darkening gradually. At its darkest it was still the color of the ocean at dawn, when the waves are rippling and the tide is low.

Again we heard the pleasant tinkle of the steward's bell as he summoned the next shift to eat their breakfast. Mama looked at me.

"You must go and eat some breakfast," she told me. "We'll ask the steward to bring something in to us."

I shook my head. "I want to eat here with both of you and listen to Papa," I declared authoritatively. "Would you like me to ring for the steward?"

Father looked from Mama to me in surprise. "Why do that?" he asked calmly. "We can all go together. There's no need to order breakfast and bother the steward. Besides, I need to do some walking. I've had very little exercise, you know."

I know that Papa did not realize how terrible he looked. I couldn't believe that he wanted to go into the public dining room. I knew instinctively that the passengers would stare at this man with his long, straggly hair and beard. Were he a priest, wearing a cassock, he'd be acceptable. But in his baggy suit and dirty, collarless shirt? I hoped that Mama could dissuade him. I tried to catch her eye.

It wasn't that I was ashamed of Papa. Heaven forbid! I would feel ashamed for the people who'd stare, unable to take their eyes off him, who'd wonder about him and us. I couldn't bear to have Papa embarrassed. He was such a gentle man, unaware now of the outside world. I found out that I didn't know my parents very well.

"Well, Serioja," Mama replied firmly, "if you want to go to the dining room, then you shall go. However, your beard is too long. I shall have to trim you up a bit and make you more presentable." Unfortunately, small sewing scissors were all she had with her.

"I knew these would come in handy some day," she declared. She made Father sit down, surveying him critically. "Mm'mm, I'm going to have to cut your hair a bit as well." She took the comb, running it through his long locks. She did the same to his beard, which curled at the ends. I sat on the lower berth, watching them both, fascinated by Papa's serenity and Mama's ingenuity. Papa saw me looking and gave me a mischievous wink. *Thank God,* I thought to myself, *he is our Papa! He has not changed!*

"I guess that Mama is bound and determined to make me into a proper gentleman," he joked.

"Stop talking." Mama straightened his head. "There, now don't move!" She began snipping away, rounding the beard carefully, shaping it to look much like the beard in my grandfather's portrait. I was amazed at the close resemblance.

"I'll shave later," Papa said when Mama had finished. He looked somewhat better, although his hair was still curling at his shoulders.

When he said that, Mama began giggling like a little girl. "You can't," she gasped. She put her hand to her mouth.

"And why not, Madame?"

"Because," she smiled ruefully. "I forgot to bring a razor with us."

Even our family predeparture ritual hadn't helped. I don't know whether this was a Russian, Bulgarian, Romanian, or Chinese custom, but before anyone in our family ever took a trip somewhere, after all the packing had been done and before a step could be taken out the door, the future travelers would have to sit down in a circle and think of what might have been forgotten. Mama had always insisted on this ritual, and we had done so that last time in Peking. For fifteen minutes Vanya, Mama, and I had sat in the bare living room thinking of all the things we had packed, thinking of all our rooms, and what was in them, taking mental inventory. Finally Mama had risen.

"I can't think of anything else we need," she had said, and we all agreed. Of course, Vanya had been using Father's razor so that was one thing that had never crossed our minds.

Father shrugged. "Then I'll just have to keep the beard," he said. "Come on, ladies, let's go." He offered us his elbows, and we walked down the narrow corridor, arm in arm.

We heard some people walking behind us. They had been talking when we came out of the cabin. Afterwards, the talking stopped. Papa gave me a playful nudge with his elbow.

"And how does it feel to have your old Papotchka back with you again?" He turned his happy face towards me.

Tears blurred my eyes. "Oh, Papa," I whispered, squeezing his arm, "it's just wonderful to have you back with us again!"

We entered the crowded dining room. Mama walked on first,

then I, then Papa followed, proudly walking behind us, his calm eyes surveying the round tables at which all the first-class passengers sat, studying with care their menus or the others who sat elsewhere. As the steward led us to our table in the corner, I saw that several people had turned to look in our direction. Of course, it was on Papa that they focused their attention. Fortunately, or maybe it was tactfully, the steward had seated Papa so that he was facing us with his back to most of the diners. Papa himself was completely oblivious to the stares and sat there contentedly, studying the menu.

"I still can't believe that I'm actually here with you two," he shook his head slowly. "And of all things, on our way to America! That to me is just incredible. Of course, I miss Vanya. If he were here with us, my cup then would surely be running over."

Mama smiled. "He said to give you hugs and kisses. But he has fallen in love; so it is good. He'll have a while longer to be with his Emily."

I wondered to myself how *Ik-Sheek* was faring. Oh, well, Dorlise would write me. Was it only yesterday that I had talked to her and said good-bye? It seemed ages ago!

We all ate heartily, Papa most of all. I thought of Mrs. Richardson's remarks about the meals. I hoped she wasn't in the room to see how Papa was wolfing down the food. And I had told her that he was seasick!

When we returned to the cabin, Papa continued his story. He seemed compelled to tell us all that had happened to him. Mama gave me a warning look.

"In time I got to know when they would be about to torture me," he told us quietly. He was now lying on the lower bunk, staring upward, his eyes reflecting the memories which now must have been flooding his mind in quick succession.

"It was some time last January when they hauled me out of the cell in the middle of the night. They made me strip, not even giving me the last bit of pride of leaving my underpants on. It was dead of night. The snow had been falling for quite some time. Then it had stopped, and the coldness and freezing wind had set in. It was the kind of cold that when you are out in it, the very marrow of your bones feels it. The soldiers who had dragged me out wore padded woolen coats on top of their woolen winter uniforms, but imagine what it was like to me—stark naked! They made me stand against a wall with my hands outstretched while they took turns pouring buckets of ice water down over me."

He smiled somewhat bitterly. "Perhaps they wished me to turn into a statue of ice, who knows?" His face regained its serenity. "For what seemed to me an eternity they did this. Soon I felt numb. I continued to fix my attention upwards to the heavens, watching the color change with the passing of time. When they had stopped this torture, the sky had become a pale blue with tinges of pink and light orange where the sun was struggling in its imperceptibly slow fashion to appear and signal the beginning of day. Then they dragged me, half-senseless, back to my cell. They left me lying in the middle of the cold cement floor. There was a tiny window in the cell, way up, almost to the level of the ceiling. As soon as their footsteps had become faint, I got up and started exercising, jumping up and down, flexing my muscles, getting my poor, nearly frozen blood to circulate once more. I did this not only then but all the other times, before the tortures and after them, no matter how weak I felt at the time.

"I am firmly convinced that this is what saved my life. Even the Japanese must have wondered how I could possibly survive their deviltry. Then one time"—he paused—"one time they made me kneel in front of my three inquisitors, who sat behind a long table, looking down at me with their hateful eyes. Behind me stood a soldier with his sword drawn and held within an inch of my neck. Once in a while he would let the cold steel touch my skin. I decided then and there, that if I had to die that I would die proudly. I thought of my great Russian heritage and you, my dear ones, all three of you. And I survived their devilish tricks!" He leaned his head against the wall. "But they thought of other ways to break me down," he said.

"They once placed me in a tiny cell. Inside it lay the most miserable Chinese man I've ever seen. He was in the last throes of tuberculosis. The poor old fellow was dying, coughing up more blood than I thought he could ever have in him! I believe their intention was to have me catch this disease too. That way they couldn't be censured if I died naturally. But again, there was a tiny window in the cell. I kept it wide open at all times, standing in front of it on my tiptoes. I did my exercises, breathing in that cold winter air. How good it felt! I even tried to make that poor devil more comfortable in his last hours of agony! Anyway, no matter what they did to me, I was able to pull through. The most difficult was the mental torture that they put me through. Thank God I had read enough of Chinese philosophy to let it take care of me. That, too, gave me strength! Through it all I never gave up hope; I was determined that I would live! I knew that I was innocent, that I'd live!"

He had talked enough. As quickly as he had started, he stopped. He was now ready to listen to Mama tell of her trials; then it would be my turn.

However, I suddenly realized how sleepy I had become. Mrs. Richardson would be wondering, again, what had happened.

"I'm going to my cabin," I told them sleepily. "We can talk some more tomorrow, but now that Papa's here, I want to go to bed and get a good sleep."

I embraced both of them, then walked quietly into the corridor, closing their cabin door softly. My cabin, thankfully, was empty. Mrs. Richardson apparently had found someone more compatible and friendly than I. For my part, I just wanted to be by myself for a little while so that I could think over the day's events and what Papa had recounted. I smiled as I gazed out the porthole down at the waves, a clear, bluish green, and thought of my precious jade bracelet. Everything was finally coming round to us Rublevs. God was in Heaven; all was right with the world!

15

On the High Seas

The MS *Tyozo Maru* was a beautiful small ship, and we enjoyed the luxury of traveling first class. The food was excellent. Fortunately, none of us became seasick, and we looked forward to mealtimes. After dessert and coffee, we always took a stroll around the deck, the three of us, arm in arm. The Yellow Sea was calm, or so it appeared to us, and we savored the wonderful sea air.

Gradually, Papa's pallor became less evident as the sun and wind swept over his face. He lay out on the deck chair, soaking in not only the sun's rays but also the air of freedom. Mama's cheeks too had taken on a rosy tint, without benefit of cosmetics. She and Papa were inseparable. I noticed a closeness between them that hadn't been there before, or perhaps it was just that I myself had matured and was looking at them now more as a happy, devoted couple than as my parents.

Early one Sunday morning we arrived in Kobe. After a sumptuous farewell breakfast, we joined the line of other passengers and debarked from the *Tyozo Maru*. Papa tipped the pleasant steward. Because Papa had spoken with him in his native tongue, he had been very attentive to our needs.

Father's attitude toward the Japanese puzzled me. I had expected him to be bitter, to avoid them, to treat them with reluctant courtesy, as I had decided to do. When I asked why he was so friendly to them after what they had done to him, he had, in his gentle manner, chided me.

"Don't judge people by what their government does," he told

263

me quietly. "The wrongs of a few don't discredit the multitude; remember that always, Tamara." His tone was emphatic. "I want you to think of the beauty that is in Japan when you see it. It is a country whose people love flowers and nature. They have expressed this with such mastery in their art and literature. Do not censure the Japanese people on my account. They are a hard-working, intelligent and sensitive people."

I listened to him, but I couldn't agree, although, of course, I didn't tell him that. For one thing, Papa hadn't been born in China; therefore, he didn't inherit that inborn antagonism towards the Japanese that somehow I had inherited. I couldn't feel friendly towards them no matter how beautifully they painted their landscapes or wrote their short-stanzaed poetry. I did admire their work, but the Chinese were more artistic, in my opinion. Anyway, I knew that the sooner we left their country, the happier I'd be. Forgive them? Yes, I had already done that. Forget what they had done to us? No!

With these thoughts in my mind I joined my parents on the pier in Kobe and promptly fell in love with this lovely city! We took pedicabs to the Pleasanton, which was described in our itinerary as "a first-class family hotel." As we rode through the streets, I contrasted it with my poor Peking. We had left a silent city, its beleaguered inhabitants hidden behind gray walls, afraid, sick, and starving. The streets we were riding on now were clean. The stores were full of colorful merchandise. Everywhere I turned I saw pots filled with yellow, lavender, or white chrysanthemums. Blaring from every radio in the open stores was music, haunting, melodic Japanese music, a magical blend of East and West. I had not heard Japanese music before, but right away, I liked it. There was one certain melody that was being broadcast everywhere we went. Initially we would hear it in one street, turn a corner, and the melody would continue on there. The refrain kept repeating itself in my mind. Even without a radio, I still kept hearing that catchy melody in my head. No wonder! When Papa asked his driver what the tune was, the driver told him that it was their national anthem. It followed us throughout every city that we visited while we were in Japan.

The people themselves, dressed in their colorful kimonos, rivaled the beauty of the flowers that grew in front of their homes or storefronts. They appeared happy as they minced their way through the streets, stopping to pass the time of day with their friends or shopping in the well-stocked stores. Their doll-like children clogged along beside them, holding on to the bottoms of their mothers' robes. Everything about these people was so pleasantly clean and picturesque that I was completely fascinated.

Henry Sanford's hotel was a large house built in Western style. He himself opened the door for us. He could easily have passed for Sidney Greenstreet, the well-known American actor, although he showed no sinister qualities insofar as I could see. He was a big man, dressed all in white, with florid cheeks and large blue eyes that constantly beamed.

"Come in; come in," he enthusiastically greeted us as he ushered us into the huge lobby. "I've been expecting you. The Bradfields and Fergusons are good friends of mine. They always stay with me when they visit Kobe."

He showed my parents into a big room containing two single beds, and other furniture; then led me into an adjoining room, smaller, but just as comfortable as the other. No wonder he called it the Pleasanton. Mama told him that we were planning to go shopping after we had freshened up. He gave us directions where we should go to shop.

"My place is right in the heart of the city, so you shouldn't have any problems," he told us. "And if, by some chance, you should get lost, just ask anyone where the Pleasanton is. They'll be able to tell you, because I've been here for thirty years."

We headed straight for a clothing store, where Papa was outfitted in a new, gray suit, shirt, tie, socks, shoes, and even a gray straw hat.

We then found a barber shop. Father, with tongue in cheek, told us that he had decided to look respectable once more. While he was getting trimmed, Mama and I walked around the area, having agreed to return to the shop within an hour.

When he finally came out of the barbershop, Mama and I couldn't believe our eyes. Papa looked completely different! Beardless, clean-shaven once more, and with his hair cut short, he looked like a much younger version of his former self. His eyes had lost their serenity; the old mischievous twinkle was there instead.

"Well," he asked us, turning around slowly like a store mannequin, "how do I look?"

Mama smiled, taking his arm. "Like you did years ago."

"And now," he said cheerfully, "we're going shopping for the two of you. We're not leaving Japan until you two get kimonos to wear in America."

Papa had regained his jaunty air and his sense of humor. He was pleased as Punch when we modeled kimono after kimono for him. Finally he chose a red one for Mama and a sky-blue one for me, as he put it, "to go with your strawberry-blonde hair. And now some 'koo-tsoo' for you also."

"What're they?" I asked curiously.

"Shoes," he laughed. "I want you and Mama to get shoes. Then some pretty hats. Since I look so snappy, my ladies also have to." He gave us both a gallant bow. We couldn't help smiling. Papa was having the time of his life.

Thus it was in Kobe that I got my first grown-up hat. It was a dainty little navy straw with a big silk rose in front. I perched it on top of my head, a bit to the side. It made me feel quite grown up. Papa, of course, was delighted.

"I can't get over her," he told Mama. "She has turned into a beauty. She's my American beauty rose!"

We spent a fortnight in Kobe. Papa soon regained his strength and some of his weight. It was a pleasant holiday. When we had visited ancient temples and various historic spots, we found out how right Papa had been. These Japanese were a most courteous and thoughtful people, so different from the ones we had encountered in Peking!

Leave it to me, though; I was still suspicious. One time we were walking over one of those picturesque bridges that are so plentiful in Japan. Two women, gaily dressed in their pretty kimonos, were walking towards us. As we were passing them, one of them stopped me and offered me a paper bag of candy.

I hesitated, even though they were smiling pleasantly.

"Take it," Papa told me.

I did as he told me. "*Arrigato*," I murmured, not too graciously, I'm afraid. They nodded cheerfully, smiling, giggling, and walked on.

"Papa, it may be poisoned," I said as he inspected it. "I sure wouldn't want to eat it."

He took one and bit into it. "Mm, it's good." He took another one and gave the bag to Mama. "They want to make us welcome," Papa explained. "That's their way. Eat one," he urged me.

In the late afternoon of May twenty-third our delightful sojourn in Japan ended. We boarded one of Japan's largest ocean liners, the MS *Hikawa Maru*. This ocean crossing was to be the giant ship's fifty-ninth trip to the United States and our first! Needless to say, we were all very excited when we stepped up from the gangplank to its deck. There were already quite a few people leaning against the ropes of the upper decks, waving down to friends at the pier or watching us and the other tourists and third-class passengers as we inched our way to the lower deck.

The steward led us past the milling crowds until he came to some gray steel stairs going downward. We followed him into the very narrow and hot corridor of the third-class compartments. I felt the pressure hit me as soon as we had reached that shiny gray area. It felt as if someone were holding something on top of my head, pressing it downward! There was also a most unpleasant smell about the whole area that, combined with the heat, made me sick at my stomach. I glanced at my parents. Papa was nonchalant as he briskly walked behind the steward. What Mama felt I didn't know, since I couldn't see her face.

The steward unlocked one of the small doors to his left and flung it open for us. Inside the tiny cabin were four narrow steel berths, quite different from our luxurious cabins on the smaller ship.

"*Arrigato*," Papa thanked the steward, bowing ceremoniously to him.

The steward smiled, showing his front gold tooth. "*Doitashi mashite*," he answered, bowing himself out.

"What was that?" I asked as I closed the cabin door behind me.

"If someone thanks you, that's what you answer," Papa laughed. "It means, 'Don't mention it.' "

Papa laid his new hat on one of the lower bunks and surveyed our small surroundings. "Well, ladies, here we are. We're on the first leg of our voyage to America."

It was close inside the cabin. Mama and I both took off our jackets, laying them on top of each other on the only straight-backed chair by the tiny sink. I inspected the cabin carefully.

"There's no bathroom," I exclaimed disappointedly.

Papa grinned. "There's probably one down the corridor," he told me. "Remember, Tamara, we're not traveling first class. We were lucky to have done that on our trip from Tanku." He then took off his suit, putting on the simple, white-and-blue cotton kimono he had bought in Kobe.

"We might just as well be comfortable here until dinner-time," he commented. He lay down on the lower berth and began reading the Japanese newspaper he'd bought before we had boarded the ship.

Mama smiled, giving me a secret wink. It was just like Papa to take everything in his stride. She, too, undressed and put on her red kimono. Papa looked at her admiringly.

"Verotchka, you certainly are beautiful," he said softly. He turned to me. "Why don't you put your blue one on and be comfortable."

"No, I think I'd rather go up on deck and see what's going on. Do you mind?" I asked. The pressure of the cabin was beginning to get to me. I was anxious to get some air before I passed out.

"Go ahead," agreed Mama. "Only don't get lost." She lay down on the lower berth across from Papa's, closing her eyes.

I walked out into the narrow corridor. The smell was awful. I had hoped it would disappear, but it hadn't. We must be near the galley, I told myself. I hurried on, almost running past the closed doors of the other cabins. I soon found the stairs to the upper deck. As soon as I reached it, I felt better.

Up here there were crowds of people. Some were standing in groups with their baggage beside their feet. Others strolled about, taking their "constitutional" or a leisurely walk, looking at everything and everyone, just as I was doing. Many were Chinese passengers; quite a few were Japanese. The latter were more formally dressed in Western outfits of the latest styles. I thought that they were rather important, like diplomats, just by the way they carried themselves.

Dorlise, still in Peking, sent me this photo of herself taken on October 30, 1939.

There were some foreigners too, but not too many. I looked to see if there was someone my own age. Unfortunately, they were either old, middle-aged, or mere children. I decided to walk around the deck.

Seeing these people, all happy and "at home" on this ship, gave me a lonely feeling. I went over to the rails and looked down at the deep waters that splashed against the sides of the big ship. Hearing the murmur of all those voices behind me made me wonder. Where were all these people going? Where were they coming from? Why? It all just seemed like one big orchestration of humanity: children yelling, mothers calling, businessmen talking, officers ordering, sailors answering, and the visitors hailing and yelling, every single one of them wanting to be heard. All this while the ocean waves sloshed gently against the ship's sides.

Then my thoughts turned to Dorlise; her big, brown eyes watching me, glowing with mischief. Oh, how much I missed her already! I hadn't thought that I would miss her this much. I recalled her on the station platform; seeing that rosy face and the forced smile as she waved and waved until our train had passed from her view. With her I had felt so sure of myself, so free! Without her I once more became another person—a lost, lonely Russian girl, homeless and very shy!

I walked back to the cabin, and sure enough my parents were sleeping soundly. I took off my clothes and climbed up in my slip to the upper berth, over Mama's. Finally I too dropped off to sleep.

The next morning the *Hikawa Maru* started on its journey to the United States. With the first lurch, Papa rolled in misery to face the wall of the cabin, hiding his face under the white sheets, pleading pitifully with us to let him alone. Mama did not last much longer. She left her berth only to stagger to the toilet a few steps from our cabin door. I was not seasick. I walked sailor fashion to the upper deck, where I made friends with a few of the other stalwart passengers. Together we commiserated about the poor souls who could not tolerate the roll and toss of this beautiful ship.

There were not many passengers who made their way to the dining room. Of course, my parents never even saw it! I brought them the ever-welcome grapefruit in the little cabin, but that was all that they dared eat, dipping the sharp little spoons into the centers, taking a few bites, then squeezing the juice onto their spoons, sipping it, and then sinking miserably back into their berths, their faces almost green with nausea. The steward brought them black coffee, which seemed to help.

As for myself, I tried to stay out of the cabin as much as possible, staying up on deck most of the time. Every hour or so I checked on them to see if they needed anything. Every time I entered, either one or the other would silently beckon to me weakly, pointing unsteadily toward the upchuck pan. I felt sorry for them; yet I stayed there for as short a time as I could, feeling myself growing nauseated at the sight of their misery. They had to keep their mouths closed tight to keep their vomit from spewing out. The steward gave them some pills, but even that didn't help. I put cold compresses on their foreheads. Then I had to leave to get fresh air. Only when the ship docked at Yokohama were they able to get up. Even then Papa seemed unstable on his feet.

We arrived in Yokohama on the thirtieth day of May and left that very same evening.

On the tenth day of June we came to Vancouver. All of us gathered excitedly at the railings, watching our ship dock. My parents, somewhat recuperated, were now able to take more nourishment than their daily diet of grapefruit and black coffee.

We watched the *Hikawa Maru* steam into the pier, where a large crowd was already waiting. Straining my eyes to look at them, I was startled to see that so many of them were foreigners. Most of the women wore white straw hats and white shoes, just like the missionary ladies of Peking did in summertime. But there were hardly any Oriental faces on the pier! Of course, how stupid of me! I had not really thought of that before, had I? I wouldn't be seeing many Asiatic faces from now on. I was no longer in Asia! The shoe was now on the other foot. I was the foreigner in this land, not they!

We had a few hours in Vancouver and that was enough. There wasn't much to see here by the pier and we didn't want to wander too far. We walked around, staring at the people and the few rather ramshackle homes on our way. The highlight of our walk was finding a drugstore.

It was large and well lighted, not at all like the dark, carbolic-smelling places in Peking where we used to buy our prescriptions. Dorlise had told me that they would be different, but I certainly had never expected this! We walked to the circular counter, where a pretty girl in a red and white smock over her dress served us ice-cream cones, with three scoops of ice cream each. Just like in my dreams!

When we walked back to our ship we found a letter waiting for us. It was from Mary Ferguson, written on the *Empress of Canada*, dated May the twenty-eighth, 1939, Kobe, Japan.

It was addressed to me. I read the letter to my parents, watching them beam in gratitude and remembrance.

Dear Tamara,

This short note must take the place of the glimpse I had hoped to have of you and your family either in Yokohama or in Kobe. Alas! We passed each other between these two ports. I was thrilled when I reached Yokohama yesterday morning to get a letter from Mr. Bradfield telling me you are all on your way to America. I have no words to express my joy at the knowledge that once more you are together and that you are now headed for a life which will seem worth living to each one of you. We will miss you as neighbors, but we are more than happy at the wonderful turn of events which are leading you to Cambridge. Truly, God is good, and surely you all deserve his goodness for the wonderful way in which you have each one in your own way borne adversity.

My warmest greeting and congratulations to your reunited parents and, to you, my love and best wishes for a good trip and a happy future. I hope your brother too will soon be on his way to America.

Always affectionately,
Mary Ferguson

With the good wishes of our good Peking friends warming our hearts, we endured one more day on the rolling Japanese ship till it finally docked in the beautiful white city of Seattle, where we would be introduced to life in America!

Part II
Cambridge, Massachusetts
June 1939–May 1944

16

At Last! My Promised Land

When we had landed in Seattle, the reality of the United States became more than I had ever imagined. From the railings at the *Hikawa Maru* we watched the great city materialize before our very eyes, its buildings modernistic and tall, its boulevards wide and impressive.

Our hotel covered almost an entire block. It was an immense, white building, some four or five stories high, with a wide circular porch on which high-backed, wooden rocking chairs, painted white, awaited tired travelers. We sat there after breakfast and watched our first American city awaken. I was completely fascinated by these well-dressed, well-fed citizens who strolled by on the sidewalks or drove past in their beautiful, shiny cars. Never in my life had I seen so many cars at one time. I could not believe that I was actually here in the United States. I felt like pinching myself to make absolutely sure that this was really not just another one of my daydreams.

All of a sudden it dawned on me that there was something else that was different. I missed the Chinese people who had been so much a part of my life. They were my countrymen, were they not? Subconsciously I still expected to see them as part of my life. I was used to their restful serenity, their unhurried, tranquil way of doing things. I realized then that I could not live in both worlds. When I had learned the customs and traditions of the United States, I would forever lose the sights and sounds of my China and its people.

The guests at the hotel were friendly, especially when they

found out that we had come from China. I found myself becoming the family spokeswoman. My parents had been used to hearing English as it was spoken by the British. The fast-paced, nasal, slangy American English was foreign to their ears. There were quite a few Americans at the hotel. Many of them were here on vacation from their own states. That confused me; America had so many states! I decided that states in the United States must be like the different provinces of China. I had a lot to learn about this strange and beautiful country.

Although my own ignorance bothered me, it was nothing as compared to that of my new-found friends. To my amazement, few Americans knew much about the Far East. Their knowledge was derived apparently from what they had seen in Charlie Chan movies.

"But you don't *look* Chinese!" was the standard answer when I told people where I had been born. "Are there blonde Chinese? But your eyes don't slant!"

Even more astonishing and shocking to me was the fact that most Americans did not even realize that China and Japan were at war! Was the Far East that isolated from the remainder of the world? These were some of the Americans' ideas about the Chinese that showed me how misinformed my new friends were: To begin with, the Chinese were either barbarians—sinister, yellow-skinned men with pigtails, who slinked along shadowy streets—or else silent, black-haired, poker-faced individuals, who stared impassively at the world through slanted eyes. They were mostly subservient men who took in dirty laundry and returned it all snow white, starched, and ironed to perfection! Listening to them, I became amused. Had I told them about my family's experiences of the past two years, I doubt if any of them would have believed my story. That, however, was no problem; Papa had given his solemn word to tell nothing! Neither would I!

Gradually we settled into what Papa once laughingly dubbed "our American way of life." Before we left Peking, Dr. Ferguson had warned Mama and me about the temptations to purchase everything in sight. He had emphasized, "When you arrive in the United States, you will find that you'll want to buy, buy, buy, especially in our five-and-ten-cent stores. *Don't,* I repeat, *don't buy!* Make that your motto. Otherwise, you will end up with a lot of junk, which eventually you'll throw out. Besides," he had chuckled to himself, "most of the stuff that Woolworth's sells comes from Japan anyway." In our Peking living room, Mama and I had smiled at his admonitions and promised that we could resist any temptations to buy.

In Seattle's large and colorful five-and-ten-cent store, however, we forgot his advice. We followed the happy, milling crowds and examined every counter, carefully inspecting the goods before us. Before we realized it, each one of us had become laden with small packages. Everything looked bright and attractive, but most of all, it cost so little. When we came back to the hotel we totaled our expenditures and were amazed that we had spent less than ten dollars! No wonder the Americans who came to China had so much. Who could resist buying at Woolworth's?

Even more fascinating to Mama and me were the dress shops. Mama had had her salon in Peking, and she had always sewed dresses for herself and me. To buy clothes in a store was a new adventure, and Papa urged us to go. "I want you to look American," he said.

While he rested and rocked on the hotel porch, Mama and I visited the dress stores. At one of them Mama found a black and white cotton dress that looked quite stylish on her. Before trying it on, however, she turned it inside out to examine the workmanship. "I can't believe it," she murmured sotto voce to me so that the saleswoman wouldn't hear. "It's beautifully made, and so inexpensive." She bought that and another dress that she thought Papa would like.

As for me, I couldn't make up my mind. Imagine! Racks and racks of dresses! I had never seen so many in my whole life. So many different styles! So many colors to choose from! It was mind-boggling; I tried several of them on and each one looked just perfect. The saleswomen who hovered over us were of no help. To her amazement, they called Mama "honey." "Is that an American custom?" she whispered to me. When they told Mama that I was a beautiful, young lady, she beamed even more. I selected two dresses. "I'd like to try on these dresses again," I told the saleslady.

"Why don't you take them both?" she asked sweetly. "They're both *you*."

How did she know? I finally decided on a two-piece outfit. It was a simple dress of white cotton with tiny, navy polka-dots. Over it went a coat of the loveliest, navy gauze. On it were white polka dots. I laughingly told the saleslady that this was *me*. I knew it would go with that navy straw hat that we had bought in Kobe.

Papa was delighted when we showed him our purchases. "*Now* you look American," he declared proudly.

We were sorry to leave Seattle but anxious to continue on with our journey. We boarded the long, shiny train that was to take us to Chicago on the first leg of our transcontinental trip. There, we were to board another train to New York City, then take our final train to Boston, Massachusetts. I couldn't believe that soon we would be in the city that would be our next home!

The American trains were luxurious. As Mama said, it was like being in her own living room.

We met some interesting people on the train. I found it easy to make friends here because people were so warm, easygoing, and sociable. Every American whom I had met so far had added to the growing store of knowledge I was collecting. I wanted to know everything about this wonderful country, mostly, about its people and their customs and traditions.

Among those we met were a mother and her children going to Chicago. Her two daughters were my age; their little brother was probably seven. We soon became friends, and all of us learned something.

In fact, when I told them that I was from China, Benjy, the young brother, had whistled. Later on, I learned that when Americans whistled it could either be a compliment or an exclamation of surprise; it all depended on the whistler. At times, it could be both.

"Oh, that's why you talk so funny," Benjy had exclaimed. "I thought you talked funnylike."

I couldn't tell them enough about my life in Peking, PAS, Vanya, Dorlise, and our daily activities. Even their mother laid down her magazine to listen. They all looked at me with awe as if I had stepped down from an outer-space vehicle or another planet! On my part, I asked them about their customs, their

278

interests, and their country. They were surprised when I asked them about their land, the United States. Their land to them was—well—it was home. *To them it is like an old shoe,* I thought to myself. It is comfortable and fits well, but not worth describing to strangers! They did know something about it, though. Each time we came to a new state they described it to me. When we passed through Idaho, they explained that this state was famous for its potatoes. It was strange to me that a state should be rated according to its potato crop.

When we had gone through endless, green potato fields, the landscape changed, and Marjorie, the elder sister, told me, "We're in Wyoming now."

I stared through my window, seeing wooly, white sheep, hundreds of them, grazing in the rich pastureland. From these pastures the train swept into the cornfields of Nebraska, past Iowa, and finally into Illinois. For days there had been nothing but endless fields—either lush green or yellow—for miles and miles around.

We talked about schools. They liked my description of PAS; they laughed when I told them about the French convent. When they started to talk about boys, I began to lose interest. To them, however, it was of utmost importance.

Janie was astonished to learn that I had never "dated." When I told them that I didn't even know what the word *dated* meant, even Benjy groaned in disgust.

"It means going out to the movies or for ice cream with a boy," explained Marjorie patiently. Both girls looked sorry for me, as if I'd missed something special in my life.

"Oh, my brother Vanya and I've gone to many affairs with boys," I told them. "I've known many boys, but to go out with them alone? I don't think I'd like that."

"You'll change your mind when you're asked," said Janie. "It's fun. With your looks you'll have no problems dating."

Even Benjy nodded vigorously at that. I smiled to myself. What if I told them that at fourteen I'd been proposed to by George An? *No, that won't do,* I cautioned myself. *Their idea of the Chinese is quite different from yours, Tamara.*

In a way I was disappointed in the girls. If all they thought about was dating boys, it was rather pathetic to me. They did not care about reading books; they knew nothing about classical music, nor were they interested. I was sure that in their eyes I, too, was quite ignorant! I didn't recognize one song that was being played on the train radio. In fact, one tune had been played so often that I was getting to like it. It was quite catchy, a rollicking, happy piece. Every time I heard it I had an urge to get up and start dancing.

Finally I asked them, and little Benjy told me, "That's *'The Beer Barrel Polka.'*" He grinned at my ignorance. "It's number one on the Hit Parade."

I was grateful to Janie for explaining to me what the Hit Parade was; I hadn't dared to ask *that*. To make our information exchange fair enough, I taught them some phrases in Chinese. They loved it!

"Now I see why you speak English the way you do," laughed their mother. "No wonder."

My most humiliating display of ignorance came quite suddenly. We had all been resting, reclining in our seats. It was nearly dusk. Most passengers had become glassy-eyed. There had been beautiful scenery, but after days of nothing but fields, no matter how picturesque, it had become tedious. Everybody was feeling tired, restless, and sleepy. I was too. In my mind's eye I was picturing all of the events in which we had taken part during these past few weeks. Then I thought of the comfortable berths on this train, how the swishing motion of the train as it noiselessly slid from one great American state into the next had lulled me to sleep. Effortlessly, it had brought us from those majestic states of the West, through the midwestern plains, toward the East. *What will Chicago be like?* I wondered. My new friends were going to visit their grandma there, they had told me. Soon, after New York, we would be taking our last train. Ah! All this traveling was fun, but it would be a relief to finally get to our new home.

A noise behind me jerked me up from my reveries. With a sudden shock, I felt, rather than saw, the enormous dark shadow of a person behind me. Mama, who was sitting across from me, had looked up; her eyes had grown larger. Suddenly, there appeared a look of alarm on her face. Already frightened, I turned around.

I shrank in horror from the apparition. Behind my seat, right in *back* of me, stood a giant. His huge hand rested on the back of my seat. I saw the immaculate white starched jacket he was wearing over black trousers. I looked at the huge, *enormous* black shoes at the side of my seat, towards the rear. Slowly I raised my eyes upwards. His head seemed to touch the ceiling of our coach, but it wasn't his height, nor his size, that made me scream out loud.

In China I had met many people from various lands. I had known Persians, Indians, Tibetans, Mongolians—even dark-skinned gypsies who roamed from city to city at different times. But this man was *different*. Seven feet tall, he had skin that shone like polished ebony! His teeth gleamed as he smiled down at me. His eyes resembled giant marbles, the black irises in stark contrast to the whites in his eyes.

Everybody was staring at *me,* not him! The giant moved forward, back into the aisle. Once in a while he rang a little bell. I watched him walk on to the next car, astonished at how graceful and fluid his movements were in spite of his size. Soon he disappeared into the next compartment.

The girls and Benjy were giggling. Even their mother had smiled at me. "Haven't you ever seen a Negro before?" Janie asked me.

I shook my head, ashamed of my behavior. "No. Are they all that big? And dark?"

Their mother laughed. "No, my dear. They come in all sizes, shapes, and forms. There are different shades, from darkest ebony even to white like us. You'll meet many Negroes here as well as Indians. We're the melting pot of the world."

I felt better then. Come to think of it, it was his size that had really frightened me. His color, once I got used to it, didn't matter.

Shortly after that, we arrived in Chicago, and I said good-bye to my new American friends and fellow passengers.

We had a few hours between trains, and Papa thought that it would be good for us to stretch our legs and see a bit of this famous windy city. We locked our small suitcases into two lockers at the train station, bought some ice-cream cones at a food counter, then walked out of the station into the city.

Perhaps if it had not been June and one of the hottest days of the year, we might have "loved" Chicago, as so many Americans had promised we would. Not so! The heat and dust of the city bore down upon us! We pounded those hot and sweltering pavements for two solid hours. All that we saw were gray streets, gray buildings, and hundreds of gleaming cars whizzing by us so fast that we barely glimpsed their drivers. Only a few people, who were as lost or crazy as us, walked in this heat. We soon returned to the station, where at least we could wait in some shade for our train to arrive.

After Chicago came New York. It was truly a magnificent, overpowering, and amazing city. We stared in wonder at the skyscrapers, ate with delight at the Automat, and visited the World's Fair.

Finally that momentous, long-awaited day dawned when we entered Grand Central Station to take our train to Boston! I was curious to see what these famous Bostonians would be like. Both Dr. Ferguson and Dorlise had said that they were different. We had met the friendly, generous midwesterners. New Yorkers had fascinated us, but they made up a melting-pot of nations with many traits and customs. What would the Bostonians be like?

Those who boarded the train were more reserved, I noted. In fact, they were very reserved and quite aloof! Were these the "proper" Bostonians? Could these be descendants of those historical figures I had read about? They were a quieter lot, more interested in their books or newspapers than in their surroundings. They certainly were not as outgoing as my midwestern companions had been. Not one person raised his head when we took our seats. Not one person even smiled in greeting.

I sat across from my parents and watched New York fade away from my window. Soon there were rolling hills with toylike, red brick houses scattered among them. Occasionally there were white church spires reaching out majestically towards the sky. We passed shipyards, mills, ironworks; large, brick factory buildings flashed by my window like a technicolor newsreel. How lovely it all is, I thought to myself. I smiled at my reflection in the glass. Tamara, you're coming home!

Soon we would be in Cambridge. I couldn't believe it. After all that had happened, after our long voyage across the Pacific

Papa's Passport Picture, May 1939

Papa—Cambridge, Massachusetts, September 1939

and the long train trip across the United States, we were finally coming to our new home: the land of the free and the home of the brave!

Now we were in Back Bay. It would not be long now. Passengers were getting up and standing in line in the narrow aisle. Soon it would be our turn. Our station would be next. I looked at my parents, noting Mama's flushed cheeks. *She, too, can't wait,* I thought. Papa, as usual, was engrossed in a book.

The conductor came down the aisle, looking to the right, then to the left. In a strange accent, he called out. "South Station, South Station. Last stop now. South Station." As the train slowed to a stop, I noticed the relief in the conductor's voice. I guessed that he, too, was happy to be going home.

Papa's mouth crinkled at the corners as he stood up, holding his valise and books. Catching my glance, he gave me a wink. "Well, my dear daughter, we're finally here. Are you happy?"

"Very," I answered. I got in line after Papa and Mama and the other passengers. We climbed down the steep steps of the train to the platform, which was already crowded. "I wonder who'll be there to meet us?" I whispered to Papa's back.

He turned his head around. "Don't worry. Someone will."

That was just like Papa. No matter what, things would turn out all right. Not to worry!

Sure enough, a tall Chinese man, dressed in a light-weight summer suit, was leaning against one of the platform columns, carefully scanning the oncoming passengers. When he saw us together, he moved forward, his hand outstretched.

"Professor Rublev?" he asked quietly. At Papa's nod, he continued, "I'm Dr. Chui from Harvard. The director asked me to meet you since he himself is out of town." He bowed to Mama, then smiled at me. "My car is outside. Let me help you with your bags."

Dr. Chui, we learned, as he drove us in his car, worked at Boylston Hall, which would be where Papa would work too. He was in charge of the Harvard-Yenching Library. As Mama and I sat in the back, we listened to his explanations, while eagerly taking in every bit of the scenery before us.

Boston was certainly a beautiful city, everything that Dr. Ferguson had described to us, and more. Most of the buildings were built of red brick. We passed several old graveyards, some old-looking churches with those beautiful, white spires. Our new friend pointed out the various buildings. There were many that belonged to history. I had not realized that Boston was such an important place, that so much of America's past had happened there. We were most privileged, Dr. Chui informed us, that we were going to make our home here. *We certainly are,* I told myself. What if we had had to live in Chicago? I shuddered involuntarily at the thought!

"Ah, there's our Esplanade," Dr. Chui pointed to a crescent building by the river. "That's where they hold many of our concerts," he explained. "Many of our students walk over the bridge in the evenings to listen. My wife and I enjoy the Pops. That's what we call the summer concerts. You sit on the grass, listen to the music, and watch the sailboats on the Charles. It's a wonderfully relaxing pastime." He looked at me through his rearview mirror. "I think that you would be interested, Tamara. Look on your left."

I looked towards the grassy slope. By the banks of the Charles sprawled two girls and a young man, engrossed in a book.

"How nice," I said, envying them already.

"You'll probably be doing that too one of these days," promised the librarian. "Students like to come here to study. It's peaceful and relaxing."

We were now entering Cambridge. I felt the excitement and strained to see everything. Dr. Chui pointed to the modern gray buildings. "That's the Massachusetts Institute of Technology," he told us. "MIT for short. There's a treasure of brains in this place. The finest scientific scholars can be found here."

"What about Harvard?" I asked him.

He laughed pleasantly, his amused eyes again eyeing me in his mirror. "Harvard is an institution that stands by itself. There is no other place like it in the United States. There never will be. There; look over yonder and you'll see what I mean." He pointed to a cluster of red-bricked buildings with rectangular chimneys on their rooftops. It was not at all what I had expected.

"*All this* is Harvard?" I asked Dr. Chui.

"All this and more," he chuckled. "And now we're coming to

Harvard Square. This is really the nucleus of Cambridge. This is where everything begins. That is," he hastened to add, "for those connected with the universities. Here's where the intellectuals meet." He slowed down, then parked beside a curved red brick wall. "I thought, Professor, that we'd stop for a moment to see where you'll be working this September," he explained.

He led us through an arched, black wrought-iron gate. Red brick buildings towered on all sides, some of them looking older than the others. In the Yard itself there were long walks criss-crossing each other in various directions. Trees shaded the Yard. Students were everywhere. Young men with evergreen book bags slung over their shoulders loped quickly along on the sidewalks, their heads bent thoughtfully downward.

"They walk so strangely," I said. "Why do they walk like that?"

"You are quite observant, young lady." He stopped for a moment. "Most students develop this gait from having to hurry from one class to another. Many classes are in different buildings and time is always valuable to a Harvard man. Since it is undig-nified to run, they lope instead. *That* fast walk has become known as the 'Harvard Stride.'" I found it intriguing to watch Harvard men as they strode by us.

Dr. Chui next pointed out Widener Library. There were even more students there, most of them laden with books. Some were on their way up to the library, mounting each third step with an easy lope. Others lightly tripped downward. Some stood, thoughtfully surveying the Yard. To each side of the steps was an enormous rectangular platform. Some students were perched on these, their long legs dangling over the edges. Dr. Chui chuckled.

"These steps and platforms," he commented, "are a favorite trysting spot for our students and the Cliffies."

"Cliffies? What are they?" I asked. Mama was curious too.

"That's another name for the girls enrolled in Radcliffe Col-lege. It's on the other end of Harvard Square," he explained. "I'll take you there one of these days." He gave me a friendly appraisal. "You look to be of college age, Tamara. Perhaps you'll decide to go there. It's one of the best women's colleges around."

I smiled hesitantly; I hadn't even thought of college for

myself. How could I when I hadn't even been able to finish eighth grade?

Across from Widener stood an unusual building with white columns and a graceful white spire. It was like many of the New England churches we had seen.

"And that building?" I couldn't believe that there would be a church on university grounds.

"That's Memorial Church," he answered. "Many of our students get married here. Now," he said, looking significantly at Papa, "let's walk over to that gray building with the green doors. See it, Professor? Way off to the right?"

We strolled leisurely down the tree-lined walk. To the left of this building stood a huge stone tortoise with an immense rectangular stone rising from its back. On its smooth surface were carved some Chinese inscriptions. Papa paused, silently reading the characters.

The Chinese was pleased. "Ah, you recognize our eighteenth-century tortoise," he said. He turned to me. "Do you know what this stylized tortoise means?"

Shamefully, I had to admit that I didn't.

"Well, this is a symbol of stability, something," he bowed courteously to Papa, "that I hope will now be a part of your own lives. This tortoise is holding up the foundations of the universe. Interesting, isn't it?"

Dr. Chui mounted the steps, reaching out for Mama's arm. "Now, this is Boylston Hall," he informed us. "This is where you and I will be working. We won't go inside now. I'm sure you're all tired after your long trip. We'll go back to the car now, and I'll take you to the rooms in the tourist home that we have rented for you. I'm sure you'll be comfortable there until you find a more permanent residence."

The next few days we spent walking around Cambridge. Our temporary quarters in the tourist home were pleasant enough, but we, especially Mama, were anxious to get settled.

Cambridge captivated the three of us. The old homes, the wide streets lined with shady trees, the historic Cambridge Commons—we liked everything about this charming town. It was also well designed, as Papa soon informed us. Its wide main thoroughfare, Massachusetts Avenue, extended all the way from one end of Cambridge to its outskirts. Off "Mass Ave,." as the locals called it, were the side residential streets, which were shaded by enormous elm and maple trees.

In a week Mama had found a house that she liked and that met with our approval. After looking at several houses, she decided on this one; it was not too far from Harvard, and was located in a pleasant-looking neighborhood with well-kept lawns.

Dr. Chui had suggested that Mama shop in Central Square for furniture. "Nathan's Used Furniture Store is the best," he said. "My wife and I have found that his prices are fair." He had grinned when he said that. "You'll find out soon enough for yourself. You see, the only similarity between Central Square and Harvard Square is that they're both 'squares.' Central is the impoverished relative of Harvard Square, but it's an interesting place."

Central Square delighted Mama, especially Nathan's. Mr. Nathan himself was a pleasant, sweet-faced man who, he told Mama, had been born in Odessa. Mama, in her youth, had visited there and knew it well. Finding that they had something in common made Mr. Nathan more talkative. He confided to us that his parents had fled the *pogrom* to seek their fortune in this land of the free. Mama had nodded in sympathy. She too had fled a kind of *pogrom*, she told him. They took to each other immediately; yet both were canny enough to know that the other was astute, clever, and probably quite adept at bargaining. Mama surveyed the contents of his store, storing in her mind the furniture she wanted to purchase without even giving him a clue. He in turn studied her every movement, noted the direction of her inspections, and calculated in his mind how high he would be able to raise the price without her balking. When they finally started to fence around the prices, they both gained a mutual respect for each other. Eventually, to my relief they reached an agreement. In the meantime, each had enjoyed the bargaining process; it had taken much thought; it was courteously done with each one appraising the other. Of course, Mama had learned from the best. Who could outwit a Chinese vendor? But Nathan was Jewish, and he had been learning the tricks of his trade from childhood.

In the end Mama firmly believed, as she told me in a whisper, that she had won the bargaining duel. Mr. Nathan had wrung his hands, telling her that she was bankrupting him. And she, gentle soul that she was, thanked him for his discount but teasingly reproached him for robbing her. Truth to tell, both of them had won. It was a fair fight, in my opinion. She purchased all her furniture from his store; he gave her a substantial discount and delivered the furniture to boot.

The first time that Mama visited a supermarket became a landmark in our lives. Mama discovered canned foods! It is impossible to describe her elation when she found that by simply opening a can of food, dumping it into a pot, and heating it, she could place a complete meal on our table, and, *mirabile dictu,* in no time at all! Canned foods became a godsend to her, especially since she was busy putting our apartment in order. By the time we all were settled in, she had become accustomed to her American kitchen. Gradually, she even began to cook on her own, buying the fresh vegetables and fruit which she had ignored in the beginning. Within several months, she had become an excellent cook. That was quite an accomplishment for her, since she had never used a stove or cooked a complete meal in her entire life until we had arrived here.

One day Papa brought home a letter he had received at the office. "It came just as I was leaving so I haven't opened it, but it's probably from Dr. Ferguson. It's from Peking." He had squinted, trying to make out the name of the sender. "I can't make out who sent this," he said, rather puzzled. "The handwriting is so minute that I can't read it." He handed it to me. "Your eyes are better. Read it to us."

I recognized the handwriting immediately. "You are right; it *is* from Dr. Ferguson," I exclaimed, happy that we finally had a letter from our friend. "He's probably writing about Vanya." I hoped so. We hadn't heard from my brother since our arrival in Cambridge, and I knew that my parents were worried. Dorlise and other friends had written, but Vanya had remained silent.

I scanned the letter, dated June 20. Papa and Mama were seated comfortably on the sofa, ready to listen to me read the unfamiliar English. "Well, go on," Papa urged.

"It's addressed to you, Papa." I began to read it out loud:

Dear Professor,

It was good news indeed to learn from your colleagues that you had arrived at your destination and that you were happy to be there. I can imagine your feelings when you saw your future home actually in front of you and realized that your long nightmare had ended. You will have received a warm welcome and hearty wishes for success in your new work, in which you will be able to forget the things that are behind and press forward to your new goal. I sent the telegram along at once to your son who was in the midst of packing and sorting the things in your former home, and as soon as I was free I went over to share his joy over the receipt of the news of your arrival. He was overjoyed when he heard that all of you liked Cambridge so much. Vanya has been quite busy tending to odds and ends, as well as saying good-bye to all his friends.

I have been helping your son clean up the house. We had packed and sent to the ex-Austrian Legation, (where Harvard-Yenching Institute still has books), all of your books and manuscripts. They can stay there until you send for them. I imagine that when you find what small quarters most people in America have for living and what splendid facilities for libraries are available to you, you will decide to have only a few of these books sent to you, but of course this is certainly a question for you to decide. The general books for children both in English and French I am sending to the American school, and the books in Russian I am trying to sell.

Your son is leaving here early in July so as to catch the MS *Hikawa Maru* leaving Kobe on the eighteenth. It will not be long after the receipt of this letter that you will once again be a united family, thank God.

I sent you a copy of my new "Catalogue of Recorded Bronzes," which I hope you will like.

My best regards to your wife and yourself and a kiss on both cheeks for Tamara.

> As ever,
> John C. Ferguson

I was pleasantly surprised that American homes were so open, not walled in like Chinese homes. Mama thought it strange. Every evening she would go from room to room, lowering shades.

"I do like Americans," she explained to me, when I asked her why she was doing that, "but I certainly don't want them to look into my life. Just look out right now. I have a feeling that many of these people have nothing better to do except sit on their porches and look in their neighbors' windows. They're good, kind people, but I like my privacy!"

In my room I kept the shades up because I enjoyed looking out to see what was going on. Not only that, but Margie Reynolds, my new friend, lived directly across from us.

Her mother owned a beauty parlor in Somerville, the township next to us. She was a tall, buxom, bleached blonde who had come to visit us on the first day we had moved in, an unwilling Margie at her heels.

She and Mama had exchanged pleasantries, while Margie and I sat and stared, sizing each other up. The next day, Margie had come over alone, and we became friends. She was fifteen, a slimmer and prettier copy of her mother. I thought her quite attractive; she reminded me of Ginger Rogers, the movie star.

To my dismay, Mama had not warmed up to either of the Reynolds women. "A girl fifteen shouldn't wear lipstick and mascara," Mama had declared. "Don't get ideas into your head, Tamara, just because Americans do that."

In three months I would turn eighteen. The only makeup I had used was a bit of Mama's rouge for my cheeks.

"It's the custom, Mama." I felt that she was making too swift a judgment. "American girls wear makeup. They did that at PAS too. Margie is a very nice girl, and we've become good friends."

Mama nodded. "She probably is. I just don't want you to get ideas in your head. You don't need makeup. You understand?"

"Yes, Mama." I reluctantly agreed.

Margie thought that I was pretty. That's the first time anyone had told me that. She took me around the neighborhood, introducing me to her friends, taking me to the little Italian grocery store around the corner. There were some boys our age loafing around a Coke machine outside the store. They had whistled at us as we were going inside.

"Why do they whistle like that?" I asked her curiously.

She gave me a strange look. "They like us; they think we're cute, nice-looking," Marjorie answered. She had carelessly tossed her blonde head around when we passed the group, looking straight ahead, completely ignoring them. I had looked at them, though rather shyly. They were just young boys, full of mischief, I decided. When one of them winked at me, I smiled.

"Tamara, don't pay any attention to them."

"Why? Why didn't you say hello to them?" I asked her.

"This store, Benidetto's," she explained, "is where most of the neighborhood kids hang out. Here is where the boys try to pick up girls."

"Pick up girls?" I hadn't heard that expression before.

She stared at me in amazement, then laughed. "I guess I'm going to have to look out for you," she explained. "Boy, are you naive!"

At Benidetto's we bought three-tiered ice-cream cones for a nickel apiece and licked them all the way home. Margie told me about her school, the Cambridge High and Latin School.

I was delighted. "Why, that's the school I'll be attending," I told her. "Mama and I went to see the assistant principal, Mr. Bliss, the other day. He suggested I try the senior class."

By then we were quite settled in Cambridge. Papa had walked to his office several times and met his associates. He was anxious to start work in September. I was eager to start school. It had been a surprise when Mr. Bliss had suggested senior class. I had told him what I had studied at both PAS and the convent. He had questioned me about literature and my knowledge of languages, and that's when he made that recommendation.

"If you feel uncomfortable with it, you can always try the junior class. I doubt though," he patted my shoulder lightly, "that you'll have any problems."

More and more, Cambridge delighted me. The atmosphere was so friendly. People waved to each other in Harvard Square, talked to strangers, helped each other with packages or books. Mama, normally shy, blossomed with this friendliness. She made friends with the wives of Papa's associates, as well as some university wives who spoke Russian. Among them was the wife of a Harvard physics professor, Hania Frank. Annitchka, as I came to call her in time, came to be one of my good friends as well. She and Philipp had no children of their own. I found her an easy, understanding adult to talk to. Mama, although gentle, was too reserved and proper for me to be able to be at ease with her or to question her about attitudes or behavior. Also, Mama was a stranger here; Annitchka had lived in America since she became a bride, many years ago. She liked young people and knew how to talk to them. She became like an aunt to me, and I became like the daughter she never had.

Our otherwise happy existence was marred by the fact that we had heard so little from Vanya. Since our arrival we had received only two letters from him. The first one had been written a week after our departure from Peking and informed us how hard he was working at packing up Papa's library. As a postscript to me he mentioned that he was having a fabulous time with his friends, especially the Hus. His second letter had been even shorter. In it he reported he would be leaving Kobe on the eighteenth of July, and please would we buy about ten pounds of chocolate bars for him and as many Del Monte products as possible. This was the sum total of his correspondence to us. Had it not been for Dr. Ferguson, Dorlise, Dr. Bradfield, and others, we would have thought that Vanya had vanished without a trace from the face of the earth!

No wonder Mama was worried. Then, thankfully, on the eighth day of August, I received this letter from another wonderful friend, Dr. Bradfield.

Dear Tamara,

It has been nice to receive your messages from points along your route to Cambridge. Before me now are your letters of June 27th and July 8th from Cambridge. By the time you receive this reply, your brother will be with you, and I can imagine how happy all of you will be. Your brother had written to me from Kobe on July 30th. He had left by the time your July 8th letter with the check enclosed reached me, so I consulted with Miss Ferguson regarding the use of the money. It appears that Dr. Ferguson had taken care of the small accounts and has written fully to your father. He does not want the check and suggests that I return it to you. I have endorsed it over to your father. It is enclosed.

Mrs. Bradfield has returned from a month at Peitahe Beach and looks fine. I was there during the first half of July. The heat here in Peking for the past three weeks has been fierce. We shall be glad for cooler weather so that we can sleep better.

We send you all our best wishes and shall look forward to seeing you on our next trip to Boston a year or so hence.

Sincerely,
Vergil Bradfield

Mama had been somewhat comforted. Then, a few days later, we received a telegram from Vanya. Papa chuckled to himself as he proceeded to read it aloud to Mama and me.

WILL ARRIVE BOSTON SOUTH STATION NINE AM EST MONDAY TWENTY FIRST STOP HAVE PLENTY OF MONEY STOP RECEIVED LETTERS STOP SPENDING NICE TIME AT VANCOUVER STOP SENDING BAGGAGE THROUGH BONDED SHIPPER STOP HAD LOVELY FAREWELL PARTY AT PEKING STOP SAW TOKYO YOKOHAMA SHIPS POET STOP VANYA STOP

"Well," Papa said, putting the telegram down, "once again we'll be one family, Verotchka." He rubbed his nose thoughtfully. He always did that when he wanted to mask his actual feelings, I recalled. Poor Papa, for him it had been a long time since he'd seen Vanya.

Monday morning we were at South Station at eight o'clock. Papa had fortified himself with books and the *Boston Globe*. Mama had filled her large purse with chocolate bars. I was empty-handed, but still excited about seeing my brother. I wondered if he had changed at all. I hoped so.

The train screeched to a stop; we scanned the faces of the arriving passengers and finally saw him. He was easy to spot.

Poor fellow! He was loaded down with books and a small, battered suitcase. He looked pale and quite unhappy as he struggled down the steps. As he landed on the platform he shifted his weight and glanced out at the milling passengers. Narrowing his eyes, he bit his lips, worried.

Mama laughed happily. "Look! There he is! Poor Kocya, he's all confused." She ran to him, mindless of the people around her.

"Kocya, my darling!" Her eyes glistened with tears as she wrapped him and his books in her arms.

When he saw her, his smile of recognition lit up his face. "Mama!" He hugged her tightly, then stepped back to look at her.

"Why you look wonderful, Mama!" he stammered. "What's happened to you?"

She positively glowed. "Am-yer-ika," she said softly.

Papa had come up to them. He had watched the two of them, his eyes blinking away the tears. His son was taller than he was; although it was now he who looked good, not Vanya.

"Vanya, it's good you've come."

"It was quite a trip, Papa, quite a trip."

And then he looked over at me. I could see him become tense. Then his face broke into a wide smile. "Ah, Tamara! Hey, Old Pal, it's good to see you. I see the good ole U.S.'A. has been good to you. You've gained a few pounds, but don't worry, you still look okay."

Papa laughed cheerfully. "She is our American beauty, isn't she? Well, Vanya, feel these muscles, will you?"

In the crowded station Vanya shifted his books to feel Papa's muscle. Then, as he always did, he rolled his eyes heavenwards and marvelled in an awed undertone, "Amazing, Papa, absolutely amazing! Those muscles feel like marble!"

I couldn't help smiling to myself. God bless America! We were finally here, together once more, in this unbelievable land of my dreams. One family, one firm unit. No matter what, we could now face the world with new confidence. We were free!

Mama by the Statue of John Harvard at
Harvard University

The First Home Mama and Papa Rented—16 Carver Street

17

Cambridge: A New Beginning

Precisely at twelve-thirty P.M. Papa strode into the kitchen, folded his jacket over his chair, and sat down. "Well, Mamotchka, and how was your day?"

"Good." Mama sounded pleased with herself. "I went to Nathan's this morning and bought a studio couch for Vanya's room." She set a bowl of soup in front of Papa. "Watch out; it's hot."

"Nathan? Who's he?" Papa hadn't heard his name before.

"He's the second-hand furniture dealer in Central Square. Bless Annitchka Frank. The other day at the Faculty Club I was complaining to her about Harvard Square's prices. That's when she told me about Central Square. Everything there is cheaper." She buttered a slice of white bread and passed it on to Papa. "Nathan's a good man. Came from Odessa originally. He's Jewish."

Papa chuckled. "So Mamotchka buys furniture from Nathan because she knows how to bargain. Eh? Tell me. Who gets the better deal, you or Nathan?"

"I do, of course, Serioja." Mama pretended to be annoyed. "He always insists that I've robbed him."

Papa and I laughed, but not Vanya. He just sat at his place, glumly scowling down at his plate. Come to think of it, he'd been rather quiet lately, brooding about something.

"Kocinka, what's wrong?" Mama eyed him anxiously.

Papa put down his soup spoon. "It's no use, Ivan," he snapped, his tone unusually harsh. He turned to Mamotchka.

297

"The Cambridge High and Latin School headmaster has suggested to me that Vanya repeat his senior year even if he is a graduate of PAS. He'll then be better prepared for taking the College Boards and entering Harvard. That is, if he passes." Papa scowled at Vanya. "Just because I work at Harvard doesn't necessarily mean that you'll get in, Vanya. You have to work for it."

So that's what the trouble was. I stared at Vanya's flushed cheeks and sensed his inner turmoil. When his angry gaze shifted to me, he startled me. "She," he almost spat the word out, "hasn't even finished the eighth grade, Papa. She will be in class with me. It's an insult; that's what it is."

I hadn't expected his outburst, but I should have. No matter what, it always had to be my fault.

Papa rose from his chair. "Tamara has nothing to do with it. You say you want to go to Harvard. All right. It's up to you to get accepted, and I'll pay your tuition. If Tamara gets into Radcliffe, I'll pay hers. But I won't support you otherwise." He turned to Mama, his voice softening, "Mamotchka, waken me at one-thirty; I have to be back at Harvard at two."

When Papa had gone, Mama tried to reason with Vanya. "Papa's right, you know. You're young. You have your whole life before you, Kocinka. Another year in school will prepare you well for the College Boards and college. I'm told the Boards are difficult."

"But, Mama, it's because of her—"

"No, Vanya." Mama laid her hand on his. "Tamara will have to study as hard, if not harder. I'm tired of you comparing yourself to her." She pointed her finger at him. "Remember that you are two individuals, as different from each other as night and day. Now stop it; stop this senseless bickering."

After that set-to, I avoided Vanya as much as possible. Something in his nature, some strange quirk in his character, made him resent me. For the life of me I couldn't fathom why. Even as a toddler in Peking I had sensed his hatred, beginning with that long-ago, moonlit night when Mama had left us alone in the guest-house bathtub. I could still feel his hands upon my head, pushing me down, down into the water. He had tried to drown me then; I was firmly convinced of that. No use trying to

298

figure him out; he was Mama's Kocinka. The best thing for me was to let him be.

September came, time for school. Vanya and I both entered the senior class at the Cambridge High and Latin School. In my wildest imagination I had not realized how large American schools were, nor that in one school there could be several senior classrooms, each with a different teacher. Both Vanya and I were delighted to find that we had been assigned separate teachers.

I had not attended a regular school since I had left the convent school in Peking at thirteen. To be at CHLS was an overwhelming experience; it was amazing to be among so many young people. I had to adjust to my new teachers, choose the right courses, and attempt to find my assigned classes in what was to me a monumental maze of doors, corridors, stairways, and corners, crowded from end to end with teeming teenagers. Even more surprising was that I myself would turn out to be a curiosity. I unwillingly found myself the cynosure of inquisitive, friendly peers who scanned my face as if I was some extraordinary alien from another planet.

"Wherever did you learn to talk like that?"

"Like what?" I asked them, in amazement.

"Your accent. Where'd you get it?"

I hadn't realized I had one. "China, I guess." More and more curious they became, hemming me in.

"No, I'm not Chinese."

"Oh, then your parents must have been missionaries."

"No, Papa, I mean *Dad* [I tried to sound American], is a sinologist."

"A what?"

One answer led to another question and still others. They had never met anyone like me. I had never been interviewed so mercilessly. I finally developed a few pat answers. "Sinologist" was not one of them. From then on, my father had just been transferred from Peking to Harvard. They could accept that. It soon dawned on me that the parents of many of my American classmates had emigrated here from foreign countries. Denise had a Greek-sounding surname. At roll call I heard names like O'Shaunessy and O'Brien, de Roode, and Denaro. And Loretta!

Loretta Ciani, daughter of Italian immigrants, took it upon herself to guide me through that bewildering year.

"Don't worry, Tamara!" Her radiant smile wrapped me round with security. "Things will get better. You just have to get used to us."

That's what Papa had assured me too.

"But why do people think I'm so different? I feel frustrated knowing that. I want to blend in with all of you, to be like you."

She had put her arm around me then. "You will," she assured me. "Don't feel bad that they think you're different. You have a cute accent." (Everything was *cute* in America.) "You have a British accent, but it's sing-songy, sort of. Didn't you tell me you'd gone to an American school in China?"

It turned out as Loretta had predicted. In a short time I got used to school in America. Everything went well, except for Mr. Sullivan's American history class.

It wasn't Mr. Sullivan's fault. The tall, round-faced Irishman was an ideal teacher—patient and interesting. He had an almost unexplainably delightful talent of being able to keep his students' rapt attention. As I explained it to Papa, it wasn't my fault either, since I had no idea of what had gone on in American history.

"Papa, I know English history from Alfred the Great down to the present, but this American stuff! . . . " I felt the lump in my throat.

Papa calmed me down. "It appears too much for you now because it's all new. I suggest you take it one day at a time. If you need extra reading material, I can get you books at Widener. You've always come through in the past, no matter what, my *dochenka* [little daughter]. *Ootro vetcherom mudrenyee"* (Morning is wiser than evening), he smiled, as he quoted one of his favorite proverbs. "I suggest you get to bed early; then you'll be fresh and ready for tomorrow's class."

I thanked him then for making me feel somewhat better, although I realized that I still had to solve this problem myself. I had to know American history backward and forward, and I hadn't yet taken even one step forward!

As it turned out, Papa didn't even have to get me extra

studying material. One day after history class, Mr. Sullivan showed that he had been well-aware of my frustration.

"You're having a difficult time with our American history, aren't you, Tamara?" He embarrassed me as he smiled and stood by his desk, studying me.

"I have a suggestion," he offered sympathetically. "I know how much it means to you to enter Radcliffe and how conscientious you are. There're no problems in your other classes, are there?"

I shook my head.

"Good," he paused, then rubbed his hands together. "Well, your only problem then is history. We'll have to take care of that, won't we?"

I nodded, not knowing what else to do.

Again, he scrutinized my face, trying to figure me out, to see just what I was made of. Had he asked me outright, I'd have told him of experiences such as he'd never known, knowledge of a very different culture, naive innocence of the facts of life, and an overwhelming ignorance of American history. Nothing like that happened; I remained painfully silent, and he could only guess.

"Well, now," he said, leaning forward toward me, "I've come up with a plan, Tamara. If you are willing to do some extra, intensive study, we'll surely pull you through. However, it'll take hard work," he warned me.

Had he not been a teacher, I'd have hugged him in gratitude. Instead, I smiled and smiled, ecstatic over my good fortune.

Then followed three solid months of intensive study and drill. Finally, I began to know American history backward and forward. In class discussion, if Mr. Sullivan turned his penetrating blue eyes towards me, I no longer got flustered or confused but usually came up with the correct answer. My classmates were amazed at my progress. When it came time to take the College Boards, I passed with flying colors, thanks to a very patient and most persistent Irishman.

Not only did I pass the College Boards, but I was also accepted for enrollment in Radcliffe College. To top it off, my friend Loretta had been accepted there as well. It seemed as if the whole wonderful world were smiling with me!

Little did I know that in another part of this wonderful

As a Radcliffe Freshman

Phyllis as a Bridesmaid

world of mine an unimpressive little man with a tiny square mustache was already planning to upset everyone's world. While I had been struggling to pass the College Boards, Adolf Hitler was taking his first steps towards eliminating the Jews in Europe. When I had first entered the Cambridge High and Latin School, his German armies had already invaded Poland. Six months later they had conquered Denmark, Norway, Holland, Belgium, and France.

However, this was all happening in Europe; these events seemed of little importance in America. As far as we were concerned, everything everywhere was "fine and dandy" (as Americans would say). We had a strong, determined, blue-blooded president who was taking care of us. Our America was in good shape. And we, in general, had little to worry about.

Family-wise, we couldn't complain. Papa liked working in the Harvard-Yenching Institute, Mama was studying to improve her English, and Vanya and I were entering two prestigious American colleges. For me, it was the *ultimate*. I couldn't wish for more.

When you stop to think about college, it is more than the completion of your official education for life. It is also the socially approved institution where you meet peers who become important in your adult life. In such a way did I meet Phyllis Olsen, who became an important link between my girlhood and adult years. She, more than any of my other peers, opened my eyes to the world around me. She called a spade a spade, no cigarette butts about it!

I first met Phyllis in Prof. Howard Mumford Jones's English I class. The cavernous lecture hall had been overflowing with chattering freshmen, brand-new notebooks clasped to their cardiganed breasts, eyes bright with anticipation, voices one octave above normal.

"Mind if I sit here?" The girl's blonde hair covered her face as she bent towards me.

"No, not at all." When I heard her husky voice, I inspected its owner more curiously. She was shifting her books from one arm to the other, trying to balance herself in the narrow space between the seat rows. She finally managed to sit down in the seat next to mine, plopping her books down on her lap. Holding one end of her jacket sleeve in her mouth, she worked at wriggling out of her jacket. Her books kept easing out of their nesting place.

"Here, let me help you." I grabbed for her books.

"Jeez," she huffed, "thanks a lot. Whew!" She turned to look at me, flashing me a smile. "I almost missed my darned bus." She smoothed out her skirt. "And to think that I'm going to have to do this every day. Jeez!"

I glanced over at her. She seemed a good sort. "Where're you from?" I whispered. I realized that the hall had quieted down. Most of the girls were seated.

"Quincy. Know where that is?" Her eyes were green. I'd never seen anyone with green eyes before.

I shook my head.

"Heck! It's about fifteen miles from here. That means I'm going to have to get up earlier than usual, gosh darn it." She groaned in good humor. "Oh well, it could be worse. One of life's great but minor tragedies, eh?" She smiled, surveying the great lecture hall. "Jeez, it's pretty crowded, isn't it? I hear old Jonesy-

boy is a tough one. Oops,"—she put her hand on my wrist—
"speak of the devil. The great man cometh!"

Silence shrouded the room as we all focused our eyes on the
tall, bespectacled man advancing toward the podium.

This English I class was to be my introduction to what went
on in college. We received a long lecture on what we were
expected to do, what to learn, and what to produce. Needless to
say, our mood was much more subdued at the end of the lecture.

When Professor Jones had folded his notes and left, Phyllis
and I silently gathered our books and walked out of class toward
Harvard Square.

"Let's stop at Hood's," Phyllis suggested, as we neared the
popular malt shop. The place was full of mostly Cliffies, who bab-
bled in excited, high-pitched voices, exchanging phone numbers
and discussing their classes and the professors.

Phyllis anxiously surveyed the room and then signaled for
me to follow her. "Good thing I'm tall," she chuckled. She spoke
in a husky, low-pitched voice.

We were fortunate to find an empty table by the window
overlooking Brattle Street. As soon as the waitress had taken
our orders, we relaxed. I looked through the plate-glass at the
passersby, most of them Cliffies or Harvard men with their green
bags slung over their shoulders.

Phyllis followed my gaze. "Gives me a good feeling to be a
part of all this." She narrowed her eyes thoughtfully, then looked
down. "Doggonit," she muttered, rummaging through her purse,
"I did bring them, I know."

Suddenly, with a huge sigh of relief, she fished out a pack of
cigarettes. "My Lucky Strikes," she cleared her throat, "I can't do
without them. Want one?"

"Thank you, but I don't smoke."

She lit her cigarette, then blew out the match. "You said you
lived in China, didn't you?"

"Yes." I then gave her my standard brief explanation of how
we came to be here in Cambridge. She seemed fascinated.

"I never realized that China and Japan were at war. I guess
it's because it's all so far away. We're safe in our own little world,
I guess, huh?" She acted as if she were embarrassed by her own
ignorance.

"I can understand your not knowing about the situation in the Far East." I told her. "If it weren't for the letters that we get, we wouldn't know what's going on over there either."

"Are your friends there okay?"

I thought of Dorlise and the Fergusons. "I don't honestly know, Phyllis." It dawned on me then that I had been so involved in my own problems here that it had been months since I'd heard from either of them. "Thanks for reminding me. I've got to write to them again. Mail is terrible these days, especially from overseas."

She nodded, smoking her cigarette. I liked her. She was a Scandinavian type, blonde, big-boned, with a healthy glow about her. "Tell me about yourself," I suggested. "You've been hearing all about me, but I know nothing about you."

"There's not much to know. I was born in Quincy, lived there all my life. My folks are of Swedish descent. I've got an older brother, and that," she said, shrugging her shoulders, "is about it." She reached for another cigarette. "Uh, what does your dad do at Harvard?"

"Well . . ." I tried to make it simple. "Pa . . . I mean, my dad, together with other scholars who are experts in the Chinese language, is working to compile a Chinese-English, English-Chinese dictionary. They develop definitions of thousands of Chinese words—we call them *characters*. It's quite a job, getting it all together; probably will take years."

"Ye gods!" Phyllis looked at me with respect. "That's impressive. He must be a genius to know Chinese. Can you speak Chinese?"

"*Yi ding wo huei shuo Chong guo hua.*" I laughed at her surprise. "Of course I know how to speak Chinese."

"I've never met anyone like you," she declared. "Jeez!" She took a last drag on her cigarette. Then she squashed the butt into her coffee cup's saucer. I must have looked quite dismayed at the sight. She burst out laughing.

"For Heaven's sake, Tamara, I haven't done anything bad! They do have to wash these dishes, you know." Then her smile turned sheepish. "I'm sorry. I didn't mean to offend you. It's just that I know smoking is a darned, dirty habit to which I happen to be totally addicted." She fished out another cigarette.

I stared out the window. Suddenly I caught sight of a familiar, round-faced girl walking towards Radcliffe. "Hey, there's my friend Loretta." I tapped on the window to get her attention. She glanced at me, waved, then, pointing to her books, hurried on.

"I guess she's going to class," I explained. "I'd have liked you two to meet. She's a terrific person. If it hadn't been for her, I'd have had a terrible time adjusting to school."

"Is she majoring in English literature too?"

"No, she's interested in the romance languages. I had hoped to see more of her in college, but we have no classes together. Still, our families are friends, so we do see each other. And her brother Manfred is our dentist. He's quite a person, Phyllis. He's not shy like Loretta."

Phyllis looked at her watch. "My Gawd," she gasped, "I've got to run, or I'll miss my train. It's been great meeting you." She hurriedly gathered her books. "Look; this is on me."

"What's on you?"

She looked amused. "I forgot. It means that I'm treating you. I'm paying the bill."

I stood up, alarmed. "Oh, no, I can't let you do that. Let's each pay our own."

She grinned at my discomfort. "Okay by me. We Americans call that 'Dutch treat.' Remember that term; it'll come in handy."

I watched her as she walked out of Hood's towards Harvard Square. I had the feeling that we would become good friends. She had an openness about her that I liked, although I knew my parents would object to her smoking and her unladylike language. Anyway, they'd have to understand. This was America.

Little did I realize then that these little worries of mine would become quite unimportant soon. The coming months were to bring new events into all our lives, changes that would affect not only the lives of Americans here but also those of most people throughout the world.

18

Of Peace and War

During my sophomore year at Radcliffe we moved to a house on Mt. Vernon Street. On this quiet, elm-shaded street the spacious single-family homes were set back on sloping, well-manicured lawns.

Mama had been ecstatic, full of plans. "This house is absolutely perfect," she cooed, as she and I roamed through it, upstairs and downstairs. "The small room in the attic will be my workroom," she told me, as her eyes scanned each corner. "I can do my ironing and sewing without having to worry about putting things away." She inspected the large, middle room. I could already see that in her mind's eye it was complete. Then she glanced into the smallest room. "Hmm, if need be, this can be a guest room." Her eyes glistened with unrestrained excitement. "Tamara, just think, you can use this big, middle room as a ballroom for entertaining your friends. You can bring your radio up here, your records . . ."—she clasped her hands together, her voice turning dreamy—"and here you and your friends can dance and dance!" She paused, her smiling face close to mine.

"I hadn't thought of that," I told her, staring at the bare room. "Papa might not . . . "

"Pfft! Papa might not what?" she interrupted me. "Papa has nothing to do with this attic. All that matters to him is that he has a study where he can work and meditate. The attic is our business." She shook her head at me, "I can't believe you hadn't thought of it first. Just look at these floors: slippery, and just perfect for dancing." She lifted up the sides of her housecoat and began to waltz around, her eyes closed, humming softly, with a Mona Lisa–like smile on her lips.

Her enthusiasm amused me, but I was still hesitant. "You really think so, Mamotchka? I still feel Papa won't like it."

Mama kept on dancing. "He'll just have to like it. You and Vanya aren't children anymore. You need a place where you can entertain your friends. This room is the ideal place; it's far enough from downstairs that he won't hear you playing dance music. Anyway," she said, with that devilish look in her eyes, "I'll talk to him. He'll see things my way."

Several days after our little talk I came home from Radcliffe to find Nathan's truck in front of our house. Nathan himself was just coming down the front porch steps, folding some bills into his wallet. When he saw me, he shook his head, "Your mother! A person just can't win with her!"

I rushed upstairs to the attic, where I found Mama moving a second-hand sofabed around. A stack of folding chairs and a card table leaned against one wall. "What are you doing, Mama?"

She wiped her forehead with the back of her hand. "Help me, Tamara. I think the sofabed is better over there."

Once we had arranged the ballroom furniture to Mama's satisfaction, she tackled me. "Now go down to your room and bring up your phonograph and records."

I protested. "Mama, I've got studying to do. Can't we do all this later?"

"Now, not later!" When Mama spoke in that tone of voice, I knew better than to argue. It took me three trips up and down those narrow stairs.

Mama looked through my records and chose one. "Now, dochenka, come here," she ordered, in a conspiratorial tone, and held out her arms. She stood in the center of the room, her back arched like a ballerina's, her head flung back. "I'll be the man. Take my hands, this way.

"Now you will learn from an expert how to waltz the proper way. The idea! A Russian *devushka* [maiden] not knowing how to waltz." Theatrically she raised her eyes in supplication to the ceiling, her mouth set with determination. "I'm going to teach you so that you'll become the best waltzer in all of Cambridge, Boston too. You'll be just like me when I was your age."

I was surprised at how simple it really was. With Mama leading I had no problem following. We danced and danced, whirling to the music of Johann Strauss. When one record ended, I ran to put on another. Mama kept laughing till tears welled up in her eyes. Soon she stopped, out of breath and panting hard.

"Oy-yoy-yoy!" she gasped. "Whew! I haven't done that in the longest time, but it's fun, isn't it? You see? That wasn't so difficult, was it?" Her eyes sparkled. "That's how we used to dance in the old days. You should have seen me then, one handsome, gallant officer after another coming up to me, bowing low to me like this, then asking for my hand to dance. And now, dochenka, it'll be happening to you."

"Was Papa a good waltzer?" I asked her.

She had a strange expression on her face, sort of amused, and yet a bit sad. "No, Papa didn't dance at all. He was always the scholar. Dancing to him, was a waste of time."

Mama had been right about the "ballroom," of course. It became a gathering place for my friends when there was nothing else to do. Everybody enjoyed dancing and contributed records, even snacks. One thing disturbed me though. Although Vanya enjoyed dancing, he stayed away.

One day I asked him why. "Vanya, you go to dances outside. Why don't you join me and my friends?"

"If I go to dances, it's to meet girls. You have your friends; I have mine. I'm not that crazy about your friends, you know."

"Okay, if that's the way you feel." It was just as well. I always felt uneasy with Vanya around, wondering what he might do or say. Since he was now in Harvard and I was in Radcliffe, we rarely saw each other, which was just fine with me.

Several times, at these "ballroom" dances, my friends and I got too carried away. If it became warm, we opened the attic windows. Unfortunately, some of our neighbors did not appreciate tangos or waltzes as much as we did. At times the doorbell rang, and I had to rush downstairs to face Officer MacIntosh at the front door. When I opened the door, he filled the doorway. He stood there, red-cheeked, puffing, and quite apologetic.

"It's that Mrs. Hollingsworth on Upland Road, my dear." He had such a melodious Irish brogue. "She's rather poorly, and your music is a wee bit merrh than she kin handle. Would ye mind closing yer windows?"

"Yes, yes, Officer MacIntosh. I'm so sorry. I didn't realize..." I'd flash him my brightest smile. "Can you wait a minute? Mama baked your favorites today." I gathered some piroshki from the dining room table into a napkin. "I know how much you like them."

It was not always smooth sailing at home. There was this one time, for instance, when Vanya's problems at Harvard had affected our whole family.

"The only time we ever get together now is at mealtimes," Mama complained. She surveyed the table with a critical eye.

"Tamara, go call Papa and Vanya. They should know by this time that we eat at seven."

At the backstairs, I yelled up to them, "Paaaapa, Vaaaanya, time to eeeat."

"Tamara, I could have done that. Tsk!" Mama gave me a disgruntled look as she sat down at the table.

"I'm sorry, Mama. What are we having?"

"Borscht."

"Is there sour cream?"

She surveyed the table, annoyed. "In the refrigerator. Get it, please."

I felt relieved when Papa and Vanya appeared, but my relief was short-lived. Both of them seemed out of sorts. Vanya was red-faced and scowling; Papa was angry, with a thundercloud look.

"Sorry, Vera," Papa apologized, "Ivan and I have been discussing his situation at Harvard. It seems that he is about to flunk Slavic I."

"Professor Cross's course?" Mama's eyes widened as she turned to Vanya. "I can't believe it, Kocinka. You yourself said that you would get an A in this course because you knew the material backward and forward. What has happened?"

Vanya, feeling cornered, got his typical, wild look. His eyes darted about the room but rarely focused on anyone's face.

311

Finally, he got control of himself. "I don't know, Mama. Cross doesn't like me."

Mama kept shaking her head in disbelief. "To fail in Russian literature! Of all subjects, to fail that one."

"Don't blame your failure on Professor Cross," Papa insisted. "As for his disliking you, I've never known him to dislike anyone. You have been going out too much with girls, Vanya, and not studying. That's your real problem. Don't think I haven't noticed. I'm not that much of a hermit."

In a way I felt sorry for my brother. Although we had never had a truly agreeable sibling relationship, I didn't like to see him humiliated. Humiliation didn't become him. He had always been, according to him, the more important child of our parents. He was older and male and therefore much smarter than I could ever be. As things were now, all he could do was stand there, red-faced, staring down at his own two feet.

"Don't be too harsh with him, Serioja," Mama said in a low tone.

"That's the trouble, Vera; I haven't been." Papa took a step towards Vanya. "I shall look into this prep-school business. Look at me when I talk to you, Ivan. And I suggest you curb your dating practices. I don't approve of the way you've been wasting your time." His lecture over, Vanya did an about-face and marched out of the kitchen.

Later that evening, I noticed that Vanya's light was still on. I tapped on his door. "Are you okay?" I asked him, opening his door a crack.

He had been sitting at his desk. His face brightened when I opened the door wider. "Come in. Yeah, I'm all right, but I feel that Papa doesn't understand my situation. He doesn't realize why I'm failing. Most guys in my classes are not doing well. Papa's getting old; that's the problem. He doesn't seem to get it through his head that there's a war going on in Europe and that we might soon have to become part of it."

"Baloney, Vanya. You're always pessimistic. That war doesn't concern us at all. Besides, what country would dare touch the United States?"

"You don't keep up with the news much, do you?" His sarcasm annoyed me, but I kept quiet. "Have you read what Germany's beloved Der Führer, that Austrian paperhanger, has done? Did you know that four months after we arrived here in the States he had invaded Poland, using his blitzkrieg tactics to tear that nation to shreds? Eventually, France and Great Britain have had to start hostilities against Germany in order to defend Poland and the smaller countries. That Il Duce, that fat despicable Benito Mussolini, has allied himself with Hitler and formed the Axis powers, to be joined later by the Japs. Can you recognize the importance of all this in your little head? Can you understand that the Germans now have control of all Western Europe except Great Britain? Can't you see why it's impossible for me to concentrate on studying old Russian literature?"

Before I could utter one word, he shushed me and continued, "Last October, Roosevelt promised American mothers that none of their sons would be sent into a foreign war. Things have changed drastically since that time. More than a year ago, Hitler crushed France. The French were supposed to have had the best modernized army in the world. Now the German Luftwaffe are bombing the British continuously. Can you imagine being bombed day in, day out?" He paused a moment.

"I know; I've been listening to Edward R. Murrow's evening news with Mama and Papa. I could hear the bombing in the background and the air-raid sirens." I wanted him to know that I knew a little about what was going on in the world.

Vanya, however, kept on lecturing. "You know, don't you, that Hitler's finally met his match in the Brits? He's getting a taste of his own damned medicine. The British have struck back with their anti-aircraft and countermeasures. They won't give up the way the French have."

"I know," I answered. "There was a picture, I think it was in *Collier's,* of English children hiding in a trench, staring up into the sky and watching war planes over London. How horrible it must be to live like that!"

Vanya turned back to his desk. "You know, Sis, we're fortunate that Roosevelt was elected for a third term."

"Why? I preferred Wendell Willkie."

"Because Roosevelt is much more experienced. He and Churchill are great leaders, and we're going to need them both. You know that we're already helping the Allies, don't you?"

"We are?" I felt ashamed of my ignorance.

"Through the Lend-Lease Act. We've been sending tanks, trucks, ammunition, food. Any materials they've needed, we've sent."

"Thanks, Vanya, for telling me all this." I closed his door softly after wishing him a good night.

A week later Papa enrolled Vanya in prep school, and I saw even less of my brother. I was grateful that he had enlightened me as to what had been going on in the world. I had been so engrossed in my classes and friends that all else had been just a blur. I now began to read the newspapers more extensively. The news had not been good. Had it not been for Papa's eternal optimism, both Mama and I might have even become depressed. Both of us had already been upset when we heard that on the twenty-second of June the Nazis had attacked Russia.

"Two years ago, in 1939, almost to the day, we arrived in this great country." Mama's eyes had filled with tears.

"The Russians will push them back, don't worry. Just wait for winter." Papa's confidence had been infectious. It continued to be so even when great cities of Russia fell into German hands. Mama counted them on her fingers: Smolensk, Kiev, Odessa, Kharkov, Rostov. "I know those places. Ach, those poor, poor people."

In November, 1941, the Germans had laid siege to Leningrad. By late November they were near Moscow. Papa still held his head high. "The Red Army is invincible," he kept insisting to us.

He was right, of course. On November 29, 1941, the Russians took the offensive on all fronts. On December 6th, they began a massive counteroffensive from Leningrad to the Sea of Azov. Cambridge had been buzzing with praise for the Russians. Friends, even strangers, stopped us on Massachusetts Avenue to discuss the war and to voice their admiration for the indomitable Russian people. Papa naturally basked in all this attention. Although it had been years since he had last seen his native land, his heart and soul were Russian to the core.

"You see! You see! No one would believe me when I said that Mother Russia is invincible." His glee knew no bounds. He even kicked up a few jiglike steps. Such behavior was totally unlike his usual dignified, scholarly self.

Time, like a woman, as the saying goes, is fickle. Shortly after the good news came the bad news. Ironically, it occurred in much the same way as it had four years ago in Peiping, China, almost to the very day.

Our family had gathered around the radio to listen to the evening news. After a slight pause, the voice of Mr. Edward R. Murrow, deadly calm but with a rare solemnity, broke in to announce his great honor and privilege to be presenting to the nation the President of the United States.

We all felt the importance of this announcement and moved even closer to the small radio, filled with apprehension.

"Yesterday, December seventh, nineteen forty-one—a date which will live in infamy...," Franklin Roosevelt began, his voice booming in a clear, ringing tone that expressed his suppressed outrage and anger.

Pearl Harbor had been sound asleep when the sneak attack had begun. *Par for the course,* I thought to myself. *That's the way the Japanese operate, just like they sneaked into our Chinese living room four years ago.*

After the broadcast Vanya had flashed me an I-told-you-so look. "Can you imagine? They sank eight battleships, three cruisers, and destroyed a hundred and eighty-eight planes." Vanya rubbed the palms of his hands together. "Boy, Roosevelt was really mad, wasn't he?"

"Do you blame him? Didn't he say that there were some two thousand and four hundred of our men killed?" It just didn't seem plausible that this could happen to Americans.

We joined Mama on the sofa, sitting there in silent shock. I felt numb too. Mama stared down at her folded hands, motionless, then slowly raised her head, her eyes full of tears.

"What now, Serioja?" she asked him softly.

Papa, his hands clutched behind his back, paced back and forth in front of her, deep in thought. "I just don't know, Verotchka. I honestly don't know. I never thought that it would be the Japanese." His voice had sounded hollow.

That same day, December the eighth, 1941, the United

States declared war on Japan. Three days later, Germany and Italy allied themselves with Japan, declaring war against the United States. It was official at last. We were now at war.

19

New Friends and Old

Mama put down the *Boston Globe*. "It gets worse every day. You know, I shudder to think what's going to happen next. That little piece of nothing, that Goebbels, now threatens that Stalingrad will fall any day. Today's paper reports that the Russians are now fighting house to house there with the Germans. You tell me, Serioja, to wait till winter comes. It has, and still the Nazis are butchering civilians, women, and children. When is all this going to end?"

"Russia will never be defeated, Verotchka." Papa rose from his chair and walked into the foyer, his head raised to look towards the top of the stairs. "Didn't you say Vanya was leaving shortly for camp?"

I heard Mama's deep sigh and tried to answer him calmly. "He's getting his stuff together, Papa. He'll be down shortly." I sat down beside Mama.

Again she took a deep breath. "He didn't have to enlist. Why would he do something like that to us? We've just become a family once again, and now this. How long is this basic training of his going to last?" She glanced up at Papa. "They might even send him to the Pacific. Who knows? I don't know who are more cruel, the Japanese or the Germans."

"It's just basic training, Mama. By the time he's gone through that, the whole war may be over." I placed my arm around her shoulders to reassure her. She said nothing, but her eyes focused on the stairs.

"Here I am, Mama." Vanya stood on the top landing of the

317

staircase, smiling down at all of us. *He looks the perfect adver-*
tisement for Colgate's toothpaste, I thought to myself. I watched
as he hurried down. He did look resplendent in his brand-new
khakis, his face flushed with excitement, and his hair all shiny
and ebony black like Rudolph Valentino's, slicked down with gobs
of brilliantine.

"How do I look?" He walked over to Mama and bent down to
give her a kiss. I noticed that his eyes looked somewhat misty,
although his voice boomed with bravado. "Just keep sending
those Baby Ruth bars, folks."

I had felt awkward at this moment, not knowing whether to
be happy or sad for him. I felt that Vanya had done the right
thing. Papa must have approved too. I watched as he and Vanya
embraced. Papa kept patting him on the back, although he didn't
say much. Over Papa's shoulder he caught my eye and grinned.
"Keep up the good work, Sis, and don't go out on too many dates."
I was relieved that he didn't hug me.

As he walked towards the front door, he tightened the strap
of his duffel bag over his right shoulder. *He looks good,* I decided.
He's even proud of himself for a change.

The three of us watched him make his way down the front
steps, shouldering his duffel bag. Just another rookie soldier boy
going off to war. There was, however, a difference. He was a member of our family; he belonged to us. He came to the corner,
turned to wave before rounding it, and then disappeared.

For a few days after Vanya's departure, Mama moped. She
walked around aimlessly, folded newspapers without reading
them, and cooked Campbell's tomato soup for Papa three days in
a row. That was not Mama's way though. In a few days she had
snapped out of her doldrums and plunged back into war relief
work. She then recruited me. What Mama had read about the
siege of Leningrad kept troubling her conscience. Here she was
basking in freedom and luxury while the people of Mother Russia were in dire need. She knew first-hand about Russia's cold
winters. Most of all, she kept remembering Dr. Ferguson's part-
ing words to us when we had said farewell to him at the Peking
railroad station.

"Whatever can we do?" She had been so full of emotion that

Prof. Henry Dana, Mama, and I at the Russian War Relief Headquarters in Cambridge, Massachusetts, 1943

day. "You have saved our lives. How can we ever repay you and the other good Americans?"

"My dear Vera," he had looked down at Mama from his great height, then had smiled at her kindly, "when you see someone whom you can help, please do so. That will repay us a hundred times over." Mama never could forget those words; neither could I.

While Mama spent her spare time at the Cambridge Russian War Relief headquarters on Dunster Street, I used my time to recruit my college classmates as volunteers. Again there were questions to be answered. Even Phyllis, who had been most enthusiastic about volunteering, wanted to know more about it. "Who's in charge of this RWR?" she asked me one day as we folded and packed donated clothing into boxes.

"Dr. Cabot is the honorary chairman."

Her eyes had become round in surprise. "You mean the Dr. Hugh Cabot of the Cabots and the Lodges?"

I thought of the sweet little old man I had met at one of our organizational meetings. I couldn't help smiling. "The very same one, the one who speaks only to God." She had been impressed.

Volunteering did involve a lot of work as we had to organize events in order to collect money and donations to send to the Russians. It was enjoyable work because more and more students kept volunteering. The headquarters happened to be on Dunster Street, where many Harvard students walked on their way either to their dorms or to their classes. Not only are Harvard students excellent academically, but they are also innately curious, especially if they happened to see, through a plate-glass window, young women bustling around. It didn't take long for us on Dunster Street to form a Junior RWR, complete with college students not only from Cambridge but from Boston proper as well.

To my delight I found that I had lost much of my shyness when I had to ask people for donations. Since I was working for a most worthwhile cause, I had convinced myself that I had a mandate to demand that others help out as well. I became known as a "go-getter," another American term that Phyllis had to define for me.

"Jeez, Tamara, how the hell do you do it?" Phyllis had been amazed when I had dialed Ruby Newman one evening and asked him if he'd mind playing for a dance we had organized. Naturally, he had agreed. It hadn't been the first time I had asked the famous Boston society bandleader to come to our rescue.

"Priorities, Phyllis. Planning and priorities. I make sure my studies come first. Otherwise, Papa would hit the ceiling. Then I schedule the other stuff."

Mama had even sewed me a special Russian Princess costume to wear at the rallies and fund-raising events. She had

A Russian Friend and I

laboriously embroidered the light blue satin front panel with pearls and other odd pieces of jewelry that she had saved.

"Look at her, Papotchka. Look at the *kakoshnik* [headdress]. That was the most difficult part to design, and then I had to cut it out of stiffened material." Mama made me pirouette in front of Papa, this way and that, stopping me in a midturn to point out some special decoration she had made.

The costume caught the attention of many and intrigued even the *Boston Globe* and the *Boston Traveller* society columnists.

One evening, I was one of the Cliffies chosen to act as usherettes at Symphony Hall to collect donations for the United War Relief during intermission. To be chosen to usher for this event was a special honor. When the person in charge told me and another Cliffie that we had been designated to work the front section on the main floor, I had been delighted.

How well I remember that evening! All of Boston society's uppercrust must have been seated in the audience that evening. Immaculately coiffed elderly dowagers, bejeweled and crowned with tiaras, swept in regal splendor over the red-carpeted aisles to their seats. Their formally clad spouses hovered nearby in elegant solicitude. It had been quite an impressive occasion, unforgettable.

It happened not long after the glittering event that Phyllis called me to have lunch with her at Schrafft's.

"Schrafft's? And to what occasion do I owe this invite? Aren't we getting up in the world, huh? What's wrong with Hood's?"

I heard the click of her lighter at the other end of the line, then a pause as she inhaled, then her amused chortle. "I just felt like splurging. Professor Johnson finally reimbursed me for that paper I had typed for him. Okay?"

Schrafft's had that cool, refined aura about its interior that makes a woman entering it straighten her back and raise her chin a notch or two. To the left of the entrance stood a long, rather ornate lunch counter. Usually older women stopped there to indulge their taste buds with delicious whipped cream and pecan-topped sundaes. To the right stood glass counters containing trays and trays of neatly arranged chocolates of all shades, shapes, and sizes, one more mouth-watering than the next.

Phyllis, already seated at a table, waved a welcoming hello. She greeted me with a large grin, pointing to the seat across from her.

"You're looking good. I've already ordered for the two of us— the Special." She laughed, shrugging her shoulders. "I'm not that flush with dough, you know."

"Okay. I'm not really hungry to tell the truth, but I did want to see you. You don't look bad yourself, Phyl." Sitting down, I glanced around the restaurant. Although the lunch counter was busy, only three other tables besides ours had customers.

Phyl followed my gaze. "We're early. Wait till one or half-past; that's when the place is packed. Hey, I noticed your photo in the paper again and the nice write-up. Congratulations, gal. That was a beautiful costume you were wearing."

I groaned, remembering. "Mama made that outfit for me. It is beautiful, but sure as heck got me in trouble with the Dean. The costume and the article, that is."

Phyl's eyes widened in surprise. "For God's sake, why?"

"Well, Mama really outdid herself when she made it. You'll have to see it when you come over. It's made of light blue satin, which she embroidered with semiprecious stones. The hem has a border of real mink. You should have seen the people at Symphony Hall that night. Many stopped me to ask about it, asking if I was a real princess. I finally told one dowager that I was. I got tired of having to explain."

Phyllis laughed in amusement. "What about the Dean?"

"Some people took photographs. How could I know that one of them was a news photographer? Even if the person had told me so, so much was going on at the same time, I wouldn't have objected. Anyway, the day after the article appeared in the paper, I got a notice that Dean Sherman wished to see me."

Phyllis pretended to gag. "I'll bet you got the heebie-jeebies, eh?"

I nodded. "Sort of. I never thought it would be about that. My grades were okay. I hadn't flunked anything. I honestly didn't know what it was she wanted."

"What did she say?"

"She was graciousness itself. Said she considered it admirable that I was doing volunteer work. Good for Radcliffe's image and all that, you know. But I had an uneasy feeling that Big Sister had her eyes upon me and that I'd better watch that my grades did not change. Anyway, she handed me the clipping and dismissed me with a nod. That was it. I couldn't walk out of her office fast enough."

Phyllis laughed, then let out a low whistle. Startled by her own audacity, she quickly looked around, heaving a sigh of relief when she realized that no one else had noticed. "Whew, I forgot where we were. Well, all's well that ends well, as old Will would say. The dean's okay. I like her. By the way, I wanted to ask you before this. How'd you like summer school? You took it, didn't you?"

"Sure did, while you chased lifeguards at the Cape. I've become a staunch believer in summer school, Phyl. Do you realize that I've got enough credits now to graduate in February instead of June? I wish I'd done it earlier. Then I might have been able to graduate in three years."

"What's your hurry? What are you planning to do after Radcliffe?"

"I'm going to New York to find me a job with a magazine. I'm going to be independent. My parents want me to live at home and find a nice position in Boston, but"—I couldn't help smiling at the thought—"the big, bad city beckons me. It says, 'Come here, little lady; let me show you around.' "

Phyllis laughed. "You've still got a year and a half to go. Who knows what can happen between then and now. Look how things are changing from day to day with world events."

Her words brought to my mind again what I'd been trying so hard to block out ever since I'd seen the article in the morning *Globe*. "You read the news too, I take it?"

She looked grim. "About what happened in Lidice? Yes, I started to read it but hadn't the stomach to finish. That Heinrich Himmler, next to Hitler, must be the most vicious monster this world has ever produced. My God, I cannot believe that people can be so damned inhuman!"

"Neither can I. Can you imagine? Just because one Gestapo official was shot they had to shoot all the men in that village. Even that did not satisfy them. That's what gets me. They had to separate mothers from their children." I shuddered. Again, in my imagination, I pictured crying children, their arms outstretched, being wrested from their mothers by those ruthless beasts.

Phyllis had blanched. "They did that? I hadn't read that part. God!"

"They placed the women in concentration camps and sent their children to so-called educational institutions. Can you believe that? Papa says these institutions are just a pretext of the Nazis, that actually they are doing scientific experiments on women and children and torturing them to see how much they can endure. Someone at Harvard had told him that. Anyway, they razed this village of Lidice. It's as if there never had been a village there."

Neither Phyllis nor I wanted dessert. I took one of her cigarettes, and we smoked for a while in silence. Then, after she had paid the bill, we walked out towards Harvard Square, where she headed for the subway station, and I made my way towards Widener Library. I needed that studious setting, the quiet and the camaraderie of those working alongside me.

In the midst of studying my notes I noticed a slip of paper being pushed slowly across the table towards me. I looked up, rather startled at this sudden intrusion into my thoughts. A young man in uniform sat directly across from me, his smiling face getting redder by the minute as he noticed my reaction. I picked up the note and unfolded it. "You are very beautiful," I read. "Please don't think me forward. I would like to know you. Can you have coffee with me at the Wursthaus? I'll wait here till you've finished studying." It was signed "Lansing Johnson." *A most unusual first name,* I thought.

I scrutinized Lansing Johnson openly, much to his discomfort. He seemed pleasant enough, although somewhat boyish and shy. In turn, I became self-conscious when he, too, examined me adoringly. I had just been curious. I nodded to him, smiling. Then on the back of his note, I wrote that I'd be through in half an hour. He read my note and grinned.

Lanny, as he had asked that I call him, reminded me of Leslie Howard, who had played Ashley in *Gone with the Wind.* He was tall and lanky, with curly blond hair and a thin, likable face, not what I could call handsome. There was, however, a certain gentleness about him that appealed to me.

On Widener's top step we properly introduced ourselves. He held my hand a bit longer than necessary. When I withdrew it, his face reddened. "Honestly, Tamara," he stammered, "I didn't mean to do that." He looked quite crestfallen.

We walked down the steps toward the Yard, his long legs mincing his stride so as to keep pace with me. "I've seen you around here going to classes. I've even seen you going into Boylston Hall. You aren't majoring in Oriental languages, are you, Tamara?"

I couldn't help smiling. "My dad does research work in Boylston Hall. I visit him sometimes or pick him up after my classes. If he's through for the day, we walk home together."

By the time we had reached the Wursthaus I felt as if I'd known Lanny all my life. That is, except for the formalities.

After we had ordered coffee, I questioned him about his family. His matter-of-fact simplicity surprised me. "My father is dead. My mother is housemother at Wellesley College. I come from Quaker stock."

"Quaker stock?"

That amused him. "It's a religious group, Tamara. We're better known as the Society of Friends."

"Interesting, hm-m." I studied his face to see if I could see anything different about him. "I've never met a Quaker before, that I know of. What are your beliefs?"

He seemed quite flattered by my attention. "They're quite simple, really. Quakers don't believe in formal church rites or that the sacraments of the church are essential. We believe that each individual will find guidance and understanding of divine truth in his own heart. And we do not believe in war."

"Why are you in an army uniform then?" I protested.

He then pointed to the insignia on his shirt. "This means that I am in ASTP, the Army Specialists Training Program. I'm training to be a medic. In other words, if I'm sent to a battlefront, it won't be to fight; I'll be helping with the wounded or doing whatever else I can do to help the men. I could never fight or kill. I feel very strongly about that."

Papa, who could never even kill a fly, would surely like Lanny, I thought to myself. In fact, I had to admit that of all the young men I had dated since entering Radcliffe, Lanny impressed me most. He appeared to be humble and gentle; yet I sensed that beneath that unassuming exterior lay other fine qualities. He could be brave, stern, and even stubborn if the need ever arose.

"A penny for your thoughts, Princess. Do you mind if I call you that? You look like one to me," he spoke in a low tone.

I laughed. "I don't accept money for my thoughts. Besides, they're worth more than a penny. To answer your other question, I don't mind at all."

"Do you like poetry?"

"Yes," I told him, "especially that of the romantic movement. I'm not too crazy about modern poetry, but that's because I haven't read that much of it."

He ordered another cup of coffee for each of us. "I enjoy writing poetry. Would you mind if I addressed one to you? I'd like to very much."

I chuckled to myself. *Boy, wait till Phyllis hears about this!* I could picture the warning signal in her eyes as she cautioned me about men's techniques; she still thought me naive and unsophisticated.

"I'd like that," I told Lanny.

He leaned forward. "I'd like to ask you something; I hope you won't be insulted, because I think it's lovely."

"Whatever could it be, Lanny?"

"Your accent. You have a charming, sing-songy manner of speaking. Your grammar is impeccable, but your accent is not American as we speak it here. It's more British."

"It's because I've been in America only since 1939. I lived in China till we came here. I've been wondering when you'd get around to asking me that. Most people do, you know."

"I knew there was something special about you."

I sipped the last of my coffee. "That tasted so good, Lanny, but it's getting late, and Mama will be worried. I'd better go now."

His disappointment was obvious. "May I see you home then?"

"I'm walking."

He rose and gathered up my books. "I'm a New Englander, remember? We're great walkers."

On the way home, as we walked through Cambridge Common, he asked if I had a steady boyfriend.

"No, I don't."

"I'm surprised at that. A pretty girl like you usually has dozens of guys after her."

"Oh, I date quite a bit," I assured him, "depending on exams and stuff along with my volunteer work. Those are important to me. Besides, Radcliffe is not a cinch." I went on to tell him about my volunteer work and laughed to myself when he, on the spur of the moment, decided he'd help the war effort too.

He kept returning to the subject of boyfriends. "You don't mean to tell me that you've never been serious about anyone. I find that hard to believe."

"No, Lanny, it shouldn't be difficult to believe when you realize that I come from a background different from yours. Don't forget that I was born in China of Russian parents—aristocratic intelligentsia, you might call them. People didn't date in China. My parents brought me up in the Euro-Asian tradition. My primary goal as an adolescent and young adult was to get the best education possible. Besides a formal education I had to be well-versed in music, art, ballet, languages, and manners. If possible, I was to go on to a university. I was to be a college graduate just like my parents. As for marriage, it will come eventually. At my age, I'm not even considering it. Anyway, with the war in China and what's happened to us in between, things have changed. We came to the States, and, as you Americans say, 'It's a totally different ballgame.' This dating business is fun. I like to dance, to meet people, but I am not planning to get serious about any man. I have my studies to finish first, and I want to be independent for a time before I get married."

Again he had studied me quizzically but said nothing, his face thoughtful.

We had approached the white house on the corner of Mt. Vernon Street. "This is my street, Lanny. It's quite different; it first goes up the hill and then winds down. We're way on the other side where it intersects Upland Road at the very end."

My description confused him, but he gamely took my hand and began singing. "It's up the hill we go; it's down the hill we go. Heigh-ho the dairy-o, to Tamara's house we go."

His boyishness amused me. "But, Lanny, first look at this house. Don't you think it looks haunted, as if there are ghosts in there? It gives me the creeps whenever I pass by it, especially in the evening if I'm by myself."

He grinned. "Yep, the broken windows, the fallen shutters, and all those hanging cobwebs. Have no fear, Princess; I'll protect you from the ghosts and goblins of Mt. Vernon Street." He squeezed my hand. "I hate to think that I'll be leaving you shortly. You don't mind if I give you a call, do you?"

I tore a sheet from my notebook and hastily scrawled my phone number. We shook hands, and he walked on down the hill. I watched his tall, retreating form round the corner. What a great guy! Happy that I had made a new friend, I ran towards our house, anxious to tell my news to Mama.

To my surprise Mama had been waiting for me inside the foyer. As soon as I had unlocked and opened the door, I saw her, sitting on the bottom step of the stairs, her face rosy with ill-concealed excitement. Mama could never hide her feelings too well, unless, of course, she was giving someone her silent treatment. This time, however, I knew that she was bursting with news, all a-shivery and smiling.

"What is it, Mama? Is the war over?" Stupid question, that. I'd have heard the whoops way back in Harvard Square!

She shook her head.

"Is Vanya home on leave?"

Again she shook her head. "Go upstairs, *dochenka*. Quickly. There's a surprise waiting for you."

I laid my books on the foyer table and ran up the stairs, two at a time; Mama was at my heels, panting and giggling to herself.

I never closed my bedroom door unless I was studying. I glanced back at Mama, who was standing behind me. Her hands clasped her cheeks as she kept waiting for me to open my door. I hesitated, not knowing what I'd find behind it.

"Well, open it, Tamara." A note of impatience had crept into her voice. So she had waited some time for me to come home.

I carefully eased the door open, taking a peek inside. "I don't know what you're up to, Mama," I began; then I noticed the familiar figure on my couch. I flung the door wide open.

"Golly Ned! Dorlise Krenz! How in the world? . . ." I stared at my old friend in amazement. She sat there yoga-style with her hands on her knees, grinning like a Cheshire cat, her brown eyes looking calm and bemused.

"How in the world?" I repeated, then ran to embrace her just as she jumped off the couch. As we hugged I could hear the familiar chuckle, so full of the promise of pranks and outlandish things to do.

"Surprised to see me, eh? What a time I had trying to con-

vince Mama not to let on. I thought you'd guess immediately."
She laughed, pleased that she'd pulled another fast one on me. I
couldn't stop looking at her. She looked a bit older but was still
the same defiant, incorrigible, lovable, and loyal Dorlise, my boon
companion and trusted friend. She and I had gone through a lot
together. She whirled me round, letting out a wolf whistle.
"Golly, Tama, you look positively like a movie star. Bee-oo-ti-ful!
Who'd have thought of it, Mama, eh?" She surveyed me from top
to toe, then turned to Mama. "Yow-ee, Mama, whatever happened to our ugly little Peking duck? I'll bet the boys are after
her, aren't they?"

Mama and I both laughed. She hadn't changed at all. Still
the same exuberant, outspoken, lovable extrovert.

Mama wiped her eyes. "She is quite popular, Dorlise. Too
many dates, but I'm sure the same thing is happening to you.
Both of you have grown into charming young women,
although"—she paused and her eyes turned slyly from Dorlise to
me— "I often wondered in Peking how you would both turn out.
Remember the time you dressed up as ricksha boys and went to
the Hus?"

We both nodded. "And on our way met the drunken Japanese soldiers? That was fun, eh?" Dorlise chortled at the
thought, then turned to me, her face curious. "What the heck
kept you so long?" She patted the couch. "Come on; let's sit. You,
Mama, in the middle, the way we used to sit in China."

"I just met a Quaker at Widener. Really pleasant but shy. He
blushed all the time."

Mama raised her eyebrows. "Quaker?"

Dorlise's expressive brown eyes rolled back dramatically as
she focused them on the ceiling. She clenched her lips tight to
keep from laughing out loud.

"Oh, Dorlise, he's not a jerk. You'd like him. Mama, Quakers
are a religious group who are better known as the Society of
Friends. They don't believe in violence or fighting or killing.
They have simple beliefs, no formal church rites, and they don't
talk much."

"Ah-h-h," Mama slowly nodded her head, as if she understood.

"Did he invite you to go to a meeting with him?" Dorlise gave

330

me an impish look. "Is he handsome? I think I could go for a Quaker if he were handsome."

"Shut up, Old Pal." I gave her a playful nudge. "He's quiet and thoughtful. He's got green eyes, Dorlise, and even though we've just met, I could tell that he likes me a lot. As we talked he would keep staring at me with a pleading expression in his eyes. Reminded me of a puppy dog. You know how they cock their heads to one side and look at a person with such soulful eyes? Well, that's Lanny!"

Dorlise snorted. "And I bet he gave you the line about how lovely you are, and he'd never met a girl like you, and he'd never acted like this before, et cetera, et cetera. Eh, Mama? Your daughter's still a baby, isn't she?"

Come to think of it Lanny had said those things to me, but not in the way that Dorlise had implied.

"You gotta watch out, old friend. I'll bet you anything that he's giving you a line. You're so damned innocent, and these American fellows, even if they're Quakers, are all wolves, believe me. Quakers or not, they're still out on the prowl."

Mama rose with a hug for each of us. "You two talk. I'll be in the kitchen."

"Can we help, Mama?" Dorlise asked, jumping up.

Mama shoved her back down. "Sit. Now that's an order. You and Tamara have much to talk about and so little time. Talk."

After Mama had left, Dorlise tucked her bare feet under her skirt. "Surprised to see me?"

"Sure am. Why didn't you write to tell us you were coming? I've written and written and not a word from anybody in Peking, not even the Fergusons. Papa said it must be the mails."

Dorlise shook her head, laying her hand across mine. "It's a long story. I've already filled Mama in on it. The thing is that after the attack on Pearl Harbor, the Japs considered us enemy, us and the British. So-o, those remaining in Peking were interned in camps. We and the Fergusons were included."

"You mean Dr. Ferguson is interned?"

"Yes, poor man. He's quite old, you know."

My dear friend! So that's why we had had no letters! Then it occurred to me, and I asked Dorlise, "How come you're here?"

She grinned, "Sheer luck, Tama. Mom had enrolled me at

Stephens so I wasn't in Peking when Pearl Harbor happened. Remember how we had hoped to be in college together? Well, I didn't have the grades for Radcliffe. Frankly, I didn't have the inclination. No blue-stocking institution for me. Much too brainy." She nudged me playfully in the ribs. "You've always had the noodle in our twosome. Me, I have the looks."

"Then why didn't you write to me to say where you were?"

"Well, you know me. I've never been much of a correspondent. Heck, I've thought of you often enough. Time sort of passed, and I traveled places. Family relatives and all. Besides I thought you'd hear about me from others."

"It doesn't really matter," I told her happily. "You're here now. Gosh, I feel so bad about Dr. Ferguson. And Mary? Is she with him? How could they arrest someone so kind and good?"

"Same thing happened to you, Tamara. Only you guys were separated and had it worse, I think. It's wartime now, Old Pal. Your family got lucky, coming to the States. Do you realize that if your Dad hadn't gotten arrested, you'd still be in China? Boy! I can't get over seeing you. Mama looks so radiant and beautiful. She used to have a pinched, concerned look all the time as if the world had eased most of its burdens on her shoulders. Her forehead has no furrows any more. I guess she's pretty happy here, huh?"

"Yep, but wait till you see Papa."

"Is he still as strict as he used to be? I remember how he used to scare me when he'd get mad, and his eyes would harden. They shone like black onyx stones, remember?"

I smiled at her vivid description of Papa. "He's mellowed a bit since then. I think his experiences with his Japanese captors taught him a lot. He's much more gentle these days, more subdued in temperament, except that time when Vanya flunked Slavic I." I told her about the incident and Vanya's subsequent enlistment in the army. Dorlise, however, wanted to hear more about Papa. "Did the Japs torture him much?"

"Yes, they tortured him. He looked pretty pathetic to us when we first saw him that morning before we sailed for the United States on the *Hikawa Maru*. He still wore the same old suit he'd worn when they arrested him. It hung loosely on him because of all the weight he had lost. His skin reminded me of antique Chinese ivory figurines, almost yellowish in shade, with minutelike brown lines. His beard was a long, straggly gray, his long, shoulder-length hair was almost snowwhite. Can you imagine Papa looking like that? He had always been so immaculate about his appearance. When he entered our cabin aboard ship, I thought that it must be some disoriented traveler, Oriental, of course, just by the way he had shuffled in, silently and with such humility. Then, when I looked into his face, I knew. No one could ever mistake those eyes, which were full of compassion, understanding, and an abundance of patience, for anyone's but Papa's."

"Papa," Dorlise's soft voice sounded husky, almost like Phyllis's.

"So, to answer your question, yes, they tortured him. One time, he told us, the guards had forced him to stand outside in the snow, naked. It had been on one of the coldest nights in January. Three of the guards had taken turns splashing him with buckets of ice water and poking him with their rifle butts to keep him from falling down. When morning dawned, they stopped their fun and dragged him, half-frozen, back to his cell."

Dorlise drew in a deep breath. "Poor little Papotchka! How terribly dreadful it must have been." Her eyes filled with tears.

"The strange thing is that the guards always gave him warning ahead of time. Knowing what would be facing him, he prepared himself for the tortures. He told us how he stood in front of the tiny window in his cell on tiptoes because it was way up. There he exercised, breathing in the cold air, trying to keep his circulation going. He's firmly convinced that that's what helped save him from certain death, that and his peace of mind."

"My God, what beasts!"

"Then there was another time when they made him kneel in front of his three inquisitors, hands outstretched, like this. One of the inquisitors, not satisfied with Papa's answers, made a sign to a soldier, who came up behind Papa, unsheathed his sword, and laid the bare steel blade against Papa's neck."

"But why? Because he was Russian?"

"They wanted him to confess to things he wasn't guilty of. They accused him of being a spy, of spreading propaganda among his students, of a whole lot of crazy stuff that hadn't a damned shred of truth in it. Papa later told us that it must have been on account of his refusal to collaborate with them. Whatever it was, they sure made him suffer for it."

"They could have killed him for it."

"If Papa hadn't been such a long resident of Peking and hadn't been so well known and respected by Americans and others, he probably would have been killed along with Mama, me, and Vanya."

Dorlise stood up and stretched out her arms as she looked around my room. "But you guys are here now, safe and sound." She smiled at me, then made a face. "I hate to think of leaving you all just when I've found you again, but I'll have to leave tomorrow. It's back to Stephens, back to the grind. Let's forget about war right now. I want to know more about your family. What about Vanya? Mama said he's in basic training."

"He flunked most of his courses at Harvard and had to go to prep school. To be fair to him, it must have been pretty hard to concentrate what with his friends being drafted and all."

"I'm surprised he enlisted. From what I remember of him he was not one of the brave."

I laughed, "But he's a romantic, remember? The army posters beckoned to him with their colorful pictures of exotic places and long-haired sirens to moon over. How could he resist such temptation? Besides, Papa had given him an ultimatum: shape up or else ship out!"

"I hope the army shapes him up."

"Why?" She had sounded so strange saying that, and the way her eyes had darkened I felt she knew something about Vanya that I didn't. "Why do you say that, Dorlise?"

She stared at me with that straightforwardness and honesty which had marked our friendship since childhood. "It's hard for me to phrase this, Tamara. Please don't get offended, but have you ever thought that your brother is off-balance? You know, not quite right in the head?"

"Of course I have, but I just thought that siblings usually feel that way about one another."

"It's more serious than that, I'm afraid." Dorlise looked at my half-closed door, got up, and shut it ever so carefully so that it wouldn't squeak in closing. Even then she lowered her voice. "He's really odd," she said, matter-of-factly, "and weird. Does he

334

still avoid looking people in the eye when he's talking to them? And does he 'dry-wash' his hands?"

" 'Dry-wash' his hands? Oh, I get it. You mean his habit of clasping his hands together, rubbing them as if he's washing them? Gee, that's a clever way of putting it. Yes, he still does. It reminds me of that David Copperfield character, remember?"

"Uriah Heep. You're absolutely right. Uriah Heep used to 'dry wash' his hands when he had some devious plan in mind."

I felt relieved. "I'm glad that I'm not the only one who thinks Vanya is strange. I've always been afraid to mention it to anyone else. Somehow I feel that my folks know it too and that they're shielding Vanya. It's almost as if he's made out of glass and might break. You know, he can't stand this new oleo that Mama buys, so what do you think we do? Because butter's rationed— sixteen points now—it's saved for him. He gets our meat rations because fish is too smelly for him. No, Vanya hasn't changed, Dorlise, but I have. I'm not afraid of him any more. We go our separate ways now."

"Too bad in a way, isn't it? I love my big brother, Henry. In fact, when you were under home arrest, I used to comfort myself that Vanya was with you so that you'd be safe."

At that I laughed scornfully. "He tried to rape me when we were under home arrest, Dorlise. First, Boy the servant, then, the next night, Vanya." Only to her could I have blurted out my dreadful secret.

"Vanya raped you?"

The image of Vanya's sleeping face, then that despicable grin when I had kicked him out of my bed and he had wakened, remembering, came back to me. Ugh! I thought that I had succeeded in blocking that hideous incident out of my head. I told Dorlise how it had happened.

She put her arms around me, clutching me. Her voice sounded raspy. "What did you do? What could you do?" She rocked me back and forth as if I were her doll.

"Every single night after that I placed a hammer under my pillow and barricaded my bedroom door with Mama's dresser."

"Sicko!" she muttered furiously, "I'd have knocked his damned block off. I had thought so often of you, even begged Dr. Ferguson to let me come and visit you, but he always refused. He said it would not help matters but might make them worse."

"That's right." I thought of poor Gavriluk, who'd come to see us and gotten arrested instead.

Dorlise laid her hand on my shoulder. "Tama, I'm going to tell you something about Vanya that I'm sure you don't know, but if you ever let on that I told you, not even God and Confucius combined would be able to help you then."

I crossed my heart and hoped to die if I told.

She smiled at me with affection. "Remember that big, tall wrought-iron stove in your living room that had the flat top where Mama used to bake sweet potatoes for us?"

"That black Russian stove? Yes, I remember."

"Well, one day your cousin Peter and Vanya were playing by themselves in your living room. It must have been summertime because the stove wasn't lit. Anyway, Vanya dared Peter to climb to the top of the stove. Remember how high it was, almost level with the top of your front door, if I remember right. Peter wouldn't do it, but Vanya kept urging and coaxing until Peter finally scrambled up on top. Then Vanya pushed him. Whether he knocked him off with a broom or scared him, I don't know. All I know is that your Aunt Raica and Mama found Peter unconscious on the floor and Vanya, of course, nowhere around."

Her recital of the incident nauseated me. If it had involved anybody but Vanya, I wouldn't have believed it.

"How did you find out about this?" I asked her.

"Peter told me just before I left to come to the States. You had a special place in his heart, he told me. He wanted you to know the truth."

So now I did know the truth. "And that's how Petya got crippled. No wonder Papa was so furious. He must have guessed that Vanya had something to do with it." I was grateful that Dorlise had finally solved the mystery for me.

"You promise not to tell?"

"Trust me; I won't. Let's go down to the kitchen now. Mama, I'll bet, needs help."

Just as we reached the bottom of the stairs we heard the lock of the front door being turned. "It's Papa," I whispered. "Stand there where he can see you." I positioned her in front of the opening door.

Papa's face underwent several quick changes: from surprise to recognition to pleasure to sheer delight. "Can it be the little American girl who used to stare at me with those big, big brown eyes?" He put down his briefcase and gallantly bent down to kiss her hand. "You're a beautiful young lady now," he announced.

We ate in the kitchen as a family.

"You made my favorite piroshki with cabbage!" Dorlise poked the rest of the Russian dumpling into her mouth and leaned over to hug Mama. "You realize I haven't had one of these since you left China?"

It was just like old times except that Papa now sat with us instead of Vanya. And as before, Dorlise and I talked about our future.

"Wouldn't it be the most wonderful thing, Tamara, if you and I found our true loves, got married, and lived right next door to each other? We'd live near Papa and Mama, of course."

Papa laughed, "Have you ever heard this Chinese proverb, Dorlise? 'When the melon is ripe, it will drop of itself.' "

"You mean we shouldn't plan for the future? I have another one for you, Papa." She thought for a minute; then, in her flawless Chinese, she quoted, "One family builds a wall; two families enjoy it."

When it came time the next morning to say good-bye, both Dorlise and I put up a brave front. Although we had talked most of the night, there remained much more to reminisce over, to plan for.

"You'll write, won't you?" I walked down to the waiting taxi with her.

"You bet I will, Old Pal. Don't worry." Hating long good-byes as always, she hurried into the cab.

Little did we both know then that once more events would change our lives. It would be years before we'd see each other again.

337

20

The Kiss

Vanya sat by the kitchen window watching Mama and me put the tea things away. "Army life isn't all that bad, Mama. It's only that they like to make me feel inferior."

His poor-poor-pitiful-me attitude was beginning to irk me. Ever since Dorlise's revelation about Vanya's active involvement in Petya's accident, everything about him repulsed me.

Any questions I asked annoyed him. "You wouldn't understand, Tamara. You're like this Sergeant Ostrowski at our basic training camp; he was always on my back. If I didn't get something done the way he had ordered, then I got KP. Either that or I had to clean the latrines."

Mama sat down, her face a mixture of love and bewilderment. "Why should they single out you, Kocinka? Don't the other soldiers have to do KP?"

"Ye-es, but not as often. I can feel his antagonism. It's because I'm Russian."

His old alibi angered me. "You can't blame your troubles on being Russian any more, Vanya. Russians are now heroes; people admire the Russians. Look how much is written about their bravery and fortitude. I'll bet you don't listen to orders."

"Tamara," Mama said, giving me a warning look, "Vanya's just come home. Please don't start an argument."

Just then the phone rang. Vanya got up. "It's probably for me. I'm expecting several calls today." With a sly grin on his face he went to the foyer.

Half an hour later he came back into the kitchen. "You'd

never guess who it was, Tamara." He laughed as he sat down, a satisfied expression on his face.

"Marlene Dietrich," I offered.

"Wrong. It was your friend, Phyllis Olsen. By the way, she said to meet her at Hood's tomorrow at eleven. Okay?" He didn't pause for my answer but continued. "I asked her to go out with me tonight. You never told me about her. I liked her sexy voice. She must be a knockout."

I stared at him in disbelief. "Why didn't you let me talk to her? She called me, Vanya; you don't even know her."

Mama thought it amusing. "Now, Tamara, don't get all riled up. Vanya meant well. Besides, what's wrong in asking your friend to go out with him?"

"Because she's not his type," I explained.

"And pray tell me, what is my type, Tamara?"

Not wanting to start an argument, I tried to keep my voice even. "The girls you date are not as fine as Phyllis." I glared at his mocking face, then noted Mama's interest. How could I let her know that his dates were, in my opinion, street-smart and cheap? I had met several of them before his enlistment and had been surprised at his choices. Perhaps my own standards were too high, but I considered such girls immoral. Mama would too; of that I was sure. However, I was not about to disillusion her; so I said nothing more.

Mama had smiled then. "Phyllis is a lovely girl, Vanya. She's blonde. Of Swedish background, isn't she, Tamara?"

"Her parents are Swedish-Americans, Mama." Then I thought of Vanya's aversion to smoking. "And she's a chain-smoker."

"That's okay; I've gotten used to that in the army. Most of the fellows in my outfit smoke."

Well, I told myself, if Phyl had been stupid enough to agree to go out with him, then what could I do? If I warned her that Vanya was a wolf, she wouldn't believe me. If she did believe me, she'd say she knew how to handle wolves. It was a no-win situation. I could see her tomorrow at Hood's anyway.

As I hurried into the malt shop, I saw Phyl waiting for me at our favorite table by the window. As usual, she was smoking and playing her favorite game of analyzing the different people around her. She smiled when I came up to the table. *Good,* I thought, *she can't have had a bad experience with Vanya.*

"I've ordered coffee for you," she told me.

"Thanks." I sat down and took a sip. "It's good and hot. Sorry I'm late, but I stopped at Boylston Hall for a sec."

Phyllis leaned back in her chair and fixed on me that contemplative look of hers. "Never in my wildest imagination, Tamara, could I have believed that two siblings, living under one roof, having the same parents, could ever turn out to be such extreme opposites." She blew a perfect smoke ring then and watched it spiral slowly upwards towards the ceiling. "It is beyond me. Why the devil didn't you tell me he was such a wolf?"

"Would you have believed me?"

"No."

"How bad was it?"

"Gruesome," Phyllis said sardonically, "but I'll live. He took me to a dance in Boston, some sort of affair for noncoms. God, Tamara, he kept dancing too close, breathing into my face, squeezing my waist. I managed to field that. Later, when we had left the dance, he began to paw me like a maniac. Would you believe it? He wanted to have sex with me. Ugh!"

"I'm sorry." It angered me that Vanya would treat a girl, moreover a friend of mine, like that. I was ashamed of him.

"It's not your fault; it's mine because I had the damned stupid idea that a brother of yours would be a prince. Boy, was I wrong about that!"

"I really feel rotten about it."

"Just forget it, will you? It's just another unpleasant episode in my life that I'll chalk up to experience. But it still amazes at me how different you two are. God!"

I told her about Dorlise's visit and then about Lanny.

"I've never met a Quaker either. Maybe we can double-date sometime, and I can meet him."

"You'll like him. He's got a good sense of humor once he's over his bashfulness."

"That'll be a welcome change."

We talked about classes and exams. Phyllis complained about the reading lists. "I'll never catch up," she moaned.

Photograph Taken by Fellow Cliffie Lillian Beresnack, February 11, 1942

Selling War Bonds, 1942

"Remember when we were freshmen and thought that the reading lists were only for reference?"

Phyl chuckled, "Yeah, then what a shock to find out that we had to read all those books listed. Remember how I'd stay overnight at your house so we could cram together and stay up all night to read what we hadn't read before? And then we'd ask your dad to make sure we were up at six? Jeez! I wouldn't want to go through that again." She glanced at her watch. "I didn't realize it's so late."

I offered to pay the bill this time. "It's the least I can do to make up for Vanya," I told her contritely. His crudeness still gnawed at me; the fact that he was my brother grated on me even more.

In spite of the war and Mama's occasional bouts of depression after Vanya's departure overseas, my junior year at Radcliffe proved to be one of my best. I found the courses I had selected for my English literature major to be most enjoyable, especially the two offered by those "Tweedledee, Tweedledum" scholars, the highly respected professors of seventeenth- and eighteenth-century poetry and prose, Sherburn and Root. Mama would have reacted in horror had she heard me refer to the two serious gentlemen of Harvard in those terms. However, in spite of their strict adherence to the times about which they taught, both of these professors were respected and admired by us students, hence their nicknames.

Theodore Spencer, the revered Shakespearean scholar, was another favorite of mine. I listened, transfixed, as he read the various soliloquies or dialogues from the Bard's masterpieces and relished the way he enunciated each bit of verse or each Shakespearean pun. Mark Shorer and Albert Guerard too, each in his individual way, revealed new thoughts and interpretations of literary works.

Volunteer work still occupied much of my spare time: there were more rallies to organize and attend; not only for the Russians but also for the Chinese and other Allied nations. I found myself planning, scheduling, and calling on Ruby Newman much more often.

Then too, of course, I was dating more young men: blond

Dick Wagner from MIT, who sent me long-stemmed red roses and, like Lanny, called me Princess. Unlike Lanny, however, he did it with tongue in cheek, and I in turn called him Sir Richard, Knight of the Valley of the Moon. Together he and I read Chinese poetry, mostly Li Po's poems, which were written with ink brush in one hand and a cup of wine in the other.

There were others, many fine young men over whom Mama exclaimed and dreamed about. Sometimes she cornered me to say, "Charlie is a fine young man, and he's in love with you. What do you think of him?" I thought Charlie handsome, witty, brilliant, and all that, but he was not for me. Just a few more months to go, then graduation, then New York and independence!

I cannot omit Jacques Dubois, the dark, handsome senior from Harvard, a member of the Free French movement who made his home in New York's Hastings-on-Hudson, and as sophisticated and enigmatic a son-in-law as any doting mother might wish for. Mama had even commented on his impeccable European manners. He had kissed her hand the first time he'd come to visit us. He showered me with flowers and gifts. On our dates he took me to nightclubs with reservations for the best seats. Jacques taught me to tango, to rhumba, and to kiss. "He is a prince," Mama had told me wistfully. "Meeting him makes me wish that I were young again."

"It" happened the evening we had come home early from a dance. He and I had sat on Mama's dragon rug in the living room, and I had turned on the radio for the evening news. On our very first date, Jacques had learned about my attitude towards kissing. Every time after that, at the end of our date, he had taken my proffered hand and ceremoniously planted a kiss on it. This time, however, he sat there on the rug, studying me with a seriousness of purpose and perplexity that puzzled me.

"What's wrong, Jacques?" I asked.

"I have pondered 'over many a quaint and curious volume of forgotten lore,'" he began in a ghostlike voice, "and I'm a-a-weary. . . ."

Smiling, I asked, in as ghostlike a voice, "And of what art thou so weary, my poor Jacques?"

With that, he had become serious. "All kidding aside, my lovely Tamarotchka." (He liked to call me by my diminutive.)

"No, I wasn't," he corrected himself, his eyes studying my face. "I've been thinking a great deal about you, Tamara," he said slowly. "You're a lovely young woman; you're beautiful, talented, intelligent. You dance like a dream, like a ballerina, except with substance. You're warm, full of life, and terribly delectable. No, don't look down in your embarrassment. You know what you are; other men have told you that, I'm sure. Why the heck are you so damned aloof? That's what I cannot understand." His voice had been gentle, as if he were talking to a child.

"I'm not aloof, Jacques. I've always been friendly."

He patted my hand. "Darling Tamarotchka, I don't mean in that way. I mean the way you act towards men. You're friendly with them to a certain point, until it's time to say good night. Out comes your hand, 'Thank you, and good night,' you say."

"You mean I have to kiss every date when I say goodnight, Jacques? Sorry, I can't do that."

"And why not?" His eyes fastened on mine, daring me to answer.

I felt rather foolish explaining why I could not. I could already see Phyllis's look of disapproval, telling me to grow up, for Heaven's (if not God's) sake. "To kiss a man, in my opinion, is to let him know that I'm serious about him, to the point of marriage. I have not thought about marriage at this time. I have other plans for my life, like going to New York and working after graduating from Radcliffe."

"I want to know why you feel like that," he had persisted, his voice most gentle. "Why?"

"Because..." I remember feeling cornered and pausing. How could I explain to him that it was the way I had been brought up, that I didn't want to have any physical contact with any man because physical things didn't happen until people got married. Not until then was it right. I knew he wouldn't understand my point of view; so I decided to be flippant. "Jacques, it's because I believe in fairy tales. Some day my prince will come to me on a white charger. He will swoop me off my feet with one mighty sweep of his arm, and he'll give me a kiss. Off we'll ride, away into the..."—I paused, thinking of how to make it more dramatic—"sunset."

He leaned towards me, laying one hand gently on my shoulder. "Are you afraid that something terrible might happen to you with a kiss? That's it, isn't it? Tamara, let me show you how harmless a kiss between a man and a woman can be. May I?"

I nodded, tired of this fencing. "You may."

I can still picture that first kiss that Jacques had planted on me. He had cradled me in his arms, then lowered his head towards mine, his eyes tender. Then, gently, he had bent his head even lower till his lips touched mine. A light press, and he had raised his head again. It had been as if a feather had brushed across my lips.

"Now, was that bad?" He took my face in his hands, smiling with amusement. "You're a woman, Tamara, and yet you're a child, aren't you?"

Without thinking I wiped my lips on the back of my hands. Realizing that Jacques had noticed my reaction, I tried to make an excuse.

"Oh, Jacques, honestly, I did enjoy your kiss. It's just that I'm not used to men kissing me."

He had laughed it off, like the perfect gentleman, who Mama had insisted he was. "Anyone else doing that would have been an insult, my Tamarotchka. With you, being you, I forgive you."

"We're friends, then?" I had been so relieved that he hadn't been insulted by my action. "I'm really glad you kissed me, Jacques. Now I realize it's not really immoral, or bad. You may kiss me good night now, whenever you want to."

At that he had grinned, then raised himself from his sitting position on the rug. He retrieved his jacket from the back of Mama's sofa. "Good night then, my darling," he whispered. Just before opening the front door, he turned and kissed me once more—this time not so lightly, or gently—on the lips.

346

21

Sammy

"What's wrong, Papa? Did you forget your key?" I had been surprised to see him at the front door, all bundled up, with his woolen scarf covering the lower part of his face.

Stomping his boots to shake off the snow, he chuckled. "Take these packages to Mama," he ordered. His scarf muffled his voice.

"Br-r-r!" Papa was just hanging up his coat when I returned to the foyer. "This must be the coldest day we've had this year. Did you give Mama the packages?"

"Indeed I did," I answered. "Why did you get us wine? It's not some special occasion, is it?"

"Haven't you been reading the newspaper?" He sat on the stairs to take off his boots. "I almost slipped in Cambridge Common. That would have been a good howdy-doody, wouldn't it?"

"Oh, Papa...." I laughed at the thought of seeing him sliding around. In his black coat he looked like a cuddly, roly-poly Russian bear. "It's not 'howdy-doody,' Papa. It's 'howd' you do.'"

Mama came out of the kitchen. "Papotchka, thanks for getting the groceries. I worried about you walking home in all this snow. It's so slippery these days. I can't believe it's still snowing."

Papa winked at me. *He surely is in a good mood today,* I thought to myself. "What's the news, Mama?"

"Look at this," Mama picked up the *Boston Globe* and pointed to the headlines: GERMANS TURNED BACK AT STALINGRAD!

No wonder Papa was so excited. The Russians had finally

347

succeeded in driving the Germans out of the city. The five months' siege had ended.

"January thirty-first, nineteen forty-three," Papa declared, as if he meant to memorialize this date forever. "I predicted it, didn't I, Mamotchka? When the Russian winter comes, I told you, the Germans will be routed. That's what I said. 'A house established by oppression cannot long enjoy its prosperity.' Eventually the Germans will be defeated on all fronts. The Japanese too. Mark my words."

Mama broke in, "I can't forget what they have done to Stalingrad. It is terrible. That beautiful city with its old buildings, its modern stores and factories . . . completely destroyed."

Papa hadn't yet finished his discourse. "The Germans, overwhelmed by the Red Army's counteroffensives, especially those of the Don Cossacks, were entrapped, thus ending the siege, just as I had predicted. Now, Mama, is dinner ready? We can't miss Eric Sevareid tonight."

"Of course. By the time you come back from washing your hands, dinner will be on the table."

Just as she had promised, dinner was ready in the kitchen, but tonight Mama had used her beautiful Chinese hand-embroidered tablecloth. "Place the napkins around, Tamara." She bustled about, ladling out the cabbage rolls, spooning her colorful and tasty vinaigrette onto smaller plates.

"Mama, you even made *banitchka*." I gave her a bear hug.

"Tsk, Tamara, I can't breathe," she protested. "I had some cottage cheese left over." She laughed, adding, "Watch out though, it's fattening, you know."

"I don't care. I love it. Besides, tonight is special."

"Oy, yoy!" she gasped. "I forgot to put Papa's sherry in the refrigerator. Whew! This excitement is too much for me."

"Don't worry, Mama. Papa won't notice. Just pour it."

Papa came down the backstairs. "Walking home tonight, I thought my nose would freeze. Ah-h, you've made cabbage rolls. They're good for a day like today." He pinched his nose, a habit of his when he was in rare, good humor, and then sat down.

It was a festive dinner, with Papa refilling our glasses even before we had had time to empty them. At dinner's end, Papa slowly got up, stood erect, put his chest out, and dramatically raised his glass, declaiming in his oratorical tones, "To the brave people of Stalingrad, *na zdorovya!*"

For the next toast, he refilled our glasses to the brim. "Now, a toast to the glorious Red Army! Here's to our brave, invincible, saber-wielding Don Cossacks!" We drank once more.

"How about our Kocinka?" Mama suggested. "We must drink to him. I wonder where he is. I only wish we knew. It is so hard, this not knowing."

"Verotchka, he's fine. His letters show that." Papa raised his glass. "To Vanya, our American soldier."

We emptied our glasses to Vanya. Papa had insisted on that. "*Do dna*" (to the bottom), he kept repeating.

Papa, inspired by the event and even more so by the wine, toasted the Red Army a second time. As he put his glass down, he turned to me and said, "The Chinese have this proverb: 'The thread cannot pass through without a needle; the boat cannot cross without water.' Do you know what that means, *dochenka?*"

"Of course. Stalingrad could not have survived without the Red Army. Right?"

My answer had pleased him. "You're a smart *dochenka.*"

Dinner over, we listened to Eric Sevareid's calm, analytical broadcast.

"Even he sounded elated," Papa observed. "I really think that we're now at the turning point of the war. Remember, Mamotchka, when the American and British forces landed in North Africa? What a mass landing that had been, troops going ashore at different places on the northern and western coasts. There had been casualties, but in the end we had won. What an immense operation that had been!"

"I can't remember all the places," Mama sighed. "There have been so many battles—in Europe, in Asia, everywhere. It's just too much for me sometimes. All I can think of is the poor mothers. How many of them have lost their sons. Ach." She placed her hand onto her breast as if it hurt, then sighed again.

"Mamotchka, take heart. Vanya writes that he's been meeting girls," Papa noted, "so he can't be in too grave danger. When he stops writing, that's when to worry—and even then, the mails can be slow."

"It's really maddening to read some of his letters with all

349

those little rectangular cut-outs," Mama complained. "Vanya, I know, wouldn't write anything that could harm America."

" 'Loose lips sink ships,' Mama," I quoted.

She became thoughtful. "Yes, I know."

Earlier, in one of his letters, Vanya had mentioned a Captain Klauber, an officer who had befriended him. He wrote that this captain would be coming to Boston on furlough and that he might be telephoning us.

"I told him all about you folks," Vanya had written to Mama. "Be sure to make him feel really welcome. He's been very good to me. He especially wants to meet Tamara, whose photograph he's seen and admired."

Mama eagerly looked forward to the captain's visit. "Now we'll be able to find out where our Kocinka is stationed." Her eyes lit up at the thought and already she was making plans. "What shall we offer this Captain Klauber to drink? What do Americans prefer, Tamara? You should know."

"Wine, maybe. Coffee or tea, I guess. I don't know, Mama. He might want something even stronger. Some Americans drink what they call 'cocktails,' or mixtures of different liquors, I think." I thought of what my friends drank. "I think you'd better make some coffee, just in case. But we haven't even heard from this friend of Vanya's."

A few days later our phone rang. I ran downstairs to answer it, knowing how much Mama disliked answering it. She was self-conscious about the way she spoke English, although I thought her accent charming and her voice quite musical.

"Is this Tamara?" The voice on the other end was soft and cozy. I almost turned around, thinking the person to be right here beside me, whispering into my ear.

"Yes?" I was still breathless from running down the stairs.

Whoever it was at the other end chuckled to himself. Then the voice became milder, rather apologetic. "I'm sorry. It's just that I feel that I already know you. Vanya has described all of his family in such detail."

"Who is this?" Then it dawned on me. "Oh, you must be Captain Klauber. My brother wrote that you were coming here on furlough."

I liked the sound of his voice, warm and friendly, as if I were not a complete stranger talking to him for the first time.

"Yes, your brother's quite a guy. I've enjoyed getting to know him. Now, Tamara, listen. Just call me Sam, will you?"

"So delighted to meet you, Sam," I said, "but really, we want to see you in person. My mother has been anxious to ask you all about Vanya."

Again, that deep chuckle. "And I'm impatiently waiting to see if the photograph your brother showed me is really you. What say you that I come," he paused, then came out with, "say in around an hour or so?"

Mama had appeared in the foyer. She waited expectantly, and I silently nodded to her. She knew at once that it was the captain.

"We'll roll out the red carpet for you," I told him. "Oh, by the way, what do you drink? Mama wants to know."

That amused him. "Anything you have in the house. If it's water, I'll drink water. I'm coming to visit you, not to drink or party. Okay? Tell your sweet mama that." With that he said good-bye.

"Mama, he sounds very nice, and he'll be here within an hour."

Mama became flustered. "Oy, my God, Tamara, we don't have much time. Do you think we should change?" She looked at her housedress. Although worn, it still looked attractive on her. I had on my long, flowered skirt and a snug-fitting green blouse. They were comfortable but not dressy. I wasn't about to change.

"Mama, we're dressed. After all, we're at home, not going out or anything. Remember that we're not in Peking now. Americans are a lot more informal. You look beautiful, just as you are."

"Oy!" Her hand flew to her mouth. "I'd better make tea. Do you think he'll like tea? Come on, Tamara. Please hurry." She pushed me into the kitchen, patting her hair on the sides of her head as she ran after me.

When the doorbell rang, I whipped off my apron and rushed to the door. When I opened it, I stared blankly for a moment at the man in uniform facing me. This was Captain Klauber! No, it couldn't be. This had to be someone else, a stranger, not the Sam whose voice had conjured up for me the image of a tall, handsome captain, who would whisper into my ear or chuckle to himself the way he had chuckled over the phone. This man was short, my height, and old, probably in his forties. He wore horn-rimmed glasses, and there was a blue-black shadow of beard. I had imagined blue eyes, deep ocean blue, swimming with tenderness and love as he would gaze into my own big brown eyes.

"Captain Klauber?" It was Mama speaking. She had come from behind me and was now extending her hand to grasp his.

He was grinning. "Thank you. May I call you Mama?" He took her hand, covering it with his other one. "Yes, indeed, I am. I'm Sam to you folks."

"Come in, Sam." Mama was graciousness itself.

"Yes, Captain, please come in," I murmured, ashamed of having stared at him, agape and speechless.

"Sam it is, not captain. Everybody who's not in the United States Army calls me Sam. Even a few who are do too.

"I don't bite, Tamara." He was amused as I stood awkwardly to the side. He patted the cushion next to him on the sofa. Then he turned to Mama. "Your son was right, Madame Rubleva. Both of you are beautiful women. I don't know which one I should choose." He fixed his eyes on me once more. "Sit here beside your Uncle Sam, my dear. Let me look to see if you're truly as lovely as you should be." I now realized that he was teasing. His flirting with Mama and me was all in fun. I relaxed, took the cushion offered, and smiled at him.

"The photograph didn't do her justice, I'd say," he told Mama, nodding his head in my direction. "You're a fortunate

352

lady indeed, Madame, to have such charming offspring. Believe me, your son is such a talented, interesting young man. I've had many enlightening discussions with him."

I could sense Mama's increasing impatience. She had been about to say something several times, then had stopped.

"Sammy," I placed my hand on his arm, feeling the rough texture of his uniform, and asked, "where did you come from? That's what Mama wants to know. She wants to know where Vanya is stationed."

He turned his kind face to Mother. "I understand. She's worried," he said. "Don't worry though. He's in North Africa now, having a ball. Mother," he took both her hands in his and rubbed them gently as he reassured her, "you have no worries. He is absolutely safe and happy. His main worry at present," he grinned, "is whom to date." *How well he knows my brother*, I thought. Those comforting words of Sam's were just what Mama needed to hear.

Sam slowly surveyed the room. "Yes, it's exactly as Vanya had described it to me. There's that RCA console and the armchair the professor sits in when he listens to the news or 'Opera of the Air' on Saturday afternoons. And all these Chinese curios of yours. They must keep your memory of China alive! What memories you people must have." He looked from Mama to me, his face full of loving sympathy.

"I'm sorry my husband isn't here to greet you, Sam, but he should be home for dinner. You'll stay, won't you?"

He took her hand. "Mama, there's nothing I'd enjoy more."

What a marvelous person he is, I thought to myself. *He's so understanding. It's his eyes. That's what it is. His eyes keep studying me as if he's trying to figure me out.* Had he done the same thing to Vanya? Was that why Vanya liked him? What did Sam really think of Vanya? Someday, when and if I got to know Sam better, I'd ask him.

Sammy was now surveying the packages on his lap, his hands feeling them, almost caressing them.

"Vanya is a good boy," he told Mama quietly, "but he has got a lot of growing up to do. Don't misunderstand me, Mama. You don't mind me calling you that, do you? It's just that when we talked about your family, that's what I learned to call you."

Mama placed her hand over his and patted it in her reassuring way. "I like it when you call me Mama. It makes me feel good."

He smiled, giving her a tender glance. "Vanya, well, he's all right, except that there's still so much that he has to learn. He has to learn about life here in the States, about army life." Seeing Mama's somewhat alarmed expression, he softened his words. "No, Mama, he's okay, really. I've seen to that."

"I myself know how it is," I told Sam. "I've had a time trying to adjust to American customs. It must be even more difficult in the army."

"It sure is." For a moment he was silent. When he crossed his short legs, I noticed his well-polished shoes. "It was very difficult for him, but one day he came to see me, extremely troubled. Everybody was on his back, he told me. After we'd talked about the possible reasons for his troubles, he calmed down, promising that he'd try to look at things more cheerfully. Several days later, he told me that our little talk had really helped him. You know how hard it is, being thrust into a new world like ours—one with a culture so different from the one you're accustomed to."

Just then I heard Papa's key turn in the front door lock, and in no time at all, Papa was hugging Sam as if he were Vanya rather than a total stranger. "I saw you through the window," Papa exclaimed. "I knew right away that you must be Sam."

At the dinner table in the dining room, Sam was the center of attention. He went on and on about his army experiences. "We had a fellow in our outfit—a corporal—whom we nicknamed Patcheye because he had lost an eye in Algiers. Well, Patcheye saw better with his one eye than I could with two." He told us about the Isle of Capri. "Before we went to North Africa, we were in Italy. Vanya and I went to the isle one time. It's a magical place. Of course, Vanya fell in love there."

We listened as if hypnotized. When he paused for breath, Mama asked, "Where is your home, Sam?"

That was when I noticed the change in him. He became subdued, as if even thinking about home made it painful.

"Mama, I come from Chelsea, Massachusetts. My beginnings were quite humble, I must say." He paused. "My parents were immigrants like you and the professor." He looked around at each of us in turn, as if to etch our features forever into his mind. Then his eyes rested on me.

"Yes," he murmured, as if to himself. He leaned forward so that his face was near mine. "You know," he seemed puzzled, "you're not at all what I had expected." At that, I smiled. Neither was he what I had expected. Mama and Papa looked amused.

"Yes," he grinned that slow, deliberate grin that was so appealing, "the way Vanya described you, I thought immediately of Pola Negri, the vamp, remember?" He laughed. "Or Clara Bow perhaps. However, you're not a bit like them." His voice softened to a purr. "You're like one of Raphael's innocent cherubs with a halo around your head."

He turned to Papa, "No?"

Papa laughed, pleasantly flattered by Sam's description of me. "But, Captain Klauber, she is a cherub," he stressed, looking at me with affection. "You can't believe how popular she is. Nearly every evening some young man calls to invite her to some function. What pleases Mama and me most is that she is not spoiled by all this attention."

"Having such a daughter makes you indeed a wealthy man."

"Captain, there is a Chinese proverb that applies to your compliment. 'There is no poverty where there is virtue, and no wealth or honor where virtue is not.'"

Sam nodded. "Professor, you're absolutely right." He gave me a knowing wink.

"Did Vanya really describe me as a vamp?" I asked Sam. I didn't like being compared to one, even as a joke.

"No, I guess I'm the one to blame." Sam slowly appraised me. "You think of a Russian woman, you think of someone exotic with manicured curved nails on long, slim fingers. [I looked down at my own stubby fingers and smiled.] Then you think of 'come-hither' eyes, inch-deep in mascara. Why you're nothing but a child; you're a lovely, delicious, and delightful child!"

I couldn't help frowning at his remarks. Papa's and Mama's amused expressions didn't help matters either. Why couldn't people see me as I really was? Couldn't they see me as a young college woman intent on getting her education and making her own way in the world? Why was it that people always judged me by my face and figure as if I were some inanimate, sculptured piece of art?

Sam must have sensed my feeling, for he cupped my face in his hands, moving it closer to his own. "You're a lovely young woman, sweetheart," he murmured. "You're one in a million, my child. Just stay as you are, always."

He left soon after, promising that he'd come back soon. Mama, of course, was smitten. Even Papa liked this kind and gentle captain. As for me, although I liked him, in a way he also annoyed me. I enjoyed his frankness, his studied thoughtfulness, and his intimate, cozy manner. However, I didn't like being called "baby" or "child." I hadn't appreciated his making fun of my innocence and treating me like an adolescent. I was a full-grown adult with ideas, thoughts, and lots more than a pretty face and an attractive figure.

One of the benefits that comes with growing old is being able to look back into one's youth and to see people as they really were without being emotionally involved. Although I did not realize it at the time, Sam eventually turned out to be a voice of reason to me. In his subtle way he advised or rebuked me, and at times even acted as my conscience. In spite of my self-denials, I was a child in so many ways, still trusting, gullible, and innocent, idealistic like the heroines of the many Victorian novels that I had ravenously read in my young adulthood. Although I was quite sure that I was mature and worldly, Sam saw me as I really was, a child-woman. He became to me what my old-fashioned parents could never have become. Like the stick that props up a young plant, he supported me at the same time that he was analyzing me. Like a guardian angel, he watched over me.

After that first visit, Sam came to see us often. In time, he met Lanny. "Tamara," he told me one day, placing a hand on my cheek and peering into my eyes, "Lanny's okay. Yes." He nodded his head like a wise, old owl. He reflected a moment and then looked at me thoughtfully, "Yes, Lanny's a good boy." Sam had a habit of repeating his phrases. "But, darling, he's not for you. No, indeed, not for you. You need,"—his brown eyes behind those hornrims studying my own eyes until, uneasy under his gaze, I lowered them—"you need someone who's stronger than you." He shook his head knowingly, and Mama, of course, agreed with him wholeheartedly.

On one occasion I did get somewhat annoyed with him. It was as if he had made himself my guardian. He always had something derogatory to say about my dates. It irritated me; yet I couldn't tell him so. It must have been my Chinese cultural upbringing that caused me to quietly disregard his solicitous intrusion. I had too much respect for his years to argue with him; yet one day I had to challenge him. "All right, Sam." I remember clenching my lips as I had him sit down on Mama's dragon rug. "You tell me. Who's the man for me? None of the men I am currently dating suit you."

His lips had slowly molded themselves into that enigmatic smile of his. "Why, me, of course," he had offered, his eyes blinking at me, half-serious, half-amused. "I'd be perfect for you." While he spoke, I saw a shadow flit across his face, but only for a moment. His eyes had smiled.

"Oh, Sammy, there you go again teasing me," I declared. "Tell me. I really want to know who the man for me is. That is, the man who fits your specifications for me."

"Ah, my sweet," he murmured, his usual self now, tenderly loving with his honeyed words. "The way I see it is this. Here's my recipe for your ideal. You've got to have a strong man, not me, or Lanny, or any of those handsome studs who've ogled you on Harvard Square. Darling, you and I have not yet found your man."

"So you don't really know?" I asked him in a mocking tone.

"No, child. You're so damned sexy and lovable. The whole world loves you, and you love it. Here's the rub to all of this; you have that damned moral code of yours that has built such a barrier between men and you. My recipe is quite a simple one. You need one night of love with one strong man to break down that barrier you hide behind. That kind of experience will free you from those terribly crazy inhibitions of yours."

The idea! To put it mildly, his words shocked me. How could he have dared to suggest that I do something like that!

I could feel my anger mounting. "And then what, Sammy-boy?" I could not conceal my sarcasm. "Once your strong man is done with me, I'd be alone, perhaps pregnant, left to combat the

357

scandal that would surely follow. What happens to him? Does he ship out to go to war? Maybe he'll be certified as a deflowering pistil for naive young girls. No, Captain, I'm determined to stick to my unpopular ideals." I could feel myself become red-faced and furious. "That's all I have left, according to you, isn't it?"

"I hope your ideals make you happy, Tamara. I certainly do hope so." I realized my outburst had saddened him. "You'll realize that some day you'll have to step down from that elevated pedestal of yours. Once you have come down off it, then a man will be able to love you as a man should. You, in turn, will love him, fully and gladly."

I stared at him. "Just what do you mean by all that, Sam?"

He shrugged his shoulders, hunching his head into the collar of his uniform. "You know damned well what I mean, Tamara. Some day, and I hope that it is soon for your own, sweet sake, you will meet a man who won't send you long boxes filled with red roses or take you by taxi to expensive night spots to dance the boogie-woogie. He won't jump at a nod of your pretty head or the bending of your lovely little pinky finger. That, my dear, will be the man for you. Pray that he comes along soon."

He spoke somewhat bitterly. I wondered to myself if the reason was that he had fallen in love with me himself and realized that I would never consider him as a husband and lover. Or was it just my Uncle Sam, the friendly doctor, who liked to see why people acted the way they did? He had taken a personal interest in Vanya, had helped him solve his problems. That done, he must have felt that it was now my turn to be helped. I looked at his thoughtful face and smiled.

"I'm not worried about myself, Sam. My life is completely happy. I have been frank about my feelings with the fellows I date. They still ask me out. A few have even asked me to marry them. They don't regard me as abnormal, the way you do. You're a man, Sam. You're the hunter. I'm satisfied to be what I am. Let me be."

22

The Lieutenant

Phyllis, Mama, and I were bustling about in the kitchen, cleaning up after supper. We had been teasing Mama unmercifully, amused to see her blush at our comments.

"You must have been some beauty when you were in college, Mama. Even now, at your advanced age, you still look glamorous. Doesn't she, Tamara?" Phyllis, her eyes sparkling with mischief, placed her hands on Mama's hips and spun her around. "Come on, Mama, let's polka."

Mama finally shook herself free, wiping her eyes with the edge of her apron. "Oy, you girls, I don't know when I've laughed so hard. Get out of my kitchen and go upstairs where you belong. I'm sure you have studying to do." She undid her apron strings. "I've about had it with the two of you. Didn't some one tell me but half an hour ago that she has exams to cram for?"

Laughingly, I gave her a playful pinch on the cheek, then darted out of her way before she could get at me. *"Oui, Maman, ma chérie,* we do have an exam." I grinned at her. "On Monday, *comprenez vous? Et demain est Samedi, n'est ce pas?"*

Mama folded her apron. "All the more time for you to study instead of aggravate me," she tried to sound stern, but her smiling eyes betrayed her.

"Aw, Mama, come on. Tell us about your days as a young girl in Russia. It has to be romantic. Tell us how you met Papa." Phyllis danced around Mama, her voice a wheedling falsetto.

"About my days in Russia . . ." Mama got that faraway look in her eyes. "Now let me see, what is it you'd like to hear about?"

"Tamara says you were very popular. Tell us about the trick

you played on that fat officer, the one who was so smitten with you."

Mama smiled in recollection. "Volodya Smolin, yes, the poor fellow. What a long time ago that was." She let out a deep sigh, "I can't believe how long. I must have been nineteen, twenty, like you are now. Let me see, you want to hear how I met Papa or about Officer Smolin? Which one?"

"The way you met Papa," I said, although I had heard the story before.

"I have to explain to Phyllis first. You see, Phyllis, in Russia, my father was considered to be a wealthy man. As a landowner, he possessed not only the great house where we lived but also estates in Lvov in western Ukraine and in Sochi on the eastern coast of the Black Sea. We were what you would call here the 'elite,' the 'cream' of society. My mother died when I was still a child, leaving my two older sisters, me, and Antosha, our baby brother. Papa had estates and servants to oversee and businesses to tend to. He had no time to worry about us children although, of course, he loved us all. He remarried soon after mother's death. We children all hated our stepmother, knowing that she had married Papa only for the position she would occupy in high society. When we were sent away to boarding schools and then the university, it was actually like an escape for us. Our happiest times, however, were when Matchexa (our stepmother) would go to visit her own kin, and we could visit with Papa alone. It was on such an occasion that I first met Serioja." She bent her head back and closed her eyes, a half-smile playing upon her lips.

"A friend of my father's recommended me as Romanian translator for our local post office. It was, you know, a part-time job during summer vacation. Well, Serioja happened to be in charge. He had recently done some graduate work at the University of Vladivostok, after already having graduated from Moscow University with a gold medal and other scholastic honors. His major had been interesting, albeit a strange one. He studied the languages of the Far East, intending to go there himself one day. I myself had just graduated from Beztuzhevsky Institute, which was considered quite an institution, like your Radcliffe. Anyway, I liked this young man; he was a contrast to the officers I went to balls with. They were, I must admit, a rather snobbish group.

360

Serioja, although he had also gone to the Military Academy, did not fit in with them. He was a serious young man, totally unskilled and uninterested in the etiquettes and flirtations of my friends. I admired him for that, and his aloofness intrigued me. Soon we started going together. Once"—her face turned rosy as she started to giggle—"he invited me for a walk on Nevsky Prospekt, something like New York's Fifth Avenue, except that it was in St. Petersburg. I got it into my head to play a trick on him. You see, he would get so involved in talking to me about his studies and ideas about China that sometimes he would walk ahead of me, not realizing that it was hard for me to keep up with him. This time I decided to let him walk on, and I hid behind a tree, watching him, laughing to myself. After he'd gone some distance, he realized that I wasn't with him. Well, he looked ahead, backwards, then retraced his steps till he came to my tree. I could no longer torment him so I came out from behind it."

"Did he mind your teasing him?" Phyllis asked.

"Not at all. He was so totally out of it all, engrossed in his Chinese philosophers and poets, that the actual world around him didn't faze him. I think that that's what I loved about him, his innate goodness and total adherence to truth. Why he fell in love with me, I'll never fathom. Anyway, he asked my father for my hand, and Papa reluctantly said yes."

"Why reluctantly?" Phyllis had been so interested in Mama's story that she had forgotten to smoke. Now she had to reach out for a Lucky.

Mama's face clouded. "Because I believe my father knew that once I married Serioja I would leave him to go to China, and he would never see me again. Traveling then was not what it is these days."

"And Mama was his favorite daughter," I explained. "My grandfather loved her very much."

Mama nodded, "My father was right, of course, He never did see me after our marriage. Serioja and I left for China, and Papa died the next year."

"How terribly tragic," Phyl said in a low tone, "but how romantic for you, meeting your husband that way, marrying him, and then going to China. That'll never happen to us."

"It will," Mama said. "In a different way perhaps, but it'll come. You're young; your lives are just beginning. If only you knew how much you have to look forward to, my dears."

The phone rang in the foyer. "Oops, I'd better get it." I hurried out of the kitchen.

Still out of breath, I picked up the receiver. "Yes?"

"Catch your breath, darling," advised the now familiar voice. "I'm not going anywhere, at least not this minute."

"Sorry, Sam. Phyl and I have just been listening to Mama talk about her romance with Papa, how she met him and so forth. We were out in the kitchen."

"Ah-h. I apologize for making you run, my sweet. I would have liked to hear Mama's story too. She's certainly a lovely lady. Now, for the reason I phoned you: It's, well, I need a favor from you. In fact, I'm glad Phyllis is with you because she's the one I'm thinking of."

Phyllis had followed me into the foyer and was now sitting at the bottom of the stairs, watching me expectantly.

"What's this all about, Sam?"

I heard his deep chuckle, "Well, to tell the truth, child, I have here with me this fine, young lieutenant, who's convinced that he is very ill, that he has sinus problems. I'm convinced that, for one thing, he's been working too hard; he's tired and probably homesick to boot. As his doctor, I've prescribed a night on the town for him. What better medicine for him and me than the company of two such delightful Cliffies as you and Phyl? What do you say? Am I right in my diagnosis and prescription? Keep in mind, though," he added hastily, "that you'll be my date."

"Why don't you talk to Phyl yourself?" I suggested. I passed the phone on to her saying, "It's about a lieutenant for you. Sam wants us to double date."

Phyllis's smile grew wider as she listened to Sam. Several times she nodded. "Sure, Sammy, we're not doing anything special tonight. In fact, we did plan to study a bit, but"—she motioned me to light her a cigarette—"we've got the whole weekend for that. No. Oh, yes. Why sure. Yep, that'll be great. Bye."

From Phyllis's monosyllabic responses I couldn't guess what Sam had told her. "C'mon, Phyl, what is it?"

She was not about to have me rush her. She first had to sit

362

down on the stairs again. "Well, apparently, from what Sam says, this lieutenant is really a fine person, very intelligent." That last part bothered her. "I hope he's not an egghead, I couldn't take that. Anyway, Tamara, they'll be here within an hour. In the meantime, we've got to figure out where they're to take us. Isn't there a dance at Memorial Hall tonight?"

"I don't know. We were going to buckle down and study this weekend, remember?"

She grinned. "Yeah, but this sounds like more fun. C'mon, let's go upstairs. I need to do my face. This lieutenant sounds okay to me. I only hope he doesn't have a girlfriend waiting for him somewhere. Wouldn't that just be my luck?" She kept on chattering as we walked upstairs. "What are you going to wear?"

"I don't know." I was in my usual long, peasant skirt and green blouse. It was comfortable, and I wasn't in the mood to get all dressed up.

"Well, you'd better get on the ball," she ordered. "Boy, it's a good thing I brought along some decent clothes and my plat-forms. Mind if I use the bathroom first?"

"Go ahead, but I suggest you'd better knock first. Papa sometimes forgets to lock the door when he's in there."

While Phyl dolled herself up in the bathroom, I lay down on my studio bed and turned on the radio. André Kostelanetz and his orchestra were playing "Night and Day." I turned up the volume hoping that she could hear. It was her favorite song.

Half an hour later, she came out and was surprised to see me still lounging. "Aren't you getting ready? They'll be here shortly."

"I like that black dress on you, Phyl. It makes your hair look lighter. Yes, I'll get ready now." I went to my dresser to comb my hair. "Sammy doesn't mind how I look; he likes me the way I am." Seeing her look of dismay, I hastened to reassure her. "I'll be changing in a sec, Phyl. Don't worry; I won't humiliate you."

Just as I started to unfasten my skirt, the doorbell rang.

"Shit!" Phyllis groaned and reached for her purse, pulling out her Lucky Strikes. Her hands shook as she lit a cigarette. "You go to the door. I'm too damned nervous."

"I will if you stop saying those words, Phyl."

"C'mon, Tamara, please?"

Mac When I First Met Him

"Especially that *s* word. It's crude to talk like that." I could be stubborn too.

Again, the doorbell rang.

"Oh, sh . . . oh, you mean shit? Okay, I won't say it," she promised. "At least not in your exalted presence. Now will you open that damned door?"

I heard Mama's bedroom door open. "Tamara? The door."

"I'm going, Mama. It's only Sam and a friend of his."

I had my hand on the top of the banisters when Phyl stopped me, panic-stricken. "Look, if this lieutenant looks like a creep or, you know, is not my type, just tell Sammy that I'm not feeling too good. Say anything, but get me out of it. Okay?"

"But, Phyl, that's not fair when they've come all this way. You promised." Her sudden change of mind annoyed me, but when I saw the look on her face, I softened. "I'll handle it." Without waiting for her reply, I ran, barefooted, down the stairs.

Again the bell sounded. This time it was Papa's voice, impatience in check, coming from the study. "Will someone please see who's at the door?"

"I'm going to, Papa," I shouted.

Breathless, I flung open the door, Phyl's desperate plea still echoing in my ears as I faced the two officers.

Sam was grinning from ear to ear. As usual, he looked neat and trim in his captain's uniform. He handed me a box of candy. "Here's something to sweeten your cruel disposition, Sweetheart."

It was then that I heard the taller officer behind Sam laugh. Curiously, I glanced up at Phyl's date, a smiling young man with rimless glasses and a sandy crewcut. Not at all the type of person Phyl usually dated. She preferred the Cary Grant type. Tempted to giggle at the thought of her predicament, I tried hard to maintain my control. I opened the door wider, motioning them to come in. "We'll be ready in a few minutes, Sam. Just go on into the living room and make yourselves at home." I didn't wait for Sam to introduce me. I made a hasty retreat to the stairs, muzzling my mouth with my fist. At the top of the stairs I could hold out no longer. Clutching my stomach, I stumbled to my room with relief, trying to keep my laughter in check. Phyllis, impatient, immediately realized the situation.

"He's that bad?" Her eyes showed her disappointment. "Tamara," she continued stubbornly, "I'm not going."

"Phyl, he's not that bad." I bit my lower lip.

"What's he like then? Tell me the truth."

I didn't know how long I could keep a straight face. The more I thought of that brief glimpse I had caught of the lieutenant, the funnier and more hilarious it became. The misery in Phyllis's face didn't help matters either. Tears welled in my eyes; my shoulders began to quiver as those uncontrollable giggles returned.

"Honestly, Phyl, I don't mean to laugh. It's just that you look so funny. Okay, I'll describe him, although I didn't get that good a look at him. He's taller than Sam; he has a crewcut; his hair is the color of sand. Eyes? Either blue or grey. It's hard to tell because he's wearing glasses." I hadn't the heart to tell her that they were the old-fashioned, rimless kind. That would have ended it for sure. Then the very thought of them set me off again. "Aw, Phyl, I can't help it. He looks like a drip." I sat on my studio couch and hid my face in my hands.

She was totally, thoroughly disgusted with me. "Well, in spite of what you've said, I'm going to be a good sport about this. I'm going down, and I'll make the best of it, drip or no drip." She gave me a scathing look, "If you decide to make yourself presentable, why don't you come down and show that you can be an adult for a change?"

With that, she marched downstairs in her platforms, looking like a sacrificial maiden going to her doom. I heard her polite hellos to both Sam and the lieutenant, and then her good-humored laughter.

Sobering up from my laughing spell, I quickly put on my black skirt and pink angora sweater. A bit of lipstick, a dab of rouge, and my mirror told me that Phyllis would approve. Gosh, she could be critical! I smiled to myself as I slipped my feet into the patent leather spikes. It had taken me barely ten minutes to do all that!

We ended up going to an officers' dance in Boston, quite a pleasant affair. The dance was already in full swing when we arrived. Still, the ever-finagling Sammy had been able to get us a table near the dance floor.

Sam had introduced the officer only as "Mac." I hadn't caught his last name, nor had Phyl. We had barely gotten settled at our table when Mac asked Phyl to dance. She laid her evening purse on the table and, giving Sam and me a radiant smile, had walked off with Mac to the dance floor. *Good,* I thought to myself, *she honestly looks as if she likes him.*

Now that they were dancing I could get a better view of Phyl's date. Sam, too, watched them dance, seemingly amused and rather pleased with himself. "What do you think, Tamara? Do they like each other?"

Phyllis looked completely relaxed, one hand lightly resting on the lieutenant's shoulder.

"Yes, I think so." I told Sam what had happened upstairs after I had opened the front door for them.

"Hmm!" Again he contemplated my face as if I puzzled him. "You're still a little girl, Princess. You know, he may not be a Prince Charming to you, this Mac, but he's one great guy; he's well-read, talented, well-educated, a fine fellow—a very fine fellow." He remained silent after that, content to watch the dancers. I watched them too but found my eyes straying back to watch Phyl and her date. Something about the man disturbed me. He had almost deliberately ignored my presence except for that brief moment when Sam had introduced us. I was not used to this.

"Your friend is not much of a dancer, Sam," I said critically, sympathizing with Phyllis. She loved the dreamy romantic music that was now being played and all that they were doing was walking around, backwards and forwards. This Mac certainly couldn't dance.

"Yes, you're right about that, but Phyllis doesn't seem to mind. She's smiling away at him, and he seems to be enjoying himself too. I'm glad." Then Sam fell silent. He seemed to be in a rather strange mood tonight, not his usual, talkative self.

When the music stopped, Mac escorted Phyl back to our table. She bubbled over with good humor; her eyes sparkled as she fastened them on Mac.

"I've learned all about Mac's hometown in Pennsylvania," she told us. "Imagine! They still use outhouses there. Isn't that quaint?"

I would have laughed with them had I known what an outhouse was. I smiled, not wishing to reveal my ignorance.

"I thought those went out of style years ago," Sam said.

"A lot of Pennsylvania is farm country," Mac informed him. "We're still a bit backward, you know, not like you New Englanders."

Both he and Phyl laughed as if sharing a private joke. Phyl reached for a cigarette. The lieutenant lit it for her and whispered something to her. She laughed, then, catching my eye, she quietly laughed again.

"What's so funny, you two?" Sam asked. "Don't leave Tamara and me out of it."

"Oh, Mac has been telling me about their midnight train in Freeport. They call it 'the Bummer.' "

"What is the significance of that?" I asked.

"It's the last train to Freeport from Pittsburgh and arrives at midnight. Many tramps and bums hitch rides on it; that's why the name. Strangers riding the train at that time of night sometimes get the impression that Freeport's a bum's town. It's exactly the opposite, quite conservative and most respectable." This was the first time that Mac had addressed himself directly to me. Was he just being considerate in explaining all this, or did he think me stupid because I had a hard time understanding American terms?

I found myself liking the sound of Mac's voice. He spoke well, enunciating his words. Sam had been right. The lieutenant was intelligent and, judging from Phyllis's spurts of laughter, he must have a good sense of humor. For a moment I wished that he had continued talking to me, but my good feelings vanished when he moved his chair closer to Phyl's. Once again their heads were close together, and they kept their voices low. Well, as far as I was concerned, I would ask no more questions. Besides, he was Phyl's date, not mine.

Sam, of course, had been delighted that Phyl and Mac had hit it off so well. He thought a lot of Phyl and apparently admired Mac a great deal. Sammy liked anybody who could think. One of his greatest pleasures was to sit with Papa in his study and listen to Papa talk about things. Now as he and I sat there watching the dancers, he kept time to the music by tapping one foot on the floor.

"They make a good couple, don't they, Tamara? Both kinda Nordic looking, aren't they? I have to admit I'm a pretty good matchmaker."

"I don't think Mac looks Swedish; he's more English- or Germanic-looking."

Sam gave me a quick appraisal. His next words left me with an instinctive desire to strangle him. He suggested we exchange dancing partners.

"Gives me a chance to talk to Phyllis," he said. "Mac . . . I know he's not your blue-blooded Harvard man, but once you get to know him you'll find out he's okay." He patted my shoulder as he nodded to Phyl.

Phyllis thought it a great idea. As usual, though, when she talked to Sam, she became sarcastic. "I guess we're stuck with each other. How did you know I am pining for you?"

"By your gruesome expression, my dear," he replied, his voice as mocking as hers. "I don't know if I can make it through one dance with you. Do you?" He winked at me, then took her by the arm. Although she was at least five inches taller than Sam, they danced beautifully together.

Left alone with the lieutenant who sat across from me made me ill at ease. I was conscious of his presence, although I avoided looking at him, having decided to remain silent. That way he wouldn't have to be forced to talk to me.

The tables around us were emptying as couples left them to step out onto the dance floor. I stared at them unseeing, only conscious of the quiet around our table. The lieutenant had not made a sound. *What a conceited, conservative snob*, I thought to myself in disgust. Any other man would have been flattered to have been in my company. No other man had ignored me so rudely, so completely. The least he could do was offer me a drink, a cigarette, or even, though heaven forbid, ask me to dance. I stole a glance at him. What a mistake that had been! He had not been watching the floor or the room; he had been watching me.

"Tamara, will you dance with me?"

I had not really expected him to ask me that or to hear such tenderness in his voice; yet there he was coming around to my chair, raising me up, taking my hand. *He's trying to be polite,* I thought to myself.

"Thank you," I remember saying in a small voice, feeling shy and uncertain of myself. I should have refused, having seen him dance with Phyl. I loved to dance, and just seeing his two-stepping in one place had been misery enough.

He took a firm grip of my arm and steered me past the moving couples until he found an uncrowded corner on the dance floor. Then he took me in his arms. "Here we are." He looked down at me. "It's not so crowded here." The way he was holding my arm so possessively bothered me; he treated me as if I belonged to him.

"What kind of dance music do you like?" he asked, looking down at me.

I had been adjusting my feet to his steps. He did not dance to the music; his feet had a rhythm all their own.

"I like Strauss waltzes," I answered, trying to look over his shoulder to see if I could spot Phyl to convey to her my agony. How could Phyllis have danced with him all this time? Now he was jerking my left hand up and down and my calf muscles were beginning to cramp. *God and Confucius, please end the music soon!* They must have heard me, for stop it did.

When I sat down again at the table with Sam, and we were alone, I shook my head at him.

"What's the matter? Didn't you like old Mac?"

"You know how much I love to dance, Sam." Under the table I slipped off my heels, wriggling my toes. "And your Mac doesn't know how to dance. That's all there is to it. If Phyl enjoys his company, that's good. He and I didn't talk much. I just didn't know what to say to him, and he must have felt the same about me. I'm surprised that Phyl likes him; he's certainly not her type. She prefers navy officers."

"Phyl likes everybody," Sammy said quietly. Whether that was a mild rebuke, I could not tell.

Back home in my room Phyl and I sat cross-legged on my studio couch, rehashing the evening.

"Mac wants us to go out again," she told me. "Isn't that great?" I felt happy for her. It was about time she met a decent guy for a change. She'd had the worst luck lately. Most of the navy fellows she had dated had been looking for one thing; worse yet, some of them had even been married. Phyl chattered excitedly, sliding off her nylons, then pressing them flat with her hands. "He's got a great sense of humor, Tamara. I know he's not my type. Sure, he isn't a guy I'd fall for, but who cares, he's fun to go out with. Didn't you like him at least a little?"

"Frankly, no. I'm sorry, but I can't understand what you see in him. He can't even dance."

"He wants to double date again. I told him it would be okay with you."

"Why the devil did you tell him that?"

Phyl reached for her pack of cigarettes, looked inside, shook it, then crumpled it and threw it into my waste basket.

"Shit!" She had missed.

Wordlessly, I retrieved the empty pack and placed it inside, silently offering her my Chesterfields.

"So you've started buying your own? Thanks." She lit the Chesterfield, inhaled, and made a face. "Well, beggars can't be

Lanny and I at the President's Ball

choosers," she conceded. "They're mild compared to Luckies. I thought you'd enjoy double dating. Believe me, if it were someone I was really interested in romantically, you can bet your bottom dollar I wouldn't double date. Mac's a good guy, clean-cut, intelligent, and he sure has a great sense of humor. Why not, Tamara? You don't really mind, do you?"

"You don't have to do a sales talk on him, Phyl. You like his company; I don't. You realize he ignored me most of the evening?"

"Oh, ho, ho, so that's it, is it? Tamara's feelings are hurt because for once she wasn't 'la belle' of the ball. Come off it, Tamara; if not for yourself, do it for me, won't you?"

"That's not it, but I'm not arguing with you. Look, Lanny and I are going to go to the President's Ball at the Copley Plaza next Friday. If he can get extra tickets, I'll let you know. It's formal; you'll need a ballgown."

"Oh, that's swell, Tamara. Gee, that sounds wonderful. I don't get much of a chance to dress up like that. Thanks."

Lanny had no problem getting tickets; so it was settled. Mama had made me a gown especially for Friday's ball.

I described it to Phyllis over the phone. "It's taffeta, a luminous lavender that changes its shade when I move around. Sometimes it's light grayish purple. Other times it looks silver blue. Mama calls it iridescent. The style is old-fashioned, you know, off-the-shoulder, with a tiny waist and a wide, voluminous skirt. I begged Mama to make it really wide so that when Lanny swings me around, it would swish, just the way Scarlett O'Hara's did in the movie, remember?"

I can still recall Lanny's face when he first saw me descending our staircase. For a moment he had gaped, then he handed me the white corsage box.

His silent compliment had delighted me. "Your eyes, Lanny, are as big as saucers."

"I have never seen you look so lovely, Princess." He had bent down to pin the pink camellia to my gown. "You do look like a princess." His voice faltered. For a moment I wished that he could mean more to me than a friend, but then I dismissed the thought. He would be my dear friend always but nothing more.

Lanny had had the table reserved for the four of us. Phyllis and Mac had not shown up as yet.

"I'll just tell the maitre d' to bring them to our table," he told me. "Let's not miss one waltz this evening, Princess."

I agreed. I loved waltzing with Lanny more than dancing with anyone else. He made me feel light as a feather whenever we glided to the music of Strauss. I forgot everything else except ourselves and our flying feet, moving in perfect unison, fast, faster, until the ballroom became waves of color flashing before my eyes. The music, the dancers, the ballroom itself became a kaleidoscope. Only Lanny and I were real. Dear Lanny, not handsome but strong and graceful as the Chinese willow tree! What a dashing partner he made in his uniform, tall, dignified, with an old-fashioned gallantry that appealed to me. Waltzing with him made me feel as if I were indeed part of a magical whirlwind, spinning round and round, at times aware that were it not for the strong hands that guided me, I would be whisked away by this very whirlwind. "Faster, please, Lanny, go faster," I begged of him. Anxious to please, caught up by my own excitement, he led me masterfully away, past the other dancers whose faces had become a blur, until miraculously he found that treasured open space where we could waltz with even more abandon. Whenever the lights dimmed and the beat changed, we stopped to rest. "Good Night, Sweetheart," always came so unexpectedly, and much too soon.

"Sorry, we're late," Phyl apologized as she and Mac came up to our table. I stared at her in surprise. She had on a beautiful aqua crepe gown that accentuated the color of her eyes. I had never seen her so lovely. She eased herself into the chair Mac had pulled out for her and then casually glanced around the ballroom. "My, but this is elegant."

"It's you who are elegant, Phyllis," corrected Lanny. "That dress is so becoming to you. You look like a Grecian goddess, doesn't she, Tamara?"

I agreed, smiling at Phyllis's evident pleasure at being the center of our admiration.

"Thank you, my kind sir." She waited till Mac sat down and then leaned over toward him, her unlit cigarette in her mouth.

"Both girls do us justice, Lanny," Mac observed. He lit Phyl's cigarette. "Tamara, that's a beautiful dress."

"Thank you," I said politely.

Just then Ruby Newman came onto the platform and bowed to the guests. Turning to his band, he raised his baton and I heard the first strains of "The Blue Danube." I reached for Lanny's hand. "Come, Lanny. Let's dance."

Once we started to waltz, I forgot about everything except Lanny and me and the music. As "The Blue Danube" came to an end, I turned to look towards our table. Phyllis and Mac, their heads together, were watching us, smiling.

When it came to rhumba time, Lanny and I walked back to

our table. As he pulled out my chair, his lips brushed against my hair. He waited till I was seated comfortably, then carefully pushed my chair forward. Then he sat down, moving his chair closer, his eyes glowing with happiness as I smiled my thanks.

Phyllis played her game with her smoke circles, watching them spiral in front of her. "I've almost got it now," she bragged. "It's taken me some time to learn how to blow a perfect smoke ring."

"You smoke too much, Phyllis," Mac said good-naturedly. "It's not too good for you, you know."

Phyl laughed. "I know. It's an ugly, dirty habit to which I am painfully addicted." She turned to me, "By the way, Mac and I have decided that you and Lanny dance beautifully together. Where'd you learn to waltz like that, Lanny?"

He blushed at her praise but not from embarrassment. The love in his gaze was obvious to all as he gestured toward me. "It's Tamara who inspires me. Dancing with her is sheer joy."

Why did he have to say that? Uneasily I glanced at Mac, suspecting that Lanny's declaration would amuse him. Instead, he was staring at me, his eyes unfathomable. *What's he thinking of?* I wondered.

"A penny for your thoughts, my princess," Lanny gave my hand a gentle squeeze. Strangely, his action irritated me, and I jerked my hand away. Mac, who had seen it all, had smiled, amused at all this byplay.

"I think I'd like a cigarette now." I reached for Phyllis's pack of Luckies.

"I thought you'd quit." She shoved the pack towards me. "Mac says smoking's not good for you."

"Lanny, would you mind?"

"Gladly, Princess," he leaned towards me with the lighter, happy that I had forgiven him.

" *'All the world's a stage and all the men and women merely players.'* " How well old Will Shakespeare had deciphered human nature! I remember darting a defiant look at Mac, then smiling at Lanny as I concentrated my attention on him and gloated with inner satisfaction as he basked in my adoration. Then, stealing a sly glance at Mac, I noted with surprise that he appeared thoughtful and quite serious and that his eyes were focused intently on me. Then Phyllis, sitting apart now, observing with interest our sport, cleverly played her continuous psychoanalytical game, much in the same way as Sam played it. Only one in our group was no actor. Lanny did not play.

That's when the band started up again. Ruby Newman, bless him, had raised his baton. He had seen me in the ballroom and smiled a greeting. He knew how much I loved Strauss waltzes, especially one in particular. When he nodded to me, I knew that this was the one, the one they would play for me. I waved my hand to thank him, then turned to Lanny. "He's going to play "The Emperor Waltz" for us," I whispered. Smiling in pleasure, Lanny moved his chair back, about to rise.

The lieutenant, however, had been faster. He stood up. "Tamara, would you dance this waltz with me?" He had sounded rather hesitant.

What could I say? He had hardly spoken to me all evening and now he wanted to ruin my favorite waltz for me. I stared at Lanny's crestfallen face; yet I couldn't be impolite and say no to Mac.

"Never mind us," Phyl patted Lanny's hand. "You guys go on. Lanny and I need to catch up on things."

There had been no out for me. Lanny, always considerate, moved his chair closer to Phyl's.

"I'll have the next one with you, Lanny," I promised, lifting up the sides of my skirt as I glided in front of Mac. Remembering his possessive hold on my arm the night we had double dated with Sam, I didn't want him to steer me to the dance floor. That once had been enough.

He took me in his arms, much too close for a waltz. Uneasily I backed off. *I should have refused him,* I thought with regret. This waltz belonged to Lanny and me.

"You enjoy waltzing, don't you?" There was an unusual tenderness in his voice as again he pulled me closer. That's what was so darned strange about everything that was happening to me right now. I hadn't wanted to waltz with him; yet it felt so right to be in his arms, as if this was where I belonged. I had never felt like this before.

I smelled the cologne on his jacket. It had a different fragrance, not at all like Papa's Mennen aftershave. Lanny didn't use any; at least, I had never noticed that about him. I liked Mac's cologne.

Naturally, the lieutenant ruined "The Emperor Waltz" for me. God and Confucius both, how he did ruin it! The strange thing was that it hadn't mattered. I found myself liking the way we were, the way he looked at me so tenderly. I didn't even mind that we moved two steps forward, two steps back while other waltzers whirled away to another tempo and a different beat. I didn't want to look away from his face.

That wasn't the way it was supposed to be, I told myself. When the music came to an end, Mac politely escorted me back to Lanny, cool and aloof as ever. He hadn't even thanked me for the dance but just set himself down and completely devoted himself to Phyllis as if what had happened on the dance floor was but a figment of my imagination. Had it happened? I stared at the two of them across the table, momentarily hurt that they didn't include me in their conversation. Only momentarily though, for Ruby Newman had raised his baton, the band started playing, and Lanny and I began to waltz.

After the ball, we took the subway home, getting off at Harvard Square. I remember how chilly it had been and having been grateful for Mama's fur coat. Neither the lieutenant nor Phyllis had minded the cold. Like silly teenagers, they ran down Mass Avenue, pelting each other with snowballs. Meanwhile, I tried to hold up my taffeta skirt, clutching Lanny's arm to keep from slipping on the icy sidewalk. Lanny squeezed my arm.

"Shall I hail us a taxi, Princess?" he asked anxiously.

I watched the other two cavorting ahead of us.

"No, I'm all right." How thoughtful of him! "We'll be home soon."

We walked quickly through the Common, then past the "haunted" house on the corner of Mt. Vernon Street. It had been vacant for some time now. More windows were broken; more shingles hanging by a nail. At this moment, with snow glistening all around and the cold moon shining, it looked ghostlier than ever before.

Lanny, winking at me, pointed it out to Mac. "Tamara says this house is haunted."

"Really?" Mac turned to look at it. "By golly, it does look

376

haunted. Have you ever met its ghost, Tamara?"

I just knew that he'd do that; make fun of me. He couldn't play along with my imagination the way Lanny had.

"No," I answered coldly. I wished now that Lanny hadn't mentioned it.

"Well, then, let's investigate, shall we?" Mac's eyes mocked me, daring me to.

Thank God for Phyl. She grabbed his sleeve. "Come on, Mac. All of us are too tired to play games. Tamara and I have a lot of studying to do; forget the old house. Let's go."

On my front porch, Lanny gave me a hug. "Bye, Princess," he whispered. "I'll call you tomorrow."

Impulsively I stood on my tiptoes and kissed him on his cheek. "Thank you for a wonderful time," I whispered back. When I reached the front door, I looked back to wave. Phyllis was standing on the porch steps, her arms entwined around the lieutenant's neck. For a moment they remained that way, oblivious to Lanny and me. Although feeling awkward, I called out a cheery good night and unlocked the front door. By the time Phyllis had come in, I was already curled up in bed, almost asleep.

The next day, over coffee and doughnuts at Hood's, Phyllis revealed to me something I could not believe at the time. As usual she had contemplated my face as if to figure out what mood I was in. Then she had cleared her throat and leaned forward. "What would you say, Tamara"—she paused, amused by what she had to tell me—"if I told you that Mac has fallen in love with you?"

I must have heard her incorrectly. I reached over for a Lucky out of her pack. She handed me her own lighted cigarette and watched my hands as I took it and nervously held it to light mine. "What was that you mentioned about your Pennsylvania lieutenant?" I too now settled back in my chair, surveying the place. The way I felt right now, for all I cared, this Mac could go out and fly a kite. Who did he think he was anyway, loving one minute and not caring the next? He hadn't even had the decency to tell me good night last night.

Phyl persisted. "He's in love with you, I'm sure of it. He's a darned nice fellow, Tamara."

"Well, he's all yours," I replied. "You two certainly looked cozy last night when we came home. By the way, when did you come in, or shouldn't I ask?"

She laughed. "We sat on the front steps talking about you, you dumbbell. Doggonit, why is it that every time I meet some nice guy, eventually I end up being his Mother Confessor? I'm not kidding, Tamara. All he did was talk about you. Honestly."

"What did you tell him?"

"Nothing much. Oh, yeah . . . that you had a lot of guys crazy about you, but that you had your damned inhibitions. You don't need to get riled up about that. It's the truth, you know. He then wanted to know how serious you are about Lanny."

"What did you tell him?"

"That Lanny and you were good friends, that's all. And, oh yes, I did say that Lanny is head over heels in love with you. Hell, anyone can see that."

"You say Mac likes me. Then why does he totally ignore me at times as if I weren't even around? That's what I can't understand about his attitude. Then sometimes . . ." I couldn't go on, afraid that I might have imagined that tender look in his eyes. It had been so brief.

Phyl seemed to understand. "Mac may be confused himself. About you, I mean. You see, Sam told him that most fellows put you up on a pedestal, that you liked being put up there." She laughed, her eyes affectionate. "You do, you know."

"Darn Sam. You know, Phyl, it hurts to know that he's talking about me behind my back. I don't like that." I made up my mind that I'd tell him a thing or two the next time he purred his way into my confidence.

"Bull!" Phyllis crushed her cigarette into the saucer, squashing it back and forth. I stared in dismay at the soggy mess of ashes and spilled coffee. When Phyllis noticed me wince at her action, she lost her cool. "Oh, come off it, Tamara. Don't be so damned disapproving. They're paid to wash dishes here. This only makes them more careful." She taunted me. "What's the matter with you? You're so damned bitchy lately. If"—her voice became sarcastic—"I'm permitted to mention that."

"I'm sorry, Phyl." Instantly I felt contrite, realizing that I had been somewhat jumpy. "I guess it's exams and too many late nights. I haven't been sleeping well lately. Guess I'm just plain tired. That's it; but of all people, to take it out on you. That wasn't fair. I'm sorry."

"Well," she conceded, somewhat mollified, "I shouldn't have gone on as I did either, but damn it, Tamara, I get so goddamn furious at you sometimes. You've got to change your attitude about things. Sure, you've had a different background, being born in China and all that, but . . . " she looked at me helplessly. "You're in America now, and you're way behind the times, my girl."

"What do you mean?"

"You know damn well what I mean. This puritanical attitude of yours. This, 'saving yourself,' for your one and only. I say bull to that crap." She quickly glanced around Hood's to see if anyone else had heard her, then lowered her voice. "You know you're missing out on a lot of fun and good times when you limit yourself like that."

"But I still have my self-respect," I told her quietly. I was not about to get into another argument with her about my so-called moralistic attitude. The more she talked, the more convinced I became that my way was the right one for me. She and Sam and the whole world could disapprove of my prudish behavior; that was their prerogative. After all, it was my life to live, not theirs.

Phyllis smiled. "Don't mind me. It's just that I'm trying to understand you better. I think I'm sometimes envious because you're so popular without trying to be. It's my green eyes, I suppose," she added lamely.

"And I get upset at you because it seems that I'm always having to explain myself to you. I can't change, Phyllis; that's just the way I am."

"I know; I know," she agreed good-naturedly. "Forget my little spiel. Friends?"

"Of course, I'm not mad at you, just stubborn." I couldn't help smiling at her, grateful she'd understood.

"Jeez, look at the time!" She grabbed her cigarette pack and dumped it into her purse. "Do me a favor, will you? I've gotta run now; promised to meet my mom. Here's my share of the bill." She threw down the change, grabbed her purse, and flew out of Hood's.

23

Mixed Emotions

"Oh, I can tell you more about how heroic our men have been when facing the enemy." Sammy Klauber, as usual, was holding us captive again, regaling us with war stories at the dinner table. "Now, when the Nazi supply lines were being bombed in North Africa, a German fighter plane, whose pilot had been killed, rammed one of our planes, aptly named the Flying Fortress. The American plane's fuselage was cut almost in two. Although other Nazi planes were attacking his plane, the American tail gunner remained firmly at his post." He paused to take a sip of his sherry. "Ah, that is good sherry," he told Papa.

"Was the American killed?" I asked.

"No, the uncanny thing about this guy..." again he hesitated, this time as if to note the effect that his words were having upon us. "This gunner routed the Nazi planes, and the pilot was able to land his plane and its crew at his own base. Both that tail gunner and the pilot were two fabulous guys."

"Yes," Papa agreed, nodding, "there have been quite amazing deeds of heroism during the war. Look what happened in Attu last May; the American forces, in spite of heavy losses, crossed over open tundra, heading inland despite continuous fire from the Japanese. We have a saying in Chinese, Sam, that 'as the pine and the cedar endure the frost and snow, so intelligence and wisdom overcome dangers and hardships.'"

"Sam, my husband has a proverb for everything," Mama warned. "In the tail gunner's case, I believe it was sheer courage for him to face the stronger enemy that had practically surrounded his plane."

380

During the war, several heroes and a Chinese heroine toured the U.S. When they came to Cambridge I was asked to accompany them on a tour. Prof. Henry Wadsworth Longfellow Dana (an old friend of Father's) came with us on a tour of Longfellow House, some of the old homes of Cambridge, and Harvard and Radcliffe colleges. From left to right: Volodia Pchelintsev, a Russian sniper who had killed over two hundred Germans; Peter Cochrane, a Scottish hero; Wang Yung, a Chinese actress who had gone behind enemy lines and saved many lives; myself; Professor Dana; Mr. Kadir, representative from the Netherlands; Nicolai Krasavchenko (seated). This photograph was taken October 12, 1942.

The Same Group on the Steps of Widener Library, Harvard

Sam nodded. "Yes, Mama. I'm amazed, Professor, at how many proverbs you can quote. How do you remember so many?"

"I collect proverbs from every country that I can. Some day I hope to publish a book of them." Pleased, Papa rubbed the tip of his nose.

"That's an excellent hobby, sir." Sam looked respectfully at Papa. "Maybe some day, after the war, I may go to a bookstore in Chelsea or Boston and find a book on proverbs. I'll recognize the author's name because it'll be yours."

"You'll be one of the first to get a complimentary copy," Mama promised, "whenever, and if ever Papa has it published. He has so many hobbies: stamps, books, music. Seriously, Sam," she asked, "when do you think this war will end? Now, with Mussolini out of the picture, won't the Germans soon be surrendering?"

"It's hard to tell," Sam's tone was grim. "General Clark had been doing well in Italy in the beginning of October. His campaign, as he goes north of Naples towards Rome, has slowed down. The Nazis have been resisting stubbornly; furthermore, it's now the rainy season there. Added to those problems is the fact that the American and British forces are not accustomed to such mountainous terrain."

"We've also been doing rather well against the Japs, haven't we, Papa?" I asked.

"Yes, indeed we have, with the help of other nations, of course. The Australian troops helped to capture Salamaua on New Guinea's northwest coast. That enabled our air force to attack Rabaul on New Britain Island."

"I read that that was an important battle, Serioja."

"Yes, Vera; Rabaul controlled ocean lanes to the south; it was a key Japanese position. They lost many ships and planes in our constant attacks; so many, in fact, that they had to abandon it a few days ago. I'm beginning to feel more confident in our Allied forces now. At first I wasn't so sure; the Japanese are shrewd, and death for their nation is an honor. They'd rather die than surrender."

"American soldiers too would rather die for their country," I interposed.

"I didn't mean that in the way you took it, *dochenka*." Papa was apologetic. "What I meant was that the Japanese don't value life so much as we do. Look at their suicide squads—the Kamikazes."

Mama turned to Papa, saying, "Why don't you and Sam go listen to the news? Tamara and I will clear the table and then join you in the living room. We can sit here all night long talking about the war. Time will tell the outcome, not talking or predictions."

After the news, my parents said goodnight and went upstairs to bed.

"Your parents are great people," Sam murmured in admiration. "You don't realize—or maybe you do, Tamara—how much both you and your brother have inherited from them." He noted my quizzical look and smiled. "I mean spiritually, not physically, dopey. No, I'm wrong; you look like Papa, although you have your mother's dark eyes. Vanya, of course, inherited your mother's olive skin and prominent Roman nose."

"If I got Papa's brains," I told him, laughing, "I'll be satisfied. The older I get the more he boggles my mind, Sam. He can talk intelligently about anything, and he really does know a lot. It's not just a bunch of hot air."

"That's what I want to do with you," Sam announced thoughtfully. "I want to talk intelligently with you." He gave me that doctor-by-the-bedside look of his.

Oh no, you don't, I thought to myself. I still remembered, and resented, what Phyllis had told me that Sam had reported to Mac. *This time,* I told myself, *Tamarotchka is going to be mighty careful. She won't fall for that sweet-talk a second time so that Captain Sammy can relay it to his snooty Yankee lieutenant.*

"Sammy, Phil Spitalny is on with his all-girl orchestra right now. I'd hate to miss the program. You've listened to it, haven't you? Would you mind if I turned on the radio?"

"Sure, dear, turn it on; but keep it soft and low, please."

I turned the volume down so that the music wouldn't disturb our conversation. I planned to turn up the volume, though, when Evelyn and her "magic violin" began to play. That part I enjoyed most of all.

"Okay, Sammy boy, now what was it that you wanted to talk

about so intelligently to me?" I gave him my full attention.

"Remember our conversation of a few weeks ago?" he began. "We were discussing your strict, as you call it, 'moral code,' which, in my opinion, is, if you'll pardon me, pure nonsense."

Remember, I cautioned myself, *keep cool; do not let him rile or confuse you. Sam's used to delving out the inner thoughts of people. He has that uncanny knack of making people confess— willingly or not—what is buried deep in their hearts. Don't let him get the better of you, Tamara,* warned my inner voice.

"I recall it," I answered, as nonchalantly as I could. "So?"

"My darling. . . . " He studied me carefully, then, in a soft, coaxing, tender voice quietly asked, "What in the world is it that you are afraid of, Tamara?"

I had not expected a question like that and felt the blood rush to my face. "Why, nothing, Sam. Whatever do you mean?" I laughed self-consciously. "If I fear anything or anybody, it's probably you, Sammy."

At that he grinned. "I know, sweetheart, I'm terribly ferocious. No." He turned serious again. "Tell me truthfully, what the devil is it? What is it that makes you afraid of men?"

"Me? Afraid of men?" It was preposterous for him to even ask me that. "Sam, if I were afraid of men I wouldn't be going out with so many of them. I'm not afraid of men."

Sammy couldn't be fooled. No, indeedy! His calm, unflinching, searching look met my own defiant one. Like stranger bulls, our eyes locked horns, eyeball to eyeball. Neither one of us gave way; neither one of us wavered.

Finally, he shifted his weight, sitting there on the floor in that yoga-lotus position, his eyes stern, dark, probing. "I've never met a person like you, Tamara, child. To me you're a puzzle all wrapped up in an enigma." He pursed his lips thoughtfully, shaking his head. "Sometimes I think I know you. Then I realize that I don't know you at all! Within you is something that holds you back. I just can't comprehend it. You have the finest parents: highly intelligent, cosmopolitan, and practical people. As for your brother . . . " He smiled indulgently. "Ah, Vanya, a bit strange perhaps, but he's a fine young fellow, nevertheless. But you? Ah, there's the rub, Tamara! What can I tell you about yourself? You, my dear sweet Russian lassie, are living in that beautiful, unrealistic dream world you built around yourself during that earlier time of your life in your beloved China. Now tell me, my darling, am I not right?"

I sensed his anger and frustration; yet I resented having to justify my attitudes and feelings to those who never could understand, especially Sam. He had no right to talk to me like that. Still, I felt compelled to explain again my beliefs and ideals.

"You must try to understand, Sam," I told him calmly. "I'm not living in a so-called dream world. It's just that I have always had these certain ideals that I am determined to live up to, no matter what. They may be old-fashioned, outmoded, absolute, or pure nonsense to you, but they are my ideals. I will live by them. That's all there is to it, Sam, nothing more."

He listened gravely, then asked, "Is that your reason for putting yourself on a pedestal?"

Well, well, shades of Phyllis Olsen! That same old refrain about Tamara and her pedestal surfaced once more. I could feel my anger mounting. "Sam, to accuse me of climbing on a pedestal is absolutely silly. Just because I hold on to my ideals does not mean that I'm erecting myself a platform for adoration. I'm surprised at you. That hurts."

At the same time as I had uttered those words, I knew that his analysis of me had been correct. I did put myself on a pedestal, but not for adoration. How could I tell him that it was for my own protection, that I had a perfectly valid reason for doing so. Good, dear friend that he had become, I still could not bring myself to share the secret of my past with him. Only Dorlise, yes, and especially Vanya, knew my secret.

"You do love to be pampered, don't you?" His words soothed me; yet I sensed the sarcasm behind them. "You are filled with delight when men crowd around you, the more the better, when they pay you homage with messenger-sent boxes of long-stemmed red roses wrapped in many, many sheets of crumpled snow-white tissue paper." He paused to take a deep breath. "You're most gratified, your serene highness, when all us poor mortals, including stupid old me, call you Princess. Fools that we men are, we just can't help calling you that, can we?" He then peered at me through those horn-rimmed glasses and gently chucked me under my chin, whispering softly, "Will you ever awaken from your impossible dream, little Princess, my snow-white pure Russian Princess?" Once more he paused to stare at me. "Will you, can you ever realize, Tamara, that there is actually a real world beyond the one which you have so easily constructed around yourself? Do you know that this real world is not made up of fairy-tale dust, but it is here—a vibrant, violent, active world, ready to welcome you into its midst?"

"Sam, I am what I am," I told him stubbornly. "You can be my friend or not, as you wish." I noticed his surprise at my curtness, although I hadn't meant to be impolite. I just wished to impress on him the fact that neither he, nor anyone else, could change my attitude. "No matter what you say, I shall keep to my ideals. I, as you so eloquently have phrased it, do put myself on a pedestal. I shall neither fall from my perch nor alight from it until I decide to. Then, and then only, shall I step down. Neither you nor Phyllis, not even Mama or Papa, can ever change the way I think." On impulse I jumped up on Papa's footstool. "See? I'm on a pedestal now. Captain, I salute you."

He began to laugh; I couldn't help joining in.

"All right, Princess, I've lost this round. Stay up on your lonely perch. I'll still remain your humble servant." He winked at me. "That's not what I really came here to talk about, Tamara. It's about old Mac. Do you remember Mac, the lieutenant I brought as a blind date for Phyl?"

"Yes." I tried to keep my voice level, although my heart skipped a beat. *Why should I feel perturbed at the mention of that name?* I wondered to myself.

"Well, darling . . ." He paused, as if trying to find the right words to use. "Ah, yes, this is what I want to tell you. Uh, Mac likes you quite a bit, you know." He raised his palm. "No, now don't interrupt me, Tamara. I tell you this, although I don't want to. I don't want you to hurt him." He looked at me intently, then went on. "The poor dope has fallen in love with you. Damn it, he's just too fine a guy, and . . . " Again, he hesitated, staring down at the dragon rug and tracing its flaming tongue with his index finger. "It's just the fact that he's such a damned special guy, Tamara, and he's fallen head over heels in love with you. That's the confounded problem in a nutshell."

It was strange to listen to Sam talk this way. I envisioned

the lieutenant again on that night, how he had steered me towards the dance floor. I could even feel his fingers again as they dug into my arm. Had I really seen that especially tender look of his or had I imagined it? Then, when the dance had ended, he had become aloof, leading me, like a stranger, back to Lanny. With pleasure I recalled how tightly he had held me in his arms, as if he could never let me go. Then there had been that scent about his jacket, the faint aroma of a mysterious cologne that had seemed to belong only to him. Never had I ever recalled my other dates in such minute detail. Worst of all, I thought to myself, he hadn't even been my date. I found myself blushing, and to my knowledge I had not blushed before. Then I heard Sam's words again. "I don't want him hurt."

What colossal impertinence! What about my own feelings in this affair? "You don't want him hurt?" I asked Sam. "What in the world do you mean? I don't hurt people, do I?"

Sam hesitated. "Tamara, he'd like to take you out." His words hit me like lightning. "He'd ask you himself..."—he watched me with that scalpel-sharp intensity—"he's afraid you will refuse him. He told me that you had been so quiet, that you hadn't talked much."

So, I thought to myself, *the offish lieutenant thinks I don't talk much. He* had plenty of chances to speak to me himself. *He* was the quiet one, not I. I was about to blow up at Sam; instead, I smiled sweetly. "So you're now Miles Standish, are you? Or John Alden? Are you asking me to go out with your good lieutenant and behave myself too? Can't he ask me himself? After all, Sam, I don't bite."

He chuckled, his lovable self once more. "In spite of your sweetness and innocence, you do intimidate people, darling."

"Well, he hasn't been that friendly to me."

"Did you give him reason to be?" Sam countered softly.

"I wasn't his date." This arguing back and forth with Sam wasn't going anywhere. Besides, the thought of dancing with Mac again didn't appeal to me in the least.

"Sam," I said, placing my hand on his arm, "let's worry about that later. I've got to stop dating for now. It's study-time; exams are coming up again. Give me a couple of weeks; we'll talk about it later, huh?"

He seemed disappointed in me. "Darling, later may not be soon enough. You forget, Tamara, that we're here for just a short duration. Soon, in fact, any day now, we'll be getting our orders for duty overseas. He's a soldier, Tamara, not one of your college boys here."

"All right, Miles Standish." I smiled reluctantly. "Tell Mac, your lieutenant, that I'll be most honored to go out with him. There's one thing, Sam, please, if you can; suggest that he not invite me to dance. Of course, you use your discretion, but I sure don't want to go dancing with him. I couldn't stand two or three whole hours of just walking about on a dance floor."

He laughed uproariously at that, then leaned over and gave me an affectionate hug. "You don't know how much this will cheer the lad up," he told me jubilantly. "He hasn't been out of Camp McKay except for his two dates with Phyllis. You'll be the best medicine for what ails him. Of that I am absolutely sure. I'm quite a good doctor, don't you agree?" He tweaked me on the cheek, elated over his success.

Why was it that I had this strange feeling that Sam and Phyllis, maybe even Mac himself, had joined together in some sort of conspiracy? I felt hemmed in on all sides.

I hadn't expected to hear from Mac so soon. The next evening he called. For a moment I didn't recognize the voice. Then I heard his infectious laugh.

"Mac?" Confused, I stopped, not knowing what else to say.

His voice sounded pleasant. "I had hoped you'd recognize my voice, Tamara." I liked the way he pronounced my name. "I would like to invite you out for dinner tomorrow evening."

"Thank you, Mac. I'd love to go." I hadn't meant to be that enthusiastic, but there was something about his voice and the way he laughed so genuinely over the phone. I wondered to myself if Sam was standing at his side, urging him on.

"You decide where you'd like to go," he had suggested. "I'm not that familiar with Cambridge, and I'm sure"—I could almost picture his smile when I heard him chuckle—"you know where all the best restaurants are."

After we had hung up, I went back to my room to study, but no matter how hard I tried, I couldn't concentrate. Our phone conversation kept intruding. I kept recalling how he had pronounced my name, his chuckle, his laugh, his hesitation in asking me out, and then I kept recalling what Sam had said.

I wasn't quite ready when Mac arrived the next evening. Mama had opened the door to let him in. From my room upstairs I heard her welcoming him, inviting him into the living room, introducing herself. Her voice sounded especially friendly; so I guessed she liked him. Then I heard him laugh. It was so pleasing, sort of shy, but spontaneous, real. I smiled to myself on hearing it, then looked in the mirror to see if the burgundy velvet suit with the bustle looked as good on me as Mama had said it would. *God and Confucius, bless her*, I thought with gratitude. It did flatter me, making my hair look reddish-gold and emphasizing my coloring. I hadn't wanted this burgundy shade, but Mama had insisted on buying it, saying, "Wait and see," and, as usual, she had been right. I glanced once more at my unsmiling image. Yes, I did look reserved and sedate enough for the lieutenant. After all, I thought, there was also something about him that was puritanical. *Remember, Tamara,* I told myself, *behave yourself. Sam wants you to, and, above all, God forbid that you place yourself on a pedestal or else you'll "hurt" his lieutenant.* I caught a last glimpse of myself in the mirror, my eyes sharp and angry. No wonder. I couldn't even be myself with this Mac fellow. I had to act out a part so that I wouldn't hurt the poor lieutenant's feelings!

I moved out into the hall, hesitant. I heard the piano being played and knew right away that it wasn't Mama playing. She always stumbled over the keys, no matter how long she had practiced a piece. Whoever was playing the piano knew how to.

Holding my high heels in my hand, I tiptoed down the stairs. Mama was seated in Papa's armchair by the fireplace, her face rapt, as she listened with a smile upon her lips. It was Mac at the piano. He played with power, moving his fingers over the keys with a sureness and dexterity that surprised me. He looked directly ahead of him, completely and totally absorbed in the music.

Mama had heard my footsteps. She placed her finger to her lips, forbidding me to speak, to break the magic that he was creating. As I knelt down on the rug beside her, she whispered,

"Ach, kakoy on chudnui" (Oh, how wonderful he is). She was as dumfounded as I was that a strange young man like this American officer could play the piano so well.

He had heard her whisper and immediately stopped playing, getting up right away from the bench. A deep flush blanketed his face when he saw me. He smiled awkwardly. Somehow he seemed different; here in our home, with Mama, he was much more likable.

I held out my hand to him. "Mama certainly enjoyed your playing. I didn't know you played the piano." He held on to my hand. It had all been so perfectly polite. Then I felt his grip tighten, and hurriedly withdrew my hand. Was that the same look I had seen at the ball that evening? I looked once more, but he had turned towards Mama. Just my imagination again!

"Thank you, Madame Rubleva. It's been a privilege meeting you." He faced me now, grinning. "While you were upstairs making yourself beautiful for me, your mother and I have become good friends."

I looked at him in amazement. Of all the audacity! "I make myself beautiful for no man," I told him curtly. "I like to look nice, but that's all."

He seemed to be enjoying himself. "Perhaps I should have put it another way, Miss Rubleva. May I tell you that you look most lovely, Miss Rubleva?"

"Shall we go now, Mac?" I still resented his first remark. "Mama, we won't be late."

"Enjoy yourselves." She patted Mac on the back. "I enjoyed your playing, Lieutenant. Anytime you wish to play our piano, do come. I, for one"—she looked pointedly at me—"would love to hear you play again." Her smile couldn't have been more gracious.

God and Confucius! I remember thinking. *What is she saying to him? She's giving him "carte blanche" to come here at any time. Glory be, how the devil can she?*

We had to wait on Mass Ave for the tram for Harvard Square. Mac had been quite polite, even attentive in a way, taking my arm to hold me as we stepped out onto the crunchy snow. I managed to wriggle free. "It's all right," I told him. "I won't slip."

He silently put his hand in his coat pocket then. I stole a

glance at him as we stood in the crowded tram car, holding on to the straps. He had not said much since we had left the house. Now, instead of facing me, he was looking at the passenger seated in front of him. He had a good profile, I observed; a nice straight nose and a firm chin. When he turned toward me, I recognized that same look. I had not imagined it after all. There it was, with all the tenderness and love that I had glimpsed before. I liked it when he looked at me that way, but I forced myself to look away, afraid of what my own eyes might reveal.

We got off at Harvard Square. I pointed across Mass Ave, saying, "We go to Brattle Street now." As we crossed the avenue, I showed him Officer Burke's booth on the corner. "He's one of the best policemen around here, except for Officer MacIntosh, who patrols our street. Officer Burke knows by name most of the 'Cliffies' who walk this way. He's really a special guy. Oh, and here on the corner is Felix's newsstand. Papa buys the *Boston Globe* and the *New York Times* here. This is the flower shop; that's where the Harvard students buy corsages for their dates. Now we're at St. Clair's. I hope you like it."

"You'd make a good tour guide for Cambridge, Tamara." He smiled down at me, "Shall we go in now?"

A pleasant waitress led us to a small table for two in the center of the restaurant. At eight o'clock most of the tables had already been filled.

"This is fine," Mac commented. "It looks like a family type restaurant."

"It is," I said.

An awkward silence followed.

"What are . . . " he started to say.

At the same time, I started to ask, "Are you? . . . "

Then we both laughed. "Phyllis tells me you're from Pennsylvania. Do you have any brothers or sisters, Mac?"

"Two sisters, Tamara. Betty is the elder, a year younger than I, and Phyllis is the younger, seventeen now. And Fuzzy, our dog is a Samoyed, all white. He's a wonderful dog. I sure miss him."

I can still picture him sitting there across from me, the candle casting shadows on his face as the flames flickered back and forth in front of us. It added a special glow to his face.

"How about your parents? What are they like?"

He had laughed then. "They're much different from yours, I suppose, although I have yet to meet your dad. They're fine, up-standing, conservative farm folks of Pennsylvania Dutch and Scottish background, who aren't as well educated as your parents."

This is a real, honest-to-goodness Yankeeman! That's just what he is, I remember thinking to myself. I could not keep my eyes away from his face. It was such a good face, now that I could observe it closely. He seemed eager that I know not only him but also get to meet his family, through his words.

"Mom"—he hesitated; had I detected an uneasiness in his mention of her?—"Mom's had a hard life, really. First were the depression years and Dad without a job, growing vegetables to sell as well as feed us. One year we had an income of only three hundred dollars for the five of us; two hundred of that went to pay my tuition at the University of Pittsburgh during my freshman year. Luckily, I was awarded a full scholarship for the next three years."

"It must have been difficult," I said sympathetically. He didn't seem like a snob or a drip anymore.

"And your dad?" I asked softly. "What's he like?"

He smiled. "Everybody thinks the world of Dad. Dad was a high-school graduate. He has read quite a bit, not classics or anything like that." He added quickly, "He reads farm magazines and magazines like the *Reader's Digest,* the *Saturday Evening Post*, and so forth. Mom is a graduate of Slippery Rock State College."

"What about other relatives? Do you have any?"

"Oh, plenty," he laughed. "Uncles Roy and Lee are both lawyers; Aunt Bertha is a schoolteacher. They're on Mom's side. Then I've got a great-aunt who's in a class all by herself, Aunt Carrie. Now that's one person I'd like you to meet." He had been so wrapped up in what he was saying that when he saw my surprised look, he stopped, somewhat embarrassed. "I'm sorry; what I really meant to say was that you'd like her if you ever met her. You see, she is known by everybody in Freeport. They all call her Aunt Carrie. She's never missed going to church or Sunday school ever since she was a little girl except, of course, when she was ill. That was rare. Aunt Carrie must be . . . Lord, she must be in her late seventies, I guess."

"You're fortunate to have so many relatives," I told him.

"What about you?" he asked. "I've been doing all the talking." He smiled. "You know, you're such a good listener that I hadn't realized I was doing all the talking."

"Well, besides Papa and Mama, I've got a brother, Vanya, the diminutive for Ivan. You know," I explained, "we Russians are great for nicknames or diminutives. It often causes foreigners to become confused."

"I can well understand." He nodded. "I've read *War and Peace*. Do you have any other relatives?"

"Oh, I guess there're some in the Soviet Union, but it has been impossible to correspond with them. Mama wrote to her sister and brother there but never got an answer. I think Papa has or had a sister with whom he used to correspond, but that was years ago." I didn't want to tell him about Aunt Raisa and the cousins. It would take much too long to explain. I changed the subject. "You must like music a lot to play the piano so well."

"I do," he told me. "I've taught myself for the most part."

"You mean you're self-taught?" I asked in amazement, thinking of the years Mother Hildebalde had spent placing coppers on the backs of my hands during our piano lessons.

"What are you smiling about?" he asked me.

I told him then about my convent days. He laughed, "That must have been quite an experience, studying with nuns. Are you Catholic?"

"No, I'm not," I answered truthfully. I hoped he wouldn't ask me what I was. I really didn't know myself, except that I did believe in God. "What are you?" I asked curiously.

"Presbyterian," he answered. "United Presbyterian."

"That's Protestant, isn't it? I know another Protestant, Dr. John Calvin Ferguson, our old neighbor in Peking. He's an Episcopalian or a Methodist, I don't know. He's now in an internment camp in Peking. Dr. Ferguson has always been a special person to me, a very special friend."

He nodded as if he understood. "He is a fortunate person to have you feel that way about him. He must be an exceptional man indeed."

"He is."

I remember we talked more, about the war, about Sam,

about Phyllis. St. Clair's had emptied by the time we were ready to leave. I can still picture his face, how earnestly he had tried to bring me into his Freeport, Pennsylvania, world. Unconsciously, I found myself drawn to him, watching his expression, examining each feature in it as if to etch it in my memory. Around us, it had then seemed to me, loomed this whole, big outside world; inside this one room there were just the two of us. For a few enchanted hours nothing else but the two of us mattered anymore.

"Don't you think we should go?" I asked him, regretfully breaking up this unusual mood.

"Oh, sure, by all means." Suddenly, he changed, once again the polite, aloof stranger. He left some dollar bills on the tray. "Ready?" He stood up, courteously waiting for me to rise from my chair.

When we left St. Clair's, it had begun to snow. With the fresh air hitting my face, I became Tamara once more. I shook my head, feeling the cold flakes stinging my cheeks. Whatever in the world had possessed me to romanticize so wildly about this Yankeeman? Lanny was one too, perhaps even more so, since he was a Quaker. I should have been worrying about exams next week, about the war, or my volunteer work. Instead, I was daydreaming of this lieutenant, wondering if he liked me or if he didn't. What in the world was happening to me? Had I gone crazy? Still, there was something very comforting about the way his hand had held mine as we walked home with the snowflakes falling down upon us.

"Thank you, Mac, for such an interesting evening." I had put out my hand for him to shake. He bent his head towards mine. Then he straightened up and took my hand in his, smiling.

"Thanks for listening to me. I hope I didn't bore you too much. You're such a good listener, Tamara." His voice had been quiet, almost caressing.

I had again withdrawn my hand quickly. Was I, as Sam had told me, afraid? Afraid of this lieutenant? Or of myself?

"Good night, Mac. And thanks again." With that I opened the front door and hurried inside.

24

Of Chaucer and Waffles

Papa and I were walking home from Harvard Square. "And how are your studies, *dochenka?*" he asked me. "It won't be long now, will it, before you graduate?"

"No, Papa, after the Christmas holidays I'll have about a month and a half to go. Then . . . "—I waved my hand into the air—"goodbychik to Radcliffe forever."

"You might decide to stay on and do some graduate work. Who knows?" Papa gave me a sidelong glance. "You might change your mind and decide to teach instead."

"No, Papa, I won't change my mind. I've already written to two places in New York, the Office of Strategic Services and the Office of War Information."

For a while we walked on in silence, both of us immersed in our own thoughts.

Then Papa sighed, "Mamotchka and I would rather that you stay in Cambridge. Think how much simpler it would be. You'd have no rent to pay, no food to buy. You could even have parties in your upstairs 'ballroom.' "

I laughed. "Papa, I can read your mind like a book. So that's why you asked me to stop by for you when I was through with my classes. Is that it? Did Mama put you up to this?" I took his arm, giving it a squeeze. "She did, didn't she?"

His positively sheepish look gave him away. He grinned, looking straight ahead, avoiding my eyes. "Mama thought you'd listen to me more. But . . . "—now he turned to me, his face serious—"I completely, wholeheartedly agree with Mamotchka. New

396

York is no place for a young woman like you, Tamara. You've lived a completely sheltered life."

"No, Papa, I have not," I contradicted him quietly. "You must remember that Vanya and I were alone those last two years in Peking, under house arrest. I was not sheltered then, and yet . . ." Suddenly, it dawned on me that he had never really asked me about those years. Perhaps he, too, had needed to blot certain experiences out of his life. "I've survived my trials as you did yours."

"You did, *dochenka*, all of you did," he agreed, again lapsing into silence.

I decided to change the subject. "Papotchka, do you realize that the Cliffies are now taking some of their classes at Harvard?"

"I've heard about that. Some of the professors are not too happy about it, either. They'd prefer that Cliffies study in Radcliffe. Some feel outraged to have women infiltrate the purely masculine halls of our fair Harvard. You know there are still some behind-the-times characters here who believe that Harvardians are quite superior . . . "

"To us lowly Cliffies! Oh, Papa, how could they?"

I had not been aware that we had walked so far already. "We're almost home, Papa. Who said that about the Cliffies? I'd like to know."

"It doesn't matter who said it, Tamara. The main thing is that you can now do graduate work at Harvard if you so wish."

"Papa, I've studied hard these three-and-a-half years. All I want to do now is to graduate. Let's not discuss this in front of Mama, please. Oh, look; there she is at the window, smiling at us." I waved as we came up to our house.

Mama opened the door, her face flushed with excitement. "Tamara, Mac called this afternoon. He'll be calling again; so hurry on in."

"What did he want? What was he calling for?" I asked.

"He wants to invite you to the Boston Symphony. I told him you'd probably want to go." She looked at me anxiously. "I told him you'd go; that is, if you weren't busy. I specified that."

"Thank you, Mama." I kept my voice impassive although I was getting that tingling feeling again. It bothered me that I, who had always been able to control my emotions, now found it difficult to do so. "I'm going upstairs to change," I told her, eager to escape her keen attention.

Just as I reached upstairs the phone rang, and I had to run down again to answer it. It was Mac. "How would you like to hear some Tchaikovsky music and Beethoven's *Emperor Concerto*?" He sounded rather pleased with himself. "Our outfit was given these tickets, and few of our fellows are interested in classical music. I knew that you'd enjoy it. Will you be able to go?"

"When?"

He chuckled. "I apologize. I was so happy to hear your pleasant voice that I got all muddled. Sorry about that, but you have to take the blame for my mental condition."

"I am to blame for your mental condition?"

"Yep, you are," he declared, and went on, "I'll pick you up tomorrow evening, say seven-thirty."

"Thank you, I'll be ready." Had I actually gotten him all muddled, or was he teasing me? It annoyed me that I was even now trying to recall all that he had said, trying to remember every single word of our conversation.

I had not realized how much I had missed Mac until the two of us stood on the subway, holding on to the straps and to each other because the train was crowded and was moving like a speeding bullet. Once, the train swerved, and I was thrown against him. He caught me, holding me for a moment close to him. His smiling face had been just a few inches from mine.

"I didn't mean to bump into you," I feebly explained, feeling myself being drawn to him like a magnet, enjoying the delicious comfort of his closeness Then, too, there was that haunting fragrance of that special cologne of his.

"I don't mind it a bit," he whispered into my ear. "I wish the train would swerve more often." His eyes fastened on mine with such a tender and loving expression that I could not turn away. Although there were people all around us, I saw only him.

Then that inner voice of mine made me move away from him and get hold of myself. Is that feeling I'd had what Sam had meant when he had asked, "What are you afraid of, Tamara?" I looked around me and now noticed the other passengers; some were staring blankly into the air, tired, depressed; others were animated, talkative; there were quite a few soldiers besides Mac. *The world is so full of wonderful things*, I thought to myself. There is so much to be done. There's a war on and, because of that, people are much more sensitive to each other's feelings. Maybe that was why I was feeling the way I did towards Mac. I felt a tenderness towards him because he was a stranger here in Boston and because soon he would be going overseas.

I felt relieved now that I understood and could suppress those damned unreasonable emotions that always seemed to take over whenever Mac happened to appear on my horizon. We had really enjoyed ourselves at the concert. When he escorted me home that evening, he asked me if I would go out with him again.

"I'd like to very much, Mac, but I've got a lot of studying to do." Seeing how disappointed he was, I reassured him. "You can phone me during the week if you'd like. I can always talk and take a break." Then we both laughed at the absurdity of that solution to the problem.

A week later, I had just arrived home and was slipping off my boots when I heard the phone ringing. I ran to answer it. "Yes; who is it?" Recognizing Mac's pleasant laugh, I felt my face flush.

"Tamara, I hoped you'd be home. You're always rushing off somewhere these days or holed up in the library. By the way, this is Mac. I didn't know if you'd remember my voice."

If he only knew. I had been waiting for his call every day, but now on the phone I spoke calmly, "Of course, I recognized your voice." As I listened, I wished so much that he could be standing here with me at this very moment, close to me. I wanted so much to inhale that mixture of him and his cologne, to feel his presence.

"May I come over to see you?" His voice was hesitant. "I'd really like to so much."

"I've got an exam on Chaucer tomorrow, Mac." I wished to see him too, terribly, and felt bad about putting him off. "Mac, I just can't; I do have to study."

"Ah, my favorite poet," he said. " 'Whan that Aprille with his shoures soote/The droghte of March hath perced to the roote.' Is it *The Canterbury Tales* that cause your cheeks to pale so?" I heard his quiet chuckle. "In that case, I may be able to helpe my vertuous mayden."

"You studied Chaucer?" I asked in surprise. "You quote him so well."

"I have a suggestion to make, Tamara. Why don't you study for a couple of hours, then I'll come by and quiz you. If you agree, I'll guarantee you an A in the course."

"I don't think that's a good idea, Mac. I just have to buckle down and do it on my own."

" 'And gladly wolde he lerne, and gladly teche.' I'm really glad I've remembered that from Chaucer, Tamara. Now tell me, where can you find this line, 'Nowher so bisy a man as he ther nas,/And yet he semed bisier than he was.' If you can tell me, then you're pretty good."

I couldn't help smiling. "That's from the Prologue to the *Canterbury Tales*. Wait a second; let me think. Ah, I know; it's about the sergeant of the lawe. Right?"

"Say, you are good." I had surprised him. "Well, how about it? Will you take me up on it?"

"All right, I will," I agreed, because I did want to see him. Besides, I did know *The Canterbury Tales* fairly well. "Come no earlier than five o'clock. You can quiz me, and afterwards stay for dinner if you'd like. Mama will want you to stay."

"And you?"

"Well, I'll have to pay you back somehow for helping me out, won't I? And Mama's cooking *kotletki* tonight."

"What's that?" he asked, curious.

"You wolde waite, my freend, have pacience." I couldn't help laughing. "I think you'll enjoy Mama's cooking. I'll see you at five, all right?" I could sense that he was intrigued.

"Okay; I'll be seeing you then, Tamara."

I ran upstairs quickly, smiling at the thought of studying Chaucer with him. Mama's bedroom door was open.

"Who was that, Tamara?" She sat at her dresser putting up her hair.

"Mac. He's coming over to help me study," I told her. It sounded ridiculous when I explained it aloud.

"Oh, so that's what he's going to do, is it? Well, I hope he can keep his mind on studying," she told my reflection in her mirror.

She bit her lips, trying hard not to smile. "And who'll be doing the teaching in this enterprise?"

"Oh, Mama." I could tell she was pleased that Mac was coming over, but I hoped she wouldn't tease me in front of him. You could never tell what Mama might do if the mood struck her. "By the way, I invited him to dinner."

"Good. Maybe he'll play the piano for us afterward."

"Well, I've got to study before he comes."

I hurried into my room. For two hours I studied frantically and busily. Not only did I want to get an A in the course, but I wanted to convince Mac that I knew Chaucer as well as he did.

When Mama opened the door for him, I was ready. He smiled, taking off his cap and coat.

"Your daughter sure is beautiful, isn't she, Mama?" He looked at me with a teasing smile. I couldn't hide my surprise at his rapport with Mama.

"When did you start calling my mother 'Mama,' may I ask?"

Mama took his coat, laying it down on the banister. "I told him he could, Tamarotchka. Sam and Phyllis both do."

Mac smiled at her, then turned to me, "Cosyn, for sothe, I tolde you I'd quiz you. Are you all set?" He was all businesslike but grinning like Alice's Cheshire cat.

"In the dining room, Mac." I sat in Papa's place and passed my notes to him. He looked through them and then let out a low whistle. "This is a lot of material to cover. Do you know it?"

"I think I do, Mac. I just can't let Professor Root down."

"You mean R. K. Root?" Mac's voice sounded full of awe.

"Yes, have you heard of him?"

"I sure as heck have. He's one of the best Chaucerian scholars. You're fortunate to have him as a teacher."

"I know. I find it fascinating to listen to him read Chaucer. He's such a nondescript kind of person in life with his gray suit, gray hair, round face, and old-fashioned, rimless glasses."

Mac smiled and asked, "Like my glasses?"

I hadn't thought of that. "I didn't mean to say that," I stammered. "Oh, anyway, he's so humble and unassuming until he starts to read or quote Chaucer. I never tire of listening to him. He made the pilgrims come to life for us; he's just superb."

"I see he's impressed you. I've read his book on Chaucer. Well, shall we begin?" He settled comfortably in Papa's red armchair by the window, laid his head back, and glanced at me from under lowered lids. His lips twitched. " 'Come closer,' Mr. Wolf told Red Riding Hood, 'So I can hear you better.' "

"Thank you, Lieutenant Wolf, I'm quite comfortable here."

"Don't be afraid, little girl. I won't bite." He had something up his sleeve. I could tell from his expression.

I was right. He patted his lap. "It would be so much more comfortable here, my dear Miss Red Riding Hood."

He doesn't think I'll do it, but I'll show him, I decided. Before he could bat an eyelid I had vaulted onto his lap.

"Ouch!" He groaned. "You didn't have to land so heavily on me, did you?"

"All the better to hear you and keep you under control, you Big, Bad Wolf. All right, Mac, quiz away."

"Not before you put your arm around my neck to hold my attention, little girl. There now, isn't that more conducive to studying? Now just relax; think hard, my darling."

Had he called me darling? He was shuffling through my notes. "All right then, here goes." Again he paused, studying my face intently, a strange gleam in his eyes. "Ah, yes, I forgot to mention a condition that goes along with my quizzing."

"No more games, Mac, please."

"It's no game, Tamara. I'm serious."

"What is this condition?"

"Well, for every mistake you make, you'll be fined one kiss. Only one. Do you agree?"

What impertinence to even suggest that! I thought to myself. *No matter,* I decided, *I won't lose.* "That's no problem, Mac. It's fine with me. Shall we begin?"

We sat there together in the armchair for more than an hour, until he had reviewed all of my notes.

"How is she doing, Mac? Is she a good student?" Mama asked when she came in to set the table. She didn't seem to be the least perturbed that I was sitting there cuddled on Mac's lap.

"She's just too smart, Mama," he told her, acting disappointed. "Would you believe she promised to kiss me for every mistake she made, but she hasn't made one yet, darn it."

"That's too bad," Mama wrung her hands in mock sympathy. "Ask her a few more questions."

"Thanks, Mama, for the suggestion. I do have a good question now for your daughter. Tamara, tell me the meaning of this quotation:

'And thereon heng a brooch of gold ful sheene,
On which ther was first write a crowned A,
And after Amor vincit omnia.'

"Now give me the meaning of the Latin phrase and tell me to which pilgrim this refers."

"That's simple," I answered, glancing at Mama, who was watching all of this byplay, thoroughly enjoying our sparring. "It's from the General Prologue and applies to the prioress. Do you want me to translate the Latin phrase, or what?"

He shifted himself in the armchair. "Pardon me; you know that you're heavy, don't you?"

If he was trying to confuse me, he wasn't succeeding, nor was I angry at his reference to my weight. "Since you are avoiding my question, I'll translate it for you: 'And there hung a shining gold brooch on which there first was written a crowned A, and after that, Love conquers all!"

"Or, better yet, Love overcomes all things," he said. "It was applicable not only to the prioress and her religious love, but it could even be applicable to a delectable, young lady such as you, Tamara. Am I not right, Mama?"

"Of course, Mac, you're absolutely right," her eyes filled with tears from laughing at our repartee.

I slid off Mac's lap. "Thanks a lot for your help, Mac. I can see Papa out on the front porch; he's just come home." I ran into the foyer to open the front door, giving Papa a big hug when he came inside.

"Ah-h, Lieutenant." Papa held out his hand. "It is such a great pleasure to meet you. My wife and Tamara have spoken highly of you."

Mac bowed, shaking Papa's hand. "It is an honor to meet you, sir." I liked the way he looked at Papa with respect.

"Now that the formalities are over, dinner is ready," Mama

announced. "If you all will hurry and wash up, we can have dinner before everything gets cold."

It had been a perfect dinner. Mac and Papa had hit it off right away, and Mac kept asking for more of Mama's *kotletki*. He had thought they would be something sweet instead of, as he termed them, "meatloaf patties." The time had passed quickly, and I had felt disappointed when Mac had to leave. Somehow he just fit into our family pattern. I couldn't believe that I had once labeled him a drip.

"He's a fine young man," Papa had declared. "A most intelligent young man."

A few days later Sam Klauber stopped by in the evening. I had opened the door for him and explained to him that the folks were in the kitchen. "Just go in there; I'm going to my room to cram for exams. Please forgive me for being so inhospitable."

"No problem, young lady. Go on and study." He patted me on the shoulder and went on towards the kitchen. A few hours later I heard a soft tapping on my door. "Tamara," Sam's head poked into my room, "may I enter your sacred inner sanctum and give my poor little recluse a 'good-night kiss'? Your folks say you've really been hitting the books."

"Come on in." I gave him a hug, then removed some books from the couch. "Sit down here. I can spare time for you, Sam."

Glancing around my messy room, he chuckled. Notebooks, textbooks, dictionaries lay scattered about, a half-empty box of saltines on my bed. Finally, his eyes rested on me. "Mm, you're pale; there're shadows under your eyes. Is this all you've been eating?" He jerked his head towards the box of crackers.

"Of course not, silly."

"Staying up too late?"

"Yes," I admitted, all of a sudden realizing how totally exhausted I felt. "I have been staying up late, but I just can't afford to fall asleep, Sam. There's so much material to cover. I've forgotten a lot of what I had read in the beginning of the term; so I have had to reread some books. I'm at the point where I've got so many facts jammed into this head of mine that they're all jumbled together, making no sense whatsoever."

"That bad, huh?" He picked at his lips, pinching them

thoughtfully. "When's this—your next exam?"

"Day after tomorrow. It makes me sick when I think how many more books I still have to scan and review."

"And you really think it'll be that difficult for you? Staying up, I mean?"

It was strange the way he was cross-examining me. Again, I told him firmly, "Yes, I do have to stay up all night."

He gazed off into space, lost for a moment in thought. I had the feeling he was up to something. Then he reached into his jacket pocket and withdrew a tiny medicine vial.

"Darling Tamara." Now he was the doctor. "I don't usually do this sort of thing, but I know you well enough to know that you do need help. These pills will do the trick. You must remember, however, that these are pills that can only be obtained through a doctor's prescription, and they must be used with caution. This is Benzedrine. It's habit forming, so be careful how you use it." He peered at me through his glasses, which had slid down his nose. "Follow those directions carefully. Take one tonight at eight o'clock. It will keep you awake and fully alert so that you can study." He gave me a fatherly pat on the cheek. "But don't, I repeat, do not, take many of these. There are directions right here for you. Remember, darling, be very, very careful with these."

He placed the vial in the palm of my hand and closed my fingers over it. "It's your magic potion," he said as he reached for the doorknob. "Well, I'd better leave you to your studies." He paused, a slow smile creasing his face. "I saw your friend, Mac, today. He sends you love."

It was strange how I got quivery inside just at the mention of Mac. I hadn't heard from him since our Chaucer quiz three weeks ago.

"Please tell that lieutenant of yours that I've passed Professor Root's course with flying colors. He'll know what I mean." I believe Sam also knew what I meant, for he smiled knowingly, then blew me a kiss.

What a sweetheart Sammy was. I forgave him for all his remarks about pedestals and ideals. He was a thoughtful person, and the pills really helped. All day long I kept at my books, even cutting one class so that I wouldn't have to leave the house. I stayed up all night too and had been pleasantly surprised at how clear and fresh my head had felt the next morning. Again, I blessed Sam for his "prescription."

In class, I was surprised at how quickly I filled up the blue exam books. Now, as I think back, I wish that I could have seen for myself what I had written in them. My goal then had been to pass the course, and that I had evidently done.

With exams over, I could now stay home and hibernate for a spell. For two straight days, I slept. Foggily, I remembered Mama bringing me a tray of food, than taking it away. Once in a while, whether in my dreams or in my waking stupor, I could hear Mama talking on the phone. In her sweet, hushed voice she was telling someone that I was sound asleep and, yes, exams were over and done with, thank goodness.

Then I awakened to hear the phone ringing again. Now fully awake, I ran downstairs.

"Hey, Tamara,"—I had forgotten how husky Phyl's voice was—"do you feel as good as I do?"

"Oh, boy, do I! As if I'd slept continuously for one whole week. I've absolutely no idea of what day or time it is."

"Me, too," Phyllis chuckled, then hesitated. "Wait a sec." I heard the match strike. "Okay, now where were we? Oh, yeah, you know my mom honestly thought I'd gone into a coma."

"I guess that's the way it was here, too," I laughed.

"Don't you think we ought to celebrate? How about a party in your 'ballroom'?"

"That's a terrific idea. It's about time, isn't it?"

"Who're we going to ask? Mac? Lanny?" Phyl asked.

I'd almost forgotten about Mac. It had been more than three weeks since I had last seen him. He hadn't even called, or Mama may have forgotten to tell me, although I doubted that.

"Phyl, you call him. I'm bashful about asking him. I'll ask Lanny, Jacques, Sam, and some of the others. I'm sure Loretta and Vicky will come, and Maria. Let's each call at least twelve people. I'll give you a list, okay?"

"Swell, Tamara. I can't wait."

It was amazing how quickly we were able to organize the party. Mama, of course, thought it a great idea.

"You know the new waffle iron Papa bought me? Well, why don't we try it out? Won't having a waffle dinner be different?"

"That's a terrific idea," Phyl had crowed, when I told her about Mama's suggestion. "Everyone whom I've invited said they'd be delighted to come."

The day of the party Lanny came earlier so that he could help move furniture and blow up the balloons.

"I'll also check out the records," he looked at me conspiratorially. "I want to make sure every other one is a Strauss waltz."

"Make sure you've got some records of Glenn Miller and Tommy Dorsey," Phyl grumbled. "Some people prefer those, you know."

By eight o'clock the party was in full swing. More than twenty-five people had eaten stacks of Mama's golden waffles with homemade, hot maple syrup. Even Papa had ventured down from his study to sample Mama's new "specialty," the American waffle.

"Any more, Professor?" It was Lanny's turn to ladle.

"Oh, no, no." Papa patted his stomach. "Thank you, but my wife already teases me about this. I must leave you young people now." He smiled at my friends, giving them a cheerful, farewell wave, and then retreated upstairs to his study.

"Doesn't your dad like to dance?" Lanny asked. "Your mom looks as if she'd love to dance sometimes."

"I've never seen Papa dance," I told him. "He likes us to enjoy ourselves, but he'd rather work in his study. You know, I sometimes think he's bashful, or maybe he feels that his presence might make us feel restrained."

"Nobody feels like that with Mama around," Phyllis interrupted, overhearing my last words. "Tamara, let's all go up, huh? Loretta and I have soaked the dishes in the kitchen sink. We'll wash them later."

"Okay," I told her. "I think some people have already gone upstairs," I said, taking Lanny's hand.

It was a great party, everyone kept saying, but still there was something lacking. In spite of everything, I didn't feel as happy as I usually did at our home parties. Sammy had told me he'd be in New York on this evening. Mac hadn't shown up either.

Perhaps Phyllis had forgotten to invite him.

"Did you tell Mac about our party?" I tried to be nonchalant about it.

"Sure thing, Tamara. I knew he'd be the one person I'd better not forget to invite," she said teasingly. "He even thanked me, saying he'd try to be here." She had shrugged her shoulders. "Maybe he couldn't make it."

I was annoyed, but I didn't know whether it was with her or with Mac. Why did anything concerning him affect me more than if it had been someone else? After all, he was just another date who had taken me out. From now on, I will positively devote myself exclusively to dear, faithful Lanny. He would never hurt me. Hurt me? I hadn't been hurt!

Again, that disquieting refrain of Sam's kept nagging and needling me, "And what are you afraid of, Tamara?"

"Come on, Lanny." I held out my arms to him. "Let's dance and dance 'til we can dance no more. All right?"

"I'm all for it, my Princess." He beamed—so much in love.

We waltzed in our stockinged feet. The floor was slippery. Lanny twirled me round and round till the room too whirled around with me. What fun it was to feel so free once more.

The doorbell rang, and my heart sank. Could it be Officer MacIntosh again? Guiltily, I questioned Lanny, "Have we been that noisy?"

"No, Princess, the windows are closed." He put his hand on my shoulder. You want me to go to the front door?"

"Thanks, Lanny, but I'll go. You'd better tend to the records."

I walked down the stairs very carefully because the talcum powder had made the stairs slippery. I opened the door, and was surprised to see Mac, bare-headed, his officer's cap in his hand, a grin on his face. He was terribly late and that stupid smirk of his as he stood there infuriated me. Apparently, he thought there was nothing wrong about being hours late to a party.

"Aren't you going to invite me in, Tamara? It's freezing cold out here on your front porch."

Without saying a word, I opened the door wider. The cold air hit my face. Br-rr. *I should let him stay out longer,* I thought angrily. Then I caught a whiff of his cologne and felt myself melting. It was good to have him here, standing so close to me.

408

Unwillingly, I had to admit to myself that I was glad he had come. Suddenly, I grew conscious of his questioning eyes on my face, that now familiar, but still evasive, tender and quizzical smile on his lips. What was I thinking of? I had completely forgotten my guests upstairs.

Here he was, this rude, unapologetic, and impertinent, to boot, young officer, standing in our foyer under the Chinese lantern, making me totally forget my dutiful obligations as a hostess. I watched him as if in a trance. Slowly he unwrapped the olive brown wool scarf from around his neck. He appeared to be thoroughly enjoying himself. When he handed me the scarf, he glanced up the stairs.

"Do I hear music? Are your guests all upstairs dancing?" Carefully, with military precision, he folded his gloves, one at a time, and put them slowly into his coat pocket.

"Yes, we're dancing upstairs," I replied icily. Insofar as I was concerned, I had been polite enough to him. Although he was an officer, I'd have to admit he was not much of a gentleman.

Curiously he looked into the dining room and then walked over to the table. The waffle iron was still there, no longer warm. One batter bowl had been emptied, washed, and put back into Mama's cupboard. Some batter still remained in the other bowl, and beside it sat the pitcher of punch, half-full.

Well, if he has few manners, I'll show him I have some. "Would you care for some punch before we go upstairs?" I asked politely.

At that he had smiled and eased himself into Papa's chair. "I'd surely like some, Tamara." He held out an empty glass towards me. Slowly, I poured out the punch, being careful not to spill any on Mama's pretty tablecloth. Upstairs, I could hear waltz music; I knew that Lanny expected me to come upstairs at any moment. Tapping my foot impatiently, I watched the lieutenant gulp down the punch. He had been thirsty.

Again, he held out his empty glass. "Do you mind?" he smiled guiltily. "It's so darned good, Tamara, and I might as well finish it up for you. That is,"—he looked at me with mocking seriousness—"if you don't want any yourself."

Silently, I ladled the punch into his glass, wishing he'd hurry so that we could go on upstairs. It would have been rude of me to leave him alone here, but he himself was in no hurry.

As he leisurely sipped at the punch, his eyes alighted on the waffle iron. "You haven't been making waffles, have you?"

What a stupid question! It had to be perfectly obvious to anyone since the bowl of batter still sat on the table.

"Yes," I determined to rub it in a bit, "they were really delicious. Everybody had two helpings or even more."

He stared at me, innocently enough. My feet were itching to dance, but I couldn't leave him there by himself. After all, he was my guest. I noticed his lips twitching. Was he about to ask me something, or was he about to laugh?

"I see there's still some batter left." His eyes fastened on my face. "I just love waffles, Tamara. You know every Sunday up on the Hill in Pennsylvania, Mom used to make us waffles."

"The Hill?" I asked.

"Yes," he answered quietly, "that's what we call my home back in Freeport."

That did it. Of course, my heart went out to him. No matter that he had been late, crude, rude, impolite, and impertinent. I felt sorry for him, poor fellow. Our home must remind him of his, I thought to myself, and like Vanya, he is so far away from home.

I turned on the waffle iron. "I'll be glad to make you a waffle if you wish." *Why in the world am I doing this?* I thought. *I should be going upstairs; I should be telling him that he can come on up later or even go back to his army base for all I care.*

Bubbles appeared, and slowly I lowered the top lid. "The secret of making good waffles," I explained to him, "is never to lower the top lid until there are bubbles."

He looked at me with respect, nodding his head. "I see exactly what you mean. I also see that you know how to cook."

He watched as I finally raised the lid and revealed a perfect waffle, colored a delicious golden brown. "There's still some of Mama's syrup left." I took the little pitcher and emptied the syrup over the waffle. "There. I hope you like it." I smiled, relieved to know that after he had eaten, we could go upstairs.

"Mm-mm, I tell you, Tamara, they're even better than Mom's, and Mom's were the very best. By golly, that was good!" He eyed the bowl.

"Would you like another one?" I reached for the ladle. "There's still some batter left."

"You mean it? Gee, thanks, I sure would." He shook his head in awe. "You make the best waffles, I swear to that!"

My patience was wearing a bit thin. I couldn't believe how quickly the second waffle had disappeared. Again he eyed the bowl, holding out his empty plate.

"Tamara, I'll be most happy to finish off this batter for you. That is"—he eyed me anxiously—"if you don't mind making me another one. You know, my Scotch-Irish and Pennsylvania Dutch parents taught me, above all, to be thrifty. I hate to see anything thrown out." He gave me a cheerful smile. "You know, one of our great philosophers in America, Ben Franklin, maximized, 'Waste not; want not.'"

"I see." I found myself neither amused nor interested in Ben Franklin's maxims just then. I poured the last ladleful of batter, scraping the bowl with a spatula so that he could see for himself how completely empty it was.

He wiped his plate of Mama's syrup with the last waffle. "Those waffles were positively superb," he told me. "Please tell Mama that for me, will you?"

"Too bad you didn't come earlier; you could have eaten many more." I couldn't help being sarcastic. "I'm going upstairs now," I told him rather curtly. "My guests are there without a hostess." Without another word he followed me to the ballroom.

"Ah, there's Phyl." I signaled to her. "Mac's here, Phyl. Introduce him around, won't you?"

Lanny welcomed me with open arms. "What kept you, my Princess?" he whispered into my ear.

I pointed towards Mac, who was now standing next to Phyl and a thin, dark-haired girl, whom I vaguely remembered having seen around Radcliffe. "He was hungry, Lanny." I was thoroughly disgusted with the lieutenant. "I had to make him three waffles. If I'd had more batter, I bet he would have eaten even more."

"I'm glad to have you back," he hugged me to him. "I missed you so much."

Everyone kept telling me how great the party was, and that made me feel good again. Jacques Dubois came over to us.

411

"Lanny, give me a chance to dance with our hostess, will you?"

"I think this is one of your best parties," Phyl commented when I joined her to smoke a cigarette. "Mac seems to be enjoying himself thoroughly, or haven't you noticed?"

"Come to think of it, I haven't, Phyl. I've been so busy. Everybody's been asking me to dance." I looked around the room. "Where is your Yankee lieutenant anyway?"

She gave me a sharp look, then blew some smoke towards me. "He's not my lieutenant. In fact, I think . . . "—she too looked around the room, then grinned—"hah, I had the feeling that he liked her the minute I introduced them."

I felt uncomfortable. "Introduced whom?"

Phyl slowly inhaled the last puff of her cigarette, then squashed it in the ashtray. "Oh, Jeanette."

"Jeanette?" The name sounded familiar, but I couldn't place the girl.

"Yeah, Jeanette Rubin. She was in Professor Schorer's class with us. Remember? We needed more girls so I invited her. She's dark-haired, rather thin, nice personality. Oh, oh, she's not around either." She grinned. "Well, well, our lieutenant friend is playing around, I'll bet." She glanced towards the small guest room where a night-light glowed. "I'll bet they're in there making out."

I should have known. Papa always said that still waters run deep. I guess the lieutenant was like that. Suddenly I wished that everybody would go away, that I could be alone, just by myself, for a while. Even Lanny, with his ever-questioning look and quivering lips, irritated me. He had held out his arms, ready to waltz again.

"Lanny, ask Phyl, will you? She loves to waltz with you."

"All right, Princess." Obediently, he left me then, looking back, his eyes still attentive with love.

I don't know what possessed me to do it. Something, a magnetism, drew me towards the guest room. Once there, I felt like a damn fool. Mac and Jeanette were sitting cozily on the bed, close together. When I appeared, they both looked up.

"Oh, I'm so sorry. I didn't realize anyone was in here. I just wanted to turn the light out." I knew just by the way he had smiled at me that the lieutenant was most amused.

412

Jeanette stood up. "Oh, I was just giving Mac my address," she explained. "I have to be leaving shortly." Mac got up too.

"Please don't leave," I objected, ever the genial hostess. "The party is just warming up."

'All the world's a stage, and all the men and women merely players,' I thought, asking myself if I too were merely playing a part, no longer being myself.

"I really do have to go," Jeanette turned to the lieutenant who looked down at her. Was it with affection? And she was absolutely faultless, cooing her appreciation, "Tamara, it's been so delightful. How can I ever thank you for inviting me?"

By leaving immediately, you dark-haired vamp, I thought angrily. I followed her and the lieutenant as they walked downstairs. In the foyer Mac slid his coat and scarf off the banister. Quickly, he wrapped the scarf around his neck. "Thanks again for the waffles," he told me, politely extending his hand. Jeanette moved next to him, her eyes glowing.

"You're going too, Mac?" I hadn't expected that he would leave with her. I had hoped, even planned, that he would accompany me upstairs, then ask me to dance. But had he done that, I would have refused and danced with Lanny instead. Oh, but I was feeling dreadfully mean that night!

"I'm taking Jeanette home." He gave her a loving, intimate glance, dismissing me.

So that was that! I let them out the front door and banged it shut behind them. I heard their laughter, then the dance music upstairs and the animated chitter-chatter of my guests. In spite of all the merriment, I felt shaken and terribly depressed.

413

25

It's Us

"Hey, Phyl," I cradled the receiver on my shoulder as I asked, "what are you doing during the holidays? Have you met anybody special?"

She snorted. "If I had, would I be talking right now to you? Hell, no. If you have anybody in mind, call me, pronto. No, I'm just messing around here, helping my Mom decorate the house and stuff. What about you?"

"Well, at first Mama didn't want us to get a tree on account of Vanya's not being here, but now that we have one she's delighted. I think it's about the most beautiful one we've had here in the States. I bought green lights for it, Phyl. After I decorated it, I wrapped angel hair all around the whole tree. Gives it an ethereal effect, and when it's lit, it's absolutely breathtaking."

"Sounds nice. I'll have to come and see it one of these days."

"Gosh, please don't come this week. I'm busy running errands for Mama. She's cooking and baking up a storm: *piroshkis, plombir,* and all sorts of Russian goodies. She won't let Papa or me taste anything. 'It's for Christmas,' she keeps saying. She also has sent Vanya a huge Christmas parcel."

"How is your brother, anyway?" I thought that really nice of her to ask, considering how he had treated her that time.

"I guess he's okay. You know, he has traveled all over: Italy, North Africa, Egypt, and other places I don't remember. In every place he has fallen in love, each girl more beautiful than the previous one."

414

"He's quite the lover boy, isn't he?"

"Yup. Sorry, I gotta go, Phyl. Just wanted to wish you and your folks a merry Christmas."

"We got your card," she laughed. "Thanks again."

"So long. I'll be seeing you," and we both hung up.

One evening, when Sam and I were sitting in the living room, talking about anything and everything, he appeared somewhat more reserved than usual, even depressed, I thought. It was uncanny how I had learned to read his mind. "What is it, Sammy-boy?" I asked him. I myself was in an unusually happy mood. My last days at Radcliffe, and I was thoroughly looking forward to my coming emancipation.

"I'm just thinking," he had started off in a low tone. "You'll be flying away pretty soon, won't you, my pretty one?" It had been both a statement and a question.

"As soon after graduation as I can," I told him. "Just imagine, Sammy, next year, nineteen hundred and forty-four, come February, I'll no longer be an overburdened undergraduate. I'll be free as a bird. And then, by golly, away I'll fly."

"To New York?" He shook his head in disapproval. "That's no place for you, Tamara."

God and Confucius both! Can't he leave me alone about that? I'm having enough problems with Mama on my back.

"Of course, I'm going, Sam." There was no doubt in my mind. Come hell or high water, I was going!

"It's a wicked place for you," he said slowly. "Tamara, I know New York. It's not, my darling, for sweet young things like you. You've been sheltered from so much. There's a big, bad wolf pit out there." He laughed a little, trying to appear lighthearted.

Had Mama put Sam up to talking me out of going to New York? She'd already been after Papa to convince me that I shouldn't go. I smiled confidently, "Sammy-boy, I've grown up. Can't you see that? Sam, I've lived through a lot more than you have; I can guarantee you that."

Again, as he sometimes had done in the past, he traced his fingers around the head and tongue of the dragon. "That's not what I mean, Princess. I know you're old, twenty-two years old. Like it or not, you're still Raphael's cherub to me with a

415

golden halo and a rounded bottom." He chuckled to himself. "Now don't get all heated up; it's just your Uncle Sam talking. I'm afraid for you in New York, Tamara. No kidding. You know nothing about places like that." He paused, hesitating as he focused his penetrating gaze on me. "Have you thought of getting married?"

I laughed to myself at this absurd question. I could count off for him the proposals I'd received. There had been two Charlies, a Jacques, one Lanny, a Claude, one Richard, and that handsome Yugoslavian student from MIT, Trian Stoyanovich. All of them had proposed marriage. *But why tell him that,* I decided.

"Sam, how many times have I told you that there is no man on this earth that I will marry right now or in the near future. There is a war on and much work for me to do. And, you of all people should know very well my viewpoint on marriage, Sam."

"I should have known. All these male bees swarming around you, buzzing away. You, that little clump of pure honey, the right bee still hasn't found you yet, has he?" Then he chuckled, "You're a tough queen bee to catch, Tamara Rubleva."

I did not like being compared to a queen bee, shades of his "princess on a pedestal." Was I really that proud and elusive?

"You know," he continued, in a more serious vein, "here you are, twenty-two years old. Many women your age have already had several babies by this time."

"Not me."

"Now there's Lanny. Why not marry him?" His voice was quietly persistent. "He really loves you."

Why was he being so insistent? I stiffened with resentment. After all, it was actually none of his business what I did with my life. He had no hold on me. I did not have to answer to him.

Again he asked. "Why don't you marry him?"

"Because I do not love him. Can you understand that, Sam? I do like him very much, but I don't love him." I took a deep breath. "Want me to spell it out for you?" I asked sarcastically.

His voice was low, barely more than a whisper. "And Mac, what about our friend Mac?"

How dare he ask about him, I thought. *What does his lieutenant friend have to do with my life?* Again, at the mention of Mac, I found myself getting mixed up, my damned flexible emo-

416

tions warping my thinking. I thought I had forgotten that Scotsman.

Sam was persistent. "Yes, I said 'Mac.' Do you think you could ever love a man like him?" His voice softened.

Sam wasn't being fair to me. He had no right to ask me such a personal question. Since the night of the party I had wiped his lieutenant completely out of my life! I had tried hard to concentrate on other things; to immerse myself in myriads of time-consuming community affairs and people. I had almost succeeded. Even Mama had now stopped inquiring about Mac.

Sam's mention of him had poured salt on the old wound. Again I pictured Mac's face as he had taken Jeanette's coat and smiled his special smile at her upturned face. Once more I felt the hurt and anger. I hadn't heard from him and the thought of him now chilled me as frigid as an ice statue.

"Mac?" I almost snorted, trying to laugh. "Never."

Sam, psychiatrist that he was, had examined me minutely like a patient. I hadn't expected him to turn his words in Mac's direction, but now that he had forewarned me, I was ready. I stared at him, knowing how open and innocent my eyes looked. I would "out-Sammy" Sam.

"Tsk, tsk!" He placed his hand on my shoulder, giving it a gentle pat. "That 'never' is too strong a word for my little girl to use. I don't like that word, Tamara."

I didn't answer him.

His hand moved around in slow motion to my cheek. Softly he patted it, then lowered his head to look into my eyes. "Do you know, dear child, that Mac loves you? Do you know, Tamara, that he loves you as much as a man can ever love a woman?"

Again I felt the old sensation return—the reeling, the delicious, weakening feeling that enveloped me and filled me with a wondrous pleasure. Why should I feel like this when I actually despised that crude, rude Yankee man? And even as I thought these thoughts, I knew they weren't true at all.

If he does love me, I thought to myself, *he certainly shows his love in a strange way, coming late to my party, eating up waffles like a half-starved refugee, and then going off with that brazen, gloating Jeanette Rubin. Not once had he asked me—his hostess—to dance.* Thinking of that waffle debacle, I really became

417

indignant. Whatever Sam was scheming in his mind, I knew that what he had told me could never come true. He had, as usual, gotten me so addled that I didn't even know my own mind, damn him! God and Confucius damn him!

Sam must have sensed my feelings, for he leaned towards me again. This time he took both my hands in his. "Little Russian princess"—he knew that I usually melted when he called me that—"you know your old Uncle Sam by now well enough to trust me, knowing how dearly I do love you, your parents, your brother Vanya. I am telling you God's truth. In fact, Tamara, I am swearing to you by all that is dear to me, that this American laddie loves you more than any other man could ever love a woman. Believe me, dear child, since that very first day when I brought him to your home. Do you remember? It was as Phyllis's date that he had come, but he left that evening in love with you. Later, that same night, he told me that you were the woman he was going to marry, or he would die trying. That, darling Tamara, is the truth, so help me God!"

He raised his hand, very solemn and properlike. I couldn't take my eyes off him, his riveting words coming much too fast for me. "That's God's honest truth," he repeated. He sounded tired now, staring at me gravely. "I've been frank with you. Take my words as you will. Manipulate Mac as much as you desire. I'm through with this case. Finished."

That had been quite a speech, even for Sam. He knew how to select his words in ways to get to me. Now, however, I knew him better. He couldn't hurt me any more.

"Sorry, Sammy-boy, I don't believe you." I smiled at him. "You say things like that to me, and you expect me to swoon? Let's see now; you say Mac loves me. Hah! He certainly hasn't acted as if he does, has he? Lanny loves me; he hasn't told me, but I can see it in his eyes and in every little thing that he does for me. That lieutenant of yours, it'll be a torrid day at the North Pole before I ever believe that he loves me. Sam, I may be naive, but I'm certainly not that stupid."

I knew that my eyes were flashing, and my voice had turned bitter. I had to have my say. It was Sam's reaction that totally unnerved me. He chuckled in delight. "Good boy! I didn't think he could pull it off." This time he laughed heartily until tears welled up in his eyes.

Had he gone mad? "What's wrong, Sam?" I asked, alarmed. This was so unlike his gentle self.

"Oh, my darling, I'm sorry," he blurted out. He became serious. "It's really all my fault, I must confess." He looked at me apologetically. "I'm the one to blame, and it's not fair for me to laugh like this at your expense."

What the devil was he ranting about? I stared at him. He had never acted like this before.

He started to explain, haltingly at first, "Believe me, Tamara," his expression grave, yet kind. "Mac actually yearned to be at your side that night of the party. God, you can't realize how difficult it was for him to act the way he did towards you."

He shook his head when I tried to interrupt. "Please, let me finish. Darling, it was all an act. You see, he and I talked all this out one day. He told me how much he worships you. He couldn't hide his feelings; I had known that in the very beginning. He had been feeling depressed, knowing how many other men were competing for you. What chance could he have, especially since he wasn't even from New England, just here for a short time, knowing that at any moment his orders might come for duty overseas. You, my beloved child," he continued, "have been so involved in your own happy little world, your safe world filled with your sweet Lannys and Dicks and Charlies, he knew you wouldn't give him the time of your day. What to do? He could see how you basked in the unswerving devotion and adulation of these ivy-leagued, young men, flashing your beautiful, sparkling brown eyes at them, smiling down at them from your throne on high, you, the golden princess on your ivory pedestal. Yes, the China doll that should be handled ever so carefully and respectfully for fear that she would break. She must be adored from afar; she must not be touched. That, in brief, is you, Tamara, whether you like it or not. Once before, I said—and I remember how displeased you were when I did—that someday you would have to climb down from that aerie abode of yours." He took a deep breath, pursing his lips. He looked at the rug, not at me. "That 'some day' has come, Tamara. It has come."

I sat perfectly still. Much of what he had told me I had already heard. What I had waited eagerly to hear was that Mac loved me, really loved me. That was the constant thought going round and round in my mind, like some haunting refrain that would not ever go away. But even as Sam's words echoed inside me, I still had some doubts. Mac himself had not expressed his love to me. I didn't care about all that other stuff, the men in my life, the pedestal, the China doll business. What mattered, what counted was the fact that Mac did love me, would even die for me! It was Sam, however, telling me all this, not Mac himself— the man from whom I wanted to hear those words.

"Thank you, Sam, thank you for telling me all that. If you are pleading Mac's case, then stop right now. If Mac loves me, then let him tell me himself. Love does not require a middle-man." I needed for Sam to leave so that I could sort all this out by myself.

Mac certainly had a strange of way of showing his love. At times he had looked lovingly at me; then he had ignored me as if I didn't even exist! From the heavens to the lower depths, if that was love "a la Mac," I would have none of it. What gall he had! Sending Sam to speak for him, to butter me up. That latest episode at my party, flirting with that black-haired dodo bird and taking her home as if he were smitten. In the end, there I was, I thought, crazily hoping that he loved me, and then full of doubts that he didn't.

"Let's not talk about this anymore, Sam." I pretended to sti-fle a yawn. If the two of them could play act, so could I. "Would you mind awfully if I said good night? Mama and I have been baking Christmas goodies all day long, and frankly, I'm tired."

He was instantaneously solicitous. "Oh, my darling, I've kept you up. That was inconsiderate, Tamara; I'm sorry."

His contrite expression made me feel guilty until I thought of his and Mac's conspiracy. I rubbed my eyes. "It's okay, Sammy." I gave him a slight pat on the back, smiled, and bade him a good night.

Several days later Mac phoned. "Tamara, how have you been?" He was acting as if nothing had happened between us, his voice calm and perfectly natural.

"Oh, Mac? Hello. . . . Why I've been fine," I told him. "I've been helping with our Christmas preparations. Also, I've been out shopping for the holidays."

"Yes, I guess you've been busy." He sounded thoughtful.

Since I had nothing more to say to him, I kept quiet.

"Are you there, Tamara?"

"Yes, I'm on the phone," I answered, regarding with pleasure the tree in the corner of the living room. I sure had done a good job on it. Everybody had liked that misty effect of the angel hair.

An uneasy laugh on the other end. I could hear him take a deep breath. "Tamara"—his voice was low—"I'd like to see you."

Well, he would, would he? "That's nice of you," I said politely. "We're usually home in the afternoons; that is, Mama and I are."

He cleared his throat, "I'd really like to see you by yourself, Tamara."

"Mac, I'm dreadfully busy right now. You know how it is." I let that sink in, then brightened my voice up a bit. "I tell you what. A few of my friends are coming over Friday evening. We're going to listen to Christmas carols, maybe even sing some ourselves. You're welcome to come if you'd like."

A brief silence followed. I smiled to myself. Well, the actor has been upstaged. If he really loves me, he'll come. I'd see him among my friends, but not alone anymore.

It had been an almost perfect evening as far as the Christmas atmosphere went. The misty tree brimful of ornaments, like a winter bride all aglow and beautiful, the familiar music, the flushed faces of my dear friends, Papa wearing his red slippers, and Mama bustling about.

"Don't forget Handel's *Messiah,* Papa," I whispered. "That's on at nine o'clock this evening."

"Don't worry, *dochenka,* I've already thought of that." He chucked me under the chin. "Are you going to dance upstairs tonight?"

"No, we're just going to talk, eat Christmas goodies, and listen to carols and, of course, the *Messiah.*"

"And tomorrow," Papa continued, "the Boston Symphony plays Tchaikovsky's *Nutcracker Suite*; then after that the Mormon Tabernacle Choir will be broadcast." He peered into the living room at my friends lounging on Mama's dragon rug, talking in low voices. "I will be seeing you young people later." He gave them a casual wave, smiling cheerfully at them.

"Why don't you stay, Serioja?" Mama asked.

"I'll come downstairs later for the *Messiah*. Verotchka, I have some important letters to write."

"I like your friends," Mama whispered to me in Russian. "They are all like family, so natural with each other."

"Oh, Mama, I'm glad you like them. Come on in and listen to the carols." Jacques, on seeing us enter, moved so that Mama and I could sit together by the fireplace. I sat at her feet, resting my head on her knee.

It had been peaceful and pleasant that night. All day it had snowed, and the temperature had dropped to twenty-eight degrees. Inside our warm house Phyllis had bustled about the kitchen, helping Mama make hot chocolate. Everybody had helped. Loretta cut the cakes; Charlie passed around cookies and helped himself at the same time. Lanny turned up wherever he had been needed.

"Where do you want the ham, Mama, the center of the table?"

"Oh, yes, Lanny," Mama told him, "right here in the center."

"It's a beautiful table, Mama," Phyl had observed.

All these voices, together with the music, how sweet and cozy it had been, listening to them all, the talking and the music. I could barely hear them now, their voices sounding so distant, too far away to make out the words. How warm it had suddenly become, how deliciously that warmth seemed to envelop me, to wrap up my whole being. My eyelids had become so heavy.

I could feel my hair being pushed gently aside from my face and heard Mama's soft voice talking to some one. How far away it seemed! At times I heard her laughter, so low and hushed. Then I heard the front door being opened and happy voices, joyous sounds of someone greeting someone. Amidst the laughter one voice stood out, a delightful, familiar, yet strange one that triggered tingling, magically warm feelings inside me. What state was I in? Awake? Asleep?

"Tamara," Mama was whispering into my ear. "Tamara,

wake up. He's here. He's finally come, your Mac. Tamarotchka dear, wake up. It's Mac."

Slowly I opened my eyes, shaking myself out of that deep sleep. It had been as if it were through a mistlike haze that I had at first noticed him, standing there beside Mama, in his American lieutenant's uniform, looking down at me.

I could see only his eyes at that moment, blue, tender and loving, just as I always imagined them to be. He, too, like Mama, was bending towards me, smiling a shy, most radiant smile. I had tried to rise, but strangely I couldn't. Seeing him that way, I felt as if my legs had crumpled underneath me. I had been unable to straighten them out. He then reached down to me, pulled me up into his arms, and I knew that he was real.

"I'm glad you came," I whispered. Somehow he moved me towards the foyer, away from Mama and the others. He led me into the dining room, where we could still hear the music, yet be alone. I heard a waltz come on the radio, and it was then that he took me in his arms.

"Shall we dance?" His mouth against my hair, his arms tight around me, his voice barely above a whisper.

"Yes," I couldn't believe how far away, how feeble my own voice sounded.

I let him steer me, my feet feeling like wood. My faithful feet, my dancing feet—they had forsaken me completely. This alien, helpless feeling I had overwhelmed me. All I wanted now was to have him hold me, forever and forever. We moved, hardly in time to the music, because neither of us could hear it now. He looked down into my eyes, as if he could see right into me, and on and on into my heart.

What could be the matter with me? Why did I act this way, so immobile, like a statue, unable to move? Why did my whole being melt with his eyes upon mine, his mouth so sweetly close to mine?

"I'm sorry," I whispered to him, afraid to hear myself speak, lest this magic disappear. "I just don't know what's wrong with me. I can't dance. My legs won't move. They just won't hold me."

"I know, my darling," he whispered back. "It's us, that's why."

When the music had ended, Mac led me back into the living room so that I could tend to my guests. Mechanically, I moved among them, noticed their bright faces, their smiles showing their sparkling, white teeth. Phyllis's blonde hair, Loretta's midnight curls, Vicky's round face and bright eyes, dear Lanny looking painfully surprised, and Jacques, sitting, smiling, always at ease. All of them then dissolved into a blurry haze along with the room and Mama and Papa and the radio with its endless music. I found myself in a strange, unbelievable trance. All that stood out in my mind were his eyes so full of love, that tender smile, and his low voice, saying to me, "It's us." What a perfectly simple and clear explanation. *It's us.*

26

The Yankee-Man

"Tamara," Mama leaned over me pulling aside my blanket, "Mac's on the phone. Wake up, *dochenka*."

I opened my eyes slowly, still dazed from my interrupted sleep. Seeing her standing there, watching me with that teasing expression of hers, wakened me up right away. "Mama?"

She shrugged her shoulders, then smiled. "It's just that Mac's on the phone and would like to talk to you. Never mind though. I can tell him that you're too sleepy to . . ."

"Why didn't you say so?" I was out of bed like a flash, running down the stairs as if a banshee had been after me. "Hello?" I panted into the phone.

"Take your time, darling," Mac laughed. "I'm sorry Mama had to waken you. I tried to wait to call, but I just couldn't wait any longer. I had to hear your voice again."

"I'm glad you did call, Mac." I loved hearing his voice too, especially when he had called me "darling." "It's just that—well—by the time that party ended last night and you . . ."

"I know." He continued my own thoughts, "Too many impressions for the two of us. It's so strange, Tamara. At first, I thought you were out of bounds for me, that you could never love me. All these Ivy League fellows. Honestly, my head swam last night when I found out that you could. I had to call to make sure. I wanted to hear you say it again."

"Say what?"

"Say, 'I love you.'"

"I do."

At that reply he laughed. "Those words come later, darling, when we're both in church. Please say, 'I love you.'"

"I love you with all my heart. I love you, Mac." How easily I was able to say those words to him.

"Ah-h, the key to my heart lies in those three little words. Thank you, my Russian darling. By the way, how do you say 'Thank you' in Russian?"

"Spasibo." I liked it that he had asked me that.

"Well, *spasibo* for your love. Now, tell me, when may I come over to see you?"

"Why not for dinner, Mac? Papa complained that he hasn't seen much of you. He told me last night, when I hugged him good night, that he'd like to know you better. As for Mama?" I smiled, thinking of her. "Mama, were she my age, would probably become my rival for your attention. Anyway, she's already told me that she thinks you're the man for me."

"Hey, that sure is swell of her. I'll have to *spasibo* her too."

"No," I corrected, "you'll have to *pob-lago-dar-it-myahkii znak* her."

"My God, I'll have to what?"

"Never mind, Mac," I laughed. "Part of that means 'to thank' and the last two words are *'myahkii znak'*, which mean the soft mark at the end of the first word. Someday, I'll teach you Russian, if you want me to."

"The same way I taught you Chaucer? I know I'll make mistake after mistake," he added slyly.

"Why don't you come over now?" I suggested. "I can cut my classes for today. After all, I'll be graduating in February."

"Today's the twenty-third of December, and you've still got two months to go before graduation. I'll not be a party to your cutting classes, my Russian darling."

"I wouldn't have cut them, not on account of your loving blue eyes or your stubborn chin, no," I teased. "I'd take you with me and show you off."

He chuckled. "Tell you what. I'll come as soon as I can, probably late afternoon. Then I'll have a chance to talk to your folks and see you whenever you get home. How about that?"

"Sounds fine to me, Mac. I'd better hurry or I'll be late to class."

"I love you, Tamara," he whispered as we hung up.

How good it felt to hear those words. A real Yankee-man had spoken them to me. At last, my dream was becoming a reality. To love him and in turn be loved by him. How sweet the very thought!

On my way to Radcliffe I had to walk through Cambridge Common. It had always held a special attraction for me with its historic statues, shaded walks, and especially the lilac and forsythia bushes that in springtime would burst into such glorious blooms of white, lilac, or yellow blossoms, inviting me to bury my face in their fragrance. Today the Common seemed even more beautiful, like a winter wonderland. The bushes looked lovely, bending their snow-laden branches as if to greet each passerby. Snow too blanketed the statues as they stood silent and ghost-like at their posts staring in solemn dignity over the heads of those who cast their eyes upon them. How much they must have witnessed. If only they could speak! I smiled at the stone soldier with the musket. What a perfectly beautiful world it was, in spite of Hitler, the war, or sad memories of China.

"Tamarotchka," a familiar calling of my name suddenly interrupted my thoughts. I turned around to see Annitchka Frank, one hand holding on to her hat, the other frantically waving, as she ran from behind me to catch up. I hurried to meet her. She was huffing and puffing from running.

"Annitchka, you might have slipped on this icy sidewalk," I chided, giving her a hug. "I'd have waited for you. Are you going to Harvard Square too?" I looked at her with great affection. Although she was Mama's friend and covolunteer, she and I had the closer friendship. Mama did not exactly approve of Annitchka's somewhat bohemian ways.

"You've been like a stranger these days, Tamarotchka." Her animated eyes examined me from my red boots to my head. "You look positively enchanting today. Ach, to have my own youth back again." She patted my cheek with her gloved hand. "Papotchka tells me you'll be graduating soon. I meet him often when I'm shopping and he's either walking to or from Harvard. He had said something about February. I thought students usually graduate in June, or am I mistaken?"

"You're not wrong, Annitchka. It's just that I wanted to

accelerate; so I took summer courses in order to get enough credits. Oh, Annitchka, I've got some wonderful news to tell you." I laid my hand on her arm. "I'm in love." I watched her face to note her reaction.

She looked surprised. "In love? But I thought Lanny and you . . ."

"No, no," I shook my head. "I've never been in love with Lanny. He loves me, poor chap, but I can't help that. Remember when he and I visited you in your apartment that day? I had told him so much about you and Dr. Frank that he had wanted to meet you both. He had been flabbergasted when I told him that we knew you. 'You are acquainted with the great physicist, Philipp Frank?' he asked me." I laughed, recalling that incident. "Annitchka, his eyes got so big, and he kept shaking his head in disbelief. I had to prove to him that I knew you."

That amused her. "What's this about being in love? Do I know the young man?"

"No. Sam Klauber brought him over one night as a blind date for Phyllis. I couldn't stand him at first. I thought him a snob because he paid no attention to me. Several days later he told me he'd fallen in love with me the moment he saw me at our front door but didn't think he had a chance because I was so popular. He had decided then to ignore me but couldn't."

At that she smiled, then linked her arm in mine. "Come on. I'll walk a ways with you. Tell me more about him."

I was happy we'd bumped into each other again. Although I loved Mama and enjoyed being with her, I could not confide in her the way I could to Annitchka. Mama was old-fashioned in many respects, and I felt ill at ease talking about my thoughts on life and love with her. Annitchka, although Mama's age, was more understanding and knew how to listen to young people without censure. Although she and Annitchka were good friends, Mama thought her bohemian.

"I'm afraid of being in love right now," I told Annitchka, as we walked out of the Common.

"Why, Tamara? Love is the most natural emotion in the world." Theatrically, she stretched out her arms, her head arched back. "It's a beautiful feeling, this closeness between man and woman. Why should you be afraid of love?"

"Because Mac will be leaving to go overseas, because he won't be back until the war is over, and who knows when that will be. And because . . . " Hot tears blurred my vision.

"Because why?"

"Because maybe he won't come back."

"And this should stop you from loving him? Don't you ever think that way, child! Use the time you have with him to enjoy your love. If your love is true, it will surmount any separation you may have. I want you to bring your Mac over sometime soon to our apartment so that Philipp and I can meet him."

"I will; I surely will." I promised. "Give my love to Dr. Frank, will you? I've got to run now. I'm late for class." With a final wave I ran past Felix's newsstand and headed towards Radcliffe.

Mac came over late that afternoon. As soon as I opened the front door, he enveloped me in his arms.

"So our lieutenant is getting romantic?" Mama's eyes teasingly surveyed us both from the top of the stairs. "It's good to see you here, Mac. This time you must play the piano for me."

"Sure thing," he agreed, taking off his coat.

"I've invited Mac for dinner, Mama," I told her. "You don't mind, do you?"

Mac grinned, "Don't you think you might be putting Mama in a spot by asking her in front of me?"

"She knows I don't mind," Mama said, "especially since you're going to entertain us with music."

"Ah, so. Well, what would you ladies like to hear? Popular music? Classical?: I'm at your service." He gallantly bowed to Mama, giving me a wink.

"How about playing 'Let It Snow?' " I sat next to him at the piano. "You do know that one, don't you?"

"Sure." He flipped through the music books that lay piled on top of the piano. "Here it is. I can't play it by ear. I need the notes." He began to play.

I hummed the tune. "I love that song, don't you?"

He nodded. When he had finished, Mama and I applauded. Mac turned to Mama. "Now what?"

"That piece you played that night you took Tamara to the restaurant, remember? You mentioned the name, something

429

about spring." Mama frowned, biting her lip in her frustration at not being able to remember the title.

Mac thought for a moment. "Oh, yes, you must mean *Rustle of Spring.*" He played a few notes. "Is that it?"

"Yes," Mama nodded, "You played that so beautifully. I have heard it before. Do you know who wrote the piece?"

"Christian Sinding," Mac answered. "He's not well-known here in the States. He was born in Norway. He's written quite a few piano and violin concertos, and some symphonies as well. I think, though, that *Rustle of Spring* is his best-known work."

When he had finished playing the piece, Mama sighed. "I would just love to play the way you do, but"—she shrugged her shoulders—"no matter how much I practice, it doesn't come out right. Then I hear someone like you, and I lose hope of ever learning to play like that. It makes me ashamed of myself."

We heard the footsteps on the front porch and then the key in the lock.

"Papa's home," I ran to the door to greet him. "Papa, Mac's here."

Papa laid down his briefcase and started taking off his overcoat.

"How could I not know it?" His eyes twinkled. "Just to see your eyes sparkling so, only your lieutenant can make them shine like that." He nodded to Mac, smiling. "It's good to see you again, Mac. You're staying for dinner, I hope."

"Both of your ladies invited me." Mac placed his arm around my waist, then turned to Mama. "Can we help you with anything?"

"No, thank you. Everything is ready. Just you all go up and wash your hands and in five minutes we'll be eating."

Mama amazed me. She had been used to servants and cooks until we came to America; yet she could whip up the best meals in a short time. How did she do it?

"Mn-mn," Mac held out his plate for seconds.

"You must like stuffed peppers," Mama observed.

"Almost as much as I like waffles," Mac answered with a grin, giving me a sly look.

"What did you do as a civilian, Mac?" Papa asked.

"I taught English literature and American history in high

school in Coraopolis, a town not far from Pittsburgh."

"Teaching is a good profession," Papa nodded with approval. "Education is so important. I have always stressed that to my students and to both Vanya and Tamara. We have a saying in Chinese: 'Learning is like rowing upstream; not to advance is to drop back.'"

"And 'Literature does not lead men astray,'" I added, giving Mama an impish glance. She shook her finger at me, her face flushing as she tried to restrain herself from giggling. Both Mama and I have always had a problem with that.

Mac noticed this interplay between Mama and me. "Am I missing something?" he asked innocently.

"No, Mac, it's just this silly girl," Mama wiped her eyes. "Papa loves to quote a proverb whenever he finds a suitable occasion. We tease him about it," she said, looking at Papa with affection, "although we actually enjoy hearing them."

Papa's face was inscrutable. "Let them entertain themselves," he told Mac. "At least they learn."

I laughed at his remark. "I agree, Papa. As you once so aptly told me, 'Learning is a treasure that follows its owner everywhere.' Am I not right?"

"Touché!" Mac was enjoying this repartee.

Papa turned his attention to Mac. His face looked serious, but I noticed the mischievous glint in his eyes. "You know, Mac, we have a Russian poet in our literature by the name of Mikhail Lermontov, whose work was greatly influenced by Lord Byron." Papa glanced at me, then pinched his nose, rubbing it thoughtfully. "Lermontov wrote a poem called 'Demon' that Tamara, as a child, learned by heart. It is a narrative poem telling of the love of a fallen angel for the mortal and beautiful Tamara."

"So, is Mac my demon?" I asked Papa.

"Translate it for Mac sometime, *dochenka*, and see what he thinks of it."

"I'd like that," Mac laid down his fork. "I'm all for anything that concerns the beauteous Tamara."

"In the poem, Mac, the demon tries to seduce Tamara," I explained.

"Then, perhaps," Mac said, throwing Mama a quick glance, and winking at me, "I should try to seduce my Tamara."

Papa looked at his watch. "Oh, we're missing the news, Mama."

"I'll do the dishes," Mac added.

"Oh, no, Mac, I'll do them later," Mama objected. "You and Tamara join us."

Mac pushed her towards the living room. "Please go. We'll do them. I always help out at home."

That pleased Mama. "In that case"—she whipped off her apron and tied it around Mac's waist—"wear this, so you won't soil your nice uniform."

It didn't take us long to clean up Mama's kitchen.

The news was almost over when we rejoined my parents. Mama laid her finger to her lips, jerking her head towards Papa. As Edward R. Murrow said good night, Papa turned the dial to "off."

"Well, Hitlerchik must be worried about the situation in the West with the Fifth Army pressing his troops on one side and Montgomery's Eighth Army pushing up the Adriatic coast."

"Does that mean we're winning?" I asked him.

"Not yet, Tamara, but we're not as vulnerable as the Germans thought we and the British were. It'll take time," Papa said. "Hitler expects the Allies to launch an offensive against the Western Front. It'll be interesting to see what happens."

"What will you be doing in the war, Mac?" Papa asked.

"I'm in the Transportation Corps." Thoughtfully, he contemplated the silent radio. "Here in Boston we're loading and unloading boxcars, loading and unloading ships, and storing ammo in the warehouses off the dock. We're being trained not only in seaport operations but also in invasion maneuvers and offshore port operations. Probably, we'll end up being invasion troops."

The word 'invasion' somehow filled me with fear. "So if the American troops launch an invasion, you'll be a part of it?" *Why,* I thought sadly to myself, *is it that just when I've found him he has to leave me?* I studied his profile as he sat next to me—what a fine, calm, honest Yankee face. How could I ever let him go? His next words, though, made me feel ashamed of having been so selfish.

"Tamara, if I'm to be part of the plan to destroy Hitler and

432

his mad followers, I shall be mighty proud of it. Even if I have to die for my country, just think how many people Hitler has slaughtered in his fanatical quest to make Germany pure, his own egotistical, inhuman ambition that has brought such suffering to so many. I'm not being heroic. I will fight for my country, my family, and"—he squeezed my hand—"most of all, for you."

I squeezed his hand too, noticing Mama's eyes, dark, unfathomable, and mysterious, fixedly staring at him. "Mac, is the place where you're stationed very far from our house?"

"You mean Camp McKay? Yes, I guess in a way it is. It's in Dorchester. I take the subway to Harvard Square, then walk to your place." He too was surprised at her question.

Mama raised her eyebrows. "You don't take the tram from Harvard Square? It's still quite a distance to our house."

Mac laughed. "It's faster when I walk," he answered cheerfully.

"Is that why you're always so on time?" Papa couldn't help asking. He had heard about the waffle fiasco.

Mac, good-naturedly, joined in our laughter. "No, that was a different matter, sir," he explained apologetically. "I had some things to attend to at camp before I could leave. I couldn't help being late that time, sir."

Mama's next words surprised me. I knew that both she and Papa liked Mac, but I had not expected this turn of events.

"Mac," Mama appeared hesitant, "my son, as you know, is overseas. His room is vacant. If you like, you're welcome to stay in his room for the night. Then you don't have to worry about hurrying back to camp. You can enjoy *this* one's company," she said, giving me a mocking glare, "although, frankly, neither Papa nor I can see why she should enchant you so much."

Papa had been reading the paper while we chatted. I heard him chuckle and noticed the paper shake a bit. Often Papa would give the appearance of being totally engrossed in music, a book, or his newspaper, but we always knew that one ear was usually tuning in to the goings-on around him. Papa never missed a thing.

Mac's mouth twitched as he turned towards me. "I don't know why I should be attracted to her either, Mme. Rubleva. She

433

is such a spoiled and ugly brat. As we Americans say, I'm just a glutton for punishment."

Papa got up from his chair to fiddle with the radio. After trying several stations, he gave up in disgust. "Nothing good on. Besides, it's getting late, Mama. I, for one, am going to turn in. How about you, Verotchka?"

"Oh, I'll be along soon," Mama said. "You go on up."

Papa paused on the stairs. "Why don't you play some of our records for Mac, Tamara? How about Beethoven's *Seventh*? You've heard the *Seventh Symphony*, haven't you?" he asked Mac.

"I don't believe so, sir. I've heard his *Fifth, Ninth*, and, of course, the *Pastoral*."

"Then, you're in for a treat, Macushla. Once you've heard the *Seventh*, you'll never be able to forget it." With that, Papa went upstairs.

"Mac, Vanya's room is all ready for you," Mama said, as she hugged us both good night.

"*Spasibo*, Mamotchka." Mac kissed her gently on the cheek.

"So, she's begun to teach you Russian," Mama said, smiling. "Well, I'm off." With that she too walked up the stairs.

"I can't get over how wonderful your parents are," Mac told me.

I had already put on the first movement of the *Seventh Symphony*. Mac patted the cushion next to him, "Come with me, my vixen," he whispered, holding out his hand. I let him pull me towards him, placing my head against his shoulder.

"Isn't it peaceful, just sitting here like this?" I asked. I felt his lips on my hair, moving on down towards my face. Embarrassed, I moved away from him. "Mac, why do you call me a vixen? Just what is a 'vixen'?"

"Exactly what you are," he tilted my chin and looked into my eyes. "You're a foxy lady. That's why I call you a 'vixen.'"

We listened to the second movement, again in silence, sitting close together.

"And what are you going to call me, little Vixen?" His voice was unusually tender.

I stared at him, loving every part of his face, everything about him. "Well-l; let me think. Don't look at me like that.

When you do, I can't think properly. I shall call you . . . I've always told myself that someday I'd find me a Yankee-man. God and Confucius bless you, Mac. You're my Yankee-man."

And I shall marry a Yankee-man. Once again I heard that persistent refrain of mine going through my head. Ever since I had been old enough, I had dreamed of marrying an American man. With a start, I contemplated him. He did not really fit into my dream pattern of a tall, dark, handsome Yankee-man. Instead, he was blond, blue-eyed, and not really handsome, but he did fit my dream even more, I decided. He was a Yankee-man who loved me.

Again he gently cupped my chin in his hands, turning me to him ever so gently so that he could look right into my face.

"You know, Vixen, your eyes are beautiful. Did anybody ever tell you that? They sparkle with such joy. And you've got a funny nose, a cute one. And I'm going to kiss you because it's about time." He sighed. "How I've wanted to kiss you ever since that moment when I first saw you, barefooted, opening your front door to Sam and me, then running back upstairs."

I moved away from him. "And Jeannette? What about her?"

He grinned. "Ah, still jealous, my little Vixen?" He shook his head. "No need to be. There never was." He took me in his arms then, and I felt his mouth on mine, pressing hard. I closed my eyes, feeling his passion, feeling myself wanting him to hold me even tighter, press his lips harder so I could feel the pain. I smelled that special fragrance of him, his own manly body smell mingled with that of his Sportsman's Cologne.

His strong arms enfolded me and never had I felt a man hold me like that, so close to his chest that I could feel both our hearts pounding in unison. There was that same tingling sensation at the pit of my stomach whenever I came near him. I felt myself relaxing, melting, giving way as he gently bent over me, pushing me down on the sofa, his lips still pressing on mine. Then I had to push him away, off me. I was afraid of what would happen if I did not. I recalled Sam's insistent demand, "And of what are you afraid, Tamara?"

"Please, Mac, don't," I whispered.

He had sat up then, his face puzzled, hurt, surprised. "What is it, my darling Vixen? Didn't you like our kissing?"

I had. I did. Never had I been kissed like that. Couldn't he understand that? Even now, though he sat far apart from me, I could still feel the imprint of his lips on mine. I felt strange emotions stirring inside me that I hadn't even known I had. Shaken, uncertain of myself, I stared at him sitting there. He in turn looked back at me, his eyes questioning, honest, and full of love.

Why did it have to be like this? I had always prided myself on my self-control, my ability to mask my emotions. Now I felt helpless and unable to overrule my own feelings. Why did I love this man and keep wishing that he would take me in his arms again and never let me go? Why did I want him to kiss and kiss me and press against me so that all of me could blend together with him? I raised my shaking hands to my swollen lips. It was as if he had placed his personal seal on me. Now I belonged to him. I had to get away from him, at least for a moment.

I jumped up from the sofa and ran upstairs to the bathroom where I stared at myself in the medicine cabinet mirror. *Do I look different?* I asked myself. My eyes glowed brightly in the reflection. There was also something in them that was not the same. Was it joy? Or was it fear? What was it that I had noticed and could not identify? So much had happened, too fast, too soon, and against my will. I liked these new emotions that churned inside me, yet I knew that they were untimely. "No time for love!" It sounded silly when said aloud, so damnably stupid. Was that it?

I ran downstairs again, not wanting to be apart from Mac. He still sat there on the sofa, his head back, his eyes closed, as he listened to the third movement. *How terribly contented he looks,* I thought to myself.

"May I sit beside you, dear sir?" I asked him gently, giving him a curtsey.

He smiled. *Strange,* I decided, as I nestled close to him, *what a short time it has been for us, yet I love him as if I had known him all my life.*

And then he turned to me, his eyes serious. Apparently he had been thinking things through while I had been upstairs. "I want to marry you, Tamara." He spoke slowly. "I just cannot imagine life without you. I love you too much." He stared at his hands. "I never thought that I could love someone so much. I just ache at the very thought of you."

He is so sure of his love, I thought, *so absolutely, unequivo-cally sure.* And I? Could I tell what my feelings were? I was too mixed up. Too many men had proposed to me, and I had not taken them seriously, not knowing or even realizing the turmoil they themselves had gone through. Had I been so unfeeling? It had been so easy before just to say, "Let us be friends, not sweet-hearts, because love is not for me. Love will come later on, not now because right now is not convenient. Ironically, now, how-ever, had become now. I must be in love because no man had ever affected me this way. "Oh, God and Confucius," I prayed, "get me out of this mess."

"And I thought you a drip," I murmured, taking his hand.

"What did you say, darling?"

"I love you too, Mac." My own words had surprised me. That was not what I had meant to say. "I do love you," I repeated, "but I cannot marry you, Mac."

I noticed the hurt, the pain in his face and felt regretful that I was the one causing it. However, my inborn, common sense finally had conquered my heart. My faithful mind had tri-umphed.

"You really don't love me, do you, Vixen?" How different and sorrowful his voice now sounded. My happy, elated Mac of a few seconds ago had disappeared.

And all this while the *Seventh Symphony* played on and on, repeating the fourth movement, since there were no more records left to drop from the spindle. Mac and I had been unaware of this until we heard Papa's voice calling down to us from the top of the stairs. "Mac and Tamara, both Mama and I enjoy listening to the *Seventh Symphony*, but we're getting rather tired of hearing the fourth movement over and over again. Don't you think it's time to stack the records on the other side? At least do it for our sakes, if not your own." Then we heard his deep chuckle as he shuffled back into the bedroom in his slippers.

"Oops," I couldn't help giggling. "As Papa says, 'we have dood it.' Now they know for sure that we haven't been listening to the music."

"I have been listening," Mac said with a smile. Then he

smiled, "Your dad's a great guy," he said. "Can you imagine him and Mama laughing as they kept listening to the fourth movement over and over again? Gee," he became thoughtful, "I wish my folks were good-humored like that. They're so conservative. Now, Vixen, I want to know why you won't marry me."

"Try to understand, Mac." I avoided looking at him. "I'm not ready for marriage yet. I know nothing about being a wife, taking care of a home, cooking, taking care of a husband or having children. Right now, the whole idea of marriage scares me. Please realize that. I have a great deal of living to do before I settle down for good. I need to work, to get this obsessive wanderlust and desire for freedom out of my system. Then I'll be ready to fulfill my promise to the man I love."

"Whew!" He shook his head, amazed. "You really have made a synopsis for your life! You actually feel that's more important? Tamara, don't you realize that love is the greatest thing in life? What else is there without love? You and I love each other. That's a fact. I have no doubts about either of us. I want to marry you. I want you to be my wife before I leave for overseas." He turned my head so that I had to look at him. "Can't you understand, Vixen, how much I need you?"

I was surprised at my own calmness and ability to reason. "Believe me, my darling, it's for the best. I've told you that I love you. I've never said that to any other man, but I've never been in love before either. The only man who has ever kissed me was Jacques. You've met him I know." I smiled, remembering the slight, breezy kiss Jacques had planted so gingerly on my lips. "You have to go fight for your country. I have to graduate. Then I'll go on to New York. After I've had my fill of independence in that big, bad city, and after the war is over, and you come back, we'll decide what to do. If you and I are still of the same mind, then we'll get married. I promise you." Quite a speech for me. Usually I wasn't so verbose with people.

Mac's dejected expression made me feel guilty. I knew that my decisions had disappointed him. "You've planned your whole life in its sequence, haven't you, Tamara?" he said sadly. "Life is not like that, my Vixen. Life cannot be sequenced, can't you understand that? Is all that so much more important than our love?"

438

"Yes, Mac, at this time it is. There's a war on and we have no way of knowing what the outcome will be. Do you know how long you'll be overseas? What should I do when you're gone? Where would I live? No, Mac, I'm sorry. That isn't the way."

My heart went out to him. I wanted to take him in my arms and kiss his hurt away. I held back, afraid I'd capitulate under his touch. I felt frustrated, heartsick that it had to be like this. In my heart, however, I knew that I was right.

"You know, I had hoped to make you my wife before I left," he told me. "Then it wouldn't have been so hard for me to leave, knowing that when I did come back, you would be here waiting for me—someone waiting for me, someone whom I love more than the world itself."

"Perhaps that someday will come," I told him gently, "and then we'll know for sure how deeply we have loved. Right now I cannot even be sure of my own true feelings. These new emotions have struck at me from all sides. I worry about you, the war, and all those other brave American boys who are even now fighting as we sit here, listening to Beethoven's *Seventh*. Then I worry about our future. Do you realize, Mac, that I don't even know your full name? Sam introduced you as Mac, and that's all that I know you by—just Mac. I want to get to know all about you."

That struck him as funny. He stood up in front of me, bowing low, then gave me a smart salute. *"Mon General,* I am John Pershing McNish, ma'am, second lieutenant, United States Army."

I saluted him in return. "Pleased to meet you, Lieutenant McNish."

He remained standing. "Born in 1918 during the First World War," he continued, "which is the reason for the middle name. Mom admired Gen. John J. Pershing, you know." He then leaned over and gave me a hearty kiss.

Ah, he is three years older than I am, I thought to myself. *Good.*

I turned off the record player. It was quite late, time for us both to go to bed. For a long moment he held me close to him, caressing my hair, kissing my eyes, then sealing my lips with his own.

"It's been good to sit just like this, hasn't it?" he whispered.

"We don't need to talk, just our two hearts beating as one. I wish it could go on like this forever and ever."

"You know it can't, Mac. There's a war going on, and it looks as if it'll be a long one."

"I know it, dear Vixen." He laid his head on my shoulder. "I'll be going on maneuvers shortly. That means I won't be seeing you for two weeks."

I was curious. "Maneuvers? What do you do when you're on them?"

"It's like playing war—getting rehearsed for the real thing," he explained.

A cold chill went through me. "Can you get hurt on maneuvers?"

He smiled. "You can get hurt anywhere, Vixen. Even in your own home, on the street. Don't worry, honey, I'll take care of myself for you. I want you only to promise to write to me, will you?"

"I promise," I whispered. Then it actually hit me. For two solid weeks I wouldn't be seeing him.

"Why such a long face, Vixen?"

"I didn't expect not to see you for two weeks," I whispered.

"Well," he said, as he patted my wrist, "that'll happen after Christmas. Oh, by the way, I want you to help me choose a tie for your Dad. I want to find him a red one on account of the Red Army. You know how he puffs up with pride at their exploits."

"I will. We can go to the Co-op on Harvard Square. They usually have a good selection."

"Oh, and another thing. I want to ask your folks and you, of course, to eat Christmas dinner with us at the base. Both Mama and Papa have been so kind to me. I'd sort of like to do something for them. Think they'll come?"

"Oh, Mama will, for sure. You know her." I laughed when Mac nodded his head. "About Papa, I have my doubts. He goes only to faculty functions, often unwillingly, or to visit old friends with whom he can converse with ease. Papa is funny about unfamiliar places. I don't think he will."

"I've noticed that he's shy with most people," Mac said.

"Have you noticed him stutter at times?"

"No," Mac paused. "Come to think of it, I remember that he

did one time when he was talking about the war. I thought then that he was trying to remember some fact or something."

"Yes, he gives that impression at times. I think he does that purposefully, to cover up the stutter. It's when he gets excited or is among people whom he's not acquainted with." I laid my head against Mac's chest, feeling secure and comfortable with his arms around me. "I think it dates from the time the Japanese tortured him in China. They beat him with bamboo rods on the back of his head. He never stuttered before his arrest."

"You've all gone through quite a bit, haven't you?" he said quietly. "No wonder you're so strong. I guess your experiences would have either strengthened or broken you. Some day, Tamara," his lips moved against my hair, "I want to hear your whole story. Will you promise me that?"

How dear he was. "Yes, some day I will," I promised him. "You know, Papa had to promise the Japanese that he would never speak of the arrest publicly. He's kept his word. I've kept it too, until I met you." I looked up into his face and tried, in vain, to wink. "But then, *I* hadn't promised them not to speak of it."

27

The Pupil of the Eye

I had been right, of course. Papa did not go with us to Camp McKay. As usual, he begged off. "Mac, I have some research work to do at home. With all the bustling around here lately, getting ready for Christmas and so forth, I have not been able to concentrate. At home alone will give me the opportunity to pursue my studies in peace and quiet." Mac, forewarned, understood.

Mama and I had been looking forward to seeing Camp McKay and having Christmas dinner with Mac where he was stationed. Mac, I remember, had been so proud of us, introducing us to his fellow officers, his company commander, and his battalion commander. After eating in the mess hall, we went to Mac's quarters, where we sat on his bed and listened to Christmas music.

"How would you like to tour the camp?" he asked us.

"Before I answer, Mac, I want to know if we have to walk." I had on high heels and did not want to tour the camp in them.

Mac grinned. "Ever ride in a jeep?"

Mama shook her head. "Not for me," she replied. "I'm too full of that wonderful dinner. You and Tamara go. I'll just rest on your bed, Mac, and listen to the music. May I?"

"Of course, Mama." Mac took my arm. "Come on, Vixen, you'll enjoy it, I guarantee. And you'll never forget it."

I did enjoy the jeep ride but only because Mac's arm held me tight, and I enjoyed watching his glee as he drove us over the rough ground. Privately, I decided that this would be the first and last ride that I'd ever take in a jeep. When we finally came back to Mac's quarters and he had lifted me out of the jeep, I felt as if my legs would collapse under me.

"See," he declared. "I told you you'd enjoy it, darling."

"Yes, Mac," I answered, trying to keep my teeth from clicking.

"There's an officers' party tonight. We'll stop there for a while, then go back home. How's that, Mama?" Mac suggested.

"If it's not too late. I don't want Papa to be all alone on Christmas night."

My first Christmas with Mac had been a joyful one. When we came home, we found that Papa had prepared his own special kind of eggnog. Catching sight of the tray with glasses and pitcher, Mama had raised her eyebrows.

"Papa, in my kitchen?" She shook her head in disbelief.

Papa had deliberately ignored her, pouring out the creamy stuff into our glasses. "We have to drink to our Demon and his Tamara," he announced, passing the tray around. He lifted up his glass and in his resonant voice toasted Mac and me. *"Za vashe zdorovye!"*

"Na zdorovye!" we echoed, clinking our glasses together.

"Pei do dna," Papa ordered Mac.

"What does that mean?" Puzzled, Mac lowered his glass.

" 'Bottoms up,' that's what it means," I explained, smiling.

"Ah, with pleasure. That certainly was good stuff, Papa. Whatever is in it?" Mac drained the contents of his glass.

"It's my special secret," Papa pinched the tip of his nose, pleased at Mac's compliment. "Let me tell you that there's plenty of brandy in it."

"And I'm sure all the whipped cream too that I have been saving to make *plombir*," Mama added. "But, Serioja, it was good."

"Let's hope that this war soon ends so that Tamara and I can get married and start our new life together." Mac had refilled our glasses.

"Bravo!" Papa shouted. "We wish you much happiness for the future. Mama and I already think of you as a son."

"Thank you, sir. You've been like real parents to me." I was surprised to see tears in Mac's eyes.

443

"And now, Papa, here's something that Mac and I picked out especially for you." I handed him the long, thin package wrapped in brightly colored Christmas paper.

He took it, smiling at the two of us. "Hmm, I don't expect presents at my age. I thought Christmas was for children and Tamara only." His eyes twinkled as he carefully folded the wrinkled paper, handing it to Mama. "Use this for next year," he said, giving me a sly look. "Now," he opened the box and pulled out the red tie. "Ach, how nice of you."

"It's to be worn in honor of the Red Army," Mac explained. "That army has done such a superb job of defending Russian soil, and I know how proud you are of it."

"I shall wear this tie proudly," Papa showed it to Mama. "Thank you, Macushla."

"Macushla?" I looked at Papa. That was the second time I had heard him refer to Mac this way.

"What better name for Mac than that?" Papa glanced mischievously at Mac, then rubbed his nose thoughtfully. "You must remember our old records in China, Tamara. You listened to them so often, to John MacCormack singing Irish love songs. There was that special one about Macushla that you played all the time. Remember? You know what Macushla means?"

Mac's face had reddened, and his eyes, behind the glasses, looked amused.

"No," I answered, "what does it mean?"

"What you, not I, should be calling Mac. It means 'my darling' in Gaelic."

"I see," I stood on my tiptoes and gave Mac a kiss. "I love you, Macushla."

It had been a wonderful holiday, but it ended all too soon for me. The time had come for Mac to go on maneuvers. It turned out, though, that it was not as bad as I had anticipated. He telephoned me once in a while, and we wrote letters. That way we learned more about each other without being overwhelmed and silenced by our physical closeness.

I read over the letter that I had just written to him as I had sat at the desk in Papa's study:

444

Dearest Macushla,

The Hour of Charm sounded beautiful tonight. They played excerpts from operas as well as "Oh, Promise Me." As I told you over the phone, I love that song. I don't think you understood me. You see, I've been thinking that if ever Papa does lead me down the aisle to you, well, that will be the time when I'd ask someone to sing that song for us.

It's very quiet and peaceful here in my dear papa's study. On his desk is *Children of the Rising Sun,* by Willard Price. John Donne is here too. He is lying in an obscure corner at the left end of this table, quite forlorn, there, all by himself. But hark! Who else is there beside him? I hadn't noticed *Chaucer*, dear poet of yet another age. Both he and Donne do not think much of you, you know. Why, you ask? Because all these brilliant poets and weavers of tales are vying for my sole attention.

There's a whole line of them waiting for my eyes to seek them out, to peruse their very thoughts, mind you. Fascinating personages like Richard Crashaw and Andrew Marvell. Poor Andrew, he was quite "a ladies' man." All of them and more are waiting for my attention so that they can then bare to me the very secrets of their souls!

As you can see, I'm not in much of a writing mood right now. Sorry, but I'm still full of impressions, too many of them coming at me in such a short time. I guess I'm just too sentimental. I like mulling over pleasant incidents, thinking about them, wondering about them, even though they have already passed.

All I can tell you right now is that I'm supremely happy, happier, I think, than I've ever been in my life. Yet, there's still the future to worry about. And yes, I do love you with all my heart.

This penpoint of mine has been wavering over this white sheet of notepaper for over five minutes, unwilling to stop writing, yet not knowing what else to say. The clock and my own sleepy eyes whisper "bedtime" to me.

And so, my darling, good night. If I had been born to dream, then my dream at this time would have you as the main attraction. But, curses, Morpheus is a powerful friend, and his influence on me is extreme.

With love,
Tamara, your Vixen

How many more letters would I be writing to him? This damned war . . . yet, had it not been for the war, Mac and I would never have met. Strange, how things happened in real life, I thought. Had Dr. Ferguson not intercepted that letter from Harvard University that day in Peking who knows where our family would have been at this time?

"Papa," I gave him the envelope, "on your way to the office, please put this in the mailbox in Harvard Square. Mail is picked up there earlier than from the one here at the corner."

Papa took the envelope and looked at the address. "You're writing letters to him already? I thought you just talked to him on the telephone."

"Oh, Papa," I watched him place the envelope in his coat pocket. "You won't forget, will you?"

"Of course not, *dochenka*. Have I ever forgotten anything you entrusted me to do?"

"No, but this is important."

He was sympathetic. "Of course, dear, you miss him already."

"I do, Papa. I don't know how I can wait for these two weeks to pass. It's such a long time."

He opened the front door and picked up his briefcase. "It is long," he kissed me on the forehead. " 'To one who waits, a moment seems a year.' But we all have to wait at one time or another. Well, it's time I took off. Tell Mamotchka that I've left."

I watched him walk down Mt. Vernon Street, a sturdy little figure, bundled up in his warm cashmere coat with the scarf almost up to his nose and his gray hat jauntily perched on his head. It must be cold outside today. My breath on the window glass had steamed it up. No matter though how cold it was, Papa always walked to Harvard, disdaining the comforts of the tram cars.

"What are you looking at, Tamara?" I hadn't heard Mama enter the dining room.

"Oh, Papa just left for Harvard," I told her. "Mama, what are you doing today?" Somehow I felt useless, lost, not knowing what to do with myself.

"Oh, we have a meeting of the war relief committee." She

gave me a calculating look. "All of which reminds me: I may not be home for lunch. So if you would warm up some soup for Papa, and heat the rest of the pilaf, you and he can have a nice lunch."

"I'll be happy to do that."

Maybe I'd invite Phyllis over. No, she had that new guy on her mind. I forget his name, Steve somebody. Gosh, I didn't even get that straight. And Sam? He was probably still in New York. He had practically forsaken us since Mac and I had fallen in love. Vicky? No, she'd be involved with family. Loretta, too.

"Did you hear me, Tamara?" Mama's voice was a trifle sharp.

"I said I'd be glad to heat the food, Mama," I said, surprised at her tone.

"I asked you if you needed anything from the store. I'll be stopping on my way home."

"No, I'm sorry, Mama. I didn't hear you." My excuse sounded lame.

She had smiled, then slipped on her gloves. "Well, I'd better go now. I'm off."

I closed the door behind her and turned to find the house deathly quiet. I walked into the living room and picked up the *Boston Globe*. As usual, there were photographs of the war. One showed an American soldier of the Fifth Army cleaning out a German mine field. A dead soldier, also American, lay a few feet away. The Nazis had laid mines and booby traps everywhere. I scanned the headlines. Monty's Eighth Army had now captured Ortona. The American Fifth Army had reached the heights before Cassino. Other war pictures: a wounded Australian soldier carried down a steep slope by native stretcher-bearers. Shaggy Ridge, what a name. Northern New Guinea. I must find it on the map sometime. So many of these places were unfamiliar. Ah, here was a photograph of Gen. Douglas MacArthur striding down a beach in Dutch New Guinea, accompanied by some soldiers and the army sector commander. *What a magnificent-looking man he is,* I thought, *except that he's always wearing those dark glasses.* I refolded the paper, not wanting to see anymore. Papa had been right. "To one who waits, a moment seems a year." Perhaps I should have gone with Mama to the Russian War Relief headquarters—anything would be better than this

447

feeling of loneliness, boredom, anxiety, or whatever. My depressed state of mind shamed me; yet I wasn't able to snap out of it. The ringing of the phone in the foyer shocked me out of my doldrums.

"Hello."

"I had hoped to catch you at home, Vixen. I've been busy on these maneuvers but had a spare moment to call you. I've just got to share a letter with you, one that I think is very beautifully written. First, I want to tell you that I love you more today than I did yesterday. Do you believe me?"

How quickly a mood can change. At the sound of his voice my depression vanished. "Of course, I believe you, Mac. And I love you so much."

I heard the chuckle. "Now that we're done with the formalities, let me tell you about Aunt Carrie. Remember, I told you about my wonderful aunt, really my father's aunt, but everyone in Freeport calls her Aunt Carrie because everyone loves and respects her? Don't ask me how old she is. In her seventies, I suppose. Anyway, I had written her about you and just got this fine letter from her in reply. I want you to hear it and see if you don't agree."

"I'd love to hear it," I told him.

"Okay. She starts out:

" 'Johnny dear,

" 'Into the quiet of my room, where I've been nursing this grippe, came a thriller, one of those letters you don't get every day. My rebound, after reading, was to say 'God loves him' and shed a wee tear. I'm highly honored that you have written me as you have. And yet, am I capable of telling you the answers? It seems but a short time ago that your own father wrote me a similar letter. And before that, I myself had a somewhat similar experience. History does repeat itself, truly. And isn't life itself strange, as human destiny weaves its web?

" 'In 1823, in a wee town in Scotland, was born a precious baby boy. In 1830, in a little home just outside Tarentum, a wee, brown-eyed girl came. In 1851 these two met in a neighborly way, and here again came the man's fall: hook, line, and sinker.

" 'Years have passed, and today I read where the great grandson of their union has found a dear little flower that blossomed in far-off China and received the fatal stroke. Do we believe in a guiding Providence?

" 'You ask, what do I think? Well, who am I, a poor old maid, to answer that, but I'll do the best I can.

" 'Knowing you, J.P., as I know you, I am sure that you will not be satisfied with superficial qualities. This is not the first girl you have known. There is something here you have not met before. Your heart tells you the answers, and if this is *the one*, there will be a mutual answer that you will both understand. Later plans will adjust themselves. If this union becomes a reality, no one will be more pleased than this aunty. If nothing more than friendship comes of it, it will still be a precious memory. I can tell you this. There's something very sweet in having beautiful hangings on memory's walls, when you sit alone at twilight.

" 'Many thanks for the splendid picture of my soldier boy. I'm glad you were having such a nice Christmas. Oh, that it may really be peace on earth long before another Yuletide.

" 'Have you gotten your First Lt. papers yet? They are too slow to please me. Wishing you the very best of a New Year.

" 'A hug and a kiss.'

"And she signed it, 'Your Aunty'."

There was a big lump in my throat. "Oh, Mac, what a beautiful, beautiful letter. Aunt Carrie must be some person."

"She is. I can't wait till you meet her. Everybody loves her. Even my mom, although I've heard her criticize Aunt Carrie often."

"Mac," I hesitated, wondering whether I should ask, but then I did. "You've never told me much about your parents. What are they like?" Strange that he hadn't mentioned them to me. Once he had been on the point of saying something about them and had stopped. There was silence on the other end. "Mac, are you still on the phone?"

"Yes, Vixen," he replied, his tone more subdued. "I've been trying to figure out how to tell you about my parents. It's not easy to explain. You see, they're so different from yours. Mama and Papa are so warm, hospitable, broadminded. Mine are, hmm, well, in the first place, they're Republicans and always have been."

"So? What's wrong with that?" It didn't matter to me what they were. They were *his* parents.

449

He sounded uneasy. "I was afraid you wouldn't understand. Remember when you first met me and thought me a drip and a snob? I have to admit it; I was a snob."

"Oh, no," I protested, "you were just shy, weren't you?" I knew him well enough by now to know that he was shaking his head.

"No, darling, I was a snob, but you and your family changed my attitudes about people drastically."

"What's so different about us?"

"You and your parents like most people; mine don't. You see, they haven't traveled widely as you people have. They aren't intellectual the way your family and friends are. They're just plain, God-fearing American farm folks, who've lived in a small town all their lives. Anyone who's not like them is not worth knowing—especially people of different nationalities—foreigners, in other words, people of different religions, races, and cultures." His voice became more gentle. "Tamara, I wrote them about you telling them that I had asked you to marry me."

"And what did they say?"

Again the painful silence. "Mom wrote me a scathing letter which broke my heart. I tore it up. You see, they don't want me marrying a 'Russky.'"

"A 'Russky'?"

"Yes, that's a Russian according to them. An Italian is a Dago, a Pole is a Polack, a Catholic is a Mickey, and so on." He sounded bitter.

This time it was my turn to be quiet. In America I couldn't believe there were people who disliked others because of their nationalities. "But, Mac, it doesn't matter who a person is. It matters what a person is. Isn't that more important? I can't help it if I was born in China, or that my parents are Russian. I'm proud of that. And I don't love you because you're a Scottish-American-Pennsylvania-Dutchman. I love you because you're you."

He laughed at that. "Funny that we should come around to talking like this, but I guess prejudice and bigotry have always existed. Besides Chaucer, I've studied Emerson's works. And just by coincidence, he lived in this Boston area. I'm sure your father has read his works."

450

"If you mean Ralph Waldo Emerson, not only Father but also your Vixen. I've read some of his essays and also part of his journal."

"Good for you," he exclaimed. "You amaze me, Tamara. Sometimes you appear so innocent and naive, and then at times, you are so knowledgeable. Are you a chameleon, perchance?"

I laughed. My depression had completely disappeared. "What were you going to tell me about Emerson?"

"Ah, yes," he paused. "Emerson has been widely quoted, you know. His definition of a bigot has stayed with me because it is so vivid and picturesque. 'The mind of the bigot is like the pupil of the eye, the more light you pour upon it, the more it will contract.' Pardon the pun, but can't you just see that in your mind's eye?"

"Papa will love that," I told him. "Will you quote it for him next time you see us? He'll write it down in his little notebook, I'm sure, if he doesn't have it already."

"That I'll be sure to do, Tamara. You know that I think you're such a sweet person. You don't have a mean bone in your body. I wish my folks and other relatives would see people the way you do. My Aunt Bertha on Mom's side also wrote me a blistering letter on my terrible choice. God! Vixen, I'm glad I found you. You've made me a better human being already."

His revelations had shaken me. I had not realized that someone as intelligent and fine as Mac had felt that way at one time, nor that his parents had already prejudged me because I had a Russian background and had been born, of all places, in China! Weren't we fighting a war against a man who thought in much the same vein, that his pure-bred Aryans were superior to any other race? How terribly sad that these prejudices existed in this freedom-loving country!

"Did you get my letter, Mac?" I decided to change the subject. "I wrote you on the twenty-ninth."

"You did! God bless you, honey." He sounded much happier. "No, I haven't gotten it yet, but I'll certainly hound the mail clerk. Sweetheart, you know that when I read your words, your sparkling eyes, your lips, and that impish smile keep crowding in between the lines."

"Flatterer."

"No, I mean every word I tell you, Vixen. Would you believe that when I crawl into bed at night I take your picture with me and lightly press a good-night kiss on those lips of yours?"

"You do?" I smiled. "And do I return your kiss?"

"Would that you did, my dearest. I hate to cut us off now, but duty calls. Good-bye, my Vixen."

His telephone call left me with much to think about. "The mind of a bigot is like the pupil of the eye." How true that was. I decided it really didn't matter. The main thing—he loved me, and I loved him. Nothing in the world could ever change that fact.

28

The Best-Laid Schemes

"Phyl, do you know what that considerate Sam Klauber wanted me to do?"

Phyl tucked her long legs under her skirt, making herself more comfortable on my studio couch. Lazily she stretched her hand towards her purse and drew out her cigarettes, offering the pack to me.

I shook my head. "Not now, thanks."

"What did Sammy want you to do?" she asked.

"Well, he knew that Mac would be on duty on New Year's so he said that I was welcome to stay at the Army dispensary and bring along some friends to boot. How about that?"

"Where would Sammy stay?" Phyl asked, looking at me through a haze of smoke.

"In New York," I answered. "I don't know why he goes to New York so often. It's a mystery to me. Anyway, he told me that I'd find nuts, candies, skis, skates, and tennis rackets there, everything except Benzedrine and him."

"Gee, that sounds like fun. You going?"

"Of course not. Stay there overnight? What would my parents say? Anyway, they would never let me."

"You might be surprised," Phyl answered. "Your folks seem pretty broad-minded to me."

She was right. In certain situations they were, but even if they had permitted me, my own self-esteem wouldn't have. It was no use rehashing the old morals attitude with Phyl. We'd never agree on that.

"Have you heard from Mac?" Phyl leaned her head against the wall. "He has been on maneuvers, hasn't he?"

"Still a few more days to go," I told her.

"Miss him?" She sounded like Sam, probing.

"Not so much as I thought I would. How about your Steve? Are you still seeing him?"

"No," she said, as she put out her cigarette, "he's been shipped overseas, damn it. But we sure had a great time while he was here." Her eyes lit up. "I wish you could have met him, Tamara. No," she corrected herself, "I don't. You'd have charmed him away from me."

"Oh, Phyl, I would never do that."

"Not on purpose. You just, oh, well, the heck with it. Next week we'll be through with exams."

"Yep; I'll be having my last exam next week. You know, I didn't touch a book all vacation. That was unusual for me."

"But, ah, you've been in love," Phyl grinned. "Pretty nice being in love, isn't it? Although," she said giving me a cursory look, "you don't seem to be pining away for Mac."

"I'm not, Phyl. I thought I'd be unable to live without him. At first I did feel blue, but I'm over it now. I guess I take things as they come. What will be will be. Oh, by the way, Mac wrote me a beautiful letter on the third. It's 1944 already. Can you believe it? Anyway, I'm going to read it to you."

"Okay; I'd like to see if he writes as well as he talks."

"He's more romantic when he writes. Listen to this, Phyl. He's writing about our future." Curled up on the studio couch, I began to read:

" 'Dearest Tamara,

" 'A Scotty is lying at my feet as I sit comfortably in my armchair reading *PM* and the *New York Times*. He yawns and stretches comfortably when Mac Junior tugs at my ear and giggles at Scotty's whiskers.

" 'Across the room sits the queen of my life. She looks up from her painting and smiles at me and Mac, Junior, and Scotty. The years have made the queen beautifully radiant. Her eyes sparkle just as they always have. Her hair is long and still shining. Her lips are just as delicate and fine as they were when she kissed her first love back in December, 1943, during the Christmas season.

Tonight she has put on Bourjois perfume to remind her Mac of those happy evenings they spent together before marriage. As she sits there and looks at the living room, tastefully furnished with oriental furniture, she remembers her dreams during the war years. Tears come to her eyes as she imagines her unhappiness had Mac not returned from the war.

" 'This is an anniversary for them. Several years ago that night they had slept together as man and wife. Tamara looked over at Mac and Mac looked over at her. Without one word they both knew what the other was thinking. Each year now they had relived their first glorious experience, and each year the experience had become more exhilarating, intensifying, and unifying. They lived, breathed, felt, and moved as one together throughout all their everyday living, but here was the culmination of that oneness. And Mac could smell the Bourjois, observed carefully the quickening rise and fall of his queen's breasts. He squirmed uncomfortably when he realized Tamara had on that grayish purple or purplish gray dress with the lace around the neck. His pulse quickened. He had to move in the chair to make himself more comfortable. Slowly he took the pipe from his mouth, knocked out the ashes, took a deep breath, and coyly whispered, "I'll put little Mac, Junior, to bed right now."

" 'Tamara smiled, quietly reached over, grasped Mac's arm firmly, and breathed deeply as she whispered, "I'll be in the bedroom."

" 'Upstairs the three of them went; Scotty went down into the cellar, and the McNishes soon were in bed for the night.

"Tonight Mac goes to bed alone, there is no little Mac, and Tamara is still Miss Rubleva. War is still here. We live in the present, and the future holds great promise for both of us.

" 'Lovingly, Your Scotty, Mac.' "

When I had finished, Phyl stared at me in awe. "Tamara," she said in a tremulous voice, "that is quite a letter. God, what wouldn't I give to have a man write to me like that. Believe me, gal, you'd better hold on to him. He's some guy."

"Not only can he write, but look at his handwriting. Have you ever seen such attractive penmanship? I always thought that Papa's handwriting was outstanding, but Mac's is perfect."

"It sure is beautiful," she agreed. "Are you going to marry him before he's shipped out?"

"No, Phyl, I've already told you that."

"But why not, Tamara? You love him, don't you?" She lit another cigarette, a Marlboro this time, I noticed.

"Since when did you change brands?" I asked her, hoping to get her off this subject.

"Oh, Steve got me on to them. They're milder than Luckies, I think. Well, what about it? Why won't you marry him now? Think how nice it would be to be his wife, not having to worry about getting a job or anything."

"That's not what I want, Phyl. You know how I've planned to live in New York on my own. I don't want to get married yet, especially to someone who'll be leaving soon. Besides, no matter how nice Mac is, I've only been serious with him for about a month. The feelings I have for him are special, Phyl, but I'm afraid."

"Of what?"

"I don't know, Phyl." She was the only one who might understand. "Sometimes I wonder if I really am in love with Mac. You know, I've always been such a romantic. I wonder if this could be merely infatuation. It's as if I don't know my own feelings anymore."

"I see." She remained silent for a moment, puffing her Marlboro, squinting her eyes, studying me. "Yep, this falling in love business is new to you. Finally, the ice statue has begun to melt, then along comes a cold spell and freezes it back into ice. How ironic!" She laughed humorlessly. "What will you tell Mac?"

"We've already discussed it," I explained. "He felt bad about it, but I think he understood. I hope so. The problem is, Phyl, why should I have doubts about my love for him? At first, it was all so heavenly, knowing that we loved each other. Being away from him these two weeks, however, has given me time to think."

"What do your folks say?" Phyl asked.

"They're glad that I'm not marrying Mac before he leaves, I guess." I smiled at the thought. "I don't discuss it much with them. I can't."

"Where's Vanya now?" Phyl blew some smoke toward me. "Does he write often?"

I made a face. "Somewhere in Italy. His V-mails are always

censored, but we're sure that's where he is. He's got an Italian girlfriend and is also teaching his commanding officer Russian. He's mad at me because I don't write him often enough. Mama writes him every day."

I turned on the radio. "Don't Sit under the Apple Tree" was just ending. Phyllis started to hum it.

"What are you wearing to the senior prom?" I asked her.

"Mom and I went to Filene's Basement one day and you wouldn't believe what we bought. We found the most beautiful blue lace gown. It just fit perfectly, and the best thing was that it wasn't at all expensive. It had been marked down and down. Now I'm all set. How about you? Mama making your dress?"

"Yes. She has this lace from France—champagne colored. She's had it since China days. She'll soon be finished with it. It's really lovely—simple, with a sweetheart neckline."

"And Mac has the tickets?"

"Yes, I sent them to him, and he told me over the phone that he's received them. Ray Tyson is delighted that Mac invited him to be your date. Mac said he's a fine person."

"Well, I should hope so," Phyl said. "God Almighty, I can't believe that we'll be graduating, you in just a few weeks. Aren't you excited? Have you heard from the places where you applied in New York City?"

"You mean the Office of Strategic Services and the Office of War Information? No, not yet. I'll probably hear from them after I graduate. We'll see."

"Well," Phyl sighed, getting up slowly. "I'd better go now." She picked up her purse. "I'll say good-bye to Mama first. Is she in the kitchen?"

"Yes, won't you stay for supper?"

"Not this time, Tamara. Your folks have been so nice to me, but I don't want to wear out my welcome. I just stopped by to check up on you. Let me know how things progress."

I walked downstairs with her. Mama heard us and came out into the foyer. "Phyllis, you're leaving so soon? You've been like a stranger lately." She gave her a hug.

"Well, with Mac around, I knew Tamara didn't need my presence." She slung her purse strap over her shoulder. "With exams next week, you'll likely be seeing me more often. And I'll be going to the senior prom with Tamara. Gee, that's in less than two weeks."

"Ah, yes," Mama clapped her hands together. "The big event. Did Tamara describe her dress to you?"

Phyllis laughed, "She sure did. I can't wait to see it, but she wouldn't allow me to until it's finished."

"Of course not," Mama agreed. "It looks almost like a wedding dress. I can't wait until Mac sees her in it."

Mama and I watched from the front porch as she walked down Mt. Vernon Street. It had started to snow again. "Come on, Tamara," Mama shivered and wrapped her woolen shawl more tightly around herself. "Let's go back in out of the cold."

Later that evening Mac phoned. "Have you missed me, Vixen?" He sounded lonely. "I tried out an experiment yesterday. That's why I didn't call you. I tried to see how I'd feel if I were to go for one whole day without hearing your voice. What a miserable day I had!"

"But you didn't see me for two weeks during your maneuvers," I teased. "You weren't miserable then."

"I spent every minute of the day working. No time for love then. But yesterday? I kept thinking of your smile; your hair; your happiness when we're together. I checked off all those beautiful virtues and aggravating faults of yours that make me love you, my Vixen."

"Oh, Mac, there you go again, romanticizing."

"I really called to see if you'd have lunch with me."

"I'd love to. Tomorrow, about noon, at St. Clair's?"

"Okay by me. Now that we've agreed on lunch, Vixen, I want you to know that I kept wondering what you were doing yesterday; whether you were thinking of me; whether you were combing that silken hair of yours. Were your lips longing for a kiss of mine? Cripes, Vixen, I can't wait till we two are one in marriage."

"Please, Mac, there's lots of time for marriage. Don't be impatient, Macushla. This war won't last forever." I wished that he didn't dwell on me so much. When he leaves, it will be so much harder to bear. "What have you been doing lately?"

"Oh, last night Ray Tyson and I saw *The Cherry Orchard*.

Throughout the play I thought of you. The actress's pronunciation of 'mamotchka' amused me. How you'd have liked it, had you sat there beside me, happy to be there with me!"

"I saw it once when it was playing at the Brattle Theater. It would have been more fun to have watched it with you, though."

"Well, someday perhaps. Anyway, then Tyson and I went to Ruby Foo's. I thought of you again. Had you been with us, you'd have ordered for us, eaten with chopsticks, and attracted everyone's attention with your beauty. How proudly I'd have strutted out of the restaurant with you. I'd have been gloriously happy."

"Mac, please get off the subject of me. I'm not beautiful. You just say that because you're in love with me. That's all there is to it. Are you trying to make me vain?"

"I tell it like it is, Vixen. As one of my fellow-Scotsmen wrote in the eighteenth century: 'O wad some Pow'r the giftie gie us to see oursels as others see us.'"

"I've heard that before; it's from one of Robert Burns's poems, isn't it? I liked the way you quoted it, like a true Scotsman."

"Well, thank ye, mae darlin'."

"Phyl was here earlier, Mac. She wanted to know if you had received the Prom tickets."

"They're safe, Tamara. Don't worry. I'm really looking forward to that event. So's Ray. How've you been doing at Radcliffe?"

"So far so good, Yankee-man. Two more exams to go and I'll be through. The ones I've already taken weren't so difficult."

"I'm proud of you, Vixen. Well, I'd better say good night. Don't forget our date for lunch tomorrow at St. Clair's."

"Sweet dreams, my laddie." I blew him a kiss and hung up.

"Where do you think they'll be sending you, Mac?"

"It'll be somewhere in Europe, of that I'm sure. I'm lucky in that respect. I'd hate to be fighting the Japanese in the Pacific. Their snipers make it so difficult for our Marines, along with the heat, the tropical downpours, and the mud. But Hill 660 on Cape Gloucester has been taken by our forces."

"That's on New Britain Island, isn't it?"

Mac nodded. "Our soldiers not only have to battle the Japs

but also the unhealthy climate conditions." He looked around St. Clair's, then rested his eyes on me. "I see you're wearing my Lieutenant's bar. That makes me feel proud, Vixen."

I looked down at the pin. "And I'm proud of you. If we weren't in a public restaurant, I'd give you a salute, and then a kiss. Anyway, congratulations, First Lieutenant McNish. I'm glad you invited me out for lunch. We can now celebrate your promotion as well as the end of my exams. Next comes the prom. You haven't forgotten it, have you?"

"Of course not. Ray and I were just talking about it. He was asking me what Phyl is like."

"And?"

"I said that she's a great gal, funloving, sexy, and has a great sense of humor. Was that a good enough build-up?"

"Yes, and what about Ray? I know Phyl is anxious to know."

"He's a quiet, shy fellow; he's well-liked and a very competent officer. I believe he's from North Dakota. He's no Clark Gable, but he's fun. She'll enjoy him."

After lunch, we strolled up Brattle Street. "There's Longfellow's home," I pointed out. "That's where our friend, Prof. Harry Dana, lives. He's Longfellow's grand-nephew and a delightful person, very knowledgeable in Russian literature. He and Papa are great friends."

"How did you folks meet him?"

I laughed. "He needed someone to help him translate the works of Constantine Simonov, one of Russia's modern playwrights. He called Radcliffe for a translator, and they recommended me. Voilà!"

"You're really something," he looked at me with admiration. "Vixen, I'm constantly learning something new about you. What else have you got hidden in that curvaceous persona of yours?"

I couldn't help smiling. "You'll find out soon enough, Yankeeman. Say," I stopped him, right there by Felix's newsstand. "Let's go home now and listen to some recordings. I want to play the *Roumanian Rhapsody* again. It was sweet of you to give me that."

His eyes were tender. "Vixen, I've got to leave you at Harvard Square and take the subway back to camp. There are things I have to do at McKay."

I felt disappointed. "I had hoped you'd stay over and visit with us."

"No such luck, darling. The army's a tough commander. Even a lovely morsel of femininity like you cannot override its orders."

"Okay, then," I stood on my tiptoes and kissed him, right there in Harvard Square. "Until tomorrow. Don't forget that the prom's at seven-thirty."

He waved his gloved hand and turned towards the subway stairs. "Ray and I won't," he shouted. "We'll be there—with bells on."

With that, he hurried down the subway stairs.

29

Gang Aft A-Gley![*]

"Papotchka," Mama said, as she stuck her head out their bedroom door, "come here for a moment and see what you think of our *dochenka*." She turned back to me and glanced critically at the hem of my gown. "Turn around so I can see if it's even. Slowly, Tamara, slowly." She straightened up, satisfied.

"It's beautiful, Mama." I looked at my image in her long mirror. Impulsively, I turned to her, hugging her tightly around the waist. "Thank you, Mamotchka."

She pushed me away from her, smiling at my delight. "I've got pins stuck on my blouse. You'll get stuck, you silly girl."

Papa came in. "Did you call me, Verotchka?" Then he saw me by the mirror. "Ah-h." He stared in silence, then nodded his head. "You've got golden hands, Mama." He came closer to examine the dress. I pirouetted in front of him watching his expression. "Hmm. . . ." He looked up at me. "The Radcliffe prom is tonight? The one you've been talking about for so long?" He was teasing me, I knew.

"Yes, Papa. Phyllis will be here shortly, then Mac and his friend."

"I'll go downstairs," Mama said. "You wait here. We'll surprise Phyllis."

"I can't wait till I hear Macushla's reaction," Papa told me when Mama had gone.

"He'll like it, I'm sure." I walked out towards the stairs,

[*] Often go awry

thinking how perfectly wonderful everything was; exams were over, graduation was around the corner, and most of all, I had Mac. What a most unusual, rare feeling it was to have someone love me the way he did. I couldn't help smiling at the thought. What else could a woman want out of life? Annitchka had been right.

I heard Phyl and Mama coming upstairs and came out to greet them. Phyl looked radiant.

"Oh, Phyl, what a lovely dress," I exclaimed. "That blue shade is so becoming to you. Doesn't Phyllis look like Lana Turner, the movie star?"

Mama laughed, cocking her head first to the right, then to the left as she examined the workmanship on Phyl's gown. "She's beautiful, and the dress is lovely; it's very well-made. I like the black gloves with it. All you need now, Phyllis, is your handsome escort and your corsage. Does your date know the color of your dress?"

"No, Mama, he didn't ask. Did Mac ask you, Tamara?"

"I told him the color, champagne. I hope he brings me roses. I love roses, don't you?" Then I glanced at my wrist. "What time is it? Darn, I forgot. My watch broke. What's the time?"

"Quarter to seven," Mama said. "Your girls had better go downstairs and wait for them. You both look lovely; don't they, Papotchka?" She walked with us to the top of the stairs.

"They sure do," he agreed. "Have a good time, and don't forget the house key. I don't want to be wakened at three o'clock in the morning."

"Good night, Papa." I gave him a kiss on the cheek. "If I forget the key, I'll crawl in through the kitchen window."

Carefully, Phyl and I made our way downstairs, holding the skirts of our gowns so as not to trip. In the living room, Phyllis withdrew a gold cigarette case. "Remnants of Steve Kent. He gave it to me before leaving for overseas. Want a cigarette?"

"No, thanks, not now." I sank into Papa's armchair. "What time is it?"

"Seven," Phyl answered. "Gee, I hope they don't forget the tickets. Is Mac forgetful?"

I shook my head. "No, you ought to hear him quote Chaucer.

463

He's got a photographic memory. Don't worry." I turned the radio on and put the volume on low so that it wouldn't bother the folks. "There, 'The White Cliffs of Dover' is being played in your honor. Your favorite song, right?"

"Huh? That?" Phyl snorted. "No more. I used to like it on account of Philip, a navy officer I dated before Christmas. The louse happened to be married! I can't stand that song now."

"You can't hate a song like that, Phyl. You might hate the association with it, but the song itself is beautiful."

"Whatever!" She walked over to the window and peered outside. "It's a good thing you've got that street lamp outside your house. Otherwise Mt. Vernon Street would be in total darkness. Say, what is keeping those guys? It's almost seven-twenty now. All I can see outside is snow."

"Don't worry. They'll be here. They might have missed the subway or had some last-minute orders. The army comes first, you know."

"Well . . ." Phyl plopped herself down on the sofa. "I guess we might as well be comfortable." She gave me a dazzling smile, slipped off her gloves, rolled them up, and stuffed them into her purse.

"I wonder who Loretta's date is," I said. Loretta didn't date much, now that I thought about it. Her parents were rather strict.

"She'll probably come with her brother Manfred or some family friend," Phyl responded. "She's shy with men, isn't she?"

"I really don't know, Phyl. I don't see that much of her, since she's majoring in Romance languages, not English lit, like us."

We heard Mama's footsteps on the stairs. Soon, her anxious face peered out at us from behind the archway. "You girls still here? What happened? Where are Mac and your date, Phyllis?"

"We don't know." Phyl attempted to smile. "Maybe they lost their way," she joked.

"It's five after eight. Didn't your prom start at seven-thirty?"

"Sure did." Phyl half turned towards the window. "Maybe they've stood us up."

"What's that?" Mama asked.

"She's joking, Mama," I explained, glaring at Phyllis. "No, Phyl, I don't think Mac would do anything like that."

Mama sat down to wait with us.

By eight-thirty, when there was still no sign of our escorts, I did begin to worry. When the clock in the dining room chimed nine, I became indignant. All the happiness and excitement that I had been waltzing around with these past few days had fizzled out. I felt disappointed and chagrined. Mama's commiserating expression and occasional "tsks" did not help.

"Are you sure he knew it was tonight?" she finally asked.

"Mama," I tried to answer calmly but couldn't keep the irritability out of my voice, "I talked to him today. He knew it was tonight."

"He'll come." She patted my knee. "Just relax. They'll be here shortly. Something has come up, I'm sure. Mac is responsible."

"He could have phoned at least," I complained. "They'd better have a darned good excuse."

Phyl's ashtray was filled with stubs. Mama, after sitting with us for a few more minutes, finally had gone upstairs.

"There they are," Phyllis whispered. "It's almost a quarter to ten." She nodded towards the window. "Look at them."

I watched them climb the four flights up to the front porch. They seemed to be having a hard time doing so, both men holding on to each other and laughing as they did so.

"What's wrong with them?" I whispered. "They're so . . . "

"Drunk." Phyl spoke out angrily. "They sure are, as drunk as they can be."

When I opened the front door for them I realized she was right. Their heightened color and the stupid, glazed look on both their faces gave them away. I smelled the liquor on Mac's breath and recoiled as he tried to kiss me, while holding on to his buddy, Ray, for support.

"Ah, m'darling Rooshian lady. Aren't you going to greet your beloved husband-to-be?" He placed one booted foot into the foyer, still holding on to Lieutenant Tyson's shoulder. "Now the other foot steps over the shreshold into my princess's domain. And look at the lady-in-waiting, sheesh, the blonde Shwede. Thash your date, me buddy, ole Ray, old pal. Ain't she a real red brick sh-shithouse, buddy ole boy?"

Ray pushed Mac inside the foyer and attempted to look dignified. He stared at Phyllis. "Sheesh! She shure is purty, me buddy. You got tasshte, if I shay sho myself. . . . Red brick shithouse, my eye! She's more than that." He leered at Phyl, who could not conceal her distaste.

I felt embarrassed for her. "Come in, please." I tried to be polite, although I could have clobbered Mac. When they both collapsed on the sofa, I stood and faced them. "What happened?" I asked coldly, then turned away when Mac held out his arms.

To my anger he looked at me with complete innocence. "Wha-what happened?" He looked at Ray for confirmation. "Nothing happened; did it, Ray? Eh, Ray? Hey, that rhymes, eh Ray? I'm a poet and don't know it." He chuckled, yawned; his eyes glazed. "How 'bout it, Ray? Ain't my Tamara booful? My Tamara. Sheesh, she is my Tamara. Ah, thash a mighty purty name, Tamara, and Tamara, and Tamara creeps on this petty pace from . . ."

"That's enough, Mac." Phyl sternly took command. "C'mon, guys. We're late. You want some black coffee or shall we go?" Taking hold of Ray's arm, she shoved him towards the door.

Ray looked at Mac for support. "But we jes' got here, li'l lady. Whash your name, li'l lady?" His eyes misted. "Ish cold outside."

"Come on, Mac, we're going too." I took his sleeve, trying to avoid his breath. Ugh, how he reeked!

Both Phyl and I realized that we'd better get them out of the house before either Mama or Papa decided to come downstairs again. I closed the door behind us quietly and, once outside, I held my hand out to Mac for the Prom tickets.

He tried in vain to focus his eyes on me. "Ticketsh? Whash you wan' ticketsh for? I shur ash hell don' hev ticketsh."

"Mac didn't bring the tickets," I told Phyllis. Disgusted, I had left his side to walk along with her. I figured the two officers could hold up each other. "You think the cold air will take some of the stupor out of them by the time we get to Radcliffe?" I whispered.

"I honestly don't know, Tamara," Phyl sounded tired. "I don't think we should go to the prom with them in the condition they're in," she said. "What's everybody going to think?"

"Aw, Phyl, this is our senior prom." I was close to tears. "At least we can see what it's like. If you're worried about getting in without tickets, don't be. Ruthie is going to be at the desk, and she's the one who sold them to me. Besides, they usually have a list of names, don't they?"

"Yeah." Phyl turned to look back at them. "That was a totally inconsiderate, despicable thing for them to do. I can't believe it of Mac, who professes to love you so much. You know"— she clutched her coat tighter against her chest—"I'm beginning to think all men are selfish boors."

I too glanced back at them. They didn't seem to have a care in the world, just two drunken officers teetering on the sidewalk, totally oblivious to the world around them.

"You should have seen Ray just now." In spite of my annoyance, I giggled. "He almost fell in the snow. Mac reached out to help him and almost fell down too."

"I wish they had," Phyl grumbled. "It'd serve them right."

We came to the tram stop on Mass Ave. "I'll pay for all of us," I told Phyl, "but we'll sit together. I just can't stand Mac's breath."

Finally, we arrived at Harvard Square and got off. I hoped that walking up Brattle Street towards Radcliffe would help clear the officers' heads. Phyllis was not so optimistic. I felt bad for her. She had really looked forward to this event, poor gal; I certainly had too.

"Do you realize they didn't bring us corsages? I just can't believe it," Phyllis shook her head. "I never thought this would happen."

"Neither did I, Phyl, but I'm glad in a way that it did; it has cleared my head. I can't imagine that I ever wanted to marry him. Thank God and Confucius that I hadn't done so before he'd gone overseas. You know, Phyl, a little voice inside me kept telling me to take my time, to be careful. Call it intuition or whatever."

She gave me a look, as if she thought I was crazy. "Something happened, Tamara." Phyl was playing her game now. "Mac hasn't acted like this before, has he? Maybe they got news at Camp MacKay that they're to be shipped out or something. Maybe that's why they got stinking drunk. You know, these guys are under a lot of stress. They realize that they may not come back. Have you thought about that, Tamara?"

"If I got bad news, I wouldn't get drunk. I'd handle it some other way, but I sure as heck wouldn't get plastered."

"C'mon, Tamara, people are different. Think of his situation a bit," she whispered.

"I am," I answered testily, "and I don't like it a bit."

By the time we arrived at Radcliffe, the prom was half over. The dance floor was crowded. My classmates, usually loafered and cardiganed, were unrecognizable in their evening finery, their faces radiant with happiness as they danced in the arms of their escorts.

"Lesh dance," Mac pressed my arm with his fingers.

"Stop that!" I turned on him with fury.

He grinned, placing a finger to his lips. "Sh-shorry, din't mean to hurt you, li'l Red Riding Hood. You are my li'l Red Riding Hood, aren't you?" He bent his face close to mine, truly lovesick and terribly drunk.

Phyllis and I tried hard to make the best of a bad situation. She suffered Ray's misguided steps and made a funny grimace when they passed close by, mouthing "phew!"

I mouthed the same in return. Mac kept insisting on dancing close, while I fought to move away. Once I glanced up into his face, then had to look away in disgust. The face I now had seen was that of a total stranger.

It must be Fate, I decided to myself. The growing horror of what I would have had to face had I actually married him made me shudder. What a monstrous mistake I would have made. Had I been so blinded by love or had it been merely physical attraction? There was certainly no physical attraction now, at least not on my part. How had I not seen him for what he was? Silently I thanked God for saving me from this man.

These thoughts that raced through my mind as I danced with him did some strange things for me. Suddenly I began to feel as if some heavy, unwelcome burden was being lifted off me; I now looked into Mac's face and felt as if I were only dancing with a passing acquaintance. I no longer experienced those over-powering emotions I had previously felt for him. He was just a nobody with whom I chanced to be dancing at my Prom. *After this prom,* I promised myself, *I'll free myself of him forever.*

The prom was ending with *Good night, Sweetheart*. Mac looked down into my face, drunk, but even then conscious of his love. I looked away. It was not good night, sweetheart for me. It was good-bye.

He and I took the tram back home, leaving Phyllis and Ray at the subway station in Harvard Square. I had ignored Mac most of the way.

When we entered the house I was relieved that he had gone immediately upstairs to Vanya's room, muttering something about having to sleep it off. I went on to my parents' bedroom, having noticed that their light was still on. Mama usually waited up for me.

"Well?" Mama waited, an expectant smile on her lips.

Only the top of Papa's head showed from underneath the blanket. I sat on the edge of their bed thinking how best I could tell them about Mac.

"It's over, Mama." It was no use to mince matters. "I'm not marrying Mac."

The blanket moved and Papa's head appeared. Awake now, he blinked his eyes at me in surprise. Mama slowly took off her glasses and put her book aside. "Why?" she asked quietly.

"Because he is not the person I thought he was." I shrugged my shoulders. "I see him differently now. It must have been infatuation on my part, I think. How should I have known? I've never been in love or infatuated." I slipped off their bed, relieved. "I just wanted to let you know." It was strange how emotionless I felt, as if all of my emotion had been drained away from me. The sound of my own voice was even stranger. Listening to myself, I couldn't get over how cold and detached I sounded.

"You've been under a great strain, Tamara." Mama was calm. "You've had exams, war work, your friends going overseas, then falling in love, which was a new experience: so many emotions and so much stress." She gave a deep sigh. "Take your time. Don't make a hasty judgment now."

"I won't regret anything, Mama," I told her grimly. "I know myself; I know what I feel. The sum total of what I feel towards Mac is nothing, absolutely and completely nothing."

Papa closed his eyes. "*Dochenka*, Mama's right. Don't make hasty judgments. Mac is a wonderful young man." With that he burrowed his face in his pillow and promptly went to sleep.

"Good night, Mama." I gave her a kiss. "I'm glad this happened. Really, I feel light-hearted and happy now, the way I used to feel before I met him."

She took up her book again. "Good night, Tamara. Sleep on it. You may feel completely different tomorrow or, rather, today," she said, as she looked at the clock on her night table. "It's two o'clock in the morning. Good night, dear."

I awakened feeling refreshed. Oh, what a sound and dreamless sleep I'd had. Why did I feel so good today? Then I glimpsed my champagne gown on the back of the chair. I groaned, remembering the night before. *I've got to face Mac this morning,* I thought to myself. *I've got to tell him now, not put it off till later.* I could see his face again as it had been last night; his idiotic grin, the glazed eyes. I could even hear the sound of his drunken voice. The very thought of it just sickened me. Better to seize the moment and go through with it right now. I slipped on my faded flowered skirt and green blouse, giving my hair a few extra whacks. Maybe he's still sleeping, I hoped. Softly, I tiptoed down the stairs, passing Vanya's room. The door was closed.

I walked into the living room, expecting to see Papa reading the morning paper. Instead, it was Mac sitting in Papa's armchair by the window, his shoulders hunched as he held his head between his hands. *Good,* I thought to myself. *He's got a bad, bad hangover. Well, he certainly deserves one.* I had no pity for him.

When he saw me, he held out his arms, looking miserable and rather sheepish. "Please, Vixen, come to me," he begged quietly.

Strange, how his calling me by that name no longer thrilled me. Looking at him now, I was surprised that I had ever held any loving feelings towards him or had been thrilled by his kisses. To me he was now a stranger I had never known. My disappointment in him, my anger, as well as my love, had by now all disappeared. Curiously, I looked at him. Then I placed myself in front of him, my hands behind my back.

"Mad at me, darling?" His voice was pathetically low. "I can't blame you one bit."

"No, Mac, I'm not mad at you. It doesn't really matter whether I'm mad or not. I just want you to know that I know now for sure that I do not love you and that I will not marry you, not

470

now nor ever. That's all I want to tell you."

At first, he had looked as if he hadn't understood what I had told him. Then, as if my words had slowly dawned on him, he stared woodenly past me. "I do one thing wrong, and you no longer love me. Have you ever loved me, darling?" His voice was dreadfully hollow.

I wasn't about to argue with him. "I don't know, Mac. I really don't know or care. You're not the man for me; that's all."

I did not wait to see how he took it, not wishing to see his misery, if it was misery, and not a bad hangover. But I did glance again at his hunched figure and lowered head as I went back upstairs. "Good-bye," I told him. "Good luck to you, Mac."

He never did answer me.

It was my parents who saw him to the front door. It was Mama who kissed him good-bye. I had gone back to sleep, happy that I had done what I had set out to do, namely, the right thing.

30

Fare Thee Well

"That, Mamotchka, was excellent coffee. Whatever did you do to it?" Papa emptied his cup and got up from the table.

"Just added a pinch of salt to the water. Would you believe it? Annitchka told me to do it," Mama confessed. "Serioja, did you read, in this morning's *Globe*, about the ingenious camouflage the Russians are using to outsmart the Nazi soldiers?"

He nodded. "That was a smart, crafty way of camouflaging themselves during the Russian winter; it was a brilliant maneuver." Papa looked over at my plate. "Are you having only a piece of toast, *dochenka*? You'll soon be wasting to nothing!"

"I'm not hungry, Papa. I want to know how the Russians outsmarted the Germans."

"I'll tell you, Tamara. Let Papa leave. He's late already. The Russians wore white uniforms that blended in with the snow. The Germans didn't realize it until it was too late."

"That was clever," I agreed. "The Red Army has been doing really well lately, hasn't it?"

"It certainly has. After they retook Stalingrad, they have been launching one offensive after another, retaking their cities; although the Germans"—Mama gritted her teeth—"have set these cities afire as they've retreated. What they've done to innocent civilians ... ach!" She heaved a deep sigh. "My heart just aches for those people ... and people everywhere. I don't know when this misery will end."

Someone was unlocking the back door. I turned to look. Mama too glanced towards the door. "Who?" Before she could continue, Papa reentered the kitchen, obviously pleased with himself. "I just happened to meet the mailman." He looked at me, grinning impishly. "Since I thought these letters might be important, I brought them swiftly to you, just like the American Pony Express."

I looked at the neat, perfectly formed script. Only one person wrote like that. "It's from Mac," I said quietly. "Strange that he's writing to me after what happened between us. Well, let's see what he has to say for himself."

I tore open the envelopes and checked the dates. "One he wrote the first of February, and this one is written on the fourth." I smiled to myself. "He's in Camp Miles Standish Hospital; he has sinus problems, poor fellow."

It amused me that he had written about that. Did he think I'd be sorry for him? Remembering how drunk he had been at the prom had hardened my feelings for him.

"Ah-h, Mama." I smiled as we sat down again at the table. He now is telling me what he thinks of me. Just listen to this.

" 'Every once in a while (every other week)—and I know you'll think me a liar when you read this—I look over your loving letters and am glad I kept them. Just think—someday, when I find that girl who will marry me, I shall show her these letters, and she'll know I showed someone the glorious road to love, but that someone with whom I'd have shared my troubles, my love, my emotions, was too afraid of being a *prisoner* to share her love, emotions, and ambitions with me. But for a time, from that night when they first kissed so happily, the calm and serene life she had enjoyed through Christmas and New Year's and on with him began to frighten her. . . . ' "

I glanced up to look at Mama.

She smiled. "I'm afraid our lieutenant is not too happy with you," she said, "but he does write beautifully."

"Yes," I read on silently, then laughed out loud.

"What's so funny?"

"Listen to what he writes now. 'For the first time in her life she was unselfish, subservient, to another person.' Mama, can you believe it? He goes on . . . " I pronounced the words dramatically as I read them aloud to her.

473

" 'She had become a prisoner of love: chained, handcuffed, and enslaved. She pitied other men who did not have the opportunity to take her out so that others might see her radiant beauty. People would envy the fortunate, young men who were privileged to have her bestow her gracious smile upon them. She felt her beauty was such that it should be shared by all, not monopolized by a certain first lieutenant, who loved her more for her character than for her beauty. However, the princess soon found that her prince had faults, that love involved sacrifices, quarrels, heartaches, disappointments. Even though she had once said, 'I love you with all my heart,' and 'If I had been born to dream—then my dreams at this time would have had you as the main attraction' she suddenly awakened from her dream, cursed her first love, called it infatuation, and expected her lover to go dash his brains out because of his broken heart. She is a vixen, though, for she hit him when he didn't feel well enough to strike back.' "

There was more in the letter, but I had to stop reading. "Can you believe his nerve, Mama? I broke it off because he didn't feel well. Hah! He was so terribly drunk that prom night that he couldn't stand up on his own two feet."

"So that's what happened," Mama murmured. "I knew that it must have been something drastic for you to break up with him so suddenly."

"Well, how would you have felt?" I demanded.

"I would probably have reacted in much the same way," she answered thoughtfully. "After all, you had known him for such a short time and under unusual circumstances. It's then that people are more prone to fall prey to their emotions."

"I'm glad you understand, Mama. I was beginning to feel that I had been as heartless as he implies. I'm not, am I?"

She laughed. "Of course not. You're a very sweet girl. That's why everybody loves you. I'm afraid that Mac is terribly bitter right now. You cannot help how you feel, either. Only time will tell how the two of you work it out."

"He sure is bitter," I had to agree. "Just listen to this. He tells me that he's lost his first love, his greatest love, and his only true love. And then he writes that our love was that great because it was never completely realized, that I'll always in my imagination be comparing my next lover to him.

"He goes on: 'Your next lover will be more handsome, devoted, worshipping, but the real things can't even begin to equal what you now have had and decided to cast off. Right now I'm a little heartsick. I'd go back to you right away if you asked, but I know better. However, I have reasons to be happy for knowing you.'

"And then, Mama, he actually numbers them! Listen:

"'One, while you were in love with me I was loved as completely as any man could hope to be loved. Two, were I to marry you, I should have to endure countless Lannies, Omars, Michaels, Dicks, Toms, and Harrys. Three, as Papa (a really wonderful man whom you already have hurt deeply) . . .'

"Mama, how have I hurt Papa? He writes that Papa told him I could probably not have been true to him had he married me. That's not true, is it, Mama? Papa couldn't have said that, could he?"

"I hardly think so, Tamara. Remember, Mac is hurt and he's lashing out at you."

"He sure is, Mama. He lists five more reasons. . . . My letters to him, 'so intense and romantic, people will know who really was in love and I can always call them exhibits one, two, and three of my Russian love affair.' Note the sarcasm, Mama. His fifth reason: 'Because of you and thanks to you, I got rid of a girl I'd have probably married and would later regret marrying. Thanks to you I know what real love is and how intensely one can love and be loved.' His sixth reason is that he has met so many interesting people through me and especially me. Seven, he declares, that thanks to me he knows what he's going to do after the war. What does he mean by that, I wonder?

"Now we come to the eighth and last reason: 'All the other officers are very curious as to why you threw me over, and when I tell them the truth, they just smile and wink knowingly.' Even after all this, he writes that he is still mine, 'happily, always, and completely.'" I laid the letter down.

Mama got up. "I can't help feeling sorry for him. He is a very fine young man and apparently his love for you is genuine."

"So is Lanny's love for me, Mama, but Lanny doesn't insult me because I don't love him. He's patient, hoping that eventually I might."

"That, too, has happened to people. Lanny is also a fine young man, but in my opinion he's not strong enough for you. I think Mac is. However, I can only stand on the sideline and observe. You alone know what is in your heart."

I scanned Mac's other letter, written on the fourth. Again, his bitterness showed through his words. *Now I am learning more about him,* I thought with amusement.

"Mama, you have to listen to this. He really does know how to write, Mama! 'I pity the other men who will inevitably swarm about you like butterflies about a brilliant, devilishly attractive flame. With singed wings and scarred bodies they will fall from heaven to be with something fantastically real. What interests me is what happens finally to that brilliant, devilishly attractive flame? There's a question for you.' "

I continued to read to myself. "You probably couldn't finish my first letter, but don't ever excuse your conduct by believing it's because 'You're you.' From one who loves you because he sees in the child Tamara One many selfish, brutal, and cruel characteristics that can be submerged in Tamara Two, deeply in love, unselfish, thoughtful of others, and not giving a damn who loves her except that she loves one who loves her just as sincerely."

I smiled, feeling his anger. "Mama, just listen to this: 'What does a child do with a shiny new toy when she first sees it? She plays all the time with it, fondles it, takes it to bed with her, and thinks she can't live without it. Bang! One day she reverts to type, throws aside the toy—if she can find it or someone else hasn't grabbed it—and cherishes it more than ever.

" 'Remember that story about Ben Franklin and Madame Helvetius I told you one day? It has no bearing on the subject, but some day old J.P. McNish will be asking Madame Tamara-Rubleva-Korsetikoff-Derriere-Wing-Loo to avenge herself on all her husbands by marrying her first and only true love. Immodest, uninteresting, average American that I am, I'm still confident that I made quite an impression on a beautiful, extraordinarily interesting, cultured Russian, Chinese, American-to-be.'

"Well!" I inserted the letters back into their envelopes. "That, at last, is that. *Fini la comédie.*"

Mama turned away from the sink, wiping her hands on her

apron. "Are you going to write back to him?"

"I don't know, Mama. I'm going to think about it. I don't want him to believe that I still love him. . . . Unbelievably, he thinks I still do. I know I did the right thing."

"You're right, Tamara. You've got your lifetime ahead of you. There'll be more men in your life, I'm sure. Maybe it'll still be Mac you eventually marry. Maybe it'll be someone else. You're wise to wait. You can afford to."

I gave Mama a hug. "You're so understanding, Mama. Thank you for listening and for your advice."

With that I ran upstairs and typed a short letter to Mac explaining that, had I known he was ill, I'd have let him down in a gentler way. I tried to be as honest as possible, ending my letter this way:

> My feelings for you may have changed because I didn't want to fall in love at this time, not with you or any other man. Of course, there are times when I do miss you. You meant so much to me these past two months.
>
> I can't see you any more unless we remain just friends. Realistically, I know that as far as you're concerned, friendship for us is now impossible. So be it.
>
> You sound bitter in your letters. Please don't be. We had a wonderful awakening to love. That I shall always treasure. Someday you will be able to reflect on all this, and, hopefully, remember me with kindness. I hope so.

I signed it, "Affectionately, Tamara," hoping that he realized that I bore him no ill will. Having done that, I decided to walk to Harvard Square and mail it there. Perhaps I'd put in some time at the Russian War Relief now that I had the time.

"Mama, you need anything? I'm going to mail this letter."

"Yes, Tamara, please mail this one that I've written to Vanya. Poor fellow, it's so difficult for him in Europe."

"You forget, Mama, that he's got a girlfriend, that he's busy teaching Russian, and that he has time to sightsee, or so he writes. It doesn't sound as if he's miserable, does it?"

She looked down at the letter, then put it in my coat pocket. "No, I just miss him, that's all."

I kissed her lightly on the cheek. "He's all right, Mama. And we're all writing to him. Don't worry. Okay?"

"Okay." Smiling, she shooed me out the door.

It felt good to walk around Harvard Square. I mailed the letters in the large mailbox near Officer Burke's booth.

"Well, if it isn't one of my favorite Cliffies." His cheerful face looked down at me. "I've missed you for a while there. Where've you been, young lady?"

I looked up at his window. "Here and there, Officer Burke. I'm graduating in two days; can you believe it?"

He nodded. "Sure can, miss. I've seen you so many times hurrying to your classes, carrying all those books. So now you'll be joining the alumnae. My congratulations to you. I bet your folks are mighty proud."

"They are." I thanked him and hurried towards Dunster Street. A few stores down was the Russian War Relief store. I looked through the plate-glass window to see who was working today. It was none other than Mrs. Levinson. Good. I liked the young wife of the physics professor. When I entered, she greeted me like a long-lost friend. "Tamara, dear, I was just wondering what had happened to you. I've seen your mother but not you. Whatever happened? We've missed you."

I took off my coat. "Well, now you'll be seeing more of me, Mrs. Levinson. I've been busy finishing up at Radcliffe."

She looked at me with admiration. "That's right. Your father told me you were accelerating. So you'll be graduating shortly. Mazeltov!" She put her arms around me and gave me a big hug. "And then what are you planning to do?" she asked.

"I've written to several places in New York. Since I know Chinese and Russian, I thought I might be of use either to the Strategic Services or the Office of War Information."

"I'm sure they could use you." She looked around the room. "I was just wishing for someone like you. This place needs some redecorating, don't you think? I know they haven't changed the articles in the window area since you were here last. How about it?"

It was fun getting back to work here. Once in a while, as I cleaned and dusted, I noticed Harvard students stopping to look through the window. Mrs. Levinson was amused. "They didn't do that when I was here alone," she pointed out.

"They're just curious," I told her, "but some of them have come in and volunteered. You've met Charlie Murray and Jonathan Wittenberg, haven't you? They've really helped out a lot here."

She nodded. "Yes, they have; especially Charlie, who does all our errands."

"And here comes another volunteer." I laid aside my dust cloth and went to the door.

"What a sight for sore eyes," I exclaimed, standing on my tip-toes. "I thought you might have been shipped out." I kissed him lightly on the cheek and took his hand.

"Mrs. Levinson, I want you to meet an old friend of mine, Lansing Johnson."

She came forward and extended her hand, saying, "Delighted to meet any friend of Tamara's."

Lanny was already blushing. Golly, it was good to see him. I hadn't realized how much I had missed him.

"What are you doing here, Lanny? Why haven't you called me?" I found myself wanting to ask him all sorts of questions, then realized why he'd stayed away. "I'm so happy to see you," I told him.

"I didn't think I'd find you back here again." He began to help me arrange the Russian toys in the show window. "This is like old times, isn't it?"

"Yes," I answered. It wasn't though, to tell the truth. There was now a barrier between us.

Lanny and I stayed at the Russian Relief quarters until lunchtime, when Annitchka came in to relieve Mrs. Levinson. She too was surprised to see the two of us together here.

"Well!" She raised her eyebrows, staring at each of us in turn. "I thought...." She stopped. "Oh, Tamarotchka, I met your papa this morning and he told me you're graduating in two days."

Silently I thanked Annitchka for changing the subject. "Yes; in two days I'll become a 'bachelorette' of arts. Isn't it wonderful?"

"Absolutely, and will you be working here this afternoon?"

"No," I told her. "Lanny and I have got to leave right now." I gave her a hug. "I'll be stopping by your apartment one of these days."

I knew there were a million questions on her mind. Taking Lanny's hand, I opened the door. "I'll be coming here more often after graduation," I told her as we left.

"Would you like to go to the Wursthaus?" He tucked my hand into the crook of his elbow as he used to. His eyes pleaded that I go with him.

"Lanny, I'd like to very much," I agreed. Maybe having a cup of coffee with him would clear the air between us.

At the Wursthaus we found our old booth unoccupied. I slid onto the bench and smiled at him as he sat across from me.

"I've missed you terribly, Princess," he said emotionally. "I was afraid that I had lost you."

I waited till the waitress had taken our order. "Lanny, I can't explain what came over me. It had never happened before."

"You couldn't help it. You fell in love." He reached out to lay his hand on mine. "I only wish it had been with me."

I thought of Mac's bitter letters. "Lanny, it's over now."

"You mean it?" It was if a burden had been lifted off him.

"Yes. Mac still loves me, or so he says." It still shocked me at how emotionless I felt when talking about him.

"So you don't mind if I call you once in a while to go out with me?"

"I'd like that, Lanny," I assured him, and meant it.

"You'll soon be leaving for New York, won't you?"

"Whenever I get a job," I told him.

"What if you don't get one?" he asked.

Phyl and I had already discussed that. "Then I'll either become a WAAC or a WAVE," I replied.

His reaction startled me. I hadn't expected that he would approve. "That's a great idea. I commend you, Princess."

"And what about you? What's next for you?"

His face had clouded over then. "I'll be leaving for South Carolina soon . . . in preparation for being shipped overseas."

"Oh, Lanny, you too?" I should have known he would be leaving as well.

It had been a pleasant afternoon. Lanny had wanted to walk home with me. "Thanks for offering, but I'm taking the tram. I

Lanny

promised Mama I'd be home by two, and it's already after that."

He looked disappointed at first, until I suggested he call me towards the end of the week. "By that time graduation will be over," I explained.

"I'll be looking forward to seeing you, dearest Princess." He blew me a kiss as I headed for the tram car stop.

When I got home Mama met me at the door. "I'm so glad you're back. The phone has not stopped ringing for you. First Mac called. We had a nice talk, and he said he'd call later. Then Phyllis. Then Professor Levinson. Whatever would he want?"

"Mrs. Levinson worked at the headquarters today. I don't

481

know. Why should her husband want to talk to me?"

She shrugged her shoulders. "He said he'd call back too."

I told Mama about Lanny. "Too bad he's leaving too," she said. "He is much too gentle for war."

The phone rang again.

"Hello?"

"Miss Rubleva?" An unfamiliar voice.

"Yes?"

"Professor Levinson here. My wife told me she'd seen you today. I was wondering whether you'd be interested in doing some typing for me."

Hallelujah! I needed some extra money to help with my trip for New York, if ever I went there. Baby-sitting did not pay well at fifty cents an hour. I promised Professor Levinson I'd get the job done as soon as I could. He agreed to leave the material with Papa in Boylston Hall.

I had no more than hung up when the phone rang again. It was Phyllis.

"I only wanted to congratulate you on your coming graduation, my friend." I heard her take a deep breath. "Well, you're a lucky bum. While you'll be flitting about in New York, I'll still be slaving away at Radcliffe."

"You don't get any sympathy from me, Phyl. Remember the happy grasshopper who flitted about while the bees stored honey for the winter? You could have accelerated as well."

"Ouch!" she laughed. "Heard from Mac yet?"

"Mama said that he had called, but I wasn't here."

"Oh." There was a pause. "I still say you shouldn't have broken up with him. He's a swell guy."

"Doggonit, Phyl; do I tell you how to act with your men?"

"I don't act the way you do," she snapped. "I've got to hang up, Tamara. Mom needs to use the phone." She said good-bye, and I heard the receiver click.

She had sensed that I was angry. Her excuse was a lame one. So be it.

Mac did not call again that day, nor the next. I tried to call Sam at the camp dispensary. When the operator asked me if the call was official, I was honest.

"Ma'am," the operator said, "I'm sorry. I cannot take any calls other than official."

Stupidly, I had remembered too late. Sam had once told me always to inform the operator that the call was official. I had wanted to invite both him and Mac to my graduation. *Too bad,* I thought to myself, not really sorry. God, what a hypocrite I was getting to be.

Mama and Papa were at my graduation, as were most of the parents of the fifty-seven Cliffies who were getting their degrees at this time. Since it was wartime, the ceremony had been brief and simple. The new Radcliffe College president, Dr. Wilbur Jordan, made a speech praising us for our diligence and welcoming us to the outside world. Then came the applause as our names were called, and then the milling of parents around their cap-and-gowned offspring. Our diplomas were not ready. They would be sent to us sometime in March. The event I had looked to for so long ended without much celebration. Vicky Sarkesian and Phyllis were both at the house after the ceremony, when Mac called.

"Hello, Tamara." I had forgotten how pleasant his voice was. "I'm calling to ask you something that will mean a great deal to me, darling."

"Hello, Mac. Yes; what is it?" Did he want us to go out again? Phyllis and Vicky sat on the steps of the staircase, watching me.

"I'd like you to come to the army base to see me off. Will you do that for me?"

"Hold on for just a minute, will you?" I laid my hand over the mouthpiece and turned to the girls. My heart had started to pound. "He wants me to come say good-bye to him at Camp McKay," I whispered. "I had already told him good-bye when he took me out the other day. What do you think? I don't want to go."

Phyllis looked at me with utter disgust. She had always been rather partial to Mac. "Oh, for God's sake, girl, grow up! He is going *overseas.* You won't be seeing him for the duration of this whole damned war. He might even be killed. Now, you tell him that you're coming."

Vicky, soft-hearted and sentimental, was tearful. "Go on, Tamara dear, tell him you're on your way. Phyl is right, honey."

"Mac"—my voice was very calm; I smiled at the girls while I was making my decision—"we'll be there in forty-five minutes to an hour. Is that all right with you?"

He sounded relieved. After his whispered, "I love you," I hung up.

"What the devil do you mean by 'we'?" Phyllis asked, surprised.

"Phyl, you're the one who said I should go see him. Besides, I don't like to go to Camp McKay alone. Please?"

They both stared at me as if I'd gone stark raving mad. Their faces looked so blank and startled that I burst out laughing. Then I shrugged my shoulders. "Don't look at me in that tone of voice. I'm right, you know."

"Oh, God, Tamara," Phyllis groaned, shaking her head. "You know, at times you're such a considerate person, but then you do something naive like this . . . playing with a person's emotions. How can you treat Mac so shabbily? You're like a child at times. I can't believe that you can be that dense. Vicky and I can't tag along everywhere with you just to get you out of your self-created jams."

"She's absolutely right, Tamara. You are sweet and charming, and we love you, but you aren't being fair to Mac. Or to yourself, for that matter."

"Okay, that settles it." I moved away from them. "We'll just forget the whole thing. I didn't want to go anyway. It's better this way, making a clean break without tearful good-byes."

Again, they stared at me in disbelief. Vicky placed her arm around my shoulder. "Tamara, honey," her brown eyes pleaded, "he loves you very much. Think of him. How would you feel if he were wounded or, worse yet, killed overseas? I can't believe you could be so cruel that you'd refuse to grant his last request to see you before he left."

Why couldn't they help me out just this once? How could I explain that I myself didn't know how I would react to Mac's departure? That I needed their physical presence for moral support? With them beside me it would be merely friends saying good-bye to a friend.

"I'm not being cruel," I protested. "I know how much he thinks of both of you. Besides, I'm not good at directions. You both know that."

And what are you afraid of, Tamara? Sam's stupid refrain again kept running through my head.

"Okay, then go, Tamara. Do it for us if not for yourself," said Phyllis. "We'll go with you. I don't want to have to listen to your regrets after it's too late."

Vicky smiled her approval, "Go. Put on his favorite dress so he can remember you as he saw you last. Make yourself beautiful for him."

I went upstairs angry and rebellious. They were all manipulating me. Why did Mac have to ask me to come? Vicky and Phyl were pressuring me. Why couldn't Mac just forget that I ever existed? It was all over and done with. Didn't he understand that I didn't want to see him? Damn them all anyway! I put on the simple gray dress with the seashell pink chiffon collar and cuffs. It had been his favorite. Then I thought of my pink hat with the long pink veil that fell down past my shoulders. Looking at my reflection, I smiled with delight at my own brilliance. I'll just keep the veil on when I see him.

I remembered Camp McKay well. The last time I had seen it was when Mac had brought Mama and me here for the Army's Christmas dinner. It seemed that years had passed since then. With a start I realized it had been only two and a half months ago. Much had happened in all that time. He and I had sat together, our feet resting on his army cot, Mama sitting at the edge of the bed ... all three of us listening to Christmas music.

"How different it is now," I told the girls. "It's like a different place."

Vicky looked at a group of men standing together, their packed duffel bags beside them. "How young they look," she said quietly. "Look at the blond fellow over there. He can't be over eighteen. Why he's just a kid."

"Yeah, poor guys; I really feel for them," Phyl flipped open her bag. "I'm glad you came, Tamara. You'd have regretted it later on." She took out her cigarette case.

"I hate good-byes," I told her. "I've said too many of them in my life, too many sad ones."

She gave me another of her blistering looks, but it didn't faze me. I knew that it was out of affection, not rancor, that she was angry with me. She and Vicky were tops.

I watched the uniformed men lugging their duffel bags, briefcases, and assorted baggage. Some of them looked sad and withdrawn. Others smiled and joked as if they were going on an excursion, not to war. Then there was Mac. There he was, coming toward us, straight and tall, smiling uncertainly. He was wearing his dress uniform and looking straight at me.

Phyllis muttered to me under her breath, "Remember, Tamara, be gentle and civil to him. He's going off to war." She didn't have to tell me that.

"Hello, Vixen." Mac peered at me through the pink veil. "You do look most lovely and mysterious." The tone of his voice was teasing; his eyes were tender, as always. "Aren't you going to lift up that delicate fabric so that I can see your beautiful face 'unveiled'?"

He actually looked handsome in his uniform, surprisingly calm, strong, and immensely sure of himself. He was watching me with that disconcerting look of his that infuriated me because it confused me and made me oblivious to everything but him and that damned cologne of his.

It was then that he noticed that Vicky and Phyl were with me. He went over and gave both of them an affectionate, brotherly embrace.

"Good of you gals to come with Tamara." His smile included me as well. "I apologize for the fact that you had to come all this distance to Dorchester. Darned inconvenient, I know, having made the trip quite a few times myself. However, I did want to get a last glimpse of you, Tamara." He came up to me and placed his hands on my waist. "One glance before I leave you. Won't you please lift that veil so that I can kiss you good-bye, my darling Vixen?"

And what are you afraid of, Tamara? This is what I am afraid of. This is why I didn't want to come, to see him, to have him touch my hands, my face, my lips. This is why the hat. I wanted him to let me go, the way I myself had set him free.

"First, kiss Phyl and Vicky good-bye. Then you may kiss me," I said stiffly.

Phyl gasped. I was not supposed to talk like that. Good God, I wasn't being nice to the first lieutenant. Damn him anyway.

Vicky went over to Mac, putting her arms around his neck. Gently she kissed him on both cheeks. "Dear Mac, good luck," she said in a low voice. "We'll both look after Tamara for you."

Phyl wiped her eyes. She gave him a tight embrace, patting his back. Over his shoulders she caught my eye, and her eyes were warning me.

Mac then came to me, holding out his arms, his eyes asking me a mute question. I looked at the serious young face, and my heart went out to him. But still, something inside me made me rigid.

"I won't lift up the veil, Mac," I whispered. "I want you to think of me this way."

He took me in his arms then, crushing me to him as if he would never let me go. Then he kissed me hard, right through the pink tulle. Having done so, he took one more long look at me. His next remark surprised me. "I suggest that you girls take Tamara to see *Lady in the Dark,*" he told Phyllis and Vicky. "It will do her a world of good."

He turned and left us then, going back to his men. The three of us walked out of Camp McKay without a backward look.

31

Breaking Away

I stared at the photographed form letter with Mac's neat handwriting filling in the blanks.

"What is it, Tamara?" Mama looked anxiously at me.

"It's Mac's new address," I explained, laying it down. "He's with the 519th Port Battalion. It's an APO number. I guess he's been shipped overseas."

"Poor Mac," Mama said as she gathered up the rest of the dishes. "Now he's gone too. One more person for you to write letters to."

"I honestly didn't believe I'd hear from him again."

"He still loves you very much, Tamara." Mama shook her head slowly. "Look at the way he has kept on writing to you every single day, in spite of the fact that you've broken off with him."

"I know, Mama. That's what disturbs me. Didn't he realize that I meant what I said to him that morning after the prom?"

"I'm sure he must have. But you know what Papa would tell you," she smiled. " 'Hope springs eternal.' Write to him, Tamara. Keep up his spirits, and above all, be gentle with him."

Of course, Mama was right. She was always right. Damn it. It irritated me how everybody felt sorry for Mac, acting as if I were the one who had done something terrible. I couldn't help it if my feelings had changed. They weren't the ones involved in this affair except as bystanders. Even Papa disapproved, remaining silent whenever Mac's name came up.

"I'll write to him," I promised dutifully. "As soon as I vacuum the house. Oh, by the way, Phyl's coming tomorrow to borrow some books from me. Can she have lunch with us?"

"Of course she can, Tamara. Why not?"

As soon as I had helped Mama clean the house, I ran upstairs to catch up on my letter writing. My list was longer these days. Most of the fellows I had known were now overseas. Shep must be somewhere in the Pacific flying bombers. Flying would always be his first love, I thought with affection. Then Dick and Charlie. Those two guys had shipped out together, both in the same outfit. They must be somewhere in northern Burma. Dick had mentioned Lieutenant General Stilwell, our former Peking neighbor. "Vinegar Joe," his men called him, Dick had written. Dave Bennett and Henry Lamont, and now Mac and Sam. Mac, in one of his letters, had written that he and Sam were in the same outfit.

It was already the thirty-first of March 1944. *My God, how time has flown, I thought to myself.*

It had been easy to write to the others. I described Cambridge, told them about funny incidents, embellishing some. Lighten their lives. Give them a laugh. That was the main idea.

With Mac it was more difficult for me to write. Several times I had to throw crumpled notepaper into my wastebasket. Finally, I succeeded in writing one that satisfied me.

"You'll be happy to know," I informed Mama at dinnertime, "that I have written Mac a very nice letter."

Mama exchanged glances with Papa.

"Besides Vanya, I also wrote letters to six people in the service."

"You have been busy," Papa nodded approvingly. "How is Professor Levinson's paper coming along?"

"Oh, I've already delivered it and gotten paid," I told him. "I'm saving that money for my trip to New York."

Mama had looked down at her plate when I mentioned the big city. Knowing her attitude towards my trip to New York, I said no more. What I had said about my trip was a slip of the tongue.

"Well, it's nice that he paid you," Papa said. With that, he got up and went into the living room to listen to the news.

April first. I wakened to feel the warm rays of the sun

489

streaming in through my window. *Oh, what a beautiful morning,* I thought to myself. Hah, it was also April Fool's. *What am I going to do today?* I asked myself lazily. *Ah yes—Phyl. It'll be great to see her.* I glanced at the clock on my desk. Jeepers, already a quarter past ten! It couldn't be that late. I sprang out of bed and flung open my door.

Absolute quiet greeted me. Either Mama was downstairs or had gone out. I called down. No answer. Nobody home.

When the doorbell rang, I thought it must be Mama. She had probably gone to the supermarket. Laden with groceries, she wasn't able to unlock the door.

Phyllis stood on the front porch, grinning. "Sorry I came a bit earlier." She held out a gaily wrapped package. "I got these Fanny Farmer chocolates for Mama. You know how she likes them," she confided, as she stepped inside.

"Mama's not here," I said. "She had already left the house by the time I got up."

"Did I waken you?" Phyl eyed my face, then muttered, "Some people have all the luck, sleeping in late."

"The rewards of accelerating in college," I countered, with a shrug.

Upstairs she looked through the books that I had piled up for her last night. "Jesus Christ, Tamara, I didn't ask for your whole library. All I need is just a couple of reference books."

"Well, take your pick. I didn't know what you might want."

She offered me a Marlboro. Laughing, I took it. "Wait a minute, Phyl. I've got to read you something Mac wrote." I shuffled through his letters on my desk. "Here it is. 'Say hello to that Quincy Quakeress, Phyllis, for me. Tell your godmother to see that you forget about smoking. Your complexion is too beautiful to ruin with weed burning.'"

Phyllis chuckled, "Boy, that's putting me in my place, huh? What else did he write besides 'I love you, darling. Will you be mine?'"

I flipped through Mac's letters. Phyl's eyes grew big, "God Almighty, you mean he's written you all those since you broke up?"

"Yep," I couldn't help smiling at her surprise. "And they're beautifully written. Listen to this: 'Often have I wondered why

490

our happiness changed into something possibly more beautiful than physical attraction; lasting and calm; a memory of how we had for a short time lived as one; forgetting others and thinking only of each other. It changed both of us into older, better, happier, and finer people.' "

"He's quite a guy," Phyl observed. "It's a shame that it's the fine fellows that often lose out and the jerks that get the best girls."

"What do you mean?"

"Well, for instance, take Lanny or Mac. Both of them are clean-cut, intelligent, fine young men. You know what? In all probability it won't be you that one of them will end up with; it'll be some gal with loose screws in her head. Worse yet, you probably will end up marrying some stuffy dodo bird." She looked at me in amusement. "That's the way it often turns out. Call it fate, or destiny, or whatever."

We heard footsteps in the kitchen. "Mama must be home," I said. "Come on downstairs."

Phyllis grabbed the box of Fanny Farmer's. "I can't wait till she sees what I brought her," she chortled, as she joined me on the landing.

Mama, her head down, was just coming up the stairs.

"Mama," Phyllis smiled broadly, holding out the package as Mama came up to join us on the landing. "Guess what I have for you."

Never in my life did I expect Mama to react the way she did. She thrust the package back at Phyllis as if it had been a venomous snake. Her eyes sparked fire, her lips twisted with rage. Then, abruptly, she pushed us both aside. "Out of my way," she intoned icily. "I want nothing to do with you, Phyllis. Nothing. Ever again!" With that she stalked off towards her bedroom.

Phyllis, aghast, tried to restrain her, "Please, Mama, what happened? What have I done?"

I too attempted to stop her. "Mama. . . . " I tried to make my voice soothing. "What is wrong? Phyllis has done nothing wrong."

She said not a word. When she reached her bedroom, she slammed the door behind her, and we heard the click in the lock.

Even in my room Mama's furious words reverberated at me. Phyl and I stared at each other in dismay.

"What could possibly have happened to make her lash out at me like that?" Tears came to Phyllis's eyes.

"I have no idea, Phyl. She was all right yesterday," I said. "I just can't understand it. I can't."

Phyl was really shaken. "I think I'd better go, Tamara. I'd like to talk to her, but . . . God . . . " She took a deep breath.

"Not when she's like that, Phyl," I didn't know what else to say to her. I too was alarmed and terribly upset. "Come on. I'll walk down with you. When I find out, I'll let you know."

Mama's temperamental tantrum at Phyllis abated into her silent treatment for me. I tried to corner Papa to find out what was wrong, but Papa had merely shaken his head, looking most troubled and unhappy.

"But, Papa," I pleaded with him, "you must know why Mama is acting like this. She acts as if I were vermin, untouchable. What could Phyllis and I possibly have done that is so horrible?"

"I don't know, Tamara." Papa looked totally miserable.

I felt that he did know, but that his loyalties belonged with Mama. If only I could find out why.

It soon became a way of life for me to live in this silent house, avoided by Mama and looked upon with uneasy sympathy by Papa. I decided to make myself scarce.

The telephone booth at the bottom of Upland Road was a godsend. I made arrangements to meet Phyl at Hood's. She was already seated when I got there. Her eyes scanned my face to see if I had any news.

I shook my head. "Phyl, she's furious at something we've done." I bit into my doughnut. "I detest that silent treatment of hers. She treats me as if I'm a nothing. . . . She talks only to Papa. She sets the table for herself and Papa. I don't even eat with them anymore. In the beginning I tried to talk to her and to help her as I used to do. I don't do it anymore. It's like talking to a statue."

"Sure is a strange way of displaying anger," Phyl mused. "I'd just as soon fly off the handle, talk, or even yell things out. . . . Maybe I'd even throw a couple of dishes at the wall. But this silence? I'd rather clear the air and get it over with."

"It's Mama's 'Russian soul,' I suppose. Russians feel deeply. They *lahv* and they *hate* with great emotional depth and feeling. I'll never be that way. I hate that silent treatment. You know, she started that technique with me when I was about five years old."

Phyl took a puff of her Marlboro. "You mean she's pulled this stunt before?"

"Yep." I couldn't help the lump in my throat. "In Peking, when I was just a kid. I remember it as clearly as if it had just happened yesterday. See, we had this guest house in front of the main house. Mama had converted it into a dress salon. Two amahs helped her do the sewing. Anyway, I was absolutely forbidden to go there without Mama. Too many sharp and dangerous things, Mama told me. Anyway, one day, when Mama was resting in the main house and the amahs had gone for the day, I sneaked in there. Mama's sewing machine fascinated me. You remember those old-fashioned Singers with the black wrought-iron treadles? Well, I monkeyed around it, turning the wheel, pretending I was Mama. The thread got all tangled up somehow, and the wheel wouldn't turn anymore, so I left the guesthouse to play with something else. Later, when Mama asked me if I had touched the sewing machine, I denied it. I don't know why I did, but I did. That's when I first found out about her silent treatment. For three days she ignored me. Believe me, that can be pretty terrifying for a five-year-old. At mealtimes, she acted as if I didn't exist. At bedtimes it was Papa who kissed me good night. Finally I couldn't stand it anymore and admitted that I had done it. That ended her silent treatment."

"Whew, I'd rather have gotten a paddling," Phyllis said. "That must have been unbearable."

"What made it even worse was Vanya's attitude. I remember sitting at the dinner table across from him. It always delighted him to see me in trouble. I couldn't stand that infuriating smirk on his face while he watched my discomfort at being ignored, but you can be sure I've never told a lie since."

"That's one hard way to learn a lesson," Phyl said soberly. "Although, frankly, I don't care for it. It must be terribly unpleasant at your house now."

"It would be if I didn't have people like you to talk to, or letters from Mac and my other friends. At times like these, it's nice to have friends."

"Oh, I'm sure it'll all work out. Your mom loves you." Phyl suddenly had an idea. "Maybe she's mad because after we became friends, you started to smoke."

"No-o. She's not mad on account of that, or she'd have said so. It's something more serious, I think."

"Perhaps it's because you want to go to New York to work."

"Thanks; you've reminded me. I've just heard from both agencies that I wrote to. The OSS is out. Their pay is too little and from what I gathered it sounded like spy work. I don't want that. But Bill White, the Director of the Russian section of the OWI, wrote me such an interesting letter. He was impressed that I'm a Radcliffe graduate, that I know Russian, French, and Chinese, besides English, and also that Papa worked at Harvard. Anyway, I'm to go for an interview as soon as I can."

"Hey, that's good news. Have you told Papa?"

"No, not yet. I thought maybe Mama would get over her anger. But I'll tell him before I leave. I've got to pack and think about where I'm going to stay. I know no one in New York. Yes, I do. I think Jacques Dubois lives there. I'll have to check on that."

"Tamara," Phyl leaned towards me. "You've got to be very careful in New York," she warned. "It's not a little university town like Cambridge, where you know a lot of folks and so forth. There are plenty of weird characters who prey on innocent and pretty girls like you."

"Baloney, Phyl. I can take care of myself."

"Like hell you can. You've got to look out for yourself, because no one else will. You don't know New York. Take my advice. I'm really concerned about you."

"I'm a big girl." I laughed at her fears.

"Okay, you are a big girl, I agree. Just take this with you." Hastily she wrote something in her address book, tore off the page, and handed it across the table.

"Barbizon Plaza. What's that?" I was curious.

"I think it's on Lexington Avenue," Phyl answered. "I'll find the correct address and give it to you before you leave. It's a place for young women to stay when they're alone in the city. It's

494

clean, safe, and inexpensive. Believe me, it's where you should go."

I thanked her. "You sure know a lot about New York."

"I was there in thirty-nine at the World's Fair," she said. "New York's a fun city, but it can be awfully evil too."

"Well, that doesn't scare me. I'm looking forward to it."

"What will you be doing in the OWI?"

"From what Mr. White wrote it'll be research work or translating from English into Russian. They're putting out two magazines; one's the size of *Life* magazine, the other, *Amerika,* is much smaller. It'll be for the Soviets so that they can learn more about American life. Sounds interesting, doesn't it?"

"Right up your alley. You're fortunate, knowing languages."

"What I liked was that Mr. White had also looked into apartments and rooms close to the OWI. My pay won't be that much, but I think I'll be able to survive."

"What will you be making?"

"About ninety-eight dollars every two weeks. He said I could get an apartment for fifty dollars a month."

"That's great, Tamara." For a moment she stared out the window, watching the people, mostly Cliffies, walk past. "I envy you, graduating and now, starting out on your own." She turned back to me. "What else does Mac write? Do you have any idea where he is?"

"I think he's in England, Phyl. You know, they aren't permitted to tell. I thought you might be interested; so I brought a couple of his letters," I grinned, rummaging in my purse. "Here's one. Listen to this. 'Last night some of us were talking of things we like, and usually simple things headed the list. There were raspberries with corn flakes, spring evenings on front porches, a ride on a summer evening.'"

"Poor Mac, he sounds homesick."

"Sure he is. He goes on. 'I don't believe any of us, if given the chance, would have turned around and gone back to the States. It's an overwhelming feeling to realize that you are a small part—a wee part, to revert to Scots—of a very huge undertaking. Little things like soap, candy bars, shoestrings, and things we used to get so easily at the nearest PX or corner drug store are now the most important things in our lives. It's a life where a

person gets down to brass tacks (if you can find any) and funda-
mental principles.'" I folded the letter, stuffing it into my purse.
"I can well understand how he feels. Living in China, those
things he says he misses had been luxuries for us. Now that I
can easily buy anything I want, they seem trivial."

"Unless you're deprived of them again. Yep"—Phyl eyed the
young man who passed our table—"and what do you write to
him?"

"Gee, but you're nosy," I ragged her. I felt my face flushing.
Sometimes I felt a flash of that old tingly feeling at the thought
of him, like just now. "Oh, I tease him because he tells me I'm
beautiful. I write him that he's again building me up into a
dream girl, putting me on a pedestal." I couldn't help ribbing her
a bit—"As you and Sam had described me. I told him that
dreams are airy stuff, very fragile. Poof, and they are gone. But I
also write how we're working for the war effort, about my selling
war bonds here. I've even written him about my dates."

"You haven't, Tamara, have you?" Phyllis was shocked.

"Phyllis, he's smart enough to know that if I ever got serious
enough about someone else, I'd not mention it to him because it
would lower his morale one hundred per cent."

She shook her head. "Either he knows you very well, or . . ."
She shrugged. "Sometimes I can't understand your attitude."

"Some day you will, Phyllis. It's simple. See? Long ago I
learned that life is a continuous waiting game. Think about it.
You wait to grow bigger, then to go to school, then you wait for
adolescence, then you can't wait till you are a young adult. I
waited for my folks to get out of Japanese prison, then waited to
come to America, then it was the College Boards, then waiting
for admission to Radcliffe, then graduation, then . . ."

"You're quite the philosopher, Tamara. Do you realize that
you fell in love without waiting?" Phyl chuckled. "That was Fate
stepping in. I see what you mean though. I'd never looked at it
from that angle before."

I was enjoying this chat. "And between all those big waitings
are the little ones. Waitings go on forever until we finally cease to
wait because we've achieved that for which we've waited since
our very beginning, the end of all waiting: death."

"Ye gads, girl, but you're morbid today."

496

"Conditions of life, Phyl. It's the truth. I'm not being morbid. I love life too much to be morbid about it."

The day before I planned to leave for New York I stopped at Papa's office. Fortunately, he was alone. He looked so small there, sitting behind his big desk, surrounded by file cabinets filled with Chinese characters and their definitions. He looked up when I entered.

"Papa, I'm leaving tomorrow for my interview," I sat down in his visitor's chair and showed him Mr. White's letter. "I would have liked to tell both you and Mama together, but since she's upset with me, I decided to come here to tell you."

Poor Papa took the letter and read it. "I see." I noticed the age lines around his mouth. "It sounds like a good job, Tamara. Perhaps it is for the best. I'll miss you, you know."

"It'll be better for Mama and you." I tried to be cheerful. "The interview will take an afternoon. I'll be back in a couple of days. This will be just to see what it's like in the city and to meet the people I'll be working with."

"It sounds good," Papa repeated.

I tried once more to find out what was wrong. "You can't tell me, Papa?"

He shook his head.

The following Monday, in New York, I checked in at the Barbizon Plaza. Afterwards, I explored the big city. I walked all the way from the Barbizon Plaza to Fifty-seventh Street, past Carnegie Hall and the Russian Tea Room. I made note of the restaurant's location because of its name.

At the OWI's Russian office, my first glance at the woman sitting at the desk nearest the door told me she had to be Russian— no makeup, a pleasant face, and intelligent, lively black eyes that looked me over with friendly interest. The wrinkles around her mouth, laughter lines, curved upwards as she smiled at me. Her hair was grayish, wispy braids intercoiled on top of her head. She held a cigarette in one hand, pinky finger extended. In fact, as I glanced beyond her, I saw that everyone was smoking. The man who stood up when I had entered was tall and thin. He surveyed me with an old-world courtesy and smiled a silent welcome.

497

A woman at another desk appraised me coolly. ERNA STEN-BUCK, SUPERVISOR, her name plate read. She was forty-five or so, not a Russian, and every single hair on her head braided in place. She wore a well-tailored gabardine suit.

"Yes? What can I do for you?"

"I'm Tamara Rubleva; I'm here for an interview with Mr. White." She looked at me with interest, smiled slightly, then got up.

Mrs. Stenbuck went into Mr. White's office and quickly returned. "If you will just go on in, Mr. White is ready for you."

The office was quite small, I thought, for a director. It had a desk, a chair behind it, and two other chairs, and a picture window through which I could see Manhattan's skyscrapers. What a view!

Bill White looked up from a sheet of paper he was reading, got up from his chair, and extended his hand. His brown eyes studied me intensely. Pat O'Brien, I thought. Just like the Irish movie star who portrayed hard-boiled but actually soft-hearted editors.

"Ye-es, Miss Rubleva." Again he scanned the paper on his desk. I recognized it as the letter I had written a few weeks ago. He smiled, and I liked him right away.

"Please sit down, Miss Rubleva. I am impressed with your qualifications. Now." He held out a small, thin magazine and said, "This is *Amerika*." He pronounced it as a Russian would.

I leafed through it. It contained beautiful photographs of American landmarks and articles about American states and artists—all in Russian.

"You see what we're trying to do, Miss Rubleva? Our purpose is to bring America into Russian living rooms. We want the Russians to know us, to see us as we are. The larger magazine, in size like *Life* magazine, will be written in the same vein as the smaller *Amerika*, only more detailed. What do you think?"

"I like the idea, Mr. White." I looked directly at him. "It's most worthwhile; it's something we have needed to do more effectively. There has been quite a bit of unfriendly propaganda against the Russians. Since they are now fighting with us as our

498

allies, we have come to realize that they're very much like us—their humor, their likes and dislikes."

Mr. White looked out his picture window, then turned back to me. "I've been to the Soviet Union," he told me. "The Russians are good people. They are like us. You are right about that." He again gave me that intense, Pat O'Brien stare. "How are you in Russian? Good? Fair?"

"I speak it well, but I'm not perfect in writing." I had to be honest with him. "My English is better."

"Well, we'll see about that when you start work. Is May the eighth all right with you? By that time you'll have had a chance to find a place to live. I sent you a list, didn't I?" His forehead had perpetual waves in it. He was a man in a hurry with millions of things on his mind, I thought, but still considerate, I could see.

"Yes, thank you."

"I see that your father's at Harvard. Tell me about yourself. You seem to have led a fascinating life."

That depends on its outcome, I thought subconsciously. Aloud, I briefly sketched my life in China and in Cambridge. When I had finished he stood up.

"I'm sure you'll be a welcome addition to our group, Miss Rubleva. Come out with me to meet your coworkers. You've met Erna already. She's my right-hand man. Pardon me,"—he grinned—"I mean woman. This pleasant lady is Natasha Ismailova. And Alex Makarov. Two of our Russian translators. Some other translators have not come in yet. Well," he said, turning expectantly to me, "do you have any questions? Anything not clear to you?"

"Thank you, Mr. White," I held out my hand to him and smiled. "Everything is perfectly clear. I know that I'll enjoy being part of your team." I smiled at the Russians, then at Mrs. Stenbuck. "Until the eighth of May, then."

"Until the eighth of May," Mr. White ushered me to the door. "Your name is Tamara, a lovely name. Your Russian poet, Lermontov, wrote about two Tamaras, didn't he?"

"Yes, he did," I answered. "The Tamara in his poem *Demon* and the Czarina of his poem *Tamara.*"

He shook my head once more. "Well, it's been a pleasure, definitely a pleasure, meeting you. Let me know if I can be of any further help when you come back."

I walked out of the building onto Fifty-seventh Street and stopped to look up at the gray skyscrapers. I was excited. New York was the place for me. I knew that I had been right. I'll become a vital part of all this frenzy and magic. I am now independent and free. All of the world is mine to survey. This was what I had come to America for, what I had studied for, what I had dreamed of.

Back at the Barbizon, I dialed Jacques' number.

"Yes?" It was good to hear that familiar voice, to know that he was here in New York. I well remembered that first kiss he had planted so carefully on my lips. I had barely felt it then, as if a tiny breeze had just wafted across my lips. If he only knew how much I had learned about kissing from Mac!

"Jacques," I couldn't hide my excitement. "This is Tamara. I'm here from Cambridge. Just had an interview at the OWI and guess what? I'll be working there come the eighth of May."

He was both surprised and delighted. "That's terrific! I can't tell you how happy I am. Where are you, and how long are you staying?"

When I told him I was leaving tomorrow, he was disappointed. "Tomorrow. You're leaving tomorrow? Look, Tamarotchka, let me take you out and show you some of my old haunts in this big, bad city. How about it?"

"Jacques, I'd love it."

"Put on your dancing slippers, darling," he said as he hung up.

"Lovely as ever, my Tamarotchka," he exclaimed when he came that evening, embracing me as I came up to him in the lobby. "If it's at all possible, you are even more ravishing than the last time I saw you." He grinned, taking my hand and holding it to him. "Let's not lose any of our precious time. I want to enjoy being with you."

Away we went in a taxi and, after he had quietly told the driver the address, he turned to me and asked, "Know where we are going?"

500

I shook my head. "Let it be a surprise," I answered. It was more of a surprise than I thought. The taxi stopped in front of the Russian Tea Room.

Jacques, like Sam Klauber, had a way with maître d's. He got us a table near the floor.

"I noted this place yesterday," I told him.

"See? I can read your mind," he teased. He ordered us a drink. "Now tell me about yourself. First of all," he said seriously, "you're not married or engaged, are you?"

"Not married, not engaged." I showed him my left hand. "See? Ringless."

We both laughed at that. Between drinks we watched men in embroidered Russian shirts swallow swords or flaming torches. Strolling violinists played songs, familiar ones that Mama used to sing.

After dinner we took a taxi to Cafe Society Downtown where we danced some more.

"Jacques, you're one of the best dancers I've danced with," I told him. "I don't usually tango or rhumba because I'm not good at it, but with you leading, I find it simple."

He smiled. "We just dance well together, Tamarotchka. What I really brought you here for is to see this extraordinary singer and dancer; she's a newcomer, but she's something. Her name is Pearl Primus."

The orchestra trumpeted her arrival on stage. Everyone cheered and applauded. A young, beautiful black woman with sparkling dark eyes danced onto the platform. She wore an off-the-shoulder blouse, a full skirt that flared out as she danced, and, to my surprise, she was barefooted. She had a rare, free-spirited quality and danced and sang with such joy and abandon that she had the audience spellbound. I could have listened to her all night long, mesmerized by her dark beauty and charm.

"Oh, Jacques, I've never seen anyone like her."

"I thought you'd enjoy seeing her. You like to dance bare-footed so much yourself that I wanted you to see a kindred soul."

It was late and I was tired, yet happy, when Jacques and I made it back to the Barbizon, where I gave him a kiss on the cheek. He bowed to me, took my right hand, and gently kissed it.

"Mademoiselle, you've given me so much pleasure tonight," he said. "I can't wait till you come here to live."

And neither could I.

32

The Evil That Men Do

I smiled to myself as I waited for the door to open. Exactly as I thought. When Annitchka saw me outside her apartment, her eyes got big, and her mouth formed into a narrow O. Then she opened the door wider and enveloped me in her arms, hugging me so close that I thought I would suffocate.

"Tamarotchka!" She took me by the hand and led me to her sofa, smiling and "oohing" and "ahing" as she did so. Then she sat down beside me, her hands clasped on her lap, her face filled with pleasure. "What a pleasant surprise. Can I get you anything: coffee, tea, some sweet liqueur perhaps? Although, it may be a bit too early for that." Catching her breath, she took my hands in her own. "You know, you're almost like a daughter to me. Philipp and I, unfortunately, couldn't have children."

"I know, Annitchka." I looked at her expressive face with affection. "I've felt close to you too, sometimes even closer than with Mama."

She nodded sympathetically, "That is not unusual, Tamarotchka, but darling, tell me all about yourself. . . . What has been happening to you?"

"Well, that's one reason I have come to see you. I'm leaving tomorrow for New York. I'm going to work in the Russian section of the OWI."

She was all ears; she was happy and excited for me. After I had told her about my interview with Mr. White and meeting my coworkers, she sighed, "How I wish that I could be in your shoes—young, beautiful, going to live and work in such a world-famous city as New York. Ach, how I love that city! Philipp sometimes is invited to lecture at different universities there. Naturally I go with him. There's so much to do in New York: concerts, ballets, shows, art galleries. Tamarotchka, I know Boston and Cambridge are cultural cities too, but there is a certain atmosphere in New York that can't be matched anywhere except maybe Paris. How I envy you, but I'm supremely happy for you."

"You're one of just a few who've encouraged me to go there," I told her.

She looked surprised. "Why? What do your parents think about your new venture?"

At that, the hurt of Mama's silent treatment returned. I couldn't help it. Annitchka's kind and sympathetic understanding had made me even more vulnerable. Tears welled up in my eyes. "That's the bad part of it, Annitchka," I sobbed. "Mama is angry with Phyllis and me." Between sobs, I told her the whole story.

After listening to me, she got up. Out of the decanter on the coffee table she poured something into one of the tiny glasses on the tray. "Here, this will make you feel better, even if it is a bit too early."

"What is it?" I asked dubiously.

"Cherry brandy, darling. Drink it. You'll feel better."

Obediently, I took a sip. The brandy, strong and sweet, made me feel warm inside. "Thank you, Annitchka. This is good."

She nodded, biting her lips as she observed me. "And now," she said, after I had put down the glass, "I want you to try these." She reached over to the end table, pulled out its top drawer and took out a pack of gold-tipped cigarettes. "Here, take one. They're Swiss cigarettes and much milder than your American ones." When I had lit it, she watched my face as I inhaled. "There. Am I not right? Aren't they more pleasant?"

I didn't want to offend her by telling her that I preferred American cigarettes. "They are different, Annitchka," I told her truthfully.

All the time we had been talking, I had an uneasy feeling that she was deliberating about telling me something. I caught her eyeing me several times, about to say something, then restraining herself. Finally, to my surprise, she placed her hand on mine. "I have heard about your mama's anger. Your papa told me about it the other day when we met on the street. I know why Verotchka is angry with you and Phyllis."

"You do? Papa told you?" In my amazement I almost screamed. "Then why couldn't she have told me? Why didn't Papa? Why was he able to tell you and not me? Annitchka, what is it? Why all this mystery? You don't know the pain and agony Phyllis and I have been through."

Again Annitchka paused, uncertain how to begin. I could not imagine what she knew nor what dastardly act Phyllis and I may have committed.

"Won't you please tell me, Annitchka?" I coaxed.

"All right, I shall. But first, Tamarotchka," she watched me closely as she said, "how much do you know about lesbianism?"

"About what?"

"Lesbianism," she repeated. "Do you know what lesbianism is?"

Should I know? I wondered to myself. I had no idea what she was driving at. "No, I don't. What is it?"

She sighed, as if with relief. "Well, dear, let me explain it in a way you might understand. On the beautiful island of Lesbos sometime around the sixth century B.C., one of the most famous of ancient Greek poets, a woman named Sappho, opened a school for young women. She fell in love with one after another of the girls in her school and wrote exquisite poetry dedicated to these women. So it is that one woman's love for another woman is termed 'lesbianism,' the word derived from the island's name."

"You mean like homosexuality, only that it has to do with women in love with each other?"

"Precisely."

"My God!" Suddenly the realization of what Mama thought hit me. "Whatever gave Mama such an idea? You mean that she thought Phyllis and I? How could she? She knows us better than that. Annitchka, why didn't she ask us? Where did she get such a terrible idea?"

"From your brother, Vanya," Annitchka smiled. "It had surprised me that he would do something like that, but I never really knew him. Even if it had been true, that was not a thing to tell his mother. You yourself know that the slightest mention of sex is taboo with her. She comes from the old school."

"But Vanya did tell her." I was still in shock over that.

"Your brother can say anything to your mother, Tamara, and she believes him. I'm sure I'm not telling you something you don't know already."

"But why?" And then it dawned on me. Vanya typically would do something like this. Phyl had rejected his advances; now he was avenging himself. I told Annitchka what I thought.

"Could well be the reason," she agreed. "Your brother is such a strange person; he's quite different from you."

"Well, what should I do now? Confront Mama? Annitchka, Mama even crosses the street if she sees me coming towards her. What can I do?"

"I suggest you do nothing right now. Mama will eventually come to her senses, believe me. Go on to New York after you've told both your parents good-bye. Whether Mama refuses to listen, she'll still hear you say it. You've done no wrong."

"Thank you, Annitchka." I gave her a hug.

"And, Tamara, don't regard lesbianism in a bad way. It is just another way of life for some people. Oscar Wilde, you know, preferred men, and he was a great writer. People are different. That's why it's so interesting to be a human being observing all aspects of life."

"I realize that, Annitchka," I told her, still smarting from her disclosure. "It's difficult for me to come to terms with that kind of living, but I'll try to understand. I cannot condone it, though."

"Now, to more pleasant subjects. Who is your man of the hour right now? Is it Mac? Lanny? Someone else?"

I laughed at her questions. "Your last name, Frank, describes you perfectly. I don't know who that man is, to be honest. Mac writes me the most beautiful letters, full of his love. He's sure I love him, but he insists I am afraid to acknowledge it. Lanny? He's my dear friend. I'm not attracted to him physically, in the way I was to Mac, though. Time will tell, I guess. I'm in no hurry to get married, Annitchka. New York comes first on my list. Maybe then I'll find someone else. Right now, though, there is no someone else."

She remained silent. That's what I liked about her; she listened to what I had to say.

It had been comforting to sit with her and talk things out. Annitchka was a people-person, somewhat like Sam Klauber, but more open. I hugged her when I was leaving.

"Tamara," she said, laying her hand on my arm, "don't tell Phyllis this. She is a fine, loyal friend to you. Even though her language at times is, shall we say, hard-core, I know she is very sensitive. It will hurt her deeply to know what Vanya told Mama. Even worse than that, it will hurt her to find out that Mama actually believed him."

When I got home, the phone was ringing. Mama was nowhere around. She's probably in her bedroom upstairs, I thought. "Hello." I hastened to answer it.

"Hello, Princess. Princess"—Lanny's voice was shaking, trembling with emotion—"I've got bad news for you. I just got my orders."

"Where will you be going?" That had been a stupid question, I suddenly realized. How would he know?

"Right now, New York, Tamara, We'll be leaving tonight, so I won't be seeing you. After that, we'll probably be going overseas."

"Oh, that is bad news." I told him, and then I remembered. "Lanny, I'll be in New York myself tomorrow. I'm leaving Cambridge tomorrow morning."

"Oh, then my bad news has become wonderful news." His mood changed right away. "Then I'll meet you at the station. You'll be coming in at Grand Central?"

"Yes, my train leaves here at eight forty-five A.M."

"I'll be there to meet you, dearest." He sounded overjoyed. "Bye for now." With that, he hung up.

On this, my last night in Cambridge, I tried to talk to Mama as she and Papa sat listening to the evening news. It had been in vain. As far as she was concerned, I didn't exist. I sat down beside her on the sofa and started to put my arms around her. Quick as a cobra thrusts out its hooded head, her arm had pushed mine away. "Stay out of my sight," she warned me.

Even Papa then tried to remonstrate, but she would have none of me. "I want nothing to do with her," she told him in a hollow voice.

I went upstairs then, too broken-hearted to plead with her anymore. It was all Vanya's making. How could we be trapped into letting him do this to us? Well, I hoped he was happy in his triumph now that he had succeeded in making so many of us miserable, all because of his damnable lie.

The next morning, Loretta's brother, Manfred, came by in his car to take me to the station. If he thought it strange that Mama wasn't there by the front door beside Papa to wave good-bye, he kept his thoughts to himself. Just before I got into the car, I ran back to Papa and hugged him once more. "Papa," I told him quietly, "I've found out why Mama is mad at me. Annitchka told me. I just want you to know before I leave that what Vanya wrote is a complete lie, an absolute untruth. I've never lied to you."

At that he had hugged me to him. "I never did believe it, *dochenka*, but I'm glad you told me. In time, Mama will realize it too. Be patient, and take care of yourself in the big city."

Phyllis was at South Station to see me off. Faithful old gal. I hugged her quickly, wishing her good luck on her finals. Then I climbed up the steel steps onto the train. Manfred struggled after me, carrying my RCA player.

"When I offered to give you a ride, I didn't expect to have to lug this darned thing," he groaned, placing it on the seat.

"I'm glad you did, though," I teased him. "Give Loretta my best, and Manfred"—I pulled him down so that I could whisper in his ear—"I am surely going to miss you as my dentist."

He grinned. Manfred was a good guy. "I'll miss you as a patient, darling, but I'll be seeing you in New York one of these days. It's one of my favorite vacation spots," he patted my cheek. "I gotta go, else I'd end up going to New York with you. I wouldn't mind that so much except that I'd have to carry your RCA again. We're all rooting for you, New Yorkie." With a wave of his hand he left the coach.

As usual, the station these days was milling with uniformed soldiers lugging their duffel bags and holding packages that loving hands had prepared for them. A few of them had let out wolf whistles and called out "hubba-hubba" when Phyllis and I had walked past them.

I smiled at the soldiers, sadly thinking to myself that some of them would not be returning home. Strong and healthy they looked, filled with bravado. And where were they all going? To New York, then overseas to fight the enemy. That was the pattern nowadays.

Manfred had just stepped off onto the platform when the train gave a violent lurch forward. I waved at him and Phyl until they had become mere specks in the distance. In the window I caught sight of my own reflection: starry-eyed, smiling back at myself. Mama, Papa, and Cambridge itself were disappearing into the past. I was now on my way to another life, a new beginning.

I looked away from the window, and my thoughts turned to Papa's face when I had said good-bye. I knew that he had been trying to hide his pain, even though he had bolstered my own spirits by bragging to Manfred that I was now his "sophisticated and worldly daughter." He had appeared so lost when I looked back at him as Manfred was pulling away. Perhaps some day, and I hoped that it would be soon, Mama would see how wrong she had been. As for Vanya? I thought of the last letter I had written to him, making it cheerful and interesting, telling him about what had been going on here in Cambridge so he could visualize it for himself. How could he have had so much evil in him?

I opened up my purse to get out my Marlboros, and pulled out Mac's letters instead. Dear, faithful Mac. I pictured him as I had last seen him, walking towards me there at Camp McKay, tall, strong, looking at me with that steady, very loving, tender look. He did love me very much. I began to reread them, one letter after another, and when the train reached Grand Central Station, I felt good again.

Part III
New York City
May 1944–October 1945

33

The Office, the War, and Information

When the train finally pulled into Grand Central Station, I noticed Lanny, tall and lanky in his uniform, standing on the platform, his eyes scanning the train windows. Frantically, I waved, and finally he saw me. He hurried towards my coach, and as soon as I appeared on the steps, he grabbed my record player.

"Here, Princess, let me take that for you."

I took my other suitcases from the landing. "Honestly, Lanny, I don't know what I'd have done without you here to meet me," I said gratefully.

He smiled. "You'd have found someone. All you would have had to do was smile. You know that." He looked down at me. "Gee, I'm glad you're here."

We checked my possessions in the station lockers and walked to an Automat for sandwiches and coffee. Afterward we hiked to Fifty-seventh Street so that he could see where I would be working. It was a long walk, but he and I were used to long walks. How often we had hiked from Cambridge over the Lars Anderson Bridge to Boston and back again. We held hands like wide-eyed children, staring up at the skyscrapers and the hurrying multitudes of pedestrians. Feet, feet, there were countless feet on the hard, cement pavements of New York's sidewalks. Some New Yorkers shuffled; others hurried; still others strolled sedately, looking over, not at, their fellow men. There were people everywhere—ugly, beautiful, pockmarked, poor, wealthy, homeless, and some with just enough to live on.

"Gosh, Lanny, can you imagine how many different nationalities there are just on this street? I've seen Chinese, Japanese, dark-skinned, and light-skinned people. This truly is a melting pot of the world, isn't it?"

He squeezed my hand, "And now there is one more among them: my dear Russian princess."

I listened to my own heels clicking and smiled up at Lanny. He smiled back, "What is it, Princess?"

"I'm just terribly happy to be here. I can't help smiling at everybody. For the first time in my life, I feel free and independent."

"I think you'd feel even more free if we found you a place to live. When I'm shipped out, I'll feel a lot more comfortable knowing that you're settled."

What a dear he was. "I've got the list of places Mr. White gave me. Let's look at this address first, since it's almost across from the OWI building."

A tiny woman with short, mouse-colored hair opened the door when I rang. She did have a room to let, but when she saw Lanny with me, she announced quite firmly that she rented to women only.

I smiled at her. "I'm the person who wishes to rent your room. I'll be working for the OWI across the street."

OWI was the magic word. She opened the door to let us in.

"Come in then. I thought that maybe the two of you wanted to rent it. I'm Miss Hindman." She stressed the Miss.

I explained that Lanny was an old friend who would be leaving soon for overseas. She nodded sympathetically. I liked her immediately for her intelligence and kindness.

The room she showed us was charming; in it were a studio couch with a flowered bedspread, frilly white curtains, and two comfortable chairs covered with the same material as the bedspread. There were a desk and bookcase along one wall. I just couldn't believe my luck, especially after she told me that the rent was forty-five dollars a month. I looked at Lanny who grinned and nodded to me. "You can't go wrong, Princess," he advised me enthusiastically. He turned to Miss Hindman, asking, "When can Miss Rubleva move in?"

514

I was amused to see her reaction when Lanny had called me princess. She then inspected me with greater interest. "You may move in whenever you'd like." She addressed herself to me. "The room is ready for immediate occupancy, as you can see," she said primly.

"I'd like to move in this evening. It's a beautiful room, Miss Hindman. I'm delighted with everything: the clothes closet, the dresser with the ruffle, and most of all, my own private bathroom. It's ideal."

She apparently was not accustomed to such praise. A pleased smile accompanied by an embarrassed shrug was her answer.

"And what do you do, Miss Hindman, if I may ask?" Lanny bent his head towards her, genuinely interested.

"Oh, young man, I teach," she answered. "I give private piano lessons." That reminded her of something. "I must tell you, Miss Rubleva, that there are no cooking privileges, you know. My kitchenette is small, and it would be inconvenient for both of us. I hope you understand."

She stood there, hands clasped, a dubious smile on her lips.

"I don't plan to cook," I assured her. "I noticed a large cafeteria next to the OWI building. I plan to eat my meals there."

"Yes, that's the Admiral. It's popular with the OWI people. Handy for them and the food, from what I hear, is good." She moved towards the door. "Any questions?"

"No, everything's perfect." I was overwhelmed with my good fortune. Then it dawned on me. "Oh, I'm dreadfully sorry." I took out my wallet and counted out the bills. Jeepers, I didn't have much left from my savings after that.

Silently she smoothed out the bills and turned them right face up. Then she handed me my key.

That evening, after we had moved my suitcases into my new lodgings, Lanny took me out for dinner to a tiny French restaurant. We ate romantically by candlelight.

"I feel better now," Lanny told me. "Now when you write to me overseas I can picture exactly where you live."

"Do you have any idea where you'll be sent, Lanny?"

He shook his head. "Nope. Wherever I'm needed, I guess."

"We're doing better in the war now, aren't we?" I had caught

515

a glimpse of the headlines. I must remember to buy the *New York Times*, I reminded myself, and catch up on the news.

"We've certainly been bombing the Nazis. The Allies have been trying to take Cassino for almost three, no, four months. In spite of the constant shelling and bombing, the Germans are still holding out."

"Why is Cassino so important? What's at Cassino?" I asked.

"It's a stronghold on the way to capturing the Eternal City. The Allies have had to fight their way up the Italian peninsula, overrunning various German positions. On top of Mount Cassino, there's a Benedictine monastery where the Nazis have firmly entrenched themselves. It's only a matter of time, though, before they will have to surrender. They are being pulverized by our air power." He paused and studied my face for a moment. "Does Mac write to you, Tamara?"

"Yes, he does, Lanny."

"You have any idea of his whereabouts?"

"He's mentioned English girls and customs. I assume he's there. He also wrote about going to hear the London Philharmonic. So far, he hasn't been fighting. He writes about sightseeing, playing the piano whenever he finds one, and seeing shows. Maybe he's just writing that because he can't write about other things that would be censored."

It had been pleasant, sitting there with Lanny, watching his dear, kind face through the flickering flame. Frequently, though, I found my thoughts focusing on another face, another restaurant, another flame.

It was the eighth day of May, 1944. I awakened bright and early and proceeded to make myself presentable. No more silk camellias in my hair. I combed it into a long but neat pageboy. A dab of lipstick, a pat of rouge on my cheeks. Surveying myself in the long mirror behind my door, I decided that I looked most professional. I was excited, and also impatient, to start on my first day of work.

Miss Hindman knocked on my door. "Are you awake, dear?"

During the weekend, she and I had become better acquainted. She had been interested in the fact that I had been born in China. Having heard her play the piano, I had decided

516

that I had indeed hit upon an unusual landlady. Perhaps this would be a good omen for me.

When I opened the door, I was surprised to find her holding out a steaming cup of coffee for me. "Thought that this would start you off in the direct direction, Tamara." Her eyes casually inspected the room. I felt good that it was tidy. "I just wanted to wish you the best of luck in the world," she said with a shy smile.

Somehow I felt sorry for this lonely, little woman. Mousy haired, gentle, talented and intelligent, she lived so alone, except for the times when her students came for their lessons. Only then did she come alive, tapping her foot on the floor as she marked their time. One-two-three-four, one-two-three-four. Then she basked in her own glory, but apart from that, how terribly lonely it must be for her to live like this.

"You're so kind. Thank you." Gratefully, I drank her coffee. Then I grabbed my purse, returning the empty cup to her. "I want to get to the office early so that I can meet everyone." I smiled at her, though inside, I felt queasy.

It was quite early. Fifty-seventh Street was not yet crowded. The lobby of the OWI building was empty except for the lone elevator man waiting at his post.

"Nineteenth floor, please," I said politely.

He nodded, studying me as he pushed the button.

"You're new here?" He was a friendly sort, middle-aged.

"Yes, how did you know?"

He laughed good-naturedly. "I know most everyone who enters through those doors, and I haven't seen you before. Who's your boss?"

Nosy old codger. "Mr. White. Do you know him?"

His smile wrinkled up his face. "Sure do, honey. One of the best guys around . . . this side of heaven. You'll like working for him. No airs about him, even though he's a big shot."

That's the way I'd felt during my interview with him. I liked hearing it from someone else, though.

The door to the office was locked, but through the frosted glass I saw that the lights were on. I knocked and soon saw the shadow of a woman coming towards the door.

A young woman opened it, welcoming me as I stepped inside.

"You must be the Tamara about whom I've been hearing so much." Her English had a Russian accent, but I'd have known that she was Russian even if I had not heard her speak. She had the grace and poise of a ballerina; her face was cleanly sculptured, with high cheekbones, a beautiful jawline, and the loveliest gray eyes framed by inch-long lashes. She did not belong in an office. Instead, she should have been on the stage where people could marvel at and applaud her beauty.

"I'm Olga; Olga Philipova." She offered me her hand. "I'm a translator. Bill told me that you're going to be quite an asset to us. Come in. I'll show you your desk."

She led me to it. I saw that it was next to Erna Stenbuck's. It was a huge desk, twice as big as mine at home. Arranged on it were a typewriter, paper, carbon paper, pencils: everything that I could possibly need.

"If there is anything else you want, just ask me." She gave me an angelic smile. "You'll like it here. Bill and Erna are the best people to work for. Tamarotchka, don't be frightened by what you see. It may all overwhelm you at first, but soon you'll find that each one of us has a part to do. When we put all our work together, it becomes a complete, well-fitted entity, a magazine. This is your first job, isn't it?"

I nodded. "I have been a bit squeamish," I admitted, "but I guess that's natural. Everyone I've met has been so kind. I'm sure it'll be interesting work. The only thing that bothers me is . . . "—funny how easy it was to talk to her—"I just hope I can live up to Mr. White's expectations and," I added, "my own."

She shook her head. "Don't worry; you will. When Bill—I mean Mr. White—comes in, he'll tell you what you're to do. In the meantime, look around; get your bearings." She then went back to her desk. I came across the latest copy of *Victory* and was still reading it when Mr. White and the others came in.

"Ah, I see that Tamarotchka is already here. Good. I have some work all ready for you." He hurried into his private office and came out holding a magazine clipping. "Will you translate this into Russian for me and bring it in when you're finished?" He turned to go, then stopped. "If you require a dictionary, ask one of the Russians." With that he went into his office.

The article that he had given me had been printed in *Time*.

Well, I'll be, I thought to myself. *It's "Boston, the Cradle of Liberty."* He must have selected it for me on purpose. When I had finished translating it, I took it in to him.

He read it over carefully, then raised his head. "That's a good job, Tamarotchka. An interesting article, wasn't it?"

"Yes, I enjoyed working on it."

"Do you think you'll like it here?"

"Mr. White, I know already that I will. You've all been so good to me. How could I feel otherwise?"

He tapped the table with the knuckles of his right hand. "I may also ask you to do some proofreading as well as interview some celebrities."

"I know how to proofread, but I've never interviewed people before." The very thought of interviewing celebrities filled me with apprehension. "However, I'll do my best."

"That's what I like to hear." He lit a cigarette, staring at me through the circle of smoke that wisped in front of his face. "We'll have you doing all sorts of things here, Tamarotchka. These Russians"—he waved his hands towards the outer office—"they're great doing the translations, but their English leaves a lot to be desired—except Olga's, of course. She's great girl, amazingly intelligent, yet modest."

He gave me another translation to do, then looked down at the papers on his desk. I stood around awkwardly, then edged towards the door. I soon learned that this was his way of dismissal.

For lunch we went to the Admiral Cafeteria. Alex Makarov had insisted on treating me. "What better way to welcome a beautiful Russian into our select group," he said, when I had protested. All three Russians—Alex, Olga, and Natasha—and Tamarotchka, the newcomer, went inside the enormous restaurant.

We were a motley group: Olga, the glamorous ballerina-type girl, who had lived in Paris for most of her life; Natasha, chain-smoking, good-hearted, and thoughtful, but cynical; Alex Makarov, a remnant of old Russia, reminiscing about his hazy past and drinking to his uncertain future; and the initiate, Tamarotchka, recent graduate of a good college, trying to find out what life was all about.

519

By the time we had finished lunch and left the cafeteria to go back to work, we had all learned about each other and become good friends. Bill and Erna were still out when we returned. I settled myself at the big desk and went back to work, certain now that I had, for sure, made the right decision.

Even though Natasha Ismailova came from the Bronx, she was usually the first one at the office. Although she was much older than I, we soon became close friends. She usually waited at Admiral's for me, letting her coffee cool, smoking one cigarette after another.

"Well, Tamarotchka," she greeted me one morning, "what have you been hearing from your American lieutenant?"

She had been impressed with Mac, as had been most of the Russian Department. Ever since Mac had found out my OWI address, he had been sending his V-mail there. At first, my coworkers had not noticed. After a month or so they did, especially when Bill one day handed me several of Mac's blue V-mail letters and told me, "This young man must have your heart, the way he writes so faithfully to you." The Russians, bless them, were an inquisitive lot. Because I was the youngest and away from home for the first time, they appointed themselves my guardian angels.

"Natasha, he writes that he's now eating out of cardboard boxes and tin cans and cellophane packages. He keeps asking for more pictures of me. In fact, yesterday I received a money order from him to have myself photographed in a studio. Twenty-five dollars. Imagine!"

"You'd better do it right away on your lunch break. I'll give you the name of a good photographer. It's just about a block away . . . a five-, maybe ten-minute walk."

"Thanks, Natasha, I'll do it Friday."

"You'll do it today." She had pursed her mouth, turned those beady, black eyes, sparking fire, upon me. "You will go, Tamara Sergeivna Rubleva, at lunchtime today. If you are delayed, I will tell Mr. White that it was an emergency. I will be telling the truth. Your lieutenant deserves it."

He was not my lieutenant, but I could not argue with Natasha, nor with any of them for that matter. Even if they had not met him, they had seen his letters come in, recognizing the small, perfect handwriting, respecting his love and loyalty to me, even in the face of war.

I did have my picture taken at lunchtime. A week later, when it was ready, Natasha made sure that I mailed it right away.

When I wrote home, I addressed both Mama and Papa, as if nothing had happened. For several weeks, it was only Papa who answered. Then one day, at the end of one of Papa's letters, there was a postscript written in Mama's larger handwriting. "You remember Olga Stepanovna, my old friend in Boston. She has moved into your old room in our house. It's nice to have company." Although she had not signed it, it had made my day for I knew that Mama finally was coming around.

Miss Hindman, like the Russians, also took it upon herself to act as my guardian, although she did it more discreetly. Every evening I found my mail neatly piled on my desk. Shortly afterwards, as regularly as clockwork, she would tap on my door.

There she would be, a shy smile, eyes questioning, a covered bowl in her hands. "Tamara, I made too much soup for myself" or "I wish you'd take this meatloaf off my hands; I always make more than I should."

One day she had two plates. "I'd like you to celebrate with me. I'm a year older today."

Poor lonely lady. Except for her pupils, she had no friends.

"Do you have family?" I asked her that day.

"My brother lives in Iowa on a farm."

"Is he married?"

"No, dear, he's not married."

She volunteered little information about herself. She did tell me that she had studied at Juilliard and had planned on becoming a concert pianist, then had decided to teach instead.

"I notice that your friend, Lansing, is now overseas. He was such a delightful young man."

"Yes, Miss Hindman, he is. He's a Quaker, you know."

"And then there's a Lieutenant McNish who writes every day to you. I hope you don't mind my curiosity. His penmanship is so unusual—almost perfect."

"He's a dear friend too," I told her and smiled to myself. *He'd be mighty amused if he heard me say that to her,* I thought. Dear friend, indeed! Conceited Yank would be more like it. The very idea of insisting in almost every letter that I did love him. How did he know?

"It certainly looks as if we're now getting the upper hand, doesn't it?" Miss Hindman had settled herself comfortably in one of her flowered armchairs in my room. Shoot, I thought in dismay, there go my plans for sitting around in my slip and finishing Mildred Walker's *Winter Wheat.* I'd been reading it for a week and still wasn't halfway through it.

"Pardon me? Oh, you mean in the war. I'm afraid I haven't kept up with it lately. We've had a deadline at the office. Had to get our magazines ready for printing. My eyes have seen so much print they're about to protest." As soon as I'd said that, I regretted it. Miss Hindman prided herself on two things: her piano-playing and her knowledge of the war.

"Well, dear, I'll be most happy to fill you in." She gave me a look of sympathy. "I know how it is when your mind is occupied with other matters. I'm so glad that our Fifth Army under General Mark Clark and the British Eighth Army under their Monty's expert leadership entered Cassino. That was shortly after you came here; May eleventh, to be exact."

I was sure she wasn't mistaken. Sitting on the desk was the box of chocolates Jacques Dubois had given me the other night. Silently I passed the open box to her.

"No, thank you, dear. I don't eat chocolates. Bad for the complexion you know. As I explained to you, the Allies then pushed towards the Hitler line, taking two cities near there. They then, yesterday it was, entered the town of Velletri, which controlled the Nazi escape route along the Via Casilina to Rome. That's where the Allies are, as far as we know. Their goal is, of course, to enter the Eternal City." Her voice became hushed at the end, almost reverent in its tone.

"Thank you, Miss Hindman. I appreciate your bringing me up to date on the Western Front. At least, I know what the Russians have been doing," I told her with a smile. "Mr. White keeps us informed about them. Between you and him I'm kept alert as to what's happening on both fronts."

"The Russians have surely been unstoppable, haven't they?

I can't get over the way they crushed the German lines at Leningrad and in the Crimea. Imagine! During the winter they've been able to push out the Germans from most of the Ukraine, Crimea, Leningrad, and other regions. They've liberated more than fifty million Russians. They certainly love their Mother Russia."

I thought of Papa's pride in the Red Army. "Yes, they do, but the Americans love their freedom too. They've fought some pretty difficult battles." I remembered the photographs of American Marines in Tarawa and other islands in the Pacific, some of the wounded or dead too horrible to look at twice. We had lost a lost of men there, but the Japanese had too.

"You're right, Tamara. Our boys are brave. We're fortunate that we're so well prepared. Do you realize that we've got the most powerful navy in the world?"

"No, I knew it was good, but . . . "

"And our army is the best equipped and trained, not to speak of our air force . . . "

"I believe you; but why then, Miss Hindman, is it taking so long? That's what bothers me. If we're so invincible and all-powerful . . . "

"Well, Tamara, the Axis Powers have been well-prepared too, but the Japanese and the Germans are losing ground. Italy, we all know, surrendered last year. I'm sure it won't be too long now." She got up from the chair, her face almost made pretty by her smile. "I hope I didn't take too much of your time." She laid her hand on the doorknob. "You know, if you ever want an extra cup of coffee, my coffee pot usually has some. I don't mind."

I thanked her, relieved that she was going, yet pleased that my being here had eased her lonely existence somewhat.

After she left, I did not read *Winter Wheat*. I sat there rereading Mac's letters, and the one from Andy Thompson. Shep, my bombardier friend, had shown my picture to Andy, who then had written to me. I had now added another fine soldier to my letter-writing list.

The next morning Natasha brought in the mail. "Two for you from Lieutenant McNish," She shook her head vigorously. "Oy-yoy-yoy, what are we going to do with you, our

Tamarotchka? How can we win the war if the American army keeps writing to you?" She said it loud enough for the others to hear. Out of the corner of my eye I noticed that even Mrs. Stenbuck had raised her head.

"Oh, Natasha, if you keep teasing me, I'll write him to send his letters to Miss Hindman's." I didn't tell her that some of them were already coming there.

"Tamarotchka." She scrunched my cheeks between the palms of her hands and looked straight into my eyes. "You know we're only teasing you. We think your Mac is wonderful."

Alex and Natasha both smiled. So did Erna. Fortunately, Bill White was in his office and hadn't heard Natasha's remark.

At lunchtime, I stayed in the office, having brought a sandwich. Natasha too stayed.

"Well." She took a sip of her coffee, then took a puff of her Camel. "What does your lieutenant have to say for himself?"

I knew she was genuinely interested in him. In spite of her cynicism, Natasha was a romantic. She could quote most of Pushkin's *Eugene Onegin* by heart. When she had talked to me for the first time, she had quoted Lermontov's *Demon*. I had hoped then that she would meet Papa some day. They would get along.

"Would you like me to read you a part of it? I can't read it all because I've got to censor it. He writes beautifully."

At that she started laughing. "That would be the part I'd like to hear; but never mind, I'll listen to the duller part. Read on, Tamarotchka." She gave me her full attention.

"This letter was written after Mac hadn't heard from me for some time. You know how the mail is. Anyway, after that he got five of my letters in one day. So this is what he writes:

" 'Dearest, so far as I'm concerned, someday, truthfully, you will be my wife. If you aren't, no one else can be. I doubt if I will change my mind on that score, either. You are, so far as military terms go, my military objective, which I intend to take by storm after an initial artillery barrage. It may be an offensive or defensive maneuver, depending upon the forces you bring into play. Just as you say (and wrongly too) that I'll be good for you, I know that you'll be good for me. You'll take away my selfishness, conceit, and false pride. In return you'll give me self-assurance and confidence. I'll keep that conceit and self-interest to brush off those people on the sidelines. I'm taking care of myself. After the war, let's take good care of each other. Love, Mac.'

"How's that for a letter?" I asked.

Natasha had tears in her eyes when I looked up from the letter but then quickly turned her head away from me. "You'll be a very stupid girl if you do not marry him," she pronounced in her loud, abrupt manner. "He's a rare young man."

In my heart I couldn't help but agree with her. I often caught myself now thinking about him, even comparing him with the men I was dating in New York. They all had their good qualities; yet Mac, I was beginning to learn through his letters, had the qualities I wanted in a man.

"He's very intelligent, Natasha, but not only that. He's a warm person, and you'd like his humor. It's dry, like yours."

"Then why don't you love him, you crazy girl? Or do you?" She placed a Camel between her lips, lighting it while looking at me with her eyelids half closed.

I recalled prom night and how repulsed I had been by his drunkenness. "I haven't known him long enough," I told her.

"You're absolutely right, Tamarotchka." Olga stood behind me, her hands resting on the back of my chair. "You have to know a person really well before you decide on marriage. After all, marriage is forever. You have sworn to God."

Natasha impatiently squashed her half-smoked cigarette. "Olga, if a woman makes a mistake and marries the wrong man, she has to stay with him and remain miserable? God forgive me for speaking my mind, but in that case, the woman should get a divorce. I'm sure our blessed Lord would agree. I'm tired of people making laws according to God." She muttered and turned back to her desk, focusing on her work.

Olga smiled at Natasha's hunched back. "Tamarotchka, what I came over for is to ask you to proofread this for me. If you have time, that is."

I liked Olga. "I'll make time," I told her, looking at the article she had translated. "George Bellows, American Artist." That's right up my alley, Olga. In fact, I've just seen an exhibit of his works at the Metropolitan. I like his work."

525

She nodded. "I do appreciate it, Tamara."

That's what I liked about working here. We were like family, helping each other out. Before she went back to her desk Olga gently tapped Natasha's shoulder. "Our views on marriage may differ, but I respect you, Natasha Ivanovna, and I do wish to apologize for butting in on your conversation."

Natasha did not raise her head. "We all have our opinions," she muttered gruffly, and continued with her writing.

It was not long after this little dispute of theirs that Bill came out of his office, his usually harried face wreathed in smiles.

"I thought you folks would like to know that the Allied forces just invaded Normandy!"

Everybody stopped working. How? When exactly did it happen? Everybody started asking questions. Mr. White raised his hand for quiet. "I just heard it on the radio...not too many details yet, except that this had been planned for a long time. Thousands of our own troops had been training precisely for this. So, under cover of darkness. American and British troops poured onto the beaches of Normandy. We'll be receiving details as they come in," he told us. "Don't worry. I'll keep all of you apprised if I hear more." With that he went back into his office.

"Well, it finally happened." Alex Makarov leaned back in his chair, his hands clasped behind his neck. "D-day! Now the Germans will see that we mean business."

"And more American and British and Canadian soldiers will be killed or maimed," grumbled Natasha.

Erna Stenbuck looked over at her. "That's why I think we all should buy an extra war bond. We can do that at least. And I expect that when we find out all the details of the invasion, we'll be writing about it in our magazines. The Russians will be pleased at the news. Finally, we've fulfilled our promise to them."

I wondered about Lanny and Mac then, and dear Shep and his friend Andy, both of whom were fliers. Were they in on this invasion? Or were they in the Pacific?

"I, for one, think we ought to celebrate." Olga danced around to my desk, her lovely grey eyes shining with joy. "Come on, Tamarotchka, let's dance." She whisked me out of my chair, and we polkaed in the middle of the office. Natasha and Erna clapped their hands, while Alex surveyed us with a benevolent air. Bill White came out, cigarette in hand. "There're more details," he said.

Olga and I went back to our desks. Natasha and Erna both lit cigarettes; Alex sat up. Bill read from his note pad: "They had five beachheads; each one with a code name: Utah was the one farthest to the west, then Omaha, and Gold, followed by Juno and Sword to the east. General Dwight Eisenhower is the Supreme Commander of Allied Forces. He and Field Marshal Montgomery are in charge. The first troops to invade Normandy were parachutists and glider troops dropping behind the enemy lines. It created sheer bedlam for the Krauts," he grinned. "Afterward, under cover of darkness, American and British troops poured onto these beaches, protected from enemy gunfire by Allied planes. All in all, four thousand ships crossed the English Channel, and they were protected by the combined Allied planes, eleven thousand of them. Can you imagine what planning must have gone into this?"

"How about our casualties?" Erna asked.

"Well, from what I heard, we lost quite a few men when they were exposed to the cross-fire from Nazi machine guns as they waded ashore from their landing boats."

Alex had been quietly listening. "The Nazis must have suffered heavy casualties."

"They did say that on the radio," Bill said, "but it's only the beginning. The Allies will have to fight their way inland. In the meantime the Allied ships are unloading tanks, trucks, ammunition, supplies, and tons of materiel. What a tremendous enterprise; I can't get over it." Smiling, he walked back into his office.

527

34

Too Damn Many Friends

"You have quite a bit of mail today," Miss Hindman told me, when I got home. "I know you've been worried about Lansing and that lieutenant with the Scottish name, McNair, is it?"

"You must mean Lieutenant McNish," I said, my heart skipping a beat. It was about time I heard from both of them.

"There were also two letters from Private Rublev. Is he a relative?" Her questioning tone annoyed me. Besides, I didn't want to explain about Vanya. I didn't feel kindly towards him.

"He's a relative," I told her. *Distant,* I should have added. It still rankled me how he had slandered Phyllis.

Once inside my room, I tore open Mac's letter, then laid it aside without reading it. I'll read what Vanya has to say first. That'll be the medicine that I have to take. Then Mac's letter will be the antidote to counteract the bitterness.

It was a good thing I had done that. The more I read of Vanya's letter, the angrier I got. I stared at the scrawly handwriting, picturing him writing to me, grinning his self-satisfied grin: He still could not understand my treatment of our mother who had done so much for me. He cautioned me that all of us make mistakes, that since we like to be pardoned so also should we learn to pardon. He sounded almost biblical. Not a word, though, about what he had done to fuel Mama's anger against Phyllis and me. I read the next lines, astonished at his audacity. Because of my terrible behavior towards Mama, he was lying awake nights! As a result of not having enough sleep, his work had suffered! *Oh, boy, Vanya,* I thought, *how like you! It's always someone else's fault. You blame me, your sister in the United States, for not doing well in the army overseas.* Par for the course; I wasn't surprised at all.

His second letter was in much the same vein except that he ordered me to send him milk chocolate, cocoa, and some *good* toffees.

There was a soft rapping on my door. It was a good thing that I hadn't taken off my street clothes yet.

"Come on in, Miss Hindman. The door's unlocked."

She came in noiselessly, holding a covered dish. "If you aren't going out tonight, I thought you might like this. I tried a new chicken recipe today."

It had been a long, tiring day for me, but her eyes had been so hopeful. She had probably slaved over this just for me, the poor thing. Her cooking was not the best, but her life was one of the loneliest.

"How terribly thoughtful of you," I exclaimed. "I was just about to read Mac's letter. If you'll just wait till I finish it? Then we can catch up on each other's doings."

She was hesitant. "You're sure I'm not in the way?"

"No," I had been scanning Mac's letter, and it looked safe enough to read out loud. "Would you like to hear what Mac has written? It's about the war."

Her eyes brightened. Anything about the war aroused her interest. "If you think . . ."

"I wouldn't offer to read it for you if I didn't want to," I told her. "Make yourself comfortable." After she had curled up in the other armchair, I explained, "This was written from 'Somewhere in France.' He'd been in England up till now. . . . Miss Hindman, I'll bet he had a part in the invasion."

"You may be right," she mused. "He may even be somewhere in Normandy."

"Well, here's what he says:

"'Another eventful day has passed here in the land of romance, knights, and castles. In my foxhole everything is hunky-dory. Improvements have been added hourly: shelves, hangers for my clothes, steps down into my cellar. A refrigeration unit has been added within the half hour.

" 'At night I try to go to sleep, and eventually do doze off. I've gotten accustomed to all the noises of the night and probably when they cease, I'll be unhappy to sleep anyway. The moles that bore underground and suddenly propel themselves out of their tunnels into the open air of our foxholes and then crawl across our faces, arms, or the rest of our bodies are an animal alarm clock that wakens the soundest sleepers among us.

" 'It's amazing how religious everyone has become around here. That there are no atheists in foxholes is right.

" 'Perhaps the most astonishing reaction of everyone to war is: *Is this all there is to it?* At night the area resembles a Fourth of July celebration with beautiful flares in the sky. It is breathtaking in the morning to see our airplanes streaming overhead to blast hell out of the devils over the hills beyond us. Yesterday, I fell asleep out in the open with very little on and got very suntanned.

" 'It's strange that when you're out here you get so damn hungry for the simplest things: hamburgers and malted milk shakes. One of the men said last night he always liked pork and beans and never got enough of them, but now that he is in the Army and came clear across the ocean, he's so damn tired of them, he isn't sure if he ever did like them.

" 'Then there is the ration of water—one canteen a day—and that is a hardship, but not one that we can't overcome. I manage to keep myself clean shaven, but it's a job. However, I feel so much better when I've shaved, it's worth the effort to keep up some semblance of the decency that supposedly goes along with civilization.

" 'Rumors—they fly around here thick and plentifully. The strangest ones too. Sometimes they turn out to be true; other times they are just fiction. The other day we listened to a war correspondent describe action up on the front line not too far away from us; it sort of gave us a weird feeling.' "

I laid the letter down. "He definitely must have been in the invasion." I was convinced. I went on, reading to myself: "He ends up asking how I like my work," I told her. I didn't tell her that Mac had asked if I'd heard from Vanya or that he'd reminded me at the end that he loved me.

"Lieutenant McNish sounds like a strong man," Miss Hindman slowly nodded her head. "He's seen some of the war. It's there, written between his lines."

"Someday I hope to find out if he really was in the invasion," I told her. "How are your piano lessons coming along? I hear that student of yours who comes on Thursdays. He or she, whoever it is,"—I smiled at her—"has been playing well. I liked that sonata that I heard the last time. What was it? It was beautiful."

"Oh, that must have been Beethoven's *Der Sturm*. Yes, Carol plays it well. She has been studying with me . . . "—she paused, counting on her fingers—"must be close to four years now. And how are things with you these days?" she asked.

Since the invasion news I had been working overtime, and

The Buddies, New York

she and I had had time only for hasty greetings. "Oh, Mr. White's been without a secretary for . . . well, ever since the second part of May. I've not only had proofreading, translating, and other things to do, but I've also had to fill in as part-time secretary for him. He's a dear, delightful person, but I've had quite a time, not knowing shorthand and trying to keep up with his speedy way of dictating."

"That's too bad," she said, her eyes full of sympathy.

"Well, I believe he's finally found a secretary. He's interviewed plenty of applicants, but it's difficult to find one who can speak and write correctly, and organize the work effectively. If he doesn't choose Miss Coleman, then he's making a big mistake. She seems very efficient, but she's also a charming, very personable young woman."

"Well then, he'll probably choose her." Miss Hindman got up, thanked me for my hospitality, and left as quietly as she had entered.

Claire Coleman was beautiful; her short, black glossy hair was naturally curly; her skin was as clear as a baby's, and her hazel eyes were fringed with long, straight lashes that cast a bluish glow across her cheekbones. She wore a navy suit with a white blouse. She was my age, perhaps, and about my height. I was delighted that Mr. White had hired her.

She spent most of the day closeted in Mr. White's office, taking notes and typing away. Bill, when we saw him, looked more relaxed and happier than he'd been in a long time.

At lunchtime we took Claire to the Admiral Cafeteria. I smiled to myself.

"What're you looking so smug about?" Natasha grumbled, giving me an affectionate look.

"I remember when all of you brought me here for the first time."

"Well, she deserves as much." Natasha picked up a tray. "She looks efficient, and besides that, she has good manners." She looked at my empty tray. "Are you broke again? You want me to lend you some money?"

I laughed, "No, I just haven't seen anything I want so far. Give me time."

Claire and I hit it off right away. It became usual for us to eat together, mostly at Admiral's, since that fit our budgets best. She told me about Moshe, the boyfriend she'd left in Washington. In turn, I told her about Mac, Lanny, Shep, and the other men to whom I wrote.

Some Sundays we splurged and went to Longchamps for brunch.

"They're famous for their popovers," Claire told me. It was fun sitting outside at a sidewalk table, watching the world stroll by. At other times we took the subway clear into the garment district where Claire introduced me to the delicatessen restaurants. There I learned to like pastrami on Jewish rye bread and prunes swimming in sour cream.

All this time Erna Stenbuck watched over us like a mother hen, smiling at our exuberance and friendship. One day she suggested, "I don't see why you two girls don't share an apartment. It would be much easier on your budgets. I've never seen two girls get along so well together. You're perfect buddies."

That name stuck. Claire became Buddy One since, she was a few months older, and I was Buddy Two.

Claire had been staying temporarily at the apartment of her cousin Dora. However, she wanted to be more independent. When she heard about a friend who was being relocated and wanted to sublet her apartment, she couldn't wait to tell me.

"I've got tremendous news, Tamara."

"What is it?"

"This gal has an apartment near Greenwich Village. She wants to sublease it. Shall we give it a try?"

"Okay; I'm willing."

We went to see the apartment after work. It was perfect. It sported a tiny kitchenette; a living room furnished with two wide couches; a deep, long closet in the hallway; a bookcase; a nice-sized bathroom, and a huge room in the back.

"That'd make a terrific guest room," Claire exclaimed.

"The good thing is that she left everything here, even dishes and linens," I said, checking out the cupboards.

"But the main thing is the rent; it's thirty dollars apiece

plus utilities halved. I think we can swing it once a month, don't you, Buddy?"

I nodded, impatient already to make the move. "But first I have to tell Miss Hindman. That's going to be the hard part."

Actually, it hadn't been. I had cornered her that very evening when I came in and saw her in her foyer. She had just come in and was removing the hat pins from her hat. When she saw me, her face brightened.

"You're a bit late, aren't you?"

Another mother hen, I thought with a pang. Well, here goes; I steeled myself for the pathetic expression that I was sure would follow my notice.

"Claire and I were looking at an apartment near the Village," I told her. "Miss Hindman, it's just perfect for the two of us." I watched her face. It had not changed, so I continued. "I'd like to give you my two weeks' notice. I'm sure you'll have no trouble renting. In fact"—the idea had just hit me—"I'll put a sign on the OWI bulletin board."

She had smiled then, "No need to do that, dear. I had been dreading to talk to *you*." She sighed, as if relieved of a heavy burden. "You see, my brother Edmund has sold the farm in Iowa and wants to move in with me . . . that is, until he can find a place of his own. I've been wondering how to tell you without hurting your feelings. Well, the good Lord solved our problem, didn't He?" She gave me a light pat on the back. "And don't worry about giving notice. You can move out whenever you'd like."

I couldn't wait to give Claire the good news. "Can you believe it?" I asked when I called her over the phone.

Of course she had been delighted. "And Tamara,"—I couldn't get over her efficiency—"if you need help in moving, I've got just the guy: Matt Tuttle. He's an architect, family friend, and very likable, a teddy-bear sort of fellow. He's got a car and will be tickled to help us out."

I had been worried about moving. During these two months my record and book library had grown quite a bit. None of my friends here owned a car.

A week later Claire and I were settled in our new apartment. Matt had turned out to be exactly how she had described him, a teddy-bear kind of guy with a heart of gold.

When I tried to thank him he had looked at me with those bulgy black eyes of his and, grinning, had patted my shoulder. "I shall be coming here for dinner, you know. Why do you think I helped you move? A man always has a motive behind his good deeds." I could not believe that about Matt. He was as sweet and dear as a lamb.

Miss Hindman did have tears in her eyes when I left, but so did I.

"You'll come to visit us, won't you, Miss Hindman?" I had already given her my new address.

"Oh, definitely, dear." She had given me a quick hug. "Take care of yourself. I'm sure you and Claire will enjoy your new apartment."

"We'll be seeing you then." I looked back at her once while hurrying towards Matt's Chevrolet.

I had not imagined how much fun it would be to live in our own apartment. Claire had the disposition of an angel. Nothing riled her. Even office deadlines didn't faze her. She was a perfect roommate.

We had been in the apartment for only one week when we got the phone call.

"Yes?" Claire had answered it. She smiled, passing the phone on to me. "Some woman," she whispered, holding her hand over the mouthpiece. "Husky voice."

"Hello; this is Tamara Rubleva."

When I heard her chuckle, I knew. "So you've moved, huh? Why the devil didn't you let me know? I had a devil of a time with that Russian woman at your office. Would you believe it? She didn't want to give me your phone number."

"Oh, Natasha?" I laughed. "She's very protective of me. Has to check everybody whom I go out with and so forth, Phyl. But tell me, where are you?"

"I'm calling from home. As you may surmise, we graduated recently. Well, I've got great news for you."

"You're coming to New York."

"How'd you guess? Yep; come eight days from now. Norma Howard; you remember her? Also an English major. Well, she and I both have secretarial jobs starting two weeks from today. Is today the sixteenth? My God, *tempus fugits* too fast for me, although I'm impatient to get there."

"Why didn't you write?" I chided her. "I wrote you three letters and got only one answer."

"You know damned well what a lousy correspondent I am." There was a pause. I heard the scratch of a match and smiled to myself. "Besides, you yourself know how hectic exams and the final days can be. Anyway, it's all over now."

"What about a place to live?" I asked her. "Can I help you in any way?"

"Uh-uh," she laughed, "we've got an apartment. A friend of Norma's owns an apartment house. It do make it nice to have rich pals, don't it? Well, I gotta go. Can't afford to talk longer." Still laughing, she said good-bye and hung up.

"You know, I'm beginning to worry," I told Claire, after I had explained to her about Phyl. "I've had good news all this time, one thing after another. Getting this apartment with you, Phyl coming, meeting such a rare person as Matt . . . sometimes I'm afraid that my good fortune can't last."

"Ah, Buddy, sure it will. You're a good person; you are happy; you've got many friends. Don't be so fatalistic. That doesn't go with your nature."

It must have been my intuition, but something did happen to cloud my happy existence. It wasn't Mama, since she had finally come around. We were now writing letters to each other as if nothing had ever happened. It was Sam's unexpected arrival in New York and the news he had brought me about Mac. I had been so elated on hearing his voice and even more delighted to see him waiting for me in the downstairs lobby of the OWI building.

He had not changed, except perhaps that his face was thinner. "What are you doing here, Sam? Have you got news of Mac? I haven't heard from him for some time. . . ."

He had patted my face in his Uncle Sam manner. "Let's find a quiet place where we can talk, darling. I don't have much time."

We went to the Russian Tea Room and found a secluded corner. Since it was daytime, they were not that crowded.

"It's about Mac," his voice was physicianlike in its composure. "I want you to deluge him with letters, encouraging ones, because he needs you now more than ever."

His seriousness alarmed me. "But what is it, Sam?"

"He's been placed in a position where he can be court martialed." Sam's eyes pierced into me. "He's been accused of something terrible; yet he's completely innocent of the charge."

"Sam, tell me please. What has he done? Where is he?" I asked, visualizing all sorts of alarming things.

"Tamara, I can't tell you. I've already told you more than I should have, but I did it because I know that only you can cheer up our Mac. If you do love him, then tell him that. He needs to know it now. His life, darling, is in danger."

"But, Sam, why?" I felt the tears clouding my eyes.

"That's the army for you. But it'll be all right, don't worry. He'll come through this; he's come through a damned lot already. You don't know what a noble, courageous person he's been throughout this hellish ordeal." He remained silent after that, lost in his own thoughts.

"Sammy, I'll write to him. Promise me one thing," I asked. "You did say that he'll be all right, that he won't be court-martialed, didn't you?" All this information was frightening and confusing, too full of intrigue for me.

He tapped his fingers on the table. "I can't promise you that. There's a five percent doubt, okay?" He smiled at me. "You're beautiful as ever, little Russian."

"When did you arrive here, Sammy?"

He put on his dark glasses. "I've been on furlough, darling. Visited Chelsea and my family, then swung by here to see you before I go back. I'll give Mac your love." He planted a kiss on my cheek and laid some money on the table. "See that that pretty waitress gets a tip. I've got to go." As I got up, he gave me a hug. "Now don't you go around moping or worrying. Just write to him right away."

Needless to say, I did worry and wonder. What could have happened for Mac to have to face court-martial? Something had happened, something very serious. I pictured Mac's face last Christmas, his eyes looking down at me—tenderly, filled with serene joy, knowing that I loved him. Could he have gotten drunk again? Was he a Dr. Jekyll and Mr. Hyde kind of person? No, Mac

The 519th Port Battalion. Mac is fourth from right (standing) and Sam Klauber is third from right (with dark glasses).

could never be that evil. Just what had happened?

I did not tell Claire or anyone else about what Sam had disclosed to me. That night I wrote a long letter to Mac. I did not find it difficult telling him that he remained constantly in my thoughts and prayers. "As God and Confucius help me on my path of life"—I smiled to myself . . . as usual, I couldn't be plainspoken—"I realize how much you mean to me." I just couldn't write him that I loved him, though, as Sam had suggested I do. I didn't really know for sure.

Several days later, somewhere around the last of June, I received a phone call at the apartment. Claire had gone out for the evening.

"Yes?"

The voice at the other end was a strange one. "Miss Rubleva? Tamara Rubleva?"

"Yes, I am Tamara Rubleva," I answered.

"This is James Martin," said the voice. "You don't know me, but I know a very fine friend of yours in the 519th Port Battalion, 305th Port Company. I think you know who it is I'm talking about: Lt. John P. McNish. I wondered if I might visit you this evening?"

My heart skipped a beat. "Lieutenant McNish? Is he all right?"

He had a hearty laugh. "Oh, yes, old J.P. is okay. That's why I'd like to see you, to explain what has happened over there. Is it all right if I come over?"

"Of course, it is. Where are you calling from?"

"I'm in the lobby of your apartment house. J.P. gave me the address."

Claire would have told me, "You're all a-dither." That's the way I felt. I was tingly, excited, and happy, all at the same time. I ran from the bathroom after combing my hair, stared into the hall mirror at myself, and checked to see if there was any Chianti left in the refrigerator. No? Yes, there it was, behind the buttermilk carton. Then I heard the doorbell.

James Martin smiled at me, then stepped in. "You're Tamara? Yes, I recognize you from your pictures. Mac has them plastered all over his foxhole." He looked around at the apartment. "Nice." He fished into his jacket pocket. "Mind if I smoke my pipe?" he asked, as he placed it in the corner of his mouth.

"No, I enjoy the smell of pipe tobacco." I looked at his insignia. "Would you like some Chianti?" Thank God we had some.

"Sure, thanks." He settled back on Claire's couch. I noticed that he wore a wide wedding band which immediately put me at ease. Some of the soldiers on furlough were wolves, and Claire and I steered clear of them.

After some polite talk he told me about Mac. "He's gone through hell and back," he told me. "Fortunately he's got so many friends among his men and commanders that he did not even have to face trial. It was a tough time, though, for him, and all of us. We sweated with him . . . for him."

I was even more impatient now to learn what the problem had been. Both he and Sam had skirted around the subject.

He dug inside his jacket pocket. "I'll leave these papers with you for you to read at your leisure. You can see they're marked CONFIDENTIAL." He handed them to me. "I think I'd better explain to you what happened. Then you'll be able to make better sense of these bureaucratic reports."

I thanked him. He took a sip of the Chianti I had poured. "Mm-m, that's good. I like it this way—cold. Now about your Lieutenant McNish. Before I start, let me tell you how overjoyed he was at the news of my departure for New York. Since I'm communications officer on a Liberty ship, I'm here in New York at regular intervals. Anyway, he told me to be sure to tell you that he loves you very much." He paused to relight his pipe.

Golly, but he was a talker. I wished he'd get on with Mac's problem, but apparently he disliked being rushed.

I refilled his glass, at which he nodded his thanks. "You know that there were five beachheads for the invasion in Normandy. I'm sure you've read about that. Well, old Mac and his two sections had been sent up the coast to a new beach that had just been opened. There he and his men were to begin unloading materiel from an English coaster that was offshore. When he and his men got aboard ship, he found out it was the same coaster on which he had served as observer during preinvasion maneuvers two months before in the Bay of Bristol."

I kept my eyes on the lieutenant, hoping he wouldn't stop.

"So actually it was a sort of reunion for him and the officers and crew. The men were unloading ammunition from the ship during the morning." Again, his damned pipe went out. He filled it with some fresh tobacco from his pouch, then tried lighting it once more. I watched the tobacco turn a glowing red. *God and Confucius be thanked,* I intoned silently. He continued, "During the afternoon, enemy shells began landing around the ship. It was now beached on dry land since the tide had gone out and therefore couldn't be moved. Moreover, two of the hatches were still filled with gasoline drums to be unloaded last."

"You mean they were on a ship loaded with gasoline below the deck, being shelled by enemy gunfire, and beached high and dry?"

"Yep. Several enemy 88-mm shells had landed on the port side and some on the starboard side. It was only minutes before one would land on the ship. Because of the shelling no more DUKWs came out to take on gasoline from the ship."

"Ducks?" I felt ashamed of my ignorance of army terms.

"Yeah, first of all, they are code-designated D-U-K-W, hence duck. They are two and one-half-ton trucks with propellers that drive them in the water and a watertight hull that keeps them afloat. Each has six wheels for travel on land. They carry materiel and/or troops on land or sea. Since there were no DUKWs, do you see the situation Mac and his troops were in?"

"You mean that they were supposed to unload gasoline drums from the ship onto DUKWs . . . only the DUKWs weren't coming out to the ship because of the shelling, right?"

"That's it in a nutshell. But the scenario gets worse. The ship's captain decided to abandon ship and shut down the boilers. That meant no power for the winches that raise the pallets of gasoline drums from below in the hatches. Even if there had been DUKWs the men couldn't have unloaded the gasoline. No steam power. It was a no-win situation: hell if you do, and hell if you don't."

I took in a deep breath. "It must have been extremely dangerous to be there with the gasoline and shells landing around the beached ship."

"You'd better believe it," he emphasized. "Well, the ship's captain and his crew left the ship, and Mac didn't have to decide what to do next. An army captain pulled up alongside the ship and told Mac that his men were to leave the ship and go ashore. They climbed overboard and went down the ladders along the ship's side onto the beach. As they walked to the shore about a quarter mile away, DUKWs came out, picked them up, and everybody made it ashore. The captain and Mac were the last to leave the ship."

"Isn't that what they were supposed to do? The captain is always the last one to abandon ship, isn't he? What was the problem?"

"You'll see. That came later. I forgot that Sam had already been here in the States and talked to you. I know I'm making this a long story, but I'll try to make it shorter. First though, Tamara, where is your bathroom? Down the hall?"

"Yes; the right," I told him.

When Jack returned, he stretched himself. "I'm sorry. I realize you're anxious to hear what happened next. Well, Mac and his men were finally ordered to go back on board ship. The captain and his crew also returned. They then proceeded to unload the gasoline."

"But what about the shelling? Weren't they still in danger?"

"Good question, Tamara. We didn't find out the answer until several days later. What happened was that a squad of our soldiers had been climbing the cliffs in the area looking for gun emplacements when suddenly, out of a cave above them shot the barrel of a German eighty-eight. They immediately hurled grenades into the cave, and that was the end of the eighty-eight, the gunners, and their ammo. It was this eighty-eight-millimeter gun that had been firing down on the beach. When it was wiped out, there was no more shelling of the beach." Jack paused to take a sip of Chianti.

"But if Mac and his men went back to the ship and the shelling stopped, and they unloaded the gasoline, what was the problem?"

"Late that afternoon, your lieutenant was placed under arrest."

"What? Why?" I couldn't believe it.

"For cowardice under enemy fire; that was the charge. He was confined to his foxhole. After a week's investigation General

Wharton ordered that the charges be dropped and no further action be taken in the matter."

"But why cowardice?" I repeated softly. In my eyes Mac had been a hero. He hadn't deserted his men. He had been the last to leave the ship. "Didn't you say that he left *after* the captain? Usually it's the captain of the ship who leaves last, isn't it?"

"Yes, very definitely. Mac had done the right thing; at least that's the way all of us saw it. Believe me, he sure had everybody rooting for him."

"Another thing I can't understand is that if Mac really had been a coward under enemy fire, then the ship's captain had been a coward too, don't you think? Hadn't he abandoned his ship? Was he charged with cowardice under enemy fire too?"

"A lot of us thought that Mac did what we would have done under the circumstances. As for the captain, the colonel who pressed the charge couldn't do a thing to him because he was British. Since Mac was American, he got charged," Lieutenant Martin explained.

"So that's why Sam told me Mac was in such danger."

"Sure thing. If he'd been found guilty as charged, he'd have been shot. Boy, you should have seen him, sitting beside his foxhole. Everybody stopped to talk to him, bring him food, books, whatever they thought might cheer him up. He was holed up like that for a week. Then the charges were dropped."

My poor Mac! How I wished that I could have been there with him and taken him in my arms, told him that I understood, that he was my hero, and always had been.

"You know the colonel who had brought the charge? That son-of-a-bitch had pressed the charge and had personally taken off Mac's bars. When he later had Mac brought to him outside his concrete stronghold on the beach, the brave colonel told Mac that the charges had been dropped because, listen to this, because he had 'too damn many friends.'

"Mac later told me that he had requested the colonel to return his bars and pin them back on his shirt since the colonel had been the one who'd removed them. Well, the bastard told his aide (who had witnessed all this) that he was to get them from his desk in the concrete headquarters where the colonel had placed them and pin them back on Mac. He then had left.

"The aide got the bars, returned, and pinned them on Mac's shirt, telling him that he was proud to so, feeling now that the wrong had been righted."

"Thank you for telling me all this," I told James, when he had finished. "The war has been horrible enough, but to go through something like that? How terrible to have it happen, especially to someone like Mac."

The lieutenant rose to leave. "I've kept you long enough, but it has been most enjoyable, meeting you and being in this cozy apartment. I have to go back to the ship now; we leave for Europe soon, and when I see Mac again, I'll tell him, 'Mission accomplished.'"

"Will you please give Mac my love and tell him also, James, that I have finally found some Sportsman's cologne here. I bought some for myself, and I'll be wearing it all the time to remind me of him."

The lieutenant laughed. "He'll be pleased to hear that, I'm sure. If Sportsman's cologne is that powerful, I'll have to get some for my wife."

35

The Eye of the Beholder

Phyllis stepped into the apartment, handing me the elegantly wrapped packages. "Something for you two," she grinned.

"Gee, thanks; but you shouldn't have spent money on us." I turned to Claire, saying, "This glamorous young lady is the very one I've been telling you about. Phyl, this is Claire Coleman, the Buddy Number One I described in my letters. Now the two of you know each other." I heaved a sigh of relief. Thank God. I hated introducing people.

They shook hands. "I hope you don't believe what Tamara told you about me," Phyl teased.

She looked terrific, a far cry from the sloppy collegiate in her loose cardigan, skirt, and loafers. Wearing a simple, black hip-hugging, shoulder-padded dress, she looked like a Fifth Avenue glamour girl. I let out a low wolf whistle. "Jeepers, Phyl, what a couple of days in New York did to you. What'll a couple of weeks do to you?"

She grinned. "You don't look so bad yourself, chum. Why don't you unwrap that long package I gave you. I spent quite some time choosing which bubbly stuff to get for this reunion."

"Isn't Norma with you?" I asked.

"She sent regrets. This guy she's been going with is being shipped out tomorrow. She wants to spend today with him since it'll be their last day together."

"More and more fellows are going overseas," Claire said softly. "It just doesn't seem fair, does it?"

Phyl glanced at her. "Yep; but, Claire, nothing's fair in

wartime." She turned to me. "Did you hear that the American Marines have landed on Saipan, Tamara? The news said that the fighting was the fiercest since Guadalcanal."

"Yes, but that happened a week ago, didn't it? They've now landed on Guam."

"I didn't know about that," Phyl smiled. "I've been swamped lately what with moving here into the new apartment and starting on a job all at once. Tonight's the first time I've been able to relax."

"It's hard to keep up with the news," Claire agreed. "We're fighting in so many places at once that I keep having to find them in the atlas."

Phyl reached into her purse, "Yes, the Pacific, the European Theater . . . "

"That's where Mac and Lanny are . . . in Europe," I told her. "And then there's Shep and his friend Andy. They're flying bombers over the Pacific."

"Ah, Shep; I remember him," Phyl said. "I didn't know he was a flier. Who's this Andy? Friend of his?"

"Shep introduced him to me via airmail," I explained. "I like his letters. I know him only through them."

"Oh," Phyl lit a cigarette, looking around the room. "I like your apartment. It's okay. It's cozy."

"Yeah; we like it; don't we, Buddy?" Claire smiled.

"Phyl, what's your apartment like?" I asked. Claire had gone to our kitchenette to open the champagne. Soon we heard the pop as the cork flew out.

"It's the best," Phyl blew out some smoke. "We're on the other side of you and have a beautiful view of the Hudson River. In fact, Norma and I took a walk yesterday after work. We watched the sun go down over the water. And, Tamara, we've got a fireplace."

"Except you can't light it now in this warm weather." Claire laughed, gingerly carrying the tray. "Look, gals, take a glass before I have an accident."

"What shall we drink to, ladies?" Phyl held up her glass.

"Why not to your success here?" suggested Claire. "The best of luck to you and Norma in your great venture in this big, bad, delightful city of New York!"

"*Skoal,*" Phyl clinked her glass with each of ours. "Mm-m, this tastes good; if I say so myself."

"And now,"—I raised my glass once more—"let's drink to our soldier boys overseas."

"Amen." Phyl said. "May this damned war end soon."

We clinked again, less boisterously than before.

"Oh, darn!" Claire gave me a guilty look, then got up, and walked over to the bookcase. "That reminds me, Tamara. I've committed a dreadful sin." She picked up the V-mail that lay beside her purse. "This came with Mr. White's mail this morning. I was going to give it to you, but I plumb forgot about it until now. Gosh, I'm sorry."

"Thanks." I took the letter. "It's from Mac. You don't mind if I read it now, do you?"

"We'd mind if you didn't," Claire assured me.

She and Phyl talked about New York while I read. They were both laughing at something when I had finished reading.

"I meant to ask you about Mac," Phyl said. "Is he still crazy enough to love you?"

"He certainly does love Tamara," Claire declared, looking at me with affection. "His letters show it. Tamara's read parts of them to you, I'm sure."

"She has, Claire, and you said it. He does love Tamara. She doesn't realize how lucky she is."

"Oh, I do, Phyl. I know that he loves me. It's only that I'm not sure of my own feelings. That's why I still date other men. Remember that I didn't start dating until I was in college. Dating wasn't done in China. I just don't know men as well as you gals do."

"Hah," Phyl snorted in amusement. "You certainly have dated more men in these three and a half years than I have since I was sixteen."

"All right, girls, now stop fighting." Claire put up her hands in mock protest. "What does your Mac say, if I may ask?"

"He tells me that he has been in the invasion. Gee, I wish I'd had this letter when I last spoke to Miss Hindman. I told her I had a feeling that he had been in it."

"What does he say about the invasion?" Phyl asked.

"I'll read you that part. Here goes.

" 'I've seen it—the biggest thing on earth—the invasion. What a sight! I had to read *Time* magazine to realize the magnitude and scope of it all. At times I just gawked, with my mouth wide open, and gazed in awe at the overwhelming striking power the Allies had massed for this great task. When we pulled in toward the beach, we were watching a destroyer shelling a town on the beach. All of us were so intent we didn't notice the naval officer purr up alongside in a PT boat and yell out through a megaphone, 'What's your cargo?'

" 'Everyone knew, but no one answered. Finally one of our wise guys yelled out, 'Hot knishes and Pepsi-Cola too!' The officer hurriedly wrote it down on a pad, and the PT zoomed away. I'll bet they are still looking for that hot-knish and Pepsi-Cola ship off Normandy.' "

Phyl guffawed at that. "Just like Mac to see the humor in things. Still, it must have been hell. Can you imagine all those men crawling ashore on the beaches with shelling all around them?" Lazily she stretched out her long legs. "Hey, Tamara, when are we going to eat? I'm starved. It's been quite a day for me."

"Wait a sec, Phyl. I just want to read this part to Claire," I said. "Remember when we went to Jones Beach, and Matt took pictures of us? I wrote about it to Mac. Here's his reply:

" 'It was sweet of you to think of me when you were riding back from Jones Beach. Perhaps I could be persuaded to go to that beach again with you when I return, but after riding on sand and out through the wet surf for almost ninety days and nights, sand, waves, surf, and ships don't seem that romantic. Thank God you can swim on a beach over in America without anti-tank obstacles studding the sand, without little wooden posts stuck in the sand with tellermines atop so that during high tide anything that hits one of them sets off the mine and, if it's a boat loaded with cargo or people, they are no more. Jones Beach has no 88's that can shell it and raise ugly splotches on the smooth stretches of sand. There are no pillboxes along the beach with silent guns pointing at you, are there? There are probably no sunken ships offshore to remind you of days past. I'm glad of that, for when you see all of these things and continue with the monotony of sight, sound, task, and scenery, it has an unerasable effect upon the memory.' "

"Boy! I can imagine how he feels." Claire shuddered.

"It's all in the eye of the beholder, isn't it?" Phyl mused.

I put the letter down. "Okay, I'll bring out the food."

"When did you have time to cook?" Phyl carried her champagne to the table.

"Last night, when we found out you were coming. It's not much, just cold cuts and salad from the deli. That's how we eat during the week, unless we're invited out. On weekends, when we have more time, we cook hot meals: roasts, and stuff. That's when our old buddy, Matt Tuttle, comes over."

At the mention of a man's name, Phyl perked up. I laughed at her awakened interest. "Forget it, Phyl; he's not your type. His first loves are architecture and photography. He likes to take photographs of us with buildings and bridges as a backdrop."

"Ah-ha," Phyl looked at the two of us, grinning.

"Honestly, Phyl," I tried to convince her, "you'll see when you meet him. He's not a wolf. He's a lamb." I got the platters out of the fridge.

Phyl's eyes got big. "God Almighty, don't expect such fancy stuff when you visit us on West End Avenue."

We made our own sandwiches with pastrami and rye bread. Phyl especially liked the kosher pickles. "I think I'm going to like it here in New York," she decided.

"It's much more enjoyable than I ever thought it would be," I told her. "I never thought an office job could be such fun."

"Tamara, our office is an exception," Claire corrected me. "It's because of the Russians, Phyllis. They're so lively, friendly, and outgoing that a person can't be stuffy around them. Now if it were only you and I with Erna and Bill, Tamara, mark my words—it would be reserved and professional. You could not polka inside the office the way you and Olga sometimes do."

While Claire washed her hair, Phyl and I cleaned up. It was a chance for us to talk privately about everybody and everything.

"I like Claire," Phyl said, wiping the glasses. "She strikes me as being very efficient and calm."

"She is," I agreed, "and she's also very tactful. Phyl, she's good for me. She makes sure I pay my bills first before spending all my salary on records or clothes."

549

"It sure do go fast, don't it?" Phyl opened a cupboard. "Where do you keep your glasses?"

"Here." I showed her. "Gee, I'm glad you're here."

"So'm I, believe me. Oh, by the way." She lowered her voice. "How's Mama? Still mad?"

"No, not any more," I told her, "but it took a long time. Finally she did write, at first only a postscript to Papa's letter, then a half-page addition. Now she's writing letters longer than Papa's. She's busy at the RWR and the Harvard Faculty Club and is even selling war bonds. She's also painting with oils again."

"I'm really glad for her and for you," Phyl said. "What about your brother? Still overseas?"

"Yes, I believe he's still in Italy. He writes regularly, mostly because he wants candy from me. That he likely gives to his girlfriends. Every letter describes still another girl with whom he's fallen in love." I didn't tell her that I wrote to him only to please the folks. Otherwise he'd complain to them, and I'd be in trouble once more. "His last letter mentions a friend, Eugene, who'll be coming to New York on furlough and wants to meet me. He saw my photo and thinks I'm pretty."

"You'd better watch out, girl," Phyl warned, "if he's a friend of Vanya's. You know the old saying: 'Birds of a feather flock together.'"

"I wish Vanya didn't flaunt my photos around," I complained. "But you know what, Phyl? He used to pull the same thing when we were in Cambridge. Passed my picture around. Then guys would butter him up in order to wangle introductions. And they were usually the greasy wolves. You know the type. Ugh! Let's change the subject. Sit down and tell me about yourself. What and who is new in your life?"

"Not much really. After you left, I had to buckle down, but it was worth it at graduation. *Cum laude* . . . what sweet words! President Jordan made a speech like the one he made for your graduation. Men? Hah! I did date Manfred several times. God, I can't get over the fact that he's Loretta's brother. She is so naive and pure, and he? Well, you know how he is, but he sure is a lot of fun to be with. We had a lot of laughs together. Then I met a couple of new guys, one was 4-F . . . bad eyesight. Poor chap, he so wished he could fight the damned Krauts instead of sitting behind a desk. I write to quite a few fellows overseas, just like you. And you? What about Lanny?"

"He writes, almost as often as Mac does. He's living in a French village, the last I heard. Phyl, he writes me such fine poetry that it hurts my conscience to read it sometimes."

The phone rang, and I grabbed the receiver. "Claire, it's for you."

She came out of the bathroom in her robe with a towel turbaned around her head. It wasn't a long conversation.

"A guy I knew in Washington, Herb Levine, on his way overseas. I'll be eating out tomorrow evening, Buddy."

Phyl chuckled. "One way of saving money, eh?" She turned to me. "Are you still as straight-laced as you were in Cambridge?"

"Hah!" Claire laughed. "I'm glad you said that, not me, Phyllis. In this day and age, to have such puritanical views about sex. You know, I have a hard time believing that she ever kissed her Mac."

"She did. I can vouch for that." She laughed, giving me a roguish look. "But I'm surprised. I thought New York would sophisticate you a bit. It's about time you got over your crazy ideas."

"To each his own," I said calmly. "As I told you before, I have my own moral standards. If a man invites me to dinner, I take it that he enjoys my company, not my lips or body. That's for engaged or married couples, and I'm neither. I don't question you about your behavior with men, do I? I could care less what you do. Please let me be."

Claire immediately apologized, "You're right. I hadn't looked at it your way. I respect your opinion, Tamara."

Phyl looked at the full ashtray. "Did I smoke all those? Yeah; I won't kid you either. Claire"—she got up to dump out the butts—"how about you? Got any special man?"

Claire tucked her feet under her. "I did like this chap in Washington, but we've drifted apart. No, I guess you can say I'm still playing the field."

The phone rang. I answered it.

"Tamara?" A man's voice was on the line, unfamiliar, pleasant, confident.

"This is Tamara." I shrugged my shoulders at the girls.

He had laughed then. "I'm Eugene Rostov. Didn't your brother write you about me?"

"Oh, yes." It dawned on me. "You're in New York?"

"Right. Could I see you tonight?"

I glanced at my watch. "I'm sorry, but I have company. Besides, it's half past ten."

"Tomorrow then?"

"Fine." I told him. "I get home from work around six. Why not come around seven?" I suggested. After I had hung up, I regretted having made the date. "Damn!"

"What's wrong?" Claire asked.

"It's his attitude: inconsiderate and demanding. He wanted me to go out tonight, at this late hour!"

"Which reminds me that I'd better get going." Phyl got up. "He probably hasn't been out with a girl for ages. That's why he talked like that. Did he just get back from overseas?"

"Could be," I decided, walking with her towards the door. "I'll call you, and we can have lunch next week. Okay?"

She smiled at Claire. "It was great meeting you." Slinging her purse over her shoulder, she left.

The next day after work I had just slipped off my heels when the doorbell rang. *Darn,* I thought to myself, *who could it be?* I ran to the door barefooted, forgetting Claire's warning not to open it unless I knew who it was.

There, taking up most of the door space, stood a young soldier. He was rather good-looking, tanned, and rosy cheeked. His long-lashed, blue eyes surveyed me boldly from head to toe. Then he let out a low wolf whistle.

"Hubba-hubba." His smile was boyish. "For the first time since I've known him, Vanya has not exaggerated. You are a beauty."

"I take it that you are Eugene." I ignored his compliment, disliking his brazen attitude. "Please come in. I hadn't expected you this early."

He made himself at home, sitting down on Claire's couch. "Nice place you got," he said, looking around the room. He took out his cigarettes. "Have one?"

"No, thank you." I went towards the hall. "If you'll just wait a moment, I'll be ready."

In the bathroom I hastily put on some fresh makeup and brushed my hair. Somehow I felt uneasy with this fellow. Perhaps it was because he was Vanya's friend.

I had suggested Asti's, one of my favorite spots. Italian-owned, it distinguished itself by having waiters and waitresses with operatic voices who, at any given moment, would break into song—from an opera or often from the more popular Rudolf Friml's operettas. It was, as usual, crowded, but Salvatore, the maître d', knew me. I had brought him some good customers.

"You sure rate, don't you?" Eugene looked at me with respect. "This is a good spot."

He enjoyed himself, something that I had not expected. He hadn't appeared to be the type who'd like classical music. In fact, here he appeared different: sensitive and courteous.

Over dinner, he told me about Vanya. "He's having a good time; he's traveled and seen quite a bit. Speaks Italian like a native. Has had to"—he looked amused—"the way he likes Italian girls. His latest is an Italian prostitute." He watched me to see what effect his words would have on me.

I didn't bat an eyelid. I had seen enough of that stuff around Times Square. Besides, Vanya's taste in women had long since ceased to surprise me. What I didn't appreciate was the way Eugene's eyes surveyed me. I asked him what he'd done before the war.

"I tried college, but it didn't pan out. Then I worked as a grease monkey."

"Grease monkey?" I hadn't heard that term.

"I worked on cars. Then I joined the army . . . after they had drafted me." He lost some of his boyishness. I detected the cynicism in his voice.

"Have you seen any fighting?"

"Nah, not really," he answered. "Vanya and I were lucky. We always happened along at the tail end."

All in all, the atmosphere was pleasant; the singing made it so. First one voice would begin, then, from the other end, another waiter would join in, until a chorus of outstanding voices was singing in perfect harmony. Because of that, we couldn't talk much.

At about half-past ten, I suggested we leave. I had had quite a day and wanted to get to bed. I talked about my day to Eugene when we walked back to the apartment.

"I did my first interview this afternoon. Mr. White, my boss, sent me out to interview Katherine Dunham."

"Katherine who?"

"She's a famous Negro dancer," I explained.

"Oh."

"She's terrific, and not only as a modern dancer," I continued. "I had told her that this was my first interviewing job and that I didn't know how to begin. She told me to get out my pad, then told me everything that I should know about her."

"Interesting," he said politely, his eyes straying to the blonde across the street.

"Miss Dunham gave me a large photograph of herself, inscribing it to me." I smiled to myself, recalling the incident. At the apartment building, he was surprised when I held out my hand. He had expected to come in with me.

"I'm sorry," I told him, "but I have to go in to the office early tomorrow. It's been a long day for me."

"Ah, just for a minute?" His eyes pleaded with me, his voice coaxing. "You're so beautiful," he whispered, then pushed open the door with his foot.

That foot action of his annoyed me more than anything. "Thanks again," I told him coldly, stepping inside the apartment.

"You mean, that's it?" Eugene's face reddened.

"Yes, that's it," I confirmed. "Good night." I tried to shut the door.

Quick as a flash, he had pushed the door wide open, turned me around, and gathered me to him in his strong arms. With animal ferocity he crushed me to him, pressing his mouth on to mine, one hand holding me and the other one caressing my buttocks and pushing my skirt upwards. With a sudden twist, I managed to free myself and slip back into the apartment, bolting the door. My heart was pounding. With shaking hands I double-locked the door.

"Darling, Tamara," he whispered. "I didn't mean to frighten

you. I'm so sorry. Open the door, please."

The better to eat you, Little Red Riding Hood! I thought.

I didn't answer him. With my heart pounding, I walked into the spare bedroom, clicking my heels loudly so that he could hear. I sat in the dark, listening to his pleadings. When I heard no more, I guessed that he had gone. I went into the bathroom and took a good hot bath, scrubbing my face to cleanse myself of his scent.

Towards midnight, when Claire returned from her date with Herb, I told her about Eugene. To my surprise, she didn't think his actions so terrible.

"After all, didn't he just come back from overseas? What do you expect him to do dating a pretty girl like you? I'd think something wrong if he didn't try something like that. It might have worked if you hadn't been you."

Phyllis too, when I talked to her by phone, had blamed it on me. "Remember what I told you about the way you look? You know how Manfred described you once to me?"

"No."

"He said that you didn't have a straight line in your body, and that's the truth. You're a damned sexy woman, and men are attracted to you. The problem, though, is"—she had paused, chuckling to herself—"you don't even realize it. You're so damned naive."

36

The Seeds of Time

"Do you realize that a month ago, on July 25, the Allies had launched the powerful offensive sweeping through France and Belgium, and largely destroying the German forces in both countries?" Natasha's black eyes sparkled. "And two days ago Paris was liberated! No wonder Olga has been so delirious." She smiled, looking at Olga's back. Olga, as usual, was conscientiously doing her translations.

Overhearing Natasha's remark, she swiveled in her chair. "Natashenka, if you'd been born in Paris and had lived there most of your life, wouldn't you be dancing with joy as well?" She pointed her pen at Natasha, "Just wait. Tease me all you want. As soon as I finish my work, I'll show you how I dance."

Natasha nodded her head, pleased with herself. "It won't be long now before those Teutonic blackguards get their due. And then, our Tamarotchka, your Mac will come home, and we'll all dance at your wedding, eh, Alexei Sergeivitch?" Her voice rose as she addressed him. Poor Alex was getting hard of hearing.

"Of course, Tamarotchka." His faded blue eyes looked watery. "I'd like to meet that lieutenant of yours someday. Where is he now, do you know?"

"Probably in Paris. He was near St. Lo in July when they bombed it. He must be in Paris now. I'm guessing, but I think I'm right."

"What does he write besides saying that he loves you?" Natasha took out her cigarettes. "You haven't said much about him lately. You haven't had a paper fight, have you?"

"I meant to tell you. In his last letter he said that he enjoyed the remarks from all of you. He said he'd try to write each one of you a separate little note."

Erna had been listening on the sidelines. She nodded approvingly. "Of all the young men you've described to us, Tamara, I'd say he's the one for you."

I smiled, fishing Mac's letter out of my pocket, "I've got to read this to you. It's apropos of what you just said. Mac writes, 'Tell all my allies in the war effort for you to keep up the good work and not to forget that I appreciate all their efforts in my behalf. Naturally, I know that you've given them a fairly good picture of me, or they wouldn't think so much of this damned Yankee. In that case, they'd be on your side, not mine.' "

"Exactly," Erna said, "I too hope to meet him some day. He sounds like a delightful young man."

That, to say the least, coming from Erna Stenbuck, was high praise. Later, when she went into Mr. White's office, I read the last part of Mac's letter to Natasha. "You'll enjoy this story, Natasha. Mac is describing his foxhole to me. Do you realize that before the war I had no idea what a foxhole was? Here's what he writes.

" 'When I built my foxhole, I made room for two people, but frogs, toads, tadpoles, glowworms, moles, wasps, bees, and lizards keep invading the privacy of my apartment. I even have etchings on the mud wall, but all the animals make me self-conscious when I need privacy most. Why the other night a lady glowworm, when I turned out the light to undress because of my shyness, turned on her light, thinking I had used up the battery for my light. She let out one unearthly yell when she realized what it was that she was seeing right before her glow, and her little glow turned red with blushing. Of course, I apologized for not telling her that my condition was what it was, but she still glows red every time she turns on her charms for me.'

"Next he writes about the wasps and bees.

" 'The wasps and bees have learned a lot from our fighter planes and bombers. They make the bomb run into a foxhole every few minutes on schedule and dive straight at the target. I let loose my newspaper anti-aircraft barrage. So far, a three-inch width of newspaper has been the most effective weapon against the dive bee bomber. We've nicknamed the bees B-29s. One dropped its bomb load right on my hand. It was a slight casualty—a piece of shrapnel entered the back of my hand, and there is only a slight swelling. For that wound received in action against the bee-enemy, I have received the burple heart!' "

Natasha broke up into hysterical laughter.

Alex looked up from his work. "What's so funny?" he asked.

Natasha shushed him. "I'll tell you later. Tamara and I were sharing something. I'm taking my break." She squashed out her cigarette, "That sure was funny."

At that moment the phone rang. Natasha answered it. "Allo? Office of War Information." She held it out to me.

"Yes?" I asked into the phone.

"It's Gene, Tamara. I just wanted to apologize for the other night."

I almost slammed down the receiver. "I have nothing to say to you," I answered coldly.

"Won't you give me another chance?" he coaxed.

The Russians were listening. "Thank you for calling," I said in my best professional voice, "but I'm not interested."

With that I gently replaced the receiver.

That evening, after we had listened to the evening news, Claire and I sat in our robes, chewing the fat. I told her about Eugene's call.

"There's something about him that gives me the 'heebie-jeebies.' " I couldn't help shivering when I visualized him that evening at the door. "Then I think of Mac, Claire, and I realize how wonderful he is, except for that one time."

"You really didn't know Mac too well in Cambridge, did you?"

"No, Claire, not when I broke up with him. I've thought about that evening time and time again. I realize now that I had been swept up by this totally new-to-me experience—the awareness of being sexually attracted to a person. I had never felt that way about anyone, before Mac, that is."

"Our innocent little Tamarotchka." Claire smiled, then seeing my hurt expression, hurriedly added, "I wasn't teasing you, Tamara. I meant it sincerely. You are so innocent compared to most American girls your age. You must have been really sheltered in China."

I smiled to myself. If she only knew. "With Mac I felt so good, Claire, knowing that he was one person in this whole world loving me for me, not for my so-called beauty or because I came from China and therefore must be a 'fascinating person.' Then when I saw him drunk that time, he turned me off as quickly as you would turn off a faucet."

"Too bad that happened," Claire murmured.

"No, I'm honestly glad it did. I saw that he was not perfect, not the way I had idealized him, because he was the Yankeeman I'd dreamed of for so long. His family had been here for generations; he has blue eyes, blond hair, speaks perfectly, is patriotic and honest. He had, I thought, all those qualities I wanted in a man."

"And then he got drunk," Claire repeated, biting her lip, "and your dreams fell apart. The apple had a worm inside. You felt you had to throw it away."

"It wasn't only that. His character changed. Like Dr. Jekyll and Mr. Hyde, he was almost vulgar that evening, completely different from the man I had fallen in love with."

"You were afraid that it would happen again?"

"I hadn't thought that far. Besides, with all these strange emotions surging inside me, I felt confused and lost. Once I broke off with Mac, I felt at peace. I could think rationally again. My life could go on as smoothly as before. I honestly thought I'd never see him again."

"But he's persistent, and he truly loves you. And you know what, Tamara?" Claire's eyes had a mischievous glint in them. "I have a feeling you still love him."

"I've asked myself that," I acknowledged. "Maybe I do in a way, but I sorely doubt it. Perhaps if I see him again in the flesh, I'll know for sure. Definitely not though, when he's oceans away from me."

It had been good to talk with someone who understood. Phyl did at times, but she was often too cynical for me.

"Unfortunately that's the way it has to be for now," Claire

yawned. "I've been writing to some of the nicest guys and their letters, although not as colorful as some of Mac's, have shown a certain sensitivity that I had not noticed in them before. It's ironic, isn't it, that in peacetime there're all these men around us, and we don't pay much attention to them. Then a war comes along and all of a sudden we realize how nice they are, but of course it's too late—they're overseas."

"How about Moshe? Why did you break up with him?" I asked.

Claire studied her fingernails. "Moshe? Too conservative for me. You know, a woman after marriage should be in the home, bear children, keep a kosher house. That's all right for some women, but I want more out of life than that. It was sort of by mutual agreement that we split up. Of course, my folks were sorry to see it happen. Moshe is what you'd call a Jewish mother's dream: handsome, a lawyer, and well-spoken. If not a rabbi, then marrying a doctor or a lawyer is the next best thing."

"That's interesting," I said. "Mac told me when we first knew each other that he'd rather I didn't work or if I wanted to, it was okay until we had children. He, and I too, feel that one parent should always be at home with the children."

"It'd be interesting to see how we do end up, wouldn't it? In the meantime, there's no place I'd rather be right now than in New York. I love it."

I agreed with her. "Some day I'd like to have an apartment here. You know, a big one, perhaps overlooking Central Park."

"You'll have to marry a darned rich man," Claire laughed. "I think Mr. White has an apartment like that. The sad thing is that his wife and son spend their summers on Saranac Lake."

"So that's why he sometimes gets that sad look on his face. I'll bet he misses them."

Claire didn't say anything for a while. Then she took a nail file out of her robe pocket and began to file her nails, examining them critically. "He's writing a book, you know. Wants us to type it for him."

"You mean you and me? What's the book about?"

"Yep, you and me. It's a mystery about some pale blonde who gets murdered...."

"Quite a change from the tame stuff we write for the Russians, eh?" I laughed. "Here's another change. Mac wrote that he's sending me three French dishes with proverbs on them. I know Papa will enjoy seeing them. Maybe he can add them to his proverb collection."

"Mac must be getting a breather now after being near St. Lo and then on to a liberated Paris. What a relief that must be for the French people."

"I think you're right," I answered. "In Mac's last letter he described how they'd been eating off white tablecloths, German silverware, and wine, but strangely, there was no music. He also told about seeing burned-out German tanks, Volkswagens, and other equipment the Germans had abandoned during the American offensive. And then, Claire, he wrote about seeing this cow lifted high up in a tree by the blast of a shell or mine. Gruesome, huh? Gee!" I shuddered at the thought.

"Sure was. It's getting to the point where I even hate to look at pictures of war any more. I don't consider myself a squeamish person, either."

"Oh, I forgot to tell you. I also got a letter from Shep today. Remember the flier I told you about? Well, he wrote that he's already flown more than seventy missions. I can't get over this, Claire. What really excites me is that I think he's in Peking! Some time ago, when we were on a date in Cambridge, I had told him about Peking, about how unusual the sky is there. It's a beautiful blue that I've seen nowhere else. And I'm not the only one who's said that. Anyway, Shep wrote me, 'The sky here is indeed the blue as you had described it to me.' Then he went on to write, 'The need for secrecy is absolute.' I have no idea what he's doing there, but I'm so happy that he's seen Peking. He's someone who'd appreciate it." I got up to start on my nighttime ritual of washing my face, brushing my teeth, and so forth.

Claire stared at me. "Sure sounds like it, doesn't it? It'd be interesting to find out—after the war, of course."

I had just finished typing "The 4-H Clubs of America" and was about to start proofreading it, when the phone rang. "Office of War Information, Russian Section," I answered in my efficient, career-woman voice.

"May I please speak to Miss Rubleva?"

My heart skipped a beat. I thought the voice sounded familiar, but it couldn't be. "Mary?" I asked hesitantly.

"Is this Tamara?"

When I heard her pronounce my name, I knew for sure. There was no mistaking the kind, clipped voice.

"How could you recognize me so quickly, my dear?" She laughed into the phone. "Your father told us that you're living here now. We are most delighted, Tamara. We've just come from visiting your folks in Cambridge."

"Really? How wonderful to hear you!"

"It's delightful, isn't it?" I could just picture her, pale blue eyes behind rimless glasses, her straight nose so like her father's, and most of all her smile; her warm, friendly smile. "Well, dear, your father told us about your successes, and we're happy for you, Father and I."

"I thought you were still in China," I exclaimed in wonder. "And how is Dr. Ferguson?" I couldn't believe that my old friend was right here now in New York City.

She sighed. "Tamara, it's a long story. We'll tell you all about it when we see you. Dear, I don't want to take up your office time. Tell me, since we're not far from the OWI building, do you think it would be possible for you to have lunch with us today? I know it's short notice, but Father does so want to see his 'Girlie' again."

I found myself catching my breath. This was the best news that I'd had in a long time! What an unexpected pleasure it would be to see my old Peking neighbors again, to hear Dr. Ferguson's voice and see his twinkling, blue eyes.

"I'm sure I can come, Mary. Oh, I can't wait to see the two of you, to find out all that's happened. Please give Dr. Ferguson my love."

Mary had said noon. I glanced up at the office clock. It was now ten to eleven. Erna Stenbuck noticed me check the time. Slowly she withdrew a Pall Mall out of her pack, placed it in her mouth. Before lighting it, she held out the pack. "Here, Tamarotchka, have one." As I took it, she smiled.

"I overheard your conversation, dear. Who called?"

I told her then. "Erna, they're just a couple of blocks away from here. I can't believe that I'll be seeing Dr. Ferguson again!"

They'd all heard me speak of Dr. Ferguson, how it had been he who'd first taught me about his country, how he had given me books about Americans who'd made this land so great. Hearing that this very fine friend of mine was now here thrilled and intrigued them.

When I got ready to leave the office, they all beamed their good wishes. Natasha narrowed her eyes, critically surveying me from top to bottom. "You look good, Tamarotchka." She nodded approval. "Enjoy your old friends and give them our regards," she drew on her cigarette. "Even if we don't know them, we love them because of you."

Alex Makarov stood up, following me with his smile. Erna too had been interested. When I was leaving, she had beckoned me to her desk. "Take your time, dear. Don't hurry back," she ordered, in a low voice.

My dear office family. Hastily I had blown them a kiss and gone to my rendezvous with my old China friends.

I had found their apartment easily, a stone's throw from the OWI. How many times I had walked by their building with no inkling that they were so nearby.

At my knock, Mary had opened the door and enveloped me in her arms. Her face had been all smiles. "Oh, my dear, let me look at you." She had held me off at arm's length to get a good look at me. "My, oh my, what a change from the last time we saw you. Five years ago? I can't wait till Father sees you. He's been so anxious to see his 'Girlie' again."

How many memories "Girlie," his name for me, evoked! I smiled at Mary, feeling like a little girl again. Mary herself had not changed much. Perhaps a few more wrinkles, a few more gray hairs. Otherwise, the eyes behind the no-nonsense spectacles, the prim graciousness, the thoughtful, kind expression in her face had remained exactly as I had remembered them in Peking.

As usual, she had been considerate. "Ah, but it's Father you want to see; isn't it? Come in, dear, into our living room. I'll go tell him you're here." She led me into the large but sparsely furnished living room. "Sit there by the window, Tamara." She pointed to an armchair next to a rocker. "That's Father's chair," she explained. "He enjoys sitting here by the window. Excuse me." With that she hurried off down the hall.

I heard them coming back and stood up to greet my dear friend, eager for my first glimpse of that beloved face. Seeing him as he first entered the room shocked me. I hadn't expected him to have changed so much. He was thinner, more stooped, and much less formidable than I remembered. Still, the noble head, with the snow-white twitching brows shading his memorable blue eyes, remained unchanged. When I saw that familiar twinkle, I went to him and nestled my face against his chest the way I had done as a little girl. As he had done then, he now patted my head.

"Well, well, well now." His voice much softer but still cheerful and loving. "I've now got my Girlie back. Let me look at you, dear, to see what America has done for you." He eased himself into the rocking chair. With a pang I noticed how strained his movements were. He still had his sense of humor, though. Winking at Mary, he said to me, "I'd take you up on my lap, Girlie, the way I used to when you were a wee Russian Girlie, but you're a woman now." He studied my face intently, the white brows knitting together. "How do you like our America, now that you're here? Does it hold up to your expectations?"

"Much, much more than I ever expected," I answered with conviction. "Oh, Dr. Ferguson, I love this country. I never thought it could be as you had described it. More important, how are you?"

"Father has to be on a special diet now," Mary broke in. "You knew, didn't you, that we had been interned by the Japanese."

"Dorlise Krenz had told me that," I told her. "I wrote to you after Pearl Harbor but never got an answer."

"That was why," she explained with a wry smile. She glanced at her father. "It was hardest on Father, being up in years. But we finally made it home." She paused, then continued, "I never dreamed that the Japanese could act like that to Americans."

"Yes," I agreed, "I had always thought that Americans were respected by all nations. I remember how safe Dorlise used to feel with the American flag on her ricksha."

"Her mother and aunt were also in the internment camp, as were many others whom I'm sure you must have known. It was quite an ordeal."

"You wouldn't happen to know about Dorlise, would you, Mary? She came to Cambridge when I was a sophomore, but I've never heard from her after that, although she promised to write."

"She went to Stephens for a while," Mary recalled. "The last I heard was that she had married and gone to Canada. You and she were good friends, weren't you?" Mary asked.

"She was my best school friend in China."

She patted my hand. "You'll be surprised one of these days. Who knows? I've had friends from China whom I hadn't seen for years suddenly pop back into my life."

"Of course, Girlie," Dr. Ferguson added, "they disappear, then reappear in your life, in the same way Mary and I have reappeared in your life." He looked at me with approval. "You've certainly grown into a lovely young lady, hasn't she, Mary?"

In the light that filtered through the curtained window, I could see how he himself had changed. The pink skin under his chin hung loosely. There were tiny bluish veins around his temples. The blue eyes that I remembered so well were now watery, and not so blue anymore. Seeing him this way, I felt a lump in my throat.

"How did you happen to move to New York?" I asked.

It was Mary who answered. That was the other change in him that hurt me to see. Mary now did most of the talking. He merely listened, nodding his head at times, content to hold my hand and look at me.

"We have relatives here in New York. My sister and Pat, my niece. Remember her? She went to PAS for a time."

How long ago that seemed. I recalled Pat: a rosy-cheeked, confident girl, who had been rather aloof.

"My brother and his wife live in Newton, Mass. We visit back and forth. It gives Father a change."

"From the work I have here," added Dr. Ferguson quietly. He stared out the bay window, his eyes squinting from the sun. "There's so much to do," he murmured. Then he turned to me. "Mary will fill you in. She's been a great help to me."

"It's the bronzes," Mary explained. "You know, of course, how Father collected all these artifacts for many years. They've had to be catalogued, and that's been a task. We're donating a portion of them to the Metropolitan Museum." She smiled indulgently at her father.

"What about you, Girlie?" Dr. Ferguson wanted to know. "Your father and mother are so proud of you."

I told them about my work. They listened with interest. Then Mary startled me by asking if I had any special young man in my life.

"Oh, quite a few," I laughed. "There's one special person that you'd like, I know." I told them about Mac, the young Scottish-American lieutenant who wouldn't let me forget him.

At that my old friend chuckled with glee. "So, you've fallen in love with a Scotsman, hae ye?" He squeezed my hand with affection. "I gie ye my blessing, wee lass, for ye hae picked a gude one." He had lapsed into his father's dialect. "Ach, aye! There's nothing, aye, I repeat, there is no one so gude as a Scotsman, especially for a bonnie lass like ye. But beware, girlie"—his eyes for a moment were stern—"we luv deeply, and for aye."

I thought of my stubborn Yankee lieutenant, bred of similar Scottish stock as Dr. Ferguson. Was that why I couldn't forget John McNish? Dr. Ferguson's given name was John too. How strange! How alike these two were—my old friend and my love. Both of them stubborn, persistent, honest, loyal, and, above all, filled with love—a deep love for the woman each had chosen for himself, a love that knew no bounds.

"I wish so much that you could meet him," I told them when I was leaving. "His name is John too."

"Who knows?" Dr. Ferguson again looked out the window. "Some day, we may meet your laddie. I really hope so, Girlie."

It was time now to embrace them both and to tell them that I'd see them again really soon.

37

Stars in the Sky

"I sent out twelve letters today," I informed Claire, as we walked home from work. Tiny snowflakes swirled about our faces, but the cold felt good and invigorating. Both of us wore high boots, warm jackets, and woolen babushkas covering our heads.

"Twelve letters? To whom? I can't believe it."

"To the boys overseas. Who else do you think I'd be writing letters to?"

"You did it in the office?" Claire's voice had a tinge of disapproval in it.

I smiled at her reaction, knowing what a stickler she could be about office rules and procedures.

"Oh, Buddy, it wasn't that awful. I just made eleven carbon copies of the original." I felt proud of my accomplishment.

"But why, for Heaven's sake?" She stopped, placing a hand on my arm. A snowflake danced into her mouth, and I laughed at the sight.

"Because I just got plumb tired of writing the same darned stuff to all of them. Carbon copies are better than no mail at all, and I haven't got time these days to write individual letters."

Claire pulled her collar up higher. "I don't think it was very kind of you; that's all." She stared ahead. "How would you like to receive a carbon-copied letter from someone you liked?"

"Aw, Claire." I didn't want her angry with me. "I made it interesting. I told them all about you and the office and the Russians. What's wrong with that?"

Claire didn't answer. I stole a look at her and felt like gig-

The Lieutenant, "Somewhere Overseas"

gling. She had pulled in her lips, pressing them together, and she was looking down at the snow-covered pavement, the ends of her eyelashes edged with snowflakes.

"It really was a good letter," I went on. "Besides, Buddy, the fellows know me. They know that I like to do crazy things."

"Well, I hope so, for your sake," Claire sighed. "I honestly hope you have some friends left after this."

"I will, Buddy, don't worry," I tried to sound convincing. "You know, sometimes my hand gets all cramped from writing so much."

"I know. I write letters too, you know." Claire walked faster.

I lengthened my stride to match hers. The snow was now coming down steadily in big, fluffy flakes.

"Isn't it just beautiful?" I cried out in sheer delight. I tore off my babushka and shook my head, feeling the flakes settle down

568

on my hair. "Claire, doesn't it feel absolutely stupendous to be out here in this weather?"

She laughed at my enthusiasm. Few people were walking today. Those who did had their faces almost hidden behind their scarves. They hurried past us, their eyes peering out at us or focused intently on the ground. Claire, caught up in my joy, danced and cavorted with me in the snow. We skipped and played about like the carefree children we once had been.

By the time we reached the apartment it was almost dark. We heated up some leftover soup and proceeded to go through our mail, our usual evening procedure that we really enjoyed.

Two letters for me, one from Mac and another in Mama's big, uneven script. Claire was already settled on her couch, yoga style, reading a V-mail.

Mac's letter had been interesting. I glanced over at Claire. She was watching me, a smile on her lips.

"Herb has finally written to me."

"Do you know where he is?" I asked.

"No," she answered, "he doesn't say. Your letter is from Mac, isn't it?"

"Yes, it is. I'll read it to you if you'd like."

"I'd like," she laughed. "I like the way he writes. He should write books when he gets out."

"Hah!" I smiled at her comment, secretly pleased. Reading his letters out loud made them even more meaningful to me.

"Okay.

" 'Now after the strains of war have left the countryside and gone far away from us, it has become quiet, too monotonous, and too unreal to think that here where we are now sleeping German snipers had once killed American troops. Here Germans had fired at paratroopers as they were dropped from the sky. We can still see an occasional shellhole where a naval gun had fired upon the Germans entrenched along the ocean's shore. The traces of their fortifications still remain. Mines still are concealed in fields that are not now being used. Long ago they removed the dead cows and horses lying feet heavenward, killed by Teller mines. That mine is the one that jumps out of the ground when triggered and either kills a soldier or makes it too horrible for him to live.' "

Claire shook her head. "I'd never heard of a Teller mine, had you?"

"No; we know so little about the weapons being used these days. I've heard of mustard gas, but that was used in the First World War, wasn't it?"

"I think so," Claire said. "I guess they've developed even more horrible weapons now. Ugh, it's awful."

"You want me to read more?"

"Yes, at least Mac's letters are more interesting than what the newspapers tell us." Claire looked thoughtful. "No, that's wrong of me to say that. I like to read Ernie Pyle. It's just the fact that you know Mac, and you feel it more intensely. That's what makes the war real to me."

"You're right," I agreed. "Well, I'll go on.

" 'Now those very same men who fought against us are prisoners, dead, or wounded. What they would have done to us had we been their prisoners, dead, or wounded, I don't know, but I'm surely glad we were able to get ashore here and to push them back as fast as the front line soldiers have.

" 'Peculiarly here for several days we either have worked or slept or eaten when we could. No one has had any time to complain. We knew the Germans were not very far away over the hills in back of us. Then the terrible storm came. That was a tense time, for we could not unload very much materiel on the beaches, and the situation looked bleak. Then one evening the skies cleared. We saw the planes over us headed out of sight to end the first phase of our battles here. Those were tense days. Those days none of us will ever forget. Strangely though, many of the details are very unclear and vague in our memories. Things moved so swiftly and changes occurred so often that the sequence of events is confused.

" 'At times there was the terrifying broken roar of German airplanes overhead along with the more terrifying anti-aircraft barrage that kept them high. Nothing was more terrifying than the terrible black shape of an airplane diving down seemingly right at my foxhole when I peered out. Three blinding red flashes, an awesome earthquake that caved in the side of my foxhole. My stomach muscles tightened up so tightly at that time that my throat became desert-dry. I couldn't swallow. There was a rawness in my throat. Everything combined to cover me like a mighty downward surge.

"'We were lucky. Everyone of us survived that dark night made more evil by the ghastly, ghostly flares that dangled suspended in the black stillness. I'm not being melodramatic. I'm just trying to explain the events that change men who are in a war and experience these happenings.'"

"Isn't that some letter?"

"I'll say," Claire's voice replied softly. "It's hard in the midst of war to think that Christmas is just around the corner."

I began to read Mama's letter and couldn't help smiling.

"What's so funny, Tamara?"

"Remember when I told you that Mama had rented my room to her friend, Olga Stepanovna? Well, it's done wonders for Mama. She now has someone her own age to chat with in the evenings. Papa usually works in his study, and she gets lonely at times, I guess. I think women need companionship more than men do, don't you?"

"It depends. I've never thought of it that way. I can see though how it would be with your father, who's a scholar. Anyway, where does the funny part come in?"

"It's not exactly funny, Claire. I've got to explain first that Olga, like many Russians—especially the older ones from the Czarist period—is deeply religious. You might even say some of them are fanatical."

"Like the Tsarina and Rasputin?"

"Indeed. Most Russians have an icon in the corner of a room with a little *lampadka*, an eternal candle, in front of it. The icons are usually placed high up, near the ceiling. One evening Olga called Mama into the room and pointed dramatically to her icon. Mama in her letter then describes what went on. I'll translate it for you.

"'Look,' Olga announced triumphantly to me. 'It's a miracle.'

"I looked, but saw nothing.

"'Can't you see what has appeared above the icon?' Olga asked me. 'Look. Don't you see?'

"This time I looked more carefully and then I noticed all the little stars on the ceiling.

"'They appeared here this morning,' Olga told me in awe.

"I just stared at her. Then I couldn't help smiling. She was just teasing me, of course.

"'Olga Stepanovna,' I scolded her, 'You pasted them up there yourself.'

"To my surprise she was deadly serious.

"'No, no, this is an act of God,' she insisted. She even got angry at me for doubting her. So I meekly congratulated her for being so blessed."

"That's quite a story," Claire responded, smiling. "You actually mean to tell me that Olga herself believed it?"

"I guess so. I don't know. I don't know her that well, but Mama does."

"What are your own ideas about religion?" she asked. "I know people consider it a breach of courtesy to mention that, but I haven't seen you going to church."

Her words took me by surprise. "I do believe in God, but you're right. I visit churches, but I don't go regularly to any particular church. I also try to abide by Confucius's words."

"He was a philosopher, wasn't he?" Claire looked puzzled by my answer. "Is that why you often say 'God and Confucius'?"

"I guess so. I mean no sacrilege to God. I learned about Him from Mama, but it was Papa who gave me books about 'the Master' as Confucius is known in China. You've heard of 'filial piety.' It is known as *Hsiao* in Chinese."

"I've heard of it," Claire admitted hesitantly, then laughed. "However, I really don't know what it means."

"It's respect towards one's parents. Confucius had many rules of behavior for men. Usually they were stated like this: 'The Master said, in serving his father and mother a man may gently remonstrate with them.' Then it ends with something like this: 'But if he can't change their opinion, he should show respect towards them and should not resent them.' Any rule of conduct always starts with 'The Master said. . . .'"

"I've learned something tonight." Claire smiled. "When I was in my teens, there was a fad of saying, 'Confucius say . . .' and then we'd have some silly saying. I never realized how important he was."

"He laid down the principles for man's behavior towards his

fellowman," I explained. "Someday I'll tell you more, if you're interested. He influenced all of China with his teachings, much in the same ways as Jesus did for Christians."

"How about your Christian beliefs? What do you believe in?"

I thought about her question before answering it. "I've had many religions in my life. Actually, it all started when I found the two icons in Mama's dresser drawer. One of them was of Mary. The other, my favorite, had her holding the baby Jesus. I liked to take them out and hold them, loving those beautiful, calm faces that stared back at me. Then, one day, Mama gave them away to her friend Anastasia just like that. It broke my heart then, but I didn't tell anyone. When I got older, Papa bought *The Children's Encyclopedia*. In it were Bible stories that I read and reread. When I was a little girl, I remember going to the Russian Orthodox church. The *batyushkis*, the priests, frightened me with their probing eyes and long black beards. I was really relieved when Papa and Mama stopped going. The services had been so long and boring to me. Then too we had to stand during the service. Russian churches don't have pews."

"Why did they stop going?"

"It was Mama's decision. Her best friend, Rebecca Poole, died of cancer. That shook Mama up so much that she became angry with God. I remember her telling Anastasia that when she gave her the icons, something about God not being merciful when he had taken such a lovely woman in her prime of life."

"Did you ever question her about it?"

"Claire,"—I couldn't help smiling at the thought—"you don't question Mama about certain things. Mama is a wonderful, special person, but she is also an amazingly private individual. Long ago I learned where to draw the line."

"You know, my mom is something like that. I guess it's their generation. They were brought up so strictly that it reflects the way they are—chained to certain beliefs, eh?"

"I guess that's it," I answered. "Then when I started going to PAS, the Peking American School, Dorlise and I visited the Union Church, where most of the missionary kids worshipped. Sometimes we even rode bikes to the Western Hills. They have Buddhist and Taoist temples there. Those were fun to visit. We would stand quietly at the entrance to watch the robed, clean-

573

shaven priests perform their rituals, listen in rapture to their melodic chants, and the beat of the great temple drums."

"How fascinating," Claire exclaimed. "What a fabulous experience for a young girl."

"That's because the pastures always seem greener on the other side," I told her. "I used to envy the American girls who had a religion to which they belonged, who went to Sunday School, then to church along with their parents. I heard them talk about this on Monday mornings. It was almost as if they belonged to a very select group when they donned their Sunday best. It was a ritual for them, saying the right prayers at the proper time."

"But you were able to choose, Tamara. I would have liked that." Claire looked pensive.

"Then I learned about the Catholic religion when Mama sent me to the convent school. I used to get the giggles listening to the Catholic girls struggle with their memorization of the catechism. That made me grateful that my folks were not Catholic. Here in the States I've visited quite a few churches, even mouthing some of their prayers. I've even gone to a synagogue and enjoyed their simple but beautiful service. You see that I have no one religion. I've embraced them all."

Claire's eyes stared at me with fascination. "I never would have thought of it, knowing you. You're so quiet and shy."

"I realize that, Claire. I've never really talked like this to anyone else. The question never came up. Basically, I believe in God. Jesus Christ, in my opinion, existed on this earth and for a definite purpose."

"I agree with you. It's how a person lives his life that's most important. I believe in goodness, truth . . . "

"Papa would have told you a proverb about that," I laughed. "I remember one: 'If you are standing upright, don't worry if your shadow is crooked.' "

"Oh, I like that. I must remember it."

"Also, what we're talking about is the Confucian *jen*, which means 'good' in the general sense of the word. I don't believe that going to church is going to make me a better person. Those are rituals fashioned by men, not God; at least that's my opinion."

"Boy, we've covered a lot of ground, haven't we?" Claire took a cigarette out of her pack.

"How about you? I've told you my innermost thoughts." I glared at her accusingly. "I haven't seen you beating a path to a synagogue."

"Touché, Buddy," Claire said with good humor. "I feel much the same way you do. I have visited Christian churches as well as different synagogues. Each religion has something to offer. Another thing we have in common, old Buddy."

Several weeks after I had sent my collective letters overseas I received one in reply. It came to the office one morning. I had to chuckle as I read it and then shared it with Claire.

"Remember when I told you about the eleven carbon-copied letters I'd sent overseas and you'd gotten mad because I did that?"

"Sure do, Buddy. I hope you got what you deserved."

I couldn't help looking triumphant. "Listen to this.

" 'Dear Alice, Betty, Cherie, Doris, Elysia, Grace, Fran, and any other of my Beloveds I might have missed, and oh, yes, Tamara.

" 'I am really worn out and so fatigued in the evenings and don't get much opportunity to write an individual letter to all of you, so you'll have to excuse my community letter. At least you'll be able to tell yourself and others, 'My darling wrote me today. He still loves me.'

" 'And believe me when I write all of you. I *do* love all of you. I miss all of you very much. Gerde and Aliecha aren't getting letters because they have a hard time reading English. However, since they are here with me off and on, I take every opportunity to teach them the language. They are so willing to learn, and I must say it's a pleasure to help them learn. You all know how good I am at teaching.

" 'As we sit by the stove in a little room in Belgium, . . . '

"My gosh, Claire, he's in Belgium now. His last letter was from France."

Claire laughed. "They do move around, you know. Go on; that's funny. Sort of puts you in your place, eh?"

"It does. What I did wasn't kosher. Shall I go on?" At her nod, I continued.

" '. . . munching an ice-cream sandwich. It's difficult to talk to them because they don't understand English that well. We prefer not to talk.

" 'Such is our life, and we make the best of it. We try to make each other happy and usually succeed. My glasses are broken so I can't write more, for my eyes are starting to ache.

" 'Cheerio, girlies, Your John, Hans, Juan, Ivan, Ian McNish.'

"There. See? He answered humor with humor." I looked at her in triumph. I opened his other letter and began to read it to myself.

"He couldn't keep it up," I chuckled. "Said he repented writing the 'collective' letter, so he wrote a nice letter to offset the other. He writes that he wants us to hang on to our apartment till he gets back. Then he wants you to vacate it for a few days so that he and I can raise Cain. Why the nerve of him!" I couldn't help smiling.

"Ho, ho, ho," Claire liked that. "He sounds pretty sure of you. Write him that I'll be delighted to vacate. Provided he finds me a nice guy to vacate with."

The stores in Manhattan, especially those on Fifth Avenue, were so beautifully decorated for Christmas that walking home after work took longer for Claire and me. We had to stop to look at our favorites: the colorful mechanical figures that looked almost lifelike as they nodded their heads, waving joyously to the passersby. Claire and I often, like little children, pressed our faces to the glass to see the holiday wonderland. What delightful gnomes, elves, and old-fashioned figures. Even old Santa Claus sometimes paused in his gift-giving to wave a mechanical hello to us mortals. People who at other times were mere strangers to one another exchanged merry smiles as they hurried along, laden with presents for those fortunate enough to be on their Christmas lists. I felt the special magic in the air: that rare, almost exalted feeling of joy and goodwill towards men.

I splurged and bought my first Christmas tree for our apartment. In Woolworth's I found some tiny green lights, angel hair, and small shiny ornaments that hadn't cost much. Laden with my purchases, I came home and phoned Phyllis.

When she responded with her deep, throaty hello, I told her, "It's only me so you don't have to use your sexy voice. Look; how about coming over tonight? Claire's in Washington for the weekend, and I'm by my lonesome. We can decorate the little tree I just bought."

Phyl couldn't have been more delighted. "God, you're a lifesaver," she chortled, her voice an octave higher. "That's almost mental telepathy. Norma's gone home for the holidays. I'm here moping around, feeling sorry for myself. I'll be over shortly."

She arrived with a bottle of Chianti, crackers, and some Brie cheese. "Like the good old days, huh?" She grinned. "Only then we couldn't afford the wine or the cheese." She eyed my purchases on the couch. "I see you got some green lights. To remind you of anyone special by chance?"

"We've always had a Christmas tree with green lights," I told her. "That is, in Cambridge. Mama and I both like the ethereal effect of green lights under a veil of angel hair. It's kinda mysterious, as if the tree is seen through a mist. I remember Mac had liked it. He told me he'd never seen a lovelier tree."

"Nor such a lovely girl as you." Phyl teased. "I guess I'm getting old, reminiscing so much; but God, weren't those terrific days, Tamara?"

"If I recall correctly, Miss Olsen, you couldn't wait till exams were over and you'd be through with Radcliffe," I told her slyly. "But those days were fun, I do admit."

"How about some Chianti? I'll fix it." Phyl took her bottle into the kitchenette.

I set up the small tree in the middle of our coffee table and began to intertwine the green lights through its branches.

"Here's to our grand old times of yesteryear," Phyl held up her glass.

I lifted up my glass, clinking it to hers, "and to the good years ahead of us, after this war," I added.

"Amen." Phyl put down her glass. "You want me to help you with the ornaments?"

"Why not? Let's finish. Then we can relax and admire our handiwork."

Carefully we hung each ornament. After that was done I

spread out the angel hair over the whole tree. Phyllis watched in fascination.

"You do it with so much patience. I'd mess up the angel hair if I did it; it always tangles up on me."

"That's because you're no angel," I smiled at my own witticism. "How about plugging in the lights?" With that I turned off the overhead light.

Phyllis took in her breath, gazing at our handiwork. "It's positively breathtaking," she sighed.

"Please turn the big light back on," I asked her. "I forgot something. Wouldn't you know that I'd forget the star?"

I went to the remaining unopened package. "Here, let me fasten it on top of the tree."

When we looked at the finished tree, it looked even more beautiful.

"A star in the sky," said Phyllis softly, "and all the little stars below it, twinkling away to a silent night." She stared thoughtfully at the tree, her eyes sad.

"What's the matter, Phyl? Does this bring back memories?"

She stretched out her long, gorgeous legs, and yawned. "It's not the company," she apologized. "No, it doesn't bring back memories of Christmases past. I was just thinking of this guy, another naval officer, whom I'd met in Boston. He and I had dated for several weeks. In fact, I had been so sure that I'd finally met Mr. Right." She shook her head. "I don't know what it is that jinxes me. Sure enough, he's married . . . and a baby on the way to boot. Had a spat with wifey and strung me along into the bargain. What a cad!"

I didn't know what to say. Finally I told her, "I'm sorry. Most of the good men are fighting overseas. Your time will come, Phyl. You've got beauty, brains . . . "

"Tra-la-la-la," Phyl shrugged her shoulders. "It's my own damned fault, I know. I shouldn't be so giving with them. Perhaps if I played hard-to-get like you do, I could find myself a decent man."

"I don't play with men," I countered. "I level with them. I think that's why they respect me."

"I didn't mean that in the way you took it," she said. "You want a Marlboro?"

"No, thanks. Mac said I shouldn't smoke."

She raised her eyebrows in mock horror. "Good heavens! Lawd amercy! Since when have you been taking orders from him?"

"It's not just him. It's such a nasty habit. I find my clothes smelling of stale cigarettes. It's hard to quit. Please don't make it more difficult for me."

"Sorry," she inhaled, blowing the smoke off to the side. She watched it swirl and disappear. "Have you heard about the Germans launching a counteroffensive against the Allies?"

"I read about that," I told her. "They did it because our forces have been trying to break through their main Siegfried defenses. What worries me is that Mac is in Belgium."

"Oh?" Phyl gave me a strange look, "I thought he was in France."

"His last letter came from Belgium. Here, wait a minute. Let me see. This letter is dated December 11, 1944. It took almost two weeks to get to me. Let's see what he says. . . . "

"Can you read it out loud?"

"Sure, except the parts that I censor."

She grinned. "Whatever," she flicked her ashes into my big ashtray. "I'm glad you bought a large one, finally."

"Here's what Mac writes.

"'We're doing all we can to bring all this mess to a close. I don't mind working if we can soon push the Germans back into the ground and bury them over with the rubble of their destroyed cities. I have no sympathy for them whatsoever. Those who want a just peace and complain about the hard-heartedness of the Morgenthau Plan ought to spend several days with any of us right where they can appreciate what war is. They'd out-Morgenthau Morgenthau then.'"

"Holy Toledo, but he sounds bitter," she said.

"Well, he knows what war is, Phyl. He goes on.

"'Whatever happens, don't ever believe that the terrible enemy we're now fighting would have surrendered more easily if they had been let off easily. I'd rather die killing all those Germans than see them get off easily this time. The only thing fit for them is unconditional surrender. I believe every soldier over here feels the same way about them. There are lots of things over here that make you think differently about the war. If we get soft about the Germans and give up, we're lost. We might as well have surrendered to them in the beginning. If I see this war out, I'm making myself a committee of one (and so will a lot of others over here) to see that the German carbuncle doesn't come to a head again in their life span. I'm convinced that they're no good, and even though I myself am descended from Germans through my maternal grandmother, nothing will change my mind on that.' "

Phyllis sat there silent, her face a study of sympathy.
I went back to the letter.

" 'I understand that some are proposing that we get together with the Germans and reach an amicable end to the conflict. What tommyrot! A lot of people think Americans are good sports. Well, forget it as far as most soldiers over here are concerned.'

"That's all except that he still loves me and dreams of me wearing his favorite pink and gray dress."
"That's a good letter. You ought to send it in to the *New York Times*. . . . Show what the common soldier feels, not what the big shot 'knows.' "
"Ernie Pyle, John Hersey and others have written about soldiers. And Bill Mauldin's cartoons always have been fair, making fun of the big shots as well as the little guy. The *Times* wouldn't publish Mac's letter, I'll bet."
"It seems to me your feelings about Mac have changed," Phyl ventured.
"In a way they have," I had to admit, "but I don't know, Phyl. I know that since we've been writing to each other, I've learned much more about him. More than that, I have come to respect him. I find myself agreeing with many of his ideas. There's a lot that's fine about him. You know me, though. I still have my doubts. I'm idealizing him because he's not here. Were he here, it might be completely different."
Phyl's only comment was, "I see." Judging by her sardonic expression, I knew that she didn't. "Mac has changed, hasn't he? You know that you too have changed a lot, Tamara."

"Oh, no, I haven't. I'm still the same."

"You've matured, old girl," Phyl declared, peering at me through cigarette smoke. "You're different from the shy girl I first met at Howard Mumford Jones's lecture to our freshman class. Remember?"

I laughed. "I wasn't that bad, was I?"

"Well, no. Maybe I'm exaggerating a bit, but the damning thing about it all was your popularity in spite of being quite different from most of us. At times I wanted to shake you out of your moralistic prudishness."

"I'm still prudish, you know. I don't consider that in any way derogatory, do you?"

"No, I guess not." She lit another Marlboro. "Now, how about that Eugene fellow? Did you go out with him any more?"

"I had a bad experience with him, Phyllis. I didn't tell anyone because I considered it much too personal. With you, I can be honest. He called me several times, and I kept refusing to go out with him. Then he started waiting by the office elevator till I came down. He just stood there watching me, not saying anything. It scared me, seeing him like that. I kept counting the days until his furlough would end. Well, I miscalculated by one day. The day before his departure he was waiting for me by the apartment. He followed me in, pushed me onto Claire's couch, jumped on top of me with his pants already unbuttoned. Whew! Was I scared! I completely forgot about being a lady and kicked him hard where it would hurt. He yelled, jumping around, grabbing himself in the crotch, finally managed to button up his trousers, and started to walk out. As he was going out the door, I yelled after him, "Don't you ever come near me again, or I'll see to it that your company commander hears of this." So far as I know, he's gone for good. And when I think that it was Vanya who introduced him to me, I boil all over."

Phyllis nodded. "It may not be completely Vanya's fault, Tamara. Eugene may have thought that if Vanya sleeps around, then his sister must too."

"Could be," I agreed, "but let's forget it now."

"What do you hear from your flier friend—I forget his name—Chad, was it?"

I couldn't place that name. Then it dawned on me. "You must

581

mean Shep. I haven't heard from him for some time. I think he is in Peking. It's hard to tell, really."

"Yes, I know. I get plenty of V-mails with stuff crossed or cut out."

"You know, Phyl, sometimes I think the censors are sadistic little twerps who gnash their teeth and eagerly snip out whatever they want, regardless. It's like a game between them and the men who write to their loved ones. The censors try to keep information from getting through to readers in the States, and the soldier boys try to slip through information casually. I know Mac mentioned the Flood family in a book he was reading, and I knew then right away that he was reading *The Sun Is My Undoing* and that he was located in Bristol, England."

Phyllis laughed, then shook her head. "Uh-unh, haven't you seen the posters everywhere? The little cocker spaniel lying on a sailor's shirt, above him a satin banner with one gold star and the words 'because somebody talked.' Then the guy drowning in ocean waters because 'Somebody talked!' No, they're doing a damned good job, these censors."

"I realize that. Mac himself censors his men's letters."

We stopped talking for a time. It felt good to sit here, watching the green lights glow through the veil of angel hair, each of us engrossed in her own thoughts. I wondered if Mama had bought a tree for the living room. It wouldn't be the same for them without a bunch of young people around. On the other hand, she might have.

I watched the snow outside the window. It was falling fast, the slanting snowflakes softly sinking to the ground. Some etched amazingly picturesque wintry scenes as they landed on the windowpanes. *Nature's very own frost brush*, I thought to myself. Again, "Silent Night" on the radio. I felt a delicious peace inside me and hoped so much that those of whom we had spoken would have that very same feeling of peace.

"You know what?" I jumped up and went over to the bookshelf, where my writing supplies were, smiling at Mac's picture that was smiling back at me. "I'm going to make a Christmas card for Mac."

"Isn't it a bit late for that?" Phyl asked. "By the time he gets it, it'll be 1945."

"That's okay," I said happily. "Russian Christmas is on January seventh. They go by the Russian Orthodox calendar." I couldn't help chuckling to myself as I curled up on my sofa-bed and began to write. Phyllis, amused by my spurt of energy, took up *Life* and her cigarettes, then began to read and smoke.

It didn't take me long after I got started. The tree and the music, as well as thoughts of Mac and the past, had put me in a nostalgic mood.

"Well?" Triumphantly, I showed her my masterpiece.

She read it slowly, then smiled, handing it back. "I think he'll like your work of art," she said. "It'll give him hope."

*   *   *

Christmas

1944

Tonight
Phyllis and Tamara
again will sit by the fireside
to recall the happy days of a year ago
thoughts spilling over with memories twirled
round a Christmastree like these word-patterns
Letters from you do not come . . . perhaps the postman
is at fault . . . or you are coming home, and will, one day
knock on our door to say, "Here I am!" It would be just too wonderful to be true! I'd be quite ready then to greet you; I mustn't be without a girdle. You know what happens to women who don't wear those tight-fitting chastity belts. We had a fine time last night. Claire went to Washington. I invited Phyl, who feels so sorry for you because you're so fine and love me as none other could. I hope it's true. She knows why I don't say yes to your important questions. Because we're young and have so much to live for and love is as lasting as is our friendship. My thoughts have turned to other things. Phyl and I will walk by the river, and we'll feel free, running on the snow with wind blowing hard in our faces; how pleasant it'll be to return to my place and turn on the radio and sit by the window, read out loud to each other, talk of endless things but mostly about life and love, men, work, and people in general, and the mysterious Future that she and I are con-

stantly wooing. How'd you like to be with us and take a look into my crystal ball to see what lies in store for you? And look into my eyes; and perhaps give me a long, long kiss, for I do need one, not from anyone, but from you. Don't you think that my letter shows a new trend in originality? It's just that the days are so long and there's always work to be done, and then more work, and though I do it, I get tired and bored. It is often the same-sized paper and words, always words; some of which make little sense, but that's my fault. I too get tired of being so good and kind and loving. Time was when you were here to show me the magic of Chaucer and the wise way to make unburned coffee. Buddy thinks we should call our place "Buddies' Asylum." I agree. You too will agree after reading this and seeing the sad state of my mind presently. Blame it on the war. And yet, at times 'tis fun to be so unworldly, like now when I reach for a cigarette to think of you. In the U.S.A., you know, cigarettes are rationed, but men are not. Therefore, 'tis time I smoked despite scoldings you so sternly apply to me. Sad 'tis when your beloved listens not. Why should I be the obedient child when you have no bonds to tie me to you? I love my freedom. I believe in independence in marriage and will definitely not obey you. If you disagree, then find yourself an obedient, pliable wife. I'm a free woman and shall love whomsoever I please. No one tells me that I must do this or will do that. I do freely love you, Mac.

Cheerio, my love
God love you.
I am always,
Your Tamara.

38

Such Sweet Sorrow

I was at the office when the letter came. For a moment I couldn't understand. The V-mail was in my own handwriting and was addressed to Lt. W. Shepard. Why was this letter of mine being returned? I checked the address. Shep's address, the same one I had been writing for several months. Then I noticed the purple stamp that the post office used when letters couldn't be delivered. Either "Not at This Address," "No Forwarding Address." I looked at the envelope closely. Opposite the check mark in dark ink was stamped one word: "Deceased."

I stared at that one word for some time, mesmerized by those eight letters. As the first hot tears slipped down my cheeks and my eyes blurred, I finally realized the meaning of this impersonal announcement. Like the monotonous, persistent sound of a moving train, the words: "Shep is dead; Shep is dead" kept resounding over and over again in my head.

I didn't even realize that Bill White was standing beside me, watching my tears stain the V-mail in my hand.

"Tamarotchka,"—his voice was gentle—"would you come into my office for a minute?"

"I'll be right there, Mr. White." Hastily, I wiped my eyes and got up from my desk. He had already gone into his office, leaving the door open.

In his office, he signaled for me to sit down, then swirled in his chair to look out that big window for a moment. Then he swirled back to me, his eyes kind, understanding.

"You know, Tamarotchka,"—he spoke slowly, as if carefully

selecting each word—"ever since you joined our department, we've all become richer in one way or another. You've had such a zest and joy for life that it has rubbed off on each one of us, even this hard-boiled Irishman . . . me. So when we see you unhappy, it makes us feel lousy too. Now, what can we do to help?"

Needless to say, I had been surprised at his remark.

"How did you know?"

"I noticed the letter on your desk and knew what it meant." He reached out to pat my hand. "Would you like to go home? Or maybe take off for a couple of hours?"

"No, thank you, Mr. White. I appreciate your understanding, but I'd better keep on with that report on American forestry. It'll help me to keep busy." I couldn't stop my tears, though.

"He must have been somebody very special to you," Mr. White said in a compassionate voice. "Would it help to talk a bit? I'm a good listener, you know."

When I looked into his kind face, it suddenly all came out. "Shep was really a man's man, Mr. White. Flying was his love. He often wrote to me about flying. I remember that he wrote once that he'd like to entertain me with stories of the heroes and legends of aviation but that those stories of the air should be told in a hangar, where 'the wings of men are sheltered.'"

"I can see what he must have been like; a true hero." Bill offered me a cigarette.

"Thank you." I thought of what Shep had written to me in his last letter. "He said that these stories should be told in hushed and solemn tones while storms raged without, told to those who had tasted the dangers, the terrors, and the treachery and glories of the high, cold air, when the skies were purple and the floor was in the clouds. He often mentioned the great fliers like Lindbergh, Doolittle, Parmentier, and others. . . . even one flier, I don't remember his name, who flew backward because he didn't give a damn where he was going but wanted to see where he'd been."

"He really did love flying," Bill remarked in a hoarse voice. He cleared his throat. "Then he died doing the thing he loved best, Tamarotchka, in a blaze of glory."

"Mr. White, he loved life so much. That's what hurts." I shook my head, trying to hold back my tears.

Bill White got up from his desk and came over to me, placing his hands on my shoulders. "Why don't you and Claire go downstairs for some coffee? It'd do you good, I think. And dry your eyes. I think Shep would be the first one to tell you not to grieve for him. He's now among the greatest of those who had flown before him."

Together we walked out into the big office where the rest of my office family gathered around me to give me comfort. And then I realized that Bill White had been right. If Shep had to die, he had died as he would have wanted to.

Shep's death, more than anything else, brought the horror of war home to me. I now thought more carefully about what I wrote to the men overseas. As I told Claire when we went for coffee that day, "Any one of them is vulnerable. Any one of them can be killed at any time."

I began to study more about the war and scanned maps, trying to figure out where my friends might be.

"I think that Lanny's still in France or maybe he's in Switzerland. He writes about snow-covered mountains with scenic villages scattered among them."

"You know what he's doing?" Claire asked.

"He works in medical wards; so I don't think he's in the danger zones. He's studying French too, he writes."

"Herb's somewhere in the Far East." Claire looked puzzled. "Psychological warfare—that's not too dangerous, is it?"

"I don't think so," I told her. "Are you serious about him?"

She smiled. "He's a fine fellow, but no, Tamara, I'm not serious about anyone these days. I'll date men, but I'm not in the marriage market. After the war maybe."

"You know, Mac writes that they've been under fire from November of forty-four to the end of March. Only one day, March seventeenth, without bombs. He's the one I'm really worried about . . . he and Andy Thompson who was with Shep in the Pacific."

"You never met Andy, did you? I mean personally."

"No, but he was Shep's buddy. I'd like to meet him some day to find out how Shep had died. Not knowing just haunts me, Claire. I just can't get Shep out of my mind."

"It'll take time, Tamara," Claire said, her voice soothing. "Of course, you think of him. You'll always have him in your heart. You weren't in love with him, were you?" She looked at me suspiciously.

"No, I've been in love only once," I answered. "You know that."

"What else has Mac written about the war?"

"Oh, he described the bombings. . . . You want me to read part of it? It's interesting, but rather scary, the way he describes it."

"I like Mac's descriptions," she told me. "He writes things as they happened, so vividly."

"All right." I took Mac's letter from my purse. "This one is dated April the second. He's now in Belgium and thanks me for my beautiful photograph. Now here's the part:

"'Those infernal, flying bombs came over in cloudy, stormy, rainy, foggy weather, shaking the buildings with the vibrations of their exhausts. Until the American anti-aircraft units (God bless them) took over from the British units, it was really horrendous here. I was told the worst night occurred when I was in Paris in January. The antiaircraft defense broke down completely, and there were more than eighty direct hits that one night.'"

"That must have been during the Battle of the Bulge," Claire said. "I read how terrible it had been."

"Yes, the Allies had Houffalize as their objective, but the Germans bitterly defended it. Bad weather made it difficult for us. This is what Mac writes about this new system of defense.

"'. . . extremely simple and brilliant in conception; it prevented most of the buzz bombs from getting through, even in cloudy weather. After that, as they approached the city from Holland and Germany, we could see them coming in at night before we heard them. They traveled terrifically fast and were over the city in a few seconds if the anti-aircraft defense didn't shoot them down. When hit by a shell, though, they exploded in the air with a great, red flash of flame. The concussion was ear-shattering, beyond anything you can imagine, even though the explosion had occurred ten or more miles away. One night the concussion from a nearby explosion blew in our French doors and knocked Dick

Finiels's clothes cupboard over on top of him while he was sleeping.'"

"Dick Finiels?"

"He and Mac shared quarters," I explained and continued reading.

"'For a moment poor Dick thought he had been shot. Most of the V-1s, however, passed right over our quarters. Four landed several hundred yards away, but we had no deaths from them in our outfit. One man lost a finger when a door slammed shut on it with the concussion from a buzz bomb. Window glass flew everywhere, to be replaced by new glass the next day, until none was left. Then plywood and particle board were used in windows and doors.'"

"I'm already a basket case hearing about that," Claire involuntarily shivered. "Imagine actually being there."

"Yes; you know, when I read the letter to myself it didn't seem so bad. Reading it aloud to you makes me feel as if I'm actually there. There's not too much more. Shall I read on?"

"Of course," Claire said. "I'd like a cigarette, though. You have any?"

I pushed my purse towards her; then, taking a deep breath, I read on.

"'The death devices had a great effect on morale. They sped up the work everywhere. Everyone was realistic; we would all die soon if the Germans weren't defeated and pushed back. There was no griping when the men had to work twelve or more hours and then, at night, from midnight on, when they were alerted for air raids and paratrooper attacks, which fortunately never did occur during the Battle of the Bulge. Those were tense days: V-1s, V-2s, air raids, threatened paratroop attacks. We felt rather lost for awhile. Antwerp became a dead city; all those civilians who could afford to leave cleared out as quickly as possible and went to Brussels or some other quiet zone.

"'Most of us stayed up as late as possible at night to get really tired so that we could drop off, exhaustedly, to sleep. Some nights, however, if I didn't get to sleep before one flew over, I'd lie there and listen for each one as it came spluttering over the apartment

589

complex and hope that it would have enough fuel to splutter on elsewhere to explode over the Scheldt River flatlands.' "

I looked up at Claire. Her eyes were intently fastened on my face; so I continued.

" 'The V-2s were too dreadfully silent and powerful. One second, there was absolute silence; the next moment, there would be a terrifying explosion, and then another, and then ruin and destruction. Several minutes later a trail of white vapor in the sky showed the tail of the missile that had already penetrated deeply into the earth and exploded there, as much as forty feet underground. They are a catastrophic weapon, but nothing like the atomic bomb.'

"He goes on about staying within a certain area to limit his chances of being hit. He writes that more than six thousand tons of ammunition have been fired at them from October through March. Can you imagine that? That is eleven hundred and sixty tons within an area of six square miles, with their barracks as the center. He got his orders to leave for Paris and writes that he was afraid he'd get hit before he got to go. Whew! That was some letter, wasn't it?"

"That was some battle," Claire declared. "He's quite some guy, your Mac is."

"He also writes"—I smiled to myself—"that the thing that worries him more than anything is that I might meet someone else. That's what bothers him, that he's not around me."

"Doesn't it bother you?" Claire's eyes looked serious.

"No. I know how much he loves me. I know that I'm still not sure of my feelings towards him. Only time will tell." He was, however, so often in my thoughts, especially since Shep's death. I knew I couldn't lose him too.

"Claire, I want you in here please." Bill White had opened his door and stuck out his head.

Claire and I had been proofreading. "I'll finish it," I whispered to her. "You'd better hurry."

"Thanks." Claire quickly got up and grabbed her pad and pencil. "I hate these deadlines," she muttered through her teeth.

"I don't like Mr. White when he's so jumpy like this. We've always come through it."

"He can't help it, Claire. It's his responsibility to see the work done. You'd be like that too if you were in charge."

"I just don't like being under pressure." She hastened towards Mr. White's office.

I finished proofreading an article about American museums. Both Claire and I had worked on it, going to the Metropolitan and the Guggenheim museums for information. Mr. White had liked the article.

"Natasha," I said, as I handed it to her, "here's the last one you have to translate."

Natasha's forehead wrinkled as she examined the article. She reached to her ashtray, where her half-smoked cigarette lay.

"This one won't take me long." She took a long, last drag of her cigarette, then snuffed it in her ashtray. She turned back to her typewriter.

Erna looked over at us. "Natasha, have you finished translating that article on museums?"

"*Chort s nei!*" (The devil with her), Natasha muttered under her breath. "I'm working on it," she said aloud.

"Good." Erna turned to me. "Are you all through with proofreading, Tamara?"

"Yes, I am." I hoped she didn't have any more for me. My eyes were beginning to blur.

"Why don't you help Mr. Makarov then? He's having a problem translating that piece about popular American music."

I started to walk over to Alex's desk when Mr. White came out of his office. Through his door I caught a glimpse of Claire, sitting in the chair opposite his desk. Her head was lowered; one hand was shading her eyes.

Bill White went to Erna's desk and stood there, clutching the edge of the desk as if to support himself. His face was ashen and his usually expressive eyes were staring vacantly in front of him. It was as if all life and energy had been drained out of him.

"*Boje moi!*" (My God!), Natasha said under her breath.

We all stared at him, knowing that something terrible must have happened to have him look like this. It seemed to me that he was trying very hard to get control of himself. His voice, when he finally spoke, sounded tired and hollow.

"Our president died today of a brain hemorrhage."

For a moment I didn't think that I had heard him correctly. Then when I saw the shock on the other faces, I knew that I had. There was not a sound in the room, until Alex coughed. I noticed him reach for a handkerchief and carefully wipe his eyes, lifting up his glasses to do so.

Mr. White continued. "Mr. Roosevelt was having his portrait painted in Warm Springs, Georgia, when he died."

"Of what?" Erna had tears in her eyes, just like the Russians and me. So that was why Claire's head had been lowered in Mr. White's office.

"Cerebral hemorrhage, Erna. He went into a coma, and that was it."

"How old was he, Mr. White?" Olga's eyes glistened.

"Sixty-three." He paused. "If any of you wish to leave now, you may do so. I doubt if any of us can concentrate on work. It is up to you." He shrugged his shoulders, head bowed. Quickly he opened his office door and went inside.

I let my own tears slide down my cheeks. In my mind I could see Mr. Roosevelt—that noble face, with the jutting jaw and the steady eyes. I could hear his voice, just as we used to during his Fireside Chats. He was my first president, and I would never hear him speak live on radio again.

How cruel and final death was. I watched Natasha reach into her worn purse and get out a new pack of Camels. She tore it open, her lips clenched tight. She got out a cigarette and passed her pack on to Alex. Olga was straightening up her desk. Quietly she put on her jacket and left. Natasha and Alex had begun to talk in low tones. Natasha looked angry. That was her way. She would not cry, but later she would ask God why He had taken FDR away from us.

"Tamarotchka." Erna's voice was low. "Why don't you also go? I'm sure Claire's finished with Bill."

I shook my head, not trusting myself to speak. Erna gathered up her purse and poked her head into Mr. White's office. "I'm leaving now, Bill," she said. As she passed me, she gave me a comforting pat on the shoulder. "Good-bye, Tamarotchka," and walked out.

"Let's go, Alexei Sergeivitch, we're not doing any good here."
Natasha spoke gruffly.

Alex Makarov slowly got up. His shoulders slumped, as if
he'd aged some twenty years. I hoped this tragedy wouldn't cause
him to take up drinking again. If he did, though, who could
blame him? It was as if all of us had lost a close friend.

I thought of that oft-quoted speech FDR had made that one
night, and the line that I couldn't forget: "There is nothing to
fear but fear itself."

Claire came out of Bill's office, her eyes a tell-tale red. "Bill
said for us to go. It's no use, Tamara. Nobody can concentrate
here." She put an arm around my shoulder. "I know, honey. He
was your first president. I loved him too."

We walked home. It was such a beautiful afternoon, a day in
which to rejoice, not to mourn. There were few people walking on
Fifty-seventh Street. Those who did pass us by looked either preoccupied or openly wept. The quick change in storefronts surprised me. Most store windows had been emptied and displayed
only a large portrait of our late President, framed in dismal
black crepe. American flags flew at half-mast from most of the
buildings. How fast sad news travels. That handsome, calm face
with the dark-circled eyes stared out at us from nearly every
window.

Claire kept shaking her head. "I just can't believe it."

"Neither can I," I said. We stopped in front of one store to
look at an unusually compelling photograph of FDR.

"Claire, is Vice-President Truman going to be president
now?" Although Mr. Sullivan had drilled me thoroughly in
American history, I still found it difficult to adapt what I'd
learned to the reality of what was happening around me.

Claire bit her lips. "Yes, I guess so. Gee, Tamara, I hadn't
thought of that. What a contrast between the two of them. Can
you imagine what's going to happen to our country now? And our
nation at war?"

I thought of Mr. Harry S. Truman, the little haberdasher who
had been FDR's vice president. How could he ever fill the president's shoes? He didn't even resemble a president. Once I had
heard him on the radio and that once had been more than enough.
He certainly hadn't talked like a president, that was for sure. And

he was now going to be in charge of this big country. What was going to happen to our boys overseas? To Lanny? To Mac?

Eventually, we arrived at our apartment, tired, depressed, and totally miserable. It was just as if Claire and I had suddenly become orphaned. On the radio, over and over again, was played Chopin's stately, haunting funeral march. Back in time, I remembered hearing it for the first time in Peking in Dr. Ferguson's white-shrouded home. I had wept then for a sweet, aged lady whom I had hardly known. Now I was weeping for a stranger whom I had loved.

Claire and I had concert tickets for April the fourteenth. We had bought them early because Serge Koussevitsky, whom my parents knew, was going to conduct. I had promised Mama that I would go backstage to meet him. Had it not been for that, Claire and I would not have gone to the concert. We surely were in no concert mood.

At the concert it was announced that Serge Koussevitsky had been too overcome with grief to conduct that evening and his young assistant, a Mr. Bernstein, would substitute.

"Gosh," whispered Claire, "if I'd known that, we could have skipped it."

"Too late for that," I whispered back. "The lights have been dimmed, and the orchestra is tuning up. Had I known this, I too would have stayed at home."

"And, Tamara, I can't believe it. They've changed the program too."

"I like the *Eroica* Symphony," I told her. "Wasn't something by Mahler scheduled?"

Claire nodded, then put her finger to her lips. The young conductor was walking towards the podium.

Claire nudged me. "Nice looking, isn't he? If you have a flair for the dramatic, that is."

He was handsome in a way; he had dark hair and somber, expressive dark eyes. There was an emotional intensity in him that he conveyed to the audience.

"Look how upset he is. He seems awfully shaken up." I could barely hear Claire's voice.

"Everybody in the audience is," I whispered.

Once the orchestra began the *Eroica* we, like the others in the audience, sat spellbound, all eyes on the young conductor. Grief, sorrow and anxiety were all temporarily forgotten, replaced by the magic of this performance.

"He's like a magician with his baton. The orchestra is playing better than I've ever heard it play." Claire shook her head in awe. "What's his name?"

I looked at the program. Under the crossed out name of Serge Koussevitsky was the replacement's name.

"Leonard Bernstein," I told her. "I've never heard of him, have you?"

Almost two weeks had passed since FDR's death. President Truman was now in the White House.

"It's difficult to think of him as our president," Claire said one evening. "FDR was so vibrant. Do you know that Eleanor Roosevelt said, after her husband's death, that she felt sorry for the American people and the world."

"In the letter I received yesterday, Mac wrote that when they heard the news in Belgium on the thirteenth, the Belgians were the ones who really mourned. All ships flew their flags at half mast. He also wrote that the people there fear for the peace that was to come."

"I know. I'll bet Hitler's gloating about it." Claire said, with a trace of bitterness.

Then the phone rang; I took the call. "Hello? Oh, Matt!"

"How would you and Buddy One like to go to Jones Beach on Sunday? I need to take some photographs."

"Okay by me; you can ask Claire." I handed her the phone.

Claire was delighted. "We haven't been to the beach in ages. Sure thing."

After she had hung up, she smiled. "It'll be good to see old Matt. I invited him for popovers. You don't mind, do you?"

"Of course not. I'm glad tomorrow's Friday. Somehow this week has been too long for me."

It was almost closing time for us at the office. Everyone seemed tired and quite ready for a restful weekend. I planned to wash my hair as soon as I got home, then catch up on *Time* and *Life*.

There was a soft knock on the office door. Since I was the one closest, I went to open it. An officer stood there, holding his cap in his hands. He looked familiar, but, try as I would, I was unable to place him.

"Tamara?" he asked in a deep, friendly voice. Then suddenly it dawned on me. He had sent me his photograph.

"You're Andy Thompson, aren't you?"

By the silence behind me I knew that my office family was eavesdropping.

"Yes." I saw the approval in his eyes. "I just got home on furlough and rushed out here, hoping I'd catch you before you left from work."

"You almost missed me," I said. "Please come in. I was just clearing my desk up for the weekend. I'll be done in a minute, and then we can leave."

"I'd like to take you out for dinner," Andy said, looking at me earnestly. "We have so much to talk about, don't we?"

I liked him. He had a strong, masculine face and his eyes, when he looked at me, were steady.

"It'll be my pleasure; thank you," I said. I wanted so much to hear about Shep.

As we walked out of the building towards the curb, Andy looked down at me. "You're prettier than your pictures," he said. "Ah, here's the car."

"I didn't know you had a car," I told him. "Not many of my friends drive in New York."

"I do," he laughed. "I could never get along without my old buddy here." He patted the front end and slid behind the wheel.

"I've got a place in mind where we can have dinner and talk," he said. "It's quite a drive, but it'll be worth it. Would you like that?"

I couldn't think of anything more pleasant. It felt good sitting in his car, not having to worry about subways, crowds, or hailing a taxi.

"I like the way you drive," I told him, imagining him as a pilot. His face looked straight ahead; his mouth firm; his eyes unflinching; his hands strong and relaxed against the wheel.

"We're now out of the city limits, Tamara." He glanced over at me, smiling. The road had become a stretch of gray surrounded on either side by lush trees and bushes.

It was getting dark. Andy turned on the radio.

"Oh, I love that song," I told him, mouthing the words along with the singer. ". . . Gonna take a Sentimental Journey . . . "

Andy took up the words, singing along. "Yeah, I like that song too," he said, then turned into a side road and parked beside a picturesque Swiss chalet look-alike.

He turned off the ignition. "Here we are, Tamarotchka. I hope you like it." He got out and came over to my side, opening the door for me and taking my hand.

"They have the best fried chicken in this place. I can't wait for you to taste it."

"It sounds good," I told him, wondering when I should ask him about Shep.

He must have read my mind. Leaning back in his chair, he watched me reflectively for a moment, then leaned forward to look into my face. "You're probably anxious to hear about Shep, aren't you?"

"Yes." I was grateful to him for asking.

"He was killed in action, Tamara. That's all I know. He had had a lot of flying missions to his credit; he was one of the bravest men in this war, always volunteering for the most dangerous missions. God, he wasn't afraid of dying. They found his plane . . . blown to bits." Andy's face had grown pale and drawn. It must have hurt him to talk about Shep. "He was my best buddy . . . and, Tamara, he loved you. Your letters meant a great deal to him."

"I know that, Andy."

"His mother received his medals, the Purple Heart among them. You know, he was an only child."

Andy ordered wine, and we drank to Shep as we had known him. I was in a somewhat better mood now that I knew about Shep, although I still could not reconcile myself to his death.

At the apartment door, I thanked Andy, "It's really been a pleasure meeting you face to face," I told him, giving him my hand, "although I feel as if I've known you longer."

He laughed. "I feel as if I know you too . . . from Shep's descriptions, and your letters."

Suddenly I had an idea. "How would you like to go to Jones

Beach with Claire, Matt, and me? Matt's a good friend of ours."

"I'd like that." He appeared quite pleased and looked at me with affection. "It's meant a lot to me, meeting Shep's girl."

Claire wasn't asleep when I came in. She looked up from the book she had been reading. "Well, how was your date?"

"He's very nice. I invited him to Jones Beach. Okay?"

"Sure thing. Oh, by the way, there's some mail for you."

"Thanks. I want to wash my face first and get into bed. Gosh, but we had fun tonight."

We all had a good time at Jones Beach. Claire and Matt both thought that Andy was fun. That pleased me no end because I liked him myself. In many ways he reminded me of Mac—they had the same sense of humor, masculinity, and, most of all, Yankee-ness.

Once we were back in the apartment, Claire had been very quiet. Several times she started to speak something, then stopped.

"What's wrong, Claire?" I finally asked her. "Something's bothering you."

She had stretched out her sunburned legs and wriggled her toes. "Ah sho' am bothehd, honey chile." She lapsed into her inimitable drawl. "Ah know that yo' felt it too. Dat's wot's worryin' yo' ole Buddy."

"What are you trying to tell me, Claire. Without the Southern accent, please!" I was losing patience. "Come on, out with it."

"Just an uneasy feeling that I got. Andy's in love with you. Matt noticed it too."

"Shoot, Claire. We've been on just two dates," I protested. You don't fall in love that quickly."

"And another thing. You are attracted to him as well."

"He was Shep's friend. I enjoy talking to him."

"Well, just be careful, hon. Remember; you've got a great guy overseas, and he's counting on you."

I didn't answer her. It was my own damned fault for sharing Mac's letters with her. I did it just because he wrote so well. I decided to keep his letters to myself from now on.

When Andy phoned the next evening, I recalled Claire's warning. I tried to act nonchalant when he asked if I'd go out; yet the sound of his deep, manly voice triggered something deep inside me. Only Mac had affected me like that before.

"Will Tamarotchka condescend to go dancing tonight?"

I liked the way he called me by my diminutive, just as Shep had done. "'Twould be an honor, sir." I smiled into the phone. It would be good to see him again.

"Claire,"—I tapped her on the shoulder—"I'm going dancing tonight."

She looked up at me from her book. "That's swell; have a good time," she said cheerfully. It surprised me that she hadn't even asked who was taking me out.

I went out several times with Andy, constantly impressed by the cozy, atmospheric, out-of-the-way places that we visited. Like Jacques Dubois, he was a good dancer and enjoyed dining by candlelight and romantic music. At first we talked mostly about Shep. Andy and he had met while training at the air base before going overseas. Then we talked about ourselves. We both loved to dance and listen to the Hit Parade.

One evening when we had returned to our table after dancing, he had reached over to take my hand. He looked unusually serious. "Remember, Tamara, when we first met and what you told me about your attitude towards men? Shep had warned me about that too, saying that you just want to be friends with men, that's all."

Could Claire have been right after all? I felt uneasy.

He continued, "I know it's wartime, when our emotions get the better of us. We hurry to enjoy life before it's cut off." He became silent, and I knew that he too had thought of Shep. "I can't help it, Tamarotchka. I've tried to look at it your way, but I can't. I am in love with you."

Earnest, steady eyes looked through the candlelight at me.

"In spite of my friendship-only rule?" I smiled at him.

He grinned. "Yep, despite that doggone rule of yours. Still friends?"

I shrugged. "Andy, it's the war, just as you said. You think you're in love. Let's just enjoy our times together. Don't let's talk of love. Please?"

"Okay," he agreed.

But when we danced again, he held me tighter, as if his confession had given him that right. I didn't protest.

When we walked back to the car, he had taken my arm.

"You're shivering, Tamarotchka. Cold?"

"No, I'm all right. Just tired, I guess."

That night he asked if he could kiss me. "I've wanted to ever since I met you," he told me quietly, "but you told me how you felt about petting and all that and I respect your feelings. The only trouble is"—his grin was infectious—"I don't feel that way."

I laughed then and, leaning over, I gave him a light kiss on his lips. "There. Shall we go now?"

He moved towards me then, took me in his arms, cradling my head. "You think you'll get away that easily? This is what I mean, my darling." He pressed his lips firmly against mine. He kissed me once more, then placed his hands on the wheel.

"I love you, Tamara, more than I've ever loved anybody. I was engaged to a girl before I went overseas, but I want you to know that it's over. I never felt about her the way I feel toward you. I want to marry you, Tamara." His eyes looked deep into mine. "Will you marry me, darling?"

It seemed to me I'd heard those words before, spoken in the same solemn, earnest manner by yet another man. Suddenly a wave of homesickness and melancholy came over me. I stared into Andy's face, studying his finely etched features, seeing in them the strength and pride of a brave and gentle man.

I then told him about Mac. I couldn't be dishonest with him or myself.

"I've got to wait until after the war, Andy. I have to see Mac before I decide anything. You see, my feelings for him were so strong. Sometimes I still think that I love him. When I'm with you, Andy, I feel different. I'm all mixed up, Andy. I can't marry you now."

He had been silent for a time. His hands, I noticed, were clenching the wheel.

"That's another quality about you that I admire," he said. "You're honest. I'll be honest too. I am going to persist, young lady, in courting you; that is, with your permission. And may the better man win."

When I came home that evening, I told Claire all about it. I realized now that she could observe better from the sideline than I, who was directly involved emotionally.

"Boy, you sure get yourself into complicated situations, don't you, Buddy?" She shook her head affectionately. "How're you going to get yourself out of this mess?"

"Oh, I'll write and explain to Mac that I've met Andy and that he wants to marry me. You know what, Claire?"

"What?"

"I could never tell Andy that I loved him, but before Mac and I broke up, it had been so easy to say 'I love you' to him. That's what boggles my mind. Andy is such a terrific person."

"You don't marry someone because he's such 'a terrific person,' Tamara. You marry him because you love him."

"I know that, Claire. I'm all muddled up right now. I can't even think clearly."

"Just relax, honey chile, yo's got yo' whole life ahaid of yo'all," Claire grinned. "But one thing I'd lak to cawshun yo," she became serious. "I wouldn't write to Mac about being in love with Andy. That's a 'Dear John' kinda letter, and it'd be awfully cruel to do a thing like that." Her tone softened. "Get what I mean, Tamara?"

"Yes." Buddy was right. I would just play it by ear. I'd go out with Andy; I'd write to Mac and the others. After all, no one was pushing me into marriage. And as Andy had already said, "May the better man win."

39

A Tangled Web

"Faster, Andy, faster!" I yelled, as we sped over the empty highway. He had the top down on his Pontiac. The wind brushed against my face, and I loved it. I felt wild and free, like a bird let out of its cage.

"I'd like to, Tamarotchka, but I can't. It's against the law to go much faster. I'm doing seventy and the speed limit is forty-five miles per hour."

"Can't you go just a bit faster?" I pleaded. "Andy, there're no other cars coming or going."

He pointed to the speedometer. It had reached seventy-five. I glanced at his calm, serene profile. There was a slight smile on his lips, but his eyes were on the road. His hand on the wheel barely moved.

"What is it, Andy? Why are you smiling like that?"

"It's you," he answered. "You make me smile. At times you're like a child, like just now. Why do you like to go so fast?"

"I don't often get to ride in a car. It makes me feel good with the wind in my hair. Besides, I love to see everything on the side of the road flash by me. It's as if it's all the trees, houses, and people that are moving past us, not us moving past them. Andy, I've been used to rickshas. Cars are a luxury for me."

That amused him. "I'd forgotten that you're my China doll. It is a great feeling to go fast. I used to feel like that when I flew my plane, way up over the clouds, all alone up there in the universe. Only," he made a wry face, "sometimes I wasn't alone."

"That must have been frightening."

His eyes were still on the road, but his lips tightened.

"Yes, Tamarotchka, it was. However, it had to be done, and we did it. We all had the best training that our country had to offer. The bad part was when some pilots, like Shep, were hit. That made us all only more determined to bomb hell out of those Nips. As for our lost buddies, they died the way they would have wished. Had it been my time, I too would have wanted to go that way."

He slowed down, lowering the volume on the radio.

"There's nothing I love more than to drive out into the country and keep on driving along an open stretch of road, listening to good music. You're alone with your thoughts—communing with nature, so to speak. Everything around is so peaceful and natural that you can't help but feel peaceful too. Except that today I'm enjoying it even more because you're with me. I love you, or have I already told you that today?"

That's what Mac used to tell me on the phone, I thought to myself. *How much like Mac Andy is.* Only Mac, if I remembered correctly, had been even more loving with me . . . except, of course, on that terrible prom night.

Later, when Andy and I danced, I thought again of Mac. He and I had never danced well together . . . always in a corner, two steps forward, to the side, and then back again. I remembered how tired my feet had felt. But Andy was a good dancer. It just seemed natural for me to slip inside his waiting arms and rest my head against his shoulder. He didn't use cologne. He had just a good, clean smell.

"You're awfully quiet tonight," he said.

"I know." I moved away from him so that I could look into his eyes. "I've been doing a lot of thinking these days."

"About us?" He sounded hopeful.

"Sort of. And Mac."

"Have you thought about what I asked you the other night?" He tilted up my chin, "I meant it when I asked you to marry me, Tamarotchka." His eyes were quite serious.

"Will you take me home, Andy? I'm tired. Let's not talk about marriage now."

"Sure thing, honey. Are you okay?" He was all concern, motioning to the waiter for the bill.

When we got to the car he hurried to open the door for me.

"Would you like the top down?"

"Yes, please. Thanks, Andy." Gosh, what a considerate person he was. "I feel better in the fresh air." We rode in silence, except for the music. I lay back with my head resting on the back of the seat, watching the darkening sky. A few stars had appeared, blinking so faintly at first that I wondered if they really were stars. I watched them and, as the sky grew darker, I realized that they were.

"Starlight, star bright . . . " I began.

"Too late, Tamarotchka." He smiled. "It's only if there is the first star in the sky that your wish will come true."

"Doesn't matter," I said nonchalantly. "My wish wouldn't have come true anyway."

He threw me an amused glance, then shook his head. "You know, little Russian girl, at times I believe I don't really know you. You mystify me."

Quite a few others had told me that. The funny part of it was that I was just being myself.

He kissed me goodnight in the car. I enjoyed being kissed by him, but I felt the difference when I compared it to being kissed by Mac. I did not have that heavenly, sinking feeling of wanting to be kissed and kissed forever, of wanting to be a part of him like I had with Mac. *You're dreaming again, Tamara*, I chided myself. Had Mac's love letters so hypnotized me that I now believed there could be no other man for me but him?

"Thanks for a great evening, Andy." I got out of the car before he had a chance to get out on his side. "Don't bother to walk up with me. Good night."

He watched me, peering out at me from the side door window until I had reached the door. I waved to him and ran inside.

"Well!" I exclaimed, as I opened the door. Claire and Matthew were sitting on the floor, examining some photographs. Matt looked up at me, a big grin on his placid face.

"How about it? How's the new boyfriend?"

I glowered at him. "It's not funny, Matt. I like him."

"But you don't love him, Buddy," Claire emphasized. "That's the difference. That's what I've been trying to get through her thick skull, Matt. She's almost ready to marry Andy."

I felt my face flushing. "I may or may not. Frankly, at this point, I don't know. What I do know is that the more I see him the more I like him."

"And Mac?" Matthew adjusted his glasses, giving Claire a quick look. I got the uneasy feeling that I had been the topic of discussion just before my arrival. It was annoying that I had to justify myself to them. On the other hand, they were friends and cared about me.

"I don't know, Matt. I'm so damned confused about everything and you guys aren't helping by your inquisition. I'm not a child."

Claire grinned, looking at Matt. "Hm-mn, sometimes I wonder about that, old Buddy." She paused. "Take a look at these pictures that Matt took of us at Jones Beach, Tamara. They're good." She must have felt remorseful for teasing me.

"Okay." I knelt down by them and sifted through the photographs. Matt knew his craft well, choosing the perfect backgrounds for his subjects. There was one of me that I would have liked to send to Mac, but I wasn't ready for more teasing. "They're good, Matt," I told him. "And now, if you'll both excuse me, I'm going into the other room to write some letters. I owe Mama one." I said goodnight and smiled at both of them to show them that I wasn't mad.

I wrote first to Mac, a long letter, which I ended "With love." To Mama I wrote about Andy and for her and Papa not to be surprised if I married him.

I never expected the storm that followed. Mama sent me a special delivery letter by return mail saying that she planned to visit us the coming weekend. Papa had added a postscript saying that both he and Mama had been shocked to learn of my change of heart. I found myself seething as I reread their letter. After all, whose problem was it? I had written them only because I felt they would like to know about my plans. I was a twenty-three-year-old working woman, not a child.

I called Andy at his home. "My mother is coming to New York. She wants to meet you."

He laughed pleasantly. "Gee, that's mighty nice of her. Let's plan on taking her out for dinner. Or, listen, perhaps she might enjoy meeting my folks."

I had already met his folks, and they had been wonderful to me. They were what I considered genuine American parents—gentle, good folks who enjoyed sports, apple pie, and hamburgers with French fries. They were friendly, hospitable, middle-class America. I shuddered when Andy mentioned going to their house with Mama. No telling what mood Mama would be in.

"Let's wait about that, honey. Let's take her to the Chalet. The drive there is scenic, and she loves fried chicken. Later on, she can meet your parents." As he agreed, I heaved a sigh of relief. That had been a narrow escape.

He sent me a kiss over the phone. "I am anxious to meet her, sweetheart. If she's anything like you, she must be swell. I love you, darling. I'm glad that you're at least thinking about marriage to me. That's mighty encouraging."

"It's still a maybe, Andy," I whispered. "Look, I can't talk now. I've got work piled sky high."

After we had hung up, I thought of his compliment about Mama. The way her letter had read, she did not resemble me at all. Already I had seen the icicles forming among her written words. Well, let her see for herself how fine Andy is, I told myself. No matter what she said or did, it was my life to lead the way I wanted to. So far, I thought, I'd done rather well.

Since Claire was going to be in Washington, my plans seemed to work out beautifully. Mama and I would have complete privacy. I groaned, already picturing her disapproving looks. Papa and she had both set their hearts on my marrying Mac. "He is the only one for you," Papa had written in his postscript. "Remember that." How could I forget when everybody else felt it their duty to remind me? Do *this*, not that. Marry *him*, not him.

"What's wrong, Tamarotchka?" One morning Natasha and I had both come in early. She came over to my desk and placed both hands at the base of my neck, massaging my back with expert strokes. "You seem so tense today. I can feel your muscles right here, all taut and hard. Relax, child, you're too young to tie yourself in knots. And, another thing"—she stopped massaging for a moment—"You've been lighting one cigarette after another. That's not good for you, my dear."

I hadn't realized it was so evident. But look who was chastising me about smoking—the office's "chimney." I looked past her at Alex Makarov who had just come in. He had been watching us. When his eyes met mine, he winked.

"Natasha Grigorievna, this is not a massage parlor. This is the OWI." He laid his hat on his desk and sat down.

"Oh, mind your own business, Alexei Sergeivitch," Natasha had snapped. "I can do whatever I want until nine o'clock, and Tamarotchka needs to relax. How can we let her Mamotchka see her this way, all nerves?" She bent her head to look into my face. "There now, feel better?"

I had felt like a piece of dough under her kneading but, once she stopped, I did feel better. "Thanks, Natasha, and don't worry," I told her. "I'll be totally relaxed with Mama around."

"What's the problem?" Alex asked, lighting a cigarette.

I let Natasha speak for me. "Her mama is coming to inspect her latest suitor, that's all."

Alex smiled. "That air force captain? A nice enough young man. I'll bet, though, that the lieutenant who writes all those letters is the one Mama will prefer. Eh, Tamarotchka?"

Just then Mr. White and Erna came in. Alex took up his pen and began to scribble away.

Natasha gave me an encouraging smile, "Don't mind him," she said in a stage whisper.

It had not been one of my best days. In fact, everything had gone wrong. Claire had gone to Washington, and I had to sub for her, which was fine with me except that Mr. White talked too fast, and I had to keep asking him to repeat. I had cleaned the apartment last night but had forgotten to check the refrigerator, so that faced me tonight. Then Erna hadn't been in a good frame of mind.

"Tamarotchka, why don't you go downstairs and visit the beauty parlor where I go? Maria could do wonders with your hair. You know, if you had her put it up in braids like mine, it would look neater, don't you think?"

No, I don't think, I told her silently, but out loud I said, "Maybe I will some time, only not while my mother's here. She likes my hair long." (This was true, in a way, since Mama had remarked once that my hair was very pretty.)

I was relieved when five o'clock finally showed on the face of my watch. This day had seemed endless.

"Well, Tamarotchka, have a good weekend, and give our regards to your Mamotchka." Natasha bustled off, clutching her worn leather purse. Everyone trooped out, all anxious to rest for the next two days. I think that I was the only one who dreaded this weekend.

Back in the apartment I made it a point to check out the refrigerator. It's a good thing I did. I'd forgotten about the spaghetti we had made last week. Mama would have been horrified. I could just hear her warning me, "Tamara, you have to be more careful. You can't leave food that long—even in the refrigerator."

Then would have followed, "Yes, Mama, I'm sorry, Mama. I'll be more careful from now on." I took out the bowl and hurriedly rushed into the bathroom and flushed the spaghetti down the toilet, reminding myself to tell Claire about it.

Then I sat down to write to Mac. I really should have done it some time ago except that I didn't know how to tell him about Andy and the possibility that I might marry him. I didn't want to hurt Mac and write him what Claire termed the "Dear John" letter, but there seemed to be no other way, and I was all confused. So I sat down and wrote him a hasty letter, then ran out of the apartment and quickly thrust it into the mailbox around the corner.

Later that evening Andy and I drove to Grand Central Station to get Mama. We were right on time. I saw her trim figure approaching, carrying her overnight case. "There she is," I said, tugging at his arm, and we hurried to greet her. Andy took her overnight case right away, although she had tried to hold on to it. "Here, let me," he told her kindly, and she had released it then.

Mama did not say much during the time we walked from the station to the car, except for the usual courtesies that are expected of introductions. She sat in the backseat with her gloved hands clasped in her lap, and looked straight ahead.

"We're taking you out for dinner, Mama," I told her. "You can rest for a bit in the apartment, get acquainted with Andy, and then we'll go out. How's that for planning?"

"Whatever you decide," she told me. "We really don't need to go out. I'm not hungry, but if you are, I certainly don't mind sitting here by myself."

Oh boy! So that's the way it's going to be. I bit my lip and stole a glance at Andy. He looked perfectly calm, but there was the hint of a smile upon his lips.

He looked into the rearview mirror at her. "Give us that pleasure, Mrs. Rubleva," he said. "Tamara has been so happy, knowing that you were coming today."

What a diplomat! I stared at him in surprise and caught his merry wink. He was thoroughly enjoying himself. And it seemed to be working. I could sense Mama relaxing. She was now looking out of the side window at the skyscrapers.

"Isn't New York beautiful, Mama?" I exclaimed. "All these bright lights blinking away. Isn't it just perfectly lovely?"

"Interesting. Yes, I can see why you like it. But, personally," she sighed, pulling at her gloves, "I prefer Cambridge's intellectual atmosphere. New York is too big, too crowded and impersonal for me."

"You'll enjoy it better when we're out of the city, Mama. Wait till you see the Chalet."

Mama didn't answer. It was as if she had suddenly remembered once more the reason for her coming.

At the apartment she freshened up. She took off her hat and smoothed her dark hair over her ears. As long as I can remember, Mama's hair style had been the same. Two waves on either side of her head, the straight white part in the middle, and the low chignon at the nape of her neck. It gave her a classical look: dignified and, at times, forbidding.

I was surprised how much at ease Andy was in her presence. As for me, I was feeling anything but. I was on pins and needles worrying about whether Mama would either explode or turn colder than the North Pole. I could sense the storm brewing. Her coming to New York had proved that to her and Papa I was still a child, unable to make my own decisions. So Mama had boarded the train to come to the rescue! *Hurrah*, I thought, rather sadly. *No matter how old I become, they'll always consider me a child.*

"Ready?" Andy looked at the two of us, smiling.

"Come on, Mama." I took hold of her arm.

Mama, at this time, was in her, what I would have labeled, "quiet-before-the-storm" mood. She could not be rude to Andy, for he had behaved like a perfect gentleman. But I knew—from the very moment when Andy had taken her overnight case and her eyes had skimmed over him—that she would never like him, much less accept him. Even before she had left Cambridge, her mind had been made up. No matter how outstanding Andy was, nothing would change Mama's already biased opinion of him.

And how was I to behave? Confucius had said that the proper behavior towards parents and elder brothers was the "trunk of Goodness." In other words, those who behaved well towards their parents and elder brothers in private life, in public life seldom showed a disposition to resist the authority of their superiors. Papa had made me memorize that passage in Chinese. This, I had been taught, was how I was to behave: to do what Mama, being my parent, wished. I was in America now, though, and the rules were different. Here my heart ruled, not Confucius.

Mama did enjoy the Chalet; she even condescended to have wine with us. After dinner, when the band had come up on stage, Andy asked Mama if she danced.

"I did, long ago."

"Would you mind if your daughter and I dance?" he asked her.

I was so proud of him then. He was courteous and considerate. I thought Mama could find nothing wrong with his behavior. Knowing her, however, she probably would. She would definitely find something bad about Andy.

Still, we did have a good time. The wine had relaxed Mama, and once she had even smiled at us. Had Andy not been courting me, she probably would have approved of him. But because he was, she would fight for me like a mother lioness for her cub.

At the apartment door, Andy kissed me goodnight. To Mama he held out his hand. "Mrs. Rubleva, it's been a pleasure." Mama had to acknowledge him. Her lips formed into a smile, but it was not her lovely, spontaneous one.

"Most kind of you, Captain," she murmured, lowering her eyes. "The dinner was delicious."

Back in the apartment, I asked her how she had liked Andy.

"Oh, he's young, good-looking," she answered frostily. "Of course, he can't compare to Mac at all. Mac has"—her voice softened—"that certain rare trait about him. That's what Papa and I like so much about him."

"But Mama." I looked at her immobile face. "You're not the one marrying him. I am the one who, supposedly, will be the bride." I couldn't help being sarcastic. It annoyed me that I had to explain my feelings to her. "Anyway, how do you know that Mac's so special? He's changed, you know. Even he has admitted that. Any person fighting in a war is apt to change. Besides, I knew Mac for only two months."

"And Captain Thompson? How long have you known him? Even less than that." Mama looked at me triumphantly. All of a sudden I saw Vanya's face in hers, grinning at me, as he did when I was in trouble at home.

It was useless to argue with Mama. I didn't want to fight with her or suffer her "silent treatment" again. "Mama, I'm going to bed," I told her, giving her a hug. "I made your bed in the spare room. Let's rest, huh?" I respected her too much to disagree with her out loud.

I heard her moving about in the spare room, then her light went out. I listened patiently and soon heard her gentle snore. How could she sleep like that, when she was messing up my life?

I got up quietly and moved a chair to the window. Lighting a cigarette, I inhaled it deeply and stared out into the still darkness. I kept trying to envision Andy with Mama's eyes. There was an uncomfortable doubt in my mind when I thought of him that way. Of course, he was good, fine, true blue. But many men were like that. In a way she was right. I should know him better. I smiled humorlessly to myself. Mama would be mighty pleased if she knew that the seed of doubt she had planted in my mind had begun to rearrange my emotions. How deeply that seed had been sown, I would find out in due time.

The next morning, Andy and I took Mama back to Grand Central Station. She had been quiet during most of the ride. At the station she was even more aloof. However, when we walked up to the train with her and helped her up the steps, she changed. Her smile was warm as she gave Andy her gloved hand.

"It would be so nice if you and Tamara visited us next weekend." She had looked straight into Andy's eyes, her smile gracious. "I'm sure you'll enjoy Cambridge, and the Professor is anxious to meet you."

She knew that I knew that it was all an act. Andy didn't. He smiled his honest smile and replied, "I'm sure we'll enjoy the visit. It is kind of you, Madame Rubleva."

Mama's eyes had that serene look as she turned to me. "Tamarotchka, make sure you come. Papa is so anxious to meet the Captain." She reached out to give me a hug. "We'll be looking forward to your visit."

"It was swell of your mom to invite us." Andy lit his pipe before taking the wheel.

I wanted to change the subject. "Do you like to drive?" I asked him.

He removed the pipe from his mouth. "Sure do, honey," he answered cheerfully. "I enjoy the feeling of power that it gives me, like piloting a plane. You realize then that it's all up to you to get yourself to where you want to go. The big machine and you." Sideways, he glanced at me. "You're upset about your mom, aren't you?"

I hadn't realized he'd noticed. "Yes," I answered. The anger I had felt all along now surfaced. "Andy, she wouldn't even give you a chance; she's so prejudiced."

"It's all right, honey. They'll come around next weekend when we see them. Don't worry. They don't scare me, because I love you very much. We'll work it out together, the two of us."

When we came back to the apartment, I nestled against his shoulder. He lit a cigarette, his eyes narrowing slightly as he blew out the smoke.

"No matter what, Tamara, I shall always love you," he said in a firm voice.

"I know that, Andy."

He then gave me a strange look, sort of puzzled. "You know, my Tamarotchka, you've never actually said 'I love you' to me, have you?"

"I realize that, Andy." That had been part of my frustration.

I could not tell him that. The words just wouldn't come out. Those words I had said to one man only, and to him I had said them with all my heart. It had been natural and right that I should do so.

Andy held me close, "You know, some day, after we've been married for a long, long time, all this that's happening right now will seem ridiculous to us."

I should have been amused at his thought, but I wasn't. "It might," I said, not too convincingly. Whether it was the aura of Mama's presence hovering over me or not, I was already beginning to feel different towards Andy.

"Good night, sweetheart," he whispered, bending his head towards me. I turned away, not wanting him to kiss me. God, but I felt irritated. . . . But I didn't know with whom.

Then my conscience pricked me. Andy was not to blame. I blew him a kiss, "Good night, Andy. Thanks for being so understanding about everything."

He had smiled in return and sped off in his car.

The apartment was as silent as a graveyard. Claire had not yet returned. I changed into pj's and turned on the radio. As if on cue, the *Roumanian Rhapsody* Number 1 came on the air. I pictured Mac's blue eyes looking tenderly into my face, his gentle smile shyly waiting to press my lips. But before doing so, I heard myself saying, "I love you, Yankeeman." And heard him whisper in reply, "It's us; that's why."

"Damn it; damn him; damn!" I turned down the volume, but still the music throbbed in my head, louder than ever, blasting my mind with its power. I quickly turned the dial to *off*.

Why should others tell me how to live? Was I bound to them by invisible chains? Bound to Mama? To Papa? To Mac? Or even Andy? At least Lanny didn't tether me to him, except with his unrequited love. It was Mac, damn him, who had the tightest hold on me. Why? The invisible chain he held around my heart tightened every time I thought of him. It just wasn't fair. God and Confucius, both, I whispered, please help me.

Enough of this silly nonsense, Tamara, I told myself. *You're being dramatic, as if you're on stage. Forget it. You're a healthy, lovable, attractive young woman with friends who love you.*

Relax. Think. You've got the whole wide world at your finger tips and time enough to think things out. Then those words Polonius spoke to his son, Laertes, came to mind: "This above all, To thine own self be true, and it shall follow . . . " Why should that refrain have come to me during a time like this? What line came next? Ah yes. "And it shall follow, as night the day, Thou canst not then be false to any man."

"Baloney!" I said loudly. This time not even Shakespeare could help me.

I must have dozed some. The next thing I knew I heard a key turn in the lock. Claire, rosy and tired, had returned.

"Well, I thought of you all weekend, wondering what Mama thought of Andy and what you three did, and so forth and so on. Fill me in, will you, Buddy? I'm dying of curiosity." She kicked off her heels and sat on her couch, yoga-style.

"Did you have a good time at home?" I asked her, stalling for time so that I could think.

"Sure did. My parents sent their love to you. Well, come on, what happened?"

I made a face. I might as well tell her everything. She nodded as I talked, commiserating, sympathizing. When I had finished, she thought for a while, then finally spoke, her words slow, as if she had first rehearsed them in her mind.

"From what you've told me about Mama, I would have expected that attitude. You'll hate me for saying this, Buddy, but I agree with her one hundred percent. Andy's a nice enough fellow, but he's not the one for you. I haven't even met Mac, but . . . " She turned to look at the framed photograph on our bookcase. "All you have to do is look at this fine, intelligent face, and then"—her eyes looked mischievously at me—"read those beautiful letters that he obviously wrote from his heart. God, Tamara, if he weren't spoken for already, I'd run after him myself—to kingdom come, if it be necessary."

The ride to Boston had been very pleasant. Andy drove at a steady pace, keeping within the speed limit. At lunchtime we stopped at a tiny restaurant, hidden beyond some trees, away from the busy highway.

"Andy, what do you plan to do after the war is over?" I asked him.

He lit his pipe, shaking the match automatically. "Oh, probably go back to the company I had worked for before the war."

"What kind of company?"

He laughed. "I should have told you, honey. I'm in advertising. That's what I've always been interested in. I was a business major in college."

"When we're in Boston and Cambridge, I'll show you where I went to college; then we can stop to see Harvard Yard. We can see the Russian War Relief headquarters on Dunster Street. It was a favorite hangout of mine, where I did volunteer work. Shep used to help me there too." It was exciting to think that I'd be seeing Cambridge again, but this time with Andy.

"Ah, sure," he said. "I'd like that."

By the sound of his voice, he didn't seem that interested. "Perhaps it'll bore you. We'll skip it."

"Whatever you wish, darling." He glanced over at me. "It's your hometown."

We drove across the Anderson Bridge that loomed over the Charles River.

"I used to bring my books and study there. See?" I pointed out the exact spot under a shading elm. He couldn't look because he was busy driving. "I have to watch the road, hon."

It didn't matter anyway. I loved it. Everything about Cambridge made me feel good inside. The lovely red-brick buildings of Harvard standing in watchful silence over the smooth waters of the Charles. The stately old homes and majestic shade trees lining the streets—my Cambridge, the city beautiful.

"I once wrote an essay about this river." I looked at him in profile. "The teacher thought it so good she had it published in our school journal. I came one evening all by myself and sat on the river banks just to watch the Charles. As it gradually became darker, getting on towards twilight, the colors of the river kept changing. The myriad colors surprised me, Andy. I sat there, enthralled, making notes on all the colors, and wrote my paper when I came home."

Some sailboats passed by.

"I used to sail with Raphael, a friend of mine. He had a boat like that one." I pointed to one, its white sails billowing against the wind. "He also played the bass fiddle."

"Fancy that."

"Oh, Andy you weren't listening, were you?" I laid my hand on his sleeve.

"Tamarotchka, you're sweet and terribly sentimental. Everything is beautiful to you, but, darling, those days are gone. You'll never recapture the past."

I will too, I told myself stubbornly. Andy could never feel that way because he was too much of a realist. He didn't care for the past because it was gone. Done with. Finished.

I stopped pointing out familiar spots to him, although my own eyes strayed through Harvard Square, noting Felix's newsstand, where Papa bought his newspapers; the Coop nearby where Mac and I had bought Papa's Christmas tie; Mass Ave itself, where so much had happened. We passed Annitchka's apartment. My conscience pricked me. I remembered I owed her a letter.

We came to Mt. Vernon Street. To the left was the "haunted house," still desolate and dilapidated as ever.

"Oh, look," I raised my hand to point, then stopped. He wouldn't be interested. Just an old house.

"What is it, hon?" He slowed down.

"We're almost home."

We drove up the hilly street, turned the corner, and drove to the end of the street. "There it is." I pointed to the last house. "It's the one with the brown-colored fascia and gray steps. That's where my parents live," I told him. I looked at the curtained windows and suddenly realized that this was no longer my home; that I was now more like a guest.

"You'll like my Dad, Andy. He's sweet." I hoped Andy wouldn't feel ill at ease. He appeared perfectly calm, though. "Mama is the one who likes or dislikes. Papa likes everyone." I knew that I was trying to convince myself as well.

"Darling, I'm anxious to meet my future in-laws," he whispered, giving me a light kiss. "I'm ready. Shall we go to brave the lions?"

We walked up the steps on to the porch, and I rang the bell.

Some time passed before I heard the lock being turned. Maybe they had been upstairs. Then the door opened, slowly at first. When he saw us, he opened the door wider. Vanya grinned at my astonishment. Then he looked over at Andy.

My heart sank when I saw Vanya. "I didn't expect you to be home," I said to him, feeling apprehensive. Mama had not mentioned Vanya. "Oh, Vanya, this is Captain Thompson. Andy, my brother, Ivan."

Andy held out his hand. Vanya gave him a quick once-over. They shook hands.

"Come on in," Vanya opened the door wider. "Mama's waiting in the living room."

Uneasily, I began to suspect that these actions were the prologue to a family production, staged and directed by Mama. Vanya would be on his best behavior and Mama the gracious hostess. She usually was, however, so why did I feel that there was a lot of play-acting going on? "Andy, how delightful to see you once more. Please, do sit down." She motioned towards the sofa. "We were certainly looking forward to your visit here."

Andy, unaware of my suspicions, basked in the warmth of their hospitality. He sat down, patting the cushion next to him, "Here, hon, come sit by me," he said. I noticed Vanya, watching us with his twisted grin.

"The Professor will be down soon," Mama told Andy; then she turned to me. "Aren't you happy to be home, dear?" Her voice was unusually solicitous, but I noticed the edge to it. I loved Mama very much, but now, as an adult, I understood what each inflection in her voice meant. Something lay behind this invitation to visit Cambridge. I realized uneasily that before this evening was over, Andy and I would find out. Why in the world was Vanya here? Neither he nor our parents had mentioned his coming home.

Papa's footsteps coming down stairs interrupted my thoughts. He soon appeared in the archway, wearing his good navy suit and the red tie that Mac had presented to him that Christmas of 'forty-three. Papa came up to us and embraced me. He looked good, I thought. In his eyes, however, I sensed a warning.

"So-o, this is Captain Thompson," he said, much too heartily for me. "So pleased to meet you, young man. Tamara has written quite a bit about you; so we feel as if we already know you. You're in the air force?" He shook hands with Andy. "Please sit down, Captain. Now"—he clasped his hands, then looked around at each one of us—"who would like a glass of sherry? I have a bottle that I've been saving for a special occasion." He smiled, but I saw that his eyes did not.

Tension, that's what I felt. To Andy, it probably all seemed very familylike and pleasant. Everyone except Vanya wanted sherry. I wanted to help Papa, but he waved me down. "Relax, dear. Let me do the family honors."

Vanya, sitting on the other side of Andy, gave me a friendly smile. Big brother, now the genial host, did the honors. "Captain, Tamara tells us you flew missions overseas."

"Yes," Andy replied, "I sure did. Quite a few missions, in fact, but, thank the good Lord, that part of it is over for me now." He took out his cigarettes and offered one to Vanya.

My brother grimaced. "Never touch them. You know it's a terrible habit, smoking. I can't abide it. I have hay fever." He sniffed, then emphasized, "Tamara is the only one who smokes in our family."

I watched Andy quietly put the pack back into his pocket. "Sorry about that, Vanya. I didn't know it affected you this way. It is a bad habit, I agree. Unfortunately, I'm addicted. It helped a lot when I flew missions."

"I suggest you drop the habit," Vanya said.

Andy glanced at me, amused, then turned back to Vanya. "Where were you stationed, Vanya?"

Vanya shrugged. "Oh, I've been all over," he waved one hand in the air. "You name it, Captain, and I'll bet that I've been there, from the China seas to the shores of North Africa." His eyes focused on the wall across the room. Now he was waxing poetic, in his element. "Ah, Italy, that magical Isle of Capri, where the young women parallel the landscape in beauty. I've been to Egypt and seen the Nile and to India—the Taj Mahal, a magnificent tribute of one man's love for his woman." He looked at Andy in triumph.

Before Andy could say a word, Vanya continued, "You should

have seen the girls I dated; they were beautiful beyond description."

"I can imagine." Andy nodded politely.

"My brother was one of the more fortunate ones," I couldn't help saying. "He did not see much of the war in the way that you did, Andy."

"But the poverty I saw in India, the misery! Then the contrast of the Taj Mahal arising like a heavenly palace in the midst. Sis, you would have enjoyed that."

"You've certainly had some experiences in your war travels," Andy said.

Vanya had not noticed his sarcasm. I didn't blame Andy, not after what he himself had gone through.

"Andy, tell me, what do you think about the war? Think it'll end soon? I'd like to hear your viewpoint."

God and Confucius, my brother could be persistent. He and his unending viewpoints. "Vanya, I don't think Andy came here to discuss the war with you. I certainly didn't." I glared at him, taking Andy's hand in mine.

Andy shot me a grateful look. "I honestly don't like to talk about the war, if you don't mind. Tamara's right. I've lost too many good buddies in it. It's not that pleasant, you must know, when you're in its path."

Fortunately Mama came out of the kitchen. "Lunch is ready. Vanya, take the Captain upstairs to wash up," she directed, taking over.

Papa had been sitting in his armchair, quietly listening to our conversation. He had not said a word, but his face had been thoughtful.

"Come on, Andy." My brother's voice sounded jovial, "I'll show you where the bathroom is." On the way up I heard him ask Andy if he really truly loved me, his little sister. Inside, I seethed. Andy's answer had been too low for me to hear.

The table in the dining room looked beautiful. Mama had gone all out to make this a festive occasion. Why didn't I feel as festive myself? Why did I keep waiting for the storm that I knew would be coming my way?

At dinner Vanya sipped his milk slowly. He didn't drink

wine. He carefully studied Andy, scrutinizing him, as if he were interviewing him for a position. I kept admiring Andy for his unbelievable calm and tact.

"What, Captain Thompson, do you know about Russian literature?"

I wanted to laugh at the absurdity of it all. I didn't dare look at Andy. Vanya's inquisitional manner of questioning Andy embarrassed me. All I heard was a silent laugh. Then Andy calmly replied, "Sorry to disappoint you, Corporal, but I know very little about Russian literature, although I have read some works by Tolstoi, Gogol, Lermontov . . . and others. I don't have that much time to read. There are other priorities in my life right now; the war, for example."

"Too bad," Vanya slid Papa a knowing glance that to me displayed triumph. I examined Papa's face, but he was now looking down at his plate. What the devil was going on?

"Do you realize that some of the world's greatest literature has been written by Russians?"

"Corporal Rublev, of course I know that. However, you must admit that the French, Italians, Spanish and English, as well as the Americans, have not done too badly in the literary field." Andy smiled at me, then rested his eyes on Vanya's flushed face. "You're so well-read and knowledgeable;" he said coolly, "I want to know from what college you have graduated?"

Touché! I could have cheered for Andy. Instead I smiled broadly, encouraging him silently in the word duel. Mama and Papa too were listening intently.

Vanya began to splutter. He hadn't expected to be questioned. "Uh, you see, the war has interrupted my studies. I'll be going back to Harvard." If not a prejudiced professor, now the war was to blame.

"What are you planning to major in?" At this point, Andy was now taking the offensive.

Andy had touched Vanya's sore spot, his nemesis. My brother hesitated. Aha, he hadn't expected Andy's question, I gloated, relishing his discomfort. "I guess that I'll be taking Slavic courses after the war. It all depends, you know, on how good the professor is. My father, since he is at Harvard, knows who they are."

Oh, God and Confucius! Please don't bring Papa into it.

"And then what?" Andy's voice serious, as if deeply interested. "What are your plans after graduation?" He gave Vanya a friendly grin, "I'm sure you have a long-term objective."

Bully for Andy. I could have hugged him right then and there. He had sized up Vanya right away, seen him for the egomaniac he really was. Vanya was being given a more than substantial dose of his own medicine.

"I'll probably teach at Harvard," Vanya replied loftily, looking at Papa for approbation. "*This* is the place for scholars to be, you know."

Ah, yes, dear Vanya, always trying to impress, aren't you?

Andy nodded pleasantly. He took Vanya's reply in his stride. "That's terrific, Vanya. I applaud your plans for your future and certainly hope you succeed." He stood up. "Ma'am, thank you. It was a delicious dinner. I'm only sorry that we have put you to so much trouble."

I could see that Mama felt flattered. In spite of her antagonism towards him, she had been delighted at his praise.

"Thank you, Captain Thompson. I recall the fine restaurant you took me to last week. This is nothing compared to that."

"But that meal there was not my cooking," Andy countered. "Your meal was made by you. That's what made it even more special."

Vanya placed his hand on Andy's sleeve. "What, Andy, if I may ask, do you know of classical music?"

So that was part of their scheme. To have Vanya put Andy in a bad light. I stared at Vanya in amazement, my anger rising. They wanted to embarrass Andy; that was it. Reveal to me how little he knew. So sorry, my dear family; you're only embarrassing me by your actions. You are hurting me, not Andy; can't you see that? It surprised me too that Papa had not interfered.

"Classical music is okay," replied Andy, "although I'm no expert on it. I take it you are. Personally I prefer the Hit Parade songs. Your sister and I listened to them while driving up here. How about you?"

Vanya's eyes stared unseeingly somewhere towards the ceiling. He bit his upper lip. "Yes, once in a while I do listen to that type of music, when there's nothing else worthwhile on the radio.

Who's your favorite classical composer?"

This amused Andy, and he laughed outright. "Boy, you ask the darndest questions, pal. I'll tell you whom I like. Bach, Beethoven, and Brahms. Satisfied? The three Bs."

Even Papa had smiled at that.

"And what is it by Brahms that you like, consider his most monumental work?" Vanya persisted.

I was taken aback by Vanya's nerve. How could Mama and Papa let him continue on like this?

"I think we'd better go now, Andy." I took his arm. "Mama, Andy and I are going to drive through Cambridge. I'm going to show him Radcliffe and other places. Is there anything we can do to help you before we go?"

"No, dear." Mama came over to us. "You and Andy have so little time here. Go and enjoy yourselves."

Vanya followed us to the car. "Andy, you never did answer my question," he asserted. "I asked you which one of Brahms's compositions you thought his best?"

Andy took out his pipe. He slowly filled it with tobacco out of his pouch. Then he lit his pipe carefully, placed it in his mouth, and puffed away till the tobacco had turned a flame red. "Mm-m." He looked at Vanya thoughtfully, as if he were mulling over this question. "To answer your question—I know it's of importance to you—let me roll it about in my mind. Ah, yes." He gave me a wink. "It's like this, Corporal Rublev. I enjoy Brahms. I believe it's his *Tiger Rag* that really sends me." He opened the car door for me, helping me inside. Puffing on his pipe, he smiled at a bewildered Vanya, waved, then got in on the driver's side.

Recalling the sight of Vanya's face gave me a great deal of pleasure for several days. Finally, he had met his match.

"I want to apologize for my brother, Andy." Puzzled by it all, I shook my head. "I had no idea this would happen or even that Vanya would be home. You kept your temper under trying circumstances; not many people could have done that."

"Think nothing of it, hon." Andy's eyes were reflective. "Once I realized what he was up to, I began to enjoy our repartee. What amazes me, though, is how two siblings can be so different. If he weren't you brother, I'd call him the most obnoxious

622

person I'd ever met. Since he is your brother, I'll do my best to tolerate him."

How understanding of Andy! As we drove around Cambridge, I kept thinking of all the things that had happened this past week: Mama's visiting us in New York, my intuitive foreboding of some unpleasant happening, crowned by this visit home. I didn't know my family any more. I had not been surprised at Vanya's behavior. However, I never believed that he could have been so rude to a stranger, especially to someone above him in military rank. Whatever. Then Mama, and, most of all, Papa? Why couldn't they have stopped this? Unless it had all been prearranged so that I could see Andy as they wanted me to see him? I was still my parents' little girl; untouched, unblemished, but disobedient. Therefore, they would save me, in their own inimitable way.

On the way home to New York, Andy and I had a long talk. He had been thoughtful at first.

"I'm afraid that your parents don't think too much of me," he said. "I guess I'm too American for them, aren't I?"

"I think Papa liked you."

"He hardly said two words to me, Tamara." Andy turned off the radio. "Does your brother act like that with everybody?"

"Surprisingly, he does, Andy. I think it's his way of trying to show his superiority, which, in fact, is his inferiority. I don't know, Andy; Vanya and I have never gotten along."

"Don't worry, hon. When we're married . . . "

"No, Andy, we're not marrying yet. You'll be going back soon, won't you?"

"Yes." His hands tightened on the wheel. "Five more days and I'll be flying bombers again. I was hoping I'd be leaving a wife behind me."

"Please, Andy, don't hurry me. When I get married it'll be forever. I can't marry you before you leave. I'd forgotten you're on furlough. Or," I laughed without humor, "I made myself forget."

"I did the same thing," Andy said. "I try not to think about leaving you. It hurts already."

"I'll write, Andy. I promise."

After that, we stopped talking, both lost in our own

thoughts. When he arrived at the apartment house he pulled me to him.

"Look at me, my Tamarotchka," he whispered gently. "I want to look into those beautiful dark eyes of yours. There." He placed his hand over my brow, moving it back over my hair. "I just want to remember you always this way, even when both of us are old and gray."

He didn't kiss me, just patted me gently on the cheek.

"I love you, darling," he murmured, his face serious. "Do you think you can tell me that you love me now?"

"Andy, I've got to think things out. I'll be talking to you." Avoiding his gaze, I grabbed my overnight case, waved to him, and ran towards the apartment door.

Strange, how, eventually, things fall back into place and confusion turns to order once more. Was it the trip home and seeing Andy through the eyes of my family? Was it the fact that Andy had reminded me so much of Mac? I don't know, but I now realized that I had not been honest with either Andy or myself. Perhaps the romantic places, the candlelight dinners and romantic music, the automobile rides in the night, had all entranced and spellbound me. Gradually, I came to know that it had been Mac all along. There was no replacement for him; there never could be.

No replacement for Mac? I remembered with horror the hasty letter I had written to him, telling him all about Andy. Oh, God and Confucius, what a mess I was making of my life.

Claire was out when I came in, apparently on a date. I sat and wrote a long letter to Mac, explaining how I had written him on impulse, without having thought things through. I had been confused, but now I had finally made up my mind. It was time that I did, I told him.

When Claire came home I told her what I had done. Her face had, at first, clouded over, until I told her that I knew now for sure that I loved Mac. "Thank God—and your Confucius—that finally you've gotten some sense into you." Once again, she became her efficient self. "Send him a cablegram. Let him know right away that he is the one you love. Poor guy, he deserves that special consideration from you; that is, if he hasn't gone off his rocker at your first news."

I would have done anything to repair the damage. Bless Claire. She dialed the Western Union number. I had hastily scrawled a message, and she read it to the operator:

"DISREGARD MY LETTER ABOUT ANDY. I SHALL ALWAYS LOVE YOU."

The operator said she'd send it right away.

It was only then that the world turned right side up for me. Once more I felt free and happy, knowing that there could be only one love in my life, and that was Mac, my Scottish Yankee-man.

In New York City, 1945

40

Wait for Me

"I can't get over how the Allies have been able to crush the Germans. Have you seen the *New York Times* this morning, Tamara?" Phyl took a sip of her coffee and made a face. "Holy Toledo, but this coffee's strong!"

"Dilute it with more cream, then." I passed the pitcher to her. "Only don't use it all. I need some too." I watched her as she poured it. "Yes, I read part of the article. Are you talking about the Allies crossing the Rhine in so many places?"

"Yep, I'm talking about the invincible Krauts. Now they're finding out how strong we are. The British Second Army and our own Ninth have crossed the Rhine River and are now occupying the Ruhr area. Even though the Germans desperately need the industrial output from its factories, they just couldn't put up enough resistance. Hallelujah!"

"It's about time," I said. "I'm wondering what the Germans are planning now. According to the *Times*, they were trying to shift their troops but couldn't since we have been attacking them on all fronts. Now the Allies are in control of 130 miles of the Rhine's east bank."

"I wouldn't be surprised if the Germans surrender soon. You know what has shaken me up though? The Germans are supposed to be using prisoners as slaves. In *Life* there was a photograph of prisoners taken by the Germans. It's unbelievable, Tamara; they looked like skeletons with skin. I can't believe the Germans would starve their prisoners."

"I'll believe anything about the Germans. I never thought

the Japanese were bad until they had arrested Papa. As for the Germans? The Russians and the Germans have never liked each other. That I know. As a child I used to sing a song in Russian about the Germans. It wasn't very nice."

"Come on, Tamara, I didn't come here to Longchamps to spend the time talking about the damned war. Thank God, though, the war news, for a change, has been good. I've come to hear the dope on Mama and Andy, and how your weekend was at home. Also, I have some good news to tell you." She smiled, immense satisfaction showing on her face.

"I know; you have inherited a million dollars from some far-away uncle or aunt." I paused, trying to think. "Whatever it is, it's made you look terrific. Ah, I know. You have lost weight."

She chuckled. "Close. I did lose weight. But why?"

I studied her. Her hair just shone and fell into soft waves around her shoulders, her face radiant. Unusual for her, she was wearing little makeup. "Elementary, my dear Watson. I can tell exactly what you are about to tell me." I laughed at her surprise. "I know, Phyl. You're in love."

"How'd you guess?" she gasped. "I know. Norma told you, huh? That . . . damn, I begged her not to let on."

"No, Norma didn't tell me, Phyl. The moment I saw you I could see that you looked different. When you said you had news for me, and the way you've been glowing, I realized that you had a new man in your life. Okay. Tell me about him."

"His name is Steven Kingsley, and he's a graduate of Annapolis. Tamara, he's a dream—six foot two, eyes of blue, blond, with the most beautiful teeth. God, he's really one swell guy. I met him—would you believe it—in Grand Central Station."

"I'm so happy for you, Phyl. It's about time you met somebody special. He's single, isn't he?"

At that Phyl grinned. "You bet he is. I made sure of that. I know a fellow who's in Steve's outfit, and he checked for me. No; Steve is handsome, loving, and single. What more could a girl like me want?" She paused. "Now tell me about you."

I gave her a full account of what had happened, from Mama's arrival in New York to Vanya's abominable behavior at home. "I can't figure out why Vanya has always delighted in tor-

627

menting me. He's done it ever since I was little. So far as I know, I've never done anything mean to him; that is, intentionally."

She looked at me as if she were deliberating whether she should or shouldn't tell me what was on her mind.

"What is it, Phyl?"

"Well, you know, I think it's because Vanya feels that you have always gotten the better end of the deal. Remember; I know him only from that one date I had with him."

"That, I recall, ended rather badly, didn't it?" I said.

Phyl lit a Marlboro, sliding the ashtray to her side. "Damn, don't they have bigger ashtrays in this joint? You'd think a place like Longchamps could afford them. Anyway, where were we? Yeah, Tamara, the way I figure it, your brother is jealous of you. How much older is he than you?"

"Two years, and he's never let me forget it, either."

Phyl nodded. "You were the one who got the good grades, the attention, and the praise. Am I right?"

I had to agree. "Vanya was bow-legged and a loner, Phyl. That was only part of the problem."

"You once told me he used to hit you," she said, letting her eyes stray around the restaurant. "Didn't you also say that he liked it when you got in trouble?"

"Oh, Phyl; yes. I know he's never liked me. I can't help that."

"There's more to it than that, I think." Phyl pursed her lips, blowing a smoke ring in front of her. "That was perfect. Did you see that?" she asked.

"You used to make those at Hood's. You *should* be making perfect smoke rings by this time," I teased. "What do you mean by 'more to it than that?'"

"He may have something wrong with him. I'm no doctor. I don't know. I believe he's paranoid—everybody's out to do him wrong. As a result, he tries to be cunning, to outfox people." Phyl stared at me, lost in thought. "I think I'm right, Tamara. That's why your parents shield him. They know that you are okay (even if, in my opinion, you do have some crazy ideas), but they honestly worry about Vanya. That's from an outsider's point of view. Do you or don't you agree with my amateur psychiatrist's diagnosis? At least partially agree with me, can't you?"

She looked so earnest and concerned. *Dear old friend. How*

honest and thoughtful she is, I thought. I recalled how Annitchka had cautioned me never to tell Phyl why Mama had been so furious with her, saying that Phyl would really be hurt. In thinking it through, though, I reasoned that I'd really hurt Phyl if I didn't tell her the truth. I knew the truth, and I wasn't going to hide it from my best friend.

"Phyl . . ." I found it difficult to begin.

She smiled. "Ah, you do agree that there's something wrong with him. You yourself told me that he flunked courses and only studied what he wanted to. That he didn't like having people ordering him to do things, not even the professors at Harvard. Right?"

"That's not what I wanted to tell you, Phyl. Don't interrupt me, because it's painful enough to have to tell you." I looked at her, and my eyes filled up. "I know why Mama was mad at you. Annitchka was the one who told me before I left Cambridge."

Phyl sighed heavily. "Finally we get to the truth. It's been bothering hell out of me, but I knew you'd tell me once you yourself found out. Well, for God's sake, what is it?"

"Vanya wrote to Mama telling her that you were a lesbian. That morning when you came to the house and she wasn't home? Well, this is what must have happened. The mailman came, and Mama got our mail. Papa had already gone; I was asleep. Mama read Vanya's letter, became infuriated, and took off, knowing that you were coming. She must have gone to Harvard to tell Papa about it. Then she came home and found us, happily traipsing down the stairs to greet her. Offering her that box of Fanny Farmer chocolates was the last straw!"

Phyl gave a derisive laugh. "I can well understand her fury, then. The lesbian queen who has sullied her innocent daughter is offering the mother a bribe. Oh, my God, what fools we mortals be! God! I can't believe it . . . but, from all I know about your brother, and I know you well enough to know that you won't lie. . . . Good heavens, so that's the reason."

I laughed, relieved that it was now all out in the open. "And Annitchka had to explain to me about lesbianism."

"I could have told you if you'd asked me," Phyl said; then she pushed her hands out in front of her. "No, not from experience, Tamara. I love men too much for that. I give you my word, I'm no

629

lesbian and have no intentions of deflowering you."

"I know that Phyl. If you were one, I'd still like you as a friend—although, I'd not ask you to spend the night with me if Claire went home to Washington."

She laughed at that. "I feel bad, because I honestly love Mama. Remember how much fun we used to have with her? The stories she would tell us about her youth? How could Vanya do something like that?"

"You spurned his advances, Phyl. You, in other words, insulted his manhood. Therefore you should be punished. An eye for an eye! Don't forget; he's punished me too. For Vanya, that was a bonus."

"Thanks for telling me, Tamara. You know, I kept thinking over each time that I had had anything to do with Mama. I just couldn't figure out what I'd done wrong. Now, what about Andy?"

"Oh, he had to leave. His furlough was up. We've written to each other. Actually, Phyl, I think that both he and I were caught up in a romantic interlude, if you can call it that. He came home after a year of hell and found me. I found someone somewhat like Mac. Both of us enjoyed listening to romantic songs and going to candlelight restaurants where we could imagine being in love. I really thought it was the real thing, Phyl. I did think of marrying him; really I did. Then, when we went to Cambridge, I saw him in a different light. I realized that even if he was a fine, upstanding Yankee, he was not for me. Vanya, in spite of his monstrous behavior, had done me a big favor."

"Ho, ho, ho, methinks that Vanya would rue it if he knew he had helped you out of a bind. Poor guy, he's a misfit in this world, isn't he? I sort of feel sorry for him."

"You're more generous than I could be, Phyl," I conceded. "I used to feel sorry for him when we were at PAS, the Peking American School. The other kids made fun of him because of his awkwardness, his ugly, black-rimmed glasses, and his bowlegged walk. But then, when he took his vengeance out on me, I lost any feelings towards him—good or bad. I haven't told you this before because I felt ashamed for him. When the Japanese jailed my parents, and Vanya and I were home alone, Vanya tried to rape me when I was asleep."

"My God!" Phyllis couldn't hide her surprise.

"I could never talk about it before because it sickened me every time I thought of it."

"No wonder." Phyl's eyes were full of compassion. "Why?"

"He had learned about sex from our servant and decided to experiment with me, knowing what a sound sleeper I was. In a way"—I couldn't help giving her a rueful smile—"that would account for my—what you and Sam call—'prim and prudish' attitude. Today, I'm able to talk about it. I think that I'm healed. I'm stronger, much stronger now than the shy little seventeen year old who came here in 'thirty-nine. I'm impatient now to get on with my own life. Is that selfish of me?"

Phyllis had tears in her eyes. "No, Tamara. My God." She reached for her Marlboros. "I wish I'd have known all this when I first knew you." She laughed. "Isn't it strange? When people meet you for the first time, they think—at least it's the way I thought—Gee, this beautiful girl with her sparkling, big brown eyes and that glorious mop of reddish-gold hair—how utterly charming and exotic. A China doll! You see, we Americans tend to think that someone who's lived in the Far East is a novelty; glamorous, unusual. Americans are like that. Truly, you do give that impression of being different. I'd never have thought that you had suffered in any way or undergone ordeals that I, a happy-go-lucky American, cannot even imagine. I'm glad you opened up to me, Tamara. I can now understand you better."

I sighed. "I'm glad too that I've leveled with you. It's been difficult to keep that secret to myself. Already it's made me feel better. Let's forget that now, okay? I don't want to dwell on the past."

"Let's dwell on the future then." Phyl's eyes gleamed. "You mind if I order another popover? They surely are out of this world."

"That's what Longchamps is famous for. Claire and I come here on Sundays for brunch. It's just a short walk from our place. Sure, order two if you wish. I'm rolling in money today. Haven't found a dress yet that I can splurge on. Go ahead."

While she ordered, I took out Mac's letter. "Knowing how much you enjoy his letters, I've brought along Mac's most recent one. I also have one of Sammy's, that you'll find interesting."

Phyl nodded, then broke out into a wide grin when the waitress brought the two golden popovers to her. "Glory be; you're sure you don't want one?"

I shook my head. "While you're eating calories, I'll read the letters to you. Okay?"

"Mm-m." Her mouth full of calories, Phyl nodded.

"Remember me telling you about writing Mac the letter about Andy and me? Then, after that, writing another one admitting how confused and wrong I had been in even thinking of marrying Andy? And then sending him the telegram to disregard everything, that I loved Mac, and only him?"

Phyllis grabbed her head in mock dismay. "Yes, yes, and yes, I do remember. I recall also how I thought that for sure you'd gone off your rocker."

"Okay; this is what he wrote after receiving all three. Now, he wrote this on the twenty-fourth of April of this year, 1945."

"Go on; I'm all ears," Phyl put a large slab of butter on her remaining popover.

" 'Dearest Tamara,

" 'How I wish that I were home now to take you in my arms, kiss your tears away, and tell you that I love you. I'm lonely, terribly lonely—for my "mean and awful" Vixen, and I can't wait until I get home once more to see you, feel you close to me, watch you laugh, hear you whisper in my ear, thrill to the touch of your lips.

" 'You tell me that I deserve someone better than you. You must be terrible. No, thanks, I'll take you. And who am I to deserve someone better than you? You'd think I was a saint with a halo. Thank God. I've become human here in this overseas theater of operations. Don't sanctify me just because I'm over here. I do love you for it though, darling. It rather makes me feel like a shining knight in an armored division riding my forty-horse-powered steed down the road to victory.

" 'First, I got your penitent letter telling me your trials and, thank God, your repentance. Second, the *terrible* letter arrived. Third, the cablegram came. Thanks to the inefficiency of the postal and telegraph system, I received the news about Andy and marriage so that I knew the outcome *before* the earlier events. Therefore, I had not worried too much.' "

"My God!" Phyl's eyes nearly popped out of her head. "What luck for both Mac and you."

"Yes," I smiled. "God and Confucius certainly were looking out for me. Mac continues.

"'However, had they been received in reverse order, I'd have probably just gone out, gotten stinko, and found me a Belgian girl who would compris, and from then on John P. McNish would have disintegrated into a hopeless shambles of the haloed saint he now is, and would *he* have been sorry! Damn it. I wish I were home so we could make up in an indecent way.'"

At that Phyl put down her fork and roared, "And I bet he would have. He's a great guy, Tamara. I sure hope you realize that now."

"He sees the humor in all this," I admitted thankfully. "Well, do you want me to read the rest? It's not that interesting."

Phyl pushed her plate away and replaced it with the ashtray. "Of course, silly. You know I've got a soft spot for Mac. Read."

"'Vixen, are you sure that I love you enough to live with you when you are old and chubby? Will we love each other as fervently as we do now? Do you love me more now than a year ago? How many times do you want me to kiss you when I return?'"

"Ah-h-h, he misses you." Phyl looked amused. "Do you love him more now? Have you thought about that?"

"I don't know." I looked at the beautiful, neat script, and pictured Mac, tongue in cheek, writing to me. "I have to see him in the flesh to really know. I can't answer you now."

I read on, smiling to myself.

"'I want you to have long hair, a hat (no damn pink veil!) shaped like an orchid...'"

Phyl interrupted, chuckling, "He sure remembers that day he left, doesn't he?"

I simply continued reading out loud as if she hadn't spoken.

"'...that gray and pink outfit, high-heeled shoes, so your

lips will be nearer mine, and no—I repeat—no girdle will be worn, so that I can feel you live and warm when I press you close to me. I hope that won't shock you, but I'm so starved for you that physical longings are just as strong as mental and spiritual longings. My dearest, when a man like me loves a girl like you, those longings increase in geometric proportion to the length of absence.

" 'Why do I have so many allies—Mama, Papa, Erna, Buddy, James Martin, Sammy, Alex Makarov, dear old Natasha, Claire, and of course, our godmother, Phyllis? All I want is you, and how I do want you. I hope I can have the patience to wait the long months. Don't worry. I'll see to it that I keep my cool. I always work harder when I begin to get impatient and downhearted. Concentration on hard work helps out a lot.

" 'Darling, I love you whether you are in my arms, in the same room with me, even in the same world with me. Now that you know what love really is and has been all along, I love you all the more.' "

"Wasn't that lucky, Phyl? Can you imagine if he'd gotten my letters and telegram in the right order? Boy. . . . I'm really going to be careful in how I handle things from now on."

"As I've said so many times before, you're damn lucky, Tamara, to have Mac. Not too many men, at least, not the ones I have met in my life, would be as sincere and faithful. Hold on to him, gal, believe me." She leaned towards me, her face amused. "Tamara, our waitress has been watching us. We've been sitting here for two hours, talking. All we've ordered are coffee and popovers. Should we leave now?"

I looked over at the waitress. When she saw me turn her way, she whipped out her pad and started to write on it. I beckoned to her. "Check, please." Then I turned to Phyl. "We'll walk to the apartment."

"Good. I'd like to see Claire again. She's such a nice person."

"She won't be there. She's visiting her cousins."

"Oh . . . well. What news did Sammy write you? I haven't heard from him for ages." Phyl watched me get out my wallet. "Let's Dutch treat, huh?"

"No, this is my treat. If I know you, you're broke."

"Okay, and you're right; I am broke. It's a good thing tomorrow's the first of May. I spent my last dollars on a carton of Marlboros." Phyl got up, slinging her purse strap over her shoulder. "This was a delicious brunch. Thanks heaps. And the conversation has been edifying. Is that the right word to use?"

"Edifying or instructive," I laughed. "I enjoyed it too. Reminds me of the times we spent at Hood's. Remember?"

"Yep, except that there we discussed poets and professors," she said. "Now we're discussing life. That's a more complex problem, isn't it?"

Back in the apartment, Phyl walked over to the bookcase. "Yep." She took up Mac's picture and studied his face. "He's the best for you. He's got such a—I don't know how to say it—but you know what I mean—just look at his eyes; how honest, kind, intelligent they look, and that smile."

I laughed at her attempt to describe Mac. "No need to do a sales talk. I agree with you, old friend."

"You mean you do love him now?"

"Seventy-five percent sure."

"And the remaining twenty-five percent?"

"I have to see him in the flesh once more. I'm being cautious, you see. If he's not the person I see in his letters, well then, we'll see, Phyl, when he returns."

She replaced the picture. "Remember 'Had we but world enough, and time, This coyness, Lady, were no crime.'"

"I sure do," I said, continuing the quote: "'We would sit down, and think which way To walk, and pass our long love's day . . .' One of my favorite poems. Do you remember the ending?"

"Yep; I do. But first, tell me who wrote it and the title." She snapped her fingers.

"Didn't think I'd know, huh?" I laughed. "Andrew Marvell, poet. 'To His Coy Mistress,' title. Now quote the ending for me." I snapped my fingers.

She grinned. "I used to think of you when I read this part: '. . . then worms shall try That long-preserved virginity, And your quaint honor turn to dust, And into ashes all my lust. The Grave's a fine and private place, but none, I think, do there embrace.' Seventeenth-century poet he may have been, but his words can be applied to our twentieth century, specifically to one certain Russian gal I know."

"Touché; to each his own," I admitted. "Let me read what Sammy wrote. I think you'll be surprised towards the end."

"I know you won't let me rest until I've heard it, so shoot."

" 'Dearest Scatterbrain Tamara . . .' "

"Well, I agree with Sammy about that," Phyl interrupted. I ignored her comment.

" 'I spoke to our mutual Mac today, and he told me of the numerous letters from you that have reached him, as well as the telegram. We looked at your picture and talked about you and came to the usual conclusions that you're a light-headed brat!' "

Phyl nodded her head in agreement. "Sam's got you pegged all right."

"Oh, be quiet and listen. That's not the part I want you to hear. Wait. Let me see. Oh, yeah, here it is.

" 'Mac let me read excerpts of your letters to him, and they surely contain some rather contradictory orders to him. Some request that Mac forget you; still others are cancellations. Then comes that telegram. And so what is poor Mac to do with his dopey Tamara?

" 'Mac has shown patience and candor during this long and painful year that places him in my highest esteem. In addition to the qualities that you and I discovered during the first week we knew him: high intelligence, profound culture, dignity, malleability, and good architecture, I came to know another man, such as you will never know even after years of marriage, if any.

" 'I have seen him under conditions of war that I cannot relate but in which he could have readily died so as to save the lives of his men. Mac was in the gravest danger of any officer in my organization. . . . Oh, if I could only tell you all I know. Yes, Mac has cleared himself honorably in all his tests, whether in the blazing fury of war or in the temptations of the flesh.' "

Phyllis broke in. "I remember you telling me about that. Didn't some colonel charge Mac with cowardice under fire, or something like that?"

"Yes, after the invasion, sometime around the middle of June of last year, it happened. Mac could have been court-martialed and shot if found guilty. As it turned out, he wasn't even brought to trial. Actually, he was a hero, since he left the ship after the ship's captain himself had already left. Imagine! The colonel in charge of the beachhead wanted his men to learn a lesson not to abandon ship, no matter what. That's something, isn't it?"

"Whew! And I thought the U.S. Army could do no wrong."

"Then Sammy writes that he became obsessed with a French girl who was the sister of a boy on whom he had operated, and he married her. He can't speak a word of French; she can't speak English."

"Well, there're other ways of communicating," Phyllis said. "Old Sammy will have no problems; of that I'm sure." She stretched her legs. "What else were you going to tell me? You had mentioned something about a poem."

"Yes; I remember now. I sent it to Mac hoping that it might cheer him up. Knowing how much you enjoy poetry, I thought you'd like to hear it. Remember when I used to help Prof. Harry Dana do Russian translations during our sophomore year? Well, one of the poems he eventually had published was this poem by a Russian writer, Konstantin Simonov. It's called 'Wait for Me.' This poem, Phyl, convinced me that I should do what I'm doing: *waiting for Mac.*"

"Okay, but first let me get a cigarette and make myself more comfortable. This damn girdle is killing me."

As soon as she got settled, I started to read.

" 'Wait for Me.

" 'Wait for me and I'll come back,
But wait with might and main!
Wait throughout the gloom and rack
Of autumn's yellow rain.
Wait when snow storms fill the way;
Wait in summer's heat.
Wait, when . . . false to yesterday
Others do not wait.
Wait when from afar at last
No letters come to you.

637

Wait when all the rest have ceased to wait, who waited too.

" 'Wait for me and I'll come back,
Do not lightly let
Those, who know so well the knack,
Teach you to forget.
Let my mother and son
Believe that I have died;
Let my friends, with waiting done,
At the fireside
Lift the wine of grief and clink
To my departed soul.
Wait, and make no haste to drink,
Alone, among them all.

" 'Wait for me and I'll come back,
Defying death. When he
Who could not wait shall call it luck
Only let it be,
They cannot know who did not wait
How in the midst of fire
Your waiting saved me from my fate,
Your waiting and desire,
Why I still am living, we
Shall know, just I and you!
You knew how to wait for me
As no other knew.'

"Never in my wildest dreams, Phyl, did it even enter my mind then that someday I'd be sending this very poem overseas to a soldier for whom I myself would be waiting."

41

The Final Accounting

When Claire and I entered the office, we found Natasha backed up against her desk, her usually pleasant face glum. She looked as if she had lost her last friend on earth. "Have you heard the latest?" she asked.

Claire and I both stopped in our tracks. "What?"

She flipped the ashes of her cigarette into her empty coffee mug. "There have been rumors for some time, but now they've been confirmed. It just came in over the radio. The British have uncovered a death camp at Bergen-Belsen with piles of bodies thrown into a huge mass grave." Her voice hardened. "Another savage monument to Nazi cruelty."

"Massacred by the Germans?" I asked in horror.

Natasha shook her head. "No, Tamara, this camp didn't specialize in massacres. Its inmates had been subjected to hard labor and purposefully starved in the process. Horrible!" She shivered at the thought, then sat on the edge of her chair. "That's not all, either. The Allies are discovering more and more of these camps in previously German-occupied territories. The terrible thing is that some of these camps have been in operation for more than a decade, since after Hitler came to power. At first, for the Poles who had resisted the Germans; then for the Czechs, Danes, and others. The Gestapo put them into 'protective custody,' so to speak, along with political prisoners, Communists, and antifascists. Protective custody indeed." Natasha angrily squashed her cigarette. "They made the inmates their slaves, forcing them to work under the most primitive conditions, giving them little to eat. And then," she said, staring at me, then turning to Claire, "if they were too feeble to work? Kaput! They let them die!"

"How could they, Natasha?" Claire's eyes filled with tears. "These were civilians, weren't they?"

"Ah," Natasha sighed, "there's still more. Their great leader, Der Führer, named his chief of police, Heinrich Himmler, the head of these camps. One of Himmler's henchmen developed a way to dispose of the inmates who had become useless. It has become known as 'The Final Solution' and was first used in labor camps that later became death camps. As the Allies move deeper into German-occupied territories, they are discovering more of these secret death camps. Few German civilians, from what I understand, even knew of their existence. So far the Allies have found them at Dachau, Auschwitz, Treblinka, Majdaneh, and elsewhere, each one more horrible than the one before it. Each camp had its own specialty—whether it was a well-built gas chamber or a special laboratory where staff members performed experiments on people." Natasha, with shaking hands, lit another cigarette. "Women and children were included."

"I cannot believe it," Claire muttered. "I cannot believe that people can be so cruel."

Natasha looked at her in pity. "You must, Claire. Had you been living in Europe, you too might have ended up in one of these camps, your arm tattooed with a number."

"Why me?" Claire asked in surprise. "What would the Germans have had against me?"

I too stared at Natasha.

Natasha's face flushed. "If your parents had been living in German-occupied territory after 1935, they would have been stripped of their German citizenship. You would have had to wear the Star of David to identify you. The 'Final Solution' was the program designed to exterminate all Jews from Europe. Herded into ghettos, they had to live there till they were deemed ready for deportation to a concentration camp."

"Natasha, are you sure?" Claire sat down in her chair, her lovely face ashen.

"I am sure," Natasha went on, almost robotlike, in a monotonous tone. "They herded the Jews like cattle, packing them into

640

box cars like sardines, and sent them on to their 'resettlement' areas, which were actually the concentration camps. All this, mind you, was done in a perfectly organized manner, with Nazi efficiency. They divided inmates into special groups, each one tattooed and then categorized according to his ability to work. Some of the more fortunate ones died en route. Others had to suffer longer before they too breathed their last."

I took a look at Buddy and saw the tears rolling down her cheeks. My own eyes blurred.

"Why, Natasha, why?" I heard my own small voice ask. Erna, Olga and Alex had come into the office and had been listening as Natasha spoke.

Erna walked over to her desk, laying down her pocketbook. "Because, Tamarotchka, they're cruel and believe that they're the superior, the 'master,' race. Anyone not a member of their race did not belong, or, as the Red Queen in *Alice in Wonderland* would say, 'Off with his head.'"

"You mean that they could arrest anyone on that pretext of not belonging to their 'race?'" Olga asked.

Natasha nodded. "Of course. You have to understand, though, that the Jews came first. After them came those who did not show absolute allegiance to Der Führer. It's been going on since 1933, maybe even earlier, but has only recently been revealed, this April, in fact. What better solution for *personae non gratae?* They—as slave labor—did the work. Dwindling German food supplies didn't have to be wasted on the prisoners. Those who died of exhaustion and starvation were replaced by living prisoners. Those too weak to work went to gas chambers."

"Don't forget the crematoriums," Alex reminded us.

Claire's eyes got bitter, "Crematoriums?"

"Yes." Alex put his arm around her waist. "They were a good way of concealing evidence. Burn the bodies. What better way to solve an annoying problem?" His usually gentle face had hardened.

"I always thought wild animals were sometimes cruel, tearing each other to pieces, but never people, human beings!" Olga put her fists to the sides of her head. "I don't want to listen to this any more. Forgive me."

Natasha gave her a disdainful look. "Olga Mihailovna, just

thank the good Lord that this nightmare is ending, at least in the European sector. There's good news too. The Russians are about to take the Reichstag building at any moment. The last I heard they were just a few miles from Berlin. Any moment we may hear that the German dogs have surrendered."

Erna nodded, agreeing. "Did anyone hear on the radio that Adolf Hitler had taken poison? I just got in on the tail end of that report."

Just then Mr. White hurried into the office, his usually harried face glowing with excitement. "Well, my friends." He stopped, looking at us in turn. "It's official now. The Russians have planted their red victory banner on top of the Reichstag dome. Herr Hitler and Eva Braun, his former mistress, both are dead, having taken poison. Would you believe it? He made her an honest woman before they died!"

"Honest woman?" I didn't understand Mr. White and was surprised when they all laughed.

Erna shushed them. "Tamarotchka," she smiled, "in America when a man marries his mistress, he makes 'an honest woman' of her. Otherwise, they'd be living in sin. Understand?"

"Oh, I see." I felt rather embarrassed at my ignorance. "I'm sorry."

Mr. White chuckled. "We all learn from language mistakes, Tamarotchka. I still make booboos in Russian, as you very well know. But to go on, what I just heard was that Goebbels, his wife, and their children are all dead too—suicide-murders. And now they're negotiating: the Russians, the British, and the Americans with the Germans. Stalin has insisted on 'unconditional surrender.'"

"That's just what Mac wrote me once," I broke in excitedly, "that all of the men in his outfit felt that Germany must surrender unconditionally, that way only, no other."

In spite of the horrible news that we had just heard about German atrocities, I felt excited and somewhat relieved. The end of the European war seemed imminent. With the German surrender, Mac would definitely be coming home.

Bill White made his way towards his office, then paused, his brow furrowed. "I feel sure that before long, we'll hear that Germany has unconditionally surrendered. We've all worked hard this week. I have an idea. . . . " He laid his hand on his doorknob. "Do you think we can finish whatever we're doing by noontime? If so, we can close up shop for the day."

Claire and I looked at each other with delight. The Russians, too, grinned.

Erna went to her desk and sat down. "We'd better get to work then and finish what we've been doing, hadn't we?" She bent her head down, staring at the papers on her desk.

Natasha sauntered to her desk, angrily fishing for a cigarette in her purse and grumbling, sotto voce, "Generalissimo! Sometimes she treats us like kindergartners. I'm several years older than she is. We know what we have to do."

"Oh, Natashenka," Olga said in Russian, her voice soothing. "She doesn't mean anything by it. After all, she's our supervisor. It's her job to issue orders."

Natasha huffily swirled her chair towards her desk. "Then why doesn't she say, 'Get to work. We have to finish by noon.' Better still, why doesn't she let us alone and be quiet?" She picked up the papers in front of her and started to read them.

Bill White peeked out of his office and beckoned to Claire, "I need you for dictation," he said, then went back in.

As Claire went by me she whispered, "Meet me at Admiral's at noon."

I nodded.

The Admiral Cafeteria was crowded, more so than usual. People kept walking around, stopping at tables to greet friends. Everyone talking about the latest news. I searched for Claire, but apparently she hadn't come in yet. Then I tried to find an unoccupied table. There were none, as far as I could see. All of the OWI apparently were here.

"Tamarotchka, over here!" I turned in the direction of the male voice and saw my old friend, Jacques Dubois, frantically waving at me. I walked over to his table, delighted to see him.

"I'm just finishing up, darling." He waved me to the opposite seat at his table and gave me a brief scrutiny. "You look great, but, then, you always do. It's good to see you. What have you been doing with yourself? I haven't seen you around these days."

I kissed him gently on the cheek. "It's good to see you,

Jacques. Where have you been hiding yourself? I haven't seen nor heard from you."

He grinned. "I'm guilty, Tamarotchka. I've been to la belle France, ma chèrie. Back and forth...all the time." He eyed me with approval. "You really look good—more sophisticated—a real career lady. Never thought you'd go through with it—living in this bad city, I mean."

"Oh, Jacques, it's a thrilling city. There's so much to see and do. You know, I'm even studying ballet here."

"I can't believe it; shy, petite, sweet little Tamarotchka." He reached out to take my hand. "Remember that first kiss I gave you? You were so afraid of being kissed."

"Ah, Jacques, I do remember." How dear he is—the rake! Then I smiled, recalling another time. "But I confess that I learned more later. Someone else gave me a more advanced course in kissing."

"So-o?" He began to laugh. "I'll never forget that day. You had been so terribly shy and afraid." Then he stared at me. "So you have learned more? Ah." He crossed himself. "Thank you, dear Lord, for letting our Tamarotchka grow up. And who, may I ask, was the great maestro who taught you how to kiss?"

I told him about Mac. Jacques was delighted.

"And all this time I have been hoping that you were pining for me," he said in a pseudodramatic voice. Then he became serious. "It's great, isn't it, that this war is finally coming to an end? It's about time that the Krauts get their due."

"They seemed to be hedging, didn't they?" I asked.

He grew thoughtful. "I had a feeling they realized they couldn't resist any more. That Russian general, Chuikov, finally got tired of negotiating and bombed the hell out of them. That was when they finally surrendered." He paused. "In fact, after that, one of their generals, who'd been doing the negotiating, committed suicide. I believe his name was Krebs." He finished his coffee. "I've got to run, darling." He stood up, smiling. "But you'll still dance with me sometime if I call you?"

"Of course, Jacques, I'd like that. So far, I'm not engaged nor married. Besides, I love dancing with you."

He came over to my side, then took my hand. "I'm glad you've found someone special, Tamarotchka. He must be, to have your love." He lifted my hand to his lips, giving it a light kiss. "To a beautiful lady," he said gallantly. Then he bowed and walked out of the cafeteria.

I had completely forgotten Claire. With Jacques' exit, I found myself searching the tables once more. Then I noticed her, hurrying towards me, squeezing past the narrow spaces separating the tables.

She plumped herself on the chair Jacques had just vacated. "Sorry, Buddy, Mr. White kept me all this time. I thought I'd never get out." She was all out of breath.

"It's okay," I told her. "Let's get some stuff and eat. I'm starved."

"Me too, I wouldn't have blamed you if you'd given up on me."

"It worked out all right." I looked at the food on display. "Either too fattening or too expensive, damn it. I sat with Jacques Dubois before you came. Remember the fellow who took me out to all the good night spots?"

"Mm, yes." Claire picked up a plate of crabmeat salad.

"I think I'll take that too. Fewer calories. Jacques was delighted that I had finally found the right man."

"I thought he liked you." Claire looked puzzled.

"Jacques?" I had to smile. "Claire, Jacques is a Casanova, the courteous and gallant Frenchman who loves all women. We've been friends ever since my sophomore days at Radcliffe. He's sort of kept an eye on me, the big brother type. We have fun together."

"I wondered about that," she said as we went back to the table. "He seems like a great guy."

"He is, but he's never been serious about any gal as far as I know. Someday, when he's middle-aged, he may settle down; although I doubt it."

"You going to the apartment after lunch?" Claire asked, getting up from the table.

"No, I thought I'd go to see the Fergusons. Take them a bouquet of flowers or something."

"Good. I've got things to do too," Claire took out her wallet. "I'll see you tonight then."

"Okay." I lingered over my coffee and watched her make her way out of Admiral's. What a graceful, elegant gal she is. And the

Germans would have tortured her, then sent her to the gas chambers, had she lived among them instead of here in this country. I couldn't get that nightmare out of my mind.

The Fergusons were delighted with my appearance.

"These roses are lovely," Mary said, "I think red roses are my favorites. Did you know we call them American Beauties?"

"That's why I got them for you," I said, watching her arrange them in a Chinese vase. "I'm sorry I didn't call beforehand."

Dr. Ferguson took my hand. "Girlie, you are welcome here any time; you know that, dear." He looked at me with affection. "You look good. How are your parents? We haven't heard from them for some time."

"They're fine. I got a letter from them just the other day. Mama met Lillian Gish at a war relief meeting. It really had thrilled her to meet such a famous actress."

Mary drew the ottoman closer. "My goodness, Lillian Gish? Why, she starred in silent movies, didn't she, Father?"

He smiled, "I believe so, Mary. Your father, Tamara, how is he?"

"Well, you know, Dr. Ferguson, if he's not at the Harvard-Yenching Institute working on the Chinese-English dictionary, he's home, either reading about Oriental philosophy or gathering more proverbs for his book."

Dr. Ferguson nodded, "I admire him immensely," he murmured. "He's gotten over his ordeal in Peking then?"

"I think so, Dr. Ferguson, except sometimes he says that the back of his head hurts. That's where the Japanese used to beat him with bamboo rods."

"That must have been terrible," Mary was sympathetic. "We were fortunate they didn't torture us. And now we're finding out about the Germans and their bestiality." She shook her head. "Honestly, I don't know what our world is coming to."

"There have been atrocities since Cain slew Abel, my dear," Dr. Ferguson recalled musingly. "In the Bible Jesus tells us, 'Ye shall hear of wars and rumors of wars. . . . Nation shall rise against nation, and kingdom against kingdom.' We are finding out now just how terrible war is, because we can communicate today with the world around us through the radio, cameras, newspapers, telegrams, telephones, and V-mail letters. We know so much more about everything good and bad everywhere."

"You're so right, Father. I can still picture our American Marines trying to land on Iwo Jima. For almost a month they struggled, not only against the constant barrage of enemy guns, but even the island itself, with its volcanic dust, which made the Marines' tractors lose traction and the trenches collapse before the Marines could even take refuge in them. In one month this year nearly seven thousand Marines died and twenty thousand were wounded, I read. Finally, they succeeded in planting the American flag there, thank God."

"And now, Mary, they're fighting at Okinawa." Dr. Ferguson stared out of the window. "Those kamikazes are a big problem to our Marines, especially our sailors. So many killed by those kamikazes. The Japanese have no fear of dying."

"Let's not dwell on the war, Father," Mary suggested gently, giving her father a look of concern.

He smiled at her. "Yes, although it's difficult not to dwell on it. All of us have relatives in the war. That reminds me, Girlie, where is Vanya now?"

"He's home on furlough. He had been in Italy. He's going to return to Harvard when the war's over."

Dr. Ferguson nodded. I looked at him anxiously. He had dozed off. Mary noticed my look of concern.

"Father, it's time for your nap." Gently, she tapped him on his shoulder.

He sat up, opening his eyes, "Ah, yes, Girlie, I wanted to ask you. You once had mentioned a Scotsman you thought a great deal of. He'll be coming home soon, I imagine."

"Yes, I hope so." I was unable to take my eyes off my old friend's face. The baby-pink skin, the white mustache, the white brows over the fading blue eyes. Even though he had aged, he looked so calm and serene.

"That's gude. He'll be faithful to you."

"I forgot." I reached into my purse. "I brought a photo of Mac to show you. And I almost didn't!"

Dr. Ferguson and Mary both examined it closely. "I like his face," Mary said. "He has a pleasant smile."

647

"It's a gude face, Tamara; an honest, intelligent face, Girlie. I'm happy for you."

"And now, Father," Mary said, taking his arm, "I'll help you up."

"May I help?" I reached for his other arm.

Dr. Ferguson smiled, "I can make it on my own, thank you." He beckoned to me and gave me a hug. "You keep writing to that Scotsman, dear. I want to meet him."

With that he took up his cane and walked out of the room. Mary accompanied me to the door.

"Mary, is your father all right?" I asked her. "He looks so pale compared to the last time I saw him."

"Dear, he's not so spry anymore. Yes; he's quite frail." Her face saddened. "He's old, and, as you know, the last few years have been hard on him. Don't worry though; Father will get over it. He's strong that way."

"You know, Tamara, it's sometimes difficult for me to believe that we're still at war," Claire said as she and I walked out of the OWI building after work. "V-E Day seems so long ago, but actually it's been only two months since it happened."

"May eighth . . . yes, it does seem long ago. I guess it's because so much has happened in the meantime. With the Germans out of the way, we were able to concentrate on the Pacific, mobilizing our forces. Remember how grim the Battle of Okinawa was? The Japanese kamikazes, those damned suicide planes, have killed more than five thousand of our sailors alone, besides sinking thirty-four ships and damaging three hundred and sixty-eight others. That was some naval battle. I believe that it was *Life* magazine that said it was the worst battle in the Pacific."

"I've read so much about the Pacific war and all the islands where our marines fought, and the awful conditions under which they fought. I'm so damned tired of this endless war," Claire sighed.

"I know." I felt the same way. "I just want to see the Japs defeated. Thank God and Confucius that they too had tremendous losses. We had some fifty thousand casualties at Okinawa, but do you realize that almost eighty-five percent of the Okinawans were either killed or committed suicide? For the Japanese, defeat is dishonor. Therefore, quite a few of them committed hara kiri."

"What's hara kiri?" Claire gave me a quizzical glance.

"Belly-cutting." I explained. "It's the Japanese traditional way to commit suicide. They started it around 1500 A.D. Take a dagger; start on the left side of your tummy; cut all the way to the right; then up . . . and, voilà, your intestines fall out, and you're dead. If that doesn't kill you, then your 'second' pulls out a sword, and beheads you. Then you're dead for sure."

"My God, how gruesome!" Claire shuddered.

"I read not long ago that some forty military men have committed hara kiri in this war . . . also some civilians. The Japanese are a mighty proud people."

"Well, I hope they surrender soon," Claire slowed down as we approached the corner newsstand. "Let's get the *Times* and find out the latest."

We stopped and bought the *New York Times*, pausing to see what the front page said.

"Hm-m." Claire held the paper so that I could read over her shoulder. "The Potsdam Proclamation." she read. "Oh-oh; now the Allies are warning Japan to choose either 'an order of peace, security, and justice,' if the Imperial government decides on unconditional surrender, or if not, then we'll bomb hell out of them till they're destroyed. Rather stiff terms, wouldn't you agree, Tamarotchka?" She chuckled with glee.

"Absolutely, Clarotchka," I answered. "It's about time we did something drastic to Tojo and his cohorts. The British and American planes have already fire-bombed their main industrial centers: Yokohama, Kobe—gosh, those were beautiful cities. I remember. We stopped there before coming to the States. Then too, Osaka, Nagoya, and Kawasaki. Most of their cities are in ruins; their people are starving, their leaders divided. Some want to surrender; others, like their General Tojo, want to fight to the bitter end. What worries me about this is what Mac wrote in his last letter. He said that he might be sent to the Pacific."

"No." Claire stopped and put her hand on my arm, her eyes full of compassion. "You did tell me that he was down in the dumps lately, but I didn't know that. Gee, that's too bad."

"Yes, that's why he's been despondent. He's also afraid I

might meet someone. In fact, in one letter he told me to go ahead and get married if I met the right man. I really felt bad for him. It was bad enough when he had been assigned to occupation forces. That meant he'd have to remain in Belgium, although many others who had been overseas for only a short time were shipped back home to the States. He wrote, 'I suppose I'm essential over here because I can read.' "

"That's rough." Claire placed the folded paper under her arm. "Shall we walk home, Buddy, or do you want to window-shop along Fifth Avenue? I have to stop at the grocery store too."

"Let's stop by the Fergusons first, if you don't mind," I suggested. "I've been worried about them. I called the other day and learned their phone has been disconnected. I don't know what's happened to them."

"Maybe they've moved."

"If they had, Mary would surely have let me know. I'm sure she would've," I told her.

When we reached the Fergusons' apartment, I rang the bell, but there was no answer.

"The only thing I can think of is to call Mama and ask her to check with Dr. Ferguson's son, Bob, in Newton, Massachusetts."

Claire agreed, then hurried on to our corner grocery store while I walked on home. When the doorbell rang, I opened the door immediately, thinking that it was either Claire or Matt. Instead, to my alarm, a Western Union boy stood by the door, holding out a yellow envelope. No telegram, in my opinion, had ever brought good news. Something bad must have happened either to Mac, my parents, or Vanya. I tipped the young messenger and came inside to read the message.

The terse telegram blinded me with its cruel brevity:

DOCTOR FERGUSON'S FUNERAL SATURDAY COME HOME FATHER

I held the telegram in my shaking hands and read it over again, letting my tears blur the words.

I hadn't even thought that it could be my old friend. In my mind people like Dr. Ferguson lived forever and ever and ever. People like him *could not die*! How could it have happened? Why

650

hadn't Mary called me to let me know? All these questions crowded into my mind.

The worst thing was that nothing I could say or do would dispel the fact that he was gone! Dr. Ferguson, my old friend, my best, best friend in life, was dead! Dead! It was the finality of it all that was so terrible. I would never, never see him again, nor place my head against his jacket, nor hear that cheerful, resounding voice say, "Ah, there's my Girlie." Even my tears, coming fast and faster, could not wash out that dreadful and numbing finality!

When Claire came back from her grocery shopping, she placed the bags on the tiny kitchen counter and stared at me in astonishment.

"What's wrong, Tamara? Whatever has happened to you?"

All I could do was hold out the telegram. She read it slowly, shaking her head in sympathy. She put her arms around me. "Tamara, look at me. You've got to take hold of yourself. Would Dr. Ferguson have wanted you to act like this? Here's a hanky. Dry your eyes and think how fortunate you were to have known him all these years. How good he was to you, and how much he did for you and your family! Tamara, he loved you like a father. Now, come on." She looked at me with concern. "You'll be going to Boston, won't you?"

It didn't take long to pack my overnight bag. I told Claire that I planned to return immediately after the funeral. She went with me to Grand Central Station, giving me a big hug. "Tamara, remember; it was his time to go," Claire told me quietly. "God planned it this way, and you have to understand. Just say good-bye to him, dear, that's all."

Yes, I would be saying good-bye, a final one. I always had hated good-byes, but this one I *had* to say.

I went on back into the coach to take a seat. How many times before had I taken this ride from Grand Central to Boston and back again to Manhattan? This trip, however, was my saddest. I sat in my black dress, staring numbly at my reflection in the window. My "stranger" face underneath the wide-brimmed, black hat was ghastly pale; my eyes, large and glassy. I hoped that the casket would be open so that I could look once more upon that beloved face. I tried to read the magazine Claire had so considerately slipped into my hands, but it made no sense. I couldn't have told anyone what the words and pictures were, although, dutifully, I had flipped the pages, absentmindedly scanning each line.

Finally the train pulled into Boston. I took the subway to Harvard Square and then the tram to Mt. Vernon Street. I noticed some people in the tram staring at me. *I must look awful,* I thought, *with my tear-stained face and dressed all in black.* It didn't matter how I looked. Nothing mattered anymore. I had come to say good-bye to the one man who had meant so much to me . . . in China as well as here. He had taught me so much. Through him I had learned about America; the beautiful, far-off land he had called home. I had discovered the beauty of the English language from reading the books he had given me. He had suggested that I try my hand at writing and had taught me to have pride in myself, to hold on to my ideals and dreams. I had formed my own conceptions of what a good person should be like by watching and listening to his words. I had admired his serenity; therefore, I too would be serene. His patience, his benevolence toward his fellowmen, his respect for that glorious starred-and-striped flag which was his own—all this, and even more, gave me the example by which I had tried to pattern myself. I associated him with the best that was *America.* So now I would be tendering him my last farewell, remembering him for those precious gifts he had given me. My sole gift to him had been my love.

My parents and I took the subway to Newton, and were met by Dr. Ferguson's son, Bob, and his wife, Marge. Together we rode to the chapel.

Thankfully, the services had been brief. The coffin was closed and covered with a large spray from the family. We sat behind Mary, Bob, Marge, and other Ferguson relatives whom we had not met before.

The music was the same as that which I had heard years ago in Dr. Ferguson's white-shrouded home in Peking. As I listened to Chopin's *Funeral March*, I felt the tears gather anew. Both Dr. Ferguson and his wife, after a long separation, were now together once more. *If there is a heaven,* I thought (and I felt that there must be one for such as they), *they're both up there with the*

God in whom they both had so strongly believed. My eyes fastened on the closed coffin. I was powerless to look away. For the very last time, I looked at him, unseeing, but loving him still.

We rode to Newtonville Cemetery in the long limousine provided by the funeral home. I watched, with my arm around Mary's waist, as they lowered the heavy bronze casket into the freshly dug grave. I marveled at Mary's composure. What a truly devoted daughter she had been! Looking at her now, I realized for the first time how very much she resembled her father.

"Ashes to ashes and dust to dust," intoned the minister, as the first spadefuls of earth were sprinkled onto the coffin. The members of the family turned away, walking slowly back to their cars. We too turned to go. As I looked for the last time at the coffin, shrouded now with black earth, I became again overwhelmed with the terrible finality of death.

I took the next train back to New York City. Mama and Papa understood. I wanted to get away from Cambridge as fast as I could; to return to the city where he had been living, not dead. Even now, as I sat in the train, staring vacantly out the coach window, I could feel his warm hand closing over my own. I heard again his voice, vibrant with the joy and exuberance of life, as he called out his special name for me, "Girlie!"

Claire was happy to see me. Bless her; she didn't question me about the funeral. I was grateful for her tact. She handed me the mail that had arrived from overseas; two from Lanny, one from Andy, and three in Mac's ever perfect script.

I sat down to read the loving words from my three most favorite men. It had been good to read what they had to write and even more comforting to know that they loved me. At this time, more than ever, I felt the need for their love; selfishly I needed all three of them right now to tell me, each in his own way, how much I meant to them. Good men they were, all three.

Deep down in my heart, however, was an empty void that no one could ever fill. It contained the pain of a complete loss; something had now gone out of my life forever and ever. It was a part of my childhood, my youth, and my womanhood for which there was no return.

It was the third time that I had come so close to Death. This third time had been the most painful.

42

Do Sveedan'ya

Those last three weeks of August 1945 had been momentous. Bill White, I recall, had come in to our big office laying the day's newspapers on Erna's desk. All of us, still in shock, had gathered round.

"Here it is," he had said. "See for yourselves. Unbelievable but true."

All the headlines, more or less, told the same story. Large, bold letters screamed: *"ATOMIC BOMB USED ON JAPS; THE EQUAL OF 20,000 TONS OF TNT!"*

Erna had pointed to one of the photographs. "There's the bomb exploding. Looks like a huge mushroom, doesn't it?" She had stared at it as if hypnotized. "My God, Bill, some seventy-eight thousand civilians, it's reported, were either maimed or killed."

Claire and I both moved closer to see for ourselves.

"August 6, 1945, will be a date to remember." Her face grave, Natasha crossed herself. "May God forgive the man who dropped that weapon of destruction on innocent people."

"A B-29 named *Enola Gay* carried the bomb." Olga had been reading a different paper. "A rather romantic name for a plane, isn't it? I'd have named it *Death*."

"*Hir-o-shi-ma* is the city we leveled," Bill had pronounced the name of the city slowly stressing the last syllable. "If the Japs refuse to surrender now, the President will order another city leveled."

"That's what is so incomprehensible to me, Bill." Erna had

straightened up to face him. "I know the militarists don't want to surrender unconditionally, but why? Their Supreme Council is in favor of it."

I had been wondering about that too.

"As I understand it," Bill explained, "under unconditional surrender, their Emperor Hirohito would no longer be their 'sovereign ruler.' The Allies are insisting on that condition."

The Japanese had ignored the Allied warnings. Then events really began to unroll. On the eighth the Soviet Union had declared war on Japan. On the ninth another B-29 had dropped an atomic bomb on Nagasaki, destroying that city and killing some twenty thousand civilians.

Still, the Japanese had remained adamant. Finally, on August fourteenth, at the urging of the Emperor himself, they agreed to accept the Allied terms, and surrendered unconditionally.

One day, just before closing time, Mr. White came out to talk to us. "I know you've been wondering about the future of our magazines. I wish I could tell you that we're going to continue." He leaned against Olga's desk. "We're closing up shop for good. These issues that we're all working on now will be our last ones." He looked around at each of us in turn.

Claire and I exchanged glances. We had just been discussing this earlier.

"What a shame," Olga had exclaimed. "Our Soviet readers have been complimenting our work; haven't they, Mr. White?"

He nodded. "They certainly have, and it's the result of the splendid teamwork in this office. If we could have, we might have been able to continue—under other auspices. Of course, that damnable funding problem stands in the way. So-o." He rubbed his hands. "That's it." He paused, as if in thought. "Oh, yes; whoever needs a recommendation, just come to me. If I can help you in any way, I'll be only too glad to do it."

Natasha popped a cigarette into the edge of her mouth and gave Alex a victorious glance. "I told you, Alexei Sergeivitch, that that's what would happen."

Bill overheard her remark. "Yes, Natasha, it was bound to

happen with the end of the war. Do any of you have plans? If so, I'd like to know about them. Maybe I can help."

Olga smiled at him, "I'm sure we do, Mr. White. What are your plans for yourself?"

"I'll probably go with *Time-Life*. They've already asked me. Also, I have a book, *The Pale Blonde of Sand Street*, coming out shortly. Ask Claire and Tamara here." He grinned at us. "They've spent several evenings in my office, typing and proofreading the final draft. I couldn't have done it without them."

Claire and I smiled like conspirators.

"We enjoyed doing it, Mr. White," I told him. "We kept hurrying to finish so that we could find out who had killed the blonde."

He laughed. "That reminds me, Tamarotchka. Have you decided what you're going to do? I'd like to get you into *Time* or *Life*, if you're interested."

"If you think so." I hadn't considered anything like that, but it sounded interesting.

"If you like, I'll make an appointment for an interview for you. If it sounds good, take it. If not," Bill smiled, "we'll find something else for you. You've already had the experience of working on magazines and doing research."

"Thank you, Mr. White, I appreciate it."

Natasha had been listening. "Mr. White, you know what's going to happen with Tamarotchka. Her lieutenant will return, and she'll end up getting married, and then babies will come."

"I may not, Natasha," I retorted. "You forget that I haven't seen Mac for almost two years. I may decide when I see him that he's not the right man for me. He writes beautiful, romantic letters that"—I looked at her teasingly—"you enjoy listening to me read, but still . . . that's not good enough reason for me to marry him."

"And you, Claire?" Mr. White turned to her.

"My folks want me to return to Washington. If I do, there's a job waiting for me."

I stared at her in surprise. "You didn't tell me, Buddy."

"I hadn't planned to return, but it's no use staying here with the OWI folding up."

"So that leaves Olga and Natasha. Erna tells me she's retir-

656

ing to rejoin the social scene. Alex says he's finishing his memoirs about old Russia. Olga?" He turned to her.

Olga looked at the copy of *Victory* on her desk. "I'm moving back to Paris with my mother. I love the United States, but I love Paris even more. Mama and I both have missed it." She sounded relieved.

How quiet it became after that! Each one of us pondered on the future. Then Natasha's cough broke the silence.

"You don't have to worry about me, Mr. White. My husband thinks I should stay home anyway. So he and I shall fight. That'll be all right. I still love that old mujik (peasant). I couldn't live without him."

We all laughed at that. In spite of her acid tongue, Natasha had a heart of gold.

"It's been a wonderful experience for all of us, hasn't it?" Erna muttered. She lit a cigarette, shoving her pack of Pall Malls towards Claire and me. "We've been like one family here. I, for one, am going to miss it a hell of a lot."

She couldn't have put it better. We all felt the same way, even dear Natasha. The sad thing was that, like many family members, we had to cut short the apron strings and, saying farewell, go our individual ways.

Several days later, after that discussion about our future, I invited Phyllis to have dinner with me. Claire had flown to Washington to see about her new job.

"That meal was certainly delicious. Where'd you learn to cook like that?" Phyl sat back on the studio couch, placing an ashtray on her lap.

I laughed. "Claire and I've been experimenting with foods. Poor Matt's our guinea pig. He'll eat anything we put before him."

Phyl hadn't even smiled at that. I took a closer look at her. She seemed withdrawn, unlike her usual effervescent self.

"What's wrong, Phyl?" I asked.

"I quit my job." She shushed me with her hand. "No, don't interrupt. I've decided to go home. Norma left two weeks ago. She never did like New York. I thought I'd stick it out, but it's getting to me. I miss New England. It's getting so that I can't stand the pace anymore. People hell-bent on whatever they're doing, not caring a damn about anyone except themselves. I'll bet you that if I fainted on the street the New Yorkers would step over or even on me to get to where they're going." She lit up a Marlboro. "I've had it up to here." She drew a line across her throat with her index finger.

"Whew!" I couldn't believe it. New York had done so much for her. Looking at her, I saw a successful, sophisticated young career woman—from the shining blonde hair that fell in soft waves to frame her Nordic face to the svelte figure draped in the black jersey sheath, to the fabulous, long gams ending in the suede, stiletto heels.

"I should have known, Phyl. Why didn't you let me know sooner? You could have moved in with us."

"Unh-uh," she cleared her throat. "That's nice of you. It's not that. At heart, I'm just a small town girl, a homebody like my mother. I thought life here would be glamorous and exciting. It was fun for a while but not anymore." She laid her head back on the cushion and smiled. "So-o, I phoned the folks, and they liked my decision. 'Your room's waiting,' they told me."

I understood her; she was right. "Can I do anything to help? Help you pack?"

"Oh, I didn't accumulate as much junk as you have." She looked around the room. "Don't worry. I'll be okay once I get home to Quincy." She flipped off some ashes that had dropped on her lap. "The next thing I'll be doing is setting myself on fire." She gave a slight chuckle. "Norma had no problem finding a job in Boston."

"I'll probably be going home too. Officially, we'll be closing up shop next Monday. Ye gods, that's four days from now! I'd better get on the ball myself."

"Can't you get a job here? I thought you liked New York."

"I love it," I told her. "Although with Claire leaving, I'd have the apartment rent to worry about. No can do. The job at *Time-Life* didn't pan out. I couldn't live on that salary by myself. So, I too will have to pack and move back to Cambridge."

"What about Mac? Is he still in the occupation forces? How long does he have to stay overseas?" she asked.

"A few more months at least. It's some sort of points system.

658

They need to have so many points before they can leave. What angers him is that some soldiers who arrived overseas much later have already been returned home."

"How come? That doesn't sound fair."

"Disorganization and influence. Some troops that arrived in Antwerp were turned around several weeks later and shipped back to the States. Seems that they had replaced veterans in two airborne divisions that were then ordered back to parade down Fifth Avenue here. Instead of the veterans returning to march in the parade, replacements who now made up the divisions were the so-called veterans who marched. Then too there are always those who know somebody who can get special orders."

"Damned shame." She paused. "At least, when he does come home, you'll be walking down the aisle, and you won't have to worry about jobs or paying bills."

"I may decide not to get married, Phyl. Everyone is so sure that I will, everyone except me. I'm not even sure that Mac's the one for me."

"God Almighty, what *do* you want in a man?" Phyl sat up in indignation. "You've certainly dated enough guys to make a choice, haven't you? First, you say you love him. Then, you're not sure. What's wrong with you, Tamara? I pity the poor guy, the way you keep him dangling on your hook."

"I'll know as soon as I see him in the flesh. I may have been building up an ideal, Phyllis."

"Have it your way," she answered in disgust. "I just feel damned sorry for Mac. Besides," she laughed, "I was hoping to be your maid of honor. Remember how we used to talk about that in Radcliffe?"

"I sure do. I very much doubt you'll be my maid of honor now, knowing the way Mama feels about you. That is, if I do get married. That's what burns me up about it. So long as I'm the obedient daughter, everything is fine and dandy. However, if I want things done differently, all hell breaks loose. My elders tell me they know better—so says Confucius—so says Mama."

"What does Mac write to you these days?" I knew she'd purposefully changed the subject to end our discussion.

"Well, even though he's been complaining about being part

of the occupation forces, he's been able to travel. He's even been to Berchtesgaden. He and another friend, Guil Worsley, traveled through Germany, and he's described the trip in his letters."

"Okay, I know what's coming next. Would I like to hear you read from his letters? Of course, you know I'll reply, 'Sure, why not?'" She plumped one of the couch pillows and laid it behind her back. "Go ahead. I'll just lie back and picture old Mac travelling throughout Germany."

" 'Dearest Sweetheart,' " I began.

"So that's what he calls you now? I thought his name for you was Vixen."

"Shut up, Phyl." I gave her a dirty look. "Just listen."

" 'They say that anyone who has not seen Berchtesgarten has not seen Bavaria. Today we toured Hitler's home, but he wasn't there. It's a bomb-wrecked and ruined house now, but at one time it must have been a really beautiful residence. The window of the movie room and theater in the front of the house is tremendous. It frames a scenic view of the mountain opposite that takes away one's breath. The remainder of the house, however, is quite ordinary and middle-class.

" 'The barracks, Goebbels', Borman's and Goering's houses, the nursery, the SS barracks, garages, administrative buildings, and greenhouses are rather well-wrecked. It felt strange to stand on the balcony and terrace where he, Chamberlain, Mussolini, and others had stood in the *good, old days* when the Germans were the Master Race.

" 'Even though we couldn't go to the *Eagle's Nest*, however, we did go into the underground bombproof shelter near Hitler's home. It was a maze of halls, interconnecting rooms, and apartments, but they had not yet been completely cleared of booby traps and debris. We had seen enough; it was an unforgettable experience for me.

" 'That night we ate in the elegant Hotel Berchtesgadenerhof. It's unbelievable that such thick carpets, exquisite furniture, beautiful drawing room, bar, and lounge could have managed to survive the Allied bombings, but they have.'

"This next part is written later."

"Can you imagine seeing Der Führer's hideout?" Phyl's eyes

660

were wide. "I wonder if Mac noticed Hitler's ghost roaming around with Eva Braun."

She seemed in a better frame of mind. It pleased me that Mac's letter had helped take her out of her doldrums. She didn't object when I read on.

" 'We are sitting in the hotel lounge now after a dinner of GI food served in an unparalleled style: hors d'oeuvres, bouillon as a consommé, salad, and hamburger with mouth-watering sauce, climaxed with ice cream and Bavarian chocolate cake. Along with all this, we had red wine, quite the thing. As soon as one course was finished, the next appeared. The dining room had sensuously soft chairs, hammered pewter sugar bowl, intricately carved wooden salt and pepper shakers, and high, lofty, wood-carved ceilings. In the midst of all this grandeur appeared a Red Cross girl who exclaimed in an air-raid siren voice, "Where the hell have you been?" to another Red Cross girl on the other side of the dining room.'

"Then he writes about listening to music played on a beautiful concert grand Steinway; the glistening candelabra, the oak-paneled walls.

" 'After having seen all the ruined cities in Germany, I can't believe that this beautiful hotel still survived. The Alps are all around: snow-covered, towering, silent, yet domineering. How Hitler could have planned or wanted war, and yet lived here is incomprehensible to me. The view from his Berghof is breathtaking. I'd have been satisfied just to have lived there and let well enough alone.'

"Isn't that a beautiful description?"

"Yes, it sure is, Tamara. He almost puts us there."

"Now I want you to listen to this; it's part of a letter written several days later, but he's still in that area.

" 'The Berchtesgadeners are going to church this warm autumn morning. The sun is shining through a slight haze into the room and over the paper on which I'm writing. That same sun will soon be shining into your room. Woodsmoke smell is everywhere, smoke curls lazily upward from the chalets on the hillside opposite. The sound of a waterfall rushing downward makes the morning even more alive. Voices in the distance sound faintly; only when I listen carefully can I pick out the many morning noises. It is peaceful here; war is remote until I remember that I am an American soldier. Below on the road 6x6's, jeeps, and weapons carriers grind or glide by.

" 'The snow high up on the peaks has an icy sheen to it in the morning sunlight; there stand the mountains, unmoved, undaunted, and seemingly unchanged. It's the kind of Sunday morning on which I'd want to get up early, get you up, and go walking in the woods. We'd look at the multi-colored leaves, thrill to the change of life into winter dress. Or we'd go down the street for Papa's newspapers, laughing, talking, keeping silent when both of us knew words were just not enough to express our happiness at being alive, in love, and together once more. War brought us together; war again separated us for a time; soon, however, we'll be together in a time of peace, love, and contentment.' "

I folded Mac's letter.

"I hope you keep that letter," Phyl told me. "It really choked me up and brought tears to my eyes."

"Oh, I'm saving all of them; not only Mac's letters but also Lanny's, Shep's, and Andy's. I enjoy rereading them."

"Yes, indeed," said Phyl, becoming thoughtful. "You know you've known some wonderful men, Tamara. I wish I could say the same, but I can't." She looked at Mac's photograph. "I still bet that he'll be the one you marry. Of course, you might meet someone new in Cambridge." She yawned, then looked at her watch. "My God! I never realized it was eleven-thirty already. I have to finish packing. Good Lord, why didn't you kick me out?"

"I didn't realize it was that late either. Tomorrow's my last day at the office, and then I'll start packing too. Claire's already taken some of her stuff to Washington."

"Well, friend." Phyl got up from the couch. "Don't say it hasn't been nice, because it really has." She gathered up her purse and cigarettes.

"How're you getting to Grand Central? Taxi?"

She smiled. "Nope, good old Matt offered to take me. I'm all set. Listen, Tamara." She paused before opening the outside door. "Call me when you get to Cambridge. I don't want to phone you at home. Okay?"

I promised. Then I gave her a big hug and closed the door before she saw my tears.

On Monday at the office we cleaned out our desks and talked about our plans for the future.

"The last issues of *Victory* and *Amerika* will be out on Wednesday." Bill White had come out of his private office. "Those of you who're leaving New York let me know, and I'll mail the copies to you." He looked around. "Claire's not back yet, Tamarotchka?"

Just as he asked me that, the door to the office opened, and Claire walked in, smiling away. "Sorry I'm late, but I just got in from Washington. Did I miss anything?"

"You would have if you'd come an hour later," Erna said. She turned to Bill. "Shall I get it now?"

He nodded, grinning. "Yes, we're all here now."

I looked at the two of them wondering what it was all about. The others looked puzzled too. Erna walked into his office. She beckoned to me. "C'mon, Tamarotchka, I need your help."

In Mr. White's office were glasses and two champagne bottles in an ice-bucket. Erna grinned. "There're some salted nuts in the large right-hand drawer." She motioned towards his desk.

I helped her carry the stuff out and arrange it on her cleared desk. The others gathered around, delighted with this surprise.

"I'd have dressed for the occasion, had I known." Natasha's eyes sparkled with good humor.

Mr. White opened a bottle and carefully poured the champagne.

All of us took a glass except Alex. When I turned to him to hand him one, he shook his head. "I've got a glass of water on my desk, dear. I'll toast with that."

It had been a memorable party for all of us, yet sad too.

We *na-zdorovye*'d our last issues, each other, and then the end of the war. I raised a silent American toast to my Yankee lieutenant and my beloved adoptive country, the land of my dreams.

Then came the hugs, the handshaking, and the tearful eyes.

663

Mr. White came over to me and took my hand. "I'm going to miss you, Tamarotchka. I'm sorry that deal with *Time-Life* didn't pan out."

"I may still come back, Mr. White." I told him. "Don't give up on me that quickly."

Natasha had overheard him. "It's her smile, Mr. White. All she has to do is smile. She's been our sunshine here."

"So have you, Natasha, in spite of your trying to be so contrary." I hugged her. "I'm really going to miss you. You've given me some excellent advice on certain occasions, and I won't ever forget that." I blinked away my tears. I had promised myself not to cry and here I was, tearful already.

I hugged them all, even Erna. There was no more left to be said except *"do Sveedan'ya."* With that, Claire and I gathered up our belongings and taking one last look at all of them, we left the office.

I can still picture them as they looked that last time, smiling and waving. After all, they had been my family here, the ones to whom I had turned for advice and comfort. I had loved them all!

Part IV

Cambridge, Massachusetts
October 1945–March 1946

43

The Waiting Game

It felt good to be home again in my own bedroom. Olga Stepanovna had moved out, and Vanya was home for good. He had reenrolled at Harvard and so far seemed content with his courses and professors. He still had no idea of what he planned to do, although when questioned, he expounded at great length on his grandiose plans for the future. I sensed that his going to the university had been merely a way of giving him time to find himself. In the meantime, with the government paying his tuition and giving him a monthly allowance, Vanya had it made. Why not take the opportunity? He walked around with a smile on his face; that was the main thing. It made Mama happy. Her face beamed these days as she bustled about in the kitchen, planning what next to cook up for her beloved "Kocinka."

My own case, I discussed with Papa one day. I had already been home for more than a month and felt restless and depressed. Even though the war was now over, I still had no idea when Mac would be coming home. His letters had become not only more despondent but also bitter.

"Papa, I think I should get a job." I sat on the couch in his study. "I just can't sit around like this. The Russian Relief doesn't really need me. I can't chase after typing or baby-sitting jobs all the time."

He put down his *maobi* (Chinese writing brush) and turned to me, his face thoughtful. "I know that, *dochenka*, but you know what the Chinese tell us. 'A hundred paths present a hundred difficulties.' That's what's happening to you, isn't it?"

"Papa, I'm thankful that you understand how I feel. I don't like living off you and Mama. I try to help Mama with the housework and cooking, but I want to start living again." I just didn't know how else to explain this restless frustration that I was feeling. "I'm just so useless. Everyone in the family except me is doing something constructive."

Papa picked up his *maobi* and carefully slanted it on his ink pad, then moved it with slow precision in several upward strokes till the tip had enough black ink for him to start writing again.

"Watch me make this character, Tamara. You yourself have practiced enough Chinese calligraphy to know that you need patience to develop a character. Each stroke is important. If you hurry, your strokes do not come out clean, and your character appears smudged. Am I not correct?"

I smiled. "In other words, Papa, I need to be patient."

"Absolutely, Tamara. First of all, you must know that Mama and I are happy to have you and Vanya home. Secondly, we do not need your financial help. You give us happiness in the knowledge that you are making something of your lives. Vanya, now at Harvard, is enough to make any parent proud. And you? I understand you're in limbo right now. You aren't sure of your feelings towards Macushla; yet you can't let him go. Am I not right in my thinking?" It was almost as if he had read my mind. Silently, I nodded in agreement.

He sighed, then continued, "You won't have long to wait. In the meantime there is plenty here in Cambridge and Boston to keep you busy: lectures, concerts, books, and your own hobbies. Why not start your oil painting again? I could use a painting here," he hinted, pointing with the *maobi* at a spot on the wall. "Or you can go to Widener and read if the books here at home don't suit you. I advise you not to look for work now. It wouldn't be fair for the person who hires you to have you leave to get married."

"I'm not that sure about marriage, Papa." I bit my lip. "I think that I love Mac, but then I'm afraid that if he comes back, I might feel towards him the way I felt at the senior prom."

"When he was drunk?" Papa looked slyly up at me. I should have guessed Mama would tell him.

"And yet I've grown to know him so well through his letters,

Papa. No other man whom I've met has had such an effect on me."

Silently he continued to form his characters. I watched him and marveled at how steadily his hand held the brush and how perfect his strokes were. "That's beautiful, Papa." I leaned over and brushed a kiss on his cheek. "Thank you, Papotchka." I'll take your advice. It's helped me by seeing it your way." I left his study then, feeling somewhat better.

Gradually, my life at home fell into a pattern. I helped Mama in the mornings, then played the piano or read or painted. In the evenings I joined the family in the living room to listen to Eric Sevareid or Edward R. Murrow, then afterwards went up to my room to write letters to Mac, Lanny, and the few other soldier-boys who were still overseas. Andy had returned to East Orange and was now a civilian. We had stopped corresponding.

Once in a while Vanya, much to my annoyance, would appear at the door of my room to ask for help in his English courses or just to talk. Although I resented his intrusion, I found it best to remain civil. He didn't know what I had learned about him, and I was not about to let him know.

One evening he told me about this new girl he'd met just before coming home. "I'm corresponding with her, Tamara. She's beautiful." By his enthusiasm I could tell that he was bursting to tell me all about her.

I wasn't particularly interested in his latest conquest.

"I love her." He glanced at himself in my full-length mirror, then smiled at his own reflection. Although anxious to get back to my letter to Mac, I waited for him to continue. "I call her 'my Pink Pebble.'" He looked so sheepish saying it that I had a hard time to refrain from laughing. "She lives in Indianapolis," he added.

"I remember you were so crazy about an Italian girl to whom you gave that amethyst ring. What about her?"

His mouth curved downward. "Her? I got fed up with her. Did Eugene tell you about her?" He looked suspiciously at me.

"Yes. She was a prostitute, wasn't she?"

"Would you believe she went back to doing it, after I had begged her not to? Anyway, she wasn't my type. Martha is."

"That's what you've said about every girl you've met, Vanya," I couldn't help saying.

He shook his head. "Honestly, this is it, the real thing. I'm asking her to marry me."

I looked directly at him. He seemed to be serious about this girl, but then he had always been serious about something or other until something else even more serious came up. I shrugged my shoulders. "How're you going to support her?"

After a significant pause he assured me. "She and I will be discussing that; don't worry. Besides," he said, shooting me a triumphant look, "Martha is most efficient. She's an executive secretary in her hometown and makes a good living. I'm sure she'll find something around here. In the meantime, Papa and Mama promised to help."

God and Confucius, I thought to myself, *he's got it all worked out already*. I stared at him in disbelief. "Well, I wish you luck." Suddenly I thought of Mac. He would never have broached marriage to me had he not known that he could support me. I hoped this "Pink Pebble" of Vanya's realized what she was getting into. On the other hand maybe I was being unfair to him. Perhaps he behaved differently with others. I turned back to my desk, hoping that he would get the hint. I had no desire to argue with him. All I wanted was for him to leave me alone.

"Excuse me, Tamara?"

Curiously, I turned to look at him and noticed at once the sly glint in his eyes. "What for, Vanya?"

"You still going to marry that Scotchman of yours?"

"In the first place, it's Scotsman, not Scotchman," I corrected. Strange how I could feel myself getting stirred up at the insinuating tones in his voice. I felt like a cat hunching its back, its fur rising, when it meets its foe. "I probably will marry Mac, if he's the man I think he is," I replied.

At that, Vanya began his despicable habit of rubbing his hands together, as if he had something devious in mind. Dorlise had termed it "dry-washing," which I thought mighty appropriate. "You know, don't you, that the folks would prefer that you marry someone of Slavic background?" He grinned, pleased again with himself. "But," he shrugged, "that's your problem, not mine."

Mac and a Friend in Wiesbaden

Simmer down, Tamara, I kept telling myself. *You know he's lying, because both Mama and Papa are crazy about Mac.*

"You mean some Slav like your friend Eugene?" I asked in a tone properly sweet and innocent. His cunning intrigued me. I wanted to see how far he would go with it.

"Yeah." He became expansive. "Gene's a great guy. You know, he told me he thinks the world of you and that you're about the sexiest broad he's ever seen."

I stared at him, my anger mounting. And to think that I had come home determined that I'd get along with him. "Yes," I answered, trying to keep my voice on an even keel, "I'd expect him to say something like that. You and he both like beautiful, sexy women, don't you?"

My reply puzzled him, I noted with satisfaction. He didn't know whether I was being sarcastic about him or not. He hadn't expected his meek baby sister to talk back to her big brother like this. I continued, still keeping my civil tongue. "Yes; you would be on Eugene's side. Did your good Slavic friend also tell you that

671

he tried to rape me? Did he? Or is raping just a way of life with people like him and you?" I thrust out my chair and clenched my fists, holding in check my revulsion.

That infernal smile froze on his lips, as he eyed me through lowered lids, not saying a word. Then, shaking his head at me, he yawned. "Boy, are you ever touchy." With that he left my room.

After he left, I took Mac's latest letter out of my robe pocket and reread it. I had to get the bad taste of Vanya out of my mind, although I knew that the letter itself would not cheer me. Most of his men were going home, he had written, except those who had seventy points or less. The points program confused me since Mac had been overseas longer than some of the men who were returning. My heart went out to him as I reread the bitter words.

What they want to do to my life I don't know, but I've never felt this way before. Disillusioned, hopeless, unambitious, uninterested. I just don't know what to do. You should have seen all us officers who have seventy or fewer points last night. No, we didn't get drunk. We went around like punch-drunk guys. One man couldn't eat his supper. What we'll be like when we do finally return I don't know, but we talked and talked of home and just about how much we could take.

One soldier had committed suicide the night before, having taken all he could. Now that a lot of men have gone home, our men of necessity must work harder so that they can see more men go home. And when will those who remain go home? When all the rest have gone. Then we'll see how disinterested everyone is in getting us back. All the jobs will be gone; clothes and other materials will be scarce. No wonder we all get bitter.

I stopped reading and closed my eyes. How terribly unfair, when he had done so much. And then my thoughts shifted back to Vanya and his scheming plans for himself. What a difference between these two men—one so upstanding and fine, and the other? I closed my eyes tight, then opened them to continue reading.

I'm just trying to show how important it is to get us home and fast. Selfish interests back home don't want us back all at once. It would, I myself realize, mean a flood on the labor market, an

672

excessive cost; but just now every month's delay is going to cause a bitterness in the hearts and minds of veterans that will take years to erase. Don't think that the cost will be small. That devotion to selfishness will cost those who had it all figured out a pretty price! To be over here one-and-a-half years, to work and slave on the beach, to sweat out buzz bombs, and then to have to see that men over here less than ten months get put on a ship for home. There's no logical explanation that makes sense to me and to others of us in this so-called 'close-out force.' What we naturally wonder is WHO IN THE HELL IS GOING TO CLOSE US OUT? It looks as though we've been closed out from going home.

Putting down the letter in my lap, I hastily wiped my eyes with the back of my hand. The last part I kept rereading to myself over and over again.

If you keep waiting, I can't help worshipping you, darling. It would be too much for me to bear if you didn't wait, what with the disillusionment, despair, and selfishness I've already had to deal with. Men come in to see me, wanting to divorce wives back home either to marry someone over here or to free the wife so that she can marry someone back home. After all I've seen, if you wait for me, I'll know that you are one extraordinary woman, rarer than a split atom. If you don't wait, I'll be better off, and you'll be happier—maybe. Darling, if you're still waiting and love me, I shall spend the remainder of my life working to make you happy, for it would rid me of that bitterness that lately has distorted and warped my thoughts and attitudes.

I finally placed that letter inside the drawer beside the others that had come from overseas, mostly from him and Lanny. Poor Lanny, he too was stranded somewhere in France.

After Thanksgiving, the weeks sped by. I had talked with Phyllis on the Upland Road pay phone several times, conscience-stricken that I had to sneak out of the house to talk to her, yet knowing that there was no other way to avoid Vanya's prying interest. One day we arranged to meet at Hood's.

"Boy, you're a sight for sore eyes," she had wise-cracked as I came up. She had chosen "our" table by the plate-glass window. "Just like Radcliffe days, eh?" She offered me a Marlboro.

"No, thanks. I'm really trying to cut down. I've been smoking like a chimney because of worrying about Mac's morale and my own situation. When I get disgusted with smoke in my room, I open the windows, but it's so cold out there; it's like an icebox. I've just got to quit." I sat back in my chair. Gee, it was good to see that grin of hers. "So you like your new job, huh?"

"Yep, I've got a terrific boss who's happily married to a doll of a wife. They're older, middle-aged, if you know what I mean. Anyway, they often invite me to their home for dinner,"—I heard the familiar chortle—"and she keeps finding me guys to date. Soo, things couldn't be better." Her face became concerned. "What's that you said about Mac? His morale? What's wrong, Tamara?"

"It's just that he's been transferring his men to the States. Some of them have fewer points than those that have to stay in Europe and that outrages him. It makes me mad too. One day he writes that they'll be getting home soon. Then it's postponed again and again. Now it looks as if he won't be home for Christmas. The army is all botched up, Phyl. One day he had fifteen men in his company; the next day there were one hundred and forty. It was ironic what he wrote about the fifteen new men. Here, I've got the letter with me: 'They're total strangers, unskilled, low I.Q. morons who have no sense or they'd be out of this mess, good fellows but helpless. Only four of the fifteen are equal to the worst men I'm losing.' "

"Pretty sickening, yep." She paused. "I'm getting the idea that marriage is not out of your plans these days. Really, you are marrying him when he gets back, aren't you?"

"I think so, Phyl. I . . . "

"Good, I always knew you loved him, even when you denied it." She stopped talking, her eyes lighting up with curiosity. "Are Mac's parents still against him marrying you?"

"I have a feeling they are although he had written that they'd asked about me. I can't understand, Phyl, how they can dislike me before they've even met me. Can you?"

"No, I can't; but, Tamara, there's something that you have to learn about this beloved country of ours. You haven't come across it until now. There are people, some even more prejudiced than Mac's parents, who hate their neighbors because either their religions are different; their race; their eyes slant; or even if, like you, they speak with an accent. I think your accent is cute, but someone else would label you a 'furriner' and want nothing to do with you, because you are, shall we say, different." She laughed laconically, adding, "And anybody who disagrees with them is an ignoramus. *Capitchi?*"

"*Capitchi,* although I find it hard to believe. I thought that that's why America was called 'the land of liberty.' I thought everyone who immigrated here became American and that it was all like one, big family. Rather stupid of me, wasn't it?"

Her voice was compassionate. "It's still the best country in the world, and we are free. You wouldn't want to go back to China, would you?"

"You're right. Besides, if Mac and I do get married I won't be marrying his family. He said once that if they wouldn't accept me, he'd disown them."

"It burns me up when people say that. Whew! That really infuriates me to have people decide whether they wish to accept someone or not. Who the hell do they think they are? Better than anybody else?"

"That's okay, Phyl. It doesn't bother me. All I want is for Mac to come home."

She grinned. "So you can make wedding plans?"

I gave her a Cheshire smile. "I'm making them already. C'mon, gal, I'll walk you down to the subway station."

I watched her go downstairs to the subway platform, sad at heart, puzzled at why life had to be this way.

"It's December 23, 1945. Do you realize, *dochenka,* that your brother will be getting married tomorrow?" Papa looked funny as he stood on the next to the top rung of the ladder.

"I wish you'd let me put up the star, Papa." I watched him anxiously.

He looked down at me, his eyes twinkling mischievously. There was a smudge on his nose. "No, no. I know how to do it. I'll bet Vanushka is getting nervous now." He couldn't help chuckling. "Finally, he's found the right girl. Well, at least I hope so." Again, he looked down at me. "It's a good thing Macushla can't see his beautiful, lovely Tamara now. How can you get so down-right messy decorating a Christmas tree?"

"The same way you can," I answered, holding the ladder. "Be careful, Papa."

He leaned over and stood on his tiptoes, stretching his arm way out to screw in the bulb in the center of the star atop the tree.

"I'm a bit taller. Please let me do it," I begged him.

"There, I done dood it." His right foot dangled down gingerly, feeling for the lower rung, then his left one came down. I heaved a sigh of relief. He should talk about me! What a sight he made in his baggy old trousers with the pockets bulging with hammers, screwdrivers, and nails. Laughing to myself, I gripped the ladder for dear life as he moved less cautiously further down.

"Half an hour to screw in a tiny light bulb," I teased him. "I'll tell Mama how slow you were."

"If you had to stand up there and have me hold the ladder, giggling and shaking it the way you have—huh!" Papa tweaked my nose, then bent down and plugged in the lights.

"Ah, Papa, how beautiful!" I exclaimed. The tiny green bulbs glowed softly through the silvery white angel hair. The light green bulb in the golden star gave it an ethereal, ghostly effect. Papa too stared at it with pride. "This is by far the prettiest tree we've ever had," he declared. "You and I make a good team, don't we?" He patted me on the back.

Just then we heard the doorbell. Papa looked towards the door, then at me. "Wait till I get upstairs, then open the door," he whispered. "I can't have people see me this way."

"Nope, you can't," I agreed, watching as he hastily climbed the stairs. What about me? Dirty, sweaty, and disheveled as I was, I still had to open the door. I caught a glimpse of myself in the foyer mirror. A smudge of white paint stood out on my nose, left over from painting the bathroom this morning.

Fortunately, it was only Sammy. When I attempted to hug him, he pushed his arms out, staring at me in mock dismay.

"Whoa, there. Who're you?" He took two steps back, his arms outstretched, backing me off. "My God, but you're breathtakingly beautiful! Too bad that Yankee lieutenant of yours can't see you now. Methinks he'd rush right back to Antwerp, Belgium."

He didn't come in right away, wanting me to step out on the

676

front porch with him. "Look," he pointed down towards the street. There, parked by the curb stood a shiny new car. "Like it, Princess? How'd you like to take a spin around the block with me?"

"Not like this, Sammy. I'd get your new car all messed up."

Mama and Papa were both happy to see him again. I, too, hoped that he might bring me news about Mac. Now that Sammy had come back to the States, perhaps Mac might even now be on his way too.

"Sammy? . . ."

He slowed me down with his hand. "Sit here beside me, my ugly duckling, but not too close. I've been in New York for the past three weeks. I just arrived here."

"Your wife?" Mama asked.

His face clouded. "She's with friends in New York. I came to welcome Vanya and his bride to Cambridge. He asked me to pick them up at the train station." He took Mama's hands in his.

"And then there may be another wedding," Papa placed his forefinger along his nose and gave me an impish glance. Sam looked at me in surprise. "Really? To Mac?"

I nodded. "When I see him, I'll know." That seemed to be my constant refrain these days.

Sam gave me a gentle smile. "As I wrote to you once, he's the man for you. I hope you marry him, darling; I truly do."

I reached out to Sam and wrapped my arms around him. "What in the world do you think I've been waiting for ever since he went overseas! My whole life I've waited for him; it's about time the wait is over!"

44

They Cannot Know Who Did Not Wait

This time Phyl and I decided to splurge. We met at St. Clair's for lunch. "You're sure Papa or Mama won't come here by chance?" She looked anxiously around the restaurant.

"Of course not, Phyl. They rarely eat out, and then only in the evening, not at noontime. If it would make you feel any better, we can sit at that table towards the back."

"Yeah; let's sit there. I'd hate to bump into Mama at this stage of the game. It's not because I'm afraid for myself, I'd hate for her to get mad at you again."

"I know." Once more, I felt thankful for her loyalty and friendship. "You're a great gal, Phyl, and believe me, I'll always be your friend."

"Baloney." Her voice was gruff. "What's wrong now? You sounded pretty upset over the phone."

I took out Mac's letter and the *Stars and Stripes* article that he'd enclosed. "Let me read you what he says here. Then you can read the article for yourself. It looks as if he won't be coming home now for some time. This letter is dated January sixth. And I was hoping so much that he'd be here shortly."

Phyl took a roll and began to butter it. "That's a damned shame, just when you've got everything ready for the wedding, everything but the groom. Hell of a way to plan a marriage, but that's the army for you, I guess." She sat back, her eyes on me. "Go ahead. I'm all ears."

"Okay," I scanned his letter quickly. "Here's what he says."

" 'More disappointments, as you can see by this article I'm enclos-
ing from the *Stars and Stripes* for you to peruse. It's an outrage to keep
those of us unwilling to remain here with no choice other than to serve
our country. Now that many with high points have gone home, they
give us another run-around. Because others don't want to serve here in
the new army, we must serve until they have enough replacements for
us irreplaceables.' "

Phyl gaped at me. "Tamara, I've never heard of something
like this happening. That is absolutely the God-awfulest thing
I've ever heard of."

"You ain't heard nothing yet," I told her. "Listen to what he
writes next.

" 'In the meantime we who *must* are not eligible for promotion
unless we *volunteer* to remain here. Meanwhile those with pull
and low points are going home as rapidly as possible by volunteering to return after forty-five days in the States. We are told
there is a critical shortage of officers. What almost breaks a man's
heart in two is to see men of a short period of service over here
and with low points going home and staying there because they
have pull.' "

"You find that everywhere," Phyl said. "It's getting to be that
it's not what you know that counts but whom you know. It's
ironic, isn't it?"

"Yep, and the worst thing is there's not much that we can do
about it. You know, I thought of writing to President Truman
about it, but Papa said that he probably wouldn't even see my
letter."

Phyl grew thoughtful. "That might be worth trying though.
Why not? You've got nothing to lose. President Truman is more
of a people's president than some others we've had."

"You may be right," I agreed. "There's just this one para-
graph that I want to read to you and then we'll order. You mind?"

"Of course not, I'm interested. I think a lot of Mac; you know
that."

I looked at her gratefully, then began to read.

" 'That's not sour grapes; there are two instances of officers doing just that here in our battalion. Morale is supposedly sky-high; everything is proceeding beautifully on the surface. Deals are being made every day by those who know *somebody*. Thank God, there is little graft in it. In the interim Vixen, forget for a while if you can about my coming home. All my friends are just ordinary people.' "

"Poor Mac and his buddies. After what they'd gone through in the invasion and the Battle of the Bulge, to be treated like this. No wonder he's bitter. But, Tamara." She paused to light a cigarette. "He's coming home . . . one of these days he'll be home and the main thing is he's whole, not wounded or hurt in any way. Be thankful for that."

Good old Phyl. I felt better already having talked to her.

"What about Vanya's bride, Tamara? What's she like?" Phyllis leaned forward, looking both amused and curious. "I can't wait to hear about them."

"She's not at all what I expected. She's totally unlike the other gals Vanya used to date. First of all, she's painfully shy, almost timid, in fact. She's pretty, with naturally curly hair, big, blue eyes, and a charming smile. Vanya walks around in a daze, as if he's sleepwalking. They stay upstairs most of the time."

"And her background?"

"I don't know, but I'd guess she's from English, perhaps Irish, background. She's not Slavic; even though, according to Vanya, Papa and Mama have hoped we'd marry Slavs. I think our family scares her a bit because we forget she's there and speak Russian. Then too, Vanya told Mama his 'Pink Pebble' doesn't like her Russian cooking. So you know what he does? He goes out and buys her hamburgers. Strange, isn't it?" I laughed, "It's strange for me to listen to Vanya these days. His voice is so gentle and for once he looks me right in the eye."

"Well, maybe she'll change him." Phyl blew a smoke ring, then laughed. "Miracles have happened, you know."

"I sure hope so." I couldn't help laughing too. "Oh, by the way, Phyl, I forgot to tell you the main thing. We're moving."

"You mean from Mt. Vernon Street? My God, why? I thought your folks liked the house."

"The landlady decided she wants to sell it. Besides, one of these days, Vanya and Martha will be getting a place of their own. And if I get married, I'll probably move too. Then it'll be too big for them. Besides, Mama, when she was out walking one day, had noticed this new apartment complex being built and out of sheer curiosity had gone to look through it. She walked through this one apartment and fell in love with it. You know Mama, once she makes up her mind about something. . . . "

Phyl grinned. "Boy, do I!"

"She found the man in charge, found out about the moderate rent, and hurried home to talk it over with Papa; she then walked right back, and rented it. Just like that!"

Phyllis chuckled. "You know, she should be running the United States Army. She'd sure get things done, wouldn't she? Mac would be home pronto, probably promoted to general!"

I shook my head. "Not unless he merited a general's stars. But one thing I'll tell you, Phyl. If things weren't done according to Mama, you know what the army'd get?"

She laughed, "The silent treatment."

"Bravo! She's a wonderful person, Phyl, but it hurts me to have her treat you like this. You remember how I'd always wanted you to be my maid of honor? Well, Martha's going to be my matron of honor, because Mama said so. She's making my dress, approving my bridesmaids, checking my guest list; sometimes I feel as if it's her wedding, not mine."

Phyl's face was sympathetic. "Listen, old gal, try to think of it this way. Your mama didn't have a wedding; she didn't even have a mother to make her wedding gown, did she? She had a stepmother who hated her. Therefore, she wants to do her best by you, and face it, Tamara, she's used to ruling the household in her own sweet, steel-like way, even though she'll inform the whole world that Papa is her lord and master. Am I wrong?"

I had never thought of it like that. "I guess . . . " Phyl pushed her half-eaten lunch to the side, then continued, "Now that she has a daughter, she wants a wedding like the one she never had but had dreamed about. You can't change her views. Frankly, when all is said and done, the actual wedding will last for a half hour to an hour. Then comes the reception, but you and Mac will be anxious to flee from all the grinning, kissing guests to be by yourselves. It'll be Mama who'll be mulling over your wedding, savoring each detail that she had planned. Give her this last bit of enjoyment, why don't you? You won't regret it, chum."

I stared at her, feeling tears blurring my eyes. "Damn it, Phyl, do you always have to psychoanalyze or whatever you call it? You're right, of course, and I'll probably abide by your wise counseling. But it still burns me up that it has to be that way."

"You won't regret it. After all, it's you and Mac who count. From your marriage on, you will have each other to turn to . . . for better, or for worse." She laughed. "To change the subject, have you seen Annitchka lately?"

"I've had coffee with her a couple of times at Schrafft's. She keeps inviting me to visit, but I've been so busy lately that I haven't had a chance."

"She's one fine lady," Phyl said slowly. "I'll always be grateful to you for introducing me to her and Philipp. You ought to go see her when you can."

"I will," I promised her, then looked at my watch. "Phyl, can you believe that we've been here for nearly two hours?"

We both grabbed our purses. "It's my turn to treat," she said, and, smiling, she paid the cashier, and we left St. Clair's. As we walked towards the subway station, I asked her if she'd ever heard "Amor."

"Sure have," she bubbled. "It's number two on the Hit Parade; it's one of my favorites."

"Well, I was listening to the radio the other night, and the announcer said something that I can't forget."

"What was it?"

"He said that it had one of the most simple, yet beautiful descriptions of love in it. When someone you love is gone, there are no days. Nights are lonesome.

"He said there was so much meaning in the song's few words. I used to listen to 'Amor,' even hummed the tune, but never really thought about the real meaning of the words. With Mac away, those lines now mean so much more to me."

We started walking again. At the station Phyl gave me a couple of taps on my shoulder. "It was good seeing you again, Tamara. And for you, remember: When the sun rises, and it's daytime again, your nights, Tamara, will no longer be lonesome."

The next day Papa came into the kitchen where Mama and I were cleaning up after lunch. "I stopped the mailman on my way to work. He gave me this letter from Macushla; I thought I'd be your mailman today." He winked at Mama as he passed the V-mail to me. "Hope it's good news, *dochenka*."

I stared at the handwriting. The letter was from Mac, but the writing did not look like his. This was large, uneven, not in the least resembling the beautiful script which I knew so well. On opening the letter, I was even more puzzled.

"What's wrong?" Papa asked. "Bad news?"

"What does 'I'm in the pipeline now' mean? He says he has been assigned to the Fortieth Amphibious Tractor Battalion and should be home before the first of March. But what does 'pipeline' mean?"

Papa read the letter, with Mama looking over his shoulder. Then he began to laugh, at first to himself, then loudly, till tears came into his eyes. "He's on orders, Tamarotchka. He'll really be home soon now!" He gave me a hug. "Congratulations! That is the best news we've had since Vanya's wedding day. Well, now I can go back to work."

After he had gone, Mama and I sat down for a cup of tea.

"It won't be long now, dochenka."

"I know, Mama. I can't wait till I see him again." I could picture him coming home, our meeting, my very first look into his eyes. Would they look as tenderly . . . then, suddenly, I remembered. I looked at Mama and began to giggle. The longer I looked at her and the more surprised she looked, the less control I had over my emotions.

"Tamara, I know how happy you must be, but try to control yourself; you're getting hysterical," Mama chided.

"I'm not laughing because I'm happy, Mama," I managed to say. "It's just that I started wondering what he'd do when he came to this house and found it vacant. He'll have a fit!"

Mama put down her teacup. "You mean to tell me that you haven't told him that we're moving? Tamara, if you were a five-year-old then, maybe, I'd understand your action, but . . . ach!" She shook her head at me, biting her lower lip. "I am surprised at you. Now you march right upstairs and write him immediately and give him our new address. The idea!"

"He'll find me, Mama." I knew he'd find me.

"Get upstairs and write!" Mama was in no mood for teasing.

I took the stairs two at a time and did as Mama had ordered. I wrote a short note to Mac telling him how happy I was and that I felt like dancing and telling the whole world that he was coming home. I wrote that we were moving into a brand new apartment house where the paint was barely dry and everything smelled new. I described it down to the minutest detail except that I didn't tell him our apartment number, only the street address. Rather tricky of me, but so what? It would be just as I had told Mama. Mac would find me. Of that I was quite certain.

Mama was in seventh heaven! Finally, we had moved into the apartment on Forest Street, and she was delighted.

"Isn't this apartment beautiful?" She kept exclaiming as she walked from room to room, planning where to hang a certain Chinese scroll or place a special chair.

Of course, the dragon rugs we laid down in front of the heavy blue-green sofa that Mama had us back up against the picture window facing Forest Street. Mama already knew where she wanted most of the furniture placed because she had frequented the apartment several times before we had actually moved in. The birchwood coffee table went in front of the sofa, and Papa had already stacked it with magazines and various newspapers, which he bought at Felix's on the way home. Against one wall stood Papa's pride and joy, the console RCA he had bought not long after we had moved to Cambridge. Mama hung her delicately embroidered silk Chinese scrolls, depicting the four seasons, above it. Directly across from the radio stood her treasured Baldwin piano, silently awaiting Mac's return so that he could bring out its magnificent tones as Mama repeatedly kept telling me only he could. In no time at all the apartment looked as if we had always lived in it.

Our first morning there had been pleasant. As usual Papa brought the mail to the breakfast table. "There are two from Macushla this time," he told me with a smile. "Who knows? Perhaps he'll be here by the end of this week. What's the news this time?"

I laid down the letters. "Nothing really that he hasn't said before, Papa. He wrote that he's excited about coming home to me." And then, right there out of the blue, tears welled up in my eyes. I had to look down so that Mama and Papa wouldn't notice.

"He'll be here before we know it," Mama sighed. "Time goes fast, and we have so much to do before your wedding. Soon, you'll be Mrs. McNish and then we'll not have our *dochenka* anymore."

"You'll always have me, both you and Papa." I put my arms around her. "Just because I'm getting married does not mean that I stop being your daughter. Besides, there's that chance that I may not marry Mac. All these preparations, the wedding dress you're making, telling friends about it . . . I don't know, Mama. What if it turns out that he isn't the one?"

Mama laid her hand over mine, patting it gently. "You'll know, my dear," she told me in a soft voice. "The minute he comes through that door, you'll know."

"How do *you* know that I'll know? *I* don't."

She poured some fresh coffee into her cup, then reached over for the sugar bowl. "Call it intuition or whatever, but I know."

I shook my head, "That's not it, Mama. *How* does one know?"

"How? Well, let me tell you how. It's because Papa and I know you so well. You're a lot like Papa, you know. You have his sunny disposition and intelligence. And like him, you're strong— in your convictions and attitude. However, in many ways, unlike your own peers, you are still a child, naive, unsophisticated." She put out her hand seeing me about to interrupt. "Please let me finish, Tamara. You asked me, so let me tell you. Think of a flower about to open its petals. Think how fragile and lovely it is. To Papa and me, that's what you are. We have watched you with the men who have courted you, rejoicing in your popularity, frightened that you might make the wrong choice. At the same time, we knew that only you could make that decision. I knew all along though, that your character would eventually pull you through."

"My character?"

"Yes. Your high ideals. Papa and I have always known, ever since we first set eyes on him, that Mac has the qualities of the man you should marry. Background so different, you say? Yes, but your interests, the way you think, your natural instincts are similar in so many ways. You thought you loved Andy, but, Tamara, think for one brief moment." Here she searched my face with a stern intensity. "Could you have lived with Andy for a life-time? Or Lanny for that matter? The look on your face answers my question as well as your silence."

"When I think about marrying any man, I think of Papa and you, how happy you've been together and how loyal you have been to him."

She continued, as if I hadn't spoken, "Your Mac has already proved how much he loves you. Every day, no matter where he was or how difficult his situation, he has always written to you reminding you of his love. Any other young woman would truly be envious of the great love he has for you." She patted my cheek, "You'll know, Tamara. As I have told you before, the moment your eyes meet his, you'll know."

45

Your Waiting Saved Me from My Fate

The air was crisp, the sky, overcast, and I instinctively knew that snowflakes would be swirling sometime soon. I could sense it as I stepped out onto Forest Street, breathing in that fresh, invigorating air. *What a truly beautiful world this is,* I thought to myself. Now that peace had come, people could once again start living normal lives, For me too it would be a new beginning, just as soon as this waiting-for-Mac game was over.

I had to get out of the apartment. Now that it was the way Mama wanted it to be she didn't need my help any more. There was nothing inside the apartment that I wanted to do. I had begun to feel confined in there, as if I had claustrophobia. I needed space for myself to think things through. A walk to Harvard Square would probably do me good. Perhaps I could even put in a couple of hours at the Russian—no longer 'War'—Relief headquarters. Whatever.

I strolled along Mass Ave., idly peeking into store windows, gazing at their crowded, dusty displays. Some of these shops had had the same window-dressings for weeks at a time. If I owned a store, I told myself, I would regularly change the displays so as to attract customers. I neared Brigham's Ice Cream Shop and almost walked in, remembering "us" that day.

"You want an ice-cream cone?" he had asked me then. That cool, crisp day had been almost like this one today. I recalled watching the girl scoop up the ice cream, packing it down, then

687

dipping it into the jimmies. (I never did find out why they were called jimmies.) And then, laughingly we had walked out, each of us licking our ice cream, happy, carefree for a while, and so very much in love. Then Mac had suddenly stopped, right there on the sidewalk, with all the people passing by. He had moved the hand holding my cone gently aside and had kissed me, right there on the sidewalk, with people watching and smiling. His kiss had tasted like black walnut ice cream.

I walked on. The Philipp Franks lived in the red brick apartment house, just before Cambridge Common, on Mass Ave. Should I stop in to say hello or just go on? I really should tell her my good news, I decided. I stepped into the apartment foyer and rang Annitchka's bell, smiling to myself at the thought of how surprised she'd be.

I dearly loved Annitchka Frank. Although Mama's age, she related more to my generation and understood our problems. With Mama I had to be careful what I said. It always depended on Mama's mood if I could confide in her or not. And ever since the Phyllis episode, I found myself withdrawing from her, even though I loved her as much as before. Some subjects I could not even dare to broach to her, especially sex. In that respect, Mama belonged, not to the 1940s, but to the Victorian age. Annitchka, and her husband Philipp too, had adapted to the times. Besides, they were genuinely interested in young people like us, how we coped with our problems and why we thought and felt as we did.

I recalled the day Lanny and I had visited her; how she had liked him, whispering to me in Russian that he—no one else— was definitely the man for me. She had sung to both of us that day, sitting at her piano, her head thrown back and her clear, untrained soprano filling the air with her emotional renditions. Only she could give those Russian gypsy love songs that special heart-rending feeling.

She and Phyl had gotten along too. Sometimes Phyllis even stopped by to see her on her own. As Phyl so aptly put it, "She's a damned good listener and knows when to give advice to us and when not to."

I heard her buzzer sound after I had rung her bell. She stood at the entrance to her apartment, wearing a black wool dress with a multicolored shawl around her shoulders. When she saw me at the door, she smiled and immediately threw her arms around me.

"Ta-mar-otch-ka!" she exclaimed, her eyes bright with pleasure. "What a delightful surprise. I had begun to suspect that you might have forgotten my existence. I know, of course, that you've been helping Mama with the apartment, but you used to visit me more often."

"I know, Annitchka," I said, feeling guilty. "I've been in such up-and-down moods these days that I haven't been good company. And with the moving . . ."

"I realize that, darling. The important thing is that you're here. Come into the living room with me." She fluffed the pillow on the sofa. "Here." She patted it. "Tell me now. How does the new apartment look?"

"Perfect," I told her. "Mama couldn't be more happy." I smiled at her. "In fact, you ought to go see it. You're like family, you know."

She smiled at my enthusiasm. "I know that, dear." She gave me an affectionate pat on my cheek. "You're like a daughter to me, and I've missed you." She put out her hand to touch my hair. "My, but you're pretty. Have you ever thought of adding a bit of peroxide to your hair or even a touch of lemon juice to make it lighter?"

"Annitchka, that's not what I came to see you for. I wanted to tell you my good news. Mac is coming home!"

Her eyes widened as she stared at me. "Really! How nice. But what about Lanny? Is he still overseas?" She passed her box of Swiss cigarettes to me. Remembering how they had tasted before, I pulled out my Chesterfields.

"Try one of mine for a change," I suggested.

For a few minutes we puffed away in silence. Then, as I watched her, a shadow momentarily flickered over her face.

"You're serious about this Mac, aren't you?" She sounded disappointed. "Why him?" she asked, in a puzzled tone.

"Because he's the man I love. Annitchka, I know you think the world of Lanny. I do too. But don't make a judgment until you've met Mac. I get goose pimples whenever I think of him. Believe me, I've never before felt this way about any other man."

Again, she was silent, puffing, blowing the smoke through

her mouth. Finally, she extinguished it, squashing it carefully into a brass ashtray.

"Poor Lanny! I'm sorry for him. He's very much in love with you, Tamarotchka," she said in a low voice. "To me and Philipp you looked like a perfect match."

I shook my head at her. "Annitchka, we're too much alike. Lanny's too gentle, too idealistic." I remembered Mama's words. "I need some one stronger. Mac is my first and last love. There is no other man in this world who could ever take his place."

"I know exactly what you're saying, Tamarotchka. Philipp's my love, and there is no other man for me."

"I hadn't wanted to fall in love when I met Mac, Annitchka. Perhaps that's why I struggled so against it. I wanted to be independent, to do exactly as I pleased. Since then I've learned a lot. I've also met enough men to know that the man I've chosen is the best man for me."

Annitchka nodded, smiling. "You have changed since that day I first met you. I remember you as such a shy, sweet, unaffected girl. Now you're confident, and know what you want out of life. I told your mama once that the best teacher for you would be experience outside the home. I don't think she liked that. She was dead set against your going to New York. And that, Tamarotchka"—she leaned forward, smiling—"that was the best thing you could possibly have done—gone there on your own."

"I think so, Annitchka." Then I thought of something. "Would you mind if I called Phyllis from your place?"

"Consider this your second home, darling. You don't need my permission to use the phone."

Phyllis was delighted with my news. "And when is the big day?" she asked.

"Whenever we can get Appleton Chapel. That also depends on when Mac arrives. You know what scares me, though, Phyl." I lowered my voice. "What if he isn't the man I've fallen in love with through his letters? What if he is more like that drunken slob who took me to the prom? Here Mama has made my gown; my maids in waiting have gotten their dresses. What if I've been wrong in my feelings? How am I going to say no to him? I get cold feet and shivers just thinking about that."

She groaned in exasperation. "Oh, God, not that again,

Tamara. Believe me, take my word for it. He is the man for you. If you don't want him, I do. Men like Mac don't grow on trees or neighborhood fences."

We made arrangements to talk again. "I'll call you soon," I promised her.

Hanging up the receiver, I felt sad and somewhat resentful towards Mama. It would have been perfect to have had Phyl with us in the new apartment, planning this wedding together, sharing my happy final days as a single girl. But Vanya's rumor-mongering had made that impossible. Why hadn't Mama believed in me? I had hardly ever given her cause to distrust me with the exception of that one time when I was five. *Well*, I thought, as I walked back to the sofa, *I hope Vanya is satisfied.* At least, I comforted myself, he could never gloat about it to me, not having the slightest idea that I now knew he had caused all this trouble with Mama. He also didn't realize that I knew he was the one who had crippled our cousin Petya by pushing him off the Russian stove.

"Phyllis will be your maid-of-honor, will she?" Annitchka held out a box of bon-bons to me.

Had Annitchka read my mind? "I always had hoped she would be. She was to be, and I, hers. With Mama's attitude, that just can't be. Mama already told me to ask Martha."

Annitchka looked at me without speaking, her eyes saying it all. "I'm sorry about that," she said slowly. "It is *your* wedding, and Mama should realize that. She must realize what good friends you are."

"I don't think she knows that Phyl and I still are friends. I have to call her at a public phone booth near us. It's a shame to sneak around, but it's the only way. As for the wedding, I'm not going against Mama's wishes, or I'll risk getting her angry again."

Annitchka gave me a strange look but remained quiet.

"It's time I walked back home, Annitchka. There's so much that I still have to do, although it's frustrating to do things without Mac." I reached for my purse, slung it over my shoulder, and embraced her, kissing her lightly on both cheeks. "You're the first friend I've told about Mac being on his way."

"Thank you, darling; I feel honored." She put her arms

around me, looking at me affectionately. "I do hope things work out for you. I'm sure they will. And . . . I'll tell Philipp when he returns. You're one of his favorite people, you know."

As we walked arm in arm towards her front door, she stopped suddenly, one hand to her mouth. "Oh, my goodness, wait a minute. I almost forgot." She opened the clothes closet door in the hallway. Reaching in, she moved aside some winter things until she found what she wanted: a beautiful shiny black fur coat.

"Look at this; it's genuine Russian karakul. I've loved this coat, but now I'm too broad to wear it. I've wanted to give it to you for some time now, but I keep forgetting. It's yours. Let's see how it fits." She took off my shoulder-purse and helped me into the coat, standing back to see the effect. She smiled her approval. "It's made for you; you look like a real Russian *devushka!*" (maiden), she exclaimed.

The coat was not only beautiful but also right in style, with the cinched waist and princess-style flared bottom. She continued, admiring my appearance. "With your blonde hair and those red boots, perfect. Ach!" her eyes shone with excitement. "Wear it in good health, my child."

I thanked her, hugging her. "Annitchka, you're the best! I love you so very much."

She smiled, closing the door behind me. I heard her humming to herself as I walked down the steps of the apartment house. As I walked out to Mass. Ave., I could hear her playing the piano. I stopped to listen. She was playing *Proschai*, one of my favorite songs that Mama used to sing to me when I was a child. She was singing in her lovely, clear soprano voice that endearing, plaintive gypsy melody: Proschai, proschai, podruga doroga-a-a-ya, Bog znayet, oovizhu li ya tebya" (Farewell, farewell, my dear friend; God knows whether I will see you). I knew that she was singing it for me.

I had walked for almost a block when I noticed my unknown friend. He was such a little man, even shorter than Papa; he was apparently quite old, but his eyes, whenever they met mine, always twinkled in salutation. I had seen him often in my undergraduate days, when I walked on Mass Ave towards Radcliffe. Somehow, I had to smile at him; he was so sweet. After a while, we even stopped to exclaim over the weather, or merely to ask how do you do? He was quite the proper gentleman with old-fashioned good manners, just like Papa's. He always greeted me first by bowing, then doffing the black hat he always wore. His clothing was rather somber, but it befit his age. I never knew his name.

On this day he stopped completely in his tracks as if my very appearance had startled him. After all, I had been away for almost two years.

"My dear young lady, I haven't seen you for a long, long time. Ach, today the sun has returned to my life, seeing your smile once more. But you look exceptionally radiant today. You must have good news perhaps?" His accent sounded European; not quite German, but close to it.

"I have indeed, sir. You see, my fiancé is coming home after two years overseas. I'm getting married then."

The old face lit up. With a dignified, courtly bow he offered me his hand. "Ach, how good to hear that. Congratulations, my child." His watery eyes glistened as he raised them towards me. "I hope the two of you are most happy. The man who marries you, he has to be a fortunate young man."

"It is I who am fortunate," I told him with a bit more confidence than I actually had. Then I smiled to myself, as he, touching his fingers to his hat, walked on. My gosh, I laughed to myself, I was even telling strangers of my love!

When I came home the phone was ringing.

"Hello, Tamara," Loretta's cheerful voice greeted me. "My sister Carrie and I want to give you a bridal shower," she said. "Think what kind you want."

I had never heard of a bridal shower. "What's a bridal shower?" I asked.

Loretta laughed. "It's sort of like a hen-party of your friends," she explained. "That's what it is. You're given gifts. If you want a linen shower, then you get linens. If you want a kitchen shower—"

"I get it," I interrupted. "What a delightful custom. Can you have a miscellaneous shower? Then anyone can bring what she wants to. Right?"

"Fine. When would you like it?"

Dear Loretta, she was such an organizer. If I hadn't had her to advise me, I would still be in a muddle.

"Let's wait till Mac gets here, huh?"

She appeared satisfied. "Let me know the minute he arrives, will you please?"

"Not 'the minute,' but when I can," I told her, smiling into the telephone. "I'd want to give him a hug first."

That evening I lay down on my narrow studio couch and tried to read. After a time I gave up; my eyes had skimmed over the words, but my mind had absorbed none of them. Instead, I thought of Mac, wondering whether he was on the high seas yet. Finally, I got up and put on the *Roumanian Rhapsody*. Wonder of wonders! How easily I now pictured him, feeling his arms around me, his lips on mine. Listening to that haunting, sensuously beautiful music, I fell fast asleep.

For me time went by slowly, even though to others the days may have flown by. I had done about everything that a bride could do without the bridegroom's presence. My wedding gown was now covered with a sheet, hanging in Mama's closet. It was exquisite, in white brocade, with seed pearls at the off-the-shoulder round neckline and bordering the long sleeves. The bridesmaids and Martha, my matron-of-honor, had their Pilgrim-like dresses stowed away in their own closets.

Loretta kept checking up on me to make sure that I was doing things a la Emily Post. She herself had been to quite a few weddings; she had even been a bridesmaid once. When she found out that I hadn't yet made arrangements with a photographer, she had been horrified.

"But, Tamara, you absolutely have to have one. You want to remember your wedding day. Besides, you don't call a photographer at the last minute." She had been all out of breath on the phone. "Here, let me give you the name of one. He's Armenian, a fine fellow by the name of Kazanjian. Want me to spell it? Okay. Now find his phone number. Look under 'PHOTOGRAPHERS.' Call him right away. Otherwise he might be too busy, and you won't get him. He's good but not too expensive."

I protested. "Loretta, I need to wait for Mac. Look, I may not even be getting married." When I heard her gasp of surprise, I burst out laughing. "I have to be sure that I love him, Loretta. After all, I knew him for only two months before he left for overseas. I may have been building up an image. I may be wrong. When I marry, it'll be forever, not for a little while."

"But if he is the one," she persisted, "it will save you both the time if everything were ready."

God and Confucius, but Loretta could be insistent! Yet even as I thought that, I realized that in my disorganized state, I needed my level-headed friend.

I hadn't heard from Mac for some time. Today was now the twenty-first of February. Tomorrow would be George Washington's birthday. And Mac was sailing to the States on the *George Washington*. How long was it going to take him to get home, anyway? I hadn't asked him, and he hadn't told me.

I felt tired and listless. Again I found myself playing that damned waiting game of mine. I had tried to keep busy, but everything to me seemed dull. As for reading, forget it. Playing the piano was frustrating; my fingers stumbled over the keys. Mother Hildebalde from the French convent in Peking would have had a stroke had she heard me play. What a long time ago that had been. Poor little French penguin, I thought with affection. I wondered whether she was still living; she had been so frail at the time I had known her.

I went to Mama's bedroom, standing by the open door. She had just finished putting up her hair. "Mama, do you need anything at the store?"

She looked at me through her mirror. "No, not really. Were you planning to take a walk?"

"No, I guess not. I just thought that if you did need something, I'd go."

"Tamara." Mama leaned over her bed and pulled the bedspread down, folding it neatly towards the base of the bed. "There, I've unmade my bed. Just change into your housecoat and lie down to rest here. It's more comfortable than your studio couch. Go to sleep if you can. You've got bags under your eyes, and you've been irritable lately. What if Macushla arrives, and you're like this?" Her eyes looked amused. "Besides, it'll make the time pass faster."

She was right. I hadn't realized how edgy I had become. She certainly was right; her bed was more comfortable. I undressed, slipped on my gray, flowered housecoat, then lay down on the cool, white sheet, pulling Mama's light blanket clear up to my chin. Already I could feel my muscles relaxing and my mind clearing itself of all those confusing, questioning thoughts that had so bedeviled me. Before I realized it, I had fallen into a deep and restful sleep.

46

Mission Accomplished

It had been between this profound sleep and a gradual reawakening when first I heard the rapping on the apartment back door. Through the obscurity of my fog-filled sleep, I could hear Mama's excited exclamations, the "ohs" and "ahs" that she kept repeating between other words. Then I thought I heard her say, "Mac," and sleepily puzzled over why she should have even mentioned his name.

I knew that it could have been only a dream. I heard him laughing—his contagious laugh, so natural and good-hearted. Strange how close it sounded and that I had remembered it so well, after not having heard it for some two long years. There was a touch of shyness about it, but there had also been a tinge of joy. Then, in my dream I heard Mama calling to me, and her voice became even more distinct as I felt her breath touch my cheek. I was conscious of her hand upon my arm and sensed that the coverlet on the bed was being lifted off me.

Mama laughed softly, "She won't waken, Macushla. She has been exhausted, poor thing. I insisted that she take a nap."

I heard him chuckle again, and all of a sudden I knew that this was no dream. I opened my eyes wide, rubbing them hard to see if the apparition at the door would disappear. No, he still stood there in his officer's uniform, smiling down at me.

With a wildness that must have startled the two of them, I jumped out of bed and flung myself into his outstretched arms. He half-carried, half-dragged me into the living room, where midway he stopped, and then his lips found mine.

"Oh, darling, I've waited a long time for this," he murmured hoarsely. There were tears in his eyes. His voice lowered to a whisper as he kissed me between words. "Oh, Vixen, my Vixen, how I've waited for these delicious moments!" He held me close to him, kissing my hair, my eyes, my cheeks, and then again, found my lips and sealed them forever with his love. Finally he let me go and went over to Mama. They embraced without words, for words weren't needed then.

The three of us sat down on the sofa, his arms around both Mama and me. *How strong he looks*, I thought to myself, shyly examining his flushed, strong face. I felt ashamed now that I had ever doubted my love for him. Looking at each beloved feature on his face, I realized how very much I did love him, how very much I always had loved him.

"Oh, how she has waited for this special day." Mama looked over at me, her eyes glistening. "And now your waiting is over. You two deserve all the happiness you get, for both of you have been so faithful in your love. Your long wait is over!"

At those words, Mac leaned over to kiss me, thanking me with his eyes. His arm around my shoulder tightened, and he heaved a deep sigh.

"Now you can begin a new life together, as one," Mama continued. Her eyes became teasing as she turned to Mac. "And tell me now, Lieutenant McNish, is your Vixen worth all that long and anxious waiting?"

Again he sighed, looking into my face as if he couldn't look enough. "Mama, she is more beautiful than I had ever dreamed possible. You don't know, my Vixen, how I've agonized, how much I dreaded losing you. It's been such a terribly long, lonely time." He turned to me, burying his head on my shoulder. I felt both his arms enclose me, his own heart beating in unison with mine as again our lips met. Finally he released me.

"I tell you, you're still, as Sam said, an irrepressible imp. Not to write me the number of your apartment. How did I find you? Your red boots, of course." He chuckled.

"The boots?" Mama looked puzzled.

He laughed, eyeing me with amusement. "Her red boots, Mama. In the little entrance there." He pointed to the backdoor.

"I came in that way and there they were. I knew right away that this had to be your apartment."

If there ever had been the slightest doubt in my mind about him, it was now dispelled forever. I felt my love grow every time my eyes met his. For certain, and forever, he was my man: the Yankee-man of my girlhood dreams and now the Yankee-man of my life.

In the midst of all this, the phone rang. I left Mac's arms to answer it. As I took up the receiver, I felt his arms enfolding me, his lips against my hair.

"Hello!" I smiled into the receiver, feeling my heart sing.

For a moment I heard only silence, then a voice that sounded distant, as if there was a bad connection.

"Princess?" How much that one word conveyed! I would have recognized his gentle voice anywhere.

"Lanny!" It was all too much for me. The two of them arriving on the same day. "How good to know you've come back!" I felt tears well up in my eyes. "Where are you, Lanny?"

Mac's arms tightened around my waist. The whiff of his Sportsman's cologne wafted me into happy remembrance.

"Oh, darling," I sensed the emotion at the other end of the receiver. "I'm home, Tamara, home! I do so want to see you, dearest. It's been such a long time, hasn't it?"

"Oh, Lanny, Mac has just come home too." Next to Mac, he was my dearest friend. Impulsively, without even thinking, I spilled out my good news. "Mac and I are getting married. He's here right now. You'll come to our wedding, won't you?"

Now that I look back on that moment in my life I wish with all my heart that I had chosen my words more carefully. I had been young and naive and had wanted to share my joy with him who had shared so much with me in the past. I forgot for that moment that he too loved me.

There had been such a long pause. Then his voice, so changed in tone, resumed. "Yes, Mac and I were on the same ship, the *George Washington*. My congratulations to both of you." His voice now sounded fainter.

"Won't you come over to see us?" I asked.

Again there was that painful pause. His voice was muffled

when he spoke again. "Tamara, I'm leaving for Wellesley to see my mother. I'll be in touch." A click, and that was it.

"He didn't even say good-bye." Disappointed and hurt, I turned to Mac, rubbing my face against his jacket.

His face was serious although his eyes looked lovingly down into my face. "Darling, no wonder he didn't. He, like me, loves you so very much. Whew! Thank God, I'm not in his place. I can well sympathize with him in his position, poor chap."

For a moment he held me to him, so closely that I could feel his body straining towards mine. I could feel myself being drawn to him as if by an invisible magnet; both of us reaching out to each other, wanting to be as one.

"Mama is out there, Mac," I whispered into his ear. "Let's go to her, darling." We walked into the living room. Mama was on her way to the kitchen, tying her apron strings behind her back. She smiled when she saw us.

"I'm going to be cooking supper. You both stay out of my way. You understand me?" She tried to look severe but looked more like the cat that had swallowed a canary.

Mac hugged me to him. "If you're thinking of cooking up a big supper, forget it, Mama. I don't think I need any supper." He squeezed me tighter. "I could eat this one right now."

Mama's eyes gleamed. "And then what, Macushla?"

"Why then she'll be a part of me forever and ever, and no war, or college prom"—he gave me an impish grin—"will ever separate us again."

At that Mama laughed. "Go on, you two. I've got too much work to do to watch the two of you mooning around in my kitchen."

"Then we'll go to see the newlyweds," I told her, then turned to Mac. "The Mt. Vernon house is still vacant, but Vanya and Martha are renting the attic part. Remember that side room?" I asked slyly.

"I sure do." He grinned, his hand around my waist, hugging me to him. "Let's go. I want to meet them. As long as we're together, I'll never let you out of my sight again. Never."

"You won't have to, Yankee-man," I promised, wrapping my arms around his neck. How good his nearness felt. I felt so right being beside him. I pulled his head down so that I could kiss him. We could have stood that way till eternity, but finally Mac let me go.

"I suggest, scandalous Vixen, that you stop tempting me and get some clothes on you if we're going out," he whispered in my ear. I had forgotten that I had on only my dressing gown.

He looked at me longingly. "Now hurry, before I rape you right here in front of Mama, God, and Confucius."

While I got dressed, I heard him at the piano. Mama had come out of the kitchen to sit beside him and listen. She liked the power with which he played, she had once told me. I smiled to myself. He looked so good: healthy, tanned, and full of energy. And too, there was that certain quality about him—that innate goodness and fortitude—something that I always had wished for in the man that I had dreamed of marrying. Those were the qualities that I had respected in Dr. Ferguson. Strange, how alike these two men were. I hadn't thought too much of that before, but it was true. Both of them of Scottish descent, both named John, both Protestants, and strangest of all, both had called me "Girlie." No wonder I loved this Mac so.

He was now playing all the old familiar tunes that had been on the "Hit Parade" when we had first met two years ago. "Let It Snow," "Till the End of Time," and others, which had been and still were our songs. When he played "If I Loved You," I felt weak at the knees. I knew that he was playing it for me.

I put on the green wool suit that I had bought on time in New York City. When I entered the living room, he stopped playing and turned to look at me, his face radiating his love.

"Vixen, I can't get over how lovely you are. Are you ready to leave?" He took a deep breath, staring at me as if hypnotized.

"My boots," I pointed towards the door. "I've got to put them on. You'd better put on your coat. It's cold outside."

As we stepped onto the sidewalk, he bent his head towards me. "I just cannot believe it, darling," he sighed. "That soon we'll be married, that I'll have you all to myself to love and to cherish." He stopped to kiss me. "Sorry, but kissing you is becoming a habit. It is better than pinching myself. Are you sure of me now?"

"I am, very sure. I love you, love you, love you." How easily those words spilled out.

Again he stopped right there on the sidewalk, heedless of

701

the smiling passersby. He took me in his arms once more; his lips on mine. I closed my eyes, wanting this thrilling feeling to go on forever. Reluctantly he let me go.

"I can't rape you right here on Massachusetts Avenue, although I'd love to shock your New England neighbors," he said abruptly. "C'mon, Vixen, let's go meet your brother and his beauteous bride."

We walked on, holding hands.

"So you found me by my boots, eh?" I couldn't help teasing him. "What if I'd worn my pink and gray dress instead of this? What would you have done?"

He laughed. "What would I have done? Hmm! Let's see. First of all I'd have given you my coat. You know that it's cold outside." He squeezed my arm. "Stop tormenting me, you Vixen. Frankly, if Mama weren't in the apartment, I'd strip you down to your birthday suit. Then you'd find out what I'd do with you."

That shut me up for a while. We came to the haunted house. He remembered it.

"Why, it's been painted and the windows replaced," he exclaimed. "What a pity!"

"Why?"

"Because it added character to your street, that's why."

We walked up Mt. Vernon Street. Curiously he looked at all the stately homes with their well-kept grounds, now covered with snow. "Are you going to miss Cambridge, Tamara?" he asked.

"No," I looked around, surprised that I felt no sadness. "I love Cambridge, but after having lived in New York, I no longer feel that this is my home. My home is going to be where my heart is."

He was silent as we walked up the gray wooden steps to our old house. Mama had given him the spare key. He unlocked the door, winking at me.

There was an eerie, ghostly stillness about the empty rooms.

"Sort of scary, isn't it?" I said, looking around.

Mac chuckled as he made his way into the dining room. "Remember the waffles you made for me that night?"

I nodded, recalling how furious I had been with him.

He looked up the stairs. "You sure they're home? It's terribly quiet," he said. "Why don't you call up to them?"

"They must not be home. They usually have the radio on if they are. Vanya!" I called out.

The rooms echoed with my voice, but there was no answer.

"Let's check anyway," Mac suggested, taking my hand. "Come on, Vixen."

I followed him up the stairs, still holding on to his hand. We entered the attic ballroom, the scene of so many dancing parties held during my college years. Memories flooded back to me. Staring now around the vacant room, I could see all the ghosts of good times past, including sweet, gentle Lanny, bending over my RCA to put on another Strauss waltz . . . turning towards me and stretching out his arms. "Princess lovely, may I please have this waltz with you?" Then the two of us, at first gently, slowly swaying, then gathering speed and spiritedly waltzing away in perfect three-quarter time.

Mac had left my side to look into the spare room that was now Vanya's and Martha's bedroom. There was a sly smile on his face as he glanced around.

I recalled the evening when I had seen him there, sitting with Jeanette, their heads so close together. How it had shaken me then, although I refused to admit it, even to myself!

I knew that he too was thinking of that night, for he chucked me under the chin, his eyes tender as he fixed them on my face. "You'll never forgive me for that evening, will you, my little Vixen?" He shook his head slowly. "If you had only known how much I had wanted to be with you, to hold you in my arms. You never knew how much I loved you then, did you?"

I couldn't answer. That had been so long ago, it seemed. It didn't matter anyway. Not now, nor ever again.

He led me out to the ballroom. There was no place to rest except on the bare floor. He lay down beside me, his face close to mine. His eyes mesmerized me with their love and tenderness. Such an exciting and joyous feeling to be so close again! His legs intertwined with mine, his face was an inch away. The hardness of him pressed against me, urging me to rise towards him, in spite of myself.

His eyes misted. "Dearest," he murmured softly, "I could never live without you. You know that, don't you? This is what

I've lived for during this war. This is why I didn't fear fighting, knowing that I had you to come home to."

As he moved on top of me, I felt myself weakening. My inhibitions were still with me although my physical self now fought back. Mentally, morally, I told myself that I shouldn't. My physical self told me that it was perfectly all right. Myself fighting myself. Again I recalled Sam's soft coaxing voice and his gentle look as he tried to probe into my very soul, "And what are you afraid of, Tamara?"

"I'm starved for you, Vixen!" I could feel the urgency of Mac's love, his need for me.

His coat he had taken off in the foyer, laying it on the banister rail as he had done two years ago. Now he was hastening to unbutton his jacket.

"I know," I whispered to him. I wanted to let go, to set myself free from these self-imposed bonds that had fettered me ever since I had become a woman. That very same womanhood, however, still bound me to its will. "Not now, Macushla. Not now. They might come upstairs at any time."

With that he sat up, cradling me in his arms. "God, but I love you so!" He cupped my face in his hands, staring into my face with that gentle smile. "I just can't look at you enough. I can't believe, darling, that finally you're in my arms, that you are my real Tamara for sure."

I smiled up at him. "You'll have me for your lifetime, darling. You might even get tired of me. We'd better leave now. Papa should be home by this time, and I know he'll be most anxious to see you. We'll leave Vanya and Martha a note. Okay?"

"I guess you're right," he answered, getting up off the floor. He lifted me up, holding me close. "That's all that I want to do right now. It's so restful, isn't it? I'll never let you go, my Tammy."

At home, Papa had poured out champagne. He toasted us, then Mac alone. "There is only one Macushla," he said, using his favorite name for Mac. He raised his glass to him triumphantly, his short proud figure erect. "We drink to your arrival, your betrothal, and your future life together with our Tamara." He chuckled, "Rightfully, Macushla, we have named you 'her Demon,' my son." Dramatically he paused, then clinked his glass

704

to Mac's, to Mama's, and then to mine. His eyes softened.

"And now, *dochenka*, are you happy?"

After dinner, we sat sipping hot tea while Mac told of his experiences overseas; then he asked us about the wedding plans. Laughing I told him about Loretta. "We don't need an Emily Post guide. Loretta is better than an etiquette book. She should make that her career. She knows everything about wedding procedures, customs, and how to do them."

"Bless her! This wedding can't be soon enough for me," Mac declared. "The sooner the better!"

"Then you should go see Dean Sperry first thing tomorrow morning," Papa suggested. "He's the Dean of the Divinity School. He'll schedule your wedding. I suggest you make an appointment tomorrow morning."

"Papotchka, I'm highly in favor of anything that will expedite matters. I do want to take this troublesome imp off your hands at the earliest possible moment."

Both my parents laughed. "That you will; you will," Papa promised, and added, happily, "with our blessing. We've worried enough about her. Now it's your turn to worry."

"Gladly, sir," Mac grinned. "Do you hear that, Vixen? Your parents don't want you anymore, but I do."

Soon after that my parents retired to their own bedroom. I silently blessed them for being so understanding. "They surely are great, honey," Mac whispered to me. His face clouded. "I wish my parents were as great and understanding."

"Don't worry, Mac. They'll understand too when they see us together."

He wasn't convinced. I kissed him. "They'll just have to accept us, Mac," I continued. I couldn't believe his parents could be mean to me just because my parents were Russian. What was so terrible about being Russian? "You know what Papa told me?" I cuddled up to him. "Papa said that if I married anyone else, I could go ahead, but I might as well elope since he and Mama wouldn't give me their blessing. That's why I have to marry you, Yankee-man. I've always wanted a wedding with all the trimmings."

"You crazy little imp." He grabbed me playfully, then bent

me backwards, trying to kiss me. Laughing, I moved my head away. "It took me a mighty long time and hundreds of letters trying to convince you." He rubbed his nose against mine. "Did you know that this is how Eskimos kiss? They really do, so I've been told."

"I know; you've been reading the *National Geographic*."

"Am I going to sleep with you, little Vixen?" he whispered.

"There's no room on my studio bed. It's too narrow," I teased. "I have to get your sheets and stuff. You're to sleep on the sofa, Mama said."

After we had made up his bed, he lay down on it, patting a place for me next to him.

"I'll lie down with you for a bit, but, Mac, we can't do anything until we are married. We mustn't," I told him gently.

He pulled me close to him. "Darling, we're going to be married soon. Don't you love me?"

"Sure I do, but the folks are here. Mac, they can hear everything. What if one of them comes out to the kitchen to get a drink of water?"

He kissed me then, hard on my lips till I could feel the pressure. "You've got the damnedest willpower of anyone I know. Boy, Heaven better help you when you become my wife."

"Heaven will, my Mac; when we're married, you can sleep with me both night and day and even in between."

He groaned. "Gee, thanks a lot. I can hardly wait."

"Would you like me to play the *Seventh* for you? I've got the album all ready for you."

He nodded, grinning. "You are a temptress, you know that? Come here, you Vixen." He reached out for me.

"Not before I start the record," I told him, sliding out of his grasp. I flipped the "on" switch of my RCA. The music began softly. I crawled in under the sheet beside him.

"My gosh!" I couldn't believe his audacity. "When did you succeed in taking off your clothes?"

"Sh-h-h!" He placed his finger against my lips, his eyes moving warningly towards the hallway. "Do you want to waken your folks?" His arms encircled me. Then one of his hands moved toward my breasts, resting there. "Mmmm," he sighed audibly. "I just love these."

Suddenly he was on top of me, his strong arms around my neck. "Oh, honey, darling, I have been dreaming so long of this moment!" He began fiddling with my robe, feverishly unzipping the front and letting it fall off my shoulders. There was just enough light coming in from the lamppost on the street.

"Whew!" He stared at my exposed breasts, cupping each one in his hands. "They're beautiful, Vixen. So perfectly formed."

He laid his head between them. "Yum, this is what I call Heaven."

I felt embarrassed. "What if..."

"What if what?" he interrupted me quietly, a teasing smile on his lips. "My God, Tamara, we love each other. We're also getting married, aren't we? Or have you again changed your mind about me? Here, let's take these damn things off." Off came my panties. "By golly, my love, you're mine, and I'm yours, now and forever more. I want you, darling; how I want you!"

My body quivered at his touch. I felt my nipples harden. "I'm not yours yet," I teased. His body strained against my own. His knees were pressing against my inner thighs, pushing them out. I felt the hardness of him against me.

"Oh, Mac!" My body rose to meet his, yearning for him. I couldn't fight my feelings any longer. "Come into me, darling," I whispered. I had to have him inside me; my body was making me yield to that which I'd been struggling against for so long.

I heard, rather than felt, that he was busy at something under the sheet. "What's the matter now?" I whispered. "What on earth are you doing?"

"This goddamned rubber," he muttered impatiently. "I'm having a hard time slipping it on."

"Slipping it on? What's a rubber?" I was really puzzled at what was going on.

"It's something..." He looked at me in surprise, then burst out laughing. "My little sweetheart! I see that I'm going to have to teach you a helluva lot about the life processes, but I don't mind. Okay; now to begin—a 'rubber' is what I slide onto my penis so you'll not get pregnant."

He was ready now. Everything was in order. He positioned himself carefully on top of me, then gently eased his penis into me. I winced at my own tightness and the pain, but he continued to push down further, penetrating deeper inside me. It hurt me, but I dared not let him see me flinch.

"Now spread your legs out wider," he ordered in a whisper. I did as he said, feeling him enter even deeper. I could feel his penis pulsating inside me, felt its warmth. The sides of my vagina were sore; yet the feeling of being a part of him filled me with such an indescribable sensation as I had never experienced before. I could never have thought that his throbbing strength submerged within me could create such an exciting, exquisite feeling.

For a moment we lay like that, two people united as one. I relished his warmth, his heart beating so close to my own; his muscular thighs nestling against mine, his toes rubbing mine. Miraculously, I couldn't feel the weight of him atop me even though he was some sixty pounds heavier than I was. Suddenly, the smooth, gentle, and passionate throbbing of his penis was interrupted.

"Damn!" Mac swore under his breath. His hands shot out, working with the sheet that covered the two of us.

"What's wrong now?" I whispered in alarm.

"Oh, this damn sheet; it's all tangled up." After a few violent movements and still inside me, he clumsily rearranged and smoothed out the sheet. Once more, he moved his head down towards me; his lips found mine, and, slowly, he began to move his hips up and down, and the overwhelming sensations carried me along with him. My body, bound to his physically, mentally, and emotionally, moved rhythmically along with nature's own cadence. I felt his strength, his passion, his love, all together, moving into an overpowering crescendo, until he had reached the utmost that was in him. With his final thrust, I felt the rush of his semen, the overwhelming throbbing and warmth filling the inside of me while his mouth moved quickly from my lips, sweeping hungrily over my face, covering my eyes, my cheeks, my ears, my neck with impassioned kisses. Finally, spent, he laid his head on my shoulder, totally exhausted from his outpouring of love.

"So this is what is called 'sleeping together,' is it?" I whispered. "If it is, I like it, darling," I murmured into his ear, giving it a playful bite.

"There's no doubt about it; I too like it," he emphasized, as

708

he moved his face closer to my breast. His tongue was licking my nipple. I could feel it hardening again. "But, Vixen, most people call it 'fucking.'"

"What?"

"F-U-C-K." He spelled it out for me. "That's what you and I have just done. We F-U-C-K-E-D." He was teasing. "Did you really like it, Vixen?"

"Yes, but I don't like that word. I'd still rather say 'sleep together' than that other word. That, to me, sounds ugly, and what we did was something beautiful. It's the long delayed climax of our love, making us one at last."

"Okay by me." He gave me a playful kiss. "It doesn't matter what we call 'it,' so long as we do it at least twice a day, or even more."

"I'd better get into my own bed now, Yankee-man. I don't want the folks to find us this way." I kissed him on the lips, hating to leave his side.

"I guess you're right, Vixen. I shall be dreaming of you tonight. The best part of it is that when I do wake up in this apartment, you will still be here. Goodnight, my love."

47

My Bridal Shower

The next morning, I jumped out of my bed, slipping my robe over my naked body. In spite of Mama's scoldings, I could never get used to wearing a nightgown. Carefully, I tiptoed into the bathroom, locking the door. It was terribly quiet in the apartment. Maybe it was too early to get up; I had no idea of the time. It surprised me that when I looked at myself in the medicine cabinet mirror, I didn't look any different. My eyes were sparkling, but Mac's homecoming yesterday had caused that brightness. My lips, as I traced their outlines with my finger, were slightly puffed. I smiled to myself, remembering how thrilling it all had been, having someone with me who loved me so, just because I was me.

I turned on the cold water and doused my face in it, feeling it wash away any left-over sleep. There was no need to put on makeup; my face was rosy enough. As for lipstick? Forget it. It would only be kissed off! I combed my hair, then brushed it with my whalebone brush, watching the gold hairs flare out from the static electricity. Then I entered the living room.

I heard laughter. Mama and Mac were eating breakfast, talking quietly. At my appearance, the two of them smiled. Mac looked at me, his eyes full of love; he held out his arms, "Come here, my Vixen, I want to say 'Good morning,' to you properly. Mama and I have been waiting for you to get up."

"Yes, it's about time. Nine o'clock already, aren't you ashamed of yourself?" Mama playfully shook her finger at me. "Come get your morning kiss."

I needed no prodding. I went to him then, easing myself onto his lap. Slowly his head bent towards me, his lips found mine, and for one blissful moment, the whole world was shut out. It was just the two of us.

Mama poured my coffee and buttered some toast. "I know that if I didn't do this, she wouldn't eat anything," she complained to Mac. "Macushla tells me, Tamara, that you two have an appointment with Dean Sperry this morning."

"Yes; we do." As far as I was concerned, he and I were already married. I wanted more of his kisses, more of that body-closeness we had had last night. I shocked myself for feeling wanton like this, but I had no regrets.

"You shouldn't stay up so late." Mama had a funny smile on her face.

"We were listening to Beethoven's *Seventh*," I explained.

"Oh, so that's what you were doing, listening to the *Seventh*." Mama winked at Mac, who smiled. Both she and Mac were heartily enjoying my embarrassment. They looked as though they shared a secret between them.

"Well, music, especially the *Seventh Symphony*, seems to do things to people in love. I know; I too was young once. Now, my dear Tamarotchka, this is what I want to know, 'Are you really sure now about Mac?' We don't want you making mistakes or wrong decisions now. Before it's too late, is he the one for you?"

Only a few days ago I had voiced my doubts to her. How could I ever have done that? All I had to do was see his face; look at his lips that were twitching now with suppressed amusement and love; those grayish blue eyes that melted with such unusual tenderness when they turned to me. Both Mac and Mama watched me, Mama's eyes teasing.

"Mama, I have no doubts now."

Mama, however, was not yet through with me. To Mac's obvious enjoyment she continued. "Then you will be wearing that wedding gown that hangs in my bedroom closet?" She was relentless.

"Yes, I will. Mac, you must see it. It's old-fashioned, simple, the way you wanted it to be, but absolutely beautiful!"

He laughed and put his hand out as if to stop me. "Whoa, there, my sweet Russian Vixen, don't you know it's bad luck for a bridegroom to see his bride in her wedding dress before the wedding? No way am I taking that chance!" He got up to help Mama clear the table.

"Thank you, Mac," Mama took off her apron. "I have a few errands to do this morning: the supermarket, the cleaners, and then I promised Annitchka I'd help her at the Russian Relief headquarters. Don't expect me until lunchtime. I'll be interested to hear about your interview with Dean Sperry when I get back." With that long announcement she picked up her purse and walked out of the apartment.

When the door had closed behind her, Mac took me in his arms, his lips on mine. Releasing me, he pushed me off so that he could look at all of me.

"Believe me, Vixen, when I tell you that I'll never let you go. You are mine, forever and ever!"

"I believe you," I whispered. "I'll always be yours, forever and ever and ever. You remind me of Soames Forsyte, the man of property," I teased him. "Have you read Galsworthy's *Forsyte Saga?* You know Soames considered the woman he loved as his property."

"Then I'm Soames Forsyte," he laughed, "for I consider you mine. When we marry, I deed myself to you, and you deed yourself to me, in permanent joint ownership."

"I'll always be yours, forever and ever and ever."

"Amen to that, my darling!" He kissed me. "That's to seal our vows."

"We're going to see Dean Sperry now, aren't we?" I asked him.

"Afterwards," he eyed me with a teasing, calculating look, an impish smile playing on his lips.

"Afterwards? After what?"

"We have to get ready, don't we?"

"Well, yes, I'd better go take my bath first, hadn't I?"

"No, you're taking a shower."

"But . . . ," I looked at him in dismay, "I'm not. I never take showers; I always take a bath in bubbly, soapy water."

"How quickly you forget." He shook his head sorrowfully. Again he looked at me in his special, teasing way. "Remember, darling, when I wrote you that letter about taking a shower? I wrote that I'd teach you how. Have you already forgotten about that?"

He led me into the bathroom, unzipping my robe on the way. It slipped down and lay in a crumpled heap around my feet. I stood in front of him, stark naked. Automatically I raised my hands to cover my breasts. Laughingly, he placed my hands back down at my sides.

"Let me look at you, my Vixen," he whispered. He let out a low whistle. "Good Lord, darling, you're—why, you're beautiful!"

It felt strange to stand like this before him, with nothing to cover me. Yet, stranger still, I felt no shame in having him look at me this way.

I watched him as he stripped. Off came the olive drab undershirt; then he unbelted his 'pinks,' those tailored officer's trousers that fit him so beautifully; then he unbuttoned the ugly olive drab undershorts that looked so ungainly on his young, muscular body. I tried not to look below his waist; yet it was that which registered itself uppermost in my mind—the brief curious glimpse I had had of his penis, that long, reddish, ugly appendage that seemed to have a life of its own, even now, hardening, lengthening, pointing itself directly towards me. This was what had been inside me last night, had made me feel so deliciously warm and glowing. He had been curiously watching me look him over and playfully gave me a spank.

"Come on, honey," he urged me. "Let's get into the tub. Let me show you the shower trick."

He helped me into the tub, his arms lifting me by my waist. His hands moved onto my thighs. Suddenly he took his hands away. "There you are. Oops, I was digressing. Pardon me, mademoiselle, but you just felt so delectable, I couldn't help it." He grinned, not at all sorry.

I had never taken a shower here. In fact, I can't remember ever having taken a shower! I thought that I would dislike having water pour on top of me, into my face and nostrils. I preferred the luxury of a tub full of warm, soapy water with plenty of bubbles to cover all of me!

He moved in beside me and pulled the curtain around us. Then he turned on the shower, lightly at first, just enough to wet us. He took the bar of soap, gently rubbing it all over my body, lingering over my breasts, pausing as he knelt in front of me, his hands inside my thighs.

"And now," he whispered, "it's time for your shampoo, my Vixen." He soaped my pubic hairs, reaching from the outside to the inside. I shivered slightly when his fingers entered my vagina. Gently he rubbed my clitoris, until I felt myself getting that fluttery, excited feeling again. He held me close to him as he continued his playing. My body was straining toward his. Suddenly, I felt that I'd scream if he didn't put his penis into me. I wanted to give myself to him, to rise up to meet him as he pounded himself into me!

"Wait, darling," Mac said hoarsely. "I'm not too good at this myself. I'm learning too, and I've never done this myself."

I was disappointed at this delay. "Then how did you know about this 'shower trick'?"

"The fellows were talking about it one evening. God," he breathed deeply, "how I wished that you had been with me that night! It was sheer agony listening to them talk about doing it with different girls. And the only one I wanted to do it with was you. And you weren't there. God, did I miss you!"

I leaned against him, feeling my soapy self slithering against his body. My pointed nipples rubbed against his chest.

"I didn't realize you had so much hair down there, Mac; and, are you sure you didn't do this 'shower trick' with anyone else?"

"Lord, no!" he placed his hands upon my shoulders, his eyes looking deeply into mine. "Vixen, I'd never want to do it with anyone but you. I couldn't sleep with anybody unless I loved her as much as I love you. The only person whom I've ever loved like this in my life is you, and this you must believe. That's why I'm telling you that I, too, am learning the 'shower trick' just as you are."

"What do we do now?"

He handed me the soap. "Now you soap me," he said quietly, "just the way I soaped you."

I rubbed his chest first, then his waist. "Turn around so that I can do your back."

I rubbed his back, thinking how nice and smooth and strong it was. Then I soaped his waist, looking at his buttocks. How small they were! I hadn't realized that men's buttocks could be

714

smaller than those of women. I had an urge to giggle as I soaped them too. I felt rather silly sliding my hands over them.

"Okay," I told him. "I'm finished. Now what?"

He turned around, looking at me appealingly. "You aren't finished yet, Vixen. You haven't soaped me here." He pointed to his penis.

I shrank from him. "I can't do that." I moved to hand him the soap.

"And why not, Vixen? It's a part of me, the most important part that becomes a part of you."

I stared at it, compelled to look yet almost repelled by its ugly exterior. "I just can't," I whispered miserably. I shook my head.

He was patient. Quietly he took my hand into his. "Here," he steered my fingers to touch it, then laid it into my open hand. "Now put some soap on it; then rub it gently."

I did as he told me. To me it appeared to be a living thing in and of itself. As I rubbed it back and forth I felt it growing in my hand. I felt the skin stretching itself taut; the hardness became harder still until it was transformed into a live, pulsating rod that quivered in my hand.

Mac's eyes did not leave my face. "You know, doing that gives me a lot of pleasure, my darling," he said softly.

"It felt good to me when you rubbed me down there too," I confessed shyly. It was strange to talk like this to each other. Never in my life had I thought I'd be doing something like this. It was so natural for us to be like this that I felt no shame.

"Now, let's shower, my Vixen." He turned on the shower and let it pour down on us, holding me close to him. Again I felt him strain towards me, his erect, hard penis searching for its haven between my thighs.

"Spread out your legs, Vixen. Let me come in," he urged, pushing my buttocks forward.

I did, again feeling the strong throbbing stranger sliding with such ease into me; the thrusts going in deeper than ever before, in and out. Suddenly I felt as if I were sinking into a deep, welcoming abyss, as if my senses were leaving my very soul. The ecstasy that came with the thrusts surmounted anything I had ever felt before.

715

He reached over and turned the shower off. "Darling, we mustn't do this without a rubber." He slipped out of me as quickly as he had entered. "Let's dry ourselves and get to bed."

He dried me off with Mama's fluffy towels. Then he dried himself.

"Now, come on to bed." He had flipped over the bedspread in a second.

Mac had mastered me completely. I let him lead me, feeling all quivery, excited, yet trusting him implicitly. I loved the feel of him inside me. I wanted him to pound away into me again and again until I could feel that special, overwhelming warmth when he came. My whole being was transformed with him inside me. I felt the stickiness between my thighs and tingled all over.

We stretched out on my studio bed, and he showed me the rubber. I was surprised at how small and fragile it looked.

"How do you use it?" I asked, fingering it gingerly.

"I unroll it over my penis like this. See?" He held his penis in his left hand, unrolling the condom down over it with his right hand until it had covered the entire organ.

"I see." I had to turn my head away. Although his penis had given me such pleasure, I still thought it ugly-looking. "I don't like the name penis for it."

He laughed good-naturedly. "Darling, that's what everybody has called it, you know, even the Romans. We call it by other names too, but they called it penis." He tweaked my nose. "And what, my dear Vixen, would you, my beloved future wife, call it?"

"I'm going to call it Little Mac," I told him. "Nobody except the two of us will know what we mean."

That amused him. "Vixen, I can see that I'm going to have a mighty interesting life with you. All right, if that's what you want, that's what we'll call this weapon of my armed forces." He took hold of his penis, looked down at it, and addressed it with mock dignity, "Private Penis, I now dub thee Little Mac."

"Now you're teasing me; I'm sorry if I know so little about sex. No," I contradicted myself, "I'm not sorry. I wouldn't want to sleep with anyone but you, and I mean it."

"Thank you, sweetness and light, the feeling and the desire are mutual." He moved atop me again, sliding in once more. "Oh, this is Heaven, isn't it?" He sighed contentedly. "Now as to Little

716

Mac's haven, I'm naming it." He paused a moment, "It's as foxy as you are, my lady. So I have the honor of dubbing it the Little Vixen." His hands traveled gently over me, finally resting on the pillow, as again he undulated, then pounded into me. I felt myself rising once more to meet him.

"Ah," his eyes teasing me, "you're an apt pupil, Miss Rubleva. I congratulate you and your Little Vixen."

When we had finished and he had uttered his last ecstatic sigh, he leaned over to look into my eyes. "Do you know that I shall be loving you forever? Are you convinced of that?"

"And I shall love you too," I laughed. I jumped out of bed and grabbed my robe. "And now, mon Capitaine, it's time for us to get dressed and go see Dean Sperry."

We both dressed in my room. He put on his uniform with the captain's insignia. I slipped into his favorite pink and gray dress. In the bathroom he combed and brushed my hair. It was fun to look at both our faces in the mirror—flushed, smiling, and full of ecstatic love.

"We do make a nice-looking couple, if I do say so myself," he remarked. He was standing in back of me, his lips brushing against my hair.

I could not answer him for my heart was much too full. Never in my whole life had I ever dreamed of being so happy.

48

Much Ado about I Do

Hand in hand, we walked to Harvard Square, oblivious to the world around us. We crossed Mass Ave and walked across Harvard Yard toward Memorial Church. Its stark, white steeple outlined against the blue of the cloudless sky was awe-inspiring.

The middle-aged secretary in the chapel office looked up from her desk with a quizzical smile and adjusted her glasses.

"We've come to see Dean Sperry," Mac told her. He hugged my arm, keeping me close to him.

The secretary opened her appointment book. "You have an appointment with the Dean?" she asked. Her tone was frosty, impersonal. I could see that she was used to dealing with all kinds of people.

"Yes, Ma'am, we do. I called and made an appointment to see the Dean. The name is McNish. John Pershing McNish, Captain, U.S. Army. And this is my fiancée, Miss Tamara Rubleva. We want to get married; the sooner the better."

She looked up at him, peering over the tops of her glasses. Then she gave me a look, more appraising than curious. I supposed it was because of my name.

"Oh, yes, here it is. I see your name, Captain McNish. If you'll kindly take seats, I'll see if the Dean can see you now." She got up from her chair and went to the door on her right, opened it quickly, then closed it behind her.

Mac smiled. "Well, Miss Rubleva, it's your last chance to reconsider whether you want to back out."

I smiled back. "I can't back out. You have slept with me."

At that, he threw back his head. "Hmn, so I did. In fact, I may do so again tonight. I hope to, if I get the opportunity."

"You think the Dean will marry us?" I asked. "What if the Dean is too busy? Who would marry us then?"

Mac patted my hand. "Of course he will, honey. Don't worry."

I marveled at how calm and patient he was. What a husband he will be! How fortunate I was to have found him; yet how strange it would be to call him husband. It was now just beginning to dawn on me that I was really, truly, finally going to be married. It was not a paper dream any more! It would be forever, not only in words but in actuality! No longer would I have single worries nor single happinesses. I would be sharing everything with this strong, steady man beside me, always and forevermore!

The door to the Dean's inner office opened, and the Dean's secretary came out, the hint of a smile on her plain face.

"Dean Sperry will see you now." Her voice sounded crisp, efficient. She ushered us into his study, closing the door softly as she went out. Dean Sperry walked around from behind his desk to greet us.

He was quite an imposing person: gray-haired with beetle-like brows over his intense eyes. In the few seconds that we had stood in front of him I was sure that he had examined us microscopically from head to toe.

"If you will sit down, please." He motioned us to the two chairs in front of his desk. Then, seating himself once more, he studied the appointment book the secretary had left with him.

"Hmm! Ah, yes; let's proceed." He inspected Mac. "Captain McNish." His eyes went to the next name below, and I saw his lips moving. The slight furrow on his brow tipped me off that he was silently trying to pronounce my name. Suppressing a giggle, I smiled at him.

"It's Tamara Rubleva, Dean Sperry. Most people have a hard time pronouncing it."

He laughed at this. "I can easily see why, young lady. Tamara Rubleva. Actually, once you hear it pronounced correctly, it's not that difficult. I've had some names that really were tongue twisters."

That broke the ice somewhat. Mac reached over, taking my hand in his, and told the Dean, "It'll be easier once she marries me." His action had not escaped the Dean's eagle eyes. He chuckled to himself, still checking his appointment book.

He leaned back in his chair so that he could look directly at the two of us. "Now when is it that the two of you would like to marry? We're really busy these days."

"I can well imagine, sir," Mac agreed. "What with all the fellows coming back from overseas."

The Dean chuckled again. "I take it you're one of them."

"Yes, sir, I just got back two and a half days ago—after two years overseas. I was with the occupation forces there as well." He squeezed my hand.

I could sense that the Dean was worried about something. His eyebrows knitted together. "And how long had you two known each other prior to that time?" He stared at each of us in turn.

Uneasily, I waited for Mac to answer. I could see that the Dean's question hadn't fazed him in the least. He was grinning from ear to ear as he looked at me, then back at the Dean.

"Two months and sixteen days, sir." Obviously Mac was enjoying this exchange. As for me, I was worried. The Dean's question made me uncomfortable.

The Dean looked stern. "Did you say two and a half months, Captain?"

"Yes, sir; that is, before I went overseas. But actually, we've known each other for two years, two months and sixteen days, sir." He leaned towards Dean Sperry. "Sir, we have corresponded almost every day since I was shipped overseas. Both of us have learned more about each other during separation than we would have had we been together all that time. We have fallen more deeply in love through our correspondence. And we want to get married as soon as possible to make up for those two lost years. We've both waited a long time, sir." He sighed and turned to me.

I would have kissed him right then and there, had I dared.

The Dean smiled. "I'm sure it has been long for you." His voice softened. He leaned forward, rubbing his chin thoughtfully. "What bothers me is the fact that nowadays many of you young folks rush into marriage without knowing just what you're letting yourselves in for. It's the aftermath of this war. More romances seem to bloom in wartime." He shuffled the papers in front of him. "Personally, I feel most strongly about the sanctity of the marriage vows. I want to make absolutely sure that the couples who come to me are not making a bad mistake. You do understand my position, don't you?"

I nodded, not really understanding. Was he telling us that he might not want to marry us? At the moment, he was making me feel like a little girl again, about to recite a lesson before a strict teacher. I surely didn't feel like a radiant, young bride-to-be!

To my surprise, Mac appeared to be thoroughly enjoying this interview. I could see that he liked, as well as respected, the man at the desk. Unlike me, he was completely at ease. I even saw his lips twitch as they did when he was amused at something and trying hard not to smile. I was even more astonished when he got up and came over to stand behind my chair, placing both his hands upon my shoulders.

"Dean Sperry," he said quietly, "Tamara and I have loved each other since the day we met. Our love has been tested for two whole years. We are absolutely certain of our love. There are no doubts in our minds at all." He bent down, his eyes intent upon me. "I love this woman more than life itself, and I'm sure she feels the same way about me."

Mac's reply apparently satisfied the Dean. He looked over at the large calendar on his desk. "The date that is available right now, that is, the earliest date that the chapel will be free, is on March sixteenth. Now, I have a wedding to perform at two-thirty; then there's one in the evening. The only time left is four o'clock on Saturday, March the sixteenth. That's four in the afternoon. How does that sound to you?"

We looked at each other, smiling. Now that there was a definite wedding date, I felt real once more; I was no longer suspended in time-space between two lives but on my way at last to the next phase of my life, that of being Mac's wife.

"Thank you, Dean Sperry." I started to get up from my chair.

"One moment, Miss Rubleva." He paused, holding up his hand. "Have you been married before?"

His question surprised me. "Of course not, Dean Sperry," I answered.

721

He turned to Mac. "And you, Captain McNish, have you been married before?"

Mac leaned a bit forward, amused at the question. His voice was quite serious as he answered the Dean.

"This, sir, shall be two marriages for me," he said calmly.

I felt a cold chill come over me. I hoped that I had heard him incorrectly. The Dean too looked up at him flustered. Once more, the bushy brows knit together, and his mouth tightened in evident disapproval.

"And how so, may I ask, sir?" he inquired icily. His whole attitude had changed towards us.

"It's simply this, Dean Sperry." Mac turned to me and gave me a tender glance. "As I told you, sir, this will be two marriages for me—my first and my last."

The Dean's face muscles relaxed. His eyes lit up with mirth. His smile broke out into a loud and hearty laugh.

"Ah, that's a good one, my boy. I'll have to remember that." He patted Mac on the back. "Just a moment, son, before you two go." He walked to the door, opening it.

"Anne," he informed his secretary, "mark four o'clock, on Saturday, March sixteenth, on the calendar. Got that? Underline that one, for I'll be marrying these young people myself."

After he had gone back inside his study, the secretary stared at us curiously. I could see that she was puzzled. Her manner too had altered. She was now smiling and quite effusive in her good wishes to us.

"You know, you are most fortunate," she told us as I wrote out my name for her. "It isn't too often that the Dean himself marries couples these days. He usually assigns assistants to perform the actual ceremony."

We left Memorial Church, walking down the stone steps into the Yard. College students, many of them with the standard green book bags slung over their shoulders, walked on the tree-lined walks, striding to their classes or mounting those many stone steps up to the imposing library across from the church.

I held on to Mac's arm, secure within myself. I too had walked into many of these buildings, had climbed those numerous steps, to seek anonymity in the tiny Radcliffe Room on the second floor of the library. That phase of my life was now over.

After March sixteenth a new phase would begin. I looked at the man beside me. Already I was looking forward to that day.

With Mac home, it was amazing how things fell right into place. The invitations were printed, then addressed, and, finally, sent to all our friends. Mac sent some to Pennsylvania to his folks and to relatives.

His folks wrote him in reply that they were not coming. I knew that he was very hurt and bitter when he told me. "You know, it wouldn't even have cost them a red cent to come here by train. Dad works on the railroad and can travel free anywhere in the United States on his railroad pass."

Seeing how his folks treated him troubled me. I still couldn't understand why his parents should feel so antagonistic toward me; they hadn't even met me. According to Mac, they were devout Christians—caring, church-going United Presbyterians.

"But the same God that made them made me," I remember protesting and shaking my head in disbelief. However, I didn't let their disapproval bother me for long. I was marrying their son, not them. Our happiness in our love soon overcame Mac's depression as well. We had too many things to do, too many people to see.

Loretta gave me the bridal shower. It surprised me that Mac couldn't come too. Loretta tried to explain.

"It's a party for you, only you. It'll be your last party as an unmarried girl, don't you see?"

I thought that silly, knowing how much fun Mac and I would have had together, but I knew better than to tell Loretta that. Mac could come later to pick me up.

It turned out to be a delightful event. Loretta shone as a hostess. She had really spent a lot of time planning this party. There were various games that we played; then the gifts were placed before me. I opened them, surprised and delighted with everything I received. *What a good custom this is*, I thought to myself. Towards the end of the evening, when Mac arrived, we were all invited into the dining room where Mrs. Ciani, Loretta's mother, had prepared a sumptuous Italian feast. Afterward, Carrie accompanied on the piano as Loretta sang in her lovely, clear soprano. They then asked Mac to play the piano.

Mac had impressed Loretta's mother. Embracing us at the front door, she invited us to come again to visit.

"Of course, we'll come back, Mama Ciani," I promised her. "We'll be returning to Cambridge soon."

Mac shook his head at me, his face serious. "We'll come if we can," he told her firmly but politely. He took my hand. "We can't promise though."

Mrs. Ciani patted him on the shoulders. Her striking, dark eyes studied him with renewed respect. "Now that's what I admire in a person. You, Captain McNish, are not one to make promises lightly. You are an honest man."

Another evening we spent with Annitchka and Philipp. When Mac sat down to play their piano, Annitchka became convinced that he was the man for me.

"*Ach, on chudnui* [he's wonderful!], Tamarotchka," she exclaimed. "I had not expected him to be such a fine young man, but that he truly is. I should have known better than to doubt your choice." Since she already had such a deep affection for Lanny, that change in her attitude was a real switch.

Philipp and Mac took to each other right away. They chatted about Philipp's past and his work and friendship with Albert Einstein. He even regaled us with his story about the doctoral robe that he had needed for the Ph.D. presentation ceremony at the Austrian Imperial Court. He brought out the robe he had purchased from Einstein for the ceremony; it was quite a thrill for both of us to see it and to learn that Philipp was working on a biography of Einstein. They talked about other physicists with whom Philipp had worked. I was surprised at Mac's knowledge of them.

"Your fiancé is a most intelligent young man," Dr. Frank observed. Mac had rejoined Annitchka at the piano, and Philipp now moved his chair closer to mine.

"But of course he is." I told him happily. "I wouldn't be marrying him otherwise."

Before we left their apartment, I phoned Phyllis to tell her about our plans. She listened quietly.

"My folks want to meet Mac," she told me when I had finished. "Name a day next week when both of you are free. We'll have a special celebration for you two."

Tears welled up in my eyes. How dear her parents were to do this! I was sure they were well aware of Mama's attitude towards Phyl.

"Tell them I love them for doing this."

Phyl laughed. "Well, my dear, that seems to be about the only way we'll be able to see you both, isn't it?"

"Yes, and the worst thing is that you're the one I most wanted to be there; to be my maid of honor; to hear Mac and me recite our vows. Phyl, you were such a big part of my growing adult years, and now this. Believe me, it makes me really unhappy with Mama. I just can't understand her."

Now as I think of that miserable day, the same bitter taste rises in my mouth. It was not only Mama's ultimatum but the fact that she couldn't deliver it herself; it had to be delivered by none other than Vanya.

Mac had gone to the store. Mama had also gone out. I was in my room alone and reading. I heard Vanya come into the apartment. Even though they didn't live here, Mama had given him a key, just "in case." I heard him sneezing; so I came into the living room.

"Hello, Vanya." I was surprised to see him here so early. "How's married life these days?"

He was sitting on the sofa, leafing through Papa's magazines. When I had entered, he had looked up, somewhat guiltily, I thought. Instinctively, I was on my guard. What could he be up to now? How well I knew that look; I became especially suspicious when he started to rub his hands together. Maybe I was wrong this time, but I wasn't.

He grinned. "I was on Mass. Ave. and saw Mac heading towards Harvard Square. Mama had asked me to tell you something privately; I thought that this would be a good opportunity; I knew you were here alone."

"I don't keep secrets from Mac," I told him coldly. "What did Mama want you to tell me?" I asked. No matter what, I made up my mind, I'm not going to argue with him. I knew that Vanya was ill at ease because he didn't look at me directly. He squirmed, studying the wall instead.

"Well." He gave me a sly glance, then looked away to hide his grin. "It's really not that important, Tamara, unless, of course, you disobey." How he was relishing this! It was that damned "holier than thou" expression that I despised most about him. "It's just that Mama wants you to know that if your friend Phyllis even shows her face at your wedding, Mama will throw herself under the tramcar. You will have her death forever on your conscience."

He delivered this speech like an actor, dramatically enunciating each word with perfect intonation. I could tell that he was thoroughly enjoying every bit of this ultimatum. It delighted him to see me in pain. My happiness had always been a bane to him!

Well, I wouldn't let him see the shock and anger that I felt, as well as the deep hurt. I could not conceal my loathing of him though. I never had had much respect for him; now I had none.

"It is kind of you to tell me that." I managed to keep calm. "You may inform Mama that you have delivered her message." Then I slowly turned, walked into my room, and closed the door. I could not trust myself to remain with him for one minute more. I heard him shut the door as he left the apartment. With relief, I knew that he was gone.

Why hadn't Mama told me that herself? Why did she have to threaten me like this? Why did she have to act this way, turning my beautiful wedding into a sham? That's what it was! A sham! It wasn't really my wedding; it was hers! I wished that I had eloped with Mac instead. Then I wouldn't have had to subject myself to her whims and desires! Why did she want to make me so miserable when this time should be the happiest of my life? The more I thought about all this, the worse I felt. I lay down on my bed, facing the wall. Slowly the hot tears fell; I sobbed into my pillow, crying my heart out.

I hadn't heard Mac return until he had quietly eased my bedroom door shut; then he hurried towards me. In a moment his strong arms encircled me. He pulled me up, cradling me in his arms.

"What's wrong, my Vixen?" His voice hushed and concerned. "Whatever happened to make you cry like this? Who hurt you?"

"Oh, it's Mama again." I could barely get the words out, but little by little I told him about Mama's terrible ultimatum. Mac drew in his breath, thoughtful for a moment.

"Darling." He raised my head so that he could look directly into my eyes. "Remember that it's 'us' from now on and forever. Now go wash your face and make yourself beautiful. We'll go out before anyone comes back here. We'll go to Cambridge Common, sit there, and watch the world go by. You'll do what you think best. And we'll enjoy Phyllis' company without them. As for 'big brother,' I think he's not all there, if you know what I mean."

I calmed down, feeling better now that he was with me. "But Mama . . . "

"Your mom may be going through a change of life. I think that's what they call it. I've heard guys in the army talk sometimes about how women change once they're into their fifties. Maybe that's why Mama sometimes acts the way she does. I honestly don't know, Vixen. Except that I love you, and when you're miserable, I am too."

As soon as I had camouflaged my face, we walked towards the Common. There we sat at the base of the Minute Man statue and talked.

"You know, it's strange when you come to think of it," Mac said, putting his arm around me. "I mean about our parents. My mom doesn't want me to marry you because you're a 'foreigner,' and your mom doesn't want Phyllis at your wedding because Vanya told her Phyl is a lesbian. Sort of sad, isn't it, how people get such warped ideas? That's a lesson for us in the future, darling. Let's resolve always to study all sides of a problem before we form an opinion or jump to a conclusion."

My mind was still on Phyllis. "What are we going to do about tomorrow evening? We were supposed to go there. What do we tell Mama?"

"Simply that we're invited out for dinner, darling. We don't have to spell out everything for her, do we? Whew! Won't it be wonderful when we're just 'us' for real?"

When we came back from our walk, Mama was cooking supper. I acted as if nothing had happened and together Mac and I set the table and filled the glasses with ice for the tea.

The next day I told Mama not to plan supper with us in mind.

"That's nice that you two are going out," she said. She

sounded pleased. "Have a good time."

I saw Mac watching me and smiled at him. I had not imagined that it would be this easy.

The Olsens were delighted that we had come and could not have been more hospitable. The dinner was superb. Phyl's parents were of Swedish stock, and her mother was not only an immaculate housekeeper but also a gourmet cook. Mr. Olsen toasted us with champagne. Both he and his wife took to Mac right away.

"May your married life be as beautiful as your love!" Mr. Olsen raised his glass. "Skoal!" he said.

"Skoal!" we all echoed, raising our glasses to his.

Mac raised his glass once more, looking into my eyes with that special, tender look reserved only for me.

Phyl then clinked her glass with ours. "Think, my friends," she said. "If you, Tamara, hadn't been around, I might have been the one sitting here in your place. After all, I was Mac's first date."

"I'm afraid not," laughed Mac. "You forget; I'm not a navy man!"

It turned out to be a pleasant evening. Phyllis had brought out their wedding presents to us. "Will you please open them?" asked Mrs. Olsen. "We're anxious to see how you like them."

The hammered-aluminum tray in the big, white box was beautiful. "Now open mine," said Phyllis. She watched patiently as I untied the pretty white satin bow and unfolded the tissue paper. Inside the white box lay the most beautiful pink glass basket that I had ever seen; it was so delicate with its ruffled edges.

"How perfectly lovely!" I exclaimed. I gave her a big hug. "Thank you, Phyl! I'll always treasure it."

Her eyes were misty. "It just sort of looked like you: delicate, pink, and rather sweet." She looked at Mac. "Agree?"

He put his arm around her. "Sure do, Phyllis. You're Tamara's best friend here. You know that, don't you? And you're mine too!" He gave her a kiss on her cheek. "And that's a 'thank you' for looking out for my best interests while I was overseas. I appreciated your loyalty, friend."

She fumbled for a cigarette. "Oh, 'twasn't that hard. I knew she loved you, even though she thought she didn't know." She looked at me affectionately.

When we were leaving, Mrs. Olsen put our gifts into a big grocery bag. "It'll be much easier carrying this on the subway."

As we approached the apartment house, Mac asked me if I had ever tried to talk to Mama about Phyllis.

"I did try at first, but now I can't," I explained to him. "She just clams up. Then she walks around with that stony look on her face. She's so wonderful most of the time, but God help the person who ever dares cross her. God and Confucius both!"

I never realized how prophetic those words were to be.

It was past eleven when we came back to the apartment. Papa had just turned off the radio after listening to the news. His face was beaming when he saw us. "Ah, the happy couple. And how, may I inquire, was the dinner-party?"

"Really excellent, sir," Mac had replied. "Boy, that roast beef was out-of-this-world; wasn't it, Tamara?"

"Sure was. You want to see our gifts?" I took out the tray, then the pink basket. Mama fingered it cautiously. "You're a lucky girl, Tamara." She placed it back in the tissue, very carefully.

They said good-night then and went into their bedroom. Mac looked at me teasingly.

"Well," he sighed, "I guess it's time to make up my lonely bachelor's bed," he whispered. "Would you help me, my love?"

"Sure I will." I went to the linen closet and brought out his sheets and pillow.

"And will you lie with me and be my love?" he asked softly, tilting my chin so that he could look into my eyes.

"I will lie with you and be your love," I whispered back to him, "but only for a moment. It's been quite a day."

We lay down on the sofa. I nestled my head in the crook of his arm, and it was as if by magic that I felt my tiredness disappear.

"I used to dream of this," Mac murmured, "just lying in bed with you by my side. Gosh! I never thought that this day would ever come, but I prayed that it would. God, how I prayed!"

"Did you dream of anything else?"

He chuckled. "You little devil! Of course, I did. What red-blooded Yankee-man, if he were in my position, wouldn't dream of you? Most of my sleeping and half my waking hours were spent in dreams about you. Even while the buzz bombs fell, I dreamed!"

"That's good." I smiled to myself.

"What did you say, Vixen?"

"I'm glad you dreamed of sleeping with me."

He gave me a prolonged kiss. "Umm, that tasted good. Let me tell you that if I hadn't dreamed of sleeping with you, I'd have gone bonkers!"

"And apple pie and motherhood." I added, laughing.

"That comes later," he countered.

49

Just You and I

The next morning I awakened with the sun streaming in through my window. I listened to the voices coming from the living room. Mac and Papa were talking in low tones. I jumped out of bed, wrapping my housecoat around me. I opened the door quietly and hurried into the bathroom to wash my face. I stared at my reflection in the mirror, smiling at myself. *What bright eyes you have, Tamarotchka,* I said to myself. *It's because I love the most wonderful man in the world,* I told myself. Enough. Time for my morning kiss from him!

"Good morning, everybody!" I sang out. I felt ready to hug the world; it was such a wonderful planet!

I hadn't expected the silence that greeted me. Papa and Mac were sitting at the dining-room table. At my appearance both of them turned towards me. Papa looked tired and depressed. Mac too was unusually subdued.

"What's the matter?" I asked in alarm. "Where's Mama?"

Never in my life did I expect to hear what I was hearing now. Papa's voice was low. "She's in the bedroom. She's not coming out. She is furious with you."

"With me?" I asked in amazement. "What did I do to make her angry?" Frantically my mind raced backwards in time to see if there was anything that I could have said that would have aroused her temper. Dumfounded, I shook my head.

"Here's the cause of all the trouble, Tamara," Mac explained. He handed me a little white card. "It fell out of the box last night when you took out the pink vase. The card must have fallen on

731

the floor. Anyway, your mother found it on the rug this morning, and that did it."

I took the card. Strange, I hadn't even noticed it. On it I saw the familiar handwriting, "To Tamara and Mac, with all my love. Phyllis."

"So?" I couldn't see anything wrong with that. "Why should Mama be angry about that?"

"Darling, she says that you lied to her. That's why she's angry." Mac's eyes were understanding.

Papa looked miserable. Poor man, he was an unwilling participant in the middle of it all! I went over to him. "Papa, I did not lie to her about this. We told both of you that we were going out to dinner. I don't think we had to tell either of you where, especially since Mama now dislikes Phyllis so. Besides, it was her parents who invited us. I did not lie."

Mac nodded. "That's what I told Papa, but I guess your mother has it in her head that we lied, and that's it."

"Why is Mama like that, Papa?" I asked him. I could feel the tears in my eyes. "You know this is supposed to be my happiest time. Mac and I deserve to be happy. We've waited so long for this. Why does she have to spoil it all for us? What's the matter with her, Papa?"

His usually cheerful face looked pained. "The Chinese have a wise saying, 'It is easy to govern a kingdom but difficult to rule one's family.' I have found that to be so true. I don't know, Tamara, why Mama gets worked up about things. I've tried to talk to her, but she shuts me out too. She's a true 'Bulgarka'; one day happy as a lark, the next day like a thunder cloud. Let her alone for a while; she'll snap out of it."

I felt sorry for Papa. "It must be awfully hard on you, isn't it?" I put my arms around him, nestling my face close to his neck. "Papa, I love you so very much. You are so understanding."

He gave me a rueful smile. "I keep on trying, *dochenka*."

He had been right, of course. Mama did snap out of it, except that it took several rather unpleasant days of silence before she became herself again. Mac now experienced first hand her 'silent treatment.' She had tried to avoid us, but that had been difficult in the small apartment. Besides, visitors came and went. She and Papa were invited out. She felt obliged to maintain her dignity and position.

A few days after the incident, Mrs. Chao, the wife of one of the Harvard professors with whom Papa was working, invited Mama for tea. When she returned, I immediately saw that she was once more her former sweet, charming self. Mac and I looked at each other with relief.

She entered the living room carrying a large white box in her arms. Smiling slyly, she laid it on the table. "Look, you two; see what a beautiful gift Mrs. Chao has given you."

We joined her on the sofa. She looked at us and smiled.

"Well, come on. What are you waiting for? Open it!"

She watched with impatience as Mac and I both started to unwrap the box. Inside the tissue paper rested some beautiful wine glasses, each one a different color.

"Oh, how beautiful," I exclaimed. "I've never seen such pretty glasses."

"I had to choose your gift," Mama laughed. "Do you really like them?"

"What do you mean that you had to choose?" Mac asked her.

Mama appeared to be pleased with herself. "This is what I mean. When I came to Bu Wei's house, she had our tea all ready for us. Of course, she wanted to know all about the wedding plans and so forth. Then just as I was about to leave, she insisted that I come into their hall. You've seen how long their hallway is, Tamara. Well, there's a cupboard there, almost the length of that hall. She slid open the doors, and there was glassware, china, and what have you, all neatly arranged."

" 'This is my gift-closet,' she told me. 'I want you to choose a gift for your daughter and her fiancé, something you think they'd like.' I thought it such an unusual idea of hers to do that. It was difficult to choose, but I finally decided on these."

"Oh, Mama," I reached over to hug her. "Thank you. They're beautiful."

Mac too thanked her. He got up and planted a kiss on her cheek. Her face turned a rosy red, and then she smiled.

The flowers had been ordered. I chose white roses and

baby's breath for my own bouquet. Bill Lawler, Mac's Army buddy, had brought his own bride's hoop skirt for me to use under my bridal dress. That would be the 'something borrowed.'

I was now wearing the diamond engagement ring that we had bought together. The wedding rings were in Mac's possession. They were simple, unpretentious gold bands, but they meant a lot to us.

The photographer was coming to the house before the wedding. He had suggested this himself, saying that usually the bridal couple were too excited and busy afterwards.

Loretta was shocked. "But Mac shouldn't see you in your wedding gown before the wedding. Tamara, that is bad luck!"

"Mr. Kazanjian knows," I told her. "He's had experience, Loretta. In fact, he is the one who suggested it."

The rehearsal had gone off without a hitch. Papa had been like a youngster with a brand-new toy. He was bubbling all over, even flirting with Vicky, who was standing up for me. Vanya was Mac's best man. Neither Mac nor I had been too thrilled about that. Sammy, whom Mac had wanted to be the best man, was in New York with his French bride. Bill Lawler was here, and Mac would have chosen him, but Mama had asked why Vanya couldn't be the one. To avoid her displeasure, we thought it best to bow to her wishes.

My bridesmaids were excited.

"I'm going to be the one to catch your bouquet," Loretta told me. Her beautiful dark eyes sparkled with anticipation. "You'll throw it in my direction, won't you?"

"No, I'm going to catch it," her sister, Carrie teased. "After all, since I'm the oldest, I should be the one married first."

I couldn't get over how peaceful and beautiful the Chapel was. There was something special about being married in this place. It was just the fact that it was all a part of Harvard and part of me—the part that I would soon be leaving behind.

"The time is drawing closer," announced Papa. Smiling, he patted my cheek. "Tomorrow is the big day. Are you ready, *dochenka*?"

I looked in turn at all their smiling faces. And I ended with a loving glance up at my beloved Yankee-man, who was standing strong and tall beside me. I used to think of him as conceited and a snob. To think, I had once called him a drip. How terribly wrong I had been! Again I looked up at that dear, dignified profile of his: the high forehead, the straight, aristocratic nose, the generous mouth that was always quick to smile and yet could set so sternly at other times as well. All that was fine, good, and upstanding this man had, and I was going to become his wife tomorrow!

I took his hand in mine, feeling the strength of him ebb into me. Mama had taken Papa's arm. "Come on, Serioja, let's go. There's still a great deal that I have to do. And Gretal Kral is coming over to help."

They walked down the concrete steps of Memorial Church, waving good-bye to all of us. Vanya and Martha, still very much in love, trailed after them. The assistant dean who had rehearsed us came down to stand beside us. He smiled beatifically, extending his hand to Mac.

"Congratulations, Captain, I have a feeling that yours will be a long and happy marriage."

We thanked him and watched him walk off. How beautiful it all was! I looked up at the simple white columns and that tall pure-white spire that reached upward towards the sky. As usual, the Yard was crowded with students, but to me now, it looked different, even alien. Once upon a time I had been a part of all this. I had belonged to Harvard, as had so many others who had trod its paths before me. No longer would I be hurrying to the Radcliffe reading room or some class in Harvard Yard. All that belonged to the past. A feeling of nostalgia swept over me; it finally dawned on me that I'd be leaving all this forever.

Then I raised my eyes to the man I loved and met the smile in his eyes.

"A penny, Vixen, for the thoughts that I know are racing through your pretty head."

"I was just thinking of the old days, Mac. This will just be a memory now. I'm getting old, I guess."

"Terribly old and gray," he grinned. Mischievously, he hugged me to him. "In fact, I'm beginning to doubt seriously the wisdom of my marrying you tomorrow," he sighed. "Look some more, my darling; cherish what you see; and remember it all, for they were memorable times for you." He lowered his face to mine. "You know, don't you, that tomorrow a new future faces you? You're getting your Yankee-man, darling, all to yourself, for keeps." With that he kissed me, right there in Harvard Yard.

We walked across the Square to the Co-op and stopped to look in the window. "Remember the time when we bought that red tie for your dad that Christmas before I went overseas?" He squeezed my hand. "I can still see his delight when he had unwrapped the box."

"He still wears it," I told him, laughing.

Suddenly, I noticed the familiar little figure walking towards us. He too had seen me right away. Even from a distance he was already taking off his hat in his gallant gesture to my womanhood. As we approached, I noticed the delight and excitement in his eyes. I hastened towards him, not wanting him to pass us by. Mac, puzzled by my action, caught up with me. The little man's face was wreathed in smiles.

"Ach, so he finally has arrived." He spoke in that thick-accented, almost guttural voice. "How happy you must be, my child!" He nodded his head in Mac's direction, extending his small hand toward him.

"Every time we've met she would tell me that she was still waiting for you to come back to her. You have a vunderful young lady here, Captain," he said, eyeing me with obvious affection.

Mac looked at me with pride. "You don't have to tell me that, sir," he replied. "I've known that for a long time, since the day I first saw her."

"Ah, so?" The little man stared at me, then at Mac.

"I'm getting married tomorrow," I told him. Looking at his sweet, old face I suddenly had a thought. For a second I hesitated. Yes, of course, I should! "Would you like to come to our wedding?" I touched the sleeve of his jacket. "We'd love to have you," I added.

Tears came into the old man's eyes. "But, my dear, it would be such a great privilege for me." He held out his hand to me, holding mine as he continued to speak. "Vere are you getting married?"

"There." I pointed to the steeple. "Memorial Church in Harvard Yard. At four o'clock." I smiled at his delight.

He thanked us, bowing, doffing his hat, then putting it on again as he walked away from us. We watched his stooped, departing figure. *What a dear, sweet person he is,* I thought to myself.

"Who is he?" Mac asked me. "What a fine old man!"

"I don't know," I answered, somewhat abashed by his question. "I'm sorry, but I really don't know who he is. You see, when I used to walk to my classes at Radcliffe, I'd often meet him, almost every day, walking on Mass Ave. In time we got to smiling at each other, then conversing a bit. He's always been like that, terribly sweet and pleasant. He's probably a retired professor. Golly, he must be terribly old, but what a dear, isn't he?"

Mac smiled at my enthusiasm. "Yes, darling, he is a dear old soul. Such a dignified and courteous person. He surely thinks a lot of you."

I smiled happily. "I think a lot of him too. I just can't help smiling at him every time I see him. He reminds me of Dr. Frank or Papa. Little, old, and very cute, in a way. Doesn't he to you?" I asked him ungrammatically.

"I guess," Mac replied, looking down at me with affectionate amusement. "You just love everybody, don't you, Vixen?"

"Why not?" I looked up at the sky overhead. There was not even one tiny cloud in it. "We live in a beautiful world, don't we; or don't you think so?"

Again he sounded amused. "Little Pollyanna, I hope you always love life the way you do right now. Is that why you invited the little man to our wedding?"

"Ye-es," I answered. "Besides, Mac, he is always alone; yet he is cheerful and pleasant. Someone like that should get a little extra happiness given to him. And I sort of thought that he'd like to see us get married."

He was thoughtful. "Tamara, you don't even know his name?"

"Nope, I don't, John Pershing." I nestled my face against his jacket, feeling the roughness of the material. Again, I smelled that exciting smell of him; his own manly body smell mixed in with a dash of Sportsman's cologne. "Does it really matter that I don't know his name? He's still my friend. After all, Mac, I didn't know your full name for a long time either."

"Get up, Tamara, get up!" My inner voice was insistent.

I opened my eyes, still sleep-filled, and stared at the ceiling overhead. So much had been happening to me these past weeks and days. Mac had come home; we'd planned the wedding; we'd seen our friends, and still there had been so much to do. And now everything was done. All the preparations had been made. For today. For TODAY! My gosh, I was getting married today! Today was March sixteenth, my wedding day! I quickly slipped out of bed, wrapping my gray flowered robe around me. I knew that Mac would be awake. Unlike me, he was an early riser, just like Papa.

"Hi ya, Vixen." He was sitting on the sofa looking at the *Boston Globe*. The folded sheets and pillow were stacked beside him. He caught my glance and grinning patted the sheets.

"Won't be needing these tonight, will I, Vixen?" He reached out for me, encircling me in his arms. "God, I can't wait till we're man and wife, can you?"

"Sure, I can. A whole year if need be!"

He pulled me to him, kissing the tip of my nose. He looked at it critically. "You do have a cute nose, come to think of it. I was so engrossed with your other attributes that I hadn't even considered that one. Vixen, can you believe that exactly at four o'clock this afternoon you will no longer be Miss Rubleva?"

"You've waited a long time for her, haven't you, Macushla?" Papa had entered without our hearing him. "Do you think it'll be worth it? All these arrangements and delays and meetings?"

"I don't know, sir. I've been checking her out to see that all the parts are there. I don't want any damaged merchandise, you know."

"I can guarantee that she's in excellent condition," said my father, rubbing his nose. "I can also tell you that we're very happy, Mama and I, that you're taking her off our hands. She's too much trouble!"

They were thoroughly enjoying themselves.

"Seriously though, Macushla, I'm glad you didn't get married before you went away. She would not have been sure that you were really her Demon. Now she knows that you are, but it took her a long time to decide. I'd say she's worth all the waiting, eh?"

"Amen to that, sir." Mac's eyes glistened. "I still can't believe that she'll really be mine."

After breakfast we helped Mama add on the extra leaves on the table. Then she placed her lovely, old lace tablecloth on it. It had been on her father's table when she had married Papa. Now it was my turn.

"Just think," she mused. "Someday you might have a daughter, and you'll be using this for her."

The morning passed quickly, what with the phone ringing, gifts arriving, people visiting. Finally Papa laid down the law.

"Time for *mertvui chas*," he said abruptly. "Come on, Mama."

"What's that?" asked Mac curiously.

"That means the 'dead hour.' When we were little, we had to have *mertvui chas* every afternoon after lunch; Papa napped. You Americans call it 'naptime.'"

"I'll be coming, Serioja," Mama looked at Mac and me. Her dark eyes sparkled. "You two are to rest too," she ordered. "After all, you are the two main characters in this drama." She raised her hand, shaking her finger at us. "And I do mean rest!"

Mac laughed heartily. "Sure, we'll rest, Mamotchka." He placed his arm around me. "Since your daughter and I are getting married today, would it be all right with you if we rested together on her bed?" He folded his hands in a prayerful attitude.

Mama shook her head in mock dismay. "Macushla, I don't know what to do with you. Just go, the two of you."

We laughed, waving a mocking farewell to her. Mac lay down on my bed, pulling me close to him, laying my head in the crook of his arm.

"From this day forward, it'll always be this way with us. This is where you belong, my Vixen."

We must have dozed off. The doorbell wakened us. Mac was up in a flash. He went to the front door. "Who is it?" he asked quietly.

"Flowers for the wedding," said a voice beyond the door.

He opened the door, and the delivery man brought in the large white boxes, stacking them against the wall.

Mac then came back into the room.

"I think we might as well get up. Let your parents sleep. I'll go in and take a shower; then you can luxuriate in the tub all you want to."

"I'd rather take a shower with you," I whispered teasingly.

"No, darling, you rest. After all, you've got to be a radiant bride today. We'll have plenty of time for showers after we're married."

I laughed to myself. God and Confucius. How lucky could I be!

When he came out of the bathroom, I was waiting for him. Holding the door open so that I could flee inside, I tore off the towel around him, leaving him standing, stark naked, in the hall.

"Why, you little Vixen, I'll get you for that!" He reached out to grab me, but I had already locked the bathroom door behind me. I heard him chuckle and go into my room.

When I came back into my room, he was already dressed in his O.D. Eisenhower jacket and his pinks. *How manly and dignified he looks*, I thought proudly. And he loved me, that was the most important thing. Amazingly, my new life was falling into place. In a few hours I would be marrying my Yankee-man.

"I think you'd better check to see if your parents are up," he suggested. "After all, time's a-passing, and the photographer will soon be here."

My parents were already awake and dressed. Papa looked most distinguished in his black tuxedo. He grinned when I exclaimed over him. And Mama in her smoke-gray gown of French lace looked more beautiful than I could ever remember seeing her. I embraced both of them. "I'm just so happy about everything. And I want to thank you for loving Mac."

"Thank him," Papa laughed. "He's the one who was so persistent. You're right, though. We've always loved him, knowing how much he loved you."

"Well, I'd better join the nervous bridegroom," Papa said. "Then Mama can help dress the bride." He patted my cheek. "I'm happy for you, *dochenka*."

Mama had already laid out my wedding gown on her bed along with Eleanor Lawler's hoop skirt. I started to put it on.

"Now the gown." Mama helped me get into it. I hadn't realized how heavy it was.

Memorial Chapel, Harvard

Mama handed me the tiara with the lace veil. She helped me pin it on. She had made the tiara herself, embroidering it with tiny seed pearls. Then she had sewed that delicate Chantilly lace on to it. Now I realized why she had saved this special lace for all these years.

When we were finished, I looked into the mirror and saw myself as a bride. In back of me, I noticed Mama's lovely reflection smiling at me, her eyes glowing.

"Mama, thank you for making this gown for me. It's just beautiful."

"You're the one who's beautiful," she said, embracing me.

There was a knock on the door, and we heard Mac's anxious voice. "Honey, everyone's here. Mr. Kazanjian is impatient to begin taking photographs. Are you ready?"

Mama gave me a final look. "Yes, we're ready." She opened the door wide; Mac came in. He just stood there, staring.

"Golly, Vixen," his voice was husky. He took my arm and led me into the living room.

They were all there waiting for me: Papa, rubbing his nose; Vanya, looking pleased with himself; the ushers, dignified and courteous; the excited bridesmaids, and Martha, shy and aloof.

Mr. Kazanjian was a tall Armenian to whom time was money. He wasted neither his nor ours. In situating us where he wanted us, either alone or as a pair, as a family, as a group, he sped through the photographic session efficiently and effectively. Satisfied, he left us, as suddenly as he had come.

Now it was time for the others to leave for Memorial Church. All of those except for Papa, me, and Manfred, who was to drive us there in his car. He smiled at me, checking the time. His dark heavy brows were twitching now as he glanced over at Papa.

"I think we'd better leave now, sir. Miss Rubleva," he pronounced my surname slowly, knowing this would be one of the last times I'd ever hear it. "Is our lovely bride ready?" He offered me his arm.

"I am," I replied. I squeezed his arm. With my other hand, I held up my train. Papa was carrying my bouquet.

All at once I felt as if I were walking on air. The apartment house, people stopping to gape on the sidewalk, the ride towards Harvard Square, then entering the massive wrought-iron gates into the Yard—all that was so hazy, as if I really were in a dream world. I do remember walking into a very small waiting room, hearing excited laughter, many voices, and then that awesome silence. Finally the majestic tones of the organ broke the hushed stillness of the chapel with the resounding first notes of the "Wedding March" from *Lohengrin*. Papa led me into the lobby to stand behind the mass of pastel colors and black and white. I watched them march slowly down the white-carpeted aisle, in step, to the cadence of that triumphal march.

"Now, *dochenka*, it's time for us." Papa offered me his arm, standing as tall and as proudly as his short stature permitted.

I held on tightly to his arm, hearing the music, seeing the sea of faces turn towards us.

Suddenly, I felt my foot step on something, blocking me from going on.

"What's wrong?" Papa whispered sideways.

"Papa, it's the hoop skirt under my dress. It's long, and it's tripping me." I realized now, with horror, that I should have shortened it. But I hadn't even tried it on, feeling sure that it would fit, forgetting that Eleanor was some five or six inches taller than I was.

Bless dear Papa. Calmly and slowly we walked as with each step I tried to make sure that I wouldn't step on the bottom of the hoop skirt. I stole a look at Papa's face. He was looking straight ahead, his gaze, as usual, quite serene.

"Do you see your Mac?" he whispered.

"Yes."

"He hasn't taken his eyes off you." I heard his low chuckle as we neared the altar, where Dean Sperry was standing, watching us approach. His ponderous form looked resplendent in the official robes of his profession. He smiled down at me, his eyes benevolent beneath the heavy brows. Papa left me then. Mac moved in to stand beside me, facing the Dean.

I heard the sonorous voice speaking to us, then to the silent congregation. I heard him firmly demand if there was any person here in this chapel who felt that we should not marry. If so, they were to speak now or forevermore hold their peace. During that pause, I trembled, lest some former boyfriend would say he did. Then I heard Mac's voice repeating after the Dean, promising to cherish me. I heard my own voice too, soft but firm, repeat the same promise. I felt Mac slip the gold band on my finger, then I took the other ring and slipped it onto his. Then the voice of the Dean rang out through the chapel so that everyone there could hear, "I now pronounce you man and wife."

Now he was smiling, nodding to the two of us. I looked at him in awe, thinking of him as an Old Testament prophet.

Once again, Mac took my arm, his head towards me, looking deep into my eyes with his love. He turned us around and down the aisle we walked, past the smiling faces staring at us, clutching at their twisted handkerchiefs.

In the receiving line people passed on by, shaking hands, kissing me, the bride, with Mac beside me, smiling, looking at me, smiling again at the guests, thanking them for saying that he was a lucky man and that I was such a lovely bride.

He had kissed me in the foyer, calling me Mrs. McNish. I realized then that he had forgotten to kiss me at the altar after we had said our vows. I hadn't remembered to either, and it didn't really matter, because now he would be kissing me always and forever.

The receiving line was endless, or so it seemed. There were just a few more people left. It was then that I saw him. He was inching his way towards us, walking with short, careful steps. As usual, he was dressed in his neat, black suit; in his hand the black hat that he always doffed when he met me. The weathered face was wreathed in a saintly smile. As he came towards us, he clasped both his hands, his hat now under his arm. Beneath the wrinkled lids, his eyes glistened mistily.

"Thank you for inviting me to see you," he said, in the now familiar voice. "Ach, I have never before seen such a radiant bride." He went over to Mac again, shaking his hand a second time. "Captain, may I wish you the very best."

Mac looked down at me, his eyes filled with tenderness. "Sir, I now have the very best."

And now my dream—the same one that had followed me from Magpie Street in Peking, China, to this land of my dreams, now mine—was at an end, for at last I had my country and my Yankee-man forever and ever.

Afterword

Never in my wildest imagination did I think that when Sam Klauber brought me to the Rublevs' home in Cambridge as a blind date for their daughter's best friend that that event would change the course of my entire life. By the end of our double date, I had made a firm decision. I was going to win the love of Tamara Rubleva with the same determination that I was fighting for my country in World War II.

What a family the Rublevs were! Reared in a conservative, Pennsylvania-Dutch–Scotch-Irish family, I had never met such a distinctive personality as their daughter. What a beauty she was! Her sparkling dark eyes highlighted a dazzling smile that enthralled the world. Her angelic innocence, mixed with an age-less wisdom, shed a magical allure about her that attracted attention, especially that of young men like me. My never-ending barrage of letters from bases overseas eventually convinced her that I was the man she should marry.

It took me years to get to know this elusive Russian girl who became my wife. Certain traits in her puzzled me although I could not pinpoint them at the time. Why was it that she always refused to answer our front doorbell when it rang? Did it recall some painful memory from the past? Why had she been so bash-ful, reticent, and inexperienced about sex? How had she learned so much about literature, music, and ballet? And how had she learned to speak Chinese, Russian, French, and English as if each were her native tongue? Why had she not gone to high school in Peking and yet had been able to enter Radcliffe with just one year of high school in Cambridge?

It was only while Tamara was writing *Wait for Me* that the pieces began to fit together for me. I have learned so much about

747

her; the reason for her feeling so insecure at times, her fierce loyalty to her adopted country, her pride in our nation's flag. We native-born Americans sometimes take for granted what others consider precious gifts.

In June, 1994, we returned to Cambridge for Tamara's fiftieth Radcliffe reunion, traveling back in time to revisit the homes in which she had lived and to see alumni classmates again.

How Cambridge had changed! Her former home at 69 Mount Vernon Street and the street itself were not the same. They were now overdeveloped, rundown, and overgrown with shrubbery. The Forest Street apartment was more attractive than before. Tamara and I stared up at the windows of the apartment where we had rekindled our love after my return from overseas.

Later, we sat with other Harvard and Radcliffe alumni in front of Memorial Church in Harvard Yard and listened to speakers welcoming alumni to the reunion. My photographic memory raced back through the years to 1946 when I had led my radiant Russian bride down those very steps we were now sitting in front of.

Ours has been a beautiful union. I have learned much from my Tamara: her interesting Russian heritage, her fascinating Chinese background, and her zest for life. In turn, she has inherited my love for my own Scottish heritage and learned to enjoy American humor and traditions. Two people of extremely different backgrounds yet bonded together by the same intellectual curiosities and their love for each other. Our marriage, as I informed Dean Sperry so many years ago, has truly been *two* marriages: our first and our last through forty-eight memorable years.

We have been fortunate to get back in touch with some of Tami's classmates. In Cambridge this summer we visited Loretta Cornell, nee Ciani. Through her thorough sleuthing, she had found dear Sam Klauber for us, he who had instigated our romance in the first place. Sammy, God bless him, is in his eighties, but, except for a bit less hair, he has hardly changed. Still active, still living in Chelsea and taking care of people, Sam is happily married to his Betty—a truly delightful couple.

Claire, Tami's "Buddy Number One" from her OWI days, is

the one who found us in our home in Miami, Florida. She and Tami correspond quite frequently these days.

Unfortunately, we don't know where Phyllis is. She was a good friend and a loyal one. Someday, perhaps, we'll find out what has happened to her.

John P. McIntyre
December, 1994
Miami, Florida